Workforce Development Theory and Practice in the Mental Health Sector

Mark Smith
Te Pou o te Whakaaro Nui: National Workforce Center for Adult Mental Health, Addiction and Disability, New Zealand

Angela F. Jury
Te Pou o te Whakaaro Nui: National Workforce Center for Adult Mental Health, Addiction and Disability, New Zealand

A volume in the Advances in Psychology, Mental Health, and Behavioral Studies (APMHBS) Book Series

IGI GLOBAL
DISSEMINATOR OF KNOWLEDGE

www.igi-global.com

Published in the United States of America by
IGI Global
Information Science Reference (an imprint of IGI Global)
701 E. Chocolate Avenue
Hershey PA, USA 17033
Tel: 717-533-8845
Fax: 717-533-8661
E-mail: cust@igi-global.com
Web site: http://www.igi-global.com

Library of Congress Cataloging-in-Publication Data

Library of Congress Cataloging-in-Publication Data

Names: Smith, Mark, 1960 March 29- editor. | Jury, Angela, 1972- editor.
Title: Workforce development theory and practice in the mental health sector / Mark Smith and Angela Jury, editors.
Description: Hershey PA : Information Science Reference, [2017] | Includes bibliographical references and index.
Identifiers: LCCN 2016046935| ISBN 9781522518747 (hardcover) | ISBN 9781522518754 (ebook)
Subjects: | MESH: Mental Health Services--manpower | Staff Development | Health Planning
Classification: LCC RA410.7 | NLM WM 30.1 | DDC 331.11/9136222--dc23 LC record available at https://lccn.loc.gov/2016046935

This book is published in the IGI Global book series Advances in Psychology, Mental Health, and Behavioral Studies (APMHBS) (ISSN: pending; eISSN: pending)

British Cataloguing in Publication Data
A Cataloguing in Publication record for this book is available from the British Library.

For electronic access to this publication, please contact: eresources@igi-global.com.

Advances in Psychology, Mental Health, and Behavioral Studies (APMHBS) Book Series

Bryan Christiansen
PryMarke, LLC, USA

ISSN:pending
EISSN:pending

Mission

The complexity of the human mind has puzzled researchers and physicians for centuries. While widely studied, the brain still remains largely misunderstood.

The **Advances in Psychology, Mental Health, and Behavioral Studies (APMHBS)** book series presents comprehensive research publications focusing on topics relating to the human psyche, cognition, psychiatric care, mental and developmental disorders, as well as human behavior and interaction. Featuring diverse and innovative research, publications within APMHBS are ideally designed for use by mental health professionals, academicians, researchers, and upper-level students.

Coverage

- Treatment & Care
- Addiction
- Socialization
- Anxiety
- Counseling & Therapy
- Cognition
- Human Interaction
- Emotional Health
- Neurological Disorders
- Mental Health & Disorders

IGI Global is currently accepting manuscripts for publication within this series. To submit a proposal for a volume in this series, please contact our Acquisition Editors at Acquisitions@igi-global.com or visit: http://www.igi-global.com/publish/.

The Advances in Psychology, Mental Health, and Behavioral Studies (APMHBS) Book Series (ISSN pending) is published by IGI Global, 701 E. Chocolate Avenue, Hershey, PA 17033-1240, USA, www.igi-global.com. This series is composed of titles available for purchase individually; each title is edited to be contextually exclusive from any other title within the series. For pricing and ordering information please visit http://www.igi-global.com/book-series/advances-psychology-mental-health-behavioral/110200. Postmaster: Send all address changes to above address.

Titles in this Series

For a list of additional titles in this series, please visit: www.igi-global.com

Improving the Quality of Life for Dementia Patients through Progressive Detection, Treatment, and Care
Jinglong Wu (Okayama University, Japan)
Medical Information Science Reference • copyright 2017 • 353pp • H/C (ISBN: 9781522509257) • US $205.00 (our price)

Police Psychology and Its Growing Impact on Modern Law Enforcement
Cary L. Mitchell (Pepperdine University, USA) and Edrick H. Dorian (Los Angeles Police Department, USA)
Information Science Reference • copyright 2017 • 345pp • H/C (ISBN: 9781522508137) • US $190.00 (our price)

Seduction in Popular Culture, Psychology, and Philosophy
Constantino Martins (Nova University of Lisbon, Portugal) and Manuel Damásio (Lusófona University, Portugal)
Information Science Reference • copyright 2017 • 332pp • H/C (ISBN: 9781522505259) • US $175.00 (our price)

Chronic Mental Illness and the Changing Scope of Intervention Strategies, Diagnosis, and Treatment
Barre Vijaya Prasad (Dharwad Institute of Mental Health and Neurosciences, India)
Medical Information Science Reference • copyright 2017 • 404pp • H/C (ISBN: 9781522505198) • US $220.00 (our price)

Identifying, Treating, and Preventing Childhood Trauma in Rural Communities
Marion Baker (Center of Hope Arizona, USA) Jacqueline Ford (Center of Hope Arizona, USA & Walden University, USA) Brittany Canfield (Center of Hope Arizona, USA & Fielding Graduate University, USA) and Traci Grabb (Arizona's Children Association, USA & Center of Hope Arizona, USA)
Information Science Reference • copyright 2016 • 306pp • H/C (ISBN: 9781522502289) • US $185.00 (our price)

Handbook of Research on Diagnosing, Treating, and Managing Intellectual Disabilities
Rejani Thudalikunnil Gopalan (Gujarat Forensic Sciences University, India)
Information Science Reference • copyright 2016 • 496pp • H/C (ISBN: 9781522500896) • US $210.00 (our price)

Neuroeconomics and the Decision-Making Process
Bryan Christiansen (PryMarke LLC, USA) and Ewa Lechman (Gdansk University of Technology, Poland)
Business Science Reference • copyright 2016 • 354pp • H/C (ISBN: 9781466699892) • US $195.00 (our price)

IGI Global
DISSEMINATOR OF KNOWLEDGE
www.igi-global.com

701 E. Chocolate Ave., Hershey, PA 17033
Order online at www.igi-global.com or call 717-533-8845 x100
To place a standing order for titles released in this series, contact: cust@igi-global.com
Mon-Fri 8:00 am - 5:00 pm (est) or fax 24 hours a day 717-533-8661

Editorial Advisory Board

List of Reviewers

Table of Contents

Detailed Table of Contents

This chapter addresses changes in the conceptualization of workforce development and its implications for mental health and addiction workers, services, and sectors. First we provide an overview of the background, historical and contextual factors impacting current approaches to workforce development. Next, an examination of systems thinking, service delivery models and goals, workforce planning, leadership and worker recruitment, retention and wellbeing are provided. Finally, theories of knowledge and innovation dissemination, learning models and theories, and emerging use of technology are examined.

Mental health and substance use conditions are among the most prominent causes of illness and disability in the U.S. Yet less than half of the individuals with these conditions receive treatment. While there are many impediments to accessing care, the absence of a workforce that is of sufficient size and adequately trained is a significant factor. This chapter provides an overview of the U.S. behavioral health workforce and describes seven strategic areas in which activity has been undertaken to strengthen it. The initiatives of the Annapolis Coalition on the Behavioral Health Workforce are presented to highlight these strategic areas, which include assessment and planning; competency identification and development; roles for persons in recovery and family members; integrated care and interprofessional collaboration; workforce development in substance use; diversity and cultural competency; and knowledge dissemination and adoption of best practices.

Working in Hawai'i and the U.S.-Affiliated Pacific Islands presents unique challenges and opportunities for mental health workforce development. This chapter presents previous, current, and future efforts aimed at not only increasing the size of the workforce but also developing a better trained workforce for existing professionals. The authors draw from their experiences at the Hawaii/Pacific Basin Area Health Education Centers (AHEC), one of the only organizations performing medical, public health, and mental health workforce development across the Pacific Region, to explore culturally appropriate initiatives and interventions. Programs targeting a range of audiences from youth to adults, students to professionals, and patients/clients to caregivers are discussed. The chapter emphasizes health career pathway programs for youth and young adults wishing to enter the health workforce and a variety of educational development and continuing education opportunities for professionals. Specific mental health workforce initiatives are described.

This chapter explores the drivers and outcomes of mental health and addiction workforce development in Australia. In contrast to many countries, these workforces remain largely separate in Australia. Large investments have been made at national, state, and local levels; with resources and programs developed that are worthy of international attention. However, many still question the outcomes of these investments in light of evidence of ongoing unmet need and variations in care. Great hopes are being placed in new workforces, including peer workers, vocationally qualified coaches, and e-mental health technicians. Much rides on the outcomes of these initiatives.

This chapter describes a nationally led approach to workforce development by analyzing three workforce development initiatives within the adult mental health and addiction sector in New Zealand. New Zealand has been on an important and critical journey with regards workforce development over the past 15 years, one which has significantly altered the way services are delivered. In order to understand this journey, some background information relevant to New Zealand will be provided covering the context of mental health, epidemiology of mental health illness, service delivery, use of evidence based treatments, as well as funding and investment in workforce development. The three workforce development initiatives are then described: 1) key knowledge, skills, values and attitudes for all people working in mental health and addiction services, 2) development of an outcomes culture, and 3) post graduate clinical training for nurses and allied health professionals.

This chapter will discuss the training of the mental health workforce in developing countries and make comparison with the developed world from where many of the systems and practices originate. All countries are different in the various factors that affect mental health care, mental health promotion, and mental health personnel training. But there are common themes. The relevancy of mental health workforce training is affected by treatment theory, the prevalence and burden of disorders in the country, the types of personnel available and involved in caring for the disabled, and the environments and resources available at country level. The realities and limitations of each country influences the types of people available for workforce training, the training approaches that are practical and can be sustained, the type of educational technologies available, and the retention of personnel once trained. These are the major themes addressed in this chapter with particular reference to the least developed countries.

Mental disorders are a major public health challenge globally, contributing to 40% of the global burden of disease. Nevertheless, it remains highly neglected by health planners and policy makers, particularly in low and middle income countries (LMIC). Bangladesh, one of the low-income countries, suffers from a severe shortage of appropriately trained and an adequate number of human resources to provide mental health care. The authors reviewed available evidence on the dynamics of mental health services in LMIC like Bangladesh, with a view to help develop appropriate policies on human resources. This chapter critically examines the current situation of human resources for mental health in Bangladesh, and explores ways to further strengthen human resources so as to enhance mental health services in the country.

services. New Zealand formally introduced the MHSW role in the early 1990's to provide non-clinical services for mental health consumers or clients through either hospital or community-based services. The work MHSWs undertake and their relationship with other health professionals is discussed. Also discussed, is the relationship that MHSWs have with mental health consumers/clients and the attributes that the MHSW brings to the relationship. Consideration is given to the debate as to whether the role of the MHSW should be regulated, what it means to be considered a health professional, and the possibilities of expanding the scope of practice for MHSWs.

Although an evidence-based practice, peer support remains an emerging discipline in mental health. Peer supporters help individuals seeking mental wellness by inspiring hope, using their recovery story, and by developing mutual relationships. Peer supporters believe in each individual's ability to recover. They know recovery is possible, because they have experienced it themselves. Understanding what peer support is, and how peer supporters work within their unique discipline is important to those wishing to include peer supporters in their service systems. Peer support is more than simply sharing stories; systems guided by licensing requirements and quality management teams require effective, well-trained individuals, with lived experience to work within peer support. With effective training, and a strong footing in their own recovery, peer supporters can be exceptional contributors within behavioral health systems of care.

Meeting the needs of people with co-existing mental health and addiction problems is a challenge faced by many mental health and addiction services and providers. A compounding factor has been the separation of mental health and addiction services which has meant that many people with co-existing mental health and addiction problems have fallen through the cracks between services or had issues not recognized or responded to, leading to poor health outcomes. This chapter describes the approach taken by New Zealand's workforce development centers to support services to improve responsiveness and workforce capability to work with people with co-existing mental health and addiction problems. International research on implementation is briefly summarized before discussion about the impact of the national approach and the barriers to implementation that have emerged. Recommendations for next steps conclude this chapter.

Chapter 13

Eating disorders are serious illnesses with both physical and psychological symptoms. In the case of anorexia nervosa, the evidence suggests the earlier one identifies and treats the illness, the greater the chance of full recovery. In 2010 the New Zealand Ministry of Health provided funding to roll out the evidence based, Family Based Therapy (also known as Maudsley Family Based Therapy [MFBT]), treatment for anorexia nervosa, to specialist eating disorders services and clinicians in child and family services. The main focus of this chapter is the planning behind the implementation and sustainability processes, the evaluation, and the initial outcomes of the implementation of MFBT. Finally, lessons learned and recommendations from the implementation process will be outlined.

Chapter 14

Online chat and email are two of the most popular ways of providing e-mental health. Online chat is synchronous communication in a virtual chat room where client and counselor meet at the same time. In contrast, email is referred to as asynchronous because it can be accessed without the synchronous presence of client and counselor. There has been a rapid increase in the demand for chat and email over recent years and much of the demand has been met by services that have traditionally provided helplines or crisis support. This chapter provides an overview of the key issues associated with the delivery of e-mental health services and workforce development. This includes an examination of the range of options for providing e-mental health and key issues to consider when working online. The chapter concludes with a brief exploration of issues associated with client suitability for e-mental health via chat and email.

Chapter 15

This chapter provides an overview of the implementation of routine outcome measurement in mental health services in Australia. It describes the preparation necessary to enable the collection of these

Foreword

The most recent findings from the Global Burden of Disease project confirm the significant impact of mental health and substance use problems. Indeed, some have described poor mental health as the non-communicable disease of the first half of the life course.

Mental health is unequivocally a major public health issue. Yet most people with such problems never receive help. This level of unmet need is particularly stark among those struggling with substance abuse problems. Indeed, if all people likely to benefit from support and/or intervention "turned up" our systems would collapse under the demand.

Research clearly tells us that most adult disorders are in fact juvenile disorders grown up. This implies that potentially up to 50% of the adult burden associated with these problems could be averted if effective interventions were applied during the juvenile years. Despite this knowledge, approximately two-thirds of mental health budgets are typically directed towards adult sufferers. The newest research reveals that mental health and substance problems are essentially the expression of several underlying vulnerabilities and that these bear little relation to the categories enshrined in DSM (Diagnostic and Statistical Manual) or ICD (International Classification of Diseases) systems. Moreover, these neurodevelopmental vulnerabilities are identifiable in the earliest years of life.

Threading this together, a future workforce seeking to effectively pre-empt or ameliorate symptoms and promote recovery needs to be well-resourced and trained (given the high levels of need); focussed and able to deliver interventions earlier in the natural history of the problems (e.g., adolescence); and committed to serious preventive efforts, beginning in utero, given that substances have a seriously toxic effect upon developing brains.

Translation of evidence into daily practice need not take decades. Success might entail acquiring new skills, and new ways of practicing, for example, by adopting massively scalable, high-fidelity and sophisticated e-interventions for mental health problems. Harnessing and harmonising the skills of more of the helping professions must also be explored.

The need to innovate is obvious; but with this comes the responsibility to rigorously evaluate new approaches to ensure we are truly making a difference. This edited volume is a valuable step in the right direction.

Richie Poulton
University of Otago, New Zealand

Preface

A number of years ago one of the co-editors had the experience of working with a group of senior managers and leaders on workforce development in the mental health context. One of those leaders summed up, inadvertently, one of the problems with understanding workforce development when they said "Workforce development, that's just training isn't it"? While training is often the focus of workforce development, it is only one aspect. In addition to training and development, workforce development may be focused on recruitment and retention, organizational development, research and evaluation, leadership, supporting systems and infrastructure (Ministry of Health, 2002). So we hope this book will make clear that there is a lot more to workforce development than the provision of training.

This preface will endeavour to provide an overview or description of:

- The subject matter of the book: *Workforce Development Theory and Practice in the Mental Health Sector*
- Where this topic fits in the mental health and addiction world today
- The target audience
- The importance of each of the chapter submissions
- How the book impacts the field and contributes to the subject matter.

OVERVIEW

Workforce development is an emerging discipline of great importance that is critical to the delivery of quality care and support. The maxim "no health without a workforce" has never seemed more apt (World Health Organization [WHO], 2014). In the 21st century, as in all areas of health, we can expect that mental health workforce development will become increasingly significant. Workforce development supports high quality practice, the development of services responsive to diverse groups and populations, and sustainability of the workforce to meet current and future needs (Roche & Skinner, 2005).

Workforce development has been variously defined but it can be seen as "a multi-faceted approach which addresses the range of factors impacting on the ability of the… workforce to function with maximum effectiveness" (Roche & Skinner, 2005, p. 4). When underpinned by strategic workforce planning, it makes efficient use of limited resources; targets development in priority or risk areas; and enables services to proactively plan for the future. The overall aim of workforce development is to support having the "right number of people, with the right skills, in the right place, at the right time, with the right work attitude, doing the right work, at the right costs, with the right work output" (WHO, 2010, p. 1).

The WHO (2014) publication, *A Universal Truth: No Health Without a Workforce,* asks three questions. "What health workforce is required to ensure effective coverage of an agreed package of healthcare benefits? What health workforce is required to progressively expand coverage overtime? How does a country produce, deploy and sustain a health workforce that is both fit for purpose and fit to practice in support of universal health coverage?" (p. v). These questions seem as relevant to mental health as to any other area of health and the chapters of this book provide a number of answers and potential solutions to these questions.

WHO (2014) propose ten steps to ensure the workforce is ready.

1. Recognising the problem.
2. Assessing how to deal with it.
3. Formulating a plan.
4. Building the data.
5. Building and sustaining policies and procedures.
6. Building political support.
7. Reform of existing workforce.
8. Assessing how to move forward.
9. Encouraging.
10. Encouraging.

As a relatively new approach to service delivery the research base for mental health workforce development is still being developed. A robust evidence base with good information and data, along with effective design and implementation are key components of workforce development. Evaluation of workforce development initiatives is also essential in understanding what works and in which contexts.

Where This Topic Fits

This book is an attempt to fill some of the gaps in our understanding around workforce development in the field of mental and behavioral health. Given the many important drivers in the health sector this has never been more appropriate or necessary. The book is broad brush in its approach, covering the range of mental health settings and interventions across the age range. The book includes a variety of international perspectives with practical examples of how workforce development initiatives have been implemented around the world.

Target Audience

The book should be of interest to a range of health professionals: planners and funders and managers of all kinds will find the chapters helpful in comparing workforce development across several jurisdictions, and what may be usefully adapted locally. Those involved in the development of policy in the area of workforce development will find it a useful text for understanding what is happening across countries and in specific programmes. Educators and training providers will find it a useful text for their courses. Clinicians from across all the mental health professions will find the approach a pleasing mix of theory and practice. Researchers and students in the mental health sector will find the book a useful introductory text to this new and exciting field.

ORGANIZATION OF THE BOOK

Section 1: Introduction to Workforce Development

The first introductory chapter provides a broad overview to the concept of workforce development. Ann Roche and Roger Nicholas set out a useful framework that seeks to explore the theory around workforce development. They analyse changes in the conceptualization of workforce development and its implications for mental health and addiction workers, services, and sectors. Firstly they provide an overview of the background, historical, and contextual factors impacting current approaches to workforce development. Next, they provide an examination of systems thinking, service delivery models and goals, workforce planning, leadership, workforce recruitment, retention and wellbeing. Roche and Nicholas highlight the need for a systems approach to workforce development, rather than primarily targeting the individual worker. The authors also reiterate the need to "grow your own" workforce rather than relying on immigration to fill staff shortages. Such an approach, as they make clear, will require leadership at many levels for this and many other initiatives in workforce development to succeed. The point is also made that training only has the potential to be effective when applied in the context of broader contextual issues, once again highlighting the need for systems thinking. Finally, Roche and Nicholas examine theories of knowledge and innovation dissemination, learning models and theories, and the emerging use of technology. All these themes find practical and specific application in the chapters which follow.

Section 2: International Perspectives on Workforce Development

Section 2 of this book considers the nature of workforce development from the perspective of various jurisdictions, and contains contributions from various countries and ethnic perspectives.

In Chapter 2 Michael Hoge and colleagues provide a U.S. perspective on some of the critical workforce issues occurring in this country. Mental health and substance use conditions are among the most prominent causes of illness and disability in the U.S., yet less than half of the people with these conditions are shown to receive treatment. An overview of the U.S. behavioral health workforce is provided along with a description of seven strategic areas in which activity has been undertaken to strengthen the U.S. behavioral workforce. The authors emphasize the need for better workforce data to base workforce analysis and decisions upon. Also highlighted is the need for a range of systems approaches to address the challenges faced by mental health and addiction services in building capacity and capability to support greater access to support for people with mental health problems. As is mentioned in many chapters in this book, the need for a greater role for people with lived experience in the delivery of care is emphasized. While developed in the U.S., the chapter includes links to a number of useful resources which have broader applicability.

Christopher Hill and Kelley Withy in Chapter 3 provide a Hawaiian and rural perspective. The authors provide an overview of U.S. licensing requirements for mental health professionals. There is a strong need for state-level coordinated workforce development efforts given the differences in licensing requirements between states. The authors describe and explore how the use of mental health services in the U.S. are generally driven by three inter-related concepts - the quality, access, and cost of mental health care. The authors draw particular attention to the health and substance use disparities experienced by native Hawaiians, recent immigrants, and people living in rural areas. The chapter goes on to show the shortage of health practitioners in many areas in Hawai'i. An overview of workforce development activities undertaken in Hawai'i and U.S.-Affiliated Pacific Islands is provided which aim to support recruitment in health careers, training and development, particularly for people from minority and disadvantaged backgrounds, and rural and underserved areas. The chapter shows how these initiatives are helping to address health disparities, in particular by using native Hawaiian cultural responses.

Chapter 4 from Rod McKay, Tim Coombs, and Julie Anderson considers workforce development in the Australian mental health and addiction context. In particular they focus on the differences between the mental health and addiction sectors in Australia. In contrast to many countries, these workforces remain largely separate in Australia even though significant investments have been made at various levels of government. In Australia, great hopes are being placed in new workforces, including peer workers, vocationally qualified coaches, and e-mental health technicians. As the authors make clear, much rides on the outcomes of these initiatives. This chapter highlights a number of critical factors, including the role of policy and funding in the mental health and addiction system being a prominent consideration, along with the need for a whole of sector approach to workforce development rather than focusing on the mental health and addiction sectors in isolation. Additionally, the need for clear leadership is emphasized, a theme which has reverberations across many of the chapters in this book.

Mark Smith and Angela Jury in Chapter 5 explore mental health workforce development in New Zealand, with a number of nationally led adult initiatives. The chapter provides an introduction to the New Zealand workforce development context, explaining how New Zealand has developed a number of national workforce centers responsible for the implementation of government policy into practice for distinct populations. The chapter focuses on the work of one of those national centers, which is responsible for adult mental health workforce development. The authors examine three national initiatives: the development of knowledge, skills, values, and attitudes for all people working in the mental health and addiction sector; the development of an outcomes culture to ensure individuals and services are focused on outcomes as much as inputs and outputs; and post graduate clinical training for nurses and allied health professionals, where the focus on the outcome of recovery is central.

Rex Billington in Chapter 6 considers workforce development from a more global perspective drawing on his extensive experience working for the WHO. This chapter discusses mental health workforce training in developing countries and makes comparisons with the developed world from where many of the systems and practices originate. As the author notes, all countries are different in the various factors that affect mental health care, mental health promotion, and workforce training. But there are common themes. The author explores the theoretical perspectives which influence workforce training, the prevalence and burden of disorders in specific countries, workforce availability, and the environments and resources available within each country which impact on workforce development. The chapter shows how the realities and limitations of each country influences the types of people available for workforce training, the training approaches that are practical and can be sustained, the type of educational technologies available, and retention of the mental health workforce once trained.

Chapter 7 by Shariful Islam and colleagues focuses on workforce development in low and middle income countries, with specific examples from Bangladesh. The authors highlight that while mental disorders are a major public health challenge globally, these are often neglected in low and middle income countries. Bangladesh, one of the low income countries, suffers from severe shortage of mental health workers, and those with appropriate training. As the chapter makes clear emigration of skilled professionals is a major problem for low and middle income countries given the loss to more developed countries. This chapter critically examines the current situation of human resources for mental health in Bangladesh, and explores ways to further strengthen the mental health workforce to enhance mental health service delivery. The authors reiterate the importance of the workforce as being the most significant resource within mental health services; that the workforce requires significant investment; and the need to look at how the available workforce can be most effectively utilized. The chapter also highlights the need for reliable data to inform workforce development, future planning and partnerships, and collaboration across sectors.

Fuimaono Karl Polotu-Endemann and Monique Faleafa in Chapter 8 discuss Pacific workforce development within a New Zealand context. The authors highlight the disparities in outcomes for Pacific people in comparison to the general population. The authors show that Pacific peoples in New Zealand have higher rates of mental illness, substance abuse, and suicide attempts, as well as disproportionately low rates of access to services when compared to the general population. Pacific families or aiga also tend to have high and complex mental health needs, and traditional cultural worldviews that are distinctly different from the dominant western mental health paradigms. Moreover, Pacific people are severely under-represented within the mental health and addiction workforce in New Zealand. An overview of innovative Pacific mental health and addiction workforce development initiatives is provided which have been led by Le Va, a national workforce center. These have been aimed at increasing the capacity and capability of the Pacific workforce in New Zealand, and enhancing the cultural competency of the "mainstream" workforce to better meet the needs of Pacific people and their families. The chapter emphasizes the importance of cultural responsiveness and how this can contribute to improving the equity of outcomes for people with experience of mental health problems. Also highlighted is how collaboration and co-design are fundamental to the successful development and implementation of workforce development initiatives.

Section 3: Specific Workforce Development Applications

Section 3 of this book focuses on specific workforce development areas, including undergraduate nursing education; mental health support workers; peer support workers; co-existing problems; eating disorders; e-competency; and routine outcome measurement.

Helen Bingham in Chapter 9 shows how undergraduate nursing education supports the development of the nursing workforce to have the right knowledge and skills to deliver effective and appropriate services to people with experience of mental health problems in all clinical settings. The importance of understanding the competencies and capabilities required so that education is relevant to practice and models of service delivery is highlighted. Also the need to take a broader biopsychosocial approach to understanding health, including the environment and early intervention. The chapter explains that traditionally nursing undergraduate education and training has focused almost exclusively on responding to clinical disorders or illness. The new emphasis is to explore connections between physical and mental health, particularly the brain itself. The chapter shows how the role of people with lived experience of mental health problems and their families is more central to undergraduate nurse education than it has been in the past. Encounters with people with lived experience are shown to be of value to nursing students and in challenging assumptions and beliefs that support stigmatizing beliefs and discriminating behaviors. Outlined in the chapter is an overview of how a nursing curriculum integrates mental health knowledge and skills.

In Chapter 10 Julia Hennessy, Liz Smythe, Max Abbott, and Frances Hughes consider how mental health support workers contribute to the recovery of people with experience of mental illness. Traditionally seen as support to mental health professionals, mental health support workers are increasingly being seen as professionals in their own right. Support workers assist people with the transition from residential or hospital services to independent living within the community. The authors describe how mental health support workers are usually based within community based non-government organisations (NGOs) within the New Zealand context. However, some support workers are also employed in acute or rehabilitation settings within secondary care services. A key initiative has been the development of a national qualification within New Zealand to prepare mental health support workers for employment into community mental health services. The chapter explores the role and significance of mental health support workers. The authors show how mental health support workers can add real value to mental health services, and support other mental health professionals in working to top of scope.

Lisa St. George in Chapter 11 considers workforce development for peer support workers, which is a growing area of interest throughout the western world. St. George makes a strong case for greater investment in peer support and the role of peer workers in supporting the recovery of individuals with mental health challenges. Drawing on a rich recovery literature and experience in delivering training from the U.S., the author shows how peer support can enhance existing services by including peer support workers within multidisciplinary teams. Recovery pathways and the value of using recovery language are emphasized. The chapter also includes an overview of peer support in New Zealand, Australia, and Scotland by Mary O'Hagan, Michael Burge, and Simon Bradstreet.

Ashley Koning and Suzette Poole in Chapter 12 explore the issue of workforce development in relation to co-existing problems for people with both mental health and addiction problems. This chapter draws on extensive theory and practice to show an implementation strategy around working with co-existing problems, involving competencies, resources, training, and other approaches. The authors highlight the importance of a set of competencies based on a three tier approach of foundational, capable, and enhanced for assisting people with co-existing problems. They emphasize the centrality of evaluation in the implementation of workforce development initiatives. Also the need for a more integrated system of care, where a more planned and co-ordinated approach is taken.

In Chapter 13, Rachel Lawson and Bronwyn Dunnachie focus on eating disorders, which are serious illnesses with both physical and psychological symptoms. In New Zealand, the evidential Maudsley Family Based Therapy has been rolled out for anorexia nervosa, to specialist eating disorder services and clinicians in child and family services. The authors outline a useful process used in this national workforce development initiative. The chapter describes key factors that need to be considered to support successful implementation of workforce development programmes, including programme characteristics; systems level factors such as funding, organizational support, and leadership; and ensuring clinicians have access to training and development opportunities to help build knowledge and skills required to deliver responsive services. It shows how having an evidence base and planning, design, implementation, and evaluation are critical to the process of workforce development.

Simone Rodda, Max Abbott, Nicki Dowling, and Dan Lubman in Chapter 14 consider workforce development and e-learning. The authors describe how there has been a rapid increase in the demand for chat and email over recent years and much of the demand has been met by services that have traditionally provided helplines or crisis support. The authors provide an overview of the key issues associated with the delivery of e-mental health services and workforce development. This includes an examination of the range of options for providing e-mental health and key issues to consider when working online. A range of practical tips that can be implemented in practice are provided. The chapter concludes with a brief exploration of issues associated with client suitability for e-mental health via chat and email. The chapter shows that e-learning can be a vehicle for therapeutic work, focusing in particular on chat and emails the authors show the advantages and potential problems of utilizing this form of therapeutic relationship. This offers the potential to reach people who might not otherwise access help.

In the final chapter of this book, Chapter 15, Tim Coombs, Philip Burgess, Rosemary Dickson, and Rod McKay provide an overview of the implementation of routine outcome measurement in mental health services in Australia from a workforce development perspective. The authors describe the preparation and development work required to enable the collection of outcome measures, including policy development. The authors explore issues related to training, benchmarking, communication, and other workforce development activities needed to initiate and sustain the collection and use of outcome measures. As more jurisdictions across the world move to outcome focused services this chapter has never been more relevant for workforce development. The chapter concludes by outlining the future development of the collection of outcome measures and the implication for continued workforce development. The authors emphasize the importance of ensuring people accessing services are at the center of workforce development initiatives, the value in benchmarking, and taking a whole of systems approach as has been emphasized throughout this book.

CONCLUSION

In conclusion, many countries are facing similar challenges with respect to workforce development in mental health. Whilst focusing on different topics, parts, and aspects of the mental health or behavioral workforce, the chapters contained in this book highlight a number of common themes.

Workforce development is critical to the delivery of quality mental health services and in achieving better outcomes for people accessing services. The workforce is the most costly but valuable resource within mental health services. As emphasized by WHO (2014), there is no health without a health workforce.

There are a number of critical drivers for changes in workforce development outlined in this book. Some of these drivers include: demographic changes, with an aging population and workforce; new technology and ways of accessing and using information; new evidence-based treatments and scientific understandings on the way the brain works; new ways of delivering services; the global demand for health workers; the need to respond to population changes and service user expectations; and a trend towards increasing empowerment of people with lived experience of mental health problems being just a few of the critical developments which the mental health sector now faces.

The challenges in building a sufficient workforce to deliver mental health and addiction services is highlighted throughout this book. Workforce shortages in many countries are shown, along with expectations of increasing demand. This necessitates a need to look at new workforces, giving thought to what is the optimal or right skill-mix, and how health professionals can be supported to work to top of scope. Both support workers, and peer support workers may well be critical workforces as Julia Hennessy and Lisa St. George indicate. Access to better information and data to inform strategic workforce planning is also required to support proactive approaches being taken to address future gaps and risks, rather than crisis driven approaches.

With the move to more recovery focused person-centered support for people with experience of mental health problems in the community, there is a need to think about the knowledge, skills, values and attitudes required of the workforce. What does the workforce currently have, what will they need in the future, what are the gaps, and how can these be addressed? As Helen Bingham shows, there is a need to also think about the workforce of tomorrow and ensure education programmes are responsive to future needs, particularly the connection between mental and physical health. This necessitates closer relationships between education and service providers to ensure education and training is both useful and relevant for the mental health workforce and service delivery.

The importance and need for greater priority and funding for development of the mental health workforce is highlighted in this book. Funding and access to resources is a real issue in low and middle income countries and developing countries as shown in both Shariful Islam's and Rex Billingham's chapters. These countries along with many others may struggle with access to on-line learning, resources and tools, therapies and support due to the technology and infrastructure required. This means the way resources and tools are developed and disseminated in many of these countries differs.

Workforce development in the mental health sector, as this book amply demonstrates, needs to take a whole of system approach. Focusing on one aspect in isolation, such as training or recruitment, will not provide the transformative changes that are needed for workforce development. In addition to training, there needs to be a focus on leadership development, organizational culture and climate, access to the right information including workforce data and outcomes information to inform workforce development, recruitment and retention, and the development of a supporting infrastructure. As is reiterated many times in the individual chapters, workforce development strategies need to target systems, organizations, teams, and individuals in a holistic manner.

Effective workforce development is shown throughout this book to be a long term investment that takes time. In order to bring about change in practice, the importance of involving stakeholders and gaining sector buy-in is emphasized. The need for clear leadership in bringing about change, including a shift towards recovery focused services, is repeatedly stressed. This is shown to be a fundamental issue which impacts on the success of workforce development initiatives.

Ultimately if the aim of mental health workforce development is to make a difference and achieve better outcomes for people accessing services, then the inclusion and leadership of people with lived experience of mental health problems and recovery is important in bringing about this change. Change can be ad hoc and ultimately fail to address the needs of the people for whom the services exist, or it can be planned and improve the well-being of the people for whom it is intended. There is a need to see the end user, the person accessing services, as central to the process of workforce development.

This book is focused on the mental health sector, both present and future workforce. We hope this book contributes towards the emerging approach of workforce development, inspires fresh thinking and practice as the mental health and addiction sector faces one of its defining periods of change.

Mark Smith
Te Pou o te Whakaaro Nui: National Workforce Center for Adult Mental Health, Addiction and Disability, New Zealand

Angela Jury
Te Pou o te Whakaaro Nui: National Workforce Center for Adult Mental Health, Addiction and Disability, New Zealand

REFERENCES

Ministry of Health. (2002). *Mental health (alcohol and other drugs) workforce development framework*. Wellington, New Zealand: Ministry of Health.

Roche, A. M., & Skinner, N. (2005). An introduction to workforce development. In N. Skinner, A.M. Roche, J. O'Connor, Y. Pollard, & C. Todd (Eds.), Workforce development TIPS (theory into practice strategies): A resource kit for the alcohol and other drugs field. Adelaide, Australia: National Centre for Education and Training on Addiction (NCETA), Flinders University.

World Health Organisation. (2014). *A universal truth: No health without a workforce*. Geneva, Switzerland: World Health Organisation Press.

World Health Organization. (2010). *Workload indicators of staffing need: User's manual*. Geneva, Switzerland: World Health Organization Press.

Acknowledgment

The editors would like to acknowledge the help of all the people involved in this project and, more specifically, to the authors and reviewers that took part in the review process. Without their support, this book would not have become a reality.

First, the editors would like to thank each one of the authors for their contributions. Our sincere gratitude goes to the chapter's authors who contributed their time and expertise to this book.

Second, the editors wish to acknowledge the valuable contributions of the reviewers regarding the improvement of quality, coherence, and content presentation of chapters. Most of the authors also served as reviewers; we highly appreciate their double task.

Finally, we would like to acknowledge Colleen Mantle, Administrator, Te Pou o te Whakaaro Nui. Also Andrew Mantle and the expertise of the Wise Group communication team.

Mark Smith
Te Pou o te Whakaaro Nui: National Workforce Center for Adult Mental Health, Addiction and Disability, New Zealand

Angela Jury
Te Pou o te Whakaaro Nui: National Workforce Center for Adult Mental Health, Addiction and Disability, New Zealand

Section 1
Introduction to Workforce Development

Chapter 1
Mental Health and Addictions Workforce Development: Past, Present, and Future

Ann M. Roche
Flinders University, Australia

Roger S. Nicholas
Flinders University, Australia

ABSTRACT

This chapter addresses changes in the conceptualization of workforce development and its implications for mental health and addiction[1] workers, services, and sectors. First we provide an overview of the background, historical and contextual factors impacting current approaches to workforce development. Next, an examination of systems thinking, service delivery models and goals, workforce planning, leadership and worker recruitment, retention and wellbeing are provided. Finally, theories of knowledge and innovation dissemination, learning models and theories, and emerging use of technology are examined.

INTRODUCTION

Over recent decades, there has been a major paradigm shift in the conceptualization of workforce development. There have also been substantial advances in the theoretical underpinnings of effective workforce development, and the dissemination and implementation of innovation. This chapter outlines key changes and their implications for mental health and addiction workers, services and sectors.

Interest in workforce development derives from concern about quality of care and provision of evidence-based, effective, and efficient services. There is now also increasing focus on treatment outcomes (in contrast to input- or output-based funding) and client and worker safety. The central tenet of this chapter is that workforce development requires a systems focus, rather than a focus on individual workers. Unlike more traditional approaches, a systems approach is broad and comprehensive, targeting individual, organizational, and structural factors, rather than addressing only the immediate education and training of individual workers (Roche, 2002).

DOI: 10.4018/978-1-5225-1874-7.ch001

While there are multiple facets to workforce development, there is no single unifying theoretical framework. Select theoretical and conceptual models related to different aspects of workforce development are therefore presented.

Currently, there is a severe global health workforce crisis (World Health Organization [WHO], 2011). Over a billion people worldwide lack access to quality healthcare resulting from critical staff shortages, imbalanced skill mixes and uneven geographical distribution of health professionals. An additional 2.4 million doctors, nurses, and midwives are needed worldwide (WHO, 2011). By 2022, Organization for Economic Co-operation and Development (OECD) countries will be facing a health workforce shortfall of approximately 22% to 29% (KPMG, 2012).

The implications of this are wide-reaching. In the Western Pacific region, for example, it has been identified that:

Disconnects still exist between health services and educational and workforce planning, contributing to inefficiencies and misalignment in training, deployment and uptake into the workforce. Limited capacity for human resource management at the national, provincial and facility levels, limited cross-sectoral and multi-stakeholder involvement and other underlying, constraining health system factors all contribute to the difficulties countries have in following through on policy-level commitments, and implementing strategies and plans. (WHO: Western Pacific Region, 2012, p.8)

The shortage of health workers is not confined to developing countries. In the U.S., there is a growing crisis in the mental health and addictions field due to unmet need for services, high worker turnover rates, worker shortages, an ageing workforce, stigma, and inadequate compensation (Hoge et al., 2013; Mojtabai & Crum, 2013; SAMHSA, 2013).

Similar problems and high levels of unmet need are also evident in other parts of the world including:

- Australia (Meadows, Enticott, Inder, Russell, & Gurr, 2015; National Mental Health Commission, 2014; Ritter et al., 2014).
- New Zealand (Mental Health Commission, 2011).
- Canada (Sunderland & Findlay, 2013; Urbanoski, Cairney, Bassani, & Rush, 2008).
- China (Liu et al., 2011; Yip et al., 2012).
- Hong Kong (Chan, Lam, & Chen, 2015).
- 58 low and middle income countries (Bruckner et al., 2011).
- The Asia-Pacific region (Ng, Herrman, Chiu, & Singh, 2009).

These problems are particularly acute among indigenous peoples (Durie, 1999; Jorm, Bourchier, Cvetkovski, & Stewart, 2012).

Compounding these issues, there is a major shortage of medical educators in the Asia-Pacific region (Hu, McColl, Thistlethwaite, Schuwirth, & Wilkinson, 2013). There have also been changes to mental health nurse education and registration in some countries. In Australia for example, nurses are now required to have a generalist qualification before specializing in mental health nursing. In addition, there is now no specialty registration for mental health nurses. These changes have led to a decrease in the number of students motivated to undertake mental health nursing as a career of choice (Hemingway, 2016).

Workforce supply and distribution is therefore a workforce development issue of central importance for a range of countries and beyond, and particularly for indigenous communities. However, these workforce supply and distribution factors comprise only one aspect of workforce development under consideration in this chapter.

Workforces in Focus

At the outset, it is important to define the workforces in question. This chapter focusses on personnel who are centrally involved in providing services to clients with addiction and/or mental health problems. The current paucity of these professionals, particularly in low and middle-income countries, is a major obstacle to adequate service provision (Buchan et al., 2013).

The workforces responding to mental health and addiction problems, and the skillsets required, overlap. However, both groups also perform unique roles and may have different professional or lived experience backgrounds, as represented diagrammatically in Figure 1.

The mental health and addiction workforces broadly comprise:

- Nurses, occupational therapists, social workers and psychologists.
- Medical practitioners including psychiatrists and general practitioners.
- Consumer carers.

Nurses are the most numerous workgroup involved in the mental health and addiction sectors. They are also the workforce group in most demand globally, which places pressure on organizations to implement workforce development measures to enhance their recruitment and retention.

Figure 1. The relationships between the workforces responding to mental health and addiction problems

The mental health workforce also includes mental health workers and indigenous mental health workers. Similarly, the addiction workforce also includes alcohol and other drug (AOD) workers, addiction medical specialists, peer workers, needle and syringe program workers, and prevention workers.

The mental health workforce may be employed in hospitals, health care and community mental health services, or correctional facilities (Mental Health Workforce Advisory Committee, 2011). Addiction workers may be employed in AOD specialist organizations or AOD programs within non-specialist organizations, the government, not-for-profit (non-government) and private sectors (Intergovernmental Committee on Drugs, 2014). Addiction workers may have degrees, specialized qualifications, or little or no formal training.

PART 1: CONTEMPORARY WORKFORCE DEVELOPMENT DEFINED

Traditionally, workforce development has been perceived as essentially synonymous with the training of individual workers. From this bottom-up perspective, workforce development involved workers attending training programs that provided content designed to enhance the skills and knowledge that would allow them to perform their roles more effectively.

In contrast, contemporary conceptualizations of workforce development highlight the importance of adopting a broader systems approach to enhancing the provision of services. However, workforce development is still often narrowly viewed in terms of worker-focused approaches intended to improve individual worker performance.

For example, in the U.S., workforce development has been described as,

... the coordination of public and private sector policies and programs that provide individuals with the opportunity for a sustainable livelihood and helps organizations achieve exemplary goals, consistent with the societal context. (Jacobs & Hawley, 2009, p.12)

In this example, emphasis is placed first on the individual worker's employment needs and secondarily on attainment of organizational goals. The crucial importance of sustainable employment notwithstanding, this example is an inherently limited and limiting perspective.

A more recent and broader definition of workforce development is:

...a set of processes that govern the identification, recruitment, assessment and training of job seekers into employment as well as the maintenance and advancement of these persons in their careers that enhance self-sufficiency and revitalise the communities in which these individuals live. (Holland, 2015, p. 55)

In Holland's definition, the issues of recruitment and retention and skill matching are embraced. Holland recognized the importance and inevitability of the need for a systems perspective and states that:

...given the complexity of how workforce development is governed under this more comprehensive definition, it becomes necessary to articulate a systems approach to ensure that the broader goal of human capital investment is met. (Holland, 2015, p. 55)

Underscoring the importance of a broader systems approach to workforce development, Canada has also recently expanded its policy approach to workforce development to include issues such as immigrant integration, social security, labor, human capital formation, and economic development policy measures (Bramwell, 2011; Wood & Klassen, 2009). The Canadian Centre for Substance Abuse's (CCSA) approach to workforce development pivots on worker competencies; an approach widely used but somewhat limited in its scope and focus to achieve higher end goals of quality care and effective, efficient service delivery (Roche, Adams, & White, 2014).

The contemporary conceptualization of workforce development, as adopted in this chapter, is:

...a multi-faceted approach which addresses the range of factors impacting on the ability of the workforce to function with maximum effectiveness in responding to mental health and addiction-related problems. Workforce development should have a systems focus. Unlike traditional approaches, this is broad and comprehensive, targeting individual, organisational, and structural factors, rather than just addressing education and training of individual mainstream workers. (Roche, 2002, p.9)

Historical Overview

The concept of workforce development is dynamic and has evolved over time. Three evolutionary workforce development phases are evident in the mental health and addictions fields.

Phase 1: Individual Workers

The first workforce development phase involved a focus on individual workers. The main strategies employed were education and training programs and resource development to enhance individual workers' knowledge and skills and, by implication, behavior change. This approach to workforce development was predicated on the assumption that providing individual workers with the requisite skills and knowledge would result in them transferring newly acquired training content to their routine practice. According to this knowledge and skill deficit approach, training is all that is required to bring about behavior change and the provision of evidence-based, quality services. By the early 2000s, the limitations of this approach were becoming increasingly apparent (Roche, Pidd, & Freeman, 2009).

Research concerning health worker training has consistently demonstrated that single-exposure training models and/or simple provision of information (e.g., manuals or guidelines) are ineffective methods of producing practitioner behavior change. Such approaches can be effective for the dissemination of information and can yield increases in knowledge, but are limited in the extent to which they produce consistent or sustained behavior change (Lyon, Stirman, Kerns, & Bruns, 2011).

There are two reasons for this. First, the effectiveness of training transfer is highly dependent on organizational culture or climate (Bennett, Lehman, & Forst, 1999; Blume, Ford, Baldwin, & Huang, 2010; Bunch, 2007). Implementing training programs without addressing organizational characteristics that may act as impediments to workers attaining/applying new knowledge and skills is unlikely to be successful. Second, even where training programs successfully increase workers' knowledge and skills, quality service delivery remains dependent on a range of organizational, structural, and systemic factors beyond the control of individual workers (Roche, Pidd, & Freeman, 2009).

Phase 2: Internal Systems Approach

Recognition of the inherent limitations in earlier workforce development efforts led to an increased focus on the systems in which individual workers function. Workforce development approaches subsequently evolved to focus more broadly on the *internal* systems within which workers were employed. This approach sought to facilitate and sustain the workforce by targeting organizational and structural factors, as well as individual factors (Baker & Roche, 2002). This systems perspective includes a diverse range of issues including:

1. Developing or changing organizational policies.
2. Developing models of care that enhance client outcomes.
3. Recruitment and retention issues.
4. Information management, knowledge transfer, and research dissemination strategies.
5. Clinical supervision, leadership, and mentoring.
6. Enhancing teamwork.
7. Education and training programs to enhance evidence-based practice.
8. Evaluating programs and projects.
9. Workplace support.
10. Professional and career development.
11. Clarification of staff roles and functions.
12. Measures to enhance workforce wellbeing (Roche & Pidd, 2010).

An internal systems focus signaled a major paradigm shift whereby education and training initiatives were still viewed as important but as a subset of a comprehensive range of workforce development activities. The essential and complementary roles of infrastructure and organizational issues relative to training are schematically illustrated in Figure 2.

Phase 3: An Integrated Human Services Systems Approach

While the internal systems approach represented a conceptual leap forward, there remained a growing appreciation of the need to address mental health and addiction problems in the context of broader physical, social and environmental issues (Roche, 2013). There was also a greater awareness of the limitations of siloed care models (Conway, McMillan, & Becker, 2006) and changing expectations of clients, the broader community and funders in regard to partnerships and client inclusion in health care.

An integrated human services systems approach entails a top-down focus.[2] It involves consideration of systems service delivery factors and identification of the service standards to provide the best quality care. This also requires needs assessments to be undertaken in the first instance to inform decisions about levels and patterns of service provision. Only then is it possible to implement workforce development strategies to meet those goals.

In summary, workforce development has shifted from:

- Identifying and responding to individual/workers' perceived knowledge and skill deficits, to
- Applying systems thinking to identify how systems, sectors and agencies should operate; identifying the nature of the workforce/s required; and developing the workforce by addressing likely impediments to, and facilitators of, change.

Figure 2. The different levels and components of workforce development
Source: Roche & Pidd, 2010

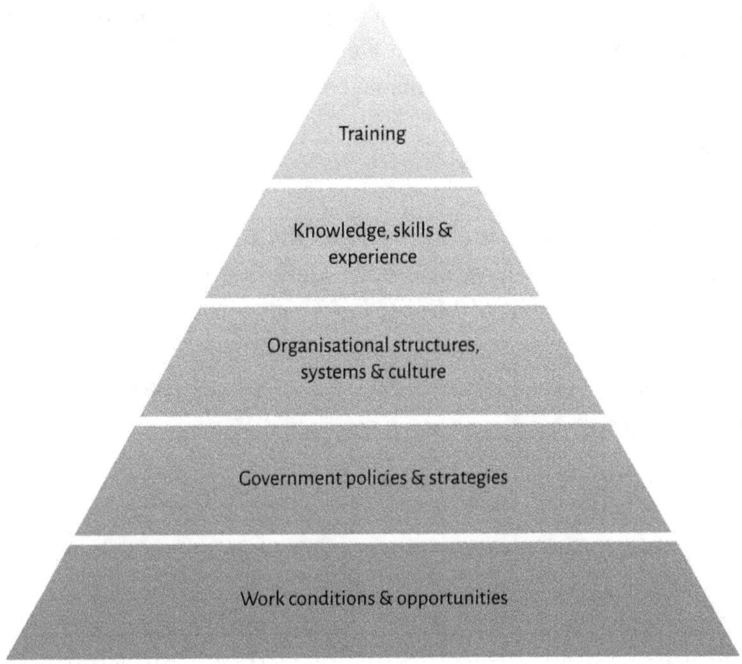

Drivers of Change

Numerous factors have provided the impetus for change and the shift towards a broader conceptualization of workforce development. Some factors are generic while others are more specific to the mental health and addiction fields.

Generic Drivers

Generic drivers of the shift towards a broader conceptualization of workforce development are outlined below.

1. *Globalization* which has resulted in unprecedented connections between markets and increased competition for skilled labor. This has meant that organizations need to work harder to attract and retain workers, including enhancing workforce development opportunities.
2. *Technology* has become more central to a range of occupations. Many health and welfare workers now need to be proficient in the use of technology, requiring the development of skills beyond those relating to direct client care.
3. *The new economy* has increased global competition and cost pressures and led to greater demands for efficiency and quality. This too, has led to a broadening of the skill base required of workers including the need to work more effectively with diminishing resources, and across agencies and sectors to improve client outcomes.

4. *Demographic shifts*. The retirement of the baby boomer generation will require a substantial workforce development replacement effort (Jacobs & Hawley, 2009).
5. *Mass migration* has facilitated the movement of people across country and regional borders in a manner that was previously inconceivable. This has resulted in unpredictable drains on human resources in developing countries and unmanageable movements in developed countries.

Mental Health and Addiction Drivers

In addition to these generic drivers, several factors specific to workforce development change within mental health and addiction services have also been identified (see Druss, 2010; Intergovernmental Committee on Drugs, 2014; New Zealand Ministry of Health, 2012; Roche & Duffield, 2007). These factors are summarized in Table 1.

As is evident, a range of generic and sector-specific factors have provided a significant impetus for change in workforce development.

Table 1. Mental health- and addiction-related drivers of a broader conceptualization of workforce development

Area	Issues
Recruitment and retention issues	• Ageing workforces mean larger numbers of workers retiring with insufficient workers to replace them • Ageing populations resulting in increased demand for services and greater competition for health and welfare workers from other sectors • Changing expectations of work-life balance including more workers choosing to work part time, requiring other workers to complete the same volume of work • Increasing expectations that workplaces will be rewarding and fulfilling, contributing to higher staff turnover if they are not • The creation of new roles for workers (particularly nurses) which can draw them away from traditional roles.
Worker wellbeing	• Increased awareness of worker wellbeing issues • A decrease in workplace safety and increased threats of violence • Increased risk of burn-out and compassion fatigue.
Changing trends in mental health and addiction problems and clinical practices	• Deinstitutionalization of mental health clients, resulting in the potential for fractured and inconsistent access to care • Earlier intervention in the life course and with at-risk families, children and adolescents • Enhanced integration across primary/secondary and mental health and addiction services using stepped care approaches • Increasing co-occurring physical and mental health and addiction problems • Increased awareness of mental health and substance use problems among the elderly • Increasing efforts to reduce inequalities in service provision and outcomes • Increasing demands for family and culturally sensitive practice • Shifting patterns of substance use, particularly poly-drug use and new psychoactive substances • New pharmacotherapies and other treatment options for substance use problems • Changes in mental health services delivery away from psychotherapy and towards psychopharmacology • Enhanced consumer input into care (e.g., client-led care) • Cutbacks in prevention activities, which may result in increased demands for treatment in the future.
Structural issues	• Greater emphasis on cost and practice efficiencies and interagency/ intersectoral collaboration • Increased emphasis by funders on program outcomes, rather than inputs or outputs • Increased requirements for program evaluation and data and other record collection • Increasing ethical concerns about addressing workforce shortfalls by bringing in workers from developing countries.

PART 2: SYSTEMS THINKING

The second part of this chapter examines broad structural issues such as systems thinking, service delivery models and goals, workforce planning (including supply and demand), leadership and worker recruitment, retention and wellbeing.

While there is no single theoretical framework to inform workforce development in the mental health and addictions fields, systems thinking offers an overarching theoretical construct.

Systems thinking is based on systems theory, which focuses on the interrelatedness of the different parts of an organization or system. Infrastructure, tasks, technologies, and resources are all deemed of equal importance. When changing one part of a system, it is important to have an appreciation of how this affects other parts of the system, as well as the relationships between systems (Rhydderch, Elwyn, Marshall, & Grol, 2004).

A system is a set of things (e.g., people, a department, an organization or a sector) that is interconnected in such a way that it produces its own pattern of behavior or outcomes over time. The system may be influenced by outside forces, but the same forces applied to different systems are likely to produce different results (Meadows & Wright, 2008).

Systems thinking is an approach in which all assumptions about how organizations and systems operate are made explicit and subjected to scrutiny. This approach is intended to improve the understanding of how systems operate and the interactions within and between different parts and systems (Aronson, 1996; Peters, 2014). Systems theory attempts to conceptualize and address the "wicked problems"[3] inherent in change processes in complex adaptive systems. This is particularly relevant to healthcare, where a problem is often the symptom of yet another problem. Further, intervening in any area of the health system will impact on many other areas in anticipated and unanticipated ways that can be both desirable and undesirable (Health Workforce Australia, 2012). It is also highly relevant to workforce development because of the myriad interconnected factors which impact on the development of workforces.

Fundamentally, systems thinking, as applied to workforce development, involves considering those aspects of workplaces, organizations, or sectors that facilitate or impede the implementation of best practice and efficient service delivery. It also encapsulates factors that make workplaces healthy or unhealthy (Senge, 1990).

Relevant factors which impact on workforce development in healthcare systems identified by Minas (2012) include:

- Inadequate infrastructure, facilities, equipment, drug distribution systems.
- Shortage of skilled mental health workers.
- Geographic maldistribution of the available workforce.
- Disciplinary imbalance: domination by physicians and nurses.
- Undeveloped information systems, with lack of high-quality local information to support planning.
- Poorly developed systems research capacity.
- No culture of evaluation or continuous quality improvement.
- Poorly organized and marginalized consumers, carers, civil society.

Workforce and Service Provision Planning

As noted above, the provision of an adequate and appropriate workforce is fundamental to good health care. The WHO has identified this in the strongest terms in a recent publication titled "*A Universal Truth: No Health Without a Workforce*" (Campbell et al., 2013) which underscored the importance of a comprehensive approach to workforce development in both developed and developing countries. The WHO report by Campbell and colleagues aimed to consolidate what is known about human resources for health services and maintains that the health workforce is central to attaining, sustaining, and accelerating progress on universal health coverage. The report recommended that three guiding questions should be asked by decision-makers:

1. What health workforce is required now?
2. What health workforce is required over time?
3. How does a country produce, deploy, and sustain a health workforce that is both fit for purpose and fit to practice?

To answer these questions, a conceptual framework was developed that addressed the right to health and minimum social protection, and the availability, accessibility, acceptability, and quality of health services. The dimensions of availability, accessibility, acceptability, and quality to the health workforce were defined as follows:

- **Availability:** The sufficient supply and stock of health workers, with the relevant competencies and skill mix that correspond to the health needs of the population.
- **Accessibility**: The equitable access to health workers, including in terms of travel time and transport, opening hours and corresponding workforce attendance, whether the infrastructure is disability-friendly, referral mechanisms and the direct and indirect cost of services, both formal and informal.
- **Acceptability**: The characteristics and ability of the workforce to treat everyone with dignity, create trust and enable or promote demand for services.
- **Quality**: The competencies, skills, knowledge and behavior of the health worker as assessed.

Further, the health workforce is seen as part of the chain of inputs, processes, outputs, outcomes, and impacts needed to supply efficient and effective health services and produce good health. Human resources (be they community-based or facility-based, clinical, administrative, managerial, education or research-oriented) cannot be considered in isolation from the infrastructure, equipment, medicines, consumables and financial resources that create an enabling or positive practice environment in which to interact with communities and individuals. All are equally essential in the complex, adaptive structures that make up health systems (Campbell et al., 2013). Nevertheless, the centrality of the health workforce in delivering health care is recognised as the core dynamic – "the backbone and limbs of the health care sector" – and hence is the starting-point for aligning supply with need and demand (Campbell et al., 2013, p.11)

Workforce Planning

Workforce planning is a continuous process of shaping and structuring the workforce to ensure there is sufficient and sustainable capability and capacity to deliver services, now and in the future. To be effective, workforce planning needs to be integrated into other planning frameworks. It also needs to clearly identify the human resource strategies required to continuously deliver the right people. That is, the people with the skills and capabilities necessary for the required work, in the right numbers, in the right place, at the right time (Australian Government: Australian Public Service Commission, 2013).

It is critical that workforce planning includes predictions of how the national situation, health needs, and delivery of services will change in the future and includes mechanisms for adjustment according to changing ongoing circumstances (WHO, 2010).

The starting point of health workforce planning is a situational analysis, which incorporates the major factors that may influence its size and shape in the future. This provides a base from which decision-makers and managers can explore the implications of internal and external changes on the need for, and supply of, human resources in the health system (WHO, 2007a). To this end, the WHO developed the Human Resources for Health Action Framework (see Figure 3).

The Action Framework includes six action fields (human resource management [HRM] systems, policy, finance, education, partnership, and leadership) and the action cycle which illustrates the steps/ phases in applying the Action Framework (situational analysis, preparation and planning, implementation, and monitoring and evaluation). To ensure a comprehensive approach to a given HRM challenge, all action fields and phases of the action cycle should be addressed, paying particular attention to critical success factors.

The ultimate aim of implementing the Framework is to achieve better health by enhancing health workforce outcomes leading to better health services. Factors specific to the country context will influ-

Figure 3. The Human Resources for Health Action Framework
Source: World Health Organization, 2010. Used with permission.

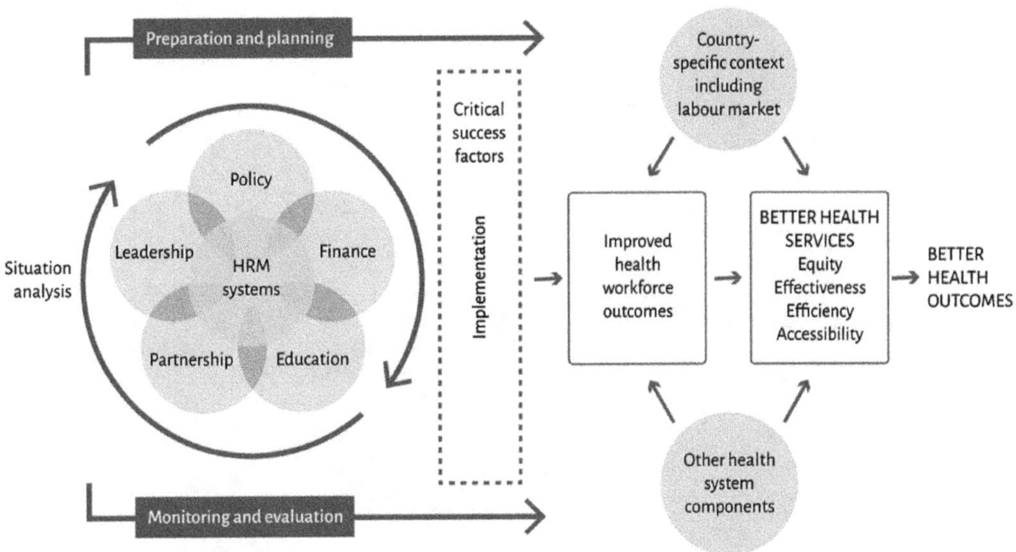

ence the degree to which this is achieved. These factors include the extent to which health is a priority for government, the economic environment, the state of the labor market support, and the available infrastructure. The ultimate success of the implementation will also be influenced by other health system components, such as the adequacy of supply of drugs, facilities, and equipment.

The WHO has also developed a theoretical framework for linking health workforce requirements and supply projections (see Figure 4).

A broad range of modelling approaches has been used to assess the demand for mental health and addiction treatment services (Clemens & Ritter, 2008; Dewit & Rush, 1996; Harris et al., 2014). The use of models is an essential feature of making projections, and provides a mechanism for defining the nature of the issues to be addressed, and testing and communicating possible solutions (WHO, 2010).

Seven steps to effective workforce planning have been identified (Cotten, 2007). These steps can be applied at organizational, sector, or systems levels. An adaptation of these steps to the mental health and addiction fields is shown in Table 2.

Figure 4. Framework for linking health workforce requirements and supply projections
Source: World Health Organization, 2010. Used with permission.

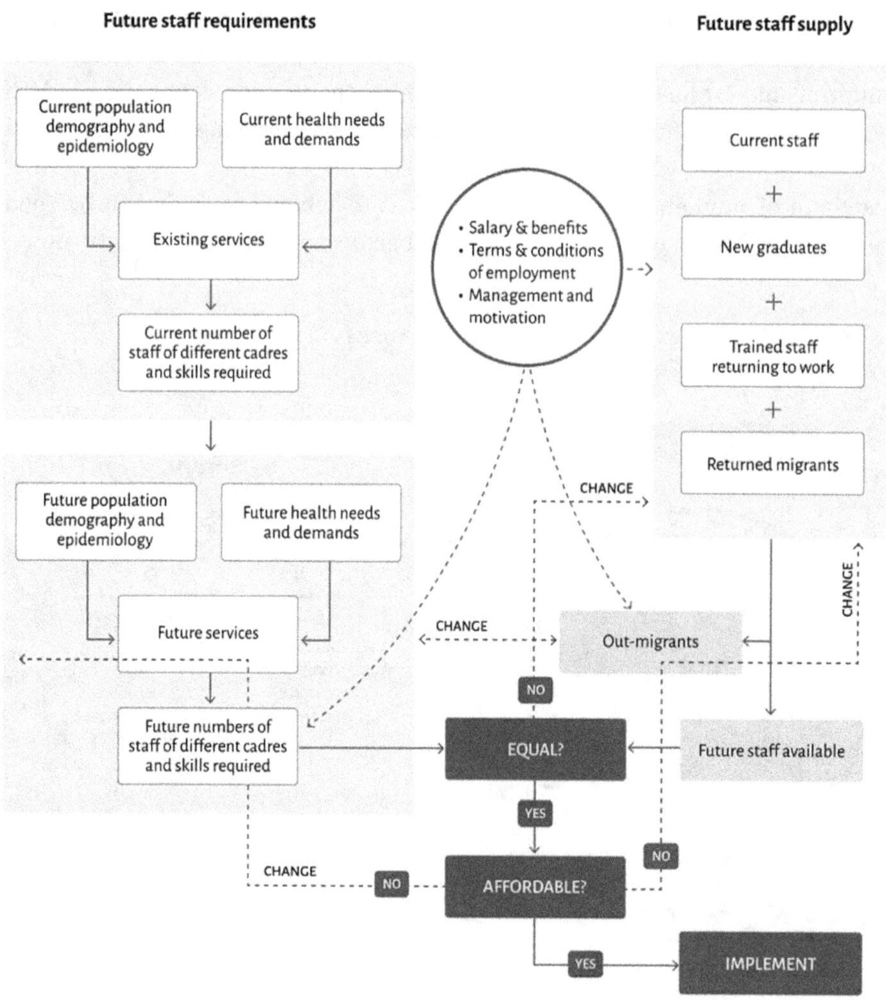

*Table 2. The seven steps to effective workforce planning**

Step	Task
Define future strategic directions for services	Document future strategic directions and identify the core or strategic skills needed
Scan internal and external environments	Assess likely service provision requirements, demographic changes among staff and clients, labor market forecasts, technology and treatment trends and workers in the educational pipeline
Model the current workforce	Model workforce demographics, characteristics, capabilities and distribution
Assess future workforce needs and project future workforce supply	Match anticipated characteristics and levels of treatment demand and compare this to projected workforce supply trends across all occupations (new workers and exiting workers)
Identify gaps and develop gap-closing strategies	Identify gaps (more workers, different skill sets or positions and work process redesign), retain workers with needed skills, recruit or develop workers, retain essential knowledge, and build worker skills
Implement gap-closing strategies	Implement chosen gap-closing strategies
Evaluate the effectiveness of gap-closing strategies and revise as needed	Check that workforce planning assumptions were valid, strategies are being implemented as planned and are having the desired impact

Adapted from Cotton (2007) for the mental health and addiction fields.

Health Worker Mobility

Severe staff and skill shortages within the health systems of developed countries have contributed to increased migration by health professionals from poorer countries (Callister, Badkar, & Didham, 2011; Connell, 2010). This migration occurs at significant economic cost, as it depletes workforces in source countries, diminishes the effectiveness of their health care delivery, and reduces the morale of the remaining workforce. There are considerable costs associated with training health care workers in developing countries and hence this migration has been perceived as perverse and as a subsidy from the poor to the rich (Connell, 2010).

New Zealand stands out among countries in the OECD in terms of the high level of movements in and out of the country of skilled professionals, including nurses. In New Zealand, much attention has been given to increasing the number of Māori and Pacific nurses as one mechanism for improving Māori and Pacific health (Callister et al., 2011).

Workforce globalization has created a major workforce supply and distribution dilemma in all health sectors, but this is particularly pronounced in the mental health and addictions sectors. This globalization trend is likely to increase. Given the ageing of the population and the very mobile workforces in most, health sector leaders and managers face major challenges in relation to attracting, retaining, and training a technically and culturally competent workforce.

Leadership and Management

Contemporary leaders of health services face a range of challenges. They are required to provide leadership for services which focus on consumer and community need, and encourage staff to engage with consumers. In addition, they must take account of the complex and adaptive nature of the health system, where making changes in one part of the system may lead to intended and unintended consequences in other parts. They face the challenge of addressing divisions between professional groups while building capacity for flexible deployment of the workforce and for multidisciplinary team care. They must also deal with high levels of cynicism and scepticism about the motivations of leaders based on experience of multiple reforms and restructures, and the perceived failure of these efforts to positively impact on clinical, preventive, and organizational outcomes (Health Workforce Australia, 2012).

Importantly, in the context of workforce development, leaders also need to:

- Provide incentives for health professionals to promote innovation that leads to improved community and patient outcomes.
- Increase the speed at which improvements and innovations are generated and spread through the health system.
- Build organizational cultures that enhance capacity and tolerance for innovation.
- Change the perspectives of health professionals who focus more strongly on the autonomy of their professions and patient or population outcomes, than on organizational or corporate outcomes (Health Workforce Australia, 2012).

Good healthcare system leadership and management involves providing direction to, and gaining commitment from, partners and staff, facilitating change, and achieving better health services through efficient, creative, and responsible deployment of people and other resources (WHO, 2007a). Leadership support and enhancement is a core component of workforce development - but one that is often overlooked.

Health care system leadership is a major issue in many low-income countries that need to significantly scale-up coverage of health services. As well as requiring additional national and international resources, better leadership and management are key to using resources effectively to achieve measurable results. While leaders set the strategic vision and mobilize efforts towards its realization, good managers ensure effective organization and utilization of resources to achieve results and meet designated goals (Asante & Hall, 2011; WHO, 2007a).

The WHO has developed a framework for building leadership and management capacity in healthcare organizations. The framework proposes that good healthcare leadership and management needs to have a balance between four areas:

1. Ensuring an adequate number of managers at all levels of the health system.
2. Ensuring managers have appropriate competencies.
3. Creating better critical management support systems.
4. Creating an enabling working environment (WHO, 2007a).

The ways in which these areas can contribute to improved health services and sector goals (such as achieving millennium development goals (MDGs) is represented diagrammatically in Figure 5.

Worker Wellbeing and Support

Worker Wellbeing

Worldwide, there is an increasing focus on occupational health and safety (WHO, 2007b). The wellbeing of the workforce is also a key factor in quality health service provision. It is important for workers

Figure 5. Leadership and management in health care systems
Source: WHO, 2007a

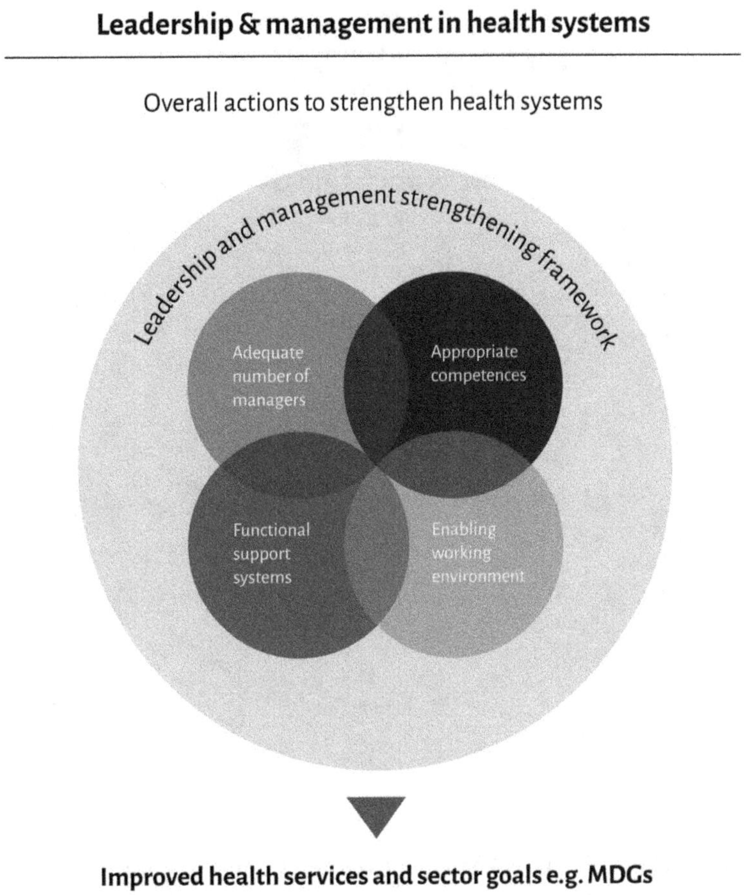

themselves, as well as for organizational functioning and client outcomes (Skinner & Roche, 2005). Enhancing workforce wellbeing is of particular relevance to the mental health and addictions workforces, as these work roles involve emotional work that can lead to elevated risk of stress and burnout (Evans et al., 2006; Ewer, Teesson, Sannibale, Roche, & Mills, 2015; Paris & Hoge, 2010; Roche et al., 2013; Rossi et al., 2012; Rössler, 2012; Volker et al., 2010). Worker well-being is also especially important among nurses who form the backbone of both the mental health and addictions sectors (Huntington et al., 2008).

Stresses associated with increasing demands, an ageing workforce, high community expectations and increased occupational exposure to aggression and violence are major issues for the well-being of mental health and addiction workers. Intensified work demands reduce the time available for workforce development activities, and may leave workers too tired to undertake them outside working hours. The intensity of work also increases the risks of burnout and loss of experienced staff (McKinnon & Cross, 2008; Mental Health Workforce Advisory Committee, 2011).

A range of factors at individual, organizational, and system levels can mitigate the likelihood of stress and burnout occurring among mental health addiction workers. These factors are summarised in Figure 6.

Figure 6. Factors impacting on stress and burnout among addiction workers
Source: Skinner & Roche, 2005

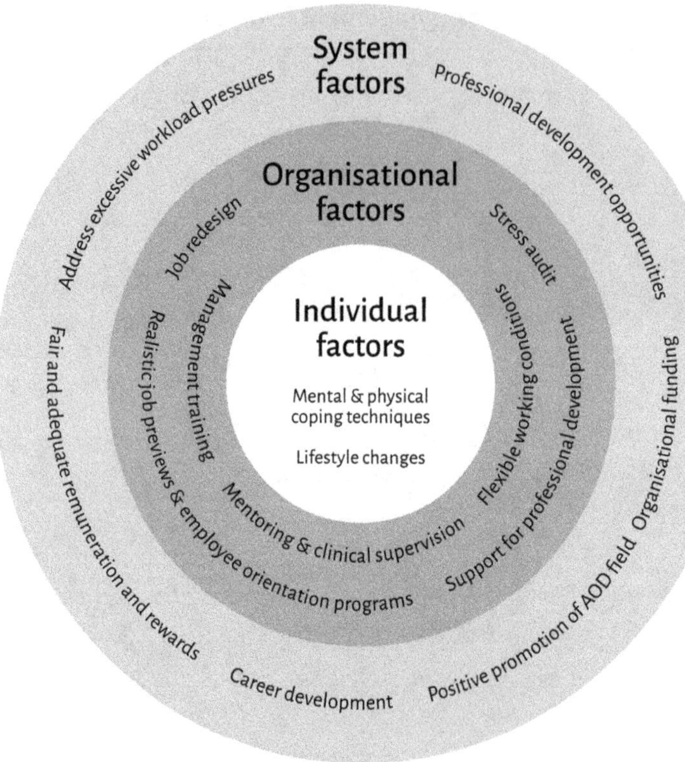

A number of strategies have similarly been identified at systems, organizational, and individual levels to reduce the risk of stress and burnout among addiction workers (Skinner & Roche, 2005). Many of these also apply to mental health workers. These strategies are summarized in Table 3.

Worker Support

Providing support for workers is also an important workforce development element. Worker support has two key functions. It enhances workers' well-being (social/emotional support) and ensures that workers are capable of effective performance (instrumental support). Support can be provided by the organization, managers/supervisors, or co-workers (Skinner, 2005), as summarized in Table 4.

Mentoring and Clinical Supervision

Mentoring and clinical supervision are particularly important workforce development strategies to enhance service provision, build capacity, ensure evidence-based practice, and prevent stress and burnout. They are strategies of central importance that are relatively inexpensive to implement and that can help retain valued workers.

Table 3. Systems-, organizational- and individual-level measures to reduce the risk of stress and burnout

Level	Strategy
System	• Providing and supporting professional development opportunities (e.g., provision of flexible learning pathways, grants and other workforce development funding arrangements) • Ensuring fair and adequate remuneration and other forms of reward • Promoting a positive image of the job roles • Addressing organizational funding issues • Developing strategies to address excessive workload pressures
Organizational	• Conducting stress audits • Ensuring that staff have realistic job expectations and adequate employee orientation programs • Support for professional and career development • Flexible working conditions • Management training • Job redesign • Recognition and rewards • Mentoring and clinical supervision programs • Measures to better support workers
Individual	• Implementing measures aimed at working smarter not harder • Maintaining a healthy lifestyle • Maintaining realistic expectations and beliefs • Seeking out a mentor or clinical supervisor

Table 4. Potential strategies to provide support for mental health and addiction workers

<table>
<tr><th></th><th>Social / emotional support</th><th>Instrumental support</th></tr>
<tr><td>Organization</td><td>• Ensuring fair treatment
• Providing valued rewards
• Ensuring supportive supervision</td><td rowspan="2">• Ensuring good job conditions (physical safety, job security, promotion paths, autonomy)
• Addressing work overload
• Addressing role ambiguity or conflict
• Providing access to high-quality resources and equipment</td></tr>
<tr><td>Managers/supervisors</td><td>• Channelling/facilitating organizational support
• Providing positive social interaction (praise, encouragement, caring, respect)
• Recognizing and rewarding good work
• Involving workers in decision-making</td></tr>
<tr><td>Co-workers</td><td>Providing positive social interaction (praise, encouragement, caring, respect)</td><td>• Providing help and advice
• Filling in when others are absent
• Assisting with heavy workloads
• Providing constructive feedback
• Appreciation and recognition
• Sharing duties and responsibilities</td></tr>
</table>

Source: Skinner, 2005

Mentoring

Mentoring is an informal and flexible approach to leadership, supervision and professional development. It involves the mentor and protégé setting goals focused on the protégé's professional and personal development needs. Mentoring relationships can occur between a mentor and a protégé or a small group of protégés, or may involve peers who act as mentors for each other. Mentoring can occur through formal or informal processes and involves encouraging protégé/s to find solutions themselves while drawing on the mentor's experience (Roche, Todd, & O'Connor, 2007).

Mentoring has a range of benefits for individual addiction and mental health workers, as well as for workforce development more broadly. These include:

- Building and sustaining skills and knowledge.
- Offering support for work practices.
- Facilitating work practice change.
- Acting as an incentive to attract skilled and qualified workers and to retain existing employees.
- Creating links between different professions and agencies.
- Offering support and accessible professional development for those working in rural and remote areas.
- Offering support during periods of change (Roche et al., 2007).

Clinical Supervision

Clinical supervision aims to develop workers' clinical practice skills via support and guidance from an experienced supervisor. This involves regular, systematic, and detailed exploration of a supervisee's work with clients or patients. While clinical supervision usually takes the form of a collaboration between an experienced practitioner and one or more less experienced practitioners, it can also involve two practitioners of equal seniority and breadth of experience (Roche et al., 2007).

Benefits of clinical supervision include:

- Availability of support for supervisees, and a forum to discuss clinical issues.
- Maintenance of clinical skills and quality practice.
- Promotion of standardized performance of core skills across the organization and/or field.
- Improvement and/or attainment of complex clinical skills.
- Increased job satisfaction and self confidence.
- Improved communication amongst workers.
- Improved worker retention.
- Reduced professional development and administration costs (Roche et al., 2007).

Recruitment and Retention

Working in the mental health and addiction sector can be a very rewarding experience. Sources of job satisfaction and reward for workers include:

- The opportunity to help and work directly with people.
- Belief in the worth of their work in terms of making a contribution to society.
- The opportunity for growth and development at a personal and professional level (Gallon, Gabriel, & Knudsen, 2003).

Nevertheless, recruitment and retention issues are some of the most prominent challenges facing contemporary addiction and mental health treatment programs.

Recruitment

With growing global demand for health workers, the recruitment of mental health and addiction workers is an increasing challenge. In both developed and developing countries, there are numerous challenges to the recruitment of mental health and addiction workers, including:

- Stigma attached to working in the mental health/addictions field.
- Perceived lower status of addiction counsellors compared to other helping professionals.
- Lack of qualified applicants.
- Lack of resources to fund service provision.
- Inadequate salary packages.
- Limited scope for advancement and promotion and lack of job security.
- High turnover, leading to a lack of role models to attract new staff.
- Remoteness of services.
- Inconsistent training and credentialing (Duraisingam, 2005a; SAMHSA, 2013).

Workforce development approaches to address these issues will be fundamental to the addiction and mental health workforces in the future.

Retention

Staff turnover among mental health and addiction workers is a major issue in some countries. A U.S. study of 27 substance use treatment organizations in 2008–2009 found an annual turnover rate of 33% for counsellors and 23% for clinical supervisors. For both groups, most turnover was voluntary (employee-initiated) (Eby, Burk, & Maher, 2010).

Minimizing avoidable turnover and retaining workers is an important workforce development component in delivering high quality mental health and addiction services. High staff turnover, combined with recruitment difficulties, can compromise the continuity and quality of care. Staff turnover can also be a major impediment to the implementation of evidence-based practices (Woltmann et al., 2008). It additionally reduces the capacity for service provision to be carried out by more experienced workers who have a higher level of job mastery and require less direct supervision.

Other workforce development implications of high staff turnover include:

- Reducing the available pool of mentors and supervisors.
- Organizations receiving less return-on-investment for formal and informal training of workers.
- Disrupting the development of cohesive work groups and teams (Mental Health Workforce Advisory Committee, 2011).

Enhancing Recruitment and Retention

Measures which can be implemented to enhance recruitment of suitable staff into mental health and addiction services include:

1. Reducing the stigma associated with working with the client groups.
2. Promoting the sectors as careers of choice.
3. Increasing opportunities for training placements.

4. Better defining career pathways.
5. Developing clear qualifications.
6. Enhancing early career exposure to mental health and substance use problems.
7. Increasing relevant teaching in undergraduate clinical and public health/policy courses (Intergovernmental Committee on Drugs, 2014).

A literature review examining factors that may assist in increasing retention in addiction services identified eight strategies with strong empirical support:

1. Maintaining good supervisor-worker relationships.
2. Providing professional development opportunities.
3. Providing challenging and varied work.
4. Ensuring adequate clinical supervision.
5. Offering rewards and recognition for good work.
6. Supporting workers' capacity to balance work and family life.
7. Providing new or potential workers with realistic work expectations in regard to promotional and professional development opportunities and career mobility.
8. Conducting exit interviews to identify organizational issues or problems (Duraisingam, 2005b).

A systems approach to workforce development has the potential to enhance capacity substantially in the addiction and mental health sectors. The focus of this chapter now turns to more proximal concerns of knowledge dissemination, innovation, knowledge generation, and information transfer, learning models and theories, and emerging use of technology.

PART 3: INNOVATION DISSEMINATION

One of the most important workforce development challenges confronting the mental health and addiction fields is the dissemination of research findings and the implementation of interventions and policies with proven efficacy (Gotham, 2006; Grimshaw & Eccles, 2004). Effective innovation dissemination requires the synthesis and dissemination of research findings, and an understanding and application of implementation science. It entails widespread acceptance that the innovation will optimize patient/client outcomes, while reducing the risk of unnecessary or harmful treatment (Buchan, Sewell, & Sweet, 2004).

Implementation science is in its infancy and its application to mental health-related practice is relatively embryonic (Tansella & Thornicroft, 2009). Nevertheless, there is an emerging literature to inform innovation implementation in this area (Brooks, Pilgrim, & Rogers, 2011; Chorpita & Regan, 2009; McHugh & Barlow, 2010; Powell et al., 2012; Proctor et al., 2009; Roche, 2009; Roche & Pidd, 2010; Roche & Duffield, 2007; Tansella & Thornicroft, 2009).

The problem of innovation dissemination in healthcare is not new. Research from the U.S. and the Netherlands estimates that 30-40% of medical treatment does not accord with current evidence and 20-25% of medical treatment is unnecessary or potentially harmful (Grimshaw & Eccles, 2004).

Ineffective innovation dissemination can contribute to large variations in clinical practice. For example, in Australia in 2013-14 there was a 75-fold difference in the rate of prescribing of attention deficit hyperactivity disorder medicines between regions with the highest and lowest rates of prescribing (Australian Commission on Safety and Quality in Health Care and National Health Performance Authority, 2015).

Barriers to Innovation Implementation

Ideally, service provision and policy should be informed by the best available evidence (Davis et al., 2003). However, multiple and complex barriers often exist to dissemination and implementation of best, or even good, practice (Uchtenhagen, Stamm, Huber, & Vuille, 2008). There is also a lack of information about strategies to promote effective and efficient innovation implementation.

Historically, implementation strategies largely focused on the distribution of paper-based manuals describing best practice guidelines (Grimshaw, Eccles, Walker, & Thomas, 2002). This approach rarely included complementary implementation resources and activities. Other strategies employed to improve the implementation of research findings have included:

- Continual professional development (Davis et al., 2003).
- Systematic reviews of research findings (Grimshaw et al., 2002).
- Implementing behavior change interventions targeting a particular practice (Michie et al., 2005).

However, such approaches rarely facilitate the real-world application of innovative, research-based practice (Metz, Blase, & Bowie, 2007). In addition, many mental health and addiction workers have not been trained to critically appraise the expanding research literature and are unlikely to be well enough resourced, or to have sufficient time, to undertake such intensive endeavors.

Grimshaw, Eccles, Lavis, Hill, and Squires (2012) summarized the findings of two Cochrane reviews that examined approaches to closing the gap between research and practice. Innovation was more likely to be successful if the strategies employed were informed by an assessment of the likely barriers and facilitators (Grimshaw et al., 2012). Multiple barriers may impede access to best practice knowledge and skills. These may include workers' low expectations of positive outcomes, lack of motivation to change, lack of confidence, skills, and resources, and lack of reinforcement for implementation (Gotham, 2006; Grol & Wensing, 2004).

Attitudinal and motivational barriers may also exist. Some workers may lack sufficient role adequacy or role legitimacy to provide mental health or addiction-related services. That is, they may not feel capable of providing services to these client groups, or do not see it is as a legitimate part of their work role (Anderson et al., 2004; Silins, Conigrave, Rakvin, Dobbins, & Curry, 2007; Skinner, Roche, Freeman, & Addy, 2005). For others, there may be a question of "deservingness", that is, whether they consider the individuals with mental health or addiction problems to be deserving of assistance (Skinner, Feather, Freeman, & Roche, 2007). The array of potential barriers can result in a failure to translate evidence into practice (Davis et al., 2003; Glasgow, Lichtenstein, & Marcus, 2003; Michie et al., 2005), and overcoming them requires a complex, nuanced, and systems-based approach (Michie et al., 2005).

What Works in Innovation Dissemination in Health Care?

Numerous theories and models pertaining to effective innovation dissemination have been developed. Findings from a systematic review of innovation, dissemination, and implementation theories and models with applicability to the addictions sector (Bywood, Lunnay, & Roche, 2008) are summarized in Table 5. Many of these theories and models are also highly relevant to the mental health sector.

Table 5. Theories and models with the greatest potential for use in the dissemination and implementation of innovations in addictions treatment

Theory/Model	Key Features
Operant conditioning	Behaviors with positive consequences for an individual are more likely to be strengthened, whereas those with negative or unpleasant consequences will diminish (Reynolds, 1975).
Social learning/ Cognitive learning theory	Knowledge acquisition can be directly related to observing others within the context of social interactions, experiences, and outside media influences.
Theory of planned behavior	Behavior is determined by beliefs about: the consequences of the behavior; the expectations of others; and the presence of facilitators or barriers (Ajzen, 1991).
Stages of change theories	The transtheoretical model (Prochaska & DiClemente, 1986) and the precaution- adoption process model (Riemsma et al., 2002)
PRECEDE-PROCEED model	A planning model that integrates theoretical constructs for designing a situation-specific intervention (Green & Kreuter, 1999).
Social marketing	Using commercial marketing techniques to influence a target population to voluntarily change their behavior.
Organizational development	Focusses on effective teamwork, with evidence supporting empowerment, communication and flexibility in successful organizational change. (Rhydderch et al., 2004)
Social worlds theory	Based on negotiation and renegotiation between two or more social worlds to implement change.
Organizational readiness for change	Integrating a number of different concepts into a model for improving practice in the substance use treatment area (Simpson & Flynn, 2007).
Adult learning theory	See below
Elaboration likelihood model	Based on the assumption that attitudes guide decisions and behaviors (Petty & Cacioppo, 1986).
Self-determination theory	A theory of motivation and personality that is grounded in the concept that people are happiest and most productive when they feel that they can control their own lives (Ryan & Deci, 2000).
Awareness-to-adherence model	Explains the cognitive and behavioral steps that practitioners use to implement clinical practice guidelines (Pathman, Konrad, Freed, Freeman, & Koch, 1996).
Diffusion of innovations	Describes the process by which an innovation is communicated through certain channels over time to members of a social system (Rogers, 1995).
Commitment-to-change model	A planning model for enabling and measuring behavioral change (Mazmanian, Johnson, Zhang, Boothby, & Yeatts, 2001).
Systems theory	Focuses on the interrelatedness of the different parts of an organization/system (Forrester, 1987).
Complexity theory	Focuses on the non-linear dynamics of adaptive systems such as health practices (Greenhalgh, Robert, Macfarlane, Bate, & Kyriakidou, 2004).
Sticky knowledge	Suggests that many of the difficulties involved in implementing innovations into practice in organizations occur because knowledge is sticky and difficult to move (Elwyn, Taubert, & Kowalczuk, 2007).
Community organisation and participatory models	Involves a process of helping a group to identify common problems, gather resources and develop and implement strategies to achieve specific mutual goals (Rimer & Glanz, 2005).

Source: Bywood et al., 2008

Bywood et al. (2008) also identified four strategies that were effective in changing the behavior of individual healthcare professionals, namely:

- Educational meetings.
- Educational outreach.
- Prompts and reminders.
- Audit and feedback.

However, Bywood et al. (2008) noted that even if staff were aware of the need to change and accepted that an innovation would fulfil this need, the organizational culture may moderate the effectiveness of strategies used to facilitate uptake. The successful uptake of innovations may be influenced by the characteristics of dissemination strategies and contextual factors that may aid or inhibit the implementation process.

While treating the available evidence with caution, Bywood et al. (2008) concluded that the most successful implementation strategies include the features as outlined in Table 6.

In summary, while there is still much to learn about implementation science, the available evidence highlights the importance of adopting a systems approach to innovation dissemination, rather than simple, one-off training approaches. Achieving practice and organizational change however is not a fast process. The successful implementation of evidence-based practices has been found to typically take two to four years (Metz et al., 2007).

Effective Training

Finally, we turn attention to the issue of training. Rather than being the focal point of workforce development, it is posited here to be a later stage, downstream consideration. That is, training only has potential to be effective when applied in the context of the broader issues addressed above.

There are numerous effective training approaches that have been identified, including:

- Academic detailing.
- Inter-professional education.
- Problem-based learning.
- Coaching.
- Reminders and guidelines.
- Self-regulated learning (Lyon et al., 2011).

Table 6. Approaches to enhance the uptake of innovation among health professionals

Issue	Recommended Approach
Characteristics of messages	• Give clear and succinct messages, providing accurate, evidence-based information • Use focused learning objectives that require small practical changes • Use an interactive format that is appealing, persuasive and encourages participation • Use tailored information that is personalized, modified to the local setting, and relevant to practitioner and client needs • Use reinforced messages, with additional materials and support • Sustain the messages over a long period • Have a reliable and credible information source
Structural factors	• Have clear identification of roles and activities • Involve systems or procedures that are accessible and easy to use, with little effort required to comply • Include an assessment of, and focus on, barriers to change • Address change at multiple levels, including the individual practitioner behavior, organizational structure and culture, and health system policy • Involve organizational changes that require practitioners to respond or take action (e.g., automatic prompts and obligatory responses)

Source: Bywood et al., 2008

These approaches stand in contrast to the lack of evidence supporting single-exposure training models that have been described as "train and hope" (Stokes & Baer, 1977) or the simple provision of information (Grimshaw et al., 2001). Evidence-based training also incorporates adult learning theory (Knowles, 1984) as one of the fundamental theoretical bases for innovation dissemination in health care. Adult learning theory is based on five assumptions as described below about how adults learn and their attitude towards, and motivation for, learning.

1. Adults are independent and self-directing.
2. They have accumulated a great deal of experience, which is a rich resource for learning.
3. They value learning that integrates with the demands of their everyday life.
4. They are more interested in immediate, problem-centered approaches than in subject-centered ones.
5. They are more motivated to learn by internal drives than by external ones (Knowles, 1984).

The Impact of Technology

Into the future, both training and service provision will be immeasurably enhanced and assisted through technological advances and their day-to-day utilization. While e-health has been well established and its efficacy continually reviewed (Meurk, Leung, Hall, Head, & Whiteford, 2016), the emergence of m-health, or mobile health, will also transform training and service delivery (Ben-Zeev et al., 2014). M-health involves the use of mobile technologies such as mobile phones to support public health and clinical care (Kahn, Yang, & Kahn, 2010). It has been flagged as holding particular scope to support Asia-Pacific countries. M-health programs could improve mental health literacy, provide greater access to mental health services, extend community-based outreach and engagement, support self-management of illness, and regulate medication distribution. They may also help to reduce stigma and discrimination commonly encountered in relation to mental health and addiction problems. However, potential barriers and limitations of m-Health for mental health, including funding, language and literacy barriers, power supply considerations, data security, and privacy issues need to be addressed. These issues form part of the current and emerging workforce development frontiers to be tackled.

WHERE TO FROM HERE?

The theoretical frameworks and conceptual models detailed in this Chapter provide some indications of the future direction of workforce development for the mental health and addiction workforces. In summary, key issues relevant to current and future workforce development initiatives are outlined below.

1. Workforce development processes should be informed by systems thinking and incorporate consideration of:
    a. The extent and nature of services to be provided.
    b. Factors that will impact service provision patterns into the future.
    c. Anticipated levels and characteristics of treatment and other required interventions.
    d. How the various treatment systems will mesh together to provide those services.
    e. The key strategic skills and knowledge required by the workforce.

2. Workforce development at organization, sector, and systems levels should be based on comprehensive workforce planning.
    a. A detailed understanding of the existing workforce (demographics, skills, future employment, intentions etc.) is required, as well as the extent and nature of workers in the pipeline. These factors need to be matched with the best available estimates of treatment demand.
3. Once the desired characteristics of the workforce have been determined, a gap analysis is required to determine what work needs to be undertaken to attain the requisite workforce profile.
    a. Inherent in this process is an examination of barriers and facilitators to achieving the required outcomes as identified in the gap analysis.
4. Evidence-based activities aimed at recruitment and retention and enhancing and maintaining the well-being of the mental health and addiction workforces are essential.
    a. There are three aspects to this:
        i. In an era of increased global competition for health workers, organizations which do not focus on the well-being of workers are likely to experience high levels of staff turnover
        ii. The mental health and addiction sectors are particularly vulnerable to problems such as stress, burnout, and compassion fatigue. Consequently, greater efforts need to be made to protect the well-being of their workforces.
        iii. Organizational performance and client outcomes are highly dependent on worker well-being.
5. Processes of innovation dissemination should be based on the best available evidence.

This is essential to ensure that the best possible use is made of workforce development resources. The evidence concerning effective innovation dissemination strategies is not strong. Nevertheless, there is sufficient evidence regarding effective approaches to innovation dissemination, as well as the structural measures that are necessary to support it, to enhance practice in this area.

There is still much to be learned about effective workforce development in general, and innovation dissemination in particular, in the mental health and addictions workforces. There is ample scope for more research examining the skills and demographics of these workforces. Also required are evaluations of the implementation of workforce development and innovation dissemination strategies.

REFERENCES

Ajzen, I. (1991). The theory of planned behavior. *Organizational Behavior and Human Decision Processes*, *50*(2), 179–211. doi:10.1016/0749-5978(91)90020-T

American Psychiatric Association. (2013). *Diagnostic and statistical manual of mental disorders: DSM-5*. Washington, DC: American Psychiatric Association.

Anderson, P., Kaner, E., Wutzke, S., Funk, M., Heather, N., Wensing, M., & Pas, L. et al. (2004). Attitudes and managing alcohol problems in general practice: An interaction analysis based on findings from a WHO collaborative study. *Alcohol and Alcoholism*, *39*(4), 351–356. doi:10.1093/alcalc/agh072 PMID:15208170

Aronson, D. (1996). *Overview of systems thinking*. Retrieved from http://resources21.org/cl/files/project264_5674/OverviewSTarticle.pdf

Asante, A., & Hall, J. J. (2011). *A review of health leadership and management capacity in Papua New Guinea*. Sydney, Australia: Human Resources for Health Knowledge Hub, University of NSW.

Australian Commission on Safety and Quality in Health Care. (2015). Australian atlas of healthcare variation. Sydney, Australia: Australian Commission on Safety and Quality in Health Care Australian Government.

Baker, A., & Roche, A. (2002). Editorial: From training to work-force development: A large and important conceptual leap. *Drug and Alcohol Review*, *21*(3), 205–207. doi:10.1080/0959523021000002642 PMID:12270069

Ben-Zeev, D., Schueller, S., Begale, M., Duffecy, J., Kane, J., & Mohr, D. (2014). Strategies for mHealth research: Lessons from 3 mobile intervention studies. *Administration and Policy in Mental Health and Mental Health Services Research*, *42*(2), 157–167. doi:10.1007/s10488-014-0556-2 PMID:24824311

Bennett, J., Lehman, W., & Forst, J. (1999). Change, transfer climate, and customer orientation: A contextual model and analysis of change driven training. *Group & Organization Management*, *24*(2), 188–216. doi:10.1177/1059601199242004

Blume, B., Ford, J., Baldwin, T., & Huang, J. (2010). Transfer of training: A meta analytic review. *Journal of Management*, *36*(4), 1065–1105. doi:10.1177/0149206309352880

Bramwell, A. (2011). *Training policy for the 21st Century. In Decentralization and workforce development programs for unemployed working-age adults in Canada*. Toronto, Canada: Mowat Centre for Policy Innovation.

Briggs, L. (2012). *Tackling wicked problems: A public policy perspective*. Retrieved from http://www.apsc.gov.au/publications-and-media/archive/publications-archive/tackling-wicked-problems

Broyles, L., Binswanger, I., Jenkins, J., Finnell, D., Faseru, B., Cavaiola, A., & Gordon, A. et al. (2014). Confronting inadvertent stigma and pejorative language in addiction scholarship: A recognition and response. *Substance Abuse*, *35*(3), 217–221. doi:10.1080/08897077.2014.930372 PMID:24911031

Bruckner, T., Scheffler, R., Shen, G., Yoon, J., Chisholm, D., Morris, J., & Saxena, S. et al. (2011). The mental health workforce gap in low-and middle-income countries: A needs-based approach. *Bulletin of the World Health Organization*, *89*(3), 184–194. doi:10.2471/BLT.10.082784 PMID:21379414

Buchan, H., Sewell, J., & Sweet, M. (2004). Translating evidence into practice. *The Medical Journal of Australia*, *180*(6Suppl), S43. PMID:15012577

Bunch, K. (2007). Training failure as a consequence of organizational culture. *Human Resource Development Review*, *6*(2), 142–163. doi:10.1177/1534484307299273

Bywood, P., Lunnay, B., & Roche, A. (2008a). *Effective dissemination: A systematic review of implementation strategies for the AOD field*. Adelaide, Australia: National Centre for Education and Training on Addiction, Flinders University.

Bywood, P., Lunnay, B., & Roche, A. (2008b). *Effective dissemination. An examination of the costs of implementation strategies for the AOD field.* Adelaide, Australia: National Centre for Education and Training on Addiction, Flinders University.

Callister, P., Badkar, J., & Didham, R. (2011). Globalisation, localisation and implications of a transforming nursing workforce in New Zealand: Opportunities and challenges. *Nursing Inquiry, 18*(3), 205–215. doi:10.1111/j.1440-1800.2011.00528.x PMID:21790871

Campbell, J., Dussault, G., Buchan, J., Pozo-Martin, F., Guerra Arias, M., Leone, C., & Cometto, G. (2013). *A universal truth: No health without a workforce.* Geneva, Switzerland: World Health Organization.

Chan, W., Lam, L., & Chen, E. (2015). Hong Kong: Recent development of mental health services. *Advances in Psychiatric Treatment, 21*(1), 71–72. doi:10.1192/apt.bp.113.012278

Clemens, S., & Ritter, A. (2008). Estimating the prevalence of individuals likely to use publicly funded alcohol treatment services: An indirect estimation technique. *Drug and Alcohol Review, 27*(5), 504–508. doi:10.1080/09595230802093752 PMID:18696297

Connell, J. (2010). *Migration of health workers in the Asia Pacific region.* Sydney, Australia: Human Resources for Health Knowledge Hub, University of New South Wales.

Conway, J., McMillan, M., & Becker, J. (2006). Implementing workforce development in health care: A conceptual framework to guide and evaluate health service reform. *Human Resource Development International, 9*(1), 129–139. doi:10.1080/13678860500522975

Cotten, A. (2007). *Seven steps of effective workforce planning.* Washington, DC: IBM Center for the Business of Government.

Davis, D., Davis, M., Jadad, A., Perrier, L., Rath, D., Ryan, D., & Wowk, M. et al. (2003). The case for knowledge translation: Shortening the journey from evidence to effect. *British Medical Journal, 327*(7405), 33–35. doi:10.1136/bmj.327.7405.33 PMID:12842955

Dewit, D., & Rush, B. (1996). Assessing the need for substance abuse services: A critical review of needs assessment models. *Evaluation and Program Planning, 19*(1), 41–64. doi:10.1016/0149-7189(95)00039-9

Duraisingam, V. (2005a). Recruitment and Selection. In N. Skinner, A.M. Roche, J. O'Connor, Y. Pollard, & C. Todd (Eds.), Workforce development TIPS (theory into practice strategies): A resource kit for the alcohol and other drugs field. Adelaide, Australia: National Centre for Education and Training on Addiction (NCETA), Flinders University.

Duraisingam, V. (2005b). Retention. In N. Skinner, A.M. Roche, J. O'Connor, Y. Pollard, & C. Todd (Eds.), Workforce development TIPS (theory into practice strategies): A resource kit for the alcohol and other drugs field. Adelaide, Australia: National Centre for Education and Training on Addiction (NCETA), Flinders University.

Eby, L., Burk, H., & Maher, C. (2010). How serious of a problem is staff turnover in substance abuse treatment? A longitudinal study of actual turnover. *Journal of Substance Abuse Treatment, 39*(3), 264–271. doi:10.1016/j.jsat.2010.06.009 PMID:20675097

Elwyn, G., Taubert, M., & Kowalczuk, J. (2007). Sticky knowledge: A possible model for investigating implementation in healthcare contexts. *Implementation Science; 2*(1), 44. doi:10.1186/1748-5908-2-44 PMID:18096040

Ergo, A., Eichler, R., Koblinsky, M., & Shah, N. (2011). *Strengthening health systems to improve maternal neonatal and child health outcomes: A framework.* Washington, DC: Maternal and Child Health Integrated Progam.

Evans, S., Huxley, P., Gately, C., Webber, M., Mears, A., Pajak, S., & Katona, C. et al. (2006). Mental health, burnout and job satisfaction among mental health social workers in England and Wales. *The British Journal of Psychiatry, 188*(1), 75–80. doi:10.1192/bjp.188.1.75 PMID:16388074

Ewer, P., Teesson, M., Sannibale, C., Roche, A. M., & Mills, K. (2015). The prevalence and correlates of secondary traumatic stress among alcohol and other drug workers in Australia. *Drug and Alcohol Review, 34*(3), 252–258. doi:10.1111/dar.12204 PMID:25355060

Forrester, J. (1987). Lessons from system dynamics modeling. *System Dynamics Review, 3*(2), 136–149. doi:10.1002/sdr.4260030205

Glasgow, R., Lichtenstein, E., & Marcus, A. (2003). Why dont we see more translation of health promotion research to practice? Rethinking the efficacy-to-effectiveness transition. *American Journal of Public Health, 93*(8), 1261–1267. doi:10.2105/AJPH.93.8.1261 PMID:12893608

Gotham, H. (2006). Advancing the implementation of evidence-based practices into clinical practice: How do we get there from here? *Professional Psychology, Research and Practice, 37*(6), 606–613. doi:10.1037/0735-7028.37.6.606

Green, L., & Kreuter, M. (1999). *The precede–proceed model. Health promotion planning: An educational approach* (4th ed.). New York: McGraw-Hill.

Greenhalgh, T., Robert, G., Macfarlane, F., Bate, P., & Kyriakidou, O. (2004). Diffusion of innovations in service organizations: Systematic review and recommendations. *The Milbank Quarterly, 82*(4), 581–629. doi:10.1111/j.0887-378X.2004.00325.x PMID:15595944

Grimshaw, J., & Eccles, M. (2004). Is evidence-based implementation of evidence-based care possible? *The Medical Journal of Australia, 180*(6), S50. PMID:15012580

Grimshaw, J., Eccles, M., Lavis, J., Hill, S., & Squires, J. (2012). Knowledge translation of research findings. *Implementation Science; 7*(50). PMID:22651257

Grimshaw, J., Eccles, M., Walker, A., & Thomas, R. (2002). Changing physicians behavior: What works and thoughts on getting more things to work. *The Journal of Continuing Education in the Health Professions, 22*(4), 237–243. doi:10.1002/chp.1340220408 PMID:12613059

Grimshaw, J., Shirran, L., Thomas, R., Mowatt, G., Fraser, C., Bero, L., & O'Brien, M. et al. (2001). Changing provider behavior: An overview of systematic reviews of interventions. *Medical Care*, II2–II45. PMID:11583120

Grol, R., & Wensing, M. (2004). What drives change? Barriers to and incentives for achieving evidence-based practice. *The Medical Journal of Australia, 180*(6Suppl), S57. PMID:15012583

Harris, M., Diminic, S., Burgess, P., Carstensen, G., Stewart, G., Pirkis, J., & Whiteford, H. (2014). Understanding service demand for mental health among Australians aged 16 to 64 years according to their possible need for treatment. *The Australian and New Zealand Journal of Psychiatry*, 1–14. PMID:24810872

Health Workforce Australia. (2012). *Leadership for the sustainability of the health system*. Adelaide: Health Workforce Australia.

Helzer, J., Bucholz, K., & Gossop, M. (2007). Dimensional option for the diagnosis of substance dependence in DSM-V. *International Journal of Methods in Psychiatric Research, 16*(S1), S24–S33. doi:10.1002/mpr.210 PMID:17623392

Hemingway, S., Clifton, A., & Edward, K.-L. (2016). The future of mental health nursing education in the United Kingdom: Reflections on the Australian and New Zealand experience. *Journal of Psychiatric and Mental Health Nursing, 23*(5), 331–337. doi:10.1111/jpm.12312 PMID:27307264

Hoge, M., Stuart, G., Morris, J., Flaherty, M., Paris, M., & Goplerud, E. (2013). Mental health and addiction workforce development: Federal leadership is needed to address the growing crisis. *Health Affairs, 32*(11), 2005–2012. doi:10.1377/hlthaff.2013.0541 PMID:24191093

Holland, B. (2015). A workforce development systems model for unemployed job seekers. *Journal of Adult and Continuing Education, 21*(2), 55–76.

Hu, W., McColl, G., Thistlethwaite, J., Schuwirth, L., & Wilkinson, T. (2013). Where is the next generation of medical educators. *The Medical Journal of Australia, 188*(1), 8–9. doi:10.5694/mja12.11654 PMID:23330743

Huntington, A., Bidewell, J., Gilmour, J., Chang, E., Daly, J., Wilson, H., & Lambert, C. et al. (2008). The relationship between workplace stress, coping strategies and health status in New Zealand nurses. *Journal of Occupational Health and Safety, 24*, 131–141.

Intergovernmental Committee on Drugs. (2014). *National alcohol and other drug workforce development strategy 2015–2018*. Canberra, Australia: Intergovernmental Committee on Drugs.

Jacobs, R., & Hawley, J. (2009). The emergence of 'workforce development': Definition, conceptual boundaries and implications. In R. MacLean & D. Wilson (Eds.), *International handbook of education for the changing world of work* (pp. 2537–2552). New York: Springer. doi:10.1007/978-1-4020-5281-1_167

Kahn, J., Yang, J., & Kahn, J. (2010). Mobilehealth needs and opportunities in developing countries. *Health Affairs, 29*(2), 252–258. doi:10.1377/hlthaff.2009.0965 PMID:20348069

Knowles, M. (1984). *Andragogy in action: Applying modern principles of adult learning*. San Francisco: Jossey-Bass.

KPMG. (2012). *Value walks: Successful habits for improving workforce motivation and productivity*. Zurich: KPMG.

Liu, J., Ma, H., He, Y., Xie, B., Xu, Y., Tang, H., & Zhang, M. et al. (2011). Mental health system in China: History, recent service reform and future challenges. *World Psychiatry; Official Journal of the World Psychiatric Association (WPA), 10*(3), 210–216. doi:10.1002/j.2051-5545.2011.tb00059.x PMID:21991281

Lyon, A., Stirman, S. W., Kerns, S., & Bruns, E. (2011). Developing the mental health workforce: Review and application of training approaches from multiple disciplines. *Administration and Policy in Mental Health and Mental Health Services Research, 38*(4), 238–253. doi:10.1007/s10488-010-0331-y PMID:21190075

Mazmanian, P., Johnson, R., Zhang, A., Boothby, J., & Yeatts, E. (2001). Effects of a signature on rates of change: A randomized controlled trial involving continuing education and the commitment-to-change model. *Academic Medicine, 76*(6), 642–646. doi:10.1097/00001888-200106000-00018 PMID:11401812

McKinnon, B., & Cross, W. (2008). Occupational violence and assault in mental health nursing: A scoping project for a Victorian Mental Health Service. *International Journal of Mental Health Nursing, 17*(1), 9–17. doi:10.1111/j.1447-0349.2007.00499.x PMID:18211399

Meadows, D., & Wright, D. (2008). *Thinking in systems: A primer*. White River Junction, VT: Chelsea Green Publishing.

Meadows, G., Enticott, J., Inder, B., Russell, G., & Gurr, R. (2015). Better access to mental health care and the failure of the Medicare principle of universality. *The Medical Journal of Australia, 202*(4), 190–194. doi:10.5694/mja14.00330 PMID:25716601

Mental Health Commission. (2011). *National indicators 2011: Measuring mental health and addiction*. Wellington, New Zealand: Mental Health Commission.

Mental Health Workforce Advisory Committee. (2011). *National mental health workforce strategy*. Melbourne, Australia: Mental Health Workforce Advisory Committee.

Metz, A., Blase, K., & Bowie, L. (2007). *Implementing evidence-based practices: Six "drivers" of success. Child Trends: Research-to-Results Brief.* Washington, DC: The Atlantic Philanthropies.

Meurk, C., Leung, J., Hall, W., Head, B., & Whiteford, H. (2016). Establishing and governing e-mental health care in Australia: A systematic review of challenges and a call for policy-focussed research. *Journal of Medical Internet Research, 18*(1), e10. doi:10.2196/jmir.4827 PMID:26764181

Michie, S., Johnston, M., Abraham, C., Lawton, R., Parker, D., & Walker, A. (2005). Making psychological theory useful for implementing evidence based practice: A consensus approach. *Quality & Safety in Health Care, 14*(1), 26–33. doi:10.1136/qshc.2004.011155 PMID:15692000

Minas, H. (2012). The Centre for International Mental Health approach to mental health system development. *Harvard Review of Psychiatry, 20*(1), 37–46. doi:10.3109/10673229.2012.649090 PMID:22335181

Mojtabai, R., & Crum, R. (2013). Perceived unmet need for alcohol and drug use treatments and future use of services: Results from a longitudinal study. *Drug and Alcohol Dependence, 127*(1), 59–64. doi:10.1016/j.drugalcdep.2012.06.012 PMID:22770461

National Mental Health Commission. (2014). *The national review of mental health programmes and services*. Sydney, Australia: National Mental Health Commission.

Ng, C., Herrman, H., Chiu, E., & Singh, B. (2009). Community mental health care in the Asia-Pacific region: Using current best-practice models to inform future policy. *World Psychiatry; Official Journal of the World Psychiatric Association (WPA)*, *8*(1), 49–55. doi:10.1002/j.2051-5545.2009.tb00211.x PMID:19293961

Paris, M., & Hoge, M. (2010). Burnout in the mental health workforce: A review. *The Journal of Behavioral Health Services & Research*, *37*(4), 519–528. doi:10.1007/s11414-009-9202-2 PMID:20013066

Pathman, D., Konrad, T., Freed, G., Freeman, V., & Koch, G. (1996). The awareness-to-adherence model of the steps to clinical guideline compliance: The case of pediatric vaccine recommendations. *Medical Care*, *34*(9), 873–889. doi:10.1097/00005650-199609000-00002 PMID:8792778

Peters, D. (2014). The application of systems thinking in health: Why use systems thinking? *Health Research Policy and Systems*, *12*(1), 51. doi:10.1186/1478-4505-12-51 PMID:25160707

Petty, R., & Cacioppo, J. (1986). *The elaboration likelihood model of persuasion*. New York: Springer.

Prochaska, J., & DiClemente, C. (1986). *Toward a comprehensive model of change*. New York: Springer. doi:10.1007/978-1-4613-2191-0_1

Public Service Commission. (2013). *Workforce planning explained*. Retrieved from http://www.apsc.gov.au/publications-and-media/current-publications/workforce-planning-guide/workforce-planning-explained

Reynolds, G. (1975). *A primer of operant conditioning*. Oxford, UK: Scott Foresman & Co.

Rhydderch, M., Elwyn, G., Marshall, M., & Grol, R. (2004). Organizational change theory and the use of indicators in general practice. *Quality & Safety in Health Care*, *13*(3), 213–217. doi:10.1136/qshc.2003.006536 PMID:15175493

Riemsma, R., Pattenden, J., Bridle, C., Sowden, A., Mather, L., Watt, I., & Walker, A. (2002). A systematic review of the effectiveness of interventions based on a stages-of-change approach to promote individual behaviour change in health care settings. *Health Technology Assessment*, *6*(24), 1–242. doi:10.3310/hta6240 PMID:12433313

Rimer, B., & Glanz, K. (2005). *Theory at a glance: A guide for health promotion practice*. Bethesda, MD: National Institutes of Health.

Ritter, A., Berends, L., Chalmers, J., Hull, P., Lancaster, K., & Gomez, M. (2014). *New Horizons: The review of alcohol and other drug treatment services in Australia*. Sydney, Australia: Drug Policy Modelling Program, National Drug and Alcohol Research Centre, University of NSW.

Roche, A., Todd, C., & OConnor, J. (2007). Clinical supervision in the alcohol and other drugs field: An imperative or an option? *Drug and Alcohol Review*, *26*(3), 241–249. doi:10.1080/09595230701247780 PMID:17454013

Roche, A. M. (2002). *Workforce development: Our national dilemma. In Catching clouds: Exploring diversity in workforce development in the alcohol and other drugs field*. Adelaide, Australia: National Centre for Education and Training on Addiction, Flinders University.

Roche, A. M. (2013). Looking to the future: The challenges ahead. *Substance*, *11*(1), 17.

Roche, A. M., Adams, V., & White, M. (2014). Up in smoke: Cannabis content in alcohol and other drug qualifications. *Drugs Education Prevention & Policy*, *21*(2), 140–146. doi:10.3109/09687637.2013.819567

Roche, A. M., Duraisingam, V., Trifonoff, A., Battams, S., Freeman, T., Tovell, A., & Bates, N. et al. (2013). Sharing stories: Indigenous alcohol and other drug workers' well-being, stress and burnout. *Drug and Alcohol Review*, *32*(5), 527–535. PMID:23675893

Roche, A. M., & Pidd, K. (2010). *Alcohol and other drugs workforce development issues and imperatives: Setting the scene*. Adelaide, Australia: National Centre for Education and Training on Addiction, Flinders University.

Roche, A. M., Pidd, K., & Freeman, T. (2009). Achieving professional practice change: From training to workforce development. *Drug and Alcohol Review*, *28*(5), 550–557. doi:10.1111/j.1465-3362.2009.00111.x PMID:19737213

Rogers, E. (1995). Diffusion of innovations: Modifications of a model for telecommunications. *Die Diffusion von Innovationen in der Telekommunikation*, *17*, 25–38. doi:10.1007/978-3-642-79868-9_2

Rossi, A., Cetrano, G., Pertile, R., Rabbi, L., Donisi, V., Grigoletti, L., & Amaddeo, F. et al. (2012). Burnout, compassion fatigue, and compassion satisfaction among staff in community-based mental health services. *Psychiatry Research*, *200*(2), 933–938. doi:10.1016/j.psychres.2012.07.029 PMID:22951335

Rössler, W. (2012). Stress, burnout, and job dissatisfaction in mental health workers. *European Archives of Psychiatry and Clinical Neuroscience*, *262*(2), 65–69. doi:10.1007/s00406-012-0353-4 PMID:22926058

Ryan, R., & Deci, E. (2000). Self-determination theory and the facilitation of intrinsic motivation, social development, and well-being. *The American Psychologist*, *55*(1), 68–78. doi:10.1037/0003-066X.55.1.68 PMID:11392867

Senge, P. (1990). *The fifth discipline: The art and practice of the learning organization*. NSW, Australia: Random House Australia Pty Ltd.

Silins, E., Conigrave, K., Rakvin, C., Dobbins, T., & Curry, K. (2007). The influence of structured education and clinical experience on the attitudes of medical students towards substance misusers. *Drug and Alcohol Review*, *26*(2), 191–200. doi:10.1080/09595230601184661 PMID:17364855

Simpson, D., & Flynn, P. (2007). Moving innovations into treatment: A stage-based approach to program change. *Journal of Substance Abuse Treatment*, *33*(2), 111–120. doi:10.1016/j.jsat.2006.12.023 PMID:17434704

Skinner, N. (2005). Workplace support. In N. Skinner, A.M. Roche, J. O'Connor, Y. Pollard, & C. Todd (Eds.), Workforce development TIPS (theory into practice strategies): A resource kit for the alcohol and other drugs field. Adelaide, Australia: National Centre for Education and Training on Addiction (NCETA), Flinders University.

Skinner, N., Feather, N., Freeman, T., & Roche, A. M. (2007). Stigma and discrimination in health-care provision to drug users: The role of values, affect, and deservingness judgments. *Journal of Applied Social Psychology*, *37*(1), 163–186. doi:10.1111/j.0021-9029.2007.00154.x

Skinner, N., Roche, A., Freeman, T., & Addy, D. (2005). Responding to alcohol and other drug issues: The effect of role adequacy and role legitimacy on motivation and satisfaction. *Drugs Education Prevention & Policy*, *12*(6), 449–463. doi:10.1080/09687630500284281

Skinner, N., & Roche, A. M. (2005). Stress and burnout: A prevention handbook for the alcohol and other drugs workforce. Adelaide, Australia: National Centre for Education and Training on Addiction (NCETA), Flinders University.

Stokes, T., & Baer, D. (1977). An implicit technology of generalization. *Journal of Applied Behavior Analysis*, *10*(2), 349–367. doi:10.1901/jaba.1977.10-349 PMID:16795561

Substance Abuse and Mental Health Services Administration. (2013). *Report to Congress on the nation's substance abuse and mental health workforce issues*. Rockville, MD: SAMHSA.

Sunderland, A., & Findlay, L. (2013). *Perceived need for mental health care in Canada: Results from the 2012 Canadian community health survey-Mental health*. Ottawa, Canada: Statistics Canada.

Tansella, M., & Thornicroft, G. (2009). Implementation science: Understanding the translation of evidence into practice. *The British Journal of Psychiatry*, *195*(4), 283–285. doi:10.1192/bjp.bp.109.065565 PMID:19794192

Uchtenhagen, A., Stamm, R., Huber, J., & Vuille, R. (2008). A review of systems for continued education and training in the substance abuse field. *Substance Abuse*, *29*(3), 95–102. doi:10.1080/08897070802219263 PMID:19042211

Urbanoski, K., Cairney, J., Bassani, D., & Rush, B. (2008). Perceived unmet need for mental health care for Canadians with co-occurring mental and substance use disorders. *Psychiatric Services (Washington, D.C.)*, *59*(3), 283–289. doi:10.1176/ps.2008.59.3.283 PMID:18308909

Volker, R., Bernhard, B., Anna, K., Fabrizio, S., Robin, R., Jessica, P., & Franz, H. et al. (2010). Burnout, coping and job satisfaction in service staff treating opioid addicts—from Athens to Zurich. *Stress and Health*, *26*(2), 149–159. doi:10.1002/smi.1276

Woltmann, E., Whitley, R., McHugo, G., Brunette, M., Torrey, W., Coots, L., & Drake, R. et al. (2008). The role of staff turnover in the implementation of evidence-based practices in mental health care. *Psychiatric Services (Washington, D.C.)*, *59*(7), 732–737. doi:10.1176/ps.2008.59.7.732 PMID:18586989

Wood, D., & Klassen, T. (2009). Bilateral federalism and workforce development policy in Canada. *Canadian Public Administration*, *52*(2), 249–270. doi:10.1111/j.1754-7121.2009.00074.x

World Health Organization. (2007a). *Towards better leadership and management in health: report on an international consultation on strengthening leadership and management in low-income countries*. Accra, Ghana: Department for Health Policy, Development and Services Health Systems and Services WHO.

World Health Organization. (2007b). *Workers' health: global plan of action. Sixtieth world health assembly*. Geneva, Switzerland: World Health Organization.

World Health Organization. (2010). *Models and tools for health workforce planning and projections*. Geneva, Switzerland: World Health Organization.

World Health Organization. (2011). *Transformative scale up of health professional education: An effort to increase the numbers of health professionals and to strengthen their impact on population health.* Geneva, Switzerland: World Health Organization.

World Health Organization. Western Pacific Region. (2012). Human resources for health: Action Framework for the Western Pacific Region (2011–2015). Geneva, Switzerland: World Health Organization.

Yip, W., Hsiao, W., Chen, W., Hu, S., Ma, J., & Maynard, A. (2012). Early appraisal of Chinas huge and complex health-care reforms. *Lancet*, *379*(9818), 833–842. doi:10.1016/S0140-6736(11)61880-1 PMID:22386036

KEY TERMS AND DEFINITIONS

Addiction Workers: Workers whose primary role involves preventing and/or responding to alcohol and other drug problems.

Mental Health Workers: Workers whose primary role involves preventing and/or responding to mental health problems.

Systems Approach: An approach to analyzing problems and developing solutions that stresses the importance of considering the full range of factors impacting on a given issue as well as the interactive and interdependent nature of those factors.

Workforce Development: A multi-faceted approach addressing the range of factors impacting on the ability of the workforce to function with maximum effectiveness.

ENDNOTES

1 Defining addiction: Although this Chapter refers to "addiction", this term is applied here to refer to any form of problematic alcohol or other drug (AOD) use. That is, various forms of problematic AOD use can cause considerable harm to individuals or to society in general, but may not necessarily fall within the traditional definitions of addiction. For example, "binge drinking" may result in substantial concerns or harms without constituting an addiction. DSM-5 criteria for alcohol and drug use disorders substantially redefined the narrower, traditional perspective of "addiction" (American Psychiatric Association, 2013; Helzer, Bucholz, & Gossop, 2007). In addition, the term "addiction" is increasingly held to have negative and stigmatizing connotations (Broyles et al., 2014).

2 This is not to imply that changes are made without consulting workers. In organizational redesign, it is essential to tap into the knowledge of the broader workforce regarding how services can be improved. A top-down approach entails a more global view of how sectors, agencies, and organizations can work more effectively to enhance services. Only then can workforce development requirements be accurately defined and measures implemented to meet those requirements.

3 The term "wicked" in this context is used, not in the sense of evil, but an issue highly resistant to resolution. Wicked problems are difficult to clearly define and have many interdependencies and are often multi-causal. There are also often internally conflicting goals or objectives within the broader wicked problem. Attempts to address wicked problems often lead to unforeseen consequences. Wicked problems are often not stable and usually have no clear solution. Since there is no definitive, stable problem there is often no definitive solution to wicked problems (Briggs, 2012).

Section 2

International Perspectives of Workforce Development

Chapter 2
Behavioral Health Workforce Development in the United States

Michael A. Hoge
Yale School of Medicine, USA & The Annapolis Coalition, USA

Leighton Y. Huey
University of Connecticut Health Sciences Center, USA & The Annapolis Coalition, USA

Gail W. Stuart
Medical University of South Carolina, USA & The Annapolis Coalition, USA

Michal T. Flaherty
Clinical Practice & The Annapolis Coalition, USA

John A. Morris
The Annapolis Coalition, USA

Manuel Paris Jr.
Yale University School of Medicine, USA & The Annapolis Coalition, USA

ABSTRACT

Mental health and substance use conditions are among the most prominent causes of illness and disability in the U.S. Yet less than half of the individuals with these conditions receive treatment (Substance Abuse and Mental Health Services Administration [SAMHSA], 2011; Office of National Drug Control Policy [ONDCP], 2013). While there are many impediments to accessing care, the absence of a workforce that is of sufficient size and adequately trained is a significant factor (Olfson, 2016). This chapter provides an overview of the U.S. behavioral health workforce and describes seven strategic areas in which activity has been undertaken to strengthen it. The initiatives of the Annapolis Coalition on the Behavioral Health Workforce are presented to highlight these strategic areas, which include assessment and planning; competency identification and development; roles for persons in recovery and family members; integrated care and interprofessional collaboration; workforce development in substance use; diversity and cultural competency; and knowledge dissemination and adoption of best practices.

INTRODUCTION

By any measure, mental health and substance use problems and the efforts to prevent and treat them are major health issues within the U.S. Data from the federal government indicates that approximately

DOI: 10.4018/978-1-5225-1874-7.ch002

45 million adults, or 1 in 5 within the population, experience a mental health condition annually. Yet less than 40% receive care for these conditions (SAMHSA, 2011). While substance use disorders are estimated to impact 10% of the U.S. population, or approximately 23 million individuals, specialty substance abuse treatment is being offered to just 1 in 10 of those individuals with a diagnosable condition (JAMA Network Journals, 2015; ONDCP, 2013). More specifically, in the last decade alone there has been a five-fold increase in deaths from heroin and a three-fold increase in deaths from prescription opioid pain relievers, with drug overdose now the number one cause of injury-related death in the U.S. (Hedegaard, Chen, & Warner, 2015).

While there are many factors that contribute to the gap between the number of individuals in the U.S. who have behavioral health conditions and the number receiving care, workforce issues appear to play a prominent role (Olfson, 2016). Difficulties recruiting and retaining a competent workforce, achieving workforce diversity, and assuring that the workforce delivers safe and effective services have been repeated sources of concern (Hoge et al, 2013).

The authors of this chapter have been addressing these issues in their role as leaders of the Annapolis Coalition on the Behavioral Health Workforce. The Coalition emerged over a decade ago from grass roots efforts to bring attention to and find solutions for the workforce crisis in this health care sector. It is a non-profit organization whose mission is to increase access to quality behavioral health care by improving the recruitment, retention, training, and performance of the mental health and addiction workforce.

The purpose of this chapter is to provide a brief overview of the behavioral health workforce in the U.S. and the educational and health care context in which it functions. With that information as background, a series of workforce strategies are reviewed, highlighting responses to key workforce challenges. The activities of the Annapolis Coalition are used to illustrate steps that have been undertaken to address these challenges. This information is supplemented by examples of the work of other groups and organizations in the country in addressing these challenges.

As the context for this review, it is important to note that, historically, there has been a clear distinction in the U.S. between the mental health workforce and the substance use workforce. This remains largely true today, though the boundaries have begun to blur given the emphasis on ensuring that all members of the workforce are competent to assess and treat persons with co-occurring mental and substance use conditions (SAMHSA, 2009). Many of the workforce challenges and workforce development strategies are common to the mental health and substance use fields, while they differ on numerous workforce dimensions. Therefore, these two fields are addressed together and, at times, separately in the analysis that follows.

BACKGROUND

The U.S. Behavioral Health Workforce

A recent primer on the mental health workforce published by the Congressional Research Service highlighted the lack of agreement within the U.S. about the composition and size of the mental health workforce, citing different definitions and statistics offered by SAMHSA, the Health Resources and Services Administration (HRSA), and the Institute of Medicine (IOM; Heisler & Bagalman, 2015). There does appear to be agreement on a set of core specialty mental health disciplines, which includes psychiatry, psychology, clinical social work, advanced practice psychiatric nursing, and mental health counseling. Other disciplines, such as psychosocial rehabilitation, school counseling, pastoral counseling, and peer supports are also often included. Data on workforce size and composition is scattered and highly variable. The federal government addressed the need for better data by creating in 2015 the Behavioral Health Workforce Research Center (https://sph.umich.edu/bhwrc/), which has undertaken its first wave of data collection and studies.

Clinical social work appears to be the largest specialty discipline, with numbers estimated between 110,000 – 193,000. Psychology is the second largest, hovering around 100,000 nationally. Estimates range from 25,000 – 62,000 for the number of marriage and family therapists and 25,000 – 40,000 for psychiatrists. Advanced practice psychiatric nursing appears to be the smallest of the specialty disciplines, with estimates ranging from 10,000 – 20,000 (Heisler & Bagalman, 2015). Social work, marriage and family therapy, and advanced practice nursing require a minimum of a master's degree to be licensed for independent practice. Psychology generally requires a doctorate for licensed independent practice, while psychiatry requires an M.D. degree and residency training. In addition to these disciplines there are approximately 133,000 registered nurses working in psychiatric care settings, though they do not have advanced specialty training in behavioral health (HRSA, 2010).

According to data submitted in a report to Congress by SAMHSA (2013), the disciplines vary greatly by gender, with females comprising 30% of the psychiatry workforce and over 80% of social workers. The report indicated that all disciplines are much less diverse than the general U.S. population, with psychology showing the least racial (non-white) diversity and psychiatry showing the greatest. Median ages range from 42.5 years of age for social workers to 55.7 for psychiatrists, with half of all male psychiatrists over the age of 60.

Mental health workforce shortages in the country are pronounced. Over half of the counties in the U.S. that are rural do not have *any* practicing psychiatrists, psychologists, or clinical social workers, while 96% of all counties have an unmet need for mental health prescribers (SAMHSA, 2013). Recruitment challenges are significant, with frequent reports from behavioral health employers of their inability to fill open positions. Once hired, retention is the next major issue, particularly for the non-degreed direct care workers, who comprise another segment of the mental health workforce that is poorly tracked and understood. It has been estimated that these workers exceed more than 145,000 in number (Hoge et al., 2007) and have annual turnover rates as high as 70% in some treatment settings (Hoge & Paris, 2006).

Determining the size of the addiction treatment workforce has been hampered by the absence of routine data collection (SAMHSA, 2013). The most recent comprehensive review of the addiction treatment workforce was published by the Addiction Technology Transfer Center (ATTC) Network. The ATTC Network, established by SAMHSA in 1993, is a nationwide training and technical assistance structure that provides a vast array of resources for professionals related to addictions treatment and recovery services (http://nattc.org). Drawing on federal survey data, the ATTC report estimated there were approximately 76,600 substance abuse and behavioral disorder counselors in the U.S. (Ryan, Murphy, & Krom, 2012). From a new survey that it conducted, the ATTC then gathered information on the characteristics of that workforce.

The ATTC survey indicated that among the direct care staff, 67% were female, 64% where white, 25% were over the age of 50, and an estimated 29% were in recovery from substance abuse. In terms of education, 13% had a high school diploma, 19% an associate's degree or some college, 24% a bachelor's degree, 36% a master's degree, 2% a doctoral degree, and 5% fell in other categories. Fifty-four percent were licensed.

Of the respondents to the ATTC survey, 49% reported recruitment difficulties in terms of finding qualified applicants and filling open positions. The source of the recruitment challenge was attributed to numerous factors, including low compensation for employees, heavy administrative burdens within these jobs, and the stigma associated with substance abuse. Among the clinical directors responding to the survey, 68% reported barriers to providing effective training and professional development for employees. These included lack of funds for these activities and the cost of release time for employees to participate. Among the workforce that was successfully recruited, turnover rates were estimated at 18.5% in the past year (Ryan et al., 2012).

In both the mental health and substance use sectors of the behavioral health field, individuals in recovery and their family members have assumed informal and formal workforce roles. Although there are distinct differences between peer-support and family support (Center for Health Care Strategies, 2013), in this chapter "peer" is used generically to refer to peer and family support approaches. Health care providers who are not behavioral health specialists, but routinely encounter and provide services to persons with mental health and substance use conditions, are another essential part of the de facto behavioral health workforce. These segments of the workforce are discussed below in the sections on planning, workforce roles for persons in recovery and families, and integrated care.

The Educational and Health Care Context

Understanding the U.S. behavioral health workforce, its development, and its deployment requires knowledge of the fragmented and decentralized nature of the country's educational system, health care system, and health care funding mechanisms (Hoge et al., 2007). It also requires some understanding of the relatively recent efforts to transform health care delivery to focus on an integrated understanding of physical and mental health, and integrated approaches to care (Kathol, Butler, McAlpine, & Kane, 2010).

As highlighted above, the core of the behavioral health specialty workforce is comprised of multiple disciplines. These tend to act independently and, to some extent, competitively as they develop future professionals. The disciplines exert only moderate influence on the populations of focus within educational programs, allowing the faculty of each institution to select the areas of emphasis. Since there also is no centralized federal or state direction regarding the training focus within the educational pipeline, population needs are often inadequately addressed. Examples include the insufficient supply of professionals adequately prepared to serve children, older adults, residents of rural and frontier areas, persons with substance use conditions, and persons with severe mental illnesses (SAMHSA, 2013).

Organized efforts at workforce planning and development are further hindered by the fragmented and uncoordinated nature of health care delivery systems in the U.S. Responsibility for the care of individuals with severe mental illnesses was historically vested with the individual states and eventually enacted as national policy, which created a segregated public system of mental health care that exists for no other health care specialty. Much later federal action created a labyrinth of county and private non-profit community provider organizations that largely function independently.

Systems of payment for behavioral health services, which in essence fund the workforce, also have been highly fragmented and decentralized. Payments for mental health and addiction treatment services have been categorically separate from payments for other health conditions, making it difficult to train and deploy the workforce to meet the comprehensive health needs of individuals. Federal health insurance programs have prohibited payments for state operated inpatient and residential services, prompting the transfer of patients *and* the workforce that serves them to community-based ambulatory services.

The federal Medicaid program, which provides health care insurance for indigent populations, has become a major funder of behavioral health services, but was established as a state/federal partnership in which each state can offer different benefit packages to recipients. Finally, the numerous managed care organizations, which function to manage cost and quality, now authorize and pay for a large percentage of the behavioral health services delivered, giving them significant influence over which portions of the workforce can be reimbursed and for which services. In building their own workforce to manage care they also draw workers out of the available pool of direct care providers.

The passage of the Affordable Care Act in 2010 has created incentives for the delivery of integrated care and for training the workforce in integrated care models, but the full impact of this legislation remains to be determined. In the interim, efforts at workforce planning and development must continue amidst this fragmented and uncoordinated web of educational, service delivery, and health care financing structures.

WORKFORCE STRATEGIES

With this background information as context, the sections below examine seven strategies that have been adopted to strengthen the mental health and addiction workforce in the U.S.

Workforce Assessment and Planning

The breadth and depth of behavioral health workforce challenges in the U.S. are often experienced as overwhelming by policy makers, state administrators, system managers, service agency and program leaders, and educators. There are many dimensions to workforce development and the responsibility for action on selected goals or objectives is often diffuse or obscure. This has led to numerous efforts within this country to assess workforce needs and to create plans to strengthen the workforce.

SAMHSA engaged the Annapolis Coalition to develop the largest ever workforce plan for behavioral health that was national in scope and encompassed both mental health and addictions. Released in 2007 (Hoge et al., 2007; Hoge et al., 2009), the process of development involved gathering input from over 5,000 individuals, including persons in recovery and their families, direct care providers, system and service managers, educators, and policy makers. The information generated was reviewed by nine expert panels, which drafted conclusions about the existing state of the workforce and the high priority strategies for strengthening it. Those panels were organized around the following topics: children and family; consumer and family/adult mental health; older adults; cultural competencies and disparities; rural health; school-based mental health; substance abuse prevention; substance use disorders treatment; and workforce financing.

A key contribution of the resulting *Action Plan for Behavioral Health Workforce Development* was to distill the diverse range of concerns and recommendations into a set of strategic goals that could guide any effort at behavioral health workforce planning. While the initial list was focused on the specialty workforce, it has evolved into a set of nine goals, known as the Annapolis Framework, with an added emphasis on interprofessional collaboration to address behavioral health needs, including the integration of behavioral health and primary care (Hoge et al., 2013).

The nine goals, which are identified in Table 1, are organized into three general areas. The first involves broadening the concept of "workforce" to include workforce roles for individuals in recovery and their families; community groups, such as anti-drug coalitions; and primary and specialty health care providers. The second area involves more traditional workforce goals, including improved efforts at recruitment and retention; increased relevance and effectiveness of training; and development of supervisors and leaders. The third area focuses on creating structures to support the workforce, including improved financing systems and worker compensation, technical assistance on workforce development, and research and evaluation of workforce practices. Within the national *Action Plan*, each goal is accompanied by a set of detailed objectives and recommended actions to meet those objectives. The stakeholder groups responsible for taking those actions are also identified (e.g., federal government, service agencies).

The Annapolis Coalition has used this planning framework to assist numerous states, associations, and organizations in their efforts to examine and address their workforce needs. For example, the framework was used to conduct a review and generate recommendations for the Iowa Division of Mental Health and Disability Services (Morris, McFaul, Madenwald, & Hoge, 2008). The framework has proven useful in both large scale and smaller, more focused, planning initiatives.

Nationally, there have been similar plans that have examined workforce needs within the addiction workforce. The ATTC National Office has played a significant role in this area, generating two recent reports: *Understanding America's Substance Use Disorders Treatment Workforce* (Murphy & Hubbard, 2009) and *Vital Signs: Taking the Pulse of the Addiction Treatment Workforce* (Ryan et al., 2012). In mental health, a unique contribution to national level planning activities has come from the federally funded efforts to identify mental health workforce shortage areas, the most recent of which was conducted by Thomas, Ellis, Konrad, Holzer and Morrissey (2009).

In reviewing all of the assessments and plans discussed above, it is clear that progress has been made on some identified problems and recommended goals, objectives, and strategies. However, it is also clear that the actions that have been taken, whether at the federal, state, or local level, have been small in comparison to the breadth and depth of the challenges. At present, the nation has many workforce plans, with far too few robust efforts to actually address current workforce needs.

Table 1. The Annapolis Framework

Broadening the Concept of "Workforce"
Goal 1: Expand the role of individuals in recovery and their families to actively participate in and influence their own care, provide care and supports to others, and educate the workforce. Goal 2: Expand the role and capacity of communities to effectively identify their needs and promote behavioral health and wellness. Goal 3: Expand the role and capacity of all health and social service providers, through interprofessional collaboration, to meet the needs of persons with mental and substance use conditions.
Strengthening the Workforce
Goal 4: Implement systematic recruitment and retention strategies at the federal, state, and local levels. Goal 5: Increase the relevance, effectiveness, and accessibility of training and education. Goal 6: Foster the development of supervisors and leaders among all segments of the workforce.
Creating Structures to Support the Workforce
Goal 7: Establish financing systems that enable employee compensation commensurate with required education and levels of responsibility. Goal 8: Build a technical assistance infrastructure that promotes adoption of workforce best practices. Goal 9: Implement a national research and evaluation program on behavioral health workforce development.

(adapted from Hoge, Morris, Daniels, Stuart, Huey & Adams, 2007)

Competency Identification and Development

Operationally defining acceptable, competent performance is one of the most challenging and essential aspects of training healthcare providers. Requirements for competent practice in the health care system have long been established by national associations and agencies, including the Joint Commission for Accreditation of Health Care Organizations (JCAHO), which holds institutional leaders accountable for ensuring that the competency of all staff is assessed, demonstrated, maintained, and continually improved (JCAHO, 1999).

Despite these accreditation processes, the quality of health care in the U.S. and the skills of the workforce delivering it have remained major concerns among payers and the general public for some time (IOM, 2001). The impact of inadequate treatment was highlighted in a major report by the IOM titled *To Err is Human: Building a Safer Health System* (IOM, 2000). The report estimated that 98,000 Americans were dying each year due to avoidable medical errors. These concerns, which were largely focused on physicians and nurses, led medical professional organizations, such as the Accreditation Council for Graduation Medical Education, to incorporate a formal focus on competencies in their training and accreditation procedures (Andolsek, Padmore, Hauer, & Holmboe, 2015). Other professions, such as nursing, had long ago established competencies in their educational programs, but specifying and measuring the application of knowledge and skill in the practice setting remained challenging (Gurvis & Grey, 1995). These issues are even more daunting within the field of behavioral health.

In 2004, as a first step in addressing the need to strengthen competencies in mental health and substance use, the Annapolis Coalition convened a federally funded conference on *Workforce Competencies in Behavioral Health*. This meeting brought together diverse leaders to share information about the state of competency development in their disciplines and to participate in educational sessions on best practices in identifying and assessing competencies. The conference resulted in a set of consensus recommendations to guide competency efforts in the field. The complete set of proceedings from the meeting are available in a special double issue of the journal *Administration and Policy in Mental Health* (Hoge, Morris, & Paris, 2005).

Since 2009, the Annapolis Coalition has been engaged in a major effort to strengthen the competencies of non-degreed direct care workers. These workers typically receive little pre-service preparation or orientation and training for their jobs, yet provide the majority of direct care in many health care settings. With funding from the Alaska Mental Health Trust Authority and in collaboration with the Western Interstate Commission for Higher Education, the Coalition developed the *Alaska Core Competencies for Direct Care Workers in Health and Human Services* (Hoge et al., 2016). This cross sector competency set was designed for direct care workers in the mental health, substance use, developmental disabilities, and long-term senior care sectors (www.annapoliscoalition.org). To support the use of the competencies, the Coalition and its partners developed a set of assessment tools for the competencies, a comprehensive curriculum, a train-the-trainer model to teach Alaskan educators to deliver the curriculum, and a coaching toolkit for use by supervisors in reinforcing the competencies on the job. This exemplifies one of the most comprehensive efforts in the U.S. to address the competence of direct care workers and illustrates the types of tools (e.g., assessments, curricula) that are needed to support adoption of competencies.

There have been many other efforts within behavioral health to strengthen the competency-based nature of workforce development and assessment. For example, competencies were developed for psychiatric-mental health nurse practitioners (National Panel for Psychiatric Mental Health NP Competencies, 2003), as well as *Essential Psychiatric, Mental Health and Substance Use Competencies for the Registered Nurse* (American Academy of Nursing, 2012). In addition, SAMSHA has developed a number of competencies, including those related to addiction counseling, substance abuse treatment, and cultural competence (www.store.samhsa.gov).

The competencies that have likely had the broadest dissemination and impact in behavioral health in the U.S. are the *Addiction Counseling Competencies*, which were funded by the SAMHSA Center for Substance Abuse Treatment (CSAT, 2006). Developed and updated since 1998 by various organizations and committees, the *Addiction Counseling Competencies* are organized around four foundational competency categories, such as knowledge about addiction and its treatment, and eight practice categories, including clinical evaluation, treatment planning, and counseling. This competency document has had enormous influence on the training, certification, and credentialing of addiction counselors within the U.S. Anecdotal information suggests that it has seen wide use in other countries as well. The publication is freely available from the SAMHSA publications website (www.store.samhsa.gov), along with a companion document, *Competencies for Substance Abuse Treatment Clinical Supervisors* (CSAT, 2007).

Over a relatively short period of time, substantial progress has been made in this country in identifying competencies in behavioral health. However, their use remains variable in educational and training programs, so dissemination and adoption of competencies is a high priority. To achieve adoption, competency sets must be practical for use in both educational programs and service organizations. Lastly, the assessment of competencies in the workforce is still methodologically challenging and remains far from prevalent as a practice. Developing practical strategies to assess competence is the next major hurdle to enhancing worker performance in the U.S.

Workforce Roles for Persons in Recovery and Family Members

As described above, a cornerstone of the national *Action Plan* was the belief that it was essential to broaden the concept of the behavioral health workforce beyond the standard professions. The Annapolis Coalition made a strategic decision to highlight as the first goal in the plan the need to significantly expand the role of individuals in recovery and their families to participate in, ultimately direct, or accept responsibility for their own care; provide care and supports to others; and educate the workforce (Hoge et al., 2007).

The overall goal has within it five objectives, which have been promoted through diverse forums and multiple media in the decade since the release of the plan. These include: providing information and education to individuals in care or recovery and their families to enable them to fully participate in or direct their own care and to assist and support each other; developing shared decision-making skills among individuals receiving care and their families and service providers; expanding peer and family-support services; increasing the employment of individuals in recovery and family members as paid staff in provider organizations; and formally engaging persons in recovery and family members in substantive roles as educators for other members of the workforce in every provider training and education program.

These objectives clarified strategic directions for future action, building on both federal and grass roots efforts to enhance the role of consumers and families in every facet of their own care. This movement had long been active within substance use disorders treatment, but in recent years has become a significant part of treatment and services for people with mental health conditions, as well.

Building on its expertise in competency development, described elsewhere in this chapter, the Annapolis Coalition was engaged in 2013 to assist in the development of competencies for persons in recovery providing peer support. Commissioned by SAMHSA and developed by the Center for Social

Innovation (www.center4si.com) under the *Bringing Recovery Supports to Scale Technical Assistance Center Strategy* (BRSS TACS) (www.samhsa.gov/brss-tacs), the Annapolis Coalition provided technical assistance on a process that involved a literature review, an expert panel, and public comment. The result was *Core Competencies for Peer Workers in Behavioral Health Services* (BRSS TACS, 2015) containing 62 individual competencies grouped into 12 competency categories.

Examining developments nationally, the emergence of certified peer-support services as reimbursable under Medicaid has had a major impact on the rise in consumer and family driven, and consumer provided services. According to a March 2014 study, 38 states had implemented peer certification as a requirement for Medicaid reimbursement, and an additional eight states planned to do so (Kaufman, Brooks, Bellinger, Steinley-Bumgarner, & Stevens-Manser, 2014). A year later, 4 of the 8 states had moved from planning to implementation, and the remaining four were still moving forward, while the Veterans Administration had employed more than 1,000 peer specialists in its programs (Wolff, Maula, & Padron, 2015).

One of the current challenges is to specify the optimal parameters of certification for peer workers. Quality assurance systems in both private and public insurance plans generally mandate some form of certification among providers, and yet there is no national consensus on the optimal characteristics of peer certification (Hendry, Hill, & Rosenthal, 2014).

SAMHSA leadership has been concerned that many traditional providers are not sufficiently knowledgeable about and supportive of recovery-based practices. To address this issue, the agency launched the *Recovery to Practice* initiative, which provides education, training and resources on: the value of recovery-oriented approaches to behavioral health care; integrating recovery into practice across service settings; and bringing together providers and people who use services. Some of the work products of the initiative include curricula on addressing recovery for the following provider types: addiction specialists, peer specialists, psychiatric nurses, psychiatrists, psychologists, and social workers. The *Recovery to Practice* initiative maintains a website (www.samhsa.gov) and produces newsletters, webinars, and other outreach activities.

As behavioral health care in the U.S. continues to evolve, it seems likely that peer- and family-driven services will play and ever larger role in comprehensive systems of care. To the extent that this projection holds true, there will be an ever-increasing need for more robust and sophisticated methods of training and credentialing these new members of the behavioral health workforce. Similarly, there will be a growing need for traditional providers to understand recovery approaches in order to develop competency in collaborating with peers and family members in the delivery of care.

Integrated Care and Interprofessional Collaboration

As mentioned above, mental health and substance use services in the U.S. have been the only two areas of health care that are systematically separated from the general health care delivery system. In this divided structure, individuals with behavioral health conditions have most often sought help in primary or specialty medical (physical) health care settings where they have too seldom received behavioral health assessments and treatment (IOM, 2006; Manderscheid & Kathol, 2014). In fact, individuals with serious mental disorders, when compared with the general population, experience greater barriers to health care; higher incidence and prevalence of preventable physical health conditions, such as cardiorespiratory diseases, diabetes, and HIV; poorer health outcomes; and higher mortality rates (Croft & Parish,

2013; Jones et al., 2004; Kathol et al., 2010; Unutzer, Schoenbaum, Druss, & Katon, 2006). Research suggests that individuals with serious mental health conditions die on average 25 years younger than peers without such conditions (Parks, Svendsen, Singer, & Foti, 2006).

Even greater medical, societal, and personal costs are reported for substance use. Personal life expectancy aside, in America today drug overdose has become the leading cause of accidental death, with 47,055 such deaths in 2014 (Centers for Disease Control and Prevention, 2015). One in 14 hospital stays in America today – about 2.3 million annually – is related to substance use (Owens, Myers, Elixhauser, & Brach, 2007). Substance use is now connected to most major health illnesses (e.g., 30% of cancer deaths, 40% of debilitating illnesses, 31% of homelessness, 60% of crime, 50-80% of child abuse) either as a cause or as a coping mechanism that makes successful treatment less likely (National Institute on Drug Abuse [NIDA], 1999). With an average societal cost of $484 billion (NIDA, 1999, 2004) and an estimated 26 million Americans struggling with substance dependence, few examples exist of a more needed and addressable "cost benefit" medical condition than the prevention, earlier intervention, and treatment of substance use.

Looked at through the lens of physical health, approximately 50% of patients with chronic medical conditions tend to have co-occurring behavioral health problems, but over 80% of these problems remain untreated or inadequately treated in primary and specialty medical care settings. These behavioral health conditions negatively affect health status, health care utilization, and total health care costs (Freeman, McGuire, Thomas, & Thayer, 2014). For the general population treated in these settings, health behaviors influence 50-60% of health outcomes (Hacker & Walker, 2013).

In response to concerns about this fragmentation of care, there has been a growing movement toward the organization and delivery of "integrated" care. SAMHSA funded the Center for Integrated Health Solutions (CIHS; www.integration.samhsa.gov) to promote integrated care through the provision of training and technical assistance. In an effort to define integration, CIHS developed a framework that outlines six levels ranging from efforts at coordination, to co-location, to actual integration of practice (Heath, Wise, & Reynolds, 2013).

The *Patient Protection and Affordable Care Act* (ACA) became law in 2010 and promotes integration. It incentivizes the creation of Accountable Care Organizations (ACOs) that use integration to achieve better outcomes and lower costs. The antecedents to this reform effort can be seen in earlier proposals focused on clinical integration (American Hospital Association, 2005), bundled payment care initiatives (Medicare Payment Advisory Commission, 2008), and accountable care (Fisher & McClellan, 2009). The workforce implications of clinical integration include: a) collaboration to improve care quality; b) performance measurement of provider practice; c) continuity of providers across an episode of care; and d) financial incentives for providers to deliver integrated care. While ACA addressed the importance of integrated care, it mandated that the funds it provided for workforce development be focused in primary care settings. More recently, the *Protecting Access to Medicare Act* (H.R. 4302) contained provisions for piloting integrated care programs in behavioral health settings (https://www.congress.gov).

Despite the growing interest in integration in the U.S., there was no well-recognized or comprehensive set of workforce competencies for this form of practice. To address this void, the Annapolis Coalition was commissioned by SAMHSA and the Center for Integrated Health Solutions to develop two sets of competencies for integrated care: one for medical providers trained to deliver primary care and one for providers trained in the specialty of behavioral health. Over the course of the project it became clear that there were few differences between the competencies for these two provider groups, so the resulting product was one set of *Core Competencies for Integrated Behavioral Health and Primary Care* (Hoge, Morris, Laraia, Pomerantz, & Farley, 2014).

The Annapolis Coalition relied on three sources to identify potential competencies: (1) a review of the recent literature on integration; (2) structured interviews with over 50 key informants with expertise germane to integrated care; and (3) a review of existing competency sets that had some relevance to this model of service delivery. With guidance from two senior content experts in integration, the project team used a qualitative, consensus driven process to distill the various sources of information into a set of nine competency categories, which were then populated with individual competencies and refined based on review and provision of feedback by the key informants. The final competency set is available online (www.integration.samhsa.gov/workforce).

Within the U.S., the SAMHSA Center for Integrated Health Solutions has assembled online many of the resources available for workforce development in integrated care (www.integration.samhsa.gov/workforce). Recruitment and retention resources include information on scholarship and loan repayment offered through the National Health Service Corps and Nurse Corps, and sample job descriptions to support job development and hiring. Performance assessment resources include an interprofessional mentoring guide for use by supervisors, staff, and students. Various sources of information focus on reimbursement and provider wage/payment strategies in integrated care settings.

While the concept of integrated care is not new, it has never before had such a prominent focus within U.S. health care. Yet the majority of the workforce is not trained in this practice and the majority of healthcare systems still do not deliver integrated care. Much remains to be done to create a workforce that is capable of and actively involved in delivering this form of care.

Workforce Development in Substance Use

The Annapolis Coalition has had a longstanding interest in promoting competency development in the prevention, identification, treatment, and recovery from substance use disorders for both the addiction and mental health workforce. In response to the White House and the Centers for Disease Control and Prevention declaring a national epidemic in opioid abuse, overdose, and deaths (The White House, 2015), members of the Board of the Annapolis Coalition have been active in developing proposed strategies and initiatives to address the workforce aspects of these problems. The efforts, which are a collaboration with faculty and trainees from Boston University, and the Universities of Toronto and Connecticut, focus on reforming how medical students, medical residents, and practicing physicians are educated about: (1) The identification of patients at risk for addiction, (2) Opioid prescribing, and (3) Treatment alternatives to pain medication. There has also been a focus on supporting the active involvement of first-responders in community-based interventions (Huey, Alford, Flaherty, & Socklingham, 2016) and in the design of joint community, treatment provider, and law enforcement efforts to reduce overdoses (Hickton & Leary, 2015).

With respect to substance use conditions more broadly, there have been workforce challenges and successes. Attempting to address the growing demand for substance use treatment, which was fueled in part by expanded insurance coverage under ACA, the U.S. has taken several steps to both expand drug interdiction and increase opportunities for treatment, especially medication-assisted treatment. Attention has been shifting to the development of a workforce that can conduct earlier screening and intervention, stronger community based prevention, and more accountable and continuous public and privately financed treatment of substance use conditions. This paradigm shift is part of this country's expanding integration of behavioral and medical care, in which substance use is assessed, treated, or referred earlier by all providers of healthcare. The integrated care model, which in its optimal form addresses substance use, calls for increased education, skills, attained competencies, and collaboration of all clinicians in both generalist and specialty settings. These efforts can be aided by new technologies that support safe and effective practice, such as the use of electronic records, mobile apps, brief screens, and medication support.

The health care workforce is being further expanded with respect to the integration of substance use treatment by adding less costly, new workers or peer and family advocates who can become certified supports to each person and family. Generalist healthcare providers (e.g., primary care physicians, nurses, dentists, social workers, counselors, first responders) are receiving enhanced training about substance abuse prevention, early intervention, and treatment in undergraduate, graduate, continuing education, and specialty education programs (http://www.samhsa.gov/recovery-to-practice/rtp-curricula). Specialty care providers, including those physicians, nurses, counselors, social workers, psychologists, and peers dedicated to providing more advanced treatment can attain certification in addictions through professional associations and state boards. Public and private organizations that pay for care have been employing health navigators and care managers to ensure continuity of care and efficient resource utilization. Criminal justice workers are receiving specialized education about substance use treatment needs in settings where clinical and legal issues need to be balanced and less costly community re-entry is possible.

Despite all these efforts, high turnover, low wages, and the aging of workers continue to hamper the development of a strong substance use workforce (Ryan et al., 2012). The country has far to go in developing an addiction workforce that can meet current demand, let alone address the needs of an aging and culturally diverse population and other populations at high risk (e.g., veterans, Native Americans, newborns, the homeless, and youth). Years of workforce neglect, underfunding, and societal stigma associated with having a substance use problem or providing health care to those with such a condition remain to be overcome (Hoge et al., 2013).

Diversity and Cultural Competency

The U.S. will soon become a majority-minority nation, with census figures projecting that by 2060 minorities will rise to an estimated 56% of the country's population (Colby & Ortman, 2014). Yet, race and ethnicity represent only two aspects of diversity. The nation's behavioral health workforce must be prepared to provide services that are sensitive, not only to racial and cultural differences, but also to diversity in age, social class, sexual orientation, gender and gender identity, religion and spirituality, physical and mental ability, national origin, immigration status, military service, and primary language.

In contrast to the diversity of the U.S. population being served, data highlights the relative absence of diversity among the behavioral health workforce. For example, only 19.2% of psychiatrists, 17.5%-37% of social workers, and 5.1%-16.4% of psychologists self-identify as members of a racial/ethnic minority group (American Psychological Association, 2015; HRSA, 2013; SAMHSA, 2013). The wide variation in estimates is indicative of an ongoing challenge to reach consensus on the data, given the large number of credentialing entities, professional trade organizations, and local, state, and federal agencies tracking the behavioral health workforce. While imperfect data exists on the racial diversity of the workforce, there is virtually no data on how many members of this workforce have the language skills necessary to provide services to those with limited proficiency in English.

In 2012, the Annapolis Coalition conducted a SAMHSA-funded review to identify workforce strategies for improving the provision of appropriate and high quality services to diverse populations (Paris & Hoge, 2012). Below are some of the promising approaches designed to meet the needs of minority groups, which are disproportionately underserved. In order to achieve long-term health equity, the use of multiple strategies to address existing health disparities is generally considered necessary.

An essential first step involves creating a workforce that is reflective of the country's diversity. There are several strategies that have been used to improve diversity within the workforce pipeline and to support those workers once they have entered the field. From an academic, pre-service perspective, the federal government invests in minority fellowships (MFP; http://www.samhsa.gov/minority-fellowship-program) and loan repayment programs (LRP; www.lrp.nih.gov; nhsc.hrsa.gov/loanrepayment/).

Both of these initiatives are dedicated to attracting and retaining talented individuals with demonstrated commitment to a clinical and/or research career related to underserved communities. The MFP provides stipends to graduate students who are receiving specialized training and supervised experience in working with diverse populations, while the LRP repays educational loans for behavioral health professionals who are willing to work in underserved areas or to conduct research on underserved populations.

While loan repayment programs are successful in attracting professionals to underserved areas, it is often difficult to retain these providers once loans are repaid. As a result, a complementary and promising "grow your own" strategy has emerged that focuses on providing training and a career ladder for individuals who live in the underserved areas and have a strong desire to work and live there over the course of their careers (Roberts et al., 2011). Grow your own strategies are most often employed with entry level positions, such as community health workers (CHW) who have been integrated into health care teams throughout the country. They are hired from within the local communities and frequently match characteristics of the population to be served on variables such as ethnicity, primary language, and lived experiences of behavioral health conditions. Research has demonstrated the potential of such workers to reduce costs and improve health disparity outcomes (Phalen & Paradis, 2015).

Ensuring diversity in the workforce is an important, but only partial solution since a match between provider and client on key characteristics will likely always be the exception rather than the rule. In order to address this gap in a feasible and more comprehensive manner, identifying cultural competencies and embedding these throughout the workforce is another prominent strategy. The U.S. has had many initiatives to identify cultural competencies.

The ATTC Network, described earlier, has four national focus area centers with two highlighting diversity and supporting the development of cultural competence in the workforce: the National Hispanic and Latino ATTC, and the National American Indian and Alaska Native ATTC. Additionally, it also has a Center of Excellence on Racial and Ethnic Minority Young Men Who Have Sex with Men and Other Lesbian, Gay, Bisexual, and Transgender Populations (YMSM+LGBT CoE). The National Network to Eliminate Disparities in Behavioral Health (NNED; http://nned.net), created by SAMHSA in 2008, has a related mission to provide workforce development resources to community-based behavioral health agencies that serve diverse racial, ethnic, and sexual minority communities.

Despite concerted efforts, the nation has struggled to standardize the concept of cultural competence or to operationalize it in clinical practice. The *Enhanced National Standards for Culturally and Linguistically Appropriate Services in Health and Health Care* from the Office of Minority Health (CLAS; U.S. Department of Health and Human Services, 2013) are "intended to advance health equity, improve quality, and help eliminate health care disparities by providing a blueprint for individuals and health and health care organizations to implement culturally and linguistically appropriate services" (p. 9). In order to provide a comprehensive set of practice guidelines, the enhanced CLAS Standards are organized around three themes and 15 standards with the explicit goal of advancing and sustaining practices that are sensitive to diverse populations.

The third strategy is to effectively train and develop the identified cultural competencies within the workforce. Training should follow a continuum that begins with awareness, transitions into knowledge, and culminates with the application of skills. Multiple teaching modalities can be utilized (e.g., classroom, web-based), but the hallmark of an effective learning approach is one in which interactive and problem-based methods are fused to build skills and improve practice (SAMHSA, 2014a; SAMHSA, 2014b).

Below are two examples of model training programs focused on educating providers to work with diverse populations. The Connecticut Latino Behavioral Health System, established in July 2007, represents a community-academic collaboration among regional behavioral health and community health providers, the Yale University Department of Psychiatry, and the Connecticut Department of Mental Health and Addiction Services. It is designed to increase access to recovery-oriented and culturally appropriate care for the monolingual Spanish-speaking community (Paris et al., 2016). Access is increased, in large part, through workforce development, including competency development among staff within a culturally and linguistically sensitive framework.

Another example is that of the Historically Black Colleges and Universities-Center for Excellence in Behavioral Health at Morehouse School of Medicine (HBCU-CFE; http://hbcucfe.net). The HBCU-CFE has three major goals, with one directly pertaining to workforce development. It is charged with promoting evidence-based and promising practices via dissemination of information, mentoring students, and providing on-site, local, and distance learning opportunities.

A final strategy for improving the relevance of services provided to diverse populations has been to provide the workforce with treatment models that have been adapted for and often tested with clients who share a specific type of diversity, such as culture or race. Evidence suggests that treatment models developed to meet the common beliefs, values, and practices of diverse groups can yield stronger therapeutic alliances, increased treatment adherence, improved health outcomes, higher levels of client satisfaction, and improved cost effectiveness (SAMHSA, 2014a). An example of an adaptation that has included practical training for the workforce is the *Promotores de Salud Initiative* launched in April 2011 by the U.S. Department of Health and Human Services Office of Minority Health as part of its *Action Plan to Reduce Racial and Ethnic Health Disparities*. One component of this is a free e-learning program titled *Promoting Healthy Choices and Community Changes* (https://promotores.thinkculturalhealth.hhs.gov/default_en.asp) geared towards training community health workers to provide health education and prevention services within underserved and uninsured communities.

The strategies to address issues of diversity are now well articulated: recruitment, identification of cultural competencies, and workforce training in those competencies and in treatments adapted for diverse populations. Further development of these approaches is certainly necessary. However, the primary challenge currently is to take these strategies to scale to increase their overall impact on the composition and competence of the workforce.

Knowledge Dissemination and Adoption of Best Practices

The fragmentation of the behavioral health system in the U.S. presents unique challenges to knowledge dissemination and adoption, which is already a complex and multifaceted process (Rogers, 1995). In his seminal paper on health reform in the U.S., Atul Gawande (2009) described the many elements of the health system as "path-dependent", tending to slip back into historical pathways whether or not they are ultimately productive. This is true in behavioral health, which had its roots in state operated asylums, has moved to community based services, and has significant participation by managed care organizations.

With no recognized single, national, or central vehicle for moving workforce innovations from pilots or demonstrations to scale across the full behavioral health spectrum, the Annapolis Coalition emerged as a non-governmental organization (NGO) committed to identifying, disseminating, and promoting the adoption of workforce innovations in behavioral health. With respect to substance use disorders, the work of the federally funded ATTCs has been impressive in its focus on knowledge transfer from the university or laboratory to routine practice. However, there is no single federally funded structure specific to mental health, nor any federally funded initiative addressing workforce development in behavioral health broadly.

The Coalition has adopted a number of strategies to acquaint the field with promising practices and encourage their adoption. The first and most consistent of these approaches has been a series of national searches for innovative workforce development practices. Innovative programs have been identified using a set of criteria developed by Harvard University's Kennedy School of Government, and adapted by the Coalition: significance, effectiveness, novelty, and transferability (O'Connell, Morris, & Hoge, 2004). In later efforts the Coalition added a category of durability, emphasizing the importance of sustaining innovation over time. Using an expert consensus methodology with a standardized set of criteria as a metric for recognizing innovation, the Coalition initially focused on educational innovations, but through a partnership with the Hitachi Foundation (www.hitachifoundation.org), recognized provider organizations for workplace innovations related to front line workers (Dailey, Morris, & Hoge, 2015).

Most recently, the Coalition created a methodology that includes anonymous student and employer surveys for evaluating a range of innovative workforce and training practices (www.annapoliscoalition.org). In each search for innovations, the Coalition has sought to disseminate the results through a variety of vehicles: peer reviewed behavioral health journals, the use of case studies in the Hitachi supported initiative, and through the use of list-serves and e-blasts in the most recent effort.

Due to the diversity of practice settings, service offerings, and reimbursement models across the U.S., disseminating standardized information about workforce practices can be helpful, but is seldom sufficient. Tailored consultation or technical assistance is often essential. To give some sense of the need for technical assistance, a survey conducted by the National Alliance on Mental Illness (NAMI) as part of its periodic *Grading the States* initiative (Aron et al., 2009), found that only 35 of the 50 states reported having any type of workforce development plan and, of those, only six had a truly comprehensive workforce plan, and five had a substantive cultural competency component in their plan. In response, the Coalition, often in partnership with other NGOs or academic partners, has offered targeted consultation to states or regions seeking to improve their behavioral health workforce practices.

The absence of a robust nationwide infrastructure within the U.S. for identifying innovative practices in behavioral health workforce development, supporting an evaluation of those practices, disseminating the findings, and promoting adoption through technical assistance remains a major problem for the country. Much can be accomplished through these practices. However, current efforts to meet this need are severely under-resourced.

Other Strategies

There are numerous other workforce strategies that have been implemented within the U.S. to which the Annapolis Coalition and its leadership have contributed. Efforts have been made to identify effective training and teaching practices that support the workforce in learning to provide evidence-based practices (Hoge, Migdole, Cannata, & Powell, 2014; Stuart, Tondora, & Hoge, 2004). Initiatives have been launched to build the skills of workforce supervisors, develop leaders who can effectively manage systems and services, and reform graduate level educational curricula (Hoge, Wolf, Migdole, Cannata, & Gregory, 2016). Managed care organizations have been striving to refine the selection of providers for their networks and to educate these providers about concepts such as evidence-based practice and recovery-focused care (Bergeson, 2015). Efforts have been made to strengthen the prevention workforce (Shea & Shern, 2011) and to train first responders, such as police officers (Walker, Pann, Shapiro, & Van Hasselt, 2016) and the general public (http://www.thenationalcouncil.org/about/mental-health-first-aid/).

SOLUTIONS AND RECOMMENDATIONS

While continued workforce assessment and planning are essential, there must be mechanisms in place to support robust implementation of high priority workforce strategies once identified. For the U.S., this inevitably means that there must be much more concerted leadership and support for workforce development demonstrated at the federal and state level (Hoge et al., 2013).

The Annapolis Framework continues to provide a clear roadmap of the path forward once action is mobilized.

- The country must define "workforce" broadly, educating all health care providers about the identification and treatment of mental health and substance use conditions and the delivery of integrated care.
- Persons in recovery and their families must assume much larger roles within the workforce and in educating the workforce.
- Community groups and organizations should be further empowered to identify and address their behavioral health needs.
- The behavioral health field must work strategically to recruit and to retain workers, provide them with relevant and effective education, and build their supervisory and leadership skills.
- Advocates must continue to press for financing systems that allow adequate compensation of workers.
- A national technical assistance infrastructure must be developed that will support the knowledge and adoption of best practices.
- Those best practices, once implemented, must then be evaluated so that the knowledge base about effective workforce development can continue to grow.

CONCLUSION

A competent behavioral health workforce of appropriate size must be an essential element of the U.S. health care system. It is clear that continuous and systematic efforts to strengthen the existing mental health and substance use segments of the workforce are required if persons in recovery and their families are to receive the health care they need. While this country has made some progress on this critical agenda, much remains to be accomplished.

ACKNOWLEDGMENT

The authors thank Sue Bergeson and DJ Ida for their comments on the organization and content of the chapter.

REFERENCES

American Academy of Nursing. (2012). Essential psychiatric, mental health and substance use competencies for the registered nurse. *Archives of Psychiatric Nursing*, *26*(2), 80–110. doi:10.1016/j.apnu.2011.12.010 PMID:22550669

American Hospital Association. (2005). Aligning hospital and physician interests: Broadening the concept of gain sharing to allow care improvement incentives. Chicago, IL: Author.

American Psychological Association. (2015). *Demographics of the U.S. psychology workforce: Findings from the American community survey*. Washington, DC: Author.

Andolsek, K., Padmore, J., Hauer, K. E., & Holmboe, E. (2015). *Clinical competency committees: A guidebook for programs*. Retrieved from https://www.acgme.org/acgmeweb/Portals/0/ACGMEClinicalCompetencyCommitteeGuidebook.pdf

Aron, L., Honberg, R., Duckworth, K., Kimball, A., Edgar, E., Carolla, B., & Fitzpatrick, M. (2009). *Grading the States 2009: A report on America's health care system for adults with serious mental illness*. Retrieved from https://www.nami.org/getattachment/About-NAMI/Publications/Reports/NAMI_GTS2009_FullReport.pdf

Bergeson, S. (2015). *Patient issues that get in the way of treatment adherence: Surprising survey findings*. Retrieved from http://slideplayer.com/slide/3885538/

BRSS TACS. (2015, November). *Core competencies for peer workers in behavioral health services*. Rockville, MD: Substance Abuse and Mental Health Services Administration.

Center for Health Care Strategies. (2013). *Family and youth peer support literature review*. Retrieved from http://www.chcs.org/media/FYPS_Literature_Review_FINAL.pdf

Center for Substance Abuse Treatment. (2006). *Addiction counseling competencies: The knowledge, skills, and attitudes of professional practice (Technical Assistance Publication Series 21, HHS Publication No. 08-4171)*. Rockville, MD: Substance Abuse and Mental Health Services Administration.

Center for Substance Abuse Treatment. (2007). *Competencies for substance abuse treatment clinical supervisors (Technical Assistance Publication Series 21-A, HHS Publication No. 12-4243)*. Rockville, MD: Substance Abuse and Mental Health Services Administration.

Centers for Disease Control and Prevention, National Center for Health Statistics System, Mortality File. (2015). *Number and age-adjusted rates of drug-poisoning deaths involving opioid analgesics and heroin: United States, 2000-2014*. Atlanta, GA: Center for Disease Control and Prevention. Retrieved from https://www.cdc.gov/nchs/data/health_policy/AADR_drug_poisoning_involving_OA_Heroin_US_2000-2014.pdf

Colby, S. L., & Ortman, J. M. (2014). *Projections of the size and composition of the U.S. population: 2014 to 2060, current population reports*. Washington, DC: U.S. Census Bureau.

Croft, B., & Parish, S. L. (2013). Care integration in the Patient Protection and Affordable Care Act: Implications for behavioral health. *Administration and Policy in Mental Health and Mental Health Services Research*, *40*(4), 258–263. doi:10.1007/s10488-012-0405-0 PMID:22371190

Dailey, W. F., Morris, J. A., & Hoge, M. A. (2015). Workforce development innovations with direct care workers: Better jobs, better services, better business. *Community Mental Health Journal*, *51*(6), 647–653. doi:10.1007/s10597-014-9798-4 PMID:25535046

Fisher, E. S., & McClellan, M. B. (2009). *Report to the Congress: Improving incentives in the Medicare program - Accountable care organizations*. Washington, DC: Medicare Payment Advisory Commission.

Freeman, E., McGuire, C. A., Thomas, J. W., & Thayer, D. A. (2014). Factors affecting costs in Medicaid populations with behavioral health disorders. *Medical Care*, *52*(3Suppl 2), S60–S66. doi:10.1097/MLR.0000000000000075 PMID:24561760

Gawande, A. (2009, January 26). Getting there from here: How should Obama reform healthcare. *Annals of Public Policy/The New Yorker.* Retrieved from http://www.newyorker.com/magazine/2009/01/26/getting-there-from-here

Gurvis, J. P., & Grey, M. T. (1995). The anatomy of a competency. *Journal of Nursing Staff Development*, *11*(5), 247–252. PMID:7562071

Hacker, K., & Walker, D. K. (2013). Achieving population health in accountable care organizations. *American Journal of Public Health*, *103*(7), 1163–1167. doi:10.2105/AJPH.2013.301254 PMID:23678910

Health Resources and Services Administration. (2010). *The registered nurse population: Findings from the 2008 national sample survey of registered nurses.* Retrieved from http://bhpr.hrsa.gov/healthworkforce/rnsurveys/rnsurveyfinal.pdf

Health Resources and Services Administration, National Center for Health Workforce Analysis. (2013, November). *The U.S. health workforce chartbook Part IV: Behavioral and allied health.* Rockville, MD: U.S. Department of Health and Human Services.

Heath, B., Wise Romero, P., & Reynolds, K. (2013, March). *A review and proposed standard framework for levels of integrated healthcare.* Washington, DC: SAMHSA-HRSA Center for Integrated Health Solutions. Retrieved from http://www.integration.samhsa.gov/integrated-care-models/CIHS_Framework_Final_charts.pdf

Hedegaard, H., Chen, L., & Warner, M. (2015, March). *Drug-poisoning deaths involving heroin: United States, 2000-2013* (NCHS Data brief, Number 190). Hyattsville, MD: National Center for Health Statistics.

Heisler, E. J., & Bagalman, E. (2015, April). *The mental health workforce: A primer.* Washington, DC: Congressional Research Service.

Hendry, P., Hill, T., & Rosenthal, H. (2014). *Peer services toolkit: A guide to advancing and implementing peer-run behavioral health services.* Retrieved from https://acmha.org/images/uploads/files/Peer_Services_Toolkit.pdf

Hickton, D. J., & Leary, M. L. (2015, December). *National heroin taskforce final report and recommendations*. Washington, DC: U.S. Department of Justice, White House Office of National Drug Control Policy.

Hoge, M. A., McFaul, M., Cauble, L. L., Craft, K. L., Paris, M., & Calcote, R. M. (2016). Building the skills of direct care workers: The Alaskan core competencies initiative. *Journal of Rural Mental Health, 40*(1), 31–39. doi:10.1037/rmh0000045

Hoge, M. A., Migdole, S., Cannata, E., & Powell, D. J. (2014). Strengthening supervision in systems of care: Exemplary practices in empirically supported treatments. *Clinical Social Work Journal, 42*(2), 171–181. doi:10.1007/s10615-013-0466-x

Hoge, M. A., Morris, J. A., Daniels, A. S., Stuart, G. W., Huey, L. Y., & Adams, N. (2007). *An action plan for behavioral health workforce development: A framework for discussion*. Rockville, MD: Substance Abuse and Mental Health Services Administration.

Hoge, M. A., Morris, J. A., Laraia, M., Pomerantz, A., & Farley, T. (2014). Core competencies for integrated behavioral health and primary care. Washington, DC: SAMHSA-HRSA Center for Integrated Health Solutions. Retrieved from http://www.integration.samhsa.gov/workforce

Hoge, M. A., Morris, J. A., & Paris, M. (Eds.). (2005). Workforce competencies in behavioral health. *Administration and Policy in Mental Health, 32*(5/6), 481–671.

Hoge, M. A., Morris, J. A., Stuart, G. W., Huey, L. Y., Bergeson, S., Flaherty, M., & Madenwald, K. (2009). A national action plan on workforce development in behavioral health. *Psychiatric Services (Washington, D.C.), 60*(7), 883–887. doi:10.1176/ps.2009.60.7.883 PMID:19564217

Hoge, M. A., & Paris, M. (2006). *Recruitment and retention in behavioral health: Background research for the national action plan on behavioral health workforce development*. Cincinnati, OH: The Annapolis Coalition on the Behavioral Health Workforce.

Hoge, M. A., Stuart, G., Morris, J., Flaherty, M. T., Paris, M., & Goplerud, E. (2013). Mental health and addiction workforce development: Federal leadership is needed to address the growing crisis. *Health Affairs, 32*(11), 2005–2011. doi:10.1377/hlthaff.2013.0541 PMID:24191093

Hoge, M. A., Wolf, J., Migdole, S., Cannata, E., & Gregory, F. (2016). Workforce development and mental health transformation: A state perspective. *Community Mental Health Journal, 52*(3), 323–331. doi:10.1007/s10597-015-9953-6 PMID:26410216

Huey, L., Alford, D., Flaherty, M., & Socklingham, S. (2016, March). *Addressing America's opioid overdose crisis through education: Breaking the cycle through workforce development at CME, GME, and UME levels*. Poster presentation at the World Congress on Continuing Professional Development, San Diego, CA.

Institute of Medicine. (2000). *To err is human: Building a safer health system*. Washington, DC: National Academy Press.

Institute of Medicine. (2001). *Crossing the quality chasm: A new health system for the 21st century*. Washington, DC: National Academy Press.

Institute of Medicine. (2006). *Improving the quality of health care for mental and substance-use conditions*. Washington, DC: The National Academies Press.

JAMA Network Journals. ScienceDaily. (2015, November). *Prevalence of lifetime drug use disorders nearly 10 percent in US*. Retrieved from http://www.sciencedaily.com/releases/2015/11/151118125314.htm

Joint Commission on Accreditation of Health Care Organizations. (1999). *Comprehensive accreditation manual for hospitals: The official handbook*. Oak Park, IL: Author.

Jones, D. R., Macias, C., Barreira, P. J., Fisher, W. H., Hargreaves, W. A., & Harding, C. M. (2004). Prevalence, severity, and co-occurrence of chronic physical health problems of persons with serious mental illness. *Psychiatric Services (Washington, D.C.)*, *55*(11), 1250–1257. doi:10.1176/appi.ps.55.11.1250 PMID:15534013

Kathol, R. G., Butler, M., McAlpine, D. D., & Kane, R. L. (2010). Barriers to physical and mental condition integrated service delivery. *Psychosomatic Medicine*, *72*(6), 511–518. doi:10.1097/PSY.0b013e3181e2c4a0 PMID:20498293

Kaufman, L., Brooks, W., Bellinger, J., Steinley-Bumgarner, M., & Stevens-Manser, S. (2014). *Peer specialist training and certification programs: A national overview*. Austin, TX: Texas Institute for Excellence in Mental Health, School of Social Work, University of Texas at Austin.

Manderscheid, R., & Kathol, R. (2014). Fostering sustainable, integrated medical and behavioral health services in medical settings. *Annals of Internal Medicine*, *160*(1), 61–65. doi:10.7326/M13-1693 PMID:24573665

Medicare Payment Advisory Commission. (2008, June). *Report to the Congress: Reforming the delivery system - A path to bundled payment around a hospitalization*. Washington, DC: Author.

Morris, J., McFaul, M., Madenwald, K., & Hoge, M. A. (2008). *Iowa mental health and disability services workforce review*. Cincinnati, OH: The Annapolis Coalition on the Behavioral Health Workforce.

Murphy, D. M., & Hubbard, R. L. (2009). *Understanding America's substance use disorders treatment workforce*. Kansas City, MO: ATTC Network Coordinating Office.

National Institute on Drug Abuse. (1999, October 25). *Magnitude*. Retrieved from http://archives.drugabuse.gov/about/welcome/aboutdrugabuse/magnitude/

National Institute on Drug Abuse. (2004, February). *Beyond the brain: The medical consequences of abuse and addiction* (NIDA Notes 18, No. 6). Retrieved from http://archives.drugabuse.gov/NIDA_Notes/NNVol18N6/DirRepVol18N6.html

National Panel for Psychiatric Mental Health NP Competencies. (2003). *Psychiatric-mental health nurse practitioner competencies*. Washington, DC: National Organization of Nurse Practitioner Faculties.

OConnell, M. J., Morris, J. A., & Hoge, M. A. (2004). Innovations in behavioral health workforce education. *Administration and Policy in Mental Health*, *32*(2), 131–165. doi:10.1023/B:APIH.0000042744.48923.8c PMID:15586848

Office of National Drug Control Policy. (2013). *National drug control strategy*. Retrieved from https://www.whitehouse.gov//sites/default/files/ondcp/policy-and-research/ndcs_2013.pdf

Olfson, M. (2016). Building the mental health workforce capacity needed to treat adults with serious mental illnesses. *Health Affairs*, *35*(6), 983–990. doi:10.1377/hlthaff.2015.1619 PMID:27269013

Owens, P., Myers, M., Elixhauser, A., & Brach, C. (2007). *Care of adults with mental health and substance abuse disorders in U.S. community hospitals, 2004*. Retrieved from Agency for Healthcare Research and Quality website: http://archive.ahrq.gov/data/hcup/factbk10/factbk10.pdf

Paris, M., & Hoge, M. (2012). *Improving workforce diversity & cultural and linguistic competency: Implications for integrated healthcare*. Unpublished report prepared for SAMHSA-HRSA Center for Integrated Health Solutions.

Paris, M., Silva, M. A., Diaz, E., Bedregal, L. E., Cole, R. A., & Añez-Nava, L. (2016). The Connecticut Latino behavioral health system: A culturally informed community-academic collaboration. *Psychological Services*, *13*(2), 140–147. doi:10.1037/ser0000065

Parks, J., Svendsen, D., Singer, P., & Foti, M. E. (2006). Morbidity and mortality in people with serious mental illness. Alexandria, VA: National Association of State Mental Health Program Directors (NASMHPD) Medical Directors Council.

Phalen, J., & Paradis, R. (2015, January 16). How community health workers can reinvent health care delivery in the US. *Health Affairs Blog*. Retrieved from http://healthaffairs.org/blog/2015/01/16/how-community-health-workers-can-reinvent-health-care-delivery-in-the-us/

Roberts, L., Smith, J., McFaul, M., Paris, M., Speer, N., Boeckmann, M., & Hoge, M. A. (2011). Behavioral health workforce development in rural and frontier Alaska. *Journal of Rural Mental Health*, *35*(1), 10–16. doi:10.1037/h0094780

Rogers, E. M. (1995). *Diffusion of innovations* (4th ed.). New York, NY: The Free Press.

Ryan, O., Murphy, D., & Krom, L. (2012). Vital signs: Taking the pulse of the addiction treatment workforce, a national report (version 1). Kansas City, MO: Addiction Technology Transfer Center National Office in residence at the University of Missouri-Kansas City.

Shea, P., & Shern, D. (2011). *Primary prevention in behavioral health: Investing in our nation's future*. Alexandria, VA: National Association of State Mental Health Program Directors.

Stuart, G. W., Tondora, J., & Hoge, M. A. (2004). Evidence-based teaching practice: Implications for behavioral health. *Administration and Policy in Mental Health*, *32*(2), 107–130. doi:10.1023/B:APIH.0000042743.11286.bc PMID:15586847

Substance Abuse and Mental Health Services Administration. (2009). *Integrated treatment for co-occurring disorders: Training frontline staff (DHHS Pub. No. SMA-08-4366)*. Rockville, MD: Author.

Substance Abuse and Mental Health Services Administration. (2011). Results from the 2010 national survey on drug use and health: Summary of national findings (NSDUH Series H-41, HHS Publication No. (SMA) 11-4658). Rockville, MD: Author.

Substance Abuse and Mental Health Services Administration. (2013). *Report to Congress on the nation's substance abuse and mental health workforce issues*. Rockville, MD: Author.

Substance Abuse and Mental Health Services Administration. (2014a). Improving cultural competence (Treatment Improvement Protocol (TIP) Series No. 59, HHS Publication No. (SMA) 14-4849). Rockville, MD: Author.

Substance Abuse and Mental Health Services Administration. (2014b). Leading change 2.0: Advancing the behavioral health of the nation 2015-2018 (HHS Publication No. [PEP] 14-LEADCHANGE2). Rockville, MD: Author.

The White House, Office of the Press Secretary. (2015, October). *Fact sheet: Obama administration announces public and private sector efforts to address prescription drug abuse and heroin use*. Retrieved from https://www.whitehouse.gov/the-press-office/2015/10/21/fact-sheet-obama-administration-announces-public-and-private-sector

Thomas, K. C., Ellis, A. R., Konrad, T. R., Holzer, C. E., & Morrissey, J. P. (2009). County-level estimates of mental health professional shortage in the United States. *Psychiatric Services (Washington, D.C.)*, *60*(10), 1323–1328. doi:10.1176/ps.2009.60.10.1323 PMID:19797371

Unutzer, J., Schoenbaum, M., Druss, B. G., & Katon, W. J. (2006). Transforming mental health care at the interface with general medicine: Report for the Presidents commission. *Psychiatric Services (Washington, D.C.)*, *57*(1), 37–47. doi:10.1176/appi.ps.57.1.37 PMID:16399961

U.S. Department of Health and Human Services. (2013). *National standards for culturally and linguistically appropriate services in health and health care: A blueprint for advancing and sustaining CLAS policy and practice*. Rockville, MD: Office of Minority Health.

Walker, L. E. A., Pann, J. M., Shapiro, D. L., & Van Hasselt, V. B. (2016). *Best practices for the mentally ill in the criminal justice system*. Springer International Publishing. doi:10.1007/978-3-319-21656-0

Wolff, J., Maula, E., & Padron, J. (2015, October). *Education pays! 2.0: Peer career development strategies*. Presentation at the Alternatives Conference, Memphis, TN.

KEY TERMS AND DEFINITIONS

Affordable Care Act: Formally known as the Patient Protection and Affordable Care Act (ACA), this law brought about major reforms of the U.S. health system centralizing accountability for care, promoting the use of technology, and fostering integration of behavioral health and primary care.

Behavioral Health: A health care sector focused on prevention, treatment, and recovery related to mental health and substance use conditions.

Behavioral Health Workforce: Individuals who are employed or volunteer to provide prevention, assessment, treatment, and recovery supports to persons with mental health and substance use conditions.

Integrated Care: The combined delivery of behavioral health and other medical care on a continuum from coordinated, to co-located, to fully integrated in a single team.

Managed Care Organizations: Public and private organizations responsible for ensuring appropriate access to safe and effective healthcare delivered by a network of qualified providers.

Peer Support: Individuals with lived experience of a mental health or substance use condition provide information, support, and inspiration to others with these conditions.

Recovery: Recovery from mental health and substance use conditions involves developing a purposeful and stable life in the community that maximizes physical and emotional health and well-being.

Chapter 3
Rural Mental Health Workforce Development in Hawai'i and the US-Affiliated Pacific Islands

Christopher W. S. Hill
University of Hawaii, USA

Kelley Withy
University of Hawaii, USA

ABSTRACT

Working in Hawai'i and the U.S.-Affiliated Pacific Islands presents unique challenges and opportunities for mental health workforce development. This chapter presents previous, current, and future efforts aimed at not only increasing the size of the workforce but also developing a better trained workforce for existing professionals. The authors draw from their experiences at the Hawaii/Pacific Basin Area Health Education Centers (AHEC), one of the only organizations performing medical, public health, and mental health workforce development across the Pacific Region, to explore culturally appropriate initiatives and interventions. Programs targeting a range of audiences from youth to adults, students to professionals, and patients/clients to caregivers are discussed. The chapter emphasizes health career pathway programs for youth and young adults wishing to enter the health workforce and a variety of educational development and continuing education opportunities for professionals. Specific mental health workforce initiatives are described.

INTRODUCTION

E Hō Mai
E hō mai
Ka `ike mai luna mai ē
`O nā mea huna no`eau
O nā mele ē
E hō mai

DOI: 10.4018/978-1-5225-1874-7.ch003

E hō mai
E hō mai
Grant us knowledge
From above
The things of knowledge
Hidden in the chants
Grant us these things

Hawaiian chant for bringing insight, clarity, and collaboration (to be sung three times, each time raising the vocal pitch one-half step) by Edith Kanaka`ole via Papa Ola Lōkahi.

Within the U.S., international and national initiatives exist aimed at improving the mental health workforce. The vast majority of regulation and impact, however, is derived from the individual states, not the federal government. Each state is responsible for the licensing and categorization of mental health providers eligible to practice in that state, and licensure requirements vary widely between the states (emphasizing the necessity of state-level coordinated workforce development efforts). The use of mental health services in the U.S. is generally driven by three inter-related concepts, which are the *quality*, *access*, and *cost* of mental health care. Furthermore, multiple dimensions influence these concepts on a workforce-level. Examples of these dimensions are licensure requirements, scopes of practice, quantity of workforce members, wages, and provider types (Heisler & Bagalman, 2015). The purpose of this chapter is to inform the reader on the types of mental health care practitioners in Hawai'i, the policies that regulate a professional's ability to practice mental health care, the psychological and behavioral health disparities of the U.S.-Affiliated Pacific Islands, and what is being done to address workforce shortages in this field. Through examining current and past programs, initiatives, and activities, recommendations are provided for workforce professionals.

BACKGROUND

Mental Health Workforce in the U.S.

The mental health workforce in the U.S. is generally divided into two main categories: providers who can prescribe medication and providers who can't, with the administration/interpretation of psychological tests falling in the scope of work for clinical psychologists almost exclusively (Heisler & Bagalman, 2015). Beyond this, unfortunately, there is no consensus on the exact provider-types that constitute the mental health workforce. The Substance Abuse and Mental Health Services Administration (SAMHSA, 2013) identifies a broad characterization of the mental health workforce, including psychiatry, clinical psychology, clinical social work, advanced practice (psychiatric) nursing, marriage and family therapy, substance abuse counseling, and counseling. The Institute of Medicine (IOM, 2012) identifies the mental health workforce as including all of the fields presented by SAMHSA and adds primary care physicians, nurses, physician assistants, peer support specialists, and family caregivers. Alternatively, the Health Resources and Services Administration (HRSA, 2015) have established a narrow view of the workforce, including psychiatrists, clinical psychologists, clinical social workers, psychiatric nurse specialists, and marriage and family therapists. SAMHSA and HRSA are subdivisions of the federal government's Department of Health and Human Services (DHHS or HHS), with HRSA managing most of the federal grant programs and providing industry-based policy development (lending significance to the strict definition of the mental health workforce which is necessary for certain grant and policy programs).

Licensing requirements for mental health professionals vary by state, but there are many themes identified that tend to be present across the nation. Table 1 describes the general U.S. licensing trends for the mental health professions described by HRSA. As of January 2016, HRSA has identified 15,990 health professional shortage areas (including 4,362 mental health professional shortage areas [MHPSAs]) and 4,208 medically underserved areas/populations in the U.S. (including all territories) and special focus is given to these regions/populations (HRSA, 2016a).

Hawai'i: Overview

The Hawaiian Islands are isolated from the rest of the U.S. as illustrated in Figure 1. The main islands of the State of Hawai'i are illustrated in Figure 2.

Hawai'i is a state of approximately 1,419,561 people living on seven inhabited islands (U.S. Census Bureau, 2015a). These are the islands of Kaua'i, O'ahu (the most populated and home to the capital city of Honolulu), Moloka'i (located 25 miles southeast of O'ahu, whose population is primarily Native Hawaiian), Lāna'i (west of Maui and was formerly a vast pineapple plantation), Maui (100 miles southeast of Honolulu with 730 square miles of land), and the Island of Hawai'i (also known as the Big Island; southeast of Maui with 4,000 square miles of land, an active volcano, and snow present most winters on the top of an inactive volcano). The name *Hawai`i* can refer to the whole State of Hawai`i or the island of Hawai`i (the Big Island), therefore, this chapter will provide a label for appropriate use of the name (if no label is provided, the reader can safely assume that the name refers to the entire State). The Native Hawaiian population totals 298,385 persons, making up 21% of the state population (Papa Ola Lokahi, 2015a). Other common ethnic groups include Caucasians (25%), mixed (23.8%), Filipino (14.4%), Japanese (13.6%), Chinese (4.1%) and other Asian (3.7% [U.S. Census Bureau, 2015b]). The State of Hawai'i currently has 17 community health centers and all islands have areas considered health professions shortage areas with medically underserved populations (DHHS, 2015).

Hawai'i: Health Disparities

Populations that experience significant health disparities in Hawai'i include the indigenous Native Hawaiians, recent immigrants, and rural residents. Native Hawaiians have the highest all-cause mortality in the state, as well as highest rates of cancer, asthma, obesity, and risky behaviors such as smoking of any ethnic group in Hawai'i. Native Hawaiians have twice the rate of diabetes as Caucasians and 40% of all childhood diabetes cases are Native Hawaiian children. The five-year survival rate for all cancers is 47% in Native Hawaiians, compared with rates of 57% for Caucasians and 55% in the general U.S. population. Participation in screening studies, such as colonoscopy and mammograms, is at or near the bottom for Native Hawaiians. In addition, 72.5% of Native Hawaiians are overweight or obese, and 13.4% of Native Hawaiians report that they have no medical coverage, the highest amongst the surveyed groups (Papa Ola Lokahi, 2015a).

More Hawaiians report smoking, drinking alcohol, or using drugs during their pregnancies than any other group, and have lower rates of prenatal care than the state average. Also, 10-14 year old Native Hawaiians make up 50% of the completed suicides in Hawai'i, and suicide rates for Native Hawaiians aged 25-44 were 72.4 per 100,000, which is seven times the national average (Papa Ola Lokahi, 2015a).

Table 1. Licensure requirements and scope of practice, by mental health provider type

	Licensure Requirements			
Provider Type[a]	Degree[c]	Supervised Practice	Exam	Scope of Practice[b]
Clinical Social Worker	Master of Social Work (MSW), which typically requires 2 years. Coursework emphasizes human and community well-being. Requires a supervised field practicum (internship).	Generally requires 3,200-3,400 post-degree supervised clinical hours, which take approximately 2 years.	Generally requires a passing score on the Clinical Exam of the Association of Social Work Boards.	• Diagnose mental disorders. • Provide psychosocial treatment for individuals, families, and groups. • Cannot prescribe medication.
Clinical Psychologist	Doctoral degree in psychology or a related field, which generally takes between 5 and 7 years to complete and requires academic coursework, clinical training, a dissertation, and an exam.	Generally requires 3,000 hours of supervised clinical training, which takes approximately 2 years.[d]	Generally requires a passing score on the Examination for Professional Practice in Psychology (EPPP).[e]	• Diagnose mental disorders. • Provide psychosocial treatment for individuals, families, and groups. • Administer and interpret psychological tests. • Generally cannot prescribe medication.[f]
Marriage & Family Therapist (MFT)	Master's degree (2-3 years), doctoral degree (3-5 years), or postgraduate clinical training (3-4 years) in marriage and family therapy or a related field.[g] Coursework emphasizes the individual's mental health in the context of interpersonal relationships (e.g., family and peers). Generally requires a field practicum or internship.	Generally requires 2 years of post-degree supervised clinical training.	Generally requires a passing score on the Association of Marital and Family Therapy Regulatory Board's Examination in Marriage and Family or the equivalent California Exam.[h]	• Diagnose mental disorders. • Provide psychosocial treatment for individuals, families, and groups. • Cannot prescribe medication.
Psychiatrist	Medical Doctorate (MD) or Doctorate of Osteopathic Medicine (DO), both of which typically require 4 years to complete (including 2 years of clinical rotations). Coursework emphasizes physical medicine.	Generally requires 3 or 4 years of post-degree supervised clinical training (residency) in the specialty of psychiatry.	Generally requires a passing score on the U.S. Medical Licensing Examination (USMLE) for MDs or DOs.[i] DOs can also elect to take the Comprehensive Osteopathic Medical Licensing Examination (COMLEX). To become board certified, an exam administered by the American Board of Psychiatry and Neurology.[j]	• Diagnose mental disorders. • Provide psychosocial treatment for individuals, families, and groups. • Can prescribe medication. • Can diagnose and treat physical conditions as well.
Advanced Practice Psychiatric Nurse (APPN)[k]	Master of Science (MS) in nursing, which generally requires 2 years of coursework and clinical hours (generally 500 or more).[l] Coursework and clinical experience focus on psychiatric mental health nursing.	No separate post-graduate clinical training is required.	Generally requires a passing score on an exam offered by the American Nurses Credentialing Center.[m]	• Diagnose mental disorders. • Provide psychosocial treatment for individuals, families, and groups. • Generally can prescribe medicine. • Can diagnose and treat physical conditions as well.[n]

Source: Heisler & Bagalman, 2015

Sources: U.S. Department of Labor, Bureau of Labor Statistics; U.S. DHHS, HRSA, and various professional associations.

Note: The degree, supervised practice, and exam indicated in the table are those generally required to obtain a license for independent practice. Licensure requirements (defined by state boards) and scope of practice (defined in state laws) vary by state. Degree requirements may vary by program. In all cases, the information provided in the table reflects what is generally true in most states and programs. Elaborating the exceptions is beyond the scope of this table.

1. The provider type may not correspond to the name of the license (which may vary by state for some provider types). The provider types correspond to HRSA's "core mental health professionals" (with the exception of advanced practice registered nurses, which HRSA calls "psychiatric nurse specialist").
2. The table focuses on the elements within scope of practice that involve diagnosing and treating mental illness. The scope of practice for most provider types includes other activities, such as preventive care, case management, and consultation with other providers.
3. The table focuses on graduate degree requirements (i.e., post-baccalaureate training requirements).
4. Generally, states require that at least 1,500 hours (of the 3,000 hours required) be a post-doctoral experience.
5. A board certified psychologist is one who has completed training in a specific specialty and has passed an examination that assesses the basic knowledge and skills in that particular area. As in psychiatry, board certification is not required, but some employers may require it. Board certification is conducted by the American Board of Professional Psychology.
6. In New Mexico, Louisiana, Guam, the U.S. Department of Defense (DoD) system, the Indian Health Service, and the U.S. Public Health Service, licensed psychologists who obtain additional training can apply to have prescription writing privileges as part of their scope of practice.
7. Related fields may include psychology, social work, nursing, education, or pastoral counseling. See American Association for Marriage and Family Therapy.
8. Marriage and Family Therapists (MFTs) who practice in California (representing more than half of all MFTs), must pass a separate California licensing exam.
9. Graduates of certain foreign medical schools may also be eligible to take the USMLE.
10. The term "board certified physician" means one who has completed the required training in a specific specialty and has passed an examination that assesses the basic knowledge and skills in a particular area (in this case psychiatry or neurology). Board certification is not required to practice as a psychiatrist but may be a condition of employment for some employers.
11. This includes mental health/psychiatric nurse practitioners and clinical nurse specialists.
12. The nursing profession is moving towards requiring doctoral degrees in these fields, which requires an additional two years of training.
13. Prior to January 1, 2014, the American Nurses Credentialing Center offered four different exams: two for Nurse Practitioners (in Adult and Family Psychiatry) and two for Clinical Nurse Specialists (in Adult or Child/Adolescent Psychiatric Nursing). In order to become an advanced practice psychiatric nurse, an individual must first be a registered nurse, which generally requires a passing score on the National Council Licensure Examination-RN (NCLEX-RN).
14. Some states may require that advanced practice psychiatric nurses be supervised by physicians.

Figure 1. The Hawaiian Islands (bottom left) are very isolated from the rest of the U.S.
Source: Adapted from Central Intelligence Agency, 2013

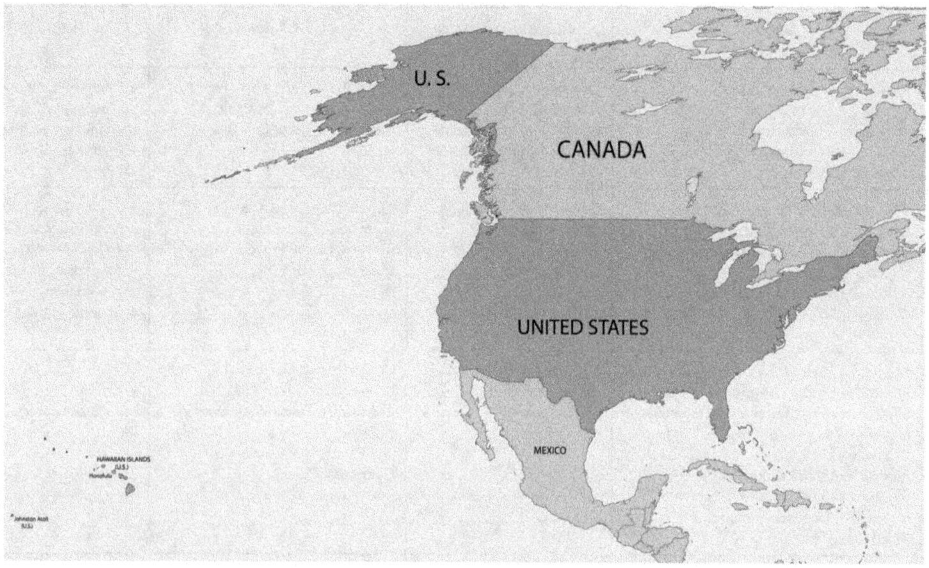

Figure 2. The main islands of the State of Hawai'i. Honolulu is the capital city. The Island of O'ahu is the most populated island. The Island of Hawai'i (the "Big Island") is the largest
Source: Adapted from Google Earth, 2015

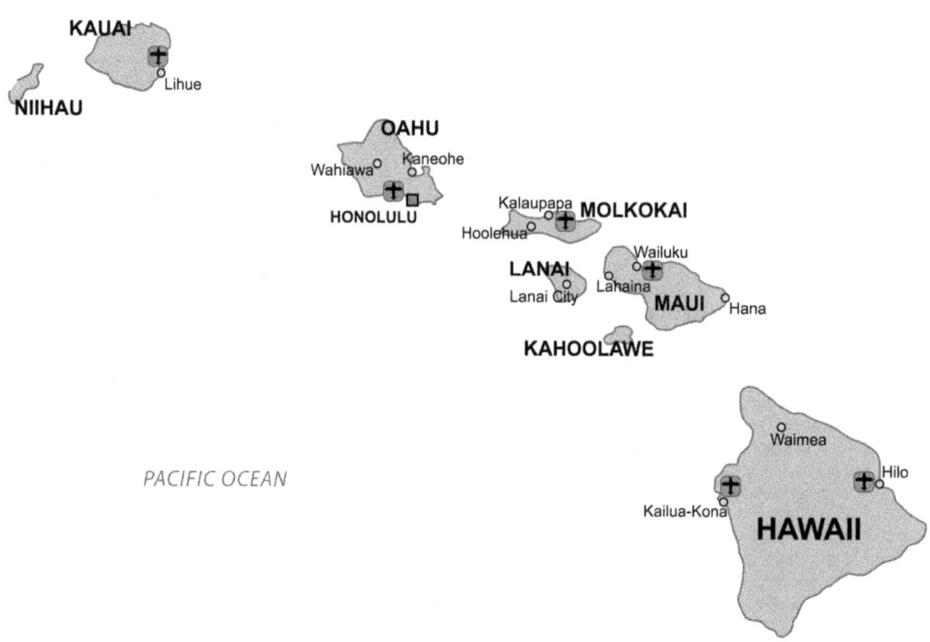

The State of Hawai'i continues to report one of the highest annual tuberculosis (TB) case rates in the country. In 2014, Hawai'i reported 136 total cases of TB, a rate of 9.6 new cases per 100,000 population and the highest in the nation that year. Although TB rates have declined over the past decade, Hawaii's 2014 rate was more than three times higher than the 2013 national TB case rate of 3.0 per 100,000 (State of Hawaii, 2015). Hawai'i has the 5th largest percentage of naturalized citizens in the U.S. at 9.4% and the 6th highest percentage of foreign-born residents at 17.6% of the population (Migration Policy Institute, 2011). Immigrants have been shown to have higher rates of infections and chronic disease than U.S. born individuals, resulting in situations such as the above mentioned TB rates. In addition, many of the immigrant families are homeless and without health insurance. Rural inhabitants of Hawai'i have the highest rates of births with less than adequate prenatal care, teen births, substance abuse, mood disorders, diabetes, unintentional injury, and mortality from cardiac, cancer, stroke and all causes combined (State of Hawaii, 2012). These factors will continue to stress the healthcare system of already underserved, isolated communities.

Selected charts showcasing various health disparities for substance use present in Hawai'i are presented below (Hawai`i State Epidemiological Outcomes Workgroup, 2014a). Notice the disparate trends among the charts broken down by ethnicity.

Figure 3 illustrates the 30 day marijuana use amongst high school students by ethnicity. Although a general decrease in marijuana use is seen over time, there was a significant increase among Other Pacific Islanders (jumping above the national average). Native Hawaiians remained above the national average with little change over time.

Figure 3. 30 day marijuana use by ethnicity (high school students)
Note. HHDW = Hawai'i Health Data Warehouse.

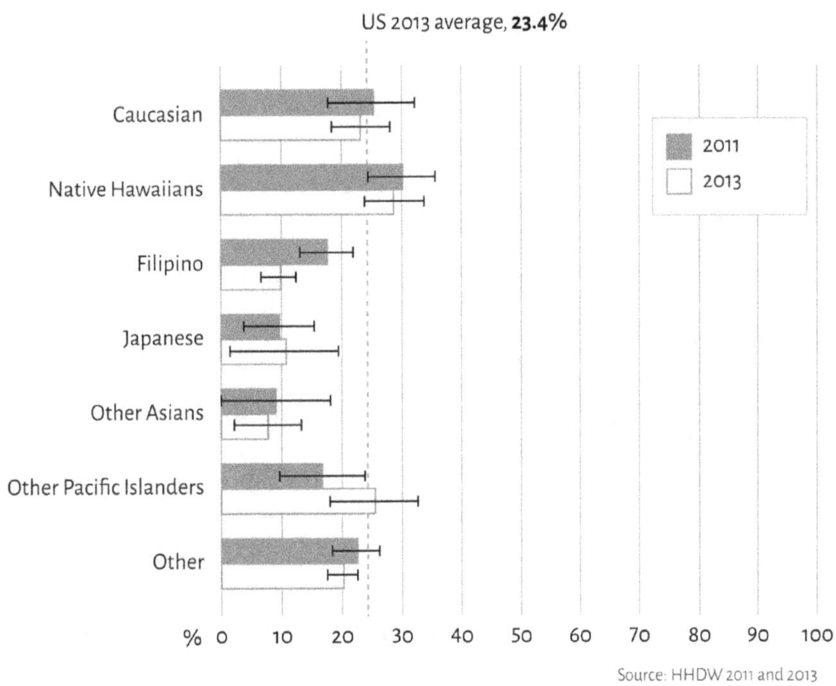

Figure 4 shows cocaine use amongst high school students by ethnicity. An increase was seen among Native Hawaiians and Japanese students, with Caucasian, Native Hawaiian, and Japanese students above the national average.

By 2013, all ethnic groups were below the national average and showed decreases in 30-day binge drinking as shown in Figure 5. Significant decreases brought Other Pacific Islanders below the national average.

Figure 6 shows Caucasian and Native Hawaiian adults were above the national average over all years with regards to adult binge drinking behavior, with Native Hawaiians consistently ranked the highest. Although below the national average, Chinese adults are the only group showing a steady increase over time.

Figure 7 shows the rate of mental health treatment among adults with any mental illness was lower than the national rate in 2009–2013 in Hawai'i. In Hawai'i, about 56,000 adults with any mental illness (30.0% of all adults with any mental illness) per year in 2009–2013 received mental health treatment or counseling within the year prior to being surveyed.

There are many efforts in place to reduce the behavioral health disparities within the substance abuse prevention and treatment field. A major funding source is derived from the SAMHSA grant programs. Table 2 describes the nine grant programs, agencies, and amount of grants awarded during the 2015 fiscal year (SAMHSA, 2015b). Although grant programs exist that benefit young people in Hawai'i, it is clear from the charts presented that anti-drug and alcohol use programs should focus their effort on the youth of Hawai'i (with additional foci on minority groups).

Figure 4. Ever used cocaine by ethnicity (high school students)

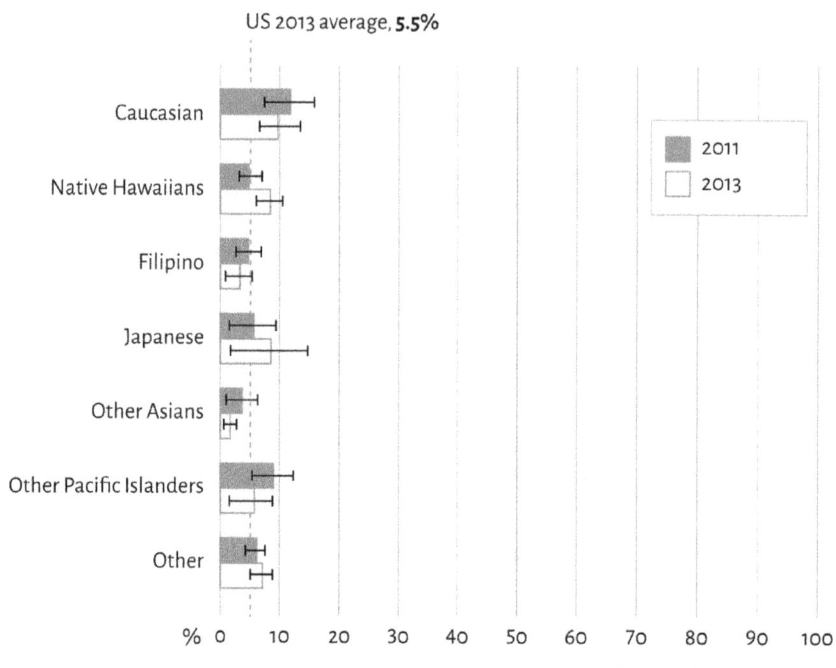

Figure 5. 30-day binge drinking by ethnicity by ethnicity (high school students)

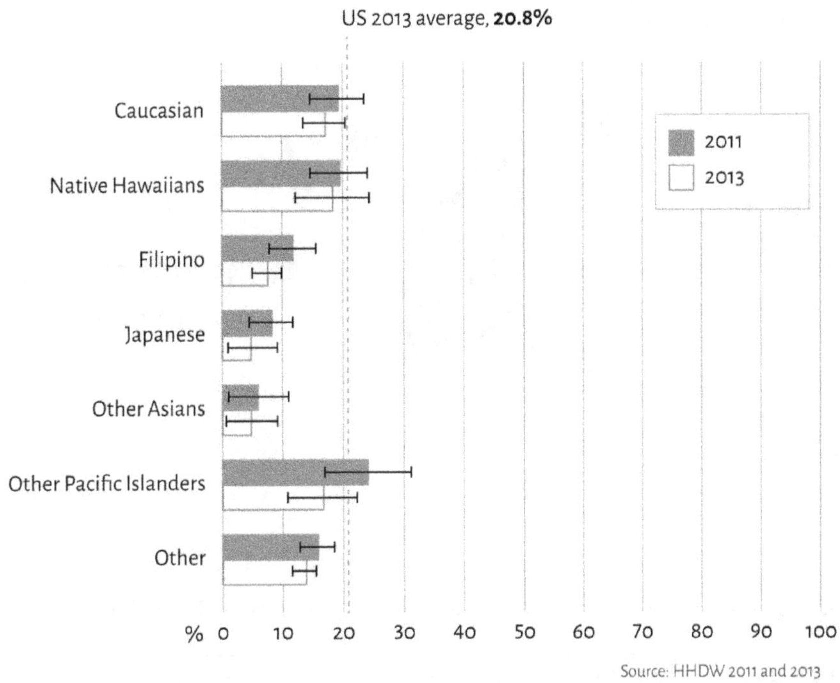

Figure 6. Adult binge drinking by ethnicity (age 18 and older)

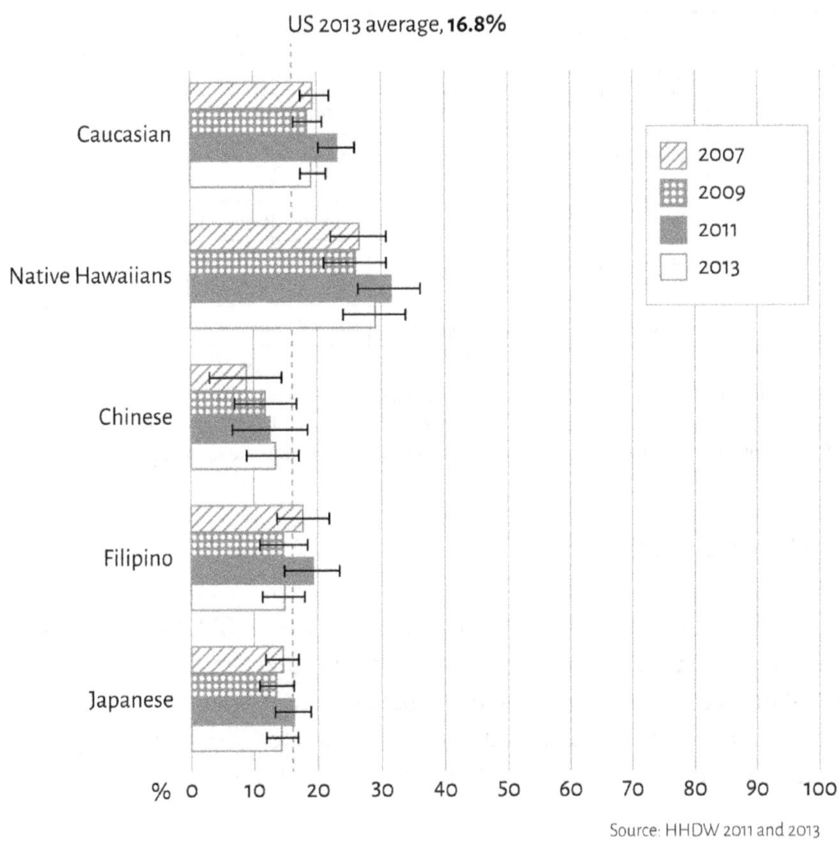

Figure 7. Past-year mental health treatment/counseling among adults aged 18 or older with Any Mental Illness (AMI) in Hawai'i (2009-2013)
Source: Adapted from SAMHSA, 2015a

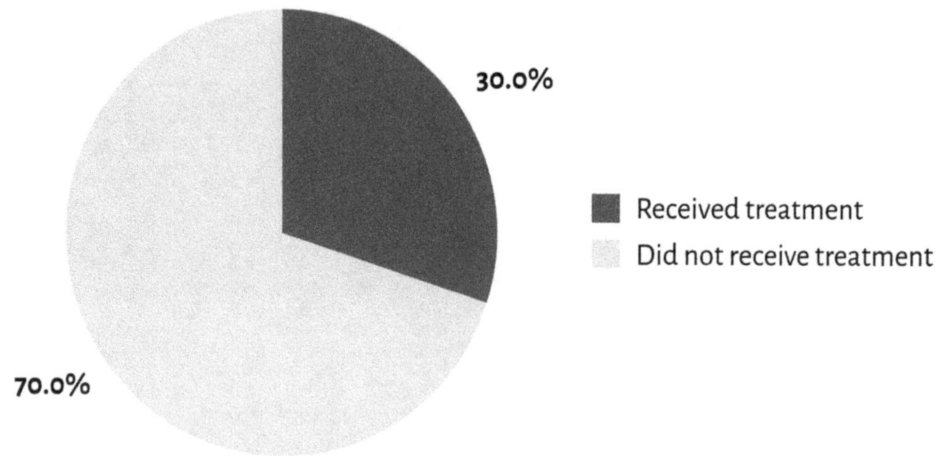

Table 2. SAMHSA grants awarded to Hawai'i agencies in fiscal Year 2015 (SAMHSA, 2015b)

SAMHSA Grant Program	Agency Awarded Grant in Hawai'i	Program to be Funded	Amount Awarded
Center for Mental Health Services (CMHS)	Hawai'i State Department of Health	Child Mental Health Initiative	$945,101
	Hawai'i State Department of Education	HI-AWARE[a]	$1,948,290
Center for Substance Abuse Prevention (CSAP)	Parents and Children Together	Drug Free Communities	$125,000
	Coalition for a Drug-Free Hawai'i	Drug Free Communities	$125,000
	Hawai'i State Department of Health	SPF-PFS[b]	$1,776,772
Center for Substance Abuse Treatment (CSAT)	Hawai'i State Department of the Judiciary	Family Drug Courts	$324,786
	University of Hawai'i at Mānoa	Offender Reentry Program	$400,000
	Hawai'i Department of Health	Cooperative Agreements to Benefit Homeless Individuals for States	$1,209,203
	Hawai'i Health Systems Corporation	SBIRT Training[c]	$190,162

Note.
1. HI-AWARE: Strengthens school-family-community partnerships in local schools
2. SPF-PFS: A Strategic Prevention Framework initiative aimed at building sustainable prevention infrastructures in Hawai'i
3. SBIRT Training: Screening, brief intervention, and referral to treatment for primary care health care providers

Hawai'i: Workforce Status

Since 2010, the Hawai'i/Pacific Basin Area Health Education Center (AHEC) has performed the Hawai'i Physician Workforce Assessment to estimate the state's supply and demand for physicians and physician assistants using full time equivalents of time spent in patient care by specialty and zip code (licensure and phone surveys were conducted). Compared with national estimates of demand by age, gender, and health status of population, Hawai'i State was found to be more than 600 physicians short with the deficiency growing by 60 physicians a year (Withy, 2015). Subsequent research completed by the Hawai'i/Pacific Basin AHEC (currently in review for publication) shows that Hawai'i has 92 less physician assistants than needed, with no school available in the State of Hawai'i to train them. The primary care workforce (including physicians, physician assistants, and nurse practitioners) is 25% smaller than is needed. The Hawai'i/Pacific Basin AHEC maintains the statewide physician supply database and will continue to monitor shortages. There is inadequate research in Hawai'i addressing supply and demand of public health, medical technology, behavioral health, and speech pathology or audiology providers. As a proxy for a full assessment (the state supported job website www.hirenethawaii.com), job openings are used to determine workforce demand. While this is an incomplete measure of demand, there is a clear need for these providers (Hawai'i/Pacific Basin AHEC, 2014).

As of 2014, the MD/DO state-wide physician workforce was experiencing shortages in many specialties, including general and family practice (34.6%), psychiatry (7.90%), and child and adolescent psychiatry (-28.1% [Hawai'i/Pacific Basin AHEC, 2014]). In the U.S., the only professionals allowed to call themselves "doctors" in the medical field are those who have either an MD (Doctor of [Allopathic] Medicine) or DO (Doctor of Osteopathic Medicine) and have completed the appropriate post-graduate training. These statistics, however, demonstrate the challenge in performing research and interpreting statistics that underlie all rural health initiatives, but is exemplified with island regions. Regarding the state-wide adult psychiatry workforce, it would initially seem that there is only a minor shortage of these psychiatrists (7.9%). This is highly misleading once the statistics are assembled per county (most of which consist of one or two islands) instead of state-wide (adult psychiatry ranges from negative shortages to 41.2%). Table 3 presents the physician shortages per county. Notice the density of physicians in Honolulu County (the seat of state government and the most populous city in Hawai'i). Not a single county's statistics are remotely close to mirroring the state-wide score. Even within the State of Hawai'i, each island requires unique approaches to remedy the physician workforce. The cost, access, and quality of care are stressed due to the added challenges of island-to-island travel, lodging, and availability of mental health professionals in that county.

It is important to note that much of the existing research in this region has been on improving the physician workforce only (not including the other mental health professions). Professionals who have earned MD or DO degrees, however, are not the only professionals trained to provide mental health services. There is insignificant research on the supply, demand, and overall quality of the mental health profession in the Pacific. Due to the lack of public health training, if research on a particular topic ex-

Table 3. Percentage of physician shortages for selected specialties, arranged by county

	General and Family Practice	Psychiatry	Child and Adolescent Psychiatry
State-wide	34.6	7.9	-28.1
Hawai'i County	0.0*	39.2	0.0*
Honolulu County	48.1	0.0*	0.0*
Kaua'i County	30.6	29.5	0.0*
Maui County	11.2	41.2	0.9

Hawai'i/Pacific Basin AHEC, 2014)

Note. *Figures presented with excess (negative shortage) but exact figures were not available

ists, it is likely to include small/unrepresentative sample sizes, bias, improper evaluation, or some other form of invalid measurement, contributing to the patchwork of ungeneralizable existing research. For non-physician mental health providers, Table 4 presents a current comparison of workforce data between national and state trends. It is easy to see that much more research is needed.

The U.S.-Affiliated Pacific Islands (USAPIs): Overview

The U.S.-affiliated Pacific islands are illustrated in Figure 8.The U.S. is directly involved in the health of seven Pacific regions (the "Pacific"), which are the State of Hawai'i and the six U.S.-Affiliated Pacific

Table 4. Mental health provider workforce trends in the state of Hawai'i

Provider Type	Statistic Type*	National	State-wide	Hawai'i County	Honolulu County	Kaua'i County	Maui County
Mental Health and Substance Abuse Social Worker	Current Employment	114,200	350	280[a]	300	130[b]	40
	Projected Employment	140,200	420	320[a]	360	150[b]	50
	Job Growth	+23%	+19.7%	N/A[d/e]	+20%	+12.4%	+21.4%
	Median Annual Wages	$41,380	$47,140[g]	$51,030[a]	$48,810	$50,710[b]	N/A[e]
Clinical Psychologist	Current Employment	145,100[c]	710[c]	70	520	N/A[e]	N/A[e]
	Projected Employment	161,500[c]	770[c]	70	570	N/A[e]	N/A[e]
	Job Growth	+11%[c]	+8.5%[c]	+12.3%	+9.2%	N/A[e]	N/A[e]
	Median Annual Wages	$68,900[c]	$102,990[c/g]	$81,760	$79,730	N/A[e]	N/A[e]
Marriage and Family Therapist	Current Employment	37,800	180	40	170	N/A[e]	N/A[e]
	Projected Employment	49,400	210	40	210	N/A[e]	N/A[e]
	Job Growth	+31%	+20.5%	+17.1%	+25.2%	N/A[e]	N/A[e]
	Median Annual Wages	$48,040	$58,300[g]	N/A[e]	$60,560	N/A[e]	N/A[e]
Psychiatrist	Current Employment	27,200	210	N/A[e]	200	N/A[e]	N/A[e]
	Projected Employment	31,6000	230	N/A[e]	220	N/A[e]	N/A[e]
	Job Growth	+16%	+10.1%	N/A[e]	+7.4%	N/A[e]	N/A[e]
	Median Annual Wages	$181,880	$135,560[g]	N/A[e]	$163,640	N/A[e]	N/A[e]
Advanced Practice Psychiatric Nurse[f]	Current Employment	N/A[e]	N/A[e]	N/A[e]	N/A[e]	N/A[e]	N/A[e]
	Projected Employment	N/A[e]	N/A[e]	N/A[e]	N/A[e]	N/A[e]	N/A[e]
	Job Growth	N/A[e]	N/A[e]	N/A[e]	N/A[e]	N/A[e]	N/A[e]
	Median Annual Wages	N/A[e]	N/A[e]	N/A[e]	N/A[e]	N/A[e]	N/A[e]

Note. * Unless otherwise noted below, year attributes and ranges are as follows: current employment (2012), projected employment (2022), job growth (2012-2022), and median annual wages (2014)

1. No data available for career field, instead used all social work sub-categories in data (wage information is averaged).
2. Data only available for child, family, & school social workers (unclear data on clinical practice).
3. Includes clinical, counseling, and school psychologists.
4. Job growth is not calculated from only 2012-2022 projections, but includes job replacements, new job openings, and other data that were not available at the time of publication.
5. Data not available at the time of publication.
6. Advanced practice psychiatric nurses are classified under registered nurse (only data for registered nurses are available).
7. 2013 annual wages (2014 unavailable).

Data Sources: O*Net Online, 2016abcde; Hawaii Workforce Infonet, 2015abcde.

Figure 8. U.S.-Affiliated Pacific islands. The Northwestern Hawaiian Islands are mostly uninhabited. One notable island in the farthest reaches of Hawai`i is Midway Atoll, now a wildlife refuge and part of the Papahānaumokuākea Marine National Monument
Source: Adapted from USA National Oceanic and Atmospheric Administration/Department of Commerce, 2015

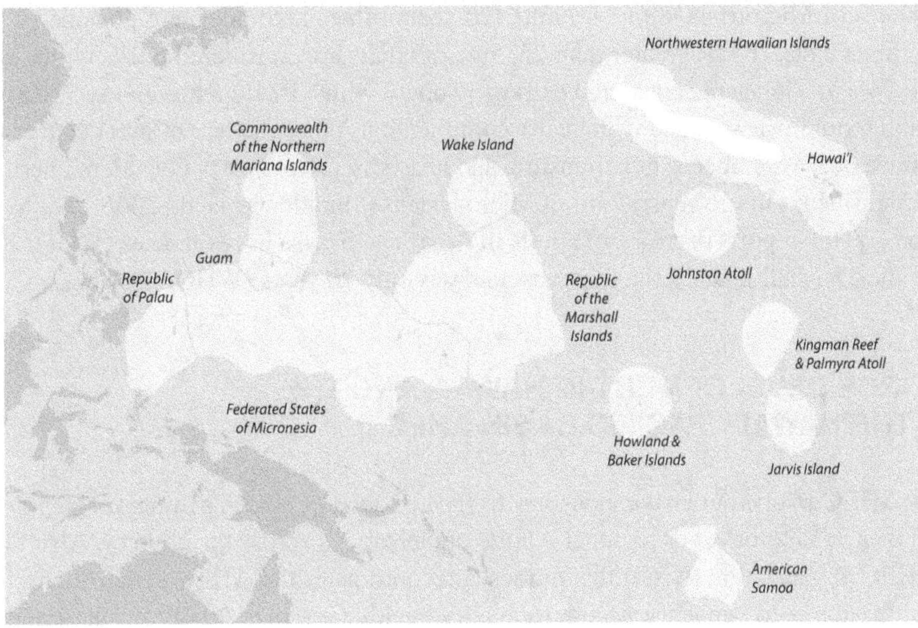

islands (USAPIs), including American Samoa, the Commonwealth of the Northern Mariana Islands (CNMI), Guam, the Federated States of Micronesia, the Republic of the Marshall Islands, and the Republic of Palau. The governments of the State of Hawai'i and the territories of American Samoa, CNMI, and Guam are all subdivisions of the U.S. Federal Government. The Federated States of Micronesia, Republic of Marshall Islands, and the Republic of Palau are independent countries but are joined with the U.S. (utilizing Compacts of Free Association) for operational support (including health, education, defense, and other essential needs). Unique agreements between each of the six USAPIs and the U.S. government delineate roles and responsibilities for all parties, making business and philanthropic efforts to these areas a form of semi-international work (for example, a passport is required to travel between Hawai'i [a U.S. state] and American Samoa [a U.S. territory]).

The USAPIs: Health Disparities

Full scale research studies in mental health status (including depression rates) have not been conducted to cover the entire Pacific, but the extreme prevalence of diabetes in the Pacific (some of the highest in the nation) is associated with depression, a topic that must be carefully and tediously approached in the collectivist cultures that Pacific Islander nations exhibit (Held, DePue, Rosen, Bereolos, Nu'usolia, Tuitele, & McGarvey, 2010). Due to the lack of space to cover the many health disparities in the USAPIs, an overview of the research will be presented together. Much of the current public health work is geared toward Native Hawaiians, which accounts for the emphasis given above.

In the Federated States of Micronesia, vitamin A deficiency and chronic diseases have emerged as serious health concerns, mostly due to dietary changes over the past 50 years (Wolanski, Richmond, & McCook, 2004). In relation to current infectious disease trends, there was a 2009 outbreak of Zika on Yap, a state of the Federated States of Micronesia (Duffy et al., 2009). In Kosrae, another state of the Federated States of Micronesia, 88% of adults (20 years of age and older) are considered overweight with a body mass index (BMI) greater than 25, 59% of adults are considered obese with a BMI greater than 30, and 24% of adults are considered extremely obese with a BMI greater than 35 (Cassels, 2006). Morbidity and mortality associated with health complications of obesity are of great concern in Kosrae, especially since obesity, diabetes, hypertension, and heart disease are party considered heritable conditions that will influence future generations of Micronesians (Shmulewitz et al., 2006). The World Health Organization (WHO) reports that 47% of adults in American Samoa have diabetes (WHO, 2010). In the Republic of the Marshall Islands, the life expectancy is only 70 years (WHO, 2015).

WORKFORCE DEVELOPMENT IN HAWAI'I AND THE USAPIs: THE HAWAI'I /PACIFIC BASIN AHEC

The national AHEC grant program is a sponsored by the U.S. DHHS, HRSA's Bureau of Health Workforce. Grants are given to state-based or regional AHEC organizations across the country. Also funded is the National AHEC Organization (NAO) that guides and coordinates the AHEC centers across the nation. The NAO's mission is to "enhance access to quality health care, particularly primary and preventive care, by improving the supply and distribution of healthcare professionals through community/academic education partnerships" (NAO, 2016). In order to be eligible, AHEC organizations must be part of a local university school of medicine (or nursing school if no school of medicine exists). Emphasis areas for the state/regional AHEC organizations are to 1) recruit and train students from minority and disadvantaged backgrounds in health careers, 2) place health professions students in community-based clinical practice settings, with a focus on primary care, 3) promote inter-professional education and collaborative teams to improve quality of care, and 4) facilitate continuing education resources and programs for health professionals, particularly in rural and underserved areas (HRSA, 2016b).

There are 10 AHEC regions in the U.S., with Region IX (nine) covering Arizona, California, Hawai'i, Nevada, and Guam (HRSA, 2016c).The Hawai'i/Pacific Basin AHEC is one of the few organizations performing health workforce research and outreach activities on this vast expanse of ocean. The goal of the Hawai'i/Pacific Basin AHEC is to facilitate access to an abundant supply of knowledgeable and culturally competent providers through training and recruitment partnerships that will improve the diversity, distribution, and quality of the health professions workforce. This includes all career fields in the health sector, including mental health professionals. Based out of the University of Hawai'i John A. Burns Schools of Medicine in Honolulu, Hawai'i, the Hawai'i/Pacific Basin AHEC operates 10 centers across the Pacific, including six in Hawai'i (on four islands), one in the Republic of Palau, one in CNMI, one in Yap (a State of the Federated States of Micronesia), and one in American Samoa. Including the additional Guam AHEC center in Region IX, the only USAPI that is not currently serviced by an AHEC center is the Republic of the Marshall Islands (although an AHEC center is not present, Republic of Marshall Islands still receives services from the Hawai'i/Pacific Basin AHEC). Due to the cultural needs of each location in the Pacific, these centers produce a multitude of independent programs for their communities under the Hawai'i/Pacific Basin AHEC umbrella, while many other grant-funded programs exist through a mix of federal, state, and local sources that are available to communities across the entire Pacific.

Due to the lack of resources, professionals, and training, much of the mental health and substance abuse activity is performed by general practitioners, especially in the USAPIs. Therefore, workforce development initiatives aimed at primary caregivers are effective at reaching the professionals responsible for the mental health of their communities in many instances. Improving the general health workforce has direct, positive effects on the mental health workforce in rural, underserved areas. Although tele-health technologies for mental health (for example, tele-psychology, tele-psychology, and tele-therapy) are becoming increasingly popular in the mainland U.S. and other technologically advanced nations, these have not spread to much of the Pacific due to a lack of technological infrastructure to support this type of health care. The remoteness of the Pacific islands make internet virtually impossible for a vast proportion of the local populations. Additionally, where internet exists, the quality may be very poor. Activities such as webinars and recorded trainings are not recommended for much of the Pacific due to the lack of bandwidth or the nonexistence of internet capabilities. Physical documents (such as DVD recordings and workbooks) as well as in-person activities (such as classes and seminars) are much preferred for the same reasons. Unfortunately, this greatly increases the cost of working in these communities (including airfare, housing, food, and supplies).

Although many challenges exist in medical and mental health workforce development in the Pacific, the financial barrier is among the greatest. Students can often not afford to attend training programs in healthcare professions, especially when other technical training programs are less expensive. Professionals are able to earn a high salary when working in a major town or city (like Honolulu, which is arguably the only major city is the U.S.-Pacific region). Conversely in the underserved areas a professional's wage is far less than their counterparts on the mainland U.S. This is especially true among the USAPIs. Compounding this is the lack of education and training programs in general. There is only one medical school in Hawai'i so students frequently travel to the mainland for their education, which is often more expensive than the local medical school. Individuals with a high level of student loan debt are logically less likely to seek employment at low-paying positions.

There is a fine line in workforce development that must be approached cautiously. On one hand, it is important to train and inspire young people and students to seek training in health careers, but this sometimes will not benefit their original community. On the other hand, it may be easier to bring in general and mental health practitioners from the mainland. However, the intercultural barrier can impede the patient-practitioner dynamic. The Hawai'i/Pacific AHEC seeks to enhance the workforce by buffering both sides of this dilemma. For instance, educational programs for K-12 and college-aged students inspire many young people to go into scientific fields. The expansion of this program over the next four years will mitigate the loss of some students to mainland schools (and possible careers) by drastically increasing the number of participants and finding mentorship activities aimed at their success in Hawai'i. Additionally, the Hawai'i/Pacific AHEC tries to bring medical and mental health professionals to Hawai'i and provide them with access to cultural resources to help them engage with their new communities.

To better understand the comprehensive work undertaken by the AHEC centers across the Pacific, examples of AHEC activities will be discussed that may be replicable and adapted for regional needs across the globe.

The Big Island AHEC collaborates with local student groups to provide volunteer experiences at a local hospital, including mini-camps lasting two days that interactively exposes the students to different departments and medicinal specialties. The center also sponsors medical and nursing students to perform rotations at local medical centers and supports student travel to Hawai'i Island for at least 10 students and residents a year from health professions training programs, including nursing, nurse practitioner, medicine, social work, physician assistants, medical technology, physical therapists, and family medicine residents performing rotations in Hilo. The Big Island AHEC recruits preceptors as needed and assists with acquiring lodging.

The Na Lei Wili AHEC (meaning "intertwining Lei" in Hawaiian) on Kaua'i focuses on youth development by implementing annual "grow our own healers" camps that introduce students to traditional Hawaiian healing practices (like lomi lomi massage and growing taro plants), as well as health skills (CPR/first aid, suture practice on rubber arms, and plaster/casting on their own arms). This center also operates a Health Occupations for Teens (HOT) Club at local schools, which is a recurring year-long program that teaches the students about health careers and educates them on medical terminology and practices. The HOT Club also provides guest speakers, comprised of current health professionals from various fields. To build leadership skills, the HOT Club allows high school seniors to be peer mentors to younger students, helping guide their interests. Additionally, the Na Lei Wili AHEC sponsors the Jr. Medical Reserve Corps, a group of young people who are trained to provide emergency preparedness training under supervision of the Kaua'i District Health Office and the Kaua'i Civil Defense Agency. This center also provides support for medical/nursing students performing rotations in local medical centers.

The Palau AHEC, the first AHEC in the USAPI, has played both a regional and local role in developing the health careers pipeline and engaging in bridging programs. The Palau AHEC works with Palau Community College (PCC) and its nursing program to assist in developing the PCC's Health Careers Initiative to encourage other PCC students to nursing or other health careers programs in the region. One of the main impediments to entry to the PCC nursing program (and all health careers programs) is high school and community college graduates' weakness in the basic sciences. To address this challenge, the Palau AHEC, along with the Pacific Island Health Officers' Association (PIHOA), developed a regional approach to initiating a "Foundation Sciences Boot Camp" process which is an intensive bridging program to ready high school and community college graduates so that they can qualify for and survive in science-based health careers programs in and outside the region. The Palau AHEC also conducts training for the public health workforce in the public health sciences (for example, epidemiology, health promotion/education, and nutrition).

The Maui County AHEC, known as Huli Au Ola (meaning "the turning point of life" in Hawaiian), serves the three-island County of Maui: Maui, Moloka'i, and Lāna'i. The AHEC Center is located on the rural, largely Native Hawaiian island of Moloka'i. In additional to implementing annual health career and science education camps similar to other AHECs, the Maui County AHEC also conducts an in-school bi-weekly health education program for K-12 students. Moloka'i offers clinical training to students when requested and is becoming an increasingly popular rotation site for medical and nursing students. Students meet monthly with the AHEC staff to learn how to develop a resume and cover letter, apply to college and training programs, improve test taking skills, locate scholarships, and discuss community service projects performed with community "kupuna" (elders). The Huli Au Ola AHEC provides regular clinical rotations for six to eight 3rd and 4th year medical and advanced practice nursing students. The Moloka'i Community Health Center staff request these rotation students and providers and offers lodging, transportation, and logistical support. Public health nursing and medical students are also drawn to Moloka'i rotations due to the proximity of "Kalaupapa", which is the historic leper colony in Hawai'i.

The Commonwealth of Northern Marianas Islands (CNMI) AHEC is sponsored by and housed at the Northern Marianas College (NMC). Achievements to date include increasing the indigenous nursing workforce by training six resident nurses who successfully passed the National Council Licensure Examination (NCLEX) certification exam, coordinating two annual health career fairs for the island of Saipan, and continuing the two-week Summer Health Careers Program for students from 10th to 12th grade who expressed interest in a health career. The CNMI AHEC provides technical assistance to the Public School System's Career and Technical Education Department to offer a nursing assistant program at the Saipan Southern High School. The Nursing Assistantship program is a secondary career technical education program for students interested in pursuing the career ladder into nursing and culminates in taking the certification exam to become a certified nurse assistant/aide.

The Federated States of Micronesia hosts the Yap AHEC in the State of Yap. The Yap AHEC conducts an annual month long summer program to promote interest in the health professions. The Future Health Providers Summer Program enrolls students in the prerequisite class for the health assistant training in College of Micronesia (COM) - Introduction to Health Sciences. In addition to the class, the students also rotate through the hospital and community health centers on preceptorships where they gain exposure to various careers in the health services. Finally the students break into groups where they complete a community health project they have designed. The Yap AHEC has implemented the COM curriculum for community health assistants (CHAs) and community health workers (CHWs) in Yap. This program is designed for the individuals that care for Yap's isolated neighboring islands. The Yap AHEC maintains the lone medical library in Yap State.

The Waimānalo AHEC is a community health center that serves an underserved Native Hawaiian population on windward coast (eastern coast) of O'ahu, Hawai'i. The Waimānalo AHEC activities include clinical training for three medical students, two family medicine residents, and two advanced practice nursing students a year, as well as an interprofessional training program and support for a culturally based in-school mentoring and health promotion program at Waimānalo Elementary/Intermediate School (called Kū I Ka Māna).

The American Samoa AHEC was established in 2006 and is located in the capital city of Pago Pago (pronounced Pahn-go Pahn-go) at the American Samoa Community College (ASCC) HHS Department. The AHEC coordinates a Health Professions Career Day for students at the high school level along with community partners. High school students can participate in a two-week summer camp program that is be modeled after the Kaua'i and Maui County AHEC programs and includes activities and discussions with nurses, physicians, medical technologists, social workers, and other health professionals from the community. The American Samoa AHEC collaborates with Kapi'olani Community College in Honolulu, Hawai'i to have visiting professors come to teach courses in emergency medical technician and respiratory therapy skills. Clinical rotations are supported for nursing, medical, public health, social work, and psychology students from elsewhere, particularly University of Hawai'i, to include community projects and clinical work.

The Waianae AHEC on O'ahu, Hawai'i, housed at the Waianae Coast Comprehensive Health Center (a federally qualified health center) is the newest and final AHEC Center within the Hawai'i/Pacific Basin AHEC program. An important factor related to the under-representation of minorities in health professions is the lack of role models and exposure to health careers during the critical K-12 school years. Community care experiences mandate the second year medical students speak about becoming a physician and demonstrate clinical skills at health fairs, career fairs, health professions classes, pre-med associations, and any academic organization that makes a request. Waianae area youth relate well to the second year medical students who inspire local youths to consider medicine or allied health careers as a realistic possibility.

The main office for the Hawai'i/Pacific Basin AHEC is located at the University of Hawai'i, John A. Burns School of Medicine in Honolulu, Hawai'i and helps coordinate and support the activities aforementioned at the local AHEC sites. A major program of the main office is the Hawai'i State Loan Repayment Program (SLRP) which provides financial incentives in the form of loan repayment to physicians, physician assistants, nurse practitioners, psychologists, social workers, and marriage and family therapists that agree to serve for two years in low-income, underserved communities in the Pacific. Additionally, the main office operates the PreHealth Career Corps (PHCC) which is a four year program designed for 11th or 12th grade high school students and/or undergraduate college students to inspire them to enter health careers. This new program, started in 2015, includes activities such as health career education, mentoring, research opportunities, and shadowing of health care providers. The activity plan for the PHCC is shown in Table 5. Starting in 2016, the main office published the first edition of the Hawai'i Health Career Navigator, a book that does not only encourage young people to enter health careers, but describes over 75 different types of health careers in Hawai'i, including expected salary, job growth information, career descriptions, types of training needed, local educational programs to fulfill these needs, and professional associations for additional resources. This free book (available for download on the Hawai'i/Pacific Basin AHEC website) is an invaluable resource for students, parents,

Table 5. Activity plan for PreHealth career corps

Area of Activity	Year 1	Year 2	Year 3	Year 4
Career Readiness	• Receive Health Career Navigator book • Participate in Teen Health Camp, UH Health Career Opportunity Program (HCOP), or AHEC Summer Camps	• Assist with improving and updating web-based Navigator book • Assist with organizing Teen Health Camp • Shadow health care providers • Assist with career presentations	• Give talks to students about health professions in Hawai'i • Write newsletter article(s)	Give health careers orientation sessions at your academic institution
Campus Exposure	Visit health professions campuses and participate in local health career or campus career fairs on their island	• Perform course shadowing at healthcare campuses •Volunteer at your local campus	Enroll in health careers training preparatory classes at local college	Volunteer to provide tours to students visiting your health career campus
Mentoring	Participate in quarterly group mentoring sessions and receive follow-up mentoring	Provide email mentoring for a new PHCC student matched by island and interests	Meet with PHCC Staff about career goals and decide career mentor	• Meet with and shadow mentor • Monthly emails with mentor
Research	Participate in health workforce research for the their interest area with AHEC	Learn to do literature searching on health research and assist with a publication for the *Hawai'i Journal of Medicine and Public Health*	• Apply to Hawai'i Pacific Health research opportunities •Apply to NIDDK STEP-UP Diabetes Research Program and other local NIH opportunities	• Apply to Hawai'i Pacific Health undergraduate research •Apply for INBRE research and other undergraduate research programs
Education Sessions	Inquiry-based case learning session at group mentoring	Email and social media etiquette training at group mentoring	Professionalism discussion at group mentoring	Graduation party

Note. PHCC = PreHealth Career Corps.

teachers, career counselors, and school administrators for supporting health careers in Hawai'i. A free student companion e-book is also available on the Hawai'i/Pacific Basin AHEC website with interactive worksheets and activities to enhance the content provided in the Hawai'i Health Career Navigator.

Workforce Development in Hawai'i and the USAPIs: Other Organizations

Papa Ola Lōkahi (pronounced *pah-pah oh-lah loh-kah-hee*) and Alu Like (pronounced *ah-lew leek-ay*) are two of the leading Native Hawaiian health organizations that focus part of their organizational strategies on workforce development, employment, and professional training. The *Native Hawaiian Health Strategy Map* illustrated in Figure 9 is a recent initiative of Papa Ola Lōkahi. After recognizing the generous work done in the community aimed at Native Hawaiians, Papa Ola Lōkahi decided to take on a coordination role. Throughout 2015, strategic planning discussion meetings were held with any and all interested parties (such as individuals, directors/staff of non-profits, and policy-makers) to explore ways to enhance their overall impact through combined and coordinated efforts. The outputs of these meetings include inter-organizational resource sharing, awareness-building of previously hidden logistical challenges, raising confidence in shared aspirations and goals, among other benefits. During a workforce development seminar sponsored by the Hawai'i Public Health Training Hui in January 2016, this plan was described by the Papa Ola Lōkahi's current executive director (Sharlene Chun-Lum) as a living, growing document. An integral aspect of developing an enduring plan is to include adaptation flexibility for progress and change over time, so although the official meetings have concluded for the development of this plan, future meetings and revisions will be implemented to provide continual revisions based on need.

Alu Like operates the Ho'omānea 'Ōiwi workforce development program (meaning "strengthening one's foundation" in Hawaiian). Sponsored by the Workforce Innovation and Opportunity Act (U.S. Department of Labor, Division of Indian and Native American Programs [DINAP]), Ho'omānea 'Ōiwi provides education and training opportunities for low-income Native Hawaiians. Ka Ipu Ka'eo (meaning "the full calabash" in Hawaiian) is a career and technical education program that Alu Like operates, with the goal of connecting Native Hawaiians with specialized training in career fields that interest them.

Another entity that provides workforce development services is the Hawai'i Public Health Training Hui (meaning "meeting" or "group" in Hawaiian) is part of the Western Regional Public Health Training Center (WRPHTC). The Public Health Training Center (PHTC) grant program is organized similarly to the AHEC grant program. Sponsored by the HRSA (part of the U.S. DHHS), the funds support a National Coordinating Center for Public Health Training as well as 10 regional PHTCs. The Region IX (nine) grant is operated by the WRPHTC, which covers Arizona, California, Nevada, Hawai'i, and USAPIs. Based at the University of Arizona, local performance sites (LPS) in the previously mentioned areas perform health workforce development activities for their own communities as well as in coordinated efforts with the region. In Hawai'i, the LPS is based out of the University of Hawai'i Office of Public Health Studies, called the Hawai'i Public Health Training Hui which delivers theme-based trainings to professionals in the health field throughout the year (at least 16 per year, at least once per month). Additionally, the Hawai'i Public Health Training Hui partners with the Healthcare Professionals Teleconference Training Series, a local organization that provides continuing education credits for healthcare professionals in Hawai'i, mostly aimed at the behavioral health counselors/therapists in Hawai'i including certified substance abuse counselors (CSACs), licensed social workers (LSWs), and licensed clinical social workers (LCSWs). The Hawai'i Public Health Training Hui is accredited to provide continuing

Figure 9. The Native Hawaiian Health Strategy Plan is a constantly-changing, living, growing document that is regularly updated. During 2015, many planning sessions and webinars further developed this plan. "Workforce development" is under "increase social equity" but is integrated throughout this strategy plan. Source: Adapted from Papa Ola Lokahi, 2015a

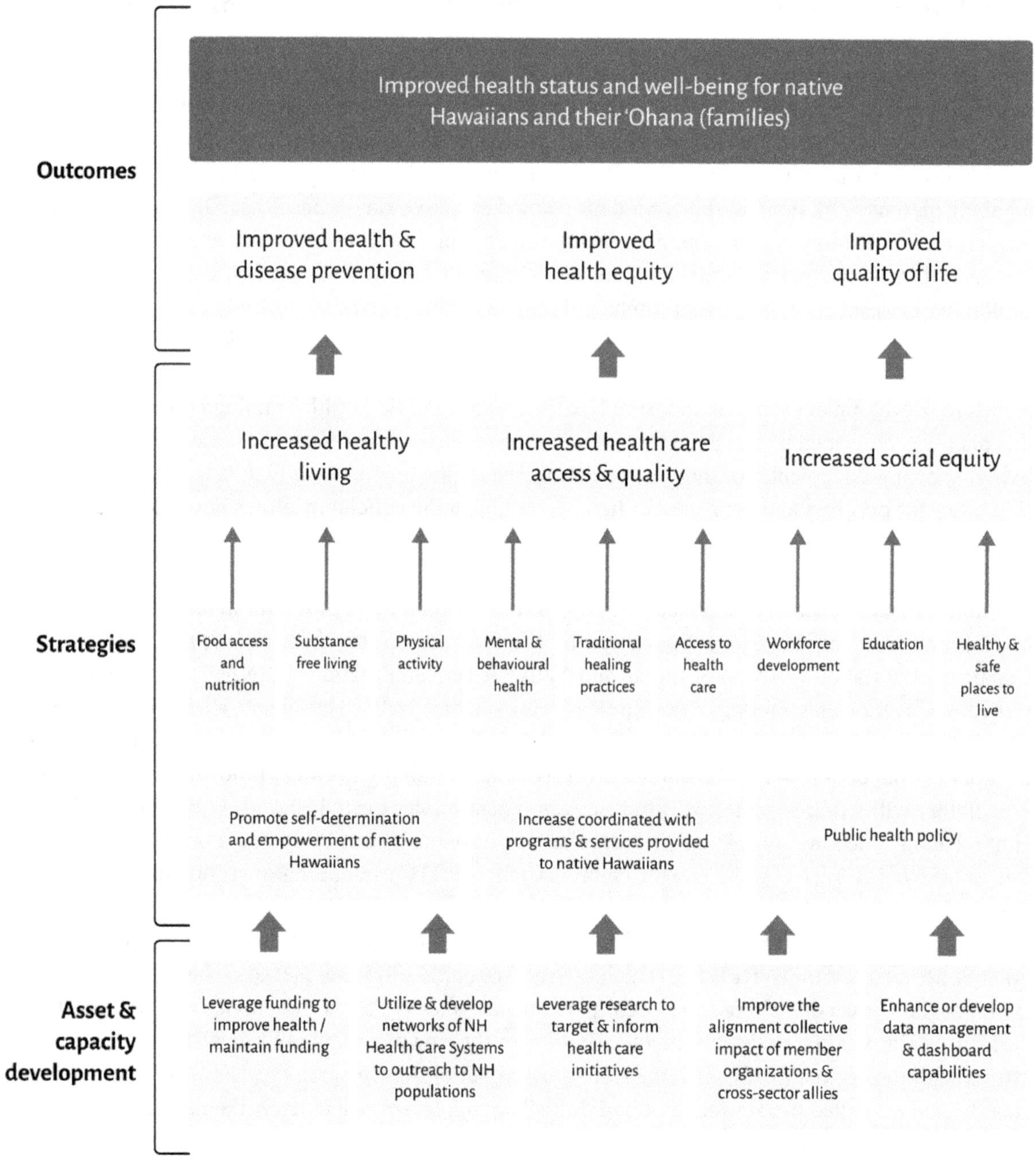

education credits for registered nurses (RNs) and certified health education specialists (CHES). These offerings are major incentives for participants of the training events who are required to gain continuing education to maintain their certifications.

The Hawai'i Public Health Training Hui events are offered free-of-charge and can be viewed remotely (from work or home) via the internet with a live webcast. The online viewers are even able to email questions to a member of the staff during the presentation and these can be answered during the question and answer session at the end of the presentation. To ease scheduling conflicts, the training events are scheduled during lunch hours and participants are invited to bring their lunch with them and eat during the presentation. Graciously, the Queen's Medical Center in Honolulu, Hawai'i donates the meeting space once a month, which helps to greatly reduce cost.

The Pacific Island Health Officers' Association (PIHOA) is a professional organization comprised of physicians, hospital medical directors, and local health officials from across the Pacific region. This influential group focuses on developing health-related policies in a collaborative and coordinated way. PIHOA also focuses on workforce development due the complicated web of licensing and certification procedures that vary between the U.S.-based systems and other international methods. Due to the highly-connected nature of PIHOA, they often write and submit grants for health departments and organizations, providing the administrative support throughout the grant's lifespan. Also, PIHOA has become a leader in the Pacific for lobbying efforts for the U.S. Federal Government. Officials from PIHOA frequently travel to Washington D.C. and other major U.S. cities to discuss health concerns with politicians and other social innovators. Additionally, PIHOA is the organization that houses the Local Performance Site for the WRPHTC grant program, so they collaborate with the Hawai'i Public Health Training Hui frequently to improve and disseminate education materials.

CONCLUSION

In rural, isolated, and/or island regions, mental health care if often provided by general practitioners. In order to effectively develop the mental health workforce, it is essential to consider the needs of all health care providers and provide education/training/resources to them. Workforce development in Hawai'i and the USAPIs is beyond the capacity of any one organization or government, but is instead a priority that requires collaboration and coordination among all sectors of medicine and public health. Generally speaking, the rich cultures of the Pacific enjoy an emphasis on family and interpersonal relationships. For these cultures, it is virtually impossible (and occasionally unethical) for outsiders to simply tell them what they should be doing. The changes need to be developed and fostered by the communities and then supported by internal and external resources. This rationale is precisely why so many successful programs in the Pacific focus on youth development and mentoring. Young people end up becoming the professionals for their own communities, and these communities become more sustainable and healthy due to the strengths that are already present in the human resources.

REFERENCES

Cassels, S. (2006). Overweight in the Pacific: Links between foreign dependence, global food trade, and obesity in the Federated States of Micronesia. *Globalization and Health*, *2*(1), 1–8. doi:10.1186/1744-8603-2-10 PMID:16834782

Central Intelligence Agency. (2013). *The world factbook 2013-14*. Washington, DC: Central Intelligence Agency.

Department of Health and Human Services. (2015). *Health Resource Service Administration, Find shortage areas: HPSA by state and county*. Retrieved from www.hpsafind.hrsa.gov

Duffy, M. R., Chen, T.-H., Hancock, W. T., Powers, A. M., Kool, J. L., Lanciotti, R. S., & Hayes, E. B. et al. (2009). Zika virus outbreak on Yap Island, Federated States of Micronesia. *The New England Journal of Medicine*, *360*(24), 2536–2543. doi:10.1056/NEJMoa0805715 PMID:19516034

Hawai`i State Epidemiological Outcomes Workgroup. (2014a). *State epidemiological profile: Selected youth and adult drug indicators*. Retrieved from http://health.hawaii.gov/substance-abuse/survey/hiepi-profile2014/

Hawai`i State Epidemiological Outcomes Workgroup. (2014b). *State epidemiological profile: Selected youth and adult alcohol indicators*. Retrieved from http://health.hawaii.gov/substance-abuse/survey/hiepi-profile2014/

Hawaii Workforce Infonet. (2015a). *State of Hawaii: Employment projections for industries & occupations 2012-2022*. Retrieved from https://www.hiwi.org/gsipub/index.asp?docid=423

Hawaii Workforce Infonet. (2015b). *Hawaii County: Employment projections for industries & occupations 2012-2022*. Retrieved from https://www.hiwi.org/gsipub/index.asp?docid=423

Hawaii Workforce Infonet. (2015c). *Honolulu County: Employment projections for industries & occupations 2012-2022*. Retrieved from https://www.hiwi.org/gsipub/index.asp?docid=423

Hawaii Workforce Infonet. (2015d). *Kauai County: Employment projections for industries & occupations 2012-2022*. Retrieved from https://www.hiwi.org/gsipub/index.asp?docid=423

Hawaii Workforce Infonet. (2015e). *Maui County: Employment projections for industries & occupations 2012-2022*. Retrieved from https://www.hiwi.org/gsipub/index.asp?docid=423

Hawaii/Pacific Basin AHEC. (2014). Report of findings from the Hawaii Physician Workforce Assessment project. Honolulu, HI: University of Hawaii, John A. Burns School of Medicine (JABSOM).

Health Resources and Services Administration. (2015). *Mental health HPSA designation criteria*. Retrieved from http://bhpr.hrsa.gov/shortage/hpsas/designationcriteria/mentalhealthhpsacriteria.html

Health Resources and Services Administration. (2016a). *Health professional shortage areas (HPSA) and medically underserved areas/populations (MUA/P)*. Retrieved from http://datawarehouse.hrsa.gov/topics/shortageareas.aspx#chart

Health Resources and Services Administration. (2016b). *Area health education centers*. Retrieved from http://bhpr.hrsa.gov/grants/areahealtheducationcenters/

Health Resources and Services Administration. (2016c). *Health workforce, area health education centers (AHEC) program directory*. Retrieved from http://datawarehouse.hrsa.gov/topics/healthprofessions.aspx

Heisler, E., & Bagalman, E. (2015). *The mental health workforce: A primer*. Washington, DC: Congressional Research Service.

Held, R. F., DePue, J., Rosen, R., Bereolos, N., Nuusolia, O., Tuitele, J., & McGarvey, S. (2010). Patient and health care provider views of depressive symptoms and diabetes in American Samoa. *Cultural Diversity & Ethnic Minority Psychology*, *16*(4), 461–467. doi:10.1037/a0020089 PMID:21058808

Institute of Medicine. (2012). *The mental health and substance abuse workforce for older adults: In whose hands?* Washington, DC: The National Academies Press.

Migration Policy Institute. (2011). *2008 American Community Survey and census data on the foreign born by State*. Retrieved from http://migrationinformation.org/dataHub/acscensus.cfm#

National AHEC Organization. (2016). *AHEC mission*. Retrieved from http://www.nationalahec.org/About/AHECMission.html

O*Net Online. (2015a). *Summary report for: 21-1023.00 mental health and substance abuse social workers*. Retrieved from http://www.onetonline.org/link/summary/21-1023.00

O*Net Online. (2015b). *Summary report for: 19-3031.02 clinical psychologists*. Retrieved from http://www.onetonline.org/link/summary/19-3031.02

O*Net Online. (2015c). *Summary report for: 21-1013.00 marriage and family therapists*. Retrieved from http://www.onetonline.org/link/summary/21-1013.00

O*Net Online. (2015d). *Summary report for: 29-1066.00 psychiatrists*. Retrieved from http://www.onetonline.org/link/summary/29-1066.00

O*Net Online. (2015e). *Summary report for: 29-1141.02 advanced practice psychiatric nurses*. Retrieved from http://www.onetonline.org/link/summary/29-1141.02

Papa Ola Lokahi. (2015a). *Hawaiian health master plan, 2013*. Retrieved from http://www.papaolalokahi.org/wp-content/uploads/2015/01/NH-Health-Overview-FINAL-Master-Planning.pdf

Papa Ola Lokahi. (2015b). *Nā leo I mauli ola – Native Hawaiian health discussion webinars*. Retrieved from http://www.papaolalokahi.org/na-leo-i-mauli-ola-native-hawaiian-health-discussion-webinars/

SAMHSA. (2013). *Behavioral health, United States, 2012. HHS Publication No. (SMA) 13-4797*. Rockville, MD: SAMHSA.

SAMHSA. (2015a). *Behavioral health barometer: Hawaii, 2014. HHS Publication No. SMA–15–4895HI*. Rockville, MD: SAMHSA.

SAMHSA. (2015b). *SAMHSA – Fiscal year 2015 discretionary funds: Hawaii*. Retrieved from http://www.samhsa.gov/grants-awards-by-state/details/Hawaii

Shmulewitz, D., Heath, S. C., Blundell, M. L., Han, Z., Sharma, R., Salit, J., … Friedman, J.M. (2006). Linkage analysis of quantitative traits for obesity, diabetes, hypertension, and dyslipidemia on the island of Kosrae, Federated States of Micronesia. *Proceedings of the National Academy of Sciences of the United States of America*, *103*(10), 3502-3509. doi:10.1073/pnas.0510156103

State of Hawaii. (2012). *Primary care needs assessment databook 2012*. Retrieved from http://health.hawaii.gov/about/files/2013/06/pcna2012databook.pdf

State of Hawaii. (2015). *Department of Health, Tuberculosis control program, data and statistics, 2014*. Retrieved from http://health.hawaii.gov/tb/data-statistics/#CaseRate_HI

University of Hawaii at Manoa. (2016). *Lokahi program*. Retrieved from http://www.hawaii.edu/shs/health_promotion/lokahi_program.php

US Census Bureau. (2015a). *American factfinder, ACD demographic and housing estimates, 2013*. Retrieved from http://factfinder.census.gov/faces/tableservices/jsf/pages/productview.xhtml?src=CF

US Census Bureau. (2015b). *American factfinder, Annual population estimates, 2014*. Retrieved from http://factfinder.census.gov/faces/nav/jsf/pages/index.xhtml

WHO. (2010). Pacific islanders pay heavy price for abandoning traditional diet. *Bulletin of the World Health Organization*, *88*(7), 481–560. Retrieved from http://www.who.int/bulletin/volumes/88/7/10-010710/en/ PMID:20616964

WHO. (2015). *Marshall Islands: WHO statistical profile (January 2015)*. Retrieved from http://www.who.int/gho/countries/mhl.pdf

Withy, K. (2015). *Hawaii Physician Workforce Assessment, Act 18, SLH, 2009. University of Hawaii system report to the Hawaii State Legislature*. Retrieved from http://ahec.hawaii.edu/workforce/html

Wolanski, E., Richmond, R. H., & McCook, L. (2004). A model of the effects of land-based, human activities on the health of coral reefs in the Great Barrier Reef and in Fouha Bay, Guam, Micronesia. *Journal of Marine Systems*, *46*(1), 133–144. doi:10.1016/j.jmarsys.2003.11.018

KEY TERMS AND DEFINITIONS

Area Health Education Centers (AHEC): A federal grant program hosted by local sites across the U.S. (usually one per state or region) with the goal of reducing workforce shortages and providing workforce development for all health care and allied health fields, with an emphasis in medical fields.

Health Disparities: The unequal distribution of health-related conditions in the general population that disproportionately affect groups of people sharing some commonality that increases their health risks (usually based on social, economic, racial/ethnic, religious, geographical, or biological factors).

Health Resources and Services Administration (HRSA): An organization (part of the U.S. Department of Health and Human Services) that provides health services, conducts research, and administers many grant programs, including the Area Health Education Centers and the Public Health Training Centers grant programs.

Public Health Training Centers (PHTC): a federal grant program hosted by local sites across the U.S. (one per region) with the goal of reducing workforce shortages and providing workforce development for all public health fields.

US-Affiliated Pacific Islands (USAPIs): The six semi-independent island groups that the United States of America has a legal authority for governing, resources, or protection. The six USAPIs include the three official US Territories of American Samoa, Guam, and the Commonwealth of the Northern Mariana Islands as well as the three nations with Compacts of Free Association with the US, which are the Federated States of Micronesia, the Republic of the Marshall Islands, and the Republic of Palau.

Workforce Development: Any combination of coordinated efforts aimed at increasing the size, quality, or efficiency of the members of a specific occupational field.

Workforce Shortage: The additional number (usually represented as a percentage of growth) of professionals in a specific occupational field needed to provide the appropriate level of services so that the entire target population is served. A positive percentage indicates the amount of growth needed and a negative percentage indicates excess.

APPENDIX

Maps of the U.S.-Affiliated Pacific Islands (USAPIs)

Figure 10. American Samoa: Adapted from Central Intelligence Agency (2013)

Figure 11. The Commonwealth of the Northern Mariana Islands (Adapted from Central Intelligence Agency, 2013)

Figure 12. The Federated States of Micronesia. Although made of up many ethnic groups, the Federated States of Micronesia is divided into four states: Chuuk, Kosrae, Pohnpei, and Yap. (Adapted from Central Intelligence Agency, 2013)

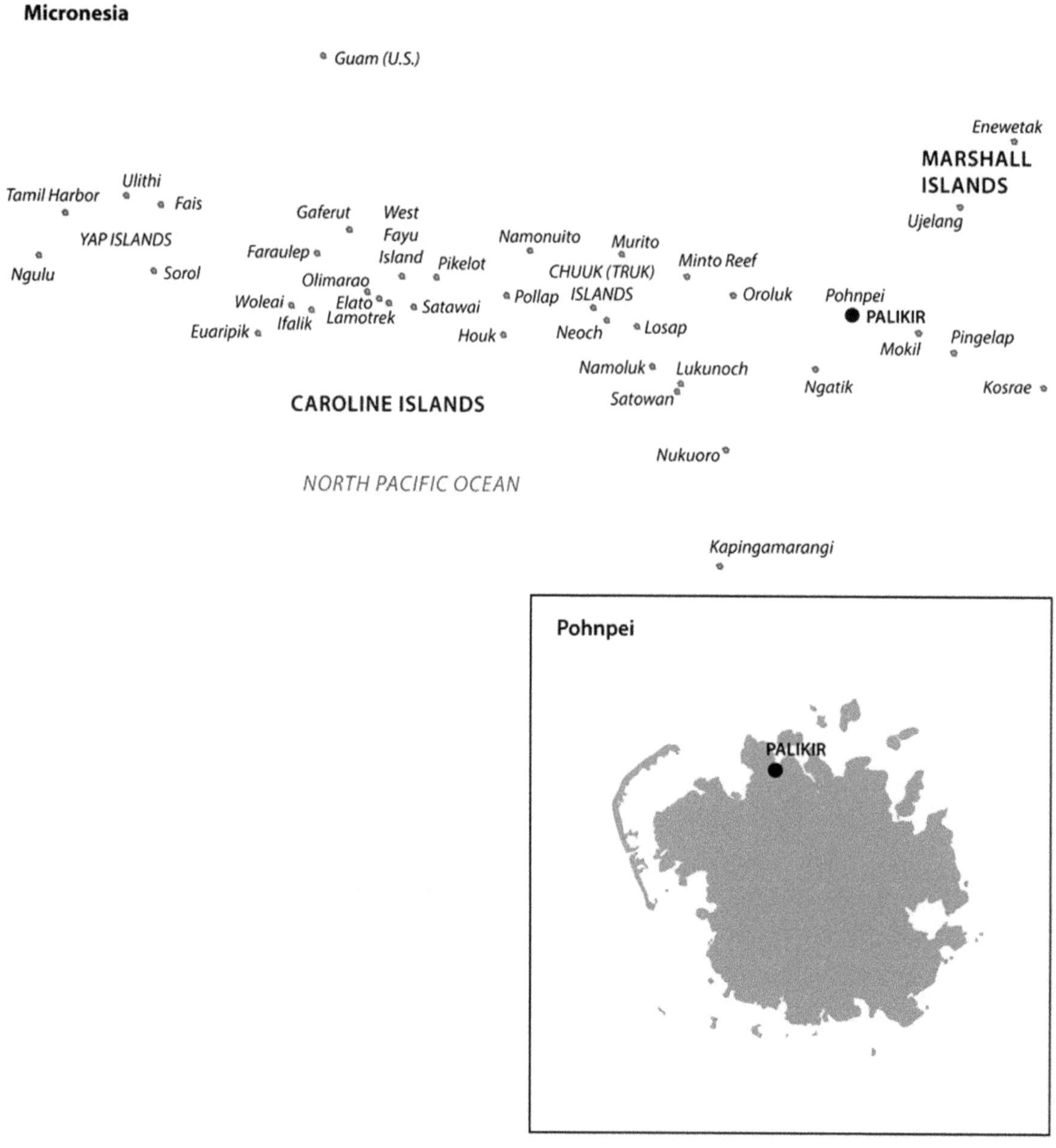

Figure 13. Guam: Adapted from Central Intelligence Agency (2013)

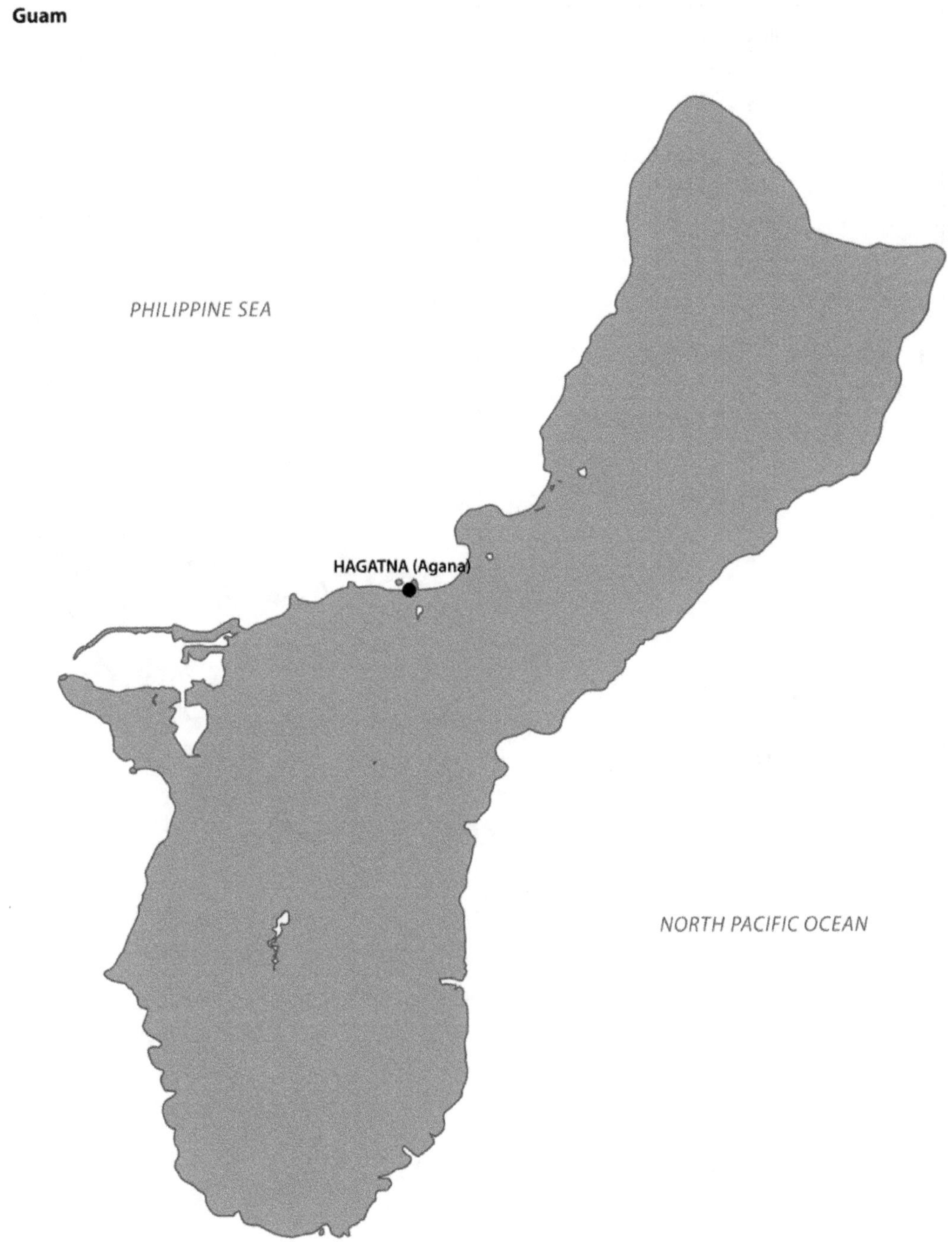

Figure 14. The Republic of Palau (Adapted from Central Intelligence Agency, 2013)

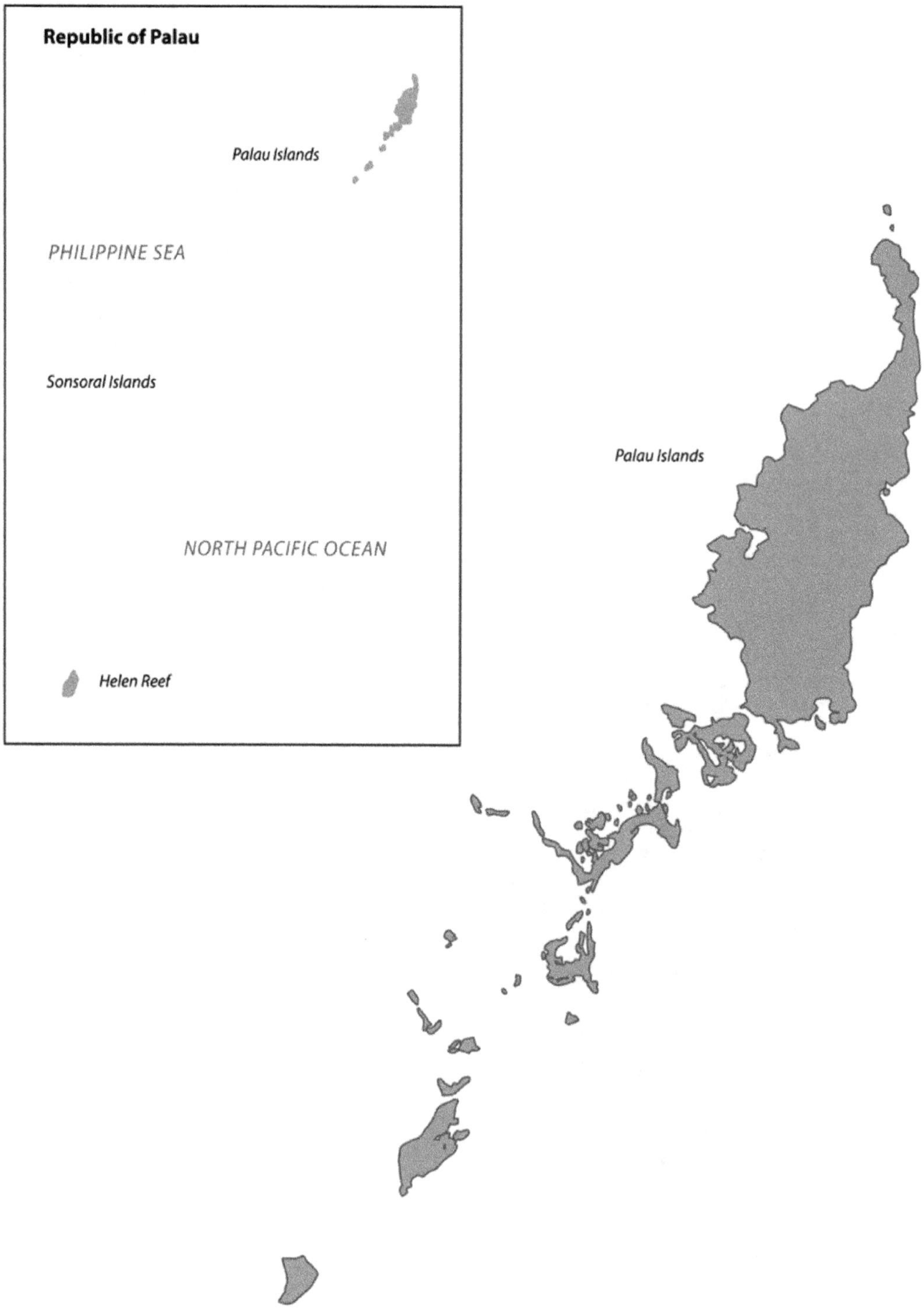

Figure 15. The Republic of the Marshall Islands (Adapted from Central Intelligence Agency, 2013)

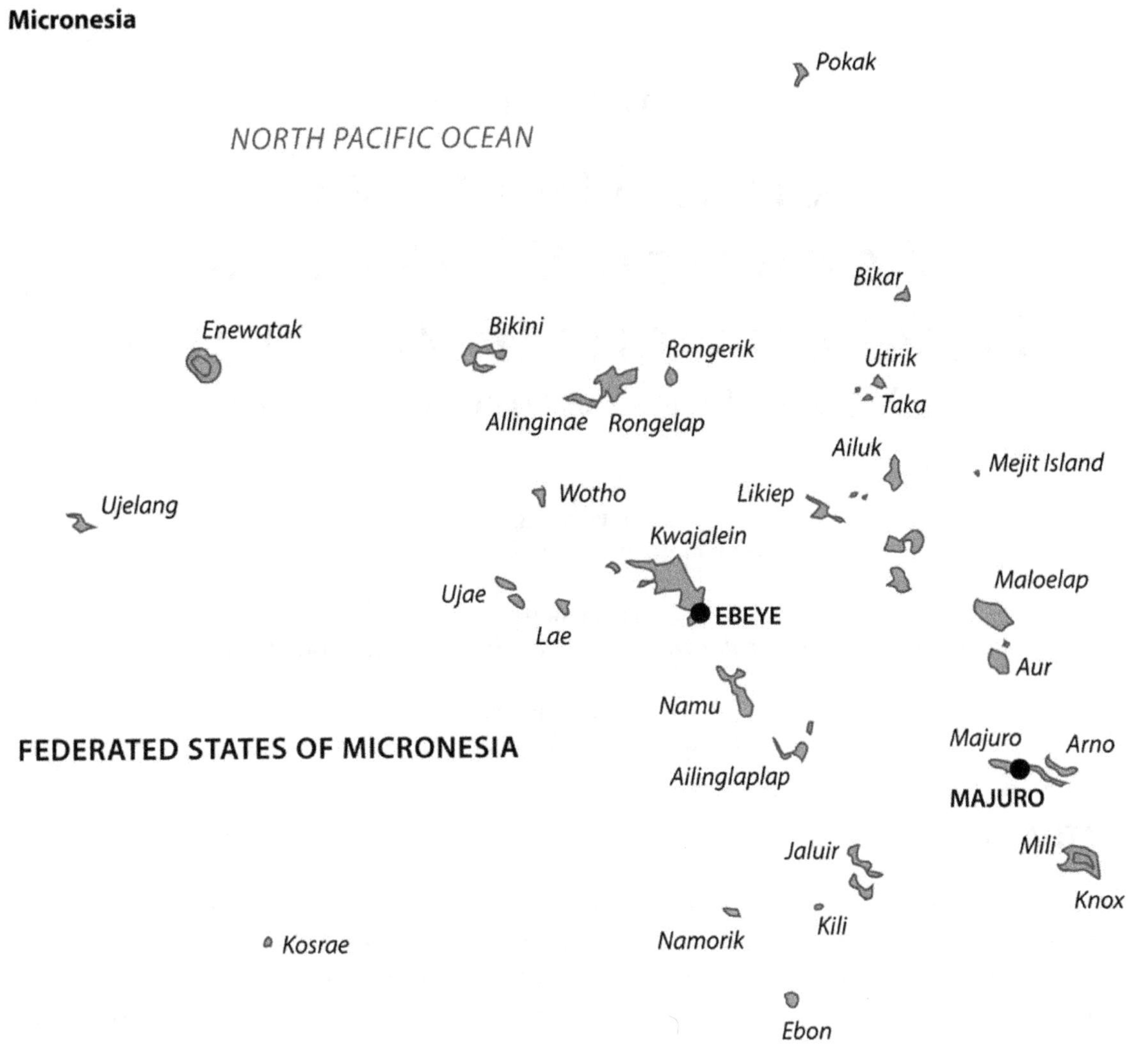

Chapter 4
Mental Health and Addiction Workforce Development in Australia:
Never the Twain to Meet?

Roderick McKay
New South Wales Institute of Psychiatry, Australia

Tim Coombs
Australian Mental Health Outcomes and Classification Network, Australia

Julie M. Anderson
National Consumer Advocate, Australia

ABSTRACT

This chapter explores the drivers and outcomes of mental health and addiction workforce development in Australia. In contrast to many countries, these workforces remain largely separate in Australia. Large investments have been made at national, state, and local levels; with resources and programs developed that are worthy of international attention. However, many still question the outcomes of these investments in light of evidence of ongoing unmet need and variations in care. Great hopes are being placed in new workforces, including peer workers, vocationally qualified coaches, and e-mental health technicians. Much rides on the outcomes of these initiatives.

INTRODUCTION

If the key goal of workforce development is to support access of the population to workers with the right skills and competencies at the right time, progress has been made in Australia but there is still much to be achieved. Structures of government, fluctuations in focus on national or local initiatives, and multiple parties with roles that impact upon workforce development potentially create duplication and lead to the premature termination of initiatives. They also create however the potential for cross fertilisation

DOI: 10.4018/978-1-5225-1874-7.ch004

of knowledge and the creation of excellent resources and strategies. The significant differences in assumptions underlying *mental health services* and *addiction services* in Australia are reflected in the respective, often separate, workforces and workforce development. Much hope is being pinned on the development of "new" workforces. Conclusions regarding the strengths and weaknesses that emerge from these initiatives will have a profound impact upon people with experience of mental illness and addiction and those currently working with them.

This chapter aims to:

- Provide an overview of:
  - The mental health and addiction workforces in Australia and the assumptions underpinning the development of relevant services.
  - The impact of key contextual factors upon workforce development, including government funding and professional organizations.
  - Key factors that have impacted upon changes in workforce composition which are predicted to drive further change.
  - Key strategies utilized to drive workforce change.
  - The key providers of education and training that support the development of the mental health and addiction workforces.
  - The impact of changes in the context in which these providers operate.
- Explore successes and limitations of programs and strategies to date.
- Highlight resources that may have international applicability.

A key theme throughout this chapter is the impact the differing emphases of mental health and addiction services have had over time on developing workforces within the health, social, and broader sectors. Consistent with the overall focus of this book, more attention will be given to initiatives within the mental health sector. This results in more detail regarding mental health workforce development, but will be placed in the context of considering the ongoing impact of this conceptual tension.

BACKGROUND

Mental health and addiction service practices in Australia were initially influenced by the U.K. and U.S., as were many of the underlying institutions that impact upon them. This includes health, social, educational, governmental, and economic structures and concepts. The predominant influences vary over time, sometimes contributing to a strengthening of unique "Australian" workforce characteristics and blending "the best of both worlds". At other times however this has led to interrupted developments after significant investments of time and money have been made. This is evident in the outcomes of the significant investments in Australia into mental health workforce development over the last decade, and less coordinated investments into developing a largely separate addiction workforce.

Within this chapter, workforce development will be considered in the context of the following definition, applied to the mental health and addiction workforces.

...a multi-faceted approach which addresses the range of factors impacting on the ability of the workforce to function with maximum effectiveness in responding to alcohol and other drug-related problems.

Workforce development should have a systems focus. Unlike traditional approaches, this is broad and comprehensive, targeting individual, organisational and structural factors, rather than just addressing education and training of individual mainstream workers. (Roche, 2002, p. 9)

MENTAL HEALTH AND ADDICTION WORKFORCE DEVELOPMENT IN AUSTRALIA

Issues, Controversies, Problems

The most publically debated controversies in mental health and addiction service provision in Australia are whether services should be separate or integrated for people who often have both mental health and addiction related problems; and the implications of differing models (De Crespigny et al., 2015). However, the workforce development implications of this debate most frequently focus upon training needs, rather than the fundamental differences in workforce conceptualizations that are discussed in this chapter.

At a broader level, the geography of Australia, with a large land mass, where most of its population live in large cities and on the eastern coastal fringe, leaves a widely dispersed rural and regional population with chronic problems in access to both services and relevant workforces (Francis, 2012). Despite a system of universal healthcare, inequity in access to services based upon individual wealth also remains a significant issue (Meadows, Enticott, Inder, Russell, & Gurr, 2015).

Whilst often not expressed overtly, there are ongoing tensions in the development of the mental health and addiction workforces regarding sufficient numbers of workers with core, relatively generic, competencies (Health Workforce Australia, 2014b); compared with meeting the needs of specific populations (Department of Developmental Disability Neuropsychiatry, University of NSW, 2016; NSW Ministry of Health, 2011; Livermore & Renu, 2011), and developing a portion of the workforce with more highly developed capabilities (Hyde, 2014; Royal Australian and New Zealand College of Psychiatrists, 2016a).

Possibly the key recurring problem arising out of the issues above, and contextual issues discussed below, is that of competing views regarding responsibility for workforce development. At multiple levels of government, the importance given to national, state, or local control of initiatives, including workforce development, has fluctuated. Whilst many good initiatives arise, their continuity is almost always open to question, impacting upon both the implementation and continuity of programs, and the sharing of lessons.

Key Contextual Influences Upon Workforce Development

It is not possible to interpret mental health workforce development in Australia without some understanding of the complex systems of funding and governance of health services in Australia, including mental health and substance abuse services.

Australia has a federal system of government in which both national and state governments have responsibilities for health funding and governance. State governments are responsible in broad terms for public hospital funding, and the national government has responsibility for non-hospital health funding (Glover, 2016; Hyde, 2014). However, both modern trends in integrated health care, and in particular for integrated mental health care, create difficulties in the application of these broad responsibilities. This is further complicated by separate responsibilities for *social* and *health* services; often (but not always) divided responsibilities for *mental health* and *substance abuse* services; and diverse approaches to clinical governance and responsibilities related to workforce development. Similar challenges arise in the education and training sectors.

One mechanism used to support coordinated service development in such an environment has been the development of national strategies and plans signed off upon by national and state governments (Ministerial Council on Drug Strategy, 1998; Whiteford & Buckingham, 2005). From a workforce development perspective, key differences are evident between the origins and implementation of the national mental health and addiction service strategies, which started from very different bases and philosophies.

Mental health services began with a large hospital base and staff from traditional health professions having to adapt to community demands to move services into the community, and improve integration with general health care services. It has only been in the early 21st century that services have moved to the incorporation of vocationally qualified staff, and engaging with more socially orientated models of care, with relevant staff. Most notable has been the Partners in Recovery initiative (Cheverton & Janamian, 2016) and the evolving role of the National Disability Insurance Scheme (Williams & Smith, 2014).

At the commencement of national plans, addiction services had limited health resources and a broad agenda across demand, supply, and harm reduction. They also had a very broad concept of workforce, including law enforcement, education, mental health, health and others; as well as "workers in treatment, prevention, health promotion and community services including AOD [alcohol and other drug] specialists, needle and syringe program workers and peer workers" (Nicholas, Adams, Roche, White, & Battams, 2013, p. 2).

In broad terms, mental health services have developed from within the domain of *healthcare* (Australian Health Ministers, 1992). Mental health services are often labelled as *private*, *primary and community care* or *public*; but these terms, and the services that sit within them, are used variably (Health Workforce Australia, 2013). It is important to note that *private* is a misnomer in many ways. Australia has a system of universal health insurance that covers some care for all people (Medicare). There are also government subsidy and tax rules that strongly encourage private health insurance for middle to high income earners, which improve their access to psychotherapies and private psychiatric care (Meadows et al., 2015). Beyond some time limited restrictions upon registration for some immigrant health professionals, there are no mechanisms that restrict the location in which health professionals practice. Non-government organizations (NGOs) are relatively small providers of services, but have increased significantly over the last 20 years. Whilst the *Fourth National Mental Health Plan* (Commonwealth of Australia, 2009) clearly expanded the scope of relevant services to "all of government", the workforce implications of this have not yet been widely explored, and data is limited (Australian Institute of Health & Welfare, 2016).

The conceptualization of services relevant to addiction, and therefore workforces, is more complicated. The *National Drug Strategy* has conceptualized supply-reduction, demand-reduction, and harm-reduction as of equal importance, and promoted partnerships between health, law-enforcement, education agencies, community-based organizations, and industry (Ministerial Council on Drug Strategy, 1998).

The Current Australian Mental Health and Addiction Workforces

As alluded to above, a key challenge in workforce development in the area of both mental health and substance misuse is defining the workforce.

Mental Health

The mental health workforce was defined nationally in 2002 in standards to guide workforce development as the disciplines of nursing, occupational therapy, psychiatry, psychology, and social work (Safety & Quality Partnerships Committee, 2013). The importance of broader workforces within services was acknowledged in the 2013 review of these standards, but were not included within the scope of the document. Work commenced to broaden the scope of disciplines relevant to the mental health workforce during the time of a national workforce agency, Health Workforce Australia. Valuable conceptualizations of the role of peer workers (Health Workforce Australia, 2014a), and expansion of the recognized role of other professions in mental health care, including other medical practitioners, Aboriginal health workers, mental health workers, consumer peer workers, carer peer workers, support and ancillary workers (Health Workforce Australia., 2014b), were published but not endorsed prior to abolishment of the agency. Since creation of these documents, further expansion of the concept of relevant workforces has occurred, with the creation of a National Disability Insurance Scheme (Green & Mears, 2014).

The initial clear definition had strengths in enabling focused data collections and the development of resources to support this workforce; but also limitations in terms of supporting workforce redesign and conceptualizing the breadth of systems and workers that may need to be included to attain the goal of developing a workforce that can function with maximum effectiveness (Roche, 2002a) in responding to the needs of people with mental health problems.

At a national level, workforce projections have been made to 2025 for psychiatrists and nurses using laborforce surveys, and modelling that is described in comparison to other OECD countries (Ono, Lafortune, & Schoenstein, 2013). Ongoing data is collected under the National Registration and Accreditation Scheme (Australian Institute of Health and Welfare, 2016). The Australian Institute of Health and Welfare provides regular reports from this data. This provides a set of reliable, reproducible data that can be compared over time; but it does not include the role of broader workers who may provide important mental health services - most notably general practitioners, clinicians in key parts of the workforce such as emergency departments, the majority of the workforce within community managed organizations, and peer workers (Australian Institute of Health & Welfare, 2016; Health Workforce Australia, 2013).

Work to improve this situation has been scoped (Health Workforce Australia, 2013; National Health Workforce Planning & Research Collaboration, 2011) but not enacted. As such, most major changes in workforce composition over the last 10 years have not been well characterized as they are out-of-scope in the collection of data on relevant registered practitioners. The latest available data (2014) shows Australia to have:

- 3,131 FTE psychiatrists (13.3/100, 000 population; 48% public practice, 46% private practice).
- 20,534 registered psychologists (87.4/100, 000; 37% private practice, 22% public practice, 18% educational practice).
- 19,351 mental health nurses (82.4/100, 000; 83% public practice).

The latest estimate of the NGO workforce was 12,000 FTE, only 43% of whom have a bachelors degree or higher qualification (National Health Workforce Planning & Research Collaboration, 2011). The most recent review has been of the psychiatric workforce (Department of Health, 2016). This highlighted potential bottlenecks in advanced training pathways in the context of increased trainee numbers.

Addiction Services

As noted above, the workforce relevant to addiction services has been conceptualized very broadly. The impact of this has been a lack of authoritative data regarding the current size of relevant workforces. Addressing this is a primary goal of the first *National Alcohol and Other Drugs Workforce Development Strategy* (Intergovernmental Committee on Drugs, 2015).

Drivers of Need for Workforce Change

Drivers of workforce change have arisen from within the mental health and addiction sector, the wider healthcare sector, and as a result of broader government and community changes.

Whilst not the focus of this book, it is important to not ignore the impact of broader changes in society that impact upon the workforces and their development. Over the last decade, policies regarding business competition, employment conditions, privatization of public businesses, and support for NGO roles have impacted both upon services that provide direct care, and those involved in workforce development such as education and training.

Major drivers of national workforce planning in the mental health workforce are in many ways similar to the broader health workforce. That is, current and predicted future workforce shortages; increasing demands for services resulting from population change, including an ageing population with an increasing burden of chronic diseases; and changing community expectations. A national health workforce agreement has highlighted the need for "funding, planning and coordinating clinical training across all health disciplines; supporting health workforce research and planning; improving international recruitment efforts; and progressing new workforce models and reforms" (Health Workforce Australia 2014a, p. 2).

Additional drivers in the mental health workforce include the demand for all relevant workforces to be equipped to support national reform agendas, particularly in the area of safety (Commonwealth of Australia, 2015); the need to establish a peer workforce (Health Workforce Australia, 2014a); continuing to increase community based care; and broadening the concepts of workforce to new disciplines and the social sector (Health Workforce Australia, 2013; Mental Health Workofrce Advisory Committee, 2011b). Whilst broader health strategies are relevant to the addiction workforce, changes in substance use and intervention techniques have been highlighted as the most important drivers (Intergovernmental Committee on Drugs, 2015). Across both sectors, the need to support recovery (Australian Health Ministers Advisory Council, 2013; Pillay, Best, & Lubman, 2014) has become a major focus of development. Changes in regulations and laws also have a major impact on the workforce (Gibson, 2015; Ryder & Ryder, 2008).

The diverse stakeholders and fluctuating dominance of different levels of government have had a significant impact on those drivers which have dominated change. This has notably resulted in the closure of Health Workforce Australia and the web archiving of many of their resources (Australian Government Department of Health, 2016a). There is still significant national workforce activity (Australian Government Department of Health, 2016b), but with less public national coordination. There are clear examples of state governments (Australian Government Department of Health, 2016ab), regional health organizations (South Estern Sydney Local Health District, 2016), community managed organizations (Mental Health Coordinating Council, 2016), and professional organizations taking more responsibility for workforce development (Australian College of Mental Health Nurses, 2016b; Royal Australian and New Zealand College of Psychiatrists, 2016a); but the consistency of such endeavours is not yet clear.

STRATEGIES USED TO SUPPORT CHANGE

Possibly because of the many factors that could drive diverse practice and standards of care, Australia has made significant investments in developing standards and strategies to drive consistency in service provision across many sectors, including mental health and addiction. However, it should be noted that developments regarding mental health and addiction have largely occurred separate to each other.

Resources that may be of international relevance are listed in Table 1, and are listed according to their main focus. Education, training, and ongoing professional development initiatives are addressed in the next section. It may seem odd to the reader to include stigma reduction initiatives, but it must be remembered that the workforce comes from the community, and therefore the community's attitude to mental illness and addiction is critical to workforce recruitment and development.

Most publically available information relates to initiatives by national and state governments, and professional organizations. However, these initiatives are often reliant upon a willingness by leaders at local levels to respond to them.

In addition to the initiatives listed in Table 1, most of which are strongly aligned to either the mental health or addiction workforces, it is important to recognize that some initiatives have been undertaken to bridge the gap between these services. These include the establishment of a Faculty of Addiction Psychiatry (Royal Australian and New Zealand College of Psychiatrists, 2016b); guidelines covering comorbidity related issues (NSW Department of Health, 2009); joint service models (Department of Health, 2008); and the first integrated state plan in 2015 (Government of Western Australia Mental Health Commission, 2015). However, to date these examples appear to highlight opportunities not explored rather than a clear path forward.

EDUCATION, TRAINING AND PROFESSIONAL DEVELOPMENT

Initial Training

In Australia, all of the traditional mental health professions except psychologists train first in their underlying profession. Psychologists undertake an undergraduate degree in psychology, but must undertake further supervision and training to undertake clinical practice without supervision. This system widens the perspectives, skills, and knowledge that can be applied to mental health care, but can lead to inter-professional rivalry and interruptions to the continuity of care. These problems are not unique to mental health, and increasing emphasis has been given to inter-professional education and practice.

Ongoing Workforce Development

Responsibility for ongoing professional development of mental health professionals is complex. Those who are in the registered professions (doctors, nurses, psychologists) must demonstrate participation in professional development for annual registration, often through activities approved by their professional organizations. Often workers of non-regulated professions participate in similar activities, but enforcement is limited, and mechanisms in the emerging workforce are still developing. There are no mechanisms for revalidation. Employers have responsibility for ensuring service safety and outcomes. This usually

Table 1. Notable Workforce Initiatives

Initiative (Further Information/Reference)
Funding
Expansion of professions eligible for Medicare rebate (Pirkis, Harris, Hall, & Ftanou, 2011)
Funding expanded training sites in expanded settings (https://www.ranzcp.org/Publications/Specialist-Training-Program.aspx)
Regulation
Establishment national health regulator (http://www.ahpra.gov.au)
Workforce Review and Planning
Central health workforce agency initiation and cessation (Mason, 2013 Section 9.2)
Mental health peer workforce review (Health Workforce Australia, 2014a)
Non-government mental health workforce review (National Health Workforce Planning & Research Collaboration, 2011)
Mental Health nursing incentive program (http://www.health.gov.au/internet/main/publishing.nsf/Content/work-pr-mhnip)
Psychiatric workforce review (Department of Health, 2016)
National mental health workforce strategy and plan (Mental Health Workforce Advisory Committee, 2011ab)
National addiction workforce strategy (Intergovernmental Committee on Drugs, 2015)
Workforce Standard Setting and Review
National mental health workforce standards (Safety and Quality Partnerships Committee, 2013)
National mental health workforce capabilities - defining four levels of capability (Health Workforce Australia, 2014b)
National competency standards for individual professions (OT Australia, 1999; Australian College of Mental Health Nurses, 2016b; Royal Australian and New Zealand College of Psychiatrists, 2016a)
A national framework for recovery-oriented mental health services (Australian Health Ministers Advisory Council, 2013)
Development of New Workforces
National certificate 4 in mental health peer work (http://training.gov.au/training/details/CHC42912)
Victorian complementary clinical and community support and workforce implementation plans (https://www2.health.vic.gov.au/mental-health/workforce-and-training)
Recovery college for community and clinical staff (http://www.seslhd.health.nsw.gov.au/Recovery_College/)
National e-mental health training resources (http://www.emhprac.org.au/)
Mental Health "coaches" (https://www.beyondblue.org.au/get-support/newaccess)
National Future Leaders (with lived experience) in Mental Health Project (http://www.mentalhealthcommission.gov.au/our-work/national-future-leaders-in-mental-health-project.aspx)
NSW Aboriginal mental health workforce program (http://www.healthinfonet.ecu.edu.au/key-resources/programs-projects?pid=139)
Aboriginal Reconciliation Action Plan and associated training resources (https://www.ranzcp.org/Publications/Indigenous-mental-health/Aboriginal-Torres-Strait-Islander-mental-health.aspx)
Stigma reduction initiatives (Jorm, 2012)
National online mental health training (Ftanou et al., 2014)

results in employers expecting, and/or supporting, employees to undertake training or other professional development activities that they consider necessary to meet such responsibilities.

HOW SUCCESSFUL HAS WORKFORCE DEVELOPMENT BEEN?

A comprehensive review of all nationally funded health workforce initiatives in 2013 reached the following conclusions that, whilst framed in the context of the entire health workforce, appear particularly relevant in considering how successful mental health and addiction workforce development has been:

The most significant health workforce issue, particularly in the area of general practice medicine, is not one of total supply but one of distribution, which is to say inadequate or non-existent service provision in some rural and remote areas, and to populations of extreme disadvantage, most particularly the Aboriginal and Torres Strait Islander communities and some outer metropolitan communities. (Mason, 2013, p. 6)

The health system exists in order to improve the health of the population and of health consumers. Health workforce programs, in turn, exist to assist in meeting patient need. While this should be self-evident, it is too easy in considering health workforce programs to become focused on whether they meet the needs of practitioners or institutions, rather than those of patients and consumer. (Mason, 2013, p. 6)

Are these harsh conclusions fair when applied to the mental health workforce? It is not possible to develop a workforce without meeting sufficient needs of practitioners to attract and retain their labor. This remains a significant challenge (Mental Health Workforce Advisory Committee, 2011b). Progress has occurred, but not as much progress as many had hoped (Commonwealth of Australia, 2015). Population mental health data has also shown limited change in national surveys (Jorm, 2014).

Of the initiatives to date, the decision to broaden access to Medicare funding to non-medical providers of mental health care has had the most dramatic influence on workforce structure, most notably in the role and number of psychologists (Mental Health Workforce Advisory Committee, 2011b). It appears to be worth asking if the inability to date of nursing and other allied health disciplines to take up this opportunity to the same degree is related to the pathway through general training before specializing in mental health. However, it has been criticized for failing to address misdistribution of access to mental health services (Meadows et al., 2015). An atlas of variation in healthcare (Australian Commision for Safety and Quality Healthcare, 2015) found marked geographic variation in the use of psychotropic medications and mental health care plans by general practitioners; but the linkage to workforce distribution is not a simple one.

SOLUTIONS AND RECOMMENDATIONS

There are no easy answers to Australia's, or any other countries', workforce development challenges. Great hope is being placed in new workforces; however these initiatives are often reliant upon a willingness by leaders at local levels to respond to them. Workforce development strategies must continue to respond to changing community expectations and demands. A combination of strategic leadership and resource development, with local leaders equipped to adapt these for local circumstances, will continue to be required. Australia's structures ensure that the needs of people with experience of mental health or addiction will always require services from a wide variety of providers and organizations; which suggests that possibly the most important element of future workforce development will be the development of innovative, responsive leaders who seek collaborative solutions to local problems. The question is how; it is easier to recognize a great leader than to create one, or a hundred.

PRACTICE DIRECTIONS

The future balance of mental health workforces in Australia is likely to be impacted upon by the ongoing call for more social interventions and supports to be available for people with experience of mental illness (Commonwealth of Australia, 2015), and decisions about whether such services should be delivered by the mental health workforce. The forthcoming national mental health service planning framework (Commonwealth of Australia, 2015) is expected to provide a basis for both reform and increased national standardization of the workforce. Associated national policy statements suggest this is likely to include projections for substantial increases in modalities of treatment, including e-health (Reynolds, Griffiths, Cunningham, Bennett, & Bennett, 2015), *low intensity* coaches using cognitive behavioural therapeutic techniques (Koivu, Drummond, Battersby, & Cromarty, 2016), and peer workers (Health Workforce Australia, 2014a), in which not all workers require a tertiary education (Commonwealth of Australia, 2015). To increase workforce capacity in a short time will be a substantial challenge; but if met, will see significant changes to mental health services and the workforce. Whilst a workforce with limited training is clearly needed in developing countries, and with increasing research support (Patel & Saxena 2014), a lot depends upon the ability to translate early research support to nationwide implementation and community acceptance in a developed country. The significance of very cautious findings of the 2013 Cochrane review regarding the efficacy of the peer workforce has been debated (Hurley, Cashin, Mills, Hutchinson, & Graham, 2016); but highlight undoubtedly a cautionary note regarding the ability to transform mental health care with new workforces. However, for many, enthusiasm is high, and with that potential it is hard to predict.

The future directions of the addiction workforce appear harder to predict. An ambitious, but broad, agenda has been set (Intergovernmental Committee on Drugs, 2015). It is now to be seen which of these agendas gains traction and at what levels. Will the focus be upon a health response, or broader governmental response?

Within the more established workforces, it appears very likely that some form of revalidation will be introduced (Archer, Nunn, & Regan de Bere, 2015). This follows on from an increasing move by relevant professional colleges to develop competency based frameworks (Hyde, 2014; Royal Australian and New Zealand College of Psychiatrists, 2016a) for training and ongoing maintenance of professional standards. There is also an increasing expectation that such professionals will embrace their roles in improving the physical health of people with mental illness.

Across both mental health and addiction workforces in Australia there is an expectation that capacity to work with Aboriginal and Torres Strait Islander people will increase; and possibly, most importantly, increasing expectation that development will occur in collaboration with people in the communities in which they work (Intergovernmental Committee on Drugs, 2015; Mental Health Workforce Advisory Committee, 2011a). Will this drive mental health and addiction services closer together?

CONCLUSION

All workforce development is complex. When a "workforce" is spread across, sometimes widely, differing sectors it becomes even more complex. Australia has made significant progress in developing mental health and addiction workforces, mostly separately, but with tantalizing opportunities for alignment. Progress has been driven by different factors at different times, and this is likely to continue into the future. At times the factors have been centralized and strategic. At other times progress has been driven by local innovation. In a democracy, where health, mental health, and addiction are often issues of political debate, this is probably inevitable. So what should this mean? Firstly, clear national direction maximizes the likelihood of effective workforce development. Secondly, we should not despair when what appear to be good programs are closed; at least some of their legacy continues and new agents for change will emerge. So whilst systems are essential, so are individuals with a passion for change. The better these individuals are equipped and supported, the more effective they will be. The development of leadership, at all levels, shared between professionals and those they serve, may well be the too often overlooked strategic imperative in workforce development.

REFERENCES

Archer, R. P., Nunn, S., & Regan de Bere, S. (2015). *The evidence and options for medical revalidation in the Australian context*. Retrieved from http://www.medicalboard.gov.au/Registration/Revalidation.aspx

Australia, O. T. (1999). *Australian competency standards for occupational therapists in mental health*. Melbourne, Australia: Occupational Therapy Australia.

Australian College of Mental Health Nurses. (2016a). *National framework for mental health nursing course accreditation*. Retrieved from http://www.acmhn.org/about-us/course-accreditation

Australian College of Mental Health Nurses. (2016b). *National framework for postgraduate mental health nursing education*. Retrieved from http://www.acmhn.org/acmhn-national-framework

Australian Commission for Safety and Quality in Healthcare. (2015). *Australian atlas of healthcare variation*. Sydney, Australia: ACSQHC. Retrieved from http://www.safetyandquality.gov.au/atlas

Australian Government Department of Health. (2016a). *Health Workforce Australia transition to the Department of Health*. Retrieved from http://www.health.gov.au/internet/main/publishing.nsf/Content/hwa-archived-publications

Australian Government Department of Health. (2016b). *Health workforce programs*. Retrieved from http://www.health.gov.au/internet/main/publishing.nsf/Content/work-prog

Australian Health Ministers. (1992). *National mental health strategy*. Canberra, Australia: Mental Health Branch, Commonwealth Department of Health and Family Services.

Australian Health Ministers' Advisory Council. (2013) *A national framework for recovery-oriented mental health services: Guide for practitioners and providers*. Retrieved from http://www.health.gov.au/internet/main/publishing.nsf/Content/mental-pubs-n-recovfra

Australian Institute of Health and Welfare. (2016). *Mental health services in Australia*. Retrieved from https://mhsa.aihw.gov.au

Cheverton, J., & Janamian, T. (2016). The Partners in Recovery program: Mental health commissioning using value co-creation. *The Medical Journal of Australia*, *204*(7), S38. doi:10.5694/mja16.00124 PMID:27078791

Commonwealth of Australia. (2009). *Fourth national mental health plan*. Retrieved from https://www.health.gov.au/internet/main/publishing.nsf/

Commonwealth of Australia. (2015). *Australian government response to Contributing Lives, Thriving Communities – Review of mental health programmes and services*. Retrieved from http://www.health.gov.au/internet/main/publishing.nsf/Content/mental-review-response

De Crespigny, C., Grønkjær, M., Liu, D., Moss, J., Cairney, I., Procter, N., & Banders, A. (2015). Service provider barriers to treatment and care for people with mental health and alcohol and other drug comorbidity in a metropolitan region of South Australia. *Advances in Dual Diagnosis*, *8*(3), 120–128. doi:10.1108/ADD-05-2015-0007

Department of Developmental Disability Neuropsychiatry, University of NSW. (2016). *The intellectual disability mental health core competency framework: A manual for mental health professionals*. NSW, Australia: Ministry of Health. Retrieved from https://3dn.unsw.edu.au/content/intellectual-disability-mental-health-core-competency-framework-%E2%80%93-download-page

Department of Health. (2008). *Kimberley mental health and drug service*. Retrieved from http://www.health.wa.gov.au/services/detail.cfm?Unit_ID=267

Department of Health. (2016). *Australia's future health workforce – Psychiatry*. Retrieved from http://www.health.gov.au/

Francis, K. (2012). Health and health practice in rural Australia: Where are we, where to from here? *Online Journal of Rural Nursing and Health Care*, *5*(1), 28–36.

Ftanou, M., Machlin, A., Nicholas, A., King, K., Fletcher, J., Harvey, C., & Pirkis, J. (2014). Mental health professional online development (MHPOD): A web-based training tool for the non-government community mental health workforce. *The Journal of Mental Health Training Education and Practice*, *9*(3), 177–189.

Gibson, N. (2015). Mental health: Mental health act 2014: Doc, are you ready? *Medicus*, *55*(9), 7–9.

Glover, L. (2016). The Australian health care system, 2015. *2015 International Profiles of Health Care Systems*, 11.

Government of Western Australia Mental Health Commission. (2015). *The Western Australian mental health, alcohol and other drug services plan 2015-2025*. Retrieved from http://www.mentalhealth.wa.gov.au/ThePlan.aspx

Green, J., & Mears, J. (2014). The implementation of the NDIS: Who wins, who loses? *Cosmopolitan Civil Societies: An Interdisciplinary Journal*, *6*(2), 25–39.

Health Workforce Australia. (2013). *Mental health workforce planning data inventory.* Retrieved from http://pandora.nla.gov.au/pan/133228/20150419-0017/www.hwa.gov.au/our-work/mental-health-workforce-reform/mental-health-workforce-study.html

Health Workforce Australia. (2014a). *Mental health peer workforce study.* Retrieved from http://pandora.nla.gov.au/pan/133228/20150419-0017/www.hwa.gov.au/our-work/mental-health-workforce-reform/mental-health-peer-workforce.html

Health Workforce Australia. (2014b). *National mental health core capabilities.* Retrieved from http://pandora.nla.gov.au/pan/133228/20150419-0017/www.hwa.gov.au/our-work/mental-health-workforce-reform/mental-health-capabilities.html

Hurley, J., Cashin, A., Mills, J., Hutchinson, M., & Graham, I. (2016). A critical discussion of Peer Workers: Implications for the mental health nursing workforce. *Journal of Psychiatric and Mental Health Nursing*, *23*(2), 129–135. doi:10.1111/jpm.12286 PMID:26914867

Hyde, J. (2014). Lessons from Australia in the public funding of mental health services. *Canadian Psychology*, *55*(2), 139–143. doi:10.1037/a0036237

Intergovernmental Committee on Drugs. (2015). *National alcohol and other drugs workforce development strategy 2015-2020.* Retrieved from http://www.nationaldrugstrategy.gov.au/internet/drugstrategy/publishing.nsf/Content/home

Jorm, A. F. (2012). Mental health literacy: Empowering the community to take action for better mental health. *The American Psychologist*, *67*(3), 231–243. doi:10.1037/a0025957 PMID:22040221

Jorm, A. F. (2014). Why hasnt the mental health of Australians improved? The need for a national prevention strategy. *The Australian and New Zealand Journal of Psychiatry*, *48*(9), 795–801. doi:10.1177/0004867414546387 PMID:25147289

Koivu, B., Drummond, A., Battersby, M., & Cromarty, P. (2016). Large reductions in depression and anxiety via low-intensity cognitive behavioural therapy delivered by novice coach. *The Australian and New Zealand Journal of Psychiatry*, *50*(6), 202. doi:10.1177/0004867415624971 PMID:26764369

Livermore, P., & Renu, A. (2011). *SMHSOP core competencies for beginning community clinicians – A clinician resource booklet to aid implementation.* Retrieved from https://www.google.com.hk/url?sa=t&rct=j&q=&esrc=s&source=web&cd=2&cad=rja&uact=8&ved=0ahUKEwiizMvEtMfMAhUGHKYKHX8HB1QQFgghMAE&url=http%3A%2F%2Fwww.health.nsw.gov.au%2Fmhdao%2Fprograms%2Fmh%2FDocuments%2Fcore-comp-measurecrit-comclinbklet.pdf&usg=AFQjCNHeEAPq4J6n5zR5F5LNETJOdzcLaw

Mason, J. (2013). *Review of Australian government health workforce programs*. Canberra, Australia: Department of Health and Ageing.

Meadows, G. N., Enticott, J. C., Inder, B., Russell, G. M., & Gurr, R. (2015). Better access to mental health care and the failure of the Medicare principle of universality. *The Medical Journal of Australia*, *202*(4), 190–194. doi:10.5694/mja14.00330 PMID:25716601

Mental Health Coordinating Council. (2016). *Sector development.* Retrieved from http://www.mhcc.org.au/sector-development.aspx

Mental Health Workforce Advisory Committee. (2011a). *National mental health workforce plan.* Melbourne, Australia: Victorian Government Department of Health. Retrieved from http://webarchive.nla.gov.au/gov/20141216070238/http://www.health.gov.au/internet/mhsc/publishing.nsf/Content/pub-mhwac-plan

Mental Health Workforce Advisory Committee. (2011b). *National mental health workforce strategy.* Melbourne, Australa: Victorian Government Department of Health Retrieved from http://webarchive.nla.gov.au/gov/20141216070240/http://www.health.gov.au/internet/mhsc/publishing.nsf/Content/pub-mhwac-strat

Ministerial Council on Drug Strategy. (1998). *The national drug strategic framework. 1998-99 to 2002-02: Building partnerships. A strategy to reduce harm caused by drugs in our community.* Canberra, Australia: AusInfo.

National Health Workforce Planning & Research Collaboration. (2011). *Mental health non-government organisation workforce project final report.* Retrieved from http://pandora.nla.gov.au/pan/133228/20150419-0017/www.hwa.gov.au/sites/uploads/Mental Health NGO Workforce Project Final Report.pdf

Nicholas, R., Adams, V., Roche, A., White, M., & Battams, S. (2013). *The development of Australia's alcohol and other drug workforce development strategy: A discussion paper.* Adelaide, Australia: National Centre for Education and Training on Addiction, Flinders University.

NSW Department of Health. (2009). *Clinical guidelines for the care of persons with comorbid mental illness and substance use disorders in acute care settings.* NSW, Australia: Better Health Centre. Retrieved from http://www.health.nsw.gov.au/mhdao/programs/mh/Publications/comorbidity-report.pdf

NSW Ministry of Health. (2011). *NSW child and adolscent mental health services (CAMHS) competency framework.* NSW, Australia: Better Health Centre.

Ono, T., Lafortune, G., & Schoenstein, M. (2013). *Health workforce planning in OECD countries. A Review of 26 Projection Models from 18 Countries, OECD Health Working Papers,* No. 62, OECD Publishing. Retrieved from http://www.oecd-ilibrary.org/docserver/download/5k44t787zcwb.pdf?expires=1472475496&id=id&accname=guest&checksum=83A91B5474CF0B62984A4A8B8F5A2E2E

Patel, V., & Saxena, S. (2014). Transforming lives, enhancing communities — Innovations in global mental health. *The New England Journal of Medicine, 370*(6), 498–501. doi:10.1056/NEJMp1315214 PMID:24428425

Pillay, I., Best, D., & Lubman, D. I. (2014). Exploring clinician attitudes to addiction recovery in Victoria, Australia. *Alcoholism Treatment Quarterly, 32*(4), 375–392. doi:10.1080/07347324.2014.949126

Pirkis, J., Harris, M., Hall, W., & Ftanou, M. (2011). *Evaluation of the better access to psychiatrists, psychologists and general practitioners through the medicare benefits schedule initiative: Summative evaluation.* Melbourne, Australia: Centre for Health Policy, Programs and Economics, University of Melbourne.

Reynolds, J., Griffiths, K. M., Cunningham, J. A., Bennett, K., & Bennett, A. (2015). Clinical practice models for the use of e-mental health resources in primary health care by health professionals and peer workers: A conceptual framework. *JMIR Mental Health*, *2*(1), e6. doi:10.2196/mental.4200 PMID:26543912

Roche, A. M. (2002). Workforce development: Our national dilemma. In *Catching clouds: Exploring diversity in workforce development in the alcohol and other drugs field* (pp. 7-16). Adelaide, Australia: Academic Press.

Royal Australian and New Zealand College of Psychiatrists. (2016a). *RANZCP 2012 (competency-based) fellowship program*. Retrieved from https://www.ranzcp.org/Pre-Fellowship/2012-Fellowship-Program.aspx

Royal Australian and New Zealand College of Psychiatrists. (2016b). *Faculty of Addiction Psychiatry*. Retrieved from https://www.ranzcp.org/Membership/Faculties-sections/Addiction-Psychiatry.aspx

Ryder, D., & Ryder, D. (2008). Political and legal institutions and their influence on drug policy: An Australian perspective. *Drug and Alcohol Review*, *27*(4), 374–379. doi:10.1080/09595230802090774 PMID:18584386

Safety and Quality Partnerships Committee. (2013). *National practice standards for the mental health workforce 2013*. Melbourne, Australia: Victorian Government Department of Health.

South Estern Sydney Local Health District. (2016). *South Eastern Sydney Recovery College*. Retrieved from http://www.seslhd.health.nsw.gov.au/Recovery_College/

Whiteford, H. A., & Buckingham, W. J. (2005). Ten years of mental health service reform in Australia: Are we getting it right? *The Medical Journal of Australia*, *182*(8), 396–400. PMID:15850436

Williams, T. M., & Smith, G. P. (2014). Can the National Disability Insurance Scheme work for mental health? *The Australian and New Zealand Journal of Psychiatry*, *48*(5), 391–394. doi:10.1177/0004867414530007 PMID:24671233

KEY TERMS AND DEFINITIONS

Australian Institute of Health and Welfare: An independent, government funded agency responsible for providing authoritative information and statistics on Australia's health and welfare.

E-Mental Health Technicians: Non-clinicians who may assist completion of e-therapy programs through scripted encouragement, support, and referral to program materials; usually with supervision.

Health Workforce Australia: A government funded agency established from 2008 to 2014 to assist government to build a sustainable health workforce through improving workforce capacity, productivity, and distribution.

Medicare: The Australian national universal health insurance scheme.

National Disability Insurance Scheme: The Australian national universal insurance scheme for support of people with disabilities.

Peer Workers: People with lived experience of mental illness (directly or as a carer) employed to assist people with mental illness (or their carers) through use of their own "peer" experience.

Professional Development: Activities undertaken by individuals to develop and maintain relevant capabilities to work within the mental health or addictions sector.

Recovery: The individually defined process of regaining hope, purpose, and quality of life; with or without the resolution of mental health or addiction disorders.

Vocationally Qualified Coach: A person with a vocational qualification (rather than mental health or addictions related tertiary education) to work to support improved mental health of individuals.

Chapter 5
Key Initiatives in New Zealand's Adult Mental Health Workforce Development

Mark Smith
Te Pou o te Whakaaro Nui, National Workforce Center for Adult Mental Health, Addiction and Disability, New Zealand

Angela F. Jury
Te Pou o te Whakaaro Nui, National Workforce Center for Adult Mental Health, Addiction and Disability, New Zealand

ABSTRACT

This chapter describes a nationally led approach to workforce development by analyzing three workforce development initiatives within the adult mental health and addiction sector in New Zealand. New Zealand has been on an important and critical journey with regards workforce development over the past 15 years, one which has significantly altered the way services are delivered. In order to understand this journey, some background information relevant to New Zealand will be provided covering the context of mental health, epidemiology of mental health illness, service delivery, use of evidence based treatments, as well as funding and investment in workforce development. The three workforce development initiatives are then described: 1) key knowledge, skills, values and attitudes for all people working in mental health and addiction services, 2) development of an outcomes culture, and 3) post graduate clinical training for nurses and allied health professionals.

INTRODUCTION

This chapter focuses on workforce development within the mental health sector in the New Zealand context. While there have been many workforce development initiatives in the past decade or so, this chapter focuses on three which have had a key role in supporting the transformation of mental health and addiction services; namely the development of core knowledge, skills, values, and attitudes for all people working in mental health (*Let's Get Real*); the development of an outcomes culture; and post

DOI: 10.4018/978-1-5225-1874-7.ch005

graduate clinical training for mental health workers (Skills Matter). These initiatives are focused on different levels of workforce development: systems level, current workers, and the future workforce based on the framework described by Roche (2001). While these initiatives are distinct developments, they are all connected by the notion that mental health and addiction services need to change. While that change is seen as evolutionary rather than revolutionary in nature, there is the determination to have a skilled and knowledgeable mental health workforce that is culturally competent, with recovery focused values and attitudes, working in services which are focused on improving outcomes.

The objectives of this chapter are to provide an overview of:

- The New Zealand context and challenges.
- Three workforce development initiatives.
- The implementation process.

BACKGROUND

Context

New Zealand is a small country in the South Pacific with a population of approximately 4.5 million people (Statistics New Zealand, 2013). It is a multi-ethnic country, particularly in the largest city of Auckland where one-third of the population lives. In total, nearly three-quarters (74%) of New Zealand's population identify as European, 15% Māori, 12% Asian, and 7% as Pacific peoples (Statistics New Zealand, 2013). While modern day New Zealand is considered a multi-cultural, multi-ethnic society, there is a statutory obligation to work towards biculturalism; that of Pakeha (New Zealanders of European descent) and Māori. Māori are the indigenous people of New Zealand who in 1840 signed a treaty (the Treaty of Waitangi) with the British crown laying the foundation for a contemporary New Zealand society (Ministry for Culture and Heritage, 2015).

Findings from *Te Rau Hinengaro: The New Zealand Mental Health Survey* (Oakley Brown, Wells & Scott, 2006) indicate 1 in 5 people in New Zealand experience a mental illness each year, similar to international survey findings (e.g., Kessler et al., 2009). Nearly 8% of the population experience two or more disorders, and 5% serious disorders (Oakley Browne et al., 2006). When sociodemographic factors are taken into account, *Te Rau Hinengaro* found Māori have a higher risk of mental illness and serious disorders. However, both Māori and Pacific peoples are less likely to seek treatment. This may reflect a range of factors including, cultural beliefs and values, barriers to access, and the responsiveness of services to Māori and Pacific peoples (Jansen, Bacal, & Crengle, 2008; Jansen, 2009). Overall, 2 in 5 people with experience of mental illness or addiction over the last year seek help from mental health or health services (Oakley Browne et al., 2006). People with a serious disorder, females, and those who are older are most likely to seek treatment (Oakley Browne et al., 2006).

Service Delivery

Until recently most of New Zealand's mental health services, like many western countries, were delivered through large institutions. These were closed in the 1990s and replaced with a range of community and day services while retaining acute inpatient facilities attached to general medical hospitals. Today, New

Zealand's publically funded mental health services are comprised of a large number of non-governmental organizations (NGOs) and primary health care services. There are also 20 state funded District Health Boards (DHBs) that provide specialist mental health services.

New Zealand's mental health services are primarily government funded. The Ministry of Health's total spending on health in 2016/17 is expected to reach $16.2 billion, of which about 8% reflects spending on mental health and addiction services (Treasury, 2016). New Zealand currently has a "ring fence" around mental health funding to protect investment and development in mental health services. That is, "mental health funding must be used for specialist mental health and addiction services for people most severely affected by a mental illness or alcohol or other drug issue" (National Service Framework Library, 2015). Approximately 30% of funding goes towards NGO services, and 70% towards DHBs (Mellsop & Smith 2010). Over the last seven years, spending on mental health services has risen by about 18% (see National Service Framework Library, 2015). There is increasing pressure for appropriate and efficient use of mental health funding which has been called for in *Rising to the Challenge: The Mental Health and Addiction Service Development Plan 2012-2017* (Ministry of Health, 2012). These are also the key priorities in the recently published *New Zealand Health Strategy* (Ministry of Health, 2016a) for health services generally.

Workforce

The workforce is the most important resource within mental health and addiction services. While the workforce is also the most costly resource within these services, the workforce is critical to the achievement of strategic goals and objectives, and the implementation of service plans. Quality health care service delivery relies on effective management and deployment of the workforce. That is, the overall performance of mental health and addiction services depends on having enough workers who are competent, productive, and responsive to the needs of people with experience of mental illness and addiction.

The mental health workforce composition has changed over time from having a strong nursing and psychiatric assistant emphasis towards one where there is a greater presence of other professionals. The recent *More Than Numbers* workforce stocktake (Te Pou & Matua Raki, 2015) estimates there are now more than 9,500 full time equivalent staff working in adult mental health and addiction services. About half of the workforce work in DHB mental health services (52%), one-third (32%) in NGO mental health services, and 16% in addiction services (7% in DHBs and 9% in NGOs). While the workforce composition varies by service type and for the addiction sector, overall the mental health and addiction workforce is comprised of 31% support workers, 28% nurses, 17% allied health, 6% psychiatrists and other medical, and 17% other (Te Pou & Matua Raki, 2015). Support workers represent nearly one-third of the overall workforce.[1] Included within the support workforce are more than 300 full-time equivalent peer and family support roles (Te Pou & Matua Raki, 2015).

Gaps in New Zealand's future supply of mental health and addiction workers are predicted. The *More Than Numbers* workforce stocktake estimated a need for a 9% increase in the workforce. However, these figures do not take into account the large proportion of the workforce which is expected to retire within the next 10-15 years. The future demand for community mental health support workers specifically is expected to rise. New Zealand has a high reliance on overseas trained health professionals, including doctors and nurses compared to other OECD countries (OECD, 2015). In order to address future workforce requirements, there is a need for long-term strategic investment in workforce planning and development. The Ministry of Health's focus is on growing the health workforce, as well as improving its performance and productivity to address some of these gaps (Ministry of Health, 2006).

Since the 1990s, there has been consistent investment in mental health workforce development. *Tauawhitia te Wero, Embracing the Challenge: National Mental Health and Addiction Workforce Development Plan 2006-2009* (Ministry of Health, 2005) was launched in December 2005. A "whole system approach" has been taken to workforce development within New Zealand's mental health services. This recognizes the fact that a range of factors impact and interact with the workforce's ability to deliver quality services which are responsive to the needs of people with experience of mental health problems. In addition to the traditional focus on training and development, other areas emphasized in this approach include organizational development, recruitment and retention, research and evaluation, and the need for a supporting infrastructure (Ministry of Health, 2002). Attention is focused on individuals, as well as the teams, services/organizations, and systems within which they operate (Skinner, Roche, O'Connor, Pollard & Todd, 2005). The ultimate goal is to build a sufficient, capable, productive, and responsive workforce that contributes to better outcomes for service users through improved service delivery. The national direction on key issues for future mental health and addiction workforce development is currently being reviewed as part of the revised workforce development plan.

New Zealand has invested in creating workforce development centers for specific parts of the mental health and addiction workforce. These workforce centers were set up to address workforce disparities for specific population groups and the need for evidence-based workforce development. Following the process of deinstitutionalization there were major gaps in these workforce areas and it has taken a concerted effort to improve efforts to grow the capacity and capability of the mental health workforce. The workforce centers also provide the supporting infrastructure or a vehicle for the implementation of national government and Ministry of Health policy into practice. There are currently five mental health and addiction workforce development centers as outlined below.

- Adult mental health workforce - Te Pou o te Whakaaro Nui (Te Pou).
- Addiction workforce - Matua Raki.
- Child and youth mental health and addiction workforce - The Werry Centre.
- Māori workforce development - Te Rau Matatini.
- Pacific workforce development - Le Va.

This chapter will focus on three significant areas of workforce development undertaken within the adult mental health and addiction sector. All three of these initiatives fall within the range of work assigned to Te Pou, the national center for adult mental health workforce development. These include:

- Knowledge, skills, values, and attitudes required of all people working in mental health and addiction services (*Let's Get Real).*
- The creation of an outcomes culture in the mental health and addiction sector.
- Post graduate clinical training for nurses and allied health professionals (Skills Matter).

WORKFORCE DEVELOPMENT INITIATIVES

Workforce development has been variously defined but it can be seen as "a multi-faceted approach which addresses the range of factors impacting on the ability of the… workforce to function with maximum effectiveness" (Roche & Skinner, 2005, p. 4). Workforce development should be aligned with strategic goals and address gaps or risks identified through workforce planning (Standards Australia, 2015).

Roche and Skinner (2005) have identified several best practice principles for workforce development including:

- Evidence-based.
- Multi-level.
- Sustainable.
- Continuously evaluated.
- Participatory and involve key stakeholders.

A four-step workforce development process has been outlined in a framework by Werner and DeSimone (2012) that includes: needs assessment/planning, design, implementation, and evaluation. This aligns with the framework developed by Damschroder and colleagues (2009) based on a review of organizational change and implementation theories. These frameworks are used to describe the three national workforce developments in adult mental health services below.

Core Knowledge, Skills, Values and Attitudes: Let's Get Real

Let's Get Real: Real Skills for People Working in Mental Health and Addiction (Ministry of Health, 2008) is a framework that describes the essential knowledge, skills, values, and attitudes required of everyone working in mental health and addiction services in New Zealand. Developed in 2008 by the Ministry of Health, Te Pou has had a role since 2009 in supporting services to implement the framework in service delivery organizational systems (such as human resources and learning and development), as well as education and training programmes.

The terms competence, capability, and capacity are often used interchangeably (Vincent, 2008). Competency models refer to the knowledge, skills, abilities, and other characteristics required for effective job performance (Campion, Fink, Ruggeberg, Carr, Phillips, & Odman, 2011). *Let's Get Real* was developed to identify the key knowledge, skills, values, and attitudes needed for service users to get the best out of services. As outlined in *Tauawhitia te Wero: Embracing the Challenge, National Mental Health and Addiction Workforce Development Plan 2006-2009* (Ministry of Health, 2005), development of the framework was expected to better align pre-service entry, orientation, and ongoing development of the mental health and addiction workforce with service delivery.

Let's Get Real aims to contribute to:

- More people having the key knowledge, skills, and attitudes on entry to working in mental health and addiction services.
- Improving recruitment and retention.
- A culture of continuous learning by influencing professional development and enhanced performance management processes.
- Improving the quality of services for service users or tangata whaiora.

The mechanisms through which these outcomes are expected to be achieved is through influencing education, human resources practices, professional development, and performance management processes.

Design and Implementation

Let's Get Real was originally modelled on the U.K.'s policy framework *The Ten Essential Shared Capabilities* (Hope, 2004). Development involved extensive stakeholder consultation, including service users, professional groups, and sector representatives. Best practice guidelines in competency modelling recommend stakeholder consultation to help ensure the acceptance and use of frameworks (Campion et al., 2011). Development considered what other industries had done to achieve good uptake of competency frameworks. This included Vodafone (a national telco company) which had a framework that included seven skills. The name *Let's Get Real* was also chosen due to its youth orientation.

As part of the development of *Let's Get Real*, people with experience of mental health problems were consulted to better understand what they wanted from the workforce to be effective. The aim was to ensure services met the essential needs of people and that the framework didn't become overly complex. The framework was intended to be easy to use and provide the essentials, whilst recognizing people may also need specialist support.

The implementation of frameworks such as *Let's Get Real* is aided by strong leadership, executive management support, service user involvement, clear planning, and integration within local initiatives (Macduff et al., 2010). In addition, a recently developed resource by SAMHSA (2011), identifies the following characteristics as important in supporting successful implementation of change plans.

- **Perceived Relevance:** Must have obvious practical application.
- **Timely:** The workforce must see the need.
- **Clear:** Language and process of implementation.
- **Credible:** Workforce confidence in the sources.
- **Multifaceted:** Use of a variety of activities and format to disseminate.
- **Continuous:** New behaviours must be continually reinforced at all levels.
- **Bi-Directional:** The workforce must be given opportunities to communicate directly with implementers.

The *Let's Get Real* framework is intended to complement profession specific competency and capability frameworks. The development involved a process of refinement which culminated in the identification of seven real skills. This process meant drawing on competency frameworks already in existence, such as:

- *Recovery Competencies for the Mental Health Workforce* (Mental Health Commission, 2001).
- Te Ao Maramatanga (New Zealand College of Mental Health Nurses) standards of practice for mental health nursing in New Zealand (2004).
- Competencies developed for professionals regulated by the Health Practitioners Competency Assurance Act (2003).
- Social Work Registration Act (2003).
- Practitioner competencies for alcohol and drug workers in Aotearoa-New Zealand (2001).

The seven real skills included in *Let's Get Real* (Ministry of Health, 2008) include:

1. Working with service users.
2. Working with Māori.
3. Working with families/whanau.
4. Working within communities.
5. Challenging stigma and discrimination.
6. Law, policy and practice.
7. Professional and personal development.

These skills are inter related and cannot be read in isolation (Te Pou, 2009a) in that the real skills influence and interact with each other. They were chosen to represent the range of skills, knowledge, values, and attitudes that the workforce would encounter and need. There is an aspirational element to the performance indicators which are associated with each of the real skills.

Each of the seven real skills has a broad definition and three levels of performance indicators.

- **Essential:** For everyone working in mental health and addiction services.
- **Practitioner:** For clinicians who have worked in a service for at least two years.
- **Leader:** For people who are in management and/or clinical leadership positions.

Let's Get Real is designed to ensure the mental health system as a whole is equipped to respond to the needs of service users. That system involves recruiting new mental health workers and managers, training new and experienced mental health workers and managers, developing organizational structures and processes, as well as actually delivering services to service users. *Let's Get Real* is designed to be a system level workforce development initiative with people who have lived experience at the centre.

Te Pou has had responsibility for implementing the *Let's Get Real* framework since it was launched in 2008. Te Pou has worked with other organizations to do this and has recognized that the level of readiness to implement *Let's Get Real* differs among organizations. SAMHSA (2011) suggests this may be due to a number of factors, and where organizations are not ready this can lead to ineffective implementation.

The implementation process has involved the inclusion of *Let's Get Real* within the national service framework since 2009, to enable contracts to include *Let's Get Real*. Additionally, the implementation of *Let's Get Real* involved engaging with tertiary education providers and providing tailored support to enable review of course content and teaching methods to reflect the framework. Most significantly, this led to the updating of the National Certificate for Mental Health and Addiction Support Work. The Skills Matter funded post graduate clinical training programme has also specified the use of *Let's Get Real* in their contracts and reporting. By working with education providers to embed *Let's Get Real* within courses and programmes, newly trained practitioners and those undertaking post graduate studies are now being exposed to the framework. *Let's Get Real* is currently reaching the majority of the workforce either directly or indirectly.

In order to ensure consistent implementation of *Let's Get Real* across the country a number of enablers were developed (see Te Pou, 2009a) to assist practitioners and services as listed below.

- **A Guide for Managers and Leaders:** A tool that supports managers and leaders to utilize *Let's Get real* and the enablers.

- **Team Planning Tool:** For services to use when developing a workforce development plan for teams in the real skills.
- **Human Resources Tool:** A tool for services to integrate *Let's Get real* into existing human resource systems and processes.
- **Learning Modules for the Seven Real Skills:** This includes 23 self-directed learning modules freely available for workers including *Getting Started, Values and Attitudes,* and a module for each of the real skills (at all three levels).
- **Education Tool:** For education and training providers to integrate *Let's Get Real* into education and training programmes.

Early implementation of *Let's Get Real* was focused on raising awareness and supporting the sector to understand how the framework could be integrated into organizational policies, processes, and systems. This included:

- Facilitation of workshops with DHB and NGO leaders and managers to identify an approach to utilize *Let's Get Real* to address service priorities.
- Sponsorship of training in the use of some of the *Let's Get Real* tools (Team Planning Tool) and in some of the real skills such as "working with families/whānau" at an essential level and practitioner level.
- Provision of values and attitudes workshops to frontline staff in DHB and NGO services.

The initial implementation and evaluation of *Let's Get Real* involved 16 pilot sites (see www.tepou.co.nz/news/lets-get-real-pilotstwo-years-on/126). The use of pilot trials is one strategy recommended as a way of garnering system wide implementation (WHO, 2006; Astho, n.d.). An evaluation of the early implementation stage was also undertaken to assess the level of awareness created through promotion and resource availability, as well as the level of uptake and utility of the *Let's Get Real* tools and learning modules. Results showed that substantial inroads towards achieving these goals had been made and that the direct engagement with services was a key contributing factor.

Recent activities have focused on refreshing *Let's Get Real.* Whilst the framework has been in existence since 2008, Te Pou recognizes that the enablers must evolve and develop to match new evidence and the changing requirements of services and the New Zealand workforce. While this will ensure *Let's Get Real* is current, Campion et al. (2011) also recommend the refreshing of models as a way of gaining greater leadership buy-in and involvement, and further supporting integration within human resource (HR) systems. The refresh will include the development of online learning modules and tools. Online learning is often more cost effective, flexible in timing, and is able to overcome geographical barriers (Bell & MacDougall, 2013; Ballew, Castro, Claus, Kittur, Brennan & Brownson, 2013). In addition, evidence suggests computer based learning can be more effective than traditional training methods (see Bluestone, Johnson, Fullerton, Carr, Alderman, & BonTempo, 2013; Ruggeri, Farrington & Brayne, 2013).

Evaluation

Evaluation is an important component of any workforce development initiative and helps ensure the greatest benefit is obtained and potential areas for improvement are identified (Skinner et al., 2005). Evaluation is a major aspect of the implementation of *Let's Get Real* (Te Pou, 2009a). The impact of the framework on the sector is continuously evaluated, reviewed, and adapted as necessary. As part of the refresh of *Let's Get Real* an evaluation framework has been developed, utilizing a programme logic process. The evaluation aims to develop a better understanding of whether the training programmes Te Pou delivers are supporting the workforce to build the right knowledge, skills, values, and attitudes; the level of knowledge, skills, values, and attitudes amongst people involved in the delivery of mental health and addiction services; the extent to which organisations are supporting and embedding the essential knowledge, skills, values, and attitudes in practice; and service users' perceptions of the knowledge, skills, and attitudes possessed by the workforce. In addition, the uptake and response from services to the online assessment tool, *Let's Get Real* learning modules and resources will be monitored.

Uptake of web resources freely available on the Te Pou website (see www.tepou.co.nz/initiatives/lets-get-real/107) has been high. *Let's Get Real* workshops have also been found to improve understanding and contribute to a greater commitment towards strengthening values and attitudes in the workplace.

Recent results from the *More than Numbers* workforce survey (Te Pou & Matua Raki, 2015) continue to indicate the importance of building the essential knowledge, skills, values, and attitudes of the workforce. One of the key challenges is in ensuring the workforce is adequately prepared to work with Māori and Pacific people. For example, the survey found around three-quarters of services perceived a need for increased knowledge and skills related to various aspects of cultural competency for working with Māori, Pacific, and Asian service users. In addition, over half to two-thirds of services indicated a need to build workforce skills in working with families, older people, and children and young people. This reiterates the need for resources, tools, and training being available to the sector.

The *Let's Get Real* framework has underpinned other subsequent frameworks designed for specific areas. These frameworks include *Real Skills Plus CAMHS* competencies for young people and children; Te Whare o Tiki, the Co-existing problems (CEP) knowledge and skills framework; *Let's Get Real: Disability*; *Real Skills Plus Seitapu: Engaging Pasifika* competency for Pacific people; and the *Takarangi Competency Framework* for the Māori workforce working with Māori. While Takarangi was initially targeted to the addiction sector, this is now being rolled out to the mental health sector as well.

Outcomes Measurement Workforce Development

New Zealand has been in the process of developing an outcomes culture within its mental health and addiction services since 2000. This is seen as a long term project. There have been a number of features to this work: development of an outcomes measurement framework; and development of an outcomes framework and commissioning framework. At the time of writing, the commissioning framework (Ministry of Health, 2016b) has been developed while work on the outcomes framework is nearing completion. The commissioning framework stresses the importance of measurement and results based accountability. The work of developing an outcomes culture is also seen as central in both the updated *New Zealand Health Strategy* (Ministry of Health, 2016a) and the mental health strategy – *Rising to the Challenge* (Ministry of Health, 2012) where measurement and the need to develop and use evidence is repeatedly stressed.

Presently mental health and addiction services are focused disproportionately on inputs and outputs, and the *funding* of mental health services is certainly focused on these aspects. Through the development of an outcomes culture the intention is to ensure outcomes become pivotal in both the funding, delivery, and accountability of services.

Design and Implementation

Central to developing an outcomes culture is the use of outcome measures (Te Pou, 2009b). New Zealand has adopted an approach to the implementation of outcome measurement which is centered on workforce development. This has meant ensuring the sector has the requisite training, resources, and understanding of outcome measurement rather than seeing it purely as research or a quality improvement initiative.

New Zealand decided to mandate the collection of certain measures, which were seen as a routine part of clinical practice. New Zealand has followed other jurisdictions, particularly the U.K. and Australia in adopting this approach.

In 2003, the Classification and Outcome Study (CAOS; Gaines, Bower, Buckingham, Eager, Burgess, & Green, 2003) identified outcome measures which could potentially be introduced into New Zealand, along with a detailed classification system. This work largely replicated the findings from the Mental Health Classification and Service Cost Study in Australia (Shane Solomon & Associates, 1996).

Following the CAOS study it was decided to add outcome measurement data to the Mental Health Information National Collection (MHINC). MHINC already collected activity data such as bed nights, referral details, and discharges. MHSMART (Mental Health Standard Measures for Assessment and Recovery initiative) was introduced in 2005 to add outcome measurement data to the MHINC activity data. A train the trainer model was used to support implementation of outcome measurement, in which Te Pou trained nominated leads, and they, in turn, trained clinicians or practitioners within their services.

New Zealand decided to focus on five areas of outcome measurement in MHSMART based on consultation with the mental health and addiction sector and work carried out in Australia. The five areas of focus are listed below.

1. Clinical symptoms.
2. Māori measure.
3. Alcohol and drug outcome measure.
4. Service user rated measure.
5. Measure of functioning.

Clinical Symptoms

HoNOS (Health of the Nation Outcome Scales) was chosen as the preferred measure and later added its various forms, such as for children (HoNOSCA), older persons (HoNOS65+), forensic (HoNOS Secure) and intellectually disabled (HoNOS LD). The symptomatology domain was chosen as the first domain to be mandated (that is, measures are required to be collected within services), since it was thought this would be the easiest to collect based on the measures available at that point. The HoNOS family of instruments were chosen because they were easy to use, acceptable to clinicians, psychometrically valid, and already widely used (Pirkis, Burgess, Coombs, Clarke, Jones-Ellis, & Dickson, 2005; Te Pou, 2012). The HoNOS family of measures were the preferred measures in 2005 and were mandated into the national collection, known as PRIMHD (Programme for the Integration of Mental Health Data) from 2008.

HoNOS is an outcome measure which was developed in the U.K. by the Royal College of Psychiatrists in the mid-1990s for adults in mental health services. John Wing (Wing, Beevor, Curtis, Park, Hadden, & Burns, 1998) an eminent psychiatrist and researcher is seen as the key figure in its development.

HoNOS is a simple outcome tool which measures symptom severity and social functioning over time, and covers 12 items. HoNOS is a clinician rated tool and is used to measure the health and social function of people with experience of severe mental health disorder. Each item can be rated from 0 (no problem) to 4 (severe problem). The information collection protocol is shown in Figure 1. This protocol has been a central feature in the training of the sector to support consistent data collection and reliability.

HoNOS is used in 22 jurisdictions around the world. However, only three countries (the U.K., Australia, and New Zealand) use it as part of a national initiative and have a memorandum of understanding underpinning collaboration and joint work in relation to HoNOS. Work is currently underway led by the U.K. which is making minor revisions to the HoNOS tool.

Figure 1. Mental Health Outcomes Information Collection Protocol
Adapted from Te Pou, 2012a

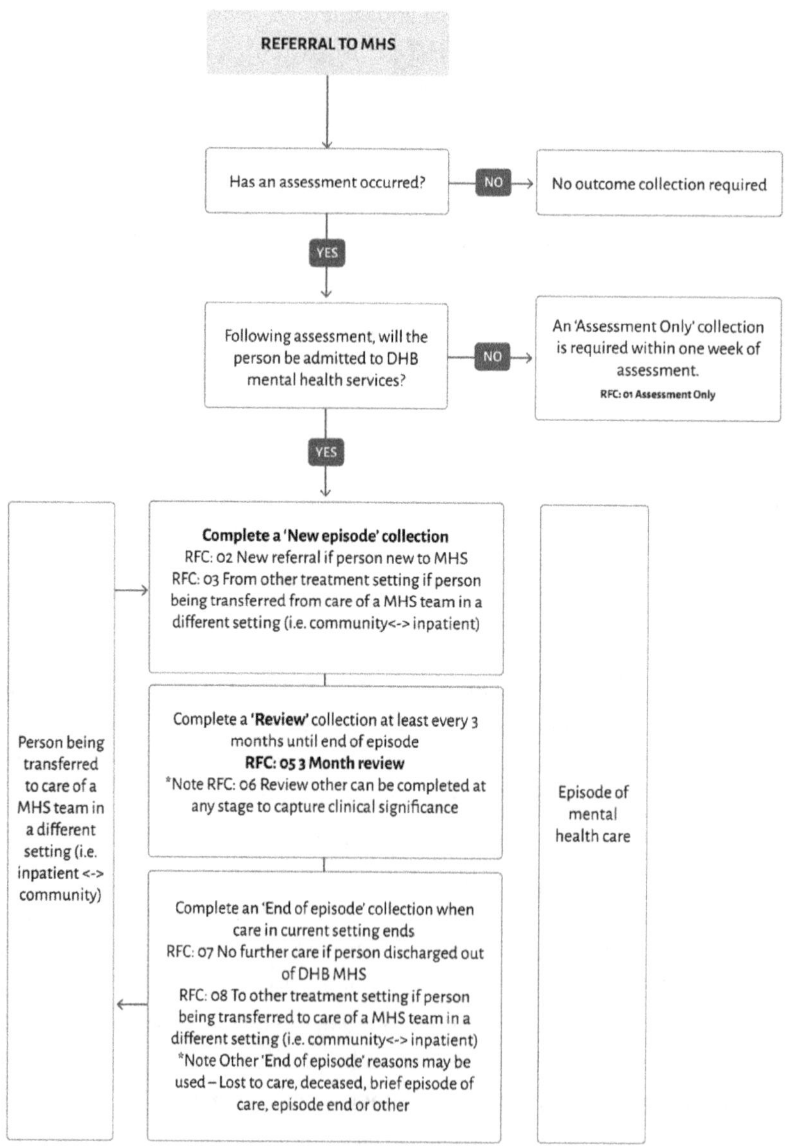

Māori Measure

Hua Oranga (Kingi & Durie, 2000) was adopted as a Māori specific outcome measure. *Hua Oranga* is informed by the *Te whare tapa wha* Māori model of mental health (Durie, 1994). This model captures the physical, mental, social, and spiritual aspects of a person's life in a holistic manner. *Hua Oranga* has been developed and piloted in a number of Māori mental health services nationwide (McClintock, Sokratov, Mellsop, & Kingi, 2013).

Alcohol and Drug Outcome Measure

After an extensive literature review of available options, New Zealand developed its own measure of alcohol and drug measurement. Initially this measure was known as the *Alcohol and Drug Outcome Project Tool* (ADOPT) and preliminary validation work was completed by Deering et al. (2009). The measure has subsequently come to be known as the *Alcohol and Drug Outcome Measure* (ADOM). The measure has three sections: frequency of use; psychosocial impact; and recovery. The ADOM is a self-rated measure for service users in community addiction services which is completed collaboratively with clinicians. The ADOM was mandated by the Ministry of Health for the national collection by community based alcohol and other drug services in July 2015.

Service User Rated Measure

Significant work informed by a literature review, ascertained that New Zealand should develop its own self rated service user outcome measure (Gordon, Ellis, Haggerty, Pere, Platz, & McLaren, 2004). This was because none of the exiting measures were thought to offer a suitable cultural match to the New Zealand context. Twelve domains were identified for the measure and this led to the development of a comprehensive instrument known as *Taku Reo, Taku Mauri Ora; My Voice My Life* (Gordon et al., 2009). Unfortunately the psychometric properties of the measure have not been established satisfactorily for aggregated use. However, the instrument remains available for individual use due to its appeal and utility. There is currently no decision on a mandated self-rated outcome measurement instrument for use in mental health services in New Zealand. However, given that service user rated outcome measures comprise one of the five identified areas in MHSMART, a self-rated measure may well be introduced into mental health services once the sector is ready.

Measure of Functioning

The selection of a measure for determining functioning in New Zealand's mental health services has proved difficult and contentious (Mellsop & Smith, 2010). Work has been undertaken to try and identify which measure(s) could be used to assess for functionality. The Personal and Social Performance (PSP) measure and the Global Assessment of Functioning (GAF) measure were both favored over the Life Skills Profile (LSP) in the New Zealand context. However, no decision has been taken on the routine introduction of a mandated functionality measure, though some NGOs voluntarily use the Camberwell Assessment of Needs (CAN).

New Zealand has had a unique approach to routine outcome measures, emphasizing the concept of standardized assessments (Mellsop & Smith, 2010), rather than simply referring to outcome measures.

This commitment to the routine use of standardized and quantified assessment allows status comparisons over time that measure progress or outcomes. The concept of assessment is one familiar to clinicians.

The use of standardized assessments remains a work in progress. However, there is practice based evidence that has assisted clinicians to see the clinical utility of the HoNOS family of measures. Also there is evidence through the emphasis in the HoNOS training on the service user/clinician conversations, and use of outcome measures within multidisciplinary teams. More work in the area of clinical utility is required, particularly in relation to the way clinicians are actually using outcome measures in their practice.

There have been a number of key challenges in the implementation of outcome measurement in New Zealand.

- **Development of a Culture Which Supports and Understands the Need for Outcome Measurement:** Traditionally the emphasis within services has been on inputs and process rather than outputs or outcomes. The work of shifting towards an outcome culture was seen to be a long term project, and some resistance to change was encountered from clinicians.
- **The Importance of Leadership at Different Levels**: Leadership has been a critical component of the implementation of outcome measurement. While pockets of resistance to measuring outcomes remain, most clinicians now accept its value. Leadership has been a major factor in achieving this buy-in.
- **Infrastructural Issues and IT Access**: Not all services have the same access to IT and infrastructure. For example an outcome measurement App was developed but most clinicians do not have access to smart phones in their workplace. Also for a small country, New Zealand has many different information systems, which make consistency in collection hard to achieve.
- **Training and Resources in Specific Outcome Measurement Tools:** The train the trainer model appears to have worked well. However, trainers move on and so sometimes services find themselves without trainers. Te Pou has developed online refresher outcome measurement training which targets clinicians directly and this has proven successful. More than 350 people have now completed the online training since its launch.

Commencing with the HoNOS measures, the process of introducing new measures has been gradual, with only the addition of ADOM in the addiction sector. Implementation essentially started with the CAOS study (Gaines et al., 2003) which replicated many of the findings from the MHCASC Australian study of 1996 (Shane Solomon & Associates, 1996), showing that outcome measurement and a classification system had value. MHSMART involved voluntary collection of specified outcome measures by a number of services and this evolved into the PRIMHD collection. In 2008, the protocol summarized in Figure 1 for collecting outcome measures was agreed.

The information collection protocol (Te Pou, 2012a) informs the way outcomes are collected into PRIMHD. PRIMHD consists of activity data, such as referral status, legal status, and demographics, as well as outcomes data. PRIMHD data can be reported at national, service, and team levels. Team level data in particular is of great interest to clinicians who can compare how their team is performing compared to others.

Building on the train the trainer model, champions have been identified across the country to assist with the overall implementation of the measures. The champions and trainers have also tried to improve buy-in by showing how the information collected can be useful at an individual, team, service, and national level. To support teams, team level videos have been developed, as well as a strategy for using outcomes information within multidisciplinary teams (Te Pou, 2009a). At the individual clinician and service user level, a HoNOS App has been developed plus a refresher e-learning module. Additionally, an online automated graph builder provides clinicians and service users with useful graphical information once basic data is entered into the system.

This work of outcome measurement has assisted in the development of a key performance indicator (KPI) framework which in turn has informed the commissioning framework and developmental work around an outcomes framework.

Evaluation

As part of the evaluation of this work on outcomes measurement, surveys have been used as well as focus group feedback to assess the development of training, resources, and reporting. A programme logic has been developed to help guide the evaluative process. This evaluative work has indicated strong support for the training approach (over 90% approval rating of workshops); the resources and quarterly reports. In addition, while community services are still working towards achieving the Ministry of Health's compliance targets of 80% for collection rates, this has been exceeded in inpatient settings (Smith & Baxendine, 2015; Te Pou, 2016a).

Skills Matter: Post Graduate Clinical Training for Nurses and Allied Health Professionals

New Zealand has experienced problems with the supply of health professionals in recent years. For example, in the 1990s many nurses left to work overseas (Rydon, Rolleston, & Mackie, 2008). While a substantial number of New Zealand trained nurses continue to work overseas, New Zealand has also become a significant importer of nurses (Whittaker, 2013). New Zealand has the highest proportion of foreign trained nurses amongst OECD countries, and is one of the highest for doctors (OECD, 2015). Moreover, future workforce shortages are predicted by adult mental health and addiction services, including those in nursing (Te Pou, 2015). The attraction and retention of mental health and addiction professionals and building a sustainable workforce in New Zealand is therefore a priority area.

In New Zealand, post entry clinical training programmes for mental health and addiction have been running for over 20 years (Te Pou, 2012c). The first new graduate programme was developed in 1994 for new graduate nurses entering mental health nursing practice (Haggerty, McEldowney, Wilson, & Holloway, 2009). The framework was subsequently used for nursing as a whole (Ministry of Health, 1998). While new graduate training was available within DHBs in some form, these were variable across the country and needed greater consistency and funding (Cassie, 2015). Nevertheless, the provision of training and educational opportunities often depends on the available funding, and when this is tight, budget cuts in workforce development are often made (Ashton, King & McRae, 2004). However, new graduate programmes for nurses and allied health (occupational therapists and social workers) have been funded in New Zealand by the Ministry of Health and up until 2008 were managed by the Clinical Training Agency (CTA).

Design and Implementation

In 2008, Te Pou took over management of the mental health and addiction post entry clinical training programmes, and had a mandate to refresh the programmes and bring about change so that they better met the needs of the mental health and addiction workforce.

In 2009, the programmes were reconfigured and the programme was rebranded Skills Matter. Skills Matter now funds programme providers on behalf of the Ministry of Health to deliver post entry clinical training in mental health and addiction. The reconfigured programmes and funding resulted in:

- Updated programme service specifications that were relevant to trainees' workplaces and aligned with national workforce development initiatives.
- Broadened access criteria to enable addiction practitioners, psychologists, and part time workers to access programmes.
- The ability to study up to post graduate diploma and masters level.
- Improved contract management and better tracking of funding and outcomes.
- Termination of former provider contracts and a request for proposal process in 2009 to identify programme providers for 2010 (Te Pou, 2012b).

Priority areas for investment in training are identified on an ongoing basis with the Ministry of Health. The funding is currently allocated across six funded programmes with two main workforce development goals:

1. Supporting people new to the mental health and addiction sector to develop the required clinical skills and knowledge. These programmes are:
    a. New Entry to Specialist Practice: Mental Health and Nursing
    b. New Entry to Specialist Practice: Allied Mental Health and Addiction.
2. Supporting existing practitioners to develop advanced or specialist knowledge, skills and leadership in priority workforce development areas. These programmes are:
    a. Core Skills for Infant, Child and Adolescent Mental Health and Addiction.
    b. Assessment and Management of Co-existing Substance Use and Mental Health.
    c. Postgraduate Certificate/Diploma in Cognitive Behavior Therapy in Mental Health and Addiction.
    d. Clinical Leadership in Nursing Practice.

These programmes are for nurses and allied health professionals in the mental health and addiction sector, including social workers, occupational therapists, psychologists, and addiction practitioners. These groups are targeted as they are seen as critical to the implementation of health, and mental health and addiction strategies, and as a way of ensuring capacity and capability of the mental health and addiction workforce is developed. Leadership has been identified as one of the key enabling factors to the implementation of quality services (Wardhani, Utarini, van Dijk, Post, & Groothoof, 2009) and this is recognised by the Clinical Leadership in Nursing Practice programme.

A key factor in Te Pou's management of Skills Matter is a focus on stakeholder engagement and fostering strong relationships with both mental health and addiction sectors. Te Pou works with the providers of programmes, DHBs, and groups such as the Directors of Mental Health Nursing, Te Ao

Māramatanga the College of Mental Health Nurses, and more recently the Directors of Allied Health, to ensure the programmes align to professional standards and reflect the Ministry of Health's mental health and addiction sector practice requirements. This helps ensure the mental health and addiction post entry clinical training programmes stay relevant, current, and reflective of workforce need. "It is not enough to simply provide particular programmes or courses: the content of these courses must also be appropriate for the needs of mental health workers" (Ashton et al., 2004, p. 17).

The programmes comprise a formal teaching (or academic) component and clinical component, which is learning undertaken in the students' workplace, and other clinical services as appropriate. The Skills Matter programme also includes mechanisms intended to enable students to apply the knowledge and skills gained through education and training into practice. Even when training is effective, a number of contextual factors determine whether training is applied in practice, including opportunities to use skills and knowledge, the support of peers and supervisors, and organizational policies (Salas, Tannenbaum, Kraiger, & Smith-Jentsch, 2012). The mechanisms included in the Skills Matter programmes to support training transfer to practice include funding for preceptors and supervisors; the requirement for clinical placements; requirements for organizational support for students; and the facilitation of strong relationships between education providers and services through programme coordination. The programme also contributes funding for release time and provides some travel assistance in order to reduce known barriers to post graduate study. These mechanisms are also some of the common elements of new graduate nurse transition programs (Rush, Adamack, Gordon, Lilly, & Janke, 2013).

With the exception of the new graduate nursing programme, programme providers are responsible for selecting students to study under the funding. Each year around 300 health professionals working in mental health and addiction are funded through Skills Matter to take part in postgraduate study (see Table 1). Currently, the demand for places exceeds available funding. For example, all three universities delivering the Clinical Leadership in Nursing Practice programme have waiting lists. In 2016, the new graduate allied mental health and addiction programme also had 22 more eligible students than available places. The final selection of candidates is made by the education provider following consultation with employers, who each have their own promotional processes. The progamme works most effectively or successfully when there is a partnership between the education provider, students, and their employers. This means the programme provider works with employers as well as individuals wanting to study to identify the candidates who receive funding.

Table 1. Summary of Skills Matter funded students from 2010 to 2016

Programme	2010	2011	2012	2013	2014	2015	2016
Clinical Leadership in Nursing Practice	47	46	51	52	59	46	44
Co-existing Substance Use and Mental Health	26	32	31	28	33	29	29
Core Skills in Infant, Child and Adolescent Mental Health and Addiction	25	28	23	26	25	28	31
New Entry to Specialist Practice: Allied Mental Health and Addiction	23	23	24	24	26	27	28
New Entry to Specialist Practice: Mental Health and Addiction Nursing	140	142	148	152	153	175	163
PG Certificate in Cognitive Behavior Therapy	20	15	20	17	18	19	18
Total	**281**	**286**	**297**	**299**	**314**	**324**	**313**

In respect to the new graduate for nursing programme, each region is set an allocated number of new graduate funded places based on population data from Statistics New Zealand. Through the Advanced Choice of Employment programme, DHBs select new graduate nurses who are then placed on the new entry to specialist practice nursing programme. Some DHBs also fund places themselves over and above what is funded by the Skills Matter. In addition, there are a set number of places managed centrally for new graduate nurses working in the NGO and primary care sector who are selected for the programme in the same way as all the other programmes.

Evaluation

Evaluation is central to the Skills Matter programme. A monitoring and evaluation framework has been developed for the programme. This includes annual student surveys, feedback from providers, and stories from students and employers sharing their experiences. In addition, several independent reviews having been undertaken of the nursing programmes funded.

The student survey design was informed by the Kirkpatrick model of training evaluation (see http://www.kirkpatrickpartners.com) and the training transfer literature (e.g., Blume, Ford, Baldwin, & Huang, 2009; Burke & Hutchins, 2007), and examines multiple factors related to training effectiveness. A five year review (Field, 2015) of the new entry to specialist practice nursing programme between 2010 and 2014 found:

- Students were satisfied with the course and considered it relevant to their work.
- Gains in values, skills, knowledge, and practice were evident.
- Most students felt well supported in their first year of practice.
- Nearly all survey respondents agreed they felt able to practice safely.
- Nearly all students were applying their learning in their workplace.
- Participation in the course enhanced development by providing employment opportunities and professional recognition.

In addition, a cohort study of new entry to specialist practice nursing students found the courses were making a positive contribution to the retention of mental health nurses, particularly in inpatient mental health services (Te Pou, 2016b). In the NESP cohort, the average retention rate for inpatient mental health nurses was 63% compared to 49% in the comparison group (Te Pou, 2016b). Moreover, in 2014 half of new graduate nurses surveyed indicated they intended working in the mental health and addiction sector for at least another 10 years (Field, 2015).

Positive results have been reported for the other Skills Matter funded programmes. A review of the Clinical Leadership in Nursing Practice programme found the sector was increasingly recognizing the value of and need for transformational change, and understanding that clinical leaders, as well as managers, were needed to drive that change. The clinical leadership in nursing programme funding is regarded as not only a valuable initiative but also vital to the advancement of best practice in mental health services in New Zealand. Post graduate study is viewed as a vehicle to raise expectations across the sector of what is seen as an acceptable level of expertise both at management level and below. It also lifts practice standards generally by helping to embed evidence-based practice.

Programme providers are surveyed each year and continue to be positive about their relationships with Skills Matter staff and the overall management and administration of the contract. There is however dissatisfaction with the short-term contract periods, which restricts providers' ability to plan for future programme delivery. Skills Matter therefore continues to advocate for longer term contract periods with the Ministry of Health (Te Pou, 2016b). Nevertheless, the above highlights the benefits of the Skills Matter programme not only to individual trainees, but also to mental health and addiction services, and people accessing services.

CONCLUSION

In conclusion, three national workforce development initiatives have been described in this chapter. These have contributed to building the capacity and capability of the workforce to deliver quality services to people that are people-centered, equitable, safe, efficient and effective (WHO, 2006). The ultimate aim is focused on improving outcomes for people with experience of mental problems and contributing to recovery. These programmes have included identifying the key knowledge, skills, values, and attitudes of all people working in mental health and addiction services (*Let's Get Real*); the development of an outcomes culture; and post graduate clinical training for nurses and allied health professionals (Skills Matter). Based on the framework outlined by Roche (2002), these initiatives each have a different focus, with *Let's Get Real* focusing on a systems level; the building of an outcomes culture focusing on the current workforce; and Skills Matter on the future workforce. While focusing on different levels, a whole of system approach to workforce development has been taken as shown in this chapter.

Roche and Skinner (2005), have identified best practice principles for workforce development: evidence-based, multi-level, sustainable, involving ongoing evaluation, and participation by stakeholders. These three national initiatives have aimed to reflect these principles. The process of implementation has taken a planned approach as has been described in this chapter. Key steps in the implementation process have included workforce planning/needs assessment, design and implementation, and evaluation (see Damschroder et al., 2009; Werner & DeSimone, 2012). Evidence has been used to inform these workforce development initiatives, including data and information to understand priority needs, issues, and risk areas. Consultation with stakeholders has been central to the process. Evaluation has also been a key component of program implementation which has helped identify areas that have been working well and those requiring improvement.

Durlak and DuPre (2008) show that the chances of successful implementation are higher when programmes are carefully implemented. These programmes have considered a range of factors which may impact on implementation. In addition to the training and development, tools and resources included within the three initiatives described in this chapter, consideration has been given to how well the programme fits with the local context (e.g., fit and adaptability), organizational capacity (e.g., leadership, climate, vision, practices and processes); and the perceived need, benefit, confidence and skills of individual workers to implement change in practice. The prioritization and funding for these initiatives by the Ministry of Health has been a critical component. However, as Durlak and DuPre (2008, p. 336) point out "funding is a necessary but insufficient condition for effective implementation". Implementation requires consideration of a range of individual, organizational, and systems factors.

Consultation with stakeholders has been a key feature included in the three initiatives implemented in this chapter. People with lived experience of mental health problems have been key to this process. Consultation has enabled a better understanding of the needs, concerns, and acceptability of programmes. Feedback from the sector is also important in the monitoring and evaluation of these initiatives.

It is important to be realistic about the implementation of initiatives. "Expecting perfect or near-perfect implementation is unrealistic" (Durlak & DuPre, 2008, p. 331). Effective implementation of workforce development initiatives takes time and is a long term investment. The initiatives described in this chapter have taken at least 8-10 years to implement and there is still more work to be done. However, the perseverance is worth it to bring about the change and transformation to services that people with lived experience of mental health problems want to support their recovery.

REFERENCES

Alcohol and Drug Treatment Workforce Development Advisory Group. (2001). Practitioner competencies for alcohol and drug workers in Aotearoa-New Zealand. Wellington, New Zealand: Alcohol Advisory Council of New Zealand (ALAC).

Ashton, T., King, D., & McRae, S. (2004). *Labour market constraints affecting the mental health sector: Report to the Mental Health Commission.* Auckland, New Zealand: Centre for Health Services Research and Policy, University of Auckland.

Astho. (n.d.). *Workforce development plan toolkit: Guidance and resources to assist state and territorial health agencies to create a workforce training and development plan.* Arlington, VA: Astho. Retrieved from http://www.astho.org/Accreditation-and-Performance/Workforce-Development-Plan-Toolkit/Home/

Ballew, P., Castro, S., Claus, J., Kittur, N., Brennan, L., & Brownson, R. C. (2013). Developing web-based training for public health practitioners: What can we learn from a review of five disciplines? *Health Education Research, 28*(2), 276–287. doi:10.1093/her/cys098 PMID:22987862

Bell, M., & MacDougall, K. (2013). Adapting online learning for Canada's Northern public health workforce. *International Journal of Circumpolar Health*, 72. PMID:23971012

Bluestone, J., Johnson, P., Fullerton, J., Carr, C., & Alderman, J., & BonTempo, J. (2013). Effective in-service training design and delivery: Evidence from an integrative literature review. *Human Resources for Health, 11*(51), 1–26. PMID:24083659

Blume, B. D., Ford, J. K., Baldwin, T. T., & Huang, J. L. (2009). Transfer of training: A meta-analytic review. *Journal of Management, 36*(4), 1065–1105. doi:10.1177/0149206309352880

Burke, L. A., & Hutchins, H. M. (2007). Training transfer: An integrative literature review. *Human Resource Development Review, 6*(3), 263–296. doi:10.1177/1534484307303035

Campion, M. A., Fink, A. A., Ruggeberg, B. J., Carr, L., Phillips, G. M., & Odman, R. B. (2011). Doing competencies well: Best practices in competency modelling. *Personnel Psychology, 64*(1), 225–262. doi:10.1111/j.1744-6570.2010.01207.x

Cassie, F. (2015). NETP: A decade of growth. *Nursing Review, 15*(4). Retrieved from http://www.nursingreview.co.nz/issue/august-2015/netp-a-decade-of-growth/#.V-TxoE0cT84

Damschroder, L. J., Aron, D. C., Keith, R. E., Kirsh, S. R., Alexander, J. A., & Lowery, J. C. (2009). Fostering implementation of health services research findings into practice: A consolidated framework for advancing implementation science. *Implementation Science; IS*, *4*(1), 50. doi:10.1186/1748-5908-4-50 PMID:19664226

Deering, D., Robinson, G., Wheeler, A., Pulford, J., Frampton, C., Dunbar, L., & Black, S. (2009). *Preliminary work towards validating a draft outcome measure for use in the alcohol and drug sector.* Auckland, New Zealand: Te Pou o te Whakaaro Nui.

Durie, M. (1994). *Whaiora: Māori health development.* Auckland, New Zealand: Oxford University Press.

Durlak, J. A., & DuPre, E. P. (2008). Implementation matters: A review of research on the influence of implementation on program outcomes and the factors affecting implementation. *American Journal of Community Psychology*, *41*(3-4), 327–350. doi:10.1007/s10464-008-9165-0 PMID:18322790

Field, A. (2015). *New entry to specialist practice: Mental health and addiction nursing.* Retrieved from http://www.tepou.co.nz/resources/an-analysis-of-the-skills-matter-new-entry-to-specialist-practice-programme/640

Gaines, P., Bower, A., Buckingham, W., Eager, K., Burgess, P., & Green, J. (2003). *New Zealand mental health classification and outcome study: Final report.* Auckland, New Zealand: Health Research Council of New Zealand.

Gordon, S., Ellis, P., Haggerty, C., O'Connor, S., Pere, L., Foster, C., & Walkey, F. (2009). *Taku reo taku mauri ora: My voice, my life.* Auckland, New Zealand: Te Pou o te Whakaaro Nui.

Gordon, S., Ellis, P., Haggerty, C., Pere, L., Platz, G., & McLaren, K. (2004). *Preliminary work towards the development of a self-assessed measure of consumer outcomes.* Auckland, New Zealand: Health Research Council of New Zealand.

Haggerty, C., McEldowney, R., Wilson, D., & Holloway, K. (2009). *Growing our own: An evaluation of nurse entry to practice programmes in New Zealand 2006-2009.* Wellington, New Zealand: Clinical Training Agency, Ministry of Health.

Health Practitioners Competency Assurance Act, 48 (2003).

Hope, R. (2004). *The ten essential shared capabilities. A framework for the whole of the mental health workforce.* London, U.K.: Sainsbury Centre for Mental Health. doi:10.1037/e543012011-001

Jansen, P. (2009). Non-financial barriers to primary health care services for Maori. *Journal of Primary Health Care*, *1*(3), 240. PMID:20690390

Jansen, P., Bacal, K., & Crengle, S. (2008). *He ritenga whakaaro: Maori experiences of health services.* Auckland, New Zealand: Mauri Ora Associates.

Kessler, R. C., Aguilar-Gaxiola, S., Alonso, J., Chatterji, S., Lee, S., Ormel, J., & Wang, P. S. et al. (2009). The global burden of mental disorders: An update from the WHO World Mental Health (WMH) Surveys. *Epidemiology and Psychiatric Sciences*, *18*(1), 23–33. doi:10.1017/S1121189X00001421 PMID:19378696

Kingi, T. K., & Durie, M. (2000). *Hua oranga: A Maori measure of mental health outcomes*. Palmerston North, New Zealand: Te Pumanawa Hauora School of Māori Studies, Massey University.

Macduff, C., Gass, J., Laing, A., Williams, H., Coull, M., Addo, M., & Mackay, R. (2010). *An evaluation of the impact of the dissemination of educational resources to support values-based and recovery-focused mental health practice*. Aberdeen, Scotland: NHS Education for Scotland.

McClintock, K., Sokratov, A., Mellsop, G., & Kingi, T. K. (2013). Hua oranga: Service utility pilot of a mental health outcome measurement for an indigenous population. *International Indigenous Policy Journal*, *4*(3), 1–14. doi:10.18584/iipj.2013.4.3.7

Mellsop, G., & Smith, M. (2010). Outcome measures in New Zealand. In T. Trauer (Ed.), *Outcome measurement in mental health: Theory and practice* (pp. 26–31). New York, NY: Cambridge University Press. doi:10.1017/CBO9780511760686.004

Mental Health Commission. (2001). *Recovery competencies for the mental health workforce*. Wellington, New Zealand: Mental Health Commission.

Ministry for Culture and Heritage. (2015). *Read the Treaty*. Retrieved from http://www.nzhistory.net.nz/politics/treaty/read-the-treaty/english-text

Ministry of Health. (1998). *Report of the Ministerial Taskforce on nursing: Releasing the potential of nursing*. Wellington, New Zealand: Ministry of Health.

Ministry of Health. (2002). *Mental health (alcohol and other drugs) workforce development framework*. Wellington, New Zealand: Ministry of Health.

Ministry of Health. (2005). *Tauawhitia te wero: Embracing the challenge: National mental health and addiction workforce development plan 2006-2009*. Wellington, New Zealand: Ministry of Health.

Ministry of Health. (2008). *Let's get real: Real skills for people working in mental health and addiction*. Wellington, New Zealand: Ministry of Health.

Ministry of Health. (2012). *Rising to the challenge: The mental health and addiction service development plan 2012-2017*. Wellington, New Zealand: Ministry of Health.

Ministry of Health. (2016a). *New Zealand health strategy: Future direction*. Wellington, New Zealand: Ministry of Health.

Ministry of Health. (2016b). *Commissioning framework for mental health and addictions: A New Zealand guide*. Wellington, New Zealand: Ministry of Health.

National Service Framework Library. (2015). *Mental health ring fence trends 2015/16*. Retrieved from http://nsfl.health.govt.nz/dhb-planning-package/201516-planning-package/supplementary-information-201516-planning-guidelines--3

Oakley Browne, M. A., Wells, J. E., & Scott, K. M. (Eds.). (2006). *Te Rau Hinengaro: The New Zealand mental health survey*. Wellington, New Zealand: Ministry of Health.

OECD. (2015). *Health at a glance 2015: OECD indicators*. Retrieved from http://www.who.int/hrh/news/2015/oecd_analysis/en/

Pirkis, J., Burgess, P., Coombs, T., Clarke, A., Jones-Ellis, D., & Dickson, R. (2005). Routine measurement of outcomes in Australias public sector mental health services. *Australia and New Zealand Health Policy*, *2*(1), 8. doi:10.1186/1743-8462-2-8 PMID:15840170

Roche, A. M. (2001). *What is this thing called workforce development?* Retrieved from nceta.flinders.edu.au/files/7712/5548/1891/EN91.pdf

Roche, A. M., & Skinner, N. (2005). An introduction to workforce development. In N. Skinner, A.M. Roche, J. O'Connor, Y. Pollard, & C. Todd (Eds.), Workforce development TIPS (theory into practice strategies): A resource kit for the alcohol and other drugs field. Adelaide, Australia: National Centre for Education and Training on Addiction (NCETA), Flinders University.

Ruggeri, K., Farrington, C., & Brayne, C. (2013). A global model for effective use and evaluation of e-learning in health. *Telemedicine Journal and e-Health*, *19*(4), 312–321. doi:10.1089/tmj.2012.0175 PMID:23472702

Rush, K. L., Adamack, M., Gordon, J., Lilly, M., & Janke, R. (2013). Best practices of formal new graduate nurse transition programs: An integrative review. *International Journal of Nursing Studies*, *50*(3), 345–356. doi:10.1016/j.ijnurstu.2012.06.009 PMID:22795800

Rydon, S. E., Rolleston, A., & Mackie, J. (2008). Graduates and initial employment. *Nurse Education Today*, *28*(5), 610–619. doi:10.1016/j.nedt.2007.10.002 PMID:18226841

Salas, E., Tannenbaum, S. I., Kraiger, K., & Smith-Jentsch, K. A. (2012). The science of training and development in organizations: What matters in practice. *Psychological Science in the Public Interest*, *13*(2), 74–101. doi:10.1177/1529100612436661 PMID:26173283

Shane Solomon & Associates. (1996). *MH-CASC study manual*. Victoria, Australia: Mental Health Research Institute.

Skinner, N., Roche, A. M., O'Connor, J., Pollard, Y., & Todd, C. (2005). *Workforce development 'TIPS': Theory into practice strategies*. Retrieved from http://nceta.flinders.edu.au/index.php?cID=111

Smith, M., & Baxendine, S. (2015). Outcome measurement in New Zealand. *International Review of Psychiatry (Abingdon, England)*, *27*(4), 276–285. doi:10.3109/09540261.2015.1023783 PMID:25832565

Social Work Registration Act, 17 (2003).

Standards Australia. (2015). *Workforce planning AS 5620:2015*. NSW, Australia: Standards Australia.

Statistics New Zealand. (2013). *2013 census*. Retrieved from http://stats.govt.nz/Census/2013-census.aspx

Substance Abuse and Mental Health Services Administration. (2011). *A provider's guide: How to use core competencies in behavioral health*. Rockville, MD: SAMHSA.

Te Ao Maramatanga NZ College of Mental Health Nurses. (2004). Standards of practice for mental health nursing in New Zealand (2nd ed.). Auckland, New Zealand: Te Ao Maramatanga (NZCMHN).

Te Pou o te Whaakaro Nui & Matua Raki. (2015). *More than numbers workforce stocktake*. Auckland, New Zealand: Te Pou.

Te Pou o te Whaakaro Nui. (2009b). *Data to information report.* Auckland, New Zealand: Te Pou.

Te Pou o te Whaakaro Nui. (2012). *Technical review of the psychometric properties of the HoNOS family of measures.* Auckland, New Zealand: Te Pou.

Te Pou o te Whaakaro Nui. (2012a). *Mental health outcomes information collection protocol.* Auckland, New Zealand: Te Pou.

Te Pou o te Whakaaro Nui. (2009). *Let's get real overview.* Auckland, New Zealand: Te Pou.

Te Pou o te Whakaaro Nui. (2012b). *Skills Matter 2012 student survey: Evaluation report.* Auckland, New Zealand: Te Pou.

Te Pou o te Whakaaro Nui. (2012c). *Briefing paper on management of post entry clinical training funding for the mental health and addiction workforce.* Auckland, New Zealand: Te Pou.

Te Pou o te Whakaaro Nui. (2015). *Adult mental health and addiction nursing roles: 2014 survey of vote health funded services.* Auckland, New Zealand: Te Pou.

Te Pou o te Whakaaro Nui. (2016a). *National PRIMHD outcomes report (September 2016).* Retrieved from www.tepou.co.nz

Te Pou o te Whakaaro Nui. (2016b). *Skills Matter provider feedback 2016.* Auckland, New Zealand: Te Pou.

Treasury. (2016). *The budget economic and fiscal update 2016.* Wellington, New Zealand: Treasury. Retrieved from http://www.treasury.govt.nz/budget/forecasts/befu2016

Vincent, L. (2008). Differentiating competence, capability and capacity. *Innovating Perspectives, 16*(3).

Wardhani, V., Utarini, A., van Dijk, J. P., Post, D., & Groothoof, J. W. (2009). Determinants of quality management systems implementation in hospitals. *Health Policy (Amsterdam), 89*(3), 239–251. doi:10.1016/j.healthpol.2008.06.008 PMID:18752866

Werner, J. M., & DeSimone, R. L. (2012). *Human resource development* (6th ed.). Mason, OH: Cengage Learning.

Whittaker, L. (2013). *New Zealand nurse migration to the United States: What makes them go? What will bring them back?* (Master's thesis). Retrieved from http://mro.massey.ac.nz/handle/10179/5471#sthash.PmH7F03a.dpuf

Wing, J. K., Beevor, A. S., Curtis, R. H., Park, S. B. G., Hadden, S., & Burns, A. (1998). Health of the nation outcomes scales (HoNOS) research and development. *The British Journal of Psychiatry, 172*(1), 11–18. doi:10.1192/bjp.172.1.11 PMID:9534825

World Health Organization. (2006). *Quality of care: A process for making strategic choices in health systems.* Geneva, Switzerland: WHO. Retrieved from http://apps.who.int/iris/handle/10665/43470

KEY TERMS AND DEFINITIONS

ADOM: Alcohol and drug outcome measure developed for use in New Zealand's community alcohol and other drug services.

CAOS: A New Zealand research study that replicated an Australian piece of work that investigated case classes for outcome measurement.

HoNOS: Health of the Nations Outcomes Scale, an outcome measure primarily focusing on clinical symptoms.

Hua Oranga: Māori mental health outcome measure based on a Māori model of mental health.

Let's Get Real: A framework setting out the knowledge, skills, and attitudes required of everyone working in in mental health and addiction services in New Zealand.

MHINC: Mental health information national collection.

MHSMART: Mental Health Standard Measures of Assessment and Recovery Initiative.

PRIMHD: Programme for the Integration of Mental Health Data, which is a national collection for activity and outcomes data in New Zealand for mental health and addiction services.

Skills Matter: Post-graduate training for nurses and allied health professionals working in mental health and addiction services.

Tangata whaiora: The Māori term for people with experience of mental illness and/or addiction.

Te Rau Hinengaro: A population survey examining the prevalence of mental disorders amongst adults living in the community in New Zealand.

Whānau: Māori term for family.

ENDNOTE

1 This is a non-regulated workforce which has a minimum requirement of a level 4 National Certificate in Mental Health and Addiction Support.

Chapter 6
A Critique on the Factors that Influence Mental Health Workforce Training in Developing Countries

Rex Billington
Auckland University of Technology, New Zealand

ABSTRACT

This chapter will discuss the training of the mental health workforce in developing countries and make comparison with the developed world from where many of the systems and practices originate. All countries are different in the various factors that affect mental health care, mental health promotion, and mental health personnel training. But there are common themes. The relevancy of mental health workforce training is affected by treatment theory, the prevalence and burden of disorders in the country, the types of personnel available and involved in caring for the disabled, and the environments and resources available at country level. The realities and limitations of each country influences the types of people available for workforce training, the training approaches that are practical and can be sustained, the type of educational technologies available, and the retention of personnel once trained. These are the major themes addressed in this chapter with particular reference to the least developed countries.

INTRODUCTION

Psychological theory, new and innovative treatments, economic realities, cultural practices, and political priorities significantly influence the composition and the training of the mental health workforce in any country. Major changes in developed countries in the past 50 years or so, have centered on the gradual de-institutionalization of psychiatric care driven by the forces of humanity and health ethics, the development of psychotropic medicines, and the desire for preventive measures to lessen the national burden of mental illness. Recent advances in technology have also supported these changes in the gathering and storing of more accurate information upon which the need for service change can be studied, and new

DOI: 10.4018/978-1-5225-1874-7.ch006

practices in care evaluated and justified. Many of these advances in the developed world have spilled over to affect changes in the care of people with experience of mental illness living in developing countries; usually for the better, but sometimes for the worse.

BACKGROUND

This chapter will focus on some of the issues important to the development of the mental health workforce globally, but particularly to developing countries. The controversial issues addressed in the chapter are ones that the author frequently faced in his international work in the World Health Organization (WHO). The relevancy and suitability to developing countries of the practices and approaches of rich countries to manage mental health workforce issues will be examined. The cost of mental health care in developed countries is substantial. But the reality is that low and mid-income countries cannot afford many of the expensive and sophisticated approaches found in these financially richer countries. And even if they could afford them, the approaches may not be suitable. The proposition being made in this chapter is that developing countries need to develop their own approaches to health care in general and mental health care more. In particular approaches that are culturally sound and that can be sustained from national and local resources without relying on wealthy country support. While there is a need for medicines to treat mental illness, which is usually beyond national production capabilities, many developing countries have a socio-cultural infrastructure to care for their mentally ill within their families and communities. Essential to this infrastructure is the production and deployment of trained primary health care workers to help support and guide families in caring for their kin in their communities.

Fortunately the capability of countries to independently develop their own health care systems is increasingly being realized and being pursued in the more stable nation states. Mental illness and the need for mental health care are now becoming more visible. Systems and innovations are being put into place to fit identified needs. A major purpose to this chapter is to examine some of the major historical influences on the structure of mental health services in developed countries and the influence this has had on the training curricula and composition of mental health care services in the developing world. Some of the effects are positive but some not so useful. Epidemiological data will be used to compare the rich and poor countries and show where gaps and inconsistencies exist.

FACTORS AFFECTING MENTAL HEALTH WORKFORCE TRAINING IN DEVELOPING COUNTRIES

Theory Affecting Workforce Development

The approaches used to treat and care for those with mental disorders in developed and developing countries reflect what was understood at the time to be the causes of mental illness. When seen to have spiritual roots, then pagan rituals were practiced as treatment. The uncontrollable were often chained and left in filth to waste away. Others had their skulls opened by quacks to release the spirits causing the dilemma. Or blood was let. The more docile were either kept in secrecy by their families or wandered the streets to be mocked. So the care for those with mental illness in these early times where ignorance was rife did not involve trained health personnel.

But by the mid-1800s, as science helped understand the empirical roots of human behavior, we saw the beginning of the study of psychology and the introduction of psychotherapy in its various forms into the Western world. As new theories developed, academic institutions introduced and adapted their teaching programmes to embrace these changes. This in turn affected the delivery of mental health care. Psychophysics and objective mental measurement led to greater understanding of physical sensation and human cognitive abilities. In turn, the field of applied statistics was significantly influenced and progressed rapidly through this association with mental measurement. New psychology departments emerged in developed country universities to embrace these developments, which in turn influenced the students in clinical and educational psychology programmes in particular, and subsequently the skills of the mental health workforce.

Freud and his acolytes at the beginning of the 20th century firmly established the psychoanalytic movement in Europe that is based on the theory that mental illness has its roots in unsatisfied natural drives and innate forces. Training programmes soon emerged in medical schools and universities in Europe to teach the skills of psychoanalysis and psychotherapy derived from these ideas. In the U.S. the humanist Abraham Maslow in the mid-20th century built on the ideas of Freud and advocated therapeutic approaches derived from the notion that humans have a hierarchy of basic needs that motivate us and have to be met for us to mature. He stressed the importance of focusing on the positive qualities in people, not the negative ones that Freud addressed. Therapy thus evolved into more cognitive approaches for clients to understand themselves and develop culturally acceptable ways to satisfy these needs. The curricula of training programmes in turn were affected to embrace these new ideas and therapeutic approaches.

John Watson coined the terms behaviorism and classical conditioning in 1918 building on the notion of reflex conditioning discovered by physiologist Ivan Pavlov. B.F. Skinner built on Watson's ideas to develop the theory of operant conditioning as being fundamental to the formation and change of behavior. These theories influenced psychotherapy and learning theory, which in turn affected both the content of curricula and the approaches to mental health workforce education.

The aftermath and consequences of World War II in Europe and the West saw an emphasis on psychotherapy in its different forms to treat war casualties. The national response influenced the direction and bias of psychology towards the treatment of mentally disturbed veterans and those in the public with mental health issues. The various categories of personnel that constitute the mental health workforce in developed countries today were largely formulated to treat and care for the mentally ill in the post-World War II era. This structure in turn was copied and still influences much of the infrastructure of mental health services in the developing world today.

In the second half of the 20th century, behaviorism was challenged by cognitive theory. From this challenge cognitive behavioral therapy has evolved. It is an approach that has been shown to be very effective in treating disorders such as some phobias, post-traumatic stress disorder, and addictions. So while behaviorism and cognitive schools of psychological thought have not agreed theoretically, they have complemented each other in practical therapeutic applications. It is not unusual now for training institutions to blend approaches derived from different theoretical bases to teach student practitioners.

In more recent times the development of health psychology and positive psychology, the latter with its roots in Maslow's ideas, have influenced the direction of mental health prevention and recovery programmes. One relatively recent theoretical approach now affecting both the roles and the makeup of the mental health workforce and consequently education curricula and training programmes is the strengths model proposed by the sociologist Charles Rapp in the 1980s (Rapp & Goscha, 2011). This approach emphasizes the central importance of social support in mental health recovery. Another theoretical approach in vogue is the study and practice of therapeutic mindfulness. It is instructive that mindfulness, which has its roots in early Asian Buddhism, is now being adapted and assimilated into modern western psychotherapy and counseling.

It is clear that both new and old theories affect training programmes both inside and outside universities and tertiary education institutions. This in turn affects workforce development and ultimately service delivery. Most modern practices in mental health care taught in developing countries have been influenced by Western theory and science. But there are other pressures influencing mental health personnel training programmes besides these two factors.

The Burden of Mental and Substance Disorders

Health services are meant to combat disease and health disorders. To what extent do mental and substance disorders contribute to the global burden of disease that health services face? The global burden of disease (GBD) data for 2010 (Whiteford H.A. et al., 2013) estimated that mental and substance abuse disorders accounted for 7.4% of the worldwide disease burden, making it the 5th leading disorder category, behind cardiovascular and circulatory diseases (1st), common infectious diseases (2nd), neonatal disorders (3rd), and cancers (4th). However, mental and substance abuse disorders were ranked highest in the years living with disability (YLD). Within the mental and substance abuse category the leading causes globally of YLD were:

- Depressive disorders 40.5%.
- Anxiety disorders 14.6%.
- Illicit drug use disorders 10.9%.
- Alcohol use disorders 9.6%.
- Schizophrenia 7.4%.
- Bipolar disorder 7.0%.
- Pervasive developmental disorders 4.2%.
- Childhood behavioral disorders 3.4%.
- Eating disorders 1.2%.

Because the breadth of the field of mental health includes broader issues such as stress management, violence, dysfunctional families, and other social ills there is some confusion where the field of mental health begins and ends. It is likely that both the Diagnostic and Statistical Manual (DSM) and the International Classification of Disease (ICD) designations of mental disorders would have been used in both developed and developing countries to help assess and classify disorders upon which the YLD rates were calculated.

Data from the Whitehead et al. (2013) paper also report that the most prevalent group with a mental disorder globally between 1990 and 2010 were 10 to 29 year olds, and that there has been a 37.6% increase in mental and substance use disorders largely due to population growth and ageing. Because population growth is greatest in least developed countries and their populations are younger and are living longer, their burden from mental and substance abuse disorders has grown faster than that of developed countries.

What implications does the distribution of mental disorders in society have for mental health workforce requirements and training? One implication is that there would need to be country level information systems to indicate what disorders are the most prevalent, where they are distributed, and who are most afflicted. The classifications of disorders using the DSM and ICD systems require specialists trained to use these tools. While these specialists are available in developed countries, poorer countries clearly do not have sufficient competent diagnosticians. A call has been made (Kakuma et al., 2011) to train more professionals so that the diagnoses and classifications of mental disorders can be made more accurately. Given the cost of this training and the problems of retaining mental health professionals in many developing countries once trained, it may be more beneficial to have the two recognized mental health classification systems simplified if necessary and made sufficient for broad national use and action. The fact that the two international classification systems differ in their criteria for some disorders, and the fact that parts of both classification systems have been modified for new versions over time, suggests the somewhat arbitrariness of these behaviorally based classification systems.

The Mental Health Workforce in Developing Countries

The mental health workforce globally today can be divided into three groups. The first is composed of specialist mental health experts, such as psychiatrists, neurologists, psychologists, psychiatric nurses, mental health social workers, and occupational therapists. The second group is formed of non-specialist mental health workers, such as doctors, nurses, pharmacists, lay health workers, and those with lived experience of mental disorders and caregivers. The third group includes other professionals outside of the health sector, such as school teachers, coaches, social workers, religious counsellors, and other community service people (adapted from Kakuma et al., 2011).

The structure of mental health services and the personnel making up the workforce in the affluent countries has been used historically as a model for mental health service structure in less affluent countries. The influence has been through colonialism, missionaries, international consultants including those from the United Nations (UN) and bilateral AID agencies. Training fellowships and the international professional literature often supports these international mental health training initiatives. A key question again is whether the systems developed and used in rich countries are suitable and appropriate for less affluent countries and cultures?

The WHO 2014 report on the human resources for mental health revealed that only 1% of the global health workforce is in mental health. Within the mental health workforce, 43% were nurses, 8% psychiatrists, 7% psychologists, 3% social workers, 1.5% occupational therapists, and 33% were classified as other.

There is one mental health worker for every 100,000 people and 45% of the world's population live in a country with less than one psychiatrist per 100,000 people (WHO, 2014). The ratio of psychiatrists to the population in some countries in Africa in 1995 was estimated as 1 per 5 million (Gureje & Alem, 2000). The median average expenditure for mental health is US$2 per person in low and lower middle-income countries (World Bank Definition) and US$50 per person in high-income countries (WHO, 2014). Both the workforce number and financial support for the mental health service(s) are totally inadequate in low and middle-income countries.

The inadequacies have persisted for years. Many mental health specialists who have been trained in developing countries migrate to more affluent countries. Others are trained there and stay on. Retention is a substantive problem. It seems a waste of money to train specialist professionals in developing countries where migration abounds. Perhaps they should be bonded to practice for a fair period of time after training. A humanitarian issue at stake however, is the right of individuals to migrate. Should developed countries accept these trained specialists at the expense of their homeland; a moral issue for affluent recruiting countries. The author is reminded of a medical school in the Sudan where in the 1980s most of its new graduates left the country soon after graduating to go to other more affluent Middle Eastern countries. How many psychiatrists and clinical psychologists soon after graduation leave their developing country and migrate to a more affluent country? The statistics suggest that many do (WHO, 2014). Whether they sent money home or not begs the question. Solutions are needed to rectify this problem.

This retention issue is a challenge to health service planners in low-income countries in particular. They need to rethink ways of delivering mental health services and to resist the tendency to plan for the utilization and training of mental health cadres similar to developed country models. Developing countries have a history of family and community care for those with mental illness. As a priority, more community nurses and mental health support workers should be trained to be involved in outreach care (WHO, 2006). Furthermore, many diagnostic, treatment, and caring tasks could be downgraded and undertaken by a lower category on the workforce hierarchy. Simpler, economical and more humanistic approaches might be pursued.

Psychotropic medicines are a major, if not the major, treatment modality for serious mental disorders in the developed world. Physicians legally prescribe them. Given the shortage of physicians in the least developed countries perhaps other trained health cadres should be permitted to prescribe some now restricted medicines. Often in some mid and low-income countries psychotropic medicines are obtainable over the chemist's counter anyhow, without medical prescription. In addition, some non-medics currently do recommend that a patient obtain and use some specific antipsychotics. It is however, beyond the scope of this chapter to recommend on this issue. Suffice to say it is important that the training of mental health care workers is based on their cultures and the realities affecting their lives, and should not be directed by the well-intentioned safety conscious systems of the developed world. Most important is the design and structure of scientifically sound mental health caring systems that suits the country and its culture(s).

The prevention of mental health disorders and the promotion of mental health and well-being is an area that is being pursued in developed countries but seldom-addressed in developing countries. This domain of activity involves inter-sectoral collaboration not only because of the socio-behavioral roots of many mental health issues but because of the influence and relevance of other sectors to educate and reduce social stressors that provoke mental illness. The 2014 WHO global mental health (WHO, 2015) report stated that globally 55% of countries reported being involved in mental health awareness and anti-stigma programmes, 2% in the promotion of maternal and child health (MCH), 11% in school based programmes, 4% in parental/family mental health promotion, 5% in women and child abuse violence prevention, 9% in workplace mental health promotion and 8% in suicide prevention. There are no reported suicide prevention strategies in low-income countries and only one-third of high-income countries. These data reflect the progress being made. But it is mostly in developed countries. Developing countries would need to devote resources to these prevention and promotion programmes where they find them relevant. The issue is one of prioritization to involve more social, recreational, education, and other sectors besides the health workforce.

The Primary Health Care Model

The WHO 2014 report indicates 90% of service contacts for mental health issues are in outpatient as opposed to inpatient services. In one WHO study published in 1995 it was reported that 60% to 90% of persons with a mental health problem first go to primary health care facilities. This suggests the importance at this level of care for those seeking help (Ustun & Von Korff, 1995).

Social inequity, the high cost of health care, and the priority of many countries to fund expensive hospital care led the WHO and UNICEF to meet with member states and international health experts to discuss and formulate a recommended course of action for the future to help rectify the situation and help bring about "health for all". The result was the Alma Ata Declaration of 1978 (WHO, 1978) that describes the principles of primary health care. The declaration remains fully relevant today. Mental health care and promotion became an implicit but unfortunately not an explicit part of the Declaration that stated that primary health care includes at least:

- Education concerning prevailing health problems and methods of preventing and controlling them.
- Promotion of food supply and proper nutrition.
- An adequate supply of safe water and basic sanitation.
- Maternal and child health care, including family planning.
- Immunization against major infectious diseases.
- Prevention and control of locally endemic diseases.
- Appropriate treatment of common diseases and injuries.
- Provision of essential drugs.

Mental health was not specifically mentioned in the Declaration.

It is difficult for political and social reasons, to give mental health promotion and care priority when the GBD data favors mortality. This remains an issue globally. Fatal disease dominates the provision of medical services while the burden of mental illness on society is not so well appreciated by the general public. Stigma and fear stifle acceptance. However, there is great flexibility within the designated priority areas in the Alma Ata Declaration for mental health to be included. There is also a variety of primary health care personnel who can be involved and responsible for mental health service when trained. The Declaration states the importance of full community participation, even ownership of some activities, and the need for inter-sectoral collaboration in attaining goals. The role of community care is explicitly stated in the Declaration.

The Declaration identified the importance of health workers including physicians, nurses, midwives, auxiliaries and community workers, as well as traditional practitioners as needed. They were to be suitably trained both technically and socially to work as a health team and to respond to the expressed health needs of the community. The approach has been pursued globally since 1978 (WHO, 2005), but it still has a long way to go to be fully effective in many countries.

A significant change took place in the health workforce of villages and rural communities in many of the least developed counties as a response to the Alma Ata Declaration. Potential primary health care workers, both men and women, were recruited and selected by their village or a cluster of villages and sent for about six months for free training in national or regional training centers. Upon graduation they returned home to serve their villages. The women were particularly responsible for maternal and child health (MCH), family health and nutrition. Men were particularly responsible for clean water and sanitation. Simple mental health care and counseling were addressed in these centers. More serious conditions were referred to hospitals and asylums if the family or community could not cope. Some primary health care centers have evolved to embrace expanded health and health related duties including community based mental health care (WHO, 2005). In a few countries some of the more able community primary health care workers were selected to continue their education and train to become nurses, midwives, medical assistants, hygiene and sanitation inspectors, and other more senior roles. Lessons from the implementation of primary health care programmes have and can guide the strengthening of mental illness and substance control programmes now being elaborated in developing countries. It is essential to have community involvement and inter-sectoral collaboration, especially because so many mental and substance abuse disorders have a large social component.

In the 1980s and 1990s it was common to have international charities and bilateral AID agencies generously financing initial primary health care training in low-income countries. The collaboration was most generous and impressive. Centers were established and staffed by trained local health care workers who commanded respect and achieved good health outcomes as evidenced by high immunization rates and reductions in child mortality. A downside of this initiative was that some bilateral donors required their financial support to be used on purchasing supplies, equipment, transport, medicines, and consultant services recruited from the donor country. Much of the financial support actually went back to the donor country, so that sustaining the operation of the centers with the necessary supplies and equipment required continuing donor country support. On the other hand, donors had to be careful that funds they provided were not deployed elsewhere in the recipient country, misused, and even embezzled. Misuse was not always of the recipients doing however. One amusing incident occurred in a poor country at a graduation ceremony where male primary health care graduates were to be provided with a small motorcycle to travel between villages. One graduate asked the generous donor if he could possibly have a donkey instead of the motorcycle because of the rugged mountainous terrain he had to cover in his work; an example of intended donor generosity being misdirected because of their naivety about local conditions.

Occasionally primary health care objectives and approaches advocated and supported by donors were not well informed. In order to reduce confusion and encourage fruitful collaboration between donor and recipient it continues to be very important to have national and district primary health care plans that include a full description of the workforce needed to deliver the services. Successful primary health care programmes require national, district, and particularly village/community control.

The Alma Ata Declaration states that primary health care "should be sustained by integrated, functional and mutually supportive referral systems, leading to progressive improvement in health care for all, and giving priority to those most in need". The term hospital is not mentioned specifically in the Declaration, but the phrase "supportive referral systems" that is used is sometimes interpreted as meaning hospitals. There is no doubt that hospitals for the seriously mentally ill are needed in all countries to care for people with experience of psychotic illnesses who are determined to willfully harm themselves and others. But the challenge is to ensure that this level of care is provided by humanitarian organizations with staff trained as carers, who are not employed solely as wardens. It is also a challenge that this care is provided without seriously under-resourcing primary mental health care services. To achieve a balance of support for both institutionalized and community mental health care services that entails well-trained personnel is a real challenge for both developed and developing countries.

In summary and as described by Kakuma (2011, p. 1654) in regard to the 2006 WHO report:

Mental health care can be delivered effectively in primary care settings, through community-based programmes and task shifting approaches that engage and support skilled non-specialist health professionals, lay workers, affected individuals, and caregivers in mental health service delivery.

Task Based and Community Oriented Education

During the 1980s and 1990s several universities in some developing and developed countries under the guidance and support of the WHO created a network of medical schools that developed task-based community orientated medical education curricula. Such schools included Gezira Medical School, Sudan; Beth Sheba University, Israel; Suez Canal University, Egypt; University of Shiraz, Iran; McMaster University, Canada and others. This approach to education practiced what many nursing and other paramedical apprentice type training programmes had been doing before formal tertiary education institutions took on this responsibility. The practice was to have students serving the public while in training. An objective was for students to be specifically prepared upon graduation to be able to treat the endemic diseases of their local communities. Too often medical education in developing countries copied developed country medical school curricula that did not use this public service approach. In essence the task based community oriented education was the re-creation of an "apprenticeship" type system for medical education. Practice in community based health facilities began soon after the student became enrolled. The approach may be contrasted with the practice of many medical and health professional education programmes in the developed world today where students learn basic science for 1-2 years before moving into structured clinical training and supervised practice.

Mental health workforce training under the apprenticeship model would have students attached to mental health care practices and services from the start of their training. Background basic science knowledge is acquired and applied while the student is learning the practical tasks and skills of their vocation. The aim is to understand and appreciate the relevancy of basic science concepts while applying it in real practice. At the same time students are serving the health care needs of the community. They learn about local diseases and their treatment concurrently. Students practice under the guidance and supervision of the local practice team. This approach appeals as being especially appropriate for the preparation of mental health professionals and support workers in both developed and developing countries. An essential requirement of this approach in training mental health personnel is the selection and training of the practice supervisor(s) to ensure students in training are allocated patients and clients in the community who are suitable for the student's level of maturity and capabilities.

An effect of the task-based learning approach has been a greater use of competency-based or criterion-referenced examinations to replace normative assessment in health training programmes. Students are graded according to their abilities to satisfy task competencies and not only on the basis of what they know. The ranking and comparison of students with each other, sometimes referred to as a norm-based approach, is not required. Levels of satisfaction against performance criteria prevail. There was some objection to the criterion-referenced approach that used just pass, fail or incomplete, because quantified results (that is, grade point averages) are often needed for the selection of graduates into a more advanced and/or specialty training where there are limited places for trainees and therefore competition for these places. The issue is resolved by having trainees awarded levels of pass based on the quality of performance that are then converted into numeric values. Therefore clear criteria are required to assess each level of success. But to fail means the student does not progress in their training until some level of competency is achieved. Many health personnel training programmes globally now opt for this method of assessing students. To assess counseling trainees and those required to interact sensitively with clients is not an easy task. A challenge is to have clients and their disorders at the desired level of difficulty to serve the purpose of the examination of students at different stages of their training. Sometimes actors are used as patients to standardize the case difficulty to help attain some control over the level of difficulty of the assessment task. Sometimes videos are used to help test diagnostic skills too. The task-based approach to learning is particularly relevant to teaching mental health personnel at all levels, but a challenge is to devise realistic and valid assessment exercises.

Selection, Qualifying, and Certification of Trainees

Factors and criteria typically used to select students for health personnel training are grade point average, academic subjects pursued, and interviews. Some academics, particularly in the selection of medical and nursing students into training programmes, have questioned the value of selection interviews. One reason is because the time and logistics involved in arranging and conducting the interviews has little payoff. Some have also suggested that interviewing criteria are too subjective. However, the situation is somewhat different for mental health workforce training, particularly in developing countries. Life experience, communication skills and personal qualities are factors that are essential for practicing psychotherapy. Selection to training programmes should take these qualities into account. It is questionable whether these qualities can be developed through training alone. Valid and reliable evaluation approaches and criteria, as well as competent interviewers are essential to the process. To be denied entry or to be dropped from an educational programme is a serious matter for a student so due diligence is required. The selection process can also provide an opportunity for some informed and able members of the community to be involved.

It is not uncommon today to find people changing their vocation or expanding their roles within their chosen vocation to become involved in counseling clients and the public. Counseling is a particularly attractive career for more mature and older persons with life experience. Potential counselors may join expensive academic training programmes to prepare themselves for the change. But others already with well-developed communication skills and a high level of social intelligence can be trained under supervision on the job while being remunerated for it. Workplace based in-service training and continuing education in counseling skills for more mature students and those coming from other careers in both developed and developing countries can keep training costs lower and provide a public service at the same time. On balance, the screening of students to assess their personal qualities to help determine their acceptance into clinical training programmes is good practice. But as above, valid and reliable evaluation instruments and criteria for this assessment are important.

How long should basic training take for different categories of mental health professional and workers? In many countries there are minimum periods in which a trainee must serve under supervision in an apprenticeship like role. For a psychological counselor in some developed countries this period can vary between 200 to 300 contact hours depending on the training institution and the licensing authorities. For a psychiatrist it is of course much longer. These times are somewhat arbitrarily established, being based on the wisdom and experience of certification boards and authorities. How appropriate are these times? Studies by Scott Miller and his colleagues (Goldberg et al., 2016; Owen, Wampold, Kopta, Rousmaniere, & Miller, 2016) suggest the time needed for training can vary significantly for trainee clinical psychologists. The implication is that time in training under supervision should be kept flexible. But high quality assessment protocols are needed to signify and decide when further formal training can be discontinued. To do this for all types comprising the mental health workforce in developing countries would be a challenge to teachers and certification authorities. But it can be done.

Cost of Health Personnel Education

Higher education was once relatively inexpensive for some students because they were supported in large part by the state. Jobs were readily available upon graduation. In recent times however tertiary education in many developed countries has become a business. In some developed countries students complete their training and qualify for employment, but there are few jobs available in their specialty. They finish their training with large financial debts to repay and few work opportunities in the field for which they were trained. For example, employment for trained counselors and community support workers in New Zealand is becoming more difficult to find. Salary levels reflect this somewhat. It is therefore important that mental health workforce requirements are monitored nationally and that students are made aware of the realities of employment before they begin training. On the other hand, knowing employment opportunities may help to inform students to train for vocations in which there are better opportunities for employment.

As noted earlier in this chapter, developing countries have a shortage at all levels of the mental health workforce and a shortage of appropriate training capability (Brucknerl et al., 2011). New Zealand, Australia, and other developed countries are responding to the shortfall while at the same time earning substantial fees from foreign students, some of whom come from emerging countries. There is the issue that continually needs to be addressed of finding suitable clinical attachments and field practice for some of the foreign trainees.

In low-income countries, where human resources for the mental health field are woefully inadequate, what is required are decisions about which parts of the workforce should be prioritized for recruitment and training action. The challenge is to give support to where service improvements are most likely to result and where personnel are most needed based on national human resource analyses, not by copying developed country ratios and priorities. Striving to copy the West is not useful. As summarized by Kakuma (2011, p. 1654) in reflecting on the WHO report (2006):

The specific composition of the mental health workforce should be expected to vary across countries, according to differing population needs, mental health service delivery systems, and resources.

As was suggested earlier in this chapter, many psychiatrists and clinical psychologists in developing countries soon upon graduation leave home and migrate to a more affluent country. Should the public funds supporting their relatively expensive training be redeployed to train other mental health personnel, because the return of the specialists through service to the public is so low? International calls are still made for an increase in these professional mental health specialists, often putting them as priority, because of the need for leadership in the health service no doubt, while ignoring the reality of their professional orientation and the fact that they migrate. Should not greater emphasis be given to recruiting and retaining people of lesser skills who will likely stay in their country of origin? Can less clinically specialized people be trained to lead? These are very difficult questions to answer, but ones that deserve thorough socio-economic and business analysis in each developing country.

Education Technology

In all countries the training of the mental health workforce has become more efficient and effective with the use of e-learning programmes particularly when in national languages. Computer based lessons increase the acquisition of information and help test students' knowledge. Interactive visual and virtual computer programmes provide simulations that students can interact with to develop some necessary analytical, diagnostic, and interactive skills as a precursor to clinical contact with clients. In the developing world these programmes are used not only in training establishments but are becoming much more accessible to students at home and in the workplace.

Mental health workforce training that uses technology is effective and efficient for both basic and continuing education. Interactive Open University type materials have helped students learn when and where they like. While these technological approaches have not replaced the need for student tutors and mentors, they have reduced the old-fashioned lecture based approach. Hopefully this will happen even more.

The costs and maintenance of a modern education technological environment can be considerable. In the mid-1980s when video was a common feature of health personnel education the author was asked by some academics in a very low-income country to provide technical equipment and supplies so they could both play and produce video learning tapes to train physicians, nurses, and paramedic students. The request was turned down because the facility that was meant to house the equipment was not dust proof, to say the least, nor were there trained people who could use and maintain the equipment. Technology requires backup and system maintenance services not just the academic expertise to manage learning. Such technical skill and capability now exist in all countries. Now, the major obstacles to mid and low-income countries are the costs and security of the equipment.

As technology was adopted in health personnel in the developing world in the 1980 and 1990s, especially audiovisual and other interactive learning approaches, so began the creation of Learning Resource Centers (LRCs) in training institutions to support this initiative. A senior academic supported by a small team of education technology personal led each LRC. At first they produced audiovisual materials, then later videos, interactive and objective assessment materials for students, and gradually they effected the modernizing of curricula. Today the use of education technology in developing countries has expanded. For example, in the training of mental health clinical personnel the video has become a vehicle for students to record, observe, and critique simulated patient interviews before they meet personally with real patients. Occasionally where it can be arranged real client interviews are used.

Several LRCs formed international collaborative networks to share and exchange ideas and materials. LRCs are now found in most leading universities and tertiary education training establishments in the world, though they may have another title. The educational programmes of most mental health personnel training embrace the services of these resource centers to serve both in-house and outreach education endeavors. They service all levels of mental health workforce training. A challenge now being met is producing suitable programmes for the training of non-academic mental health support workers, community, and family caregivers. In summary, this area of educational technology is one where some poorer countries have emulated the richer ones and benefitted.

CONCLUSION

Despite significant international effort and support the mental health workforce in all low and most middle income countries remains inadequate. The situation in these countries is likely to worsen unless substantial national investments are made and more effective strategies are implemented. It has been shown that mental health care can be delivered effectively in primary care settings, through community-based programmes and task based approaches that engage and support both skilled and non-specialist health professionals and caregivers in mental health services. Mental health specialists, where they are available, continue to have essential roles in the delivery of services and in the training, supervision, and mentoring of these non-specialists. The specific composition of the mental health workforce should be expected to vary across countries, according to differing population needs, mental health service delivery systems, and resources. Standard international training programmes need to be cognizant of this need and design training activities and preparations to fit. This is perhaps a challenge to the business and commercial interests of many developed country higher education institutions. Finally, effective leadership and the management of human resources for mental health is essential to address key challenges, including the mobilization of financial resources, and the recruitment, training, retention, and equitable distribution of the workforce.

REFERENCES

Bruckner, I., Scheffler, R. M., Shen, G., Yoon, J., Chisholm, D., Morris, J., & Saxena, S. et al. (2011). The mental health workforce gap in low- and middle-income countries: A needs-based approach. *Bulletin of the World Health Organization*, *89*(3), 184–194. doi:10.2471/BLT.10.082784 PMID:21379414

Goldberg, S. B., Rousmaniere, T., Miller, S. D., Whipple, J., Nielsen, S. L., Hoyt, W. T., & Wampold, B. E. (2016). Do psychotherapists improve with time and experience? A longitudinal analysis of outcomes in a clinical setting. *Journal of Counseling Psychology*, *63*(1), 1–11. doi:10.1037/cou0000131 PMID:26751152

Gureje, O., & Alem, A. (2000). Mental health policy development in Asia. *Bulletin of the World Health Organization*, *78*(4), 475–482. PMID:10885166

Kakuma, R., Minas, H., van Ginneken, N., Dal Poz, M. R., Desiraju, K., Morris, J. E., & Scheffler, R. W. et al. (2011). Human resources for mental health care: Current situation and strategies for action. *Lancet*, *378*(9803), 1654–1663. doi:10.1016/S0140-6736(11)61093-3 PMID:22008420

Owen, J., Wampold, B. E., Kopta, M., Rousmaniere, T., & Miller, S. D. (2016). As good as it gets? Therapy outcomes of trainees over time. *Journal of Counseling Psychology*, *63*(1), 12–19. doi:10.1037/cou0000112 PMID:26751153

Rapp, C. A., & Goscha, R. J. (2011). *The strengths model: A recovery-oriented approach to mental health service* (3rd ed.). Oxford University Press.

Ustun, B. D., & Von Korff, M. (1995). Primary mental health service access and provision of care. In T. B. Ustun & N. Sartorius (Eds.), *Mental Illness in general health care: An international study*. Chichester, UK: John Wiley.

Whiteford, H. A., Degenhardt, L., Rehm, J., Baxter, A. J., Ferrari, A. J., Erskine, H. E., & Vos, T. et al. (2013). Global burden of disease attributable to mental and substance disorders: Findings from the Global Burden of Disease *Study 2010*. *Lancet*, *382*(9904), 1575–1586. doi:10.1016/S0140-6736(13)61611-6 PMID:23993280

World Health Organization. (1978). Declaration of Alma-Ata. *International Conference on Primary Health Care.* Retrieved from http://www.who.int/publications/almaata_declaration_en.pdf

World Health Organization. (2005). *Human resources and training for mental health: Mental Health Policy and Guidance Package*. Geneva, Switzerland: WHO.

World Health Organization. (2006). *The world health report: Working together for health.* Geneva, Switzerland: WHO. Retrieved from http://www.who.int/whr/2006/whr06

World Health Organization. (2015). *Mental health atlas 2014*. Geneva, Switzerland: WHO.

KEY TERMS AND DEFINITIONS

Alma Ata Declaration: This was written and agreed at the end of an international conference sponsored by WHO and UNICEF that was held in Alma Ata, USSR from Sept 6 -11, 1978. The declaration became a major milestone in the pursuit of primary health care in order to attain the global goal of health for all.

Community Based Mental Health: Posits that mental health care services should be pursued where possible at community or village level using local expertise and involving not only health but also other sectors.

Competency Assessment: Refers to education assessment that focuses on testing examinees performing essential tasks of their work. It is also referred as criterion referenced testing where particular standards of performance are required in order to pass the test.

Education Technology: A general term used to encompass audio-visual, computer, sophisticated communication technology and other interactive technical gadgetry to facilitate teaching and learning.

Developing Countries: Countries classified according to the World Bank based on economic criteria and eligibility for financial loans. In this chapter, developing countries include low and lower middle-income countries.

Global Burden of Disease or GBD: A measure using the disability life years (DALY) concept to calculate the mortality rate for a disease category combined with the difficulty in living with that disease.

Primary Health Care: As defined in the Alma Ata Declaration, refers to the first level of health care and disease prevention services that can be delivered by trained health care personal and involves the community and inter-sectoral collaboration.

Task Based Community Oriented Education: A term that was used to describe medical and health care professional training where students learned simple skills early in their professional training while providing services in community health practices to treat prevalent common disease and disorders.

World Health Organization or WHO: Is the specialized agency of the United Nations that is concerned with international public health.

Years Living with a Disease or YLD: Is as the name implies and is used to measure morbidity.

Chapter 7
Human Resources for Mental Health in Low and Middle Income Countries:
Evidence from Bangladesh

Sheikh Mohammed Shariful Islam
International Center for Diarrhoeal Diseases Research, Bangladesh

Reshman Tabassum
Macquarie University, Australia

Paolo C Colet
Shaqra University, Saudi Arabia

Jonas Preposi Cruz
Shaqra University, Saudi Arabia

Sukhen Dey
Bellamarine University, USA

Lal B. Rawal
International Center for Diarrhoel Diseases Research, Bangladesh

Anwar Islam
York University, Canada

ABSTRACT

Mental disorders are a major public health challenge globally, contributing to 40% of the global burden of disease. Nevertheless, it remains highly neglected by health planners and policy makers, particularly in low and middle income countries (LMIC). Bangladesh, one of the low-income countries, suffers from a severe shortage of appropriately trained and an adequate number of human resources to provide mental health care. The authors reviewed available evidence on the dynamics of mental health services in LMIC like Bangladesh, with a view to help develop appropriate policies on human resources. This chapter critically examines the current situation of human resources for mental health in Bangladesh, and explores ways to further strengthen human resources so as to enhance mental health services in the country.

DOI: 10.4018/978-1-5225-1874-7.ch007

INTRODUCTION

Non-communicable diseases including mental disorders are the leading cause of morbidity and mortality globally (S. Islam et al., 2014). The Global Burden of Disease study reported that between 1990 and 2010, the burden of mental and substance use disorders increased by 37·6% (Whiteford et al., 2013). In 2010, mental health and substance use disorders were the leading cause of years lived with disability (YLDs) worldwide, posing a striking and growing challenge to health systems in both developed and developing regions. The World Health Organization (WHO) estimated that mental health conditions contribute to 14% of all of the world's premature deaths (Bruckner et al., 2011). Mental health disorders impose huge financial burdens on people, families, health systems, and nations. Yet, mental health remains neglected in global health priorities and donor agenda, and seriously compromises access to care for people who need it the most.

A great majority of the people with mental health disorders live in low-and-middle income countries (LMIC) where the health systems are inadequate to provide the minimal necessary services. More than two-thirds of people with serious mental disorders in LMICs do not receive treatment and are often undiagnosed (Demyttenaere et al., 2004). While the mental health issues are escalating in developing countries, the growing shortage of trained health care providers is adversely affecting the quality of mental health of the general population. The *World Health Report 2006* drew global attention to the shortage of health workers in LMICs (WHO, 2006). Many LMIC face a serious crisis of adequately trained human resources for mental health (Kakuma et al., 2011).

Bangladesh, one of the developing countries, suffers from a severe shortage of mental health workers. The lack of reliable data on the prevalence of mental illness and the resultant burden of morbidity in Bangladesh makes it difficult to develop and introduce effective preventative measures and appropriate health care interventions (Islam & Tabassum, 2015). Since mental well-being is clearly associated with physical well-being (Saxena, Thornicroft, Knapp, & Whiteford, 2007), it is critically important to assess the mental health and well-being of the people of Bangladesh. It should be noted that emphasis is being placed on the issue of human resources for health in LMIC with special focus on mental health. Clearly growing evidence from these countries strongly suggests the need for the development of effective strategies for human resources in mental health. Bangladesh is no exception in this regard.

The authors reviewed the available evidence on mental health services with a view to better understand the need for human resources for mental health in LMIC. Evidence gained from developing countries could be used to inform the development of appropriate policies in Bangladesh. This chapter examines the current situation of human resources for mental health in Bangladesh, and explores the potential solutions to improving mental health services in Bangladesh with respect to human resources for mental health care.

BACKGROUND

According to the WHO (1948, p. 1), "health is a state of complete physical, mental and social well-being and not merely the absence of disease and infirmity". Mental health is an integral part of human health and well-being. In 2005, the WHO endorsed the phrase "no health without mental health" (Prince et al.,

2007). The WHO (World Health Organization, 2004) classification of mental and behavioral disorders include:

- Organic, including symptomatic, mental disorders (dementia, delirium, and brain injury).
- Mental and behavioral disorders due to use of psychoactive substances (alcohol-use and substance-use syndromes, including harmful use, dependence, and withdrawal).
- Schizophrenia, and schizotypal and delusional disorders.
- Mood (affective) disorders (mania, hypomania, bipolar affective disorder, and depressive episodes).
- Neurotic, stress-related, and somatoform disorders (phobic anxiety disorder, panic disorder, generalized anxiety disorder, obsessive-compulsive disorder, post-traumatic stress disorder, adjustment disorder, dissociative disorder, and somatization disorder).
- Behavioral syndromes associated with physiological disturbances and physical factors (eating disorders, sleep disorders, sexual dysfunction).
- Disorders of adult personality and behavior.
- Mental retardation.
- Disorders of psychological development.
- Behavioral and emotional disorders with onset usually in childhood and adolescence (hyperkinetic disorders, emotional disorders, and conduct disorders).
- Unspecified mental disorders.

The World Mental Health surveys, which includes nationally or regionally representative surveys in 28 countries, reflecting all regions of the world, demonstrated that mental disorders are highly prevalent throughout the world; the lifetime prevalence figures ranged from 12.0% to 47.4%, with a median of 26% (Kessler et al., 2009). Mental health and neuropsychiatric conditions contributed to 28% of the total global burden of disability-adjusted life-years worldwide in 2005 (Whiteford, Ferrari, Degenhardt, Feigin, & Vos, 2015). There is a complex web of interrelated issues linking mental disorders with physical ailments making them both important public health concerns (Prince et al., 2007). It is disconcerting to note that about half of all lifetime mental disorders start by the mid-teens, and three-quarters by the mid-twenties (Kessler et al., 2007).

The burden of neuropsychiatric disorders varies across regions of the world: disability-adjusted life-years and years lived with disability are highest in high-income countries and lowest in low-income countries (Okpaku, 2014). More than 85% of the world's population lives in the 153 countries classified as LMIC, according to the World Bank criteria (Jacob et al., 2007). Scarcity of mental health resources, inequity in resource distribution across service sectors, as well as geographical regions (rural and urban), and the inefficiency in use of such resources plague most LMIC (Saxena et al., 2007). However, there is growing evidence that many of these countries do not have effective interventions for the treatment and prevention of mental disorders (Prince et al., 2007). Major deficits in effective provision of health care services in LMIC include a scarcity of appropriately trained personnel and a lack of proper training facilities. Moreover, there is a need to assess innovative, scalable models of care delivery, and to ensure there is a strong political will to support policy, research, training, and infrastructure development as explicit priorities at the national level (Becker & Kleinman, 2013).

In many regions of the world, mental disorders often remain undiagnosed and untreated. In addition, those who receive treatment have often delayed their treatment for years (Wang et al., 2007). Reasons for the delay in treatment include failing to seek help because the problem is not acknowledged, perceiving treatment will not be effective, believing the problem will go away by itself, and desiring to deal with the problem without outside help (Okpaku, 2014). In addition, a lack of knowledge about mental disorders and stigma remain major barriers to care. Factors that are direct barriers to care also preclude treatment, including financial considerations and issues of accessibility, as well as the limited or lack of availability of services in many countries (Kohn, Saxena, Levav, & Saraceno, 2004; Saldivia, Vicente, Kohn, Rioseco, & Torres, 2004). As a result, mental health imposes huge financial burdens on individuals, societies, and nations.

As a low income country, Bangladesh has made significant progress in several health indicators over recent decades including reducing maternal and child deaths, increasing immunization coverage, and improving the overall life-expectancy at birth. However, the country still faces several health challenges, including increasing burden of several chronic diseases like diabetes (Biswas, Islam, Rawal, & Islam, 2016; Sal-sabil, Islam, & Islam, 2016), hypertension (Islam, Mainuddin et al., 2015), cardiovascular diseases (Karim et al., 2015), stroke, respiratory diseases, and cancer (Islam & Niessen, 2014; Islam et al., 2014c). The health system remains inadequate for the provision of essential services for chronic diseases and mental health. Bangladesh has 536 public hospitals with 37,387 beds that deliver inpatient care services for a population of 160 million (Islam & Biswas, 2014). Nevertheless, there is only one 500-bedded mental hospital in Dhaka, the capital city of the country for inpatient care services. On the other hand, there are only a few tertiary-level psychiatric care facilities which are mostly concentrated in the major metropolitan areas. Although Dhaka has five times more psychiatric beds than the rest of the country, few publicly funded facilities are available, including medicines, clinical facilities, and emergency care services for people with mental illness. At the same time, there is a serious lack of mental health rehabilitation and community support (Islam, Rahman, Aleem, & Islam, 2016).

According to WHO, more than 15 million people are suffering from severe mental disorders in Bangladesh (Hosman, Jané Llopis, & Saxena, 2004). Even though a significant decline was observed in the rate of mental disorders in Bangladesh between 1974 (31.4%) and 2005 (16.1%), it was still shockingly high in 2005. The first WHO national survey on mental health conducted in Bangladesh in 2003-2005 demonstrated that 16.1% of the population had some form of mental disorder, and the prevalence of mental disorders was higher among women (19%) than men (12.9%) (WHO, 2006). Additionally, a community-based survey conducted in 2009 in Bangladesh found the prevalence of mental disorders among children was 18.4% (Gausia, Fisher, Ali, & Oosthuizen, 2009). Previous studies in Bangladesh have also reported a high prevalence of depression in patients with diabetes or post stroke (Islam et al., 2016; Islam, Ferrari, Seissler, Niessen, & Lechner, 2015; S. Islam, Rawal, & Niessen, 2015). Mental illnesses are predominantly deemed as the result of being possessed by malicious spirits. The victims of mental illnesses are often neglected, abused, or their care delayed if it takes place at all in Bangladesh (Adams et al., 2014; S. Islam et al., 2015d).

HUMAN RESOURCES FOR MENTAL HEALTH IN BANGLADESH

Global Human Resources for Health

Human resources are the main pillars of the health system. The WHO Global Health Workforce Alliance endorsed that there is "no health without a workforce" (Campbell et al., 2013). Data on human resources for health are not available for all countries. The WHO Global Health Observatory reports workforce data for 186 countries. But 53% of these countries have fewer than 7 annual data points on midwives, nurses, and physicians across the past 20 years. Furthermore, of the 57 countries identified in 2006 with low human resources for health in density and low service coverage, 17 of these countries have no data point in the past five years (Campbell et al., 2013). The report showed that 118 countries (63%) fall below the threshold of 59.4 skilled health professionals per 10,000 population. Two-thirds of the world's countries may therefore face considerable challenges in addressing deficits below this indicative threshold. Reports of the Second Global Forum on Human Resources for Health, Bangkok, Thailand in 2011 found that the supply and availability of qualified health workers in many countries remained insufficient to deliver an effective package of essential health services, and ensure poor and marginalized people have equitable access to the health workforce and to health services (Global Health Workforce Alliance, 2011).

Current State of Global Human Resources for Mental Health

A total of 130 countries, representing two-thirds of all the WHO member states, were able to provide at least partial estimates of known mental health workers in their country. The median number of mental health workers per 100,000 population are shown for different WHO regions and for countries at different income levels in Figure 1. The global median is 9 per 100,000 population, or less than one mental health worker for every 10,000 people (WHO, 2015). However, based on these data, rates are projected to vary from below 1 per 100,000 population in low-income countries to over 50 in high-income countries.

The *Mental Health Atlas 2014* provides information on different staff categories across countries. Results indicate the proportion of workers in different staff categories is quite stable across countries and different income levels, with nurses comprising the single largest group of workers (40% to 60%). However, the absolute number of workers per 100,000 population varies enormously; for example, there were 6.6 psychiatrists per 100,000 population in the sampled high-income countries, compared to less

Figure 1. Mental health workforce per 100,000 populations, by World Bank income group
Source: WHO, 2015

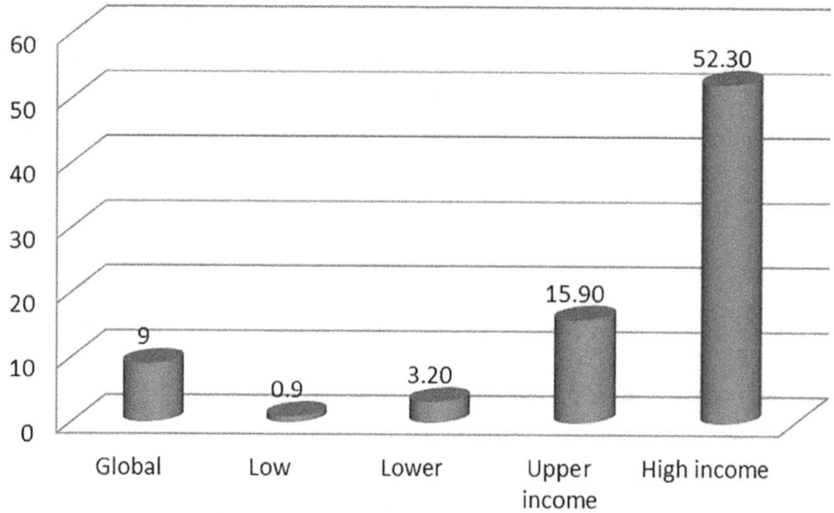

than 0.5 per 100,000 population in LMIC. Similarly, there are over 30 nurses working in mental health per 100,000 population in high-income country settings compared to 0.4 in low-income countries, 2.5 in LMIC, and 7.1 in upper-middle income countries. Across all WHO regions, a large majority of mental health workers surveyed by the *Mental Health Atlas 2014* survey are working in inpatient and day care services (82% globally).

There has been a slight decline (of 6%) in the overall reported number of psychiatrists between 2011 and 2014, as shown in Table 1. This finding may reflect under-reporting in the 2014 survey of psychiatrists working in private practice (particular emphasis had been given to this in the 2011 survey). In the South-East Asian and African Regions, the reported number of psychiatrists has increased by more than 25% (albeit from a very low baseline rate in 2011) (WHO, 2014). However, training programmes for psychiatrists are present in only 55% of low-income countries, 69% of LMIC, and 60% of upper middle income countries (World Psychiatric Association & WHO, 2005). The median number of nurses working in mental health globally has increased by 37%, with particularly notable increases in the American (63%) and Eastern Mediterranean Regions (46%) (WHO, 2015). The positive change in the number of nurses working in mental health is greatest in low-income countries and least in high-income countries. However, the absolute number of nurses working in mental health in high-income countries is still a lot higher than that in lower income countries (WHO, 2015).

Hospital Beds and Admissions

Globally, there was a slight decrease of 5% in the number of mental hospitals between 2011 and 2014. There has been a more significant decrease in the number of mental hospital beds, which has dropped by nearly 30% compared to 2011 (WHO, 2014). In all WHO regions, there was a decline in the number of beds, particularly in the region of the Americas (a 45% decrease) (WHO, 2014). When countries were grouped according to income level, all except the lower middle-income category showed a reduction in both the number of hospitals and number of mental hospital beds. At the global level, the number of beds available in psychiatric wards in general hospitals has increased significantly by 60% between 2011 and 2014 (WHO, 2015).

Despite the global decrease in the number of beds, as shown in Table 2 there was an increase of over 20% in the median rate of admission to mental hospitals globally, indicative of a higher patient turnover

Table 1. Change in number of psychiatrists and nurses working in mental health from 2011 to 2014

	Psychiatrists (Median Rate Per 100,000 Population)				Nurses (Median Rate Per 100,000 Population)			
	N	2014	2011	Change	*N*	2014	2011	Change
Global	118	0.93	0.99	−6%	106	5.31	3.89	37%
Income								
Low	24	0.05	0.05	−2%	23	0.36	0.26	41%
Lower-middle	33	0.38	0.33	15%	30	2.73	2.26	20%
Upper-middle	34	1.39	1.61	−13%	32	8.2	7.09	16%
High	27	7.47	8.18	−8%	21	33.24	30.76	8%

Source: WHO, 2015

Table 2. Change in admissions to mental hospital and psychiatric wards in general hospitals

		Mental Hospital Admission (Median Rate Per 100,000 Population)			General Hospital Admission (Median Rate Per 100,000 Population)			
	N	2014	2011	Change	*N*	2014	2011	Change
Global	94	41.15	33.75	22%	94	43.79	23.74	84%
Income								
Low	16	9.36	9.19	2%	10	3.62	4.57	−21%
Lower-middle	20	15.98	19.36	−17%	14	5.97	4.74	26%
Upper-middle	27	41.89	55.7	−25%	16	50.86	27.36	86%
High	31	128.32	159.11	−19%	23	121.89	164.98	−26%

Source: WHO, 2014

rate. The trends across WHO regions are mixed; for example, the Western Pacific Region shows a decline of more than 50%, while the Eastern Mediterranean and South-East Asian Regions show an increase of 25%. In high-income countries there was a 19% decline in admission rates to mental hospitals while there was a slight increase (of 2%) in low-income countries (WHO, 2014).

Human Resources for Health in Bangladesh

Bangladesh is one of the countries with a stark shortage of health workers, especially in rural areas. A nationally representative survey conducted in 2007 reported that there were approximately 5 physicians and 2 nurses per 10 000 population, the ratio of nurse to physician being only 0.4 (Ahmed, Hossain, RajaChowdhury, & Bhuiya, 2011). This ratio is far below the WHO minimum recommended levels. The distribution of human resources in Bangladesh varied substantially among different divisions, with a gross imbalance favoring urban areas. There were around 12 unqualified village doctors and 11 sales people at local medicine retail shops per 10,000 population. The number of community health workers (CHWs) from the non-governmental organization (NGO) sector was almost double compared to the government sector and an overwhelming number of traditional birth attendants with no medical training. The village doctors (predominantly males) and the CHWs (predominantly females) were mainly concentrated in rural areas, while the paraprofessionals were concentrated in urban areas. The number of faith/traditional healers, homeopaths (qualified and non-qualified) and basic care providers are still high in rural and hard to reach areas, and form the first level of contact for several diseases including mental health (S. Islam & Moreau, 2009).

In summary, Bangladesh is suffering from a severe human resources for health crisis in terms of a shortage of qualified providers, has an inappropriate skills-mix, and inequity in distribution, compared to international recommendations which demands priority action from policy makers (Ahmed et al., 2011).

Human Resources for Mental Health in Bangladesh

Like many other developing countries, Bangladesh is also faced with a range of daunting and interlocking mental health issues, especially an acute shortage of skilled and qualified human resources for mental health. There are only 0.49 skilled human resources and 0.07 psychiatrists per 100,000 population (WHO,

2011). These figures clearly highlight the crisis of human resources for mental health in the country. The *Mental Health Atlas 2011* (WHO, 2011) reports existing categories of human resources for mental health per 100,000 population in Bangladesh as follows:

- Medical doctors (not specialized in psychiatry) 0.19.
- Nurses 0.20.
- Psychologists 0.01.
- Social workers 0.002.
- Occupational therapists 0.002.
- Other mental health workers 0.04.

The human resource situation in Bangladesh, as noted earlier, remains critical. Table 3 shows the health facilities for available mental health patients. It should be noted that a total of only 47 psychiatrists are actively involved in service provision – 10 in outpatient facilities, 33 in community-based inpatient psychiatric units, and 4 in mental hospitals. On the other hand, 70 medical doctors (general practitioners) work in outpatient facilities; 140 in community-based psychiatric inpatient units, and 15 in mental hospitals. As for nurses, 21 work in outpatient facilities, 220 in community-based psychiatric inpatient units, and 140 in mental hospitals. Furthermore, four psychosocial professionals are engaged in outpatient services; three in community-based psychiatric inpatient units, and three in mental hospitals (A. Islam & Biswas, 2015).

Table 4 shows the number of human resources for mental health in Bangladesh. Most of the psychiatrists (54%) deliver services in public or private sector mental health facilities, while 46% of practitioners work for NGOs or are involved in private practice (Barkat & Maksud, 2003). Moreover, 62% and 26% of psychosocial professionals work for government funded mental health facilities and NGOs, or in private practice respectively. The remaining 12% of psychosocial professionals are involved in public or private sector mental health practice. Additionally, the psychiatrists practicing in government hospitals or facilities are permitted to work simultaneously in the private sector, which triggers the culture of dual practice in the mental health care sector (A. Islam & Biswas, 2015).

Table 3. Health facilities available for mental health patients in Bangladesh

	Total Number of Facilities/ Beds	Rate Per 100,000 Population	Number of Facilities/ Beds Reserved for Children and Adolescents Only	Rate Per 100,000 Population
Mental health outpatient facilities	60	0.04	2	0.001
Day treatment facilities	0	0.0	NA	NA
Psychiatric beds in general hospitals	900	0.55	20	0.01
Community residential facilities	11	0.01	0	NA
Beds/places in community residential facilities	1283	0.78	936	0.57
Mental hospitals	1	0.0001	0	0
Beds in mental hospitals	500	0.3	0	0

Source: WHO, 2011

Table 4. The number of human resources for mental health in Bangladesh

	Health Professionals Working in the Mental Health Sector Rate Per 100,000	Training of Health Professions in Educational Institutions Rate Per 100,000
Psychiatrists	0.07	0.03
Medical doctors, not specialized in psychiatry	0.19	3.04
Nurses	0.20	0.25
Psychologists	0.01	0.02
Social workers	0.002	0.12
Occupational therapists	0.002	0.18
Other health workers	0.04	NA

Source: WHO, 2011

Since the 1990s, growing emphasis has been placed on health promotion and preventative services in Bangladesh by the health sector. Nevertheless, a large number of people in rural areas have little access to healthcare services compared to their urban counterparts (A. Islam & Biswas, 2014). There are 0.04 psychiatrists per bed in community-based inpatient psychiatric units, whereas in hospitals the psychiatrist-bed ratio is only 0.01. However, nurses are almost evenly distributed between the community-based inpatient psychiatric units (0.27 per bed) and mental hospitals (0.028 per bed) (Islam & Biswas, 2015). The urban-rural disparity is most pronounced in the incidence of mental illness with rural areas accounting for the largest number of cases as more than 70% of the population live in rural Bangladesh. Needless to say, human resources for mental health is disproportionately distributed across the country with rural areas facing a critical shortage (Joint Learning Initiative, 2004; WHO, 2004).

Key Challenges in Developing Human Resources for Mental Health in Bangladesh

The paucity of human resources for health has undoubtedly affected the provision of services for people experiencing mental illness in Bangladesh. Developing, training, and retaining human resources for mental health in primary healthcare has received little attention from policy makers. Although the burden of mental illness is growing in Bangladesh, it has a low profile on the national public health agenda. Firstly, there is lack of national policy and strategy guidelines on mental health that can assist in planning. Secondly, insufficient funding for mental health resources, especially health personnel, hinders the process of further enhancing the prevention and treatment services for people with experience of mental illness in Bangladesh. Thirdly, healthcare workers, especially primary health care workers, seldom receive adequate training, supervision, and institutional support for sustainable skills growth. Fourthly, Bangladesh has a paucity of leaders in mental health, who have the appropriate skills to carry out multifaceted tasks and responsibilities, for instance, development of human resource policy for mental illness, reinforcing mental health related health services, and advising on population-level intermediations to prevent mental health problems. Finally, Bangladesh still lacks a coherent national surveillance and monitoring system for mental illness. Progress towards prevention has not kept pace with the rising burden of neuropsychiatric diseases, primarily because of a lack of prudent priority setting. The absence of effective interventions as well as non-adherence to international standards or frameworks (i.e., WHO Health Systems Framework and Health Workforce 2030) for surveillance and monitoring of mental illnesses have also put burden on developing human resources for mental health. As a result, the responsible government departments have largely been unsuccessful in planning and successfully carrying out multifaceted programs aimed at further strengthening the development of human resources for mental health.

SOLUTIONS AND RECOMMENDATIONS

Outlined below are strategies for increasing human resources for mental health based on lessons from LMIC.

Capacity Building and Task Shifting

Ongoing development of the workforce with appropriate skills is essential to strengthen the necessary human resources for mental health. Training should be relevant to the mental health needs of the population and include in-service training as well as the strengthening of institutional capacity to conduct effective training programmes. Approaches to psychiatric education also vary across countries (Savin, 2000; Singh & Ng, 2008). In Nigeria, a specialist training programme in psychiatry has been in place for more than 25 years, yet only half of the country's tertiary mental health facilities have enough psychiatrists to provide accredited training (World Psychiatric Association & WHO, 2005). Overall short-term training by specialist mental health professionals with ongoing monitoring and supervision can improve confidence, detection, treatment, and treatment adherence amongst people with experience of mental disorders and reduce caregiver burden. Academic programs for capacity development of mental health professionals are needed. At the same time there is a need to produce mental health leaders with appropriate advocacy and resource mobilization skills.

Task shifting, referred to as delegating tasks to less trained health workers with supervision, has been widely recognized as an efficient method to deliver healthcare in low resource settings. A high proportion of mental health services can be delivered in primary care settings by non-specialists. Primary level health staff need to be better trained and supported to identify and manage mental disorders. However, Bangladesh is lagging behind in providing appropriate training to primary health care personnel, which seriously affects the quality of mental health services. The sustainability of knowledge and skills gained remains uncertain, and further examination of effective supervision and mentorship is needed. With the increasing prevalence of chronic diseases and an aging population (S. Islam, 2010), the need for mental health professionals in Bangladesh is likely to increase in the future. Training mid-level health workers will help to improve the delivery of health services for health (L. Rawal et al., 2016), including mental health.

Effective Human Resources Policies for Mental Health

Despite extensive evidence and agreement on what are effective mental health practices for people experiencing severe mental illness, research shows that routine mental health programs do not provide these evidence-based practices to the great majority of people (Drake et al., 2001). National health policies and plans often fail to include human resources for mental health. Developing countries need to adopt both short-term and long-term policies for mental health workforce development based on the needs of health systems and national capacities. A recent report concluded that Bangladesh needs more effective policies and provisions designed specifically for attraction, deployment, and retention of human resources for health in rural areas, and the execution of these policies and provisions must be monitored and evaluated effectively (L. B. Rawal, Joarder, Islam, Uddin, & Ahmed, 2015).

Financial Management

Scaling up of human resources and training will incur huge costs. Mobilization of financial resources to develop human resources for mental health care is one of the biggest challenges in fashioning effective mental health systems (Saxena, Sharan, & Saraceno, 2003; Saxena et al., 2007). All LMIC have inadequate funding for mental health. Cost-effectiveness studies for the scaling-up of skills and the development of non-specialist health workers are scarce (Chisholm, Lund, & Saxena, 2007). Clearly, further studies are necessary to inform planners and policy makers on the required human resources for mental health. Strategic changes in payment systems are as important as financing in bringing about system change (Chisholm, 2007). For example, increasing the role of psychiatrists as supervisors and trainers, and boosting the number of other mental health workers, will need payment arrangements that recognize changes in these roles. These alterations will also be important for shifting practice from institutions to community settings.

Financial resources are an apparent requirement for developing and maintaining mental health services and moving towards programme goals (WHO, 2015). Based on *Mental Health Atlas 2014* data, it is possible to generate reliable information on the extent of government spending on mental health in both developed and developing countries. Figure 2 illustrates median government mental health spending per capita for countries at different levels of income. Expenditure levels in low and LMIC groups is very low (less than US $2), and falls far below levels estimated for high-income countries (over US$ 50 per capita) (WHO, 2015). Nevertheless, mental health expenditures by the government in Bangladesh represents less than 1% (0.44%) of the total health budget. Furthermore, mental hospital expenditurecomprises 35.6% of the total mental health budget, which is lower than that in many developing countries (A. Islam & Biswas, 2015).

Figure 2. Median mental health expenditure per capita (US$), by World Bank income group in 2013
Source: WHO, 2015

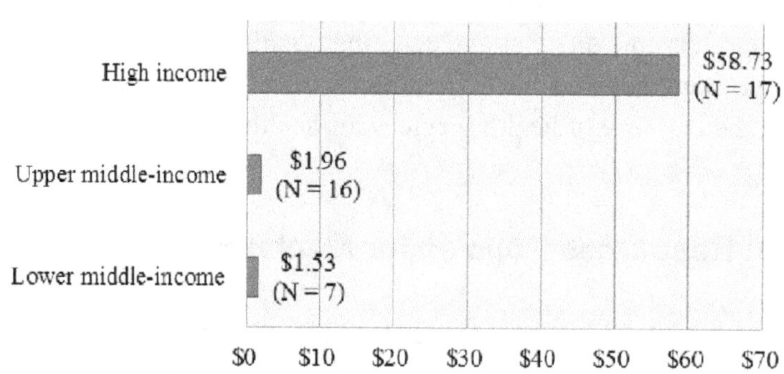

	Lower middle-income	Upper middle-income	High income
Mental health expenditure per capita	$1.53	$1.96	$58.73

Leadership

Effective leadership is critically important for scaling-up the mental health workforce (Schiffbauer, O'Brien, Timmons, & Kiarie, 2008; Sherk, Nauseda, Johnson, & Liston, 2009). However, there is a scarcity of research and/or evidence that addresses this issue adequately. A case example from India highlighted the implications of good leadership when funding for mental health was increased substantially. The University of Melbourne has been conducting an international mental health leadership programme since 2001 (Beinecke, Minas, Goldsack, & Peters, 2010). This 4-week course provides training in mental health policy and systems, mental health workforce, and mental health and human rights for researchers, psychiatrists, mental health professionals, and decision makers. Shorter 2-week leadership courses have been developed subsequently in many countries, including Indonesia, India, and Nigeria. Anecdotal evidence suggests that the courses and ongoing support for alumni have a positive effect in their home countries. In contrast, political will in taking decisive action to bring about change, is rare in the context of mental health services in Bangladesh. Thus, policymakers often miss the mark to develop incentive programmes for human resources for mental health in Bangladesh.

Information Technology for Mental Health Workforce Development

In recent years, with the growing use of mobile phones, their application in health is increasing at a rapid pace. Mobile phone technologies have been shown to improve medication adherence, glycemic control (Islam, Niessen, Ferrari, Ali, Seissler & Lechner, 2015), decrease blood pressure (Bobrow et al., 2016), and overall help to reduce the burden of chronic diseases and thus to build a healthier nation (Chow et al., 2015). The use of telemedicine for mental health could be used to provide a range of services to patients and healthcare providers including training for the mental health workforce working in rural and remote regions.

Brain Drain

The migration of mental health professionals from LMIC (Jenkins et al., 2010), and rural-to-urban migration, seriously affects the development of human resources for mental health. Professional isolation, social facilities, insecurity, and lack of better training and career opportunities are key reasons for emigration (Gureje et al., 2009). The U.K., the U.S., New Zealand, and Australia collectively employ almost 9,000 psychiatrists from India, the Philippines, Pakistan, Bangladesh, Nigeria, Egypt, and Sri Lanka (Jenkins et al., 2010). Without such migration, many source countries would have more than doubled their number of psychiatrists per 100,000 population.

Establishment of local training programmes is especially important to reduce the likelihood of out-migration of health professionals. International development partners could help develop and implement effective strategic collaborations and in scaling-up human resources for mental health (Hauff, 1996). It is encouraging to note that following the launching of effective training programmes in Ethiopia, the number of psychiatrists rose from 11 to 34 between 2003 and 2009 (Alem, Pain, Araya, & Hodges, 2010). The success of the initiative has led to its expansion to cover 14 different health programmes (see http://taaac.com/). However, Bangladesh lacks effective strategies in retaining available human resources for mental health. Clearly there is a need to further strengthen the official capacity building efforts that can stimulate career development opportunities for health workers, especially those in the mental health field.

Role of Mental Health Nurses

Mental health nursing is built on a philosophy of holistic care and a client-centered approach, where the nurse strives to empower the client to regain control of their lives (Barker & Buchanan-Barker, 2011). Mental health nurses should have the interpersonal skills to communicate effectively with clients, based on mutual trust and respect (Ross, Clarke, & Kettles, 2014). Fundamentally, they have the core duty of maintaining patient well-being, and the promotion of mental and physical health to its optimum, including the prevention of mental illness (WHO & International Concil of Nurses, 2007). In LMIC, mental health nurses often act as the primary providers of care for people with mental disorders due to the insufficiency of other mental health professionals in these countries. In addition to their role of providing direct care, mental health nurses often have administrative and policy-making responsibilities, prescribing, and medication management roles, as well as managing patient wards and performing follow-up care in the community (Barrett et al., 2009; WHO & International Council of Nurses, 2007).

Despite these significant roles for mental health nurses, the importance of mental health nursing care and the critical role nurses have in providing mental health care is largely unrecognized. Therefore, there is a serious need to develop nursing professionals for mental health in LMIC, empower nurses with proper delegation, incentives, and prescribing authority. A previous study suggested that nurse prescribing is perceived to enhance care and offer better delivery of services (Devane & Leahy-Warren, 2015). Furthermore, mental health nurses have indicated that obtaining prescriptive authority would simply legalize what nurses are already doing in everyday practice (Devane & Leahy-Warren, 2015). In addition, there is a need to clarify the role of nurses within a nursing care model in order to improve mental health services. It has also been recommended that basic and graduate nursing curriculum on mental health education be enhanced to have more hours focused on mental health, prioritizing psychiatry, standardizing training curriculum on a global level, and including multidisciplinary influences in nursing curriculum (Barrett et al., 2009).

Role of Other Mental Health Workers

Psychosocial workers have an important role in the delivery of mental health services as well. For example, in India, social workers have facilitated support groups for patients and caregivers as part of a multidisciplinary mental health team (Murthy et al., 2005). Chile has provided psychosocial education to patients and other relevant parties about mental illness, its treatment, relapse prevention, and monitoring (Araya et al., 2003). Psychologists have also applied effective psycho-social education interventions to reduce caregiver burden and improve their attitudes in Chile (Gutiérrez-Maldonado & Caqueo-Urízar, 2007; Gutiérrez-Maldonado, Caqueo-Urízar, & Ferrer-García, 2009). Hence, psychosocial education for caregivers of individuals with experience of mental illness (Kulhara, Chakrabarti, Avasthi, Sharma, & Sharma, 2009) can result in better mental health and well-being outcomes. A recent study in Bangladesh reported that among people with a drug addiction, psychological factors were associated with an increased likelihood of relapse (Rahman, Rahaman, Hamadani, Mustafa, & Shariful Islam, 2016). Therefore, the training of clinical psychologists to support people with a drug dependence or mental illness should be considered by policy makers.

Recommendations

Multifaceted approaches that address the paucity of human resources for mental health and staff supply in underserved areas will help ensure accessibility of health care facilities for poor people of Bangladesh. The barriers to progress in developing human resources for mental health can be overcome by the generation of strong political support to improve the number of appropriately trained health workers and actively engaging them in unconventional solutions for further strengthening the workforce. This will require highly skilled public health specialists in mental health leadership positions, and collaboration with stakeholders/donors to address the human resources crisis. This will pave the way for financial support for sustainable human resources for mental health, appropriate legislation and policies, and their alignment with national health policies. The changeability in roles of different mental health workers across LMIC settings stresses the significance of aiming for a skill-mix rather than a staff-mix approach in further enhancing human resources for mental health (Fulton et al., 2011).

A well suited national human resource for mental health strategy, as well as programs tailored to the local context and consistent with the WHO Health Systems Framework and Health Workforce 2030 will ensure the availability of trained staff and well equipped health facilities for mental health. Hence, surveillance and monitoring of human resources for mental health are crucial in better understanding and overcoming key challenges to developing human resources for mental health and in improving mental health services in Bangladesh. Professional certification and life-long learning for mental health workers will support better quality of care (Dey, Standing, & Islam, 2009).

FUTURE RESEARCH DIRECTIONS

There have been global efforts to develop a practical framework to support governments and health administrators to work on and implement a comprehensive plan to achieve sustainable health workforce development in response to widespread shortages (WHO, 2006). The Human Resources for Health Action Framework (Dal Poz et al., 2006) encompasses six interlinked elements necessary for human resource development (policy, health workforce management, finance, education, partnerships, and leadership), could provide an expedient approach to effectively addressing the challenge of scarcity in human resources for mental health.

Stronger collaborations and cross country comparisons presented in this chapter will also contribute to lessening the shortages in human resources for mental health in Bangladesh (Skeen et al., 2010). However, further research is needed to better understand the dynamics and complexity of the issues underlying the scarcity of human resources for mental health. Developing simple effective models of care for mental health human resources should be explored. The newer models could involve task shifting of specialist care to junior doctors and general practitioners in primary health care. It could involve nurses, psychologists, social workers, and community health workers diagnosing and referring cases to primary health care. Following evidence from other countries, there is a need to explore the models of mental health service integration into existing primary care and community services. Future research on policies and operational programs for rural retention of human resources are also recommended.

The authors did not identify any literature related to the role of community resources, for example, alternative mental health care providers. This issue requires further investigation as in many LMIC, especially in Bangladesh, alternative care is generally sought before that from a mental health specialist or practitioner. While task shifting has been suggested as a mechanism to address the human resources shortage, a sustainable model based on the local needs deserves to be tested and evaluated.

CONCLUSION

There is an urgent need to improve the mental health workforce in LMIC. Human resources are recognized as the most significant asset of mental health services. The WHO and governments have endorsed the need to strengthen human resources for mental health globally. In spite of this, human resources for mental health continue to be inadequate in most countries. The scarcity is likely to worsen unless significant investments are made to train a broader range of mental health workers in LMIC. Scaling up and training entails substantial investment, rigorous planning, and effective leadership. Training programs must be tailored to the needs of the local population and countries. Ensuring ongoing career development opportunities and task shifting will a play a crucial role in the development of human resources for mental health. The generation of reliable data on mental health systems and workforce will also aid future planning. Effective policies, planning, and investment for human resources development and retention are vital. The authors recommend a systemic multidisciplinary approach with strong partnerships among government ministries, NGOs, health practitioners, and communities to ensure improved mental health services in Bangladesh with appropriately skilled and an adequate number of human resources for mental health.

REFERENCES

Adams, A. M., Ahmed, T., El Arifeen, S., Evans, T. G., Huda, T., & Reichenbach, L. (2014). Innovation for universal health coverage in Bangladesh: A call to action. *Lancet*, *382*(9910), 2104–2111. doi:10.1016/S0140-6736(13)62150-9 PMID:24268605

Ahmed, S. M., Hossain, M. A., Chowdhury, A. M. R., & Bhuiya, A. U. (2011). The health workforce crisis in Bangladesh: Shortage, inappropriate skill-mix and inequitable distribution. *Human Resources for Health*, *9*(1), 3. doi:10.1186/1478-4491-9-3 PMID:21255446

Alem, A., Pain, C., Araya, M., & Hodges, B. D. (2010). Co-creating a psychiatric resident program with Ethiopians, for Ethiopians, in Ethiopia: The Toronto Addis Ababa Psychiatry Project (TAAPP). *Academic Psychiatry*, *34*(6), 424–432. doi:10.1176/appi.ap.34.6.424 PMID:21041465

Araya, R., Rojas, G., Fritsch, R., Gaete, J., Rojas, M., Simon, G., & Peters, T. J. (2003). Treating depression in primary care in low-income women in Santiago, Chile: A randomised controlled trial. *Lancet*, *361*(9362), 995–1000. doi:10.1016/S0140-6736(03)12825-5 PMID:12660056

Barkat, A., & Maksud, A. (2003). Private sector health services in Bangladesh: An exploratory study. Dhaka, Bangladesh: Human Development Research Centre (HDRC), EngenderHealth.

Barker, P. J., & Buchanan-Barker, P. (2011). Mental health nursing and the politics of recovery: A global reflection. *Archives of Psychiatric Nursing*, *25*(5), 350–358. doi:10.1016/j.apnu.2011.03.009 PMID:21978803

Barrett, T., Boeck, R., Fusco, C., Ghebrehiwet, T., Yan, J., & Saxena, S. (2009). Nurses are the key to improving mental health services in low-and middle-income countries. *International Nursing Review*, *56*(1), 138–141. doi:10.1111/j.1466-7657.2008.00687.x PMID:19239528

Becker, A. E., & Kleinman, A. (2013). Mental health and the global agenda. *The New England Journal of Medicine*, *369*(1), 66–73. doi:10.1056/NEJMra1110827 PMID:23822778

Beinecke, R., Minas, H., Goldsack, S., & Peters, J. (2010). Global mental health leadership training programmes. *International Journal of Leadership in Public Services*, *6*(0suppl), 63–72. doi:10.5042/ijlps.2010.0575

Biswas, T., Islam, A., Rawal, L., & Islam, S. (2016). Increasing prevalence of diabetes in Bangladesh: A scoping review. *Public Health*, *138*, 4–11. doi:10.1016/j.puhe.2016.03.025 PMID:27169347

Bobrow, K., Farmer, A. J., Springer, D., Shanyinde, M., Yu, L.-M., Brennan, T., & Tarassenko, L. et al. (2016). Mobile phone text messages to support treatment adherence in adults with high blood pressure (SMS-text adherence support [StAR]): A single-blind, randomized trial. *Circulation*, *133*(6), 592–600. PMID:26769742

Bruckner, T. A., Scheffler, R. M., Shen, G., Yoon, J., Chisholm, D., Morris, J., & Saxena, S. et al. (2011). The mental health workforce gap in low-and middle-income countries: A needs-based approach. *Bulletin of the World Health Organization*, *89*(3), 184–194. doi:10.2471/BLT.10.082784 PMID:21379414

Campbell, J., Dussault, G., Buchan, J., Pozo-Martin, F., Guerra Arias, M., Leone, C., & Cometto, G. (2013). *A universal truth: No health without a workforce*. Geneva, Switzerland: World Health Organization.

Chisholm, D. (2007). Mental health system financing in developing countries: Policy questions and research responses. *Epidemiology and Psychiatric Sciences*, *16*(04), 282–288. PMID:18333422

Chisholm, D., Lund, C., & Saxena, S. (2007). Cost of scaling up mental healthcare in low-and middle-income countries. *The British Journal of Psychiatry*, *191*(6), 528–535. doi:10.1192/bjp.bp.107.038463 PMID:18055957

Chow, C. K., Redfern, J., Hillis, G. S., Thakkar, J., Santo, K., Hackett, M. L., & Barry, T. et al. (2015). Effect of lifestyle-focused text messaging on risk factor modification in patients with coronary heart disease: A randomized clinical trial. *Journal of the American Medical Association*, *314*(12), 1255–1263. doi:10.1001/jama.2015.10945 PMID:26393848

Dal Poz, M. R., Quain, E. E., ONeil, M., McCaffery, J., Elzinga, G., & Martineau, T. (2006). Addressing the health workforce crisis: Towards a common approach. *Human Resources for Health*, *4*(1), 1–4. doi:10.1186/1478-4491-4-21 PMID:16887029

Demyttenaere, K., Bruffaerts, R., Posada-Villa, J., Gasquet, I., Kovess, V., Lepine, J., & Morosini, P. et al. (2004). Prevalence, severity, and unmet need for treatment of mental disorders in the World Health Organization World Mental Health Surveys. *Journal of the American Medical Association*, *291*(21), 2581–2590. doi:10.1001/jama.291.21.2581 PMID:15173149

Devane, M., & Leahy-Warren, P. (2015). Mental health nurses on prescribing in Ireland: Although in its infancy in Ireland, nurse prescribing has helped patients. Here, Michelle Devane and Patricia Leahy-Warren discuss conflicting views and practical concerns. *Mental Health Practice*, *19*(3), 14–22. doi:10.7748/mhp.19.3.14.s16

Dey, S., Standing, C., & Islam, S. (2009). A framework for offering professional certifications worldwide. *INTED2009 Proceedings*, 1227-1235.

Drake, R. E., Goldman, H. H., Leff, H. S., Lehman, A. F., Dixon, L., Mueser, K. T., & Torrey, W. C. (2001). Implementing evidence-based practices in routine mental health service settings. *Psychiatric Services (Washington, D.C.)*, *52*(2), 179–182. doi:10.1176/appi.ps.52.2.179 PMID:11157115

Fulton, B. D., Scheffler, R. M., Sparkes, S. P., Auh, E. Y., Vujicic, M., & Soucat, A. (2011). Health workforce skill mix and task shifting in low income countries: A review of recent evidence. *Human Resources for Health*, *9*(1), 1–11. doi:10.1186/1478-4491-9-1 PMID:21223546

Gausia, K., Fisher, C., Ali, M., & Oosthuizen, J. (2009). Antenatal depression and suicidal ideation among rural Bangladeshi women: A community-based study. *Archives of Womens Mental Health*, *12*(5), 351–358. doi:10.1007/s00737-009-0080-7 PMID:19468825

Global Health Workforce Alliance. (2011). *Outcome statement of the second global forum on human resources for health.* Geneva, Switzerland: WHO.

Gureje, O., Hollins, S., Botbol, M., Javed, A., Jorge, M., Okech, V., & Jenkins, R. et al. (2009). Report of the WPA task force on brain drain. *World Psychiatry; Official Journal of the World Psychiatric Association (WPA)*, *8*(2), 115–118. doi:10.1002/j.2051-5545.2009.tb00225.x PMID:19516936

Gutiérrez-Maldonado, J., & Caqueo-Urízar, A. (2007). Effectiveness of a psycho-educational intervention for reducing burden in Latin American families of patients with schizophrenia. *Quality of Life Research: An International Journal of Quality of Life Aspects of Treatment, Care and Rehabilitation*, *16*(5), 739–747. doi:10.1007/s11136-007-9173-9 PMID:17286192

Gutiérrez-Maldonado, J., Caqueo-Urízar, A., & Ferrer-García, M. (2009). Effects of a psychoeducational intervention program on the attitudes and health perceptions of relatives of patients with schizophrenia. *Social Psychiatry and Psychiatric Epidemiology*, *44*(5), 343–348. doi:10.1007/s00127-008-0451-9 PMID:18982233

Hauff, E. (1996). The Cambodian mental health training programme. *Australasian Psychiatry*, *4*(4), 187–188. doi:10.3109/10398569609080486

Hosman, C., Jané-Llopis, E., & Saxena, S. (2004). *Prevention of mental disorders: Effective interventions and policy options: Summary report.* Geneva, Switzerland: WHO.

Islam, A., & Biswas, T. (2014). Health system in Bangladesh: Challenges and opportunities. *American Journal of Health Research*, *2*(6), 366–374. doi:10.11648/j.ajhr.20140206.18

Islam, A., & Biswas, T. (2015). Mental health and the health system in Bangladesh: Situation analysis of a neglected domain. *Journal of Psychiatry & Neuroscience*, *3*(4), 57–62. doi:10.11648/j.ajpn.20150304.11

Islam, M. A., Rahman, A., Aleem, M. A., & Islam, S. M. S. (2016). Prevalence and associated factors of depression among posts-stroke patients in Bangladesh. *International Journal of Mental Health and Addiction, 14*(2), 154–166. doi:10.1007/s11469-015-9582-x

Islam, S. (2010). *Demographic situation of population ageing in Bangladesh.* Paper presented at the Asian Population Association. Geneva: World Health Organization.

Islam, S., & Moreau, A. (2009). Traditional healers in preventing HIV/AIDS: Roles and scopes. UNDP program on HIV/AIDS prevention in Bangladesh. *Bulletin of Medicus Mundi Switzerland, 2009*(113), 39-43.

Islam, S. M. S., Ferrari, U., Seissler, J., Niessen, L., & Lechner, A. (2015). Association between depression and diabetes amongst adults in Bangladesh: A hospital based case–control study. *Journal of Global Health, 5*(2), 020406. doi:10.7189/jogh.05.020406 PMID:26649173

Islam, S. M. S., Mainuddin, A., Islam, M. S., Karim, M. A., Mou, S. Z., Arefin, S., & Chowdhury, K. N. (2015). Prevalence of risk factors for hypertension: A cross-sectional study in an urban area of Bangladesh. *Global Cardiology Science & Practice, 2015*(4), 43. doi: 10.5339/gcsp.2015.43

Islam, S. M. S., & Niessen, L. W. (2014). Population based cancer registry in the developing countries: A first step towards cancer control programs and research. *Journal of Cancer Therapeutics and Research, 11*(4), 1044. doi:10.4103/0973-1482.140989 PMID:26881677

Islam, S. M. S., Niessen, L. W., Ferrari, U., Ali, L., Seissler, J., & Lechner, A. (2015). Effects of mobile phone SMS to improve glycemic control among patients with type 2 diabetes in Bangladesh: A Prospective, Parallel-Group,Randomized Controlled Trial. *Diabetes Care, 38*(8), 112–113. doi:10.2337/dc15-0505

Islam, S. M. S., Purnat, T. D., Phuong, N. T. A., Mwingira, U., Schacht, K., & Fröschl, G. (2014). Non-communicable diseases (NCDs) in developing countries: A symposium report. *Globalization and Health, 10*(1), 1–8. doi:10.1186/s12992-014-0081-9 PMID:25498459

Islam, S. M. S., Rawal, L. B., & Niessen, L. W. (2015). Prevalence of depression and its associated factors in patients with type 2 diabetes: A cross-sectional study in Dhaka, Bangladesh. *Asian Journal of Psychiatry, 17*, 36–41. doi:10.1016/j.ajp.2015.07.008 PMID:26259893

Islam, S. M. S., & Tabassum, R. (2015). Implementation of information and communication technologies for health in Bangladesh. *Bulletin of the World Health Organization, 93*(11), 806–809. https://dx.doi.org/10.2471/BLT.15.153684 doi:10.2471/BLT.15.153684 PMID:26549909

Jacob, K., Sharan, P., Mirza, I., Garrido-Cumbrera, M., Seedat, S., Mari, J. J., & Saxena, S. et al. (2007). Mental health systems in countries: Where are we now? *Lancet, 370*(9592), 1061–1077. doi:10.1016/S0140-6736(07)61241-0 PMID:17804052

Jenkins, R., Kydd, R., Mullen, P., Thomson, K., Sculley, J., Kuper, S., & Brownie, S. et al. (2010). International migration of doctors, and its impact on availability of psychiatrists in low and middle income countries. *PLoS ONE, 5*(2), e9049. doi:10.1371/journal.pone.0009049 PMID:20140216

Joint Learning Initiative. (2004). *Human resources for health: Overcoming the crisis.* Retrieved from http://www.who.int/hrh/documents/JLi_hrh_report.pdf

Kakuma, R., Minas, H., van Ginneken, N., Dal Poz, M. R., Desiraju, K., Morris, J. E., & Scheffler, R. M. et al. (2011). Human resources for mental health care: Current situation and strategies for action. *Lancet*, *378*(9803), 1654–1663. doi:10.1016/S0140-6736(11)61093-3 PMID:22008420

Karim, M. A., Majumder, A. A. S., Islam, K. Q., Alam, M. B., Paul, M. L., Islam, M. S., & Islam, S. M. S. et al. (2015). Risk factors and in-hospital outcome of acute ST segment elevation myocardial infarction in young Bangladeshi adults. *BMC Cardiovascular Disorders*, *15*(73). PMID:26197888

Kessler, R. C., Aguilar-Gaxiola, S., Alonso, J., Chatterji, S., Lee, S., Ormel, J., & Wang, P. S. et al. (2009). The global burden of mental disorders: An update from the WHO World Mental Health (WMH) surveys. *Epidemiologia e Psichiatria Sociale*, *18*(01), 23–33. doi:10.1017/S1121189X00001421 PMID:19378696

Kessler, R. C., Matthias, A., Anthony, J. C., De Graaf, R., Demyttenaere, K., Gasquet, I., & Haro, J. (2007). *Lifetime prevalence and age-of-onset distributions of mental disorders in the World Health Organization's World Mental Health Survey Initiative*. Geneva, Switzerland: World Health Organization.

Kohn, R., Saxena, S., Levav, I., & Saraceno, B. (2004). The treatment gap in mental health care. *Bulletin of the World Health Organization*, *82*(11), 858–866. PMID:15640922

Kulhara, P., Chakrabarti, S., Avasthi, A., Sharma, A., & Sharma, S. (2009). Psychoeducational intervention for caregivers of Indian patients with schizophrenia: A randomised-controlled trial. *Acta Psychiatrica Scandinavica*, *119*(6), 472–483. doi:10.1111/j.1600-0447.2008.01304.x PMID:19032700

Murthy, R. S., Kumar, K. K., Chisholm, D., Thomas, T., Sekar, K., & Chandrashekar, C. (2005). Community outreach for untreated schizophrenia in rural India: A follow-up study of symptoms, disability, family burden and costs. *Psychological Medicine*, *35*(03), 341–351. doi:10.1017/S0033291704003551 PMID:15841870

Okpaku, S. O. (2014). *Essentials of global mental health*. Cambridge: University Press. doi:10.1017/CBO9781139136341

Prince, M., Patel, V., Saxena, S., Maj, M., Maselko, J., Phillips, M. R., & Rahman, A. (2007). No health without mental health. *Lancet*, *370*(9590), 859–877. doi:10.1016/S0140-6736(07)61238-0 PMID:17804063

Rahman, M. M., Rahaman, M. M., Hamadani, J. D., Mustafa, K., & Islam, S. M. S. (2016). Psycho-social factors associated with relapse to drug addiction in Bangladesh. *Journal of Substance Use*, *21*(6), 1–4. doi:10.3109/14659891.2015.1122099

Rawal, L., Mahmud, K., Islam, S., Mahumud, R., Nuruzaman, M., & Ahmed, S. (2016). Training mid-level health cadres to improve health service delivery in rural Bangladesh. *Primary Health Care Research and Development*, *17*(5), 503–513. doi:10.1017/S1463423616000104 PMID:27029790

Rawal, L. B., Joarder, T., Islam, S. M. S., Uddin, A., & Ahmed, S. M. (2015). Developing effective policy strategies to retain health workers in rural Bangladesh: A policy analysis. *Human Resources for Health*, *13*(1), 1–10. doi:10.1186/s12960-015-0030-6 PMID:25990240

Ross, J. D., Clarke, A., & Kettles, A. (2014). Mental health nurse prescribing: Using a constructivist approach to investigate the nurse–patient relationship. *Journal of Psychiatric and Mental Health Nursing, 21*(1), 1–10. doi:10.1111/jpm.12039 PMID:23413877

Sal-sabil, T., Islam, A., & Islam, S. M. S. (2016). Risk factors for type 2 diabetes in Bangladesh: A systematic review. *Journal of Diabetology, 2*(4), 1–12.

Saldivia, S., Vicente, B., Kohn, R., Rioseco, P., & Torres, S. (2004). Use of mental health services in Chile. *Psychiatric Services (Washington, D.C.), 55*(1), 71–76. doi:10.1176/appi.ps.55.1.71 PMID:14699204

Savin, D. (2000). Developing psychiatric training and services in Cambodia. *Psychiatric Services (Washington, D.C.), 51*(7), 935–935. doi:10.1176/appi.ps.51.7.935 PMID:10875964

Saxena, S., Sharan, P., & Saraceno, B. (2003). Budget and financing of mental health services: Baseline information on 89 countries from WHO's Project Atlas. *The Journal of Mental Health Policy and Economics, 6*(3), 135–143. PMID:14646006

Saxena, S., Thornicroft, G., Knapp, M., & Whiteford, H. (2007). Resources for mental health: Scarcity, inequity, and inefficiency. *Lancet, 370*(9590), 878–889. doi:10.1016/S0140-6736(07)61239-2 PMID:17804062

Schiffbauer, J., OBrien, J. B., Timmons, B. K., & Kiarie, W. N. (2008). The role of leadership in HRH development in challenging public health settings. *Human Resources for Health, 6*(1), 1–7. doi:10.1186/1478-4491-6-23 PMID:18983671

Sherk, K. E., Nauseda, F., Johnson, S., & Liston, D. (2009). An experience of virtual leadership development for human resource managers. *Human Resources for Health, 7*(1), 1–3. doi:10.1186/1478-4491-7-1 PMID:19133140

Singh, B., & Ng, C. H. (2008). Psychiatric education and training in Asia. *International Review of Psychiatry (Abingdon, England), 20*(5), 413–418. doi:10.1080/09540260802397362 PMID:19012125

Skeen, S., Kleintjes, S., Lund, C., Petersen, I., Bhana, A., & Flisher, A. J.The Mental Health and Poverty Research Programme Consortium. (2010). Mental health is everybodys business: Roles for an intersectoral approach in South Africa. *International Review of Psychiatry (Abingdon, England), 22*(6), 611–623. doi:10.3109/09540261.2010.535510 PMID:21226649

Wang, P. S., Angermeyer, M., Borges, G., Bruffaerts, R., Chiu, W. T., De Girolamo, G., & Huang, Y. (2007). *Delay and failure in treatment seeking after first onset of mental disorders in the World Health Organization's World Mental Health Survey Initiative*. Geneva, Switzerland: World Health Organization.

Whiteford, H. A., Degenhardt, L., Rehm, J., Baxter, A. J., Ferrari, A. J., Erskine, H. E., & Vos, T. et al. (2013). Global burden of disease attributable to mental and substance use disorders: Findings from the Global Burden of Disease Study 2010. *Lancet, 382*(9904), 1575–1586. doi:10.1016/S0140-6736(13)61611-6 PMID:23993280

Whiteford, H. A., Ferrari, A. J., Degenhardt, L., Feigin, V., & Vos, T. (2015). The global burden of mental, neurological and substance use disorders: An analysis from the global burden of disease study 2010. *PLoS ONE, 10*(2), e0116820. doi:10.1371/journal.pone.0116820 PMID:25658103

World Health Organization. (1948). *Constitution of the World Health Organization.* Retrieved from http://www.who.int/about/mission/en/

World Health Organization. (2004). *International statistical classification of diseases and related health problems* (Vol. 1). Geneva, Switzerland: World Health Organization.

World Health Organization. (2006). *The world health report: 2006: Working together for health.* Geneva, Switzerland: WHO.

World Health Organization. (2011). mental health atlas 2011. Geneva, Switzerland: WHO.

World Health Organization. (2014). *Global status report on alcohol and health.* Geneva, Switzerland: World Health Organization.

World Health Organization. (2015). *mental health atlas 2014.* Geneva, Switzerland: WHO.

World Health Organization & International Council of Nurses. (2007). *Atlas: Nurses in mental health 2007.* Geneva, Switzerland: World Health Organization.

World Psychiatric Association & World Health Organization. (2005). *Atlas: Psychiatric education and training across the world: 2005.* Geneva, Switzerland: World Health Organization.

KEY TERMS AND DEFINITIONS

Capacity Building: Activities aimed to increase the ability of individuals, institutions, and societies to perform optimally to achieve its objectives in a sustainable manner.

Human Resources: All people who make up the workforce of an organization.

Low and Middle Income Countries (LMIC): Countries with per capita gross national income from $1,045 or less to $12,736 are defined by the World Bank as LMIC.

Mental Illness: A health problem that significantly affects how a person thinks, behaves and interacts with other people and is diagnosed according to standardized criteria.

Primary Health Care: The first level of contact individuals, families and communities have with the health care system.

Task Shifting: A process of delegation whereby tasks are moved, where appropriate, to less specialized health workers.

Chapter 8
Developing a Culturally Competent Workforce that Meets the Needs of Pacific People Living in New Zealand

Fuimaono Karl Pulotu-Endemann
Independent Consultant, New Zealand

Monique Faleafa
Le Va, New Zealand

ABSTRACT

This chapter provides an overview of innovative Pacific workforce development initiatives. Pacific people have higher rates of mental illness, substance abuse, and suicide attempts, as well as lower rates of service access compared to New Zealand's general population. Pacific families also tend to have high and complex mental health needs, traditional cultural worldviews that are different from the dominant western mental health paradigms, and a workforce with severe under-representation of Pacific people. National non-government organization (NGO) Le Va, was established to reduce ethnic disparities in the access to, and quality of mental health and addictions services, through a targeted workforce development strategy to achieve better outcomes for Pacific people. This chapter specifically describes three of Le Va's programmes designed to increase Pacific workforce capacity and capability, and cultural competency of the "mainstream" workforce. These include cultural competency training, effective upskilling and growth through scholarships and support, and leadership development.

INTRODUCTION

This chapter marks the first documented overview of New Zealand's first and only national Pacific mental health and addiction workforce development programme. The objective is to describe how the not-for-profit organisation, Le Va, is addressing the challenges of over-representation of Pacific people with mental illness and addiction issues through workforce development solutions. In order to do this,

DOI: 10.4018/978-1-5225-1874-7.ch008

context is required to give perspective of the historical issues, current social, economic and health profile, and potentially contrasting cultural worldviews of health and well-being.

I am not an individual,
I am an integral part of the cosmos.
I share divinity with my ancestors, the land, the seas and the skies.
I am not an individual because
I share a tofi with my family, my village, my nation.
I belong to my family and my family belongs to me.
I belong to my village and my village belongs to me.
I belong to my nation and my nation belongs to me.
This is the essence of my sense of belonging.
Tui Atua Tupua Tamasese, (2002)

BACKGROUND

Pasifika People in New Zealand

As tāngata whenua (people of the land), Māori are the first settlers, and indigenous to Aotearoa, New Zealand. As Polynesian cousins, the distinct considerations afforded to Māori are firmly embedded and recognized in Pacific health processes. Under Article 3 of the Treaty of Waitangi, Māori are guaranteed and entitled to equitable health-related access and outcomes when seeking health care services (Durie, 1998).

Pacific populations hold special relations in New Zealand not only through shared Polynesian whakapapa (ancestry) to Māori, but through strong government relationships and moral obligations between New Zealand and its neighboring countries in the South Pacific. This unique relationship has been influenced by many factors such as: the historical relationships between New Zealand and Pacific nations; the geographic relationships and proximity between New Zealand and the Pacific homelands; the constitutional links that continue to exist between New Zealand and a number of Pacific nations; and New Zealand's identity in the 21st century as a Pacific nation. These intersecting factors mean that the place of Pacific people, both individually and collectively, in New Zealand society, is unique, and that New Zealand has particular moral responsibilities vis a vis its Pacific people (Ministry of Justice and Ministry of Pacific Island Affairs, 2000). With a vibrant history of residing in New Zealand for over 150 years, Pasifika people now contribute to its international identity and economy in a significant way.

Health status is influenced by socio demographic factors for Pacific people in New Zealand. So it is important to highlight the history that has led to the over-representation of Pacific people in negative social indicators and determinants of health. The New Zealand government actively sought labor workforce recruitment from the South Pacific nations with chronic labour shortages due to the industrial boom periods between the 1940s and 70s. However, a downturn in the economy in the mid-1970s resulted in high unemployment amongst the waves of Pacific communities that had migrated. With jobs scarce, and Pacific people "taking New Zealander's jobs", Pacific people's presence in New Zealand was racialized in a way that led to "overstayer" campaigns (illegal immigrants who have overstayed their temporary or work visas) and the infamous "dawn raids" (when special police squads raided Pacific Islander's houses at dawn – the raids received widespread criticism from human rights organizations for being racially motivated).

Migrating to "the land of milk and honey" did not turn out to be all that it appeared for most Pacific people. Increasing statistical evidence supports the view that, overall, Pacific peoples are disadvantaged compared with other populations in New Zealand across a range of socio-economic factors, with marked differences in the health status of Pacific New Zealanders and Palagi New Zealanders well documented, showing decades of disparity and continuing negative trends (Wright & Hornblow, 2008).

Despite structural oppression, Pacific people have continued to provide a constant and reliable workforce and contributed to New Zealand's economic growth, politics, success in sporting arenas, achievements in creative arts, and more recently in health, education, and business.

New Zealand's Pacific population is now just under 300,000 people (7.4% of the overall population) and is highly diverse made up of many different ethnic groups. The Samoan community is the largest ethnic group (48.7%), followed by Cook Islands (20.6%), Tongan (20.4%), Niuean (8.1%), Fijian (4.9%), Tokelauan (2.4%), and Tuvaluan (1.2%) (Statistics New Zealand, 2014). These nations have their own specific languages, beliefs, customs, values, traditions, and lifestyles. Youthfulness is a defining characteristic of the New Zealand Pacific population with 54% of Pacific people under the age of 25, and a median age of 21 years compared to 36 years for the total New Zealand population. Almost two-thirds of Pacific people are now born in New Zealand and are highly urbanized, with 97 per cent living in urban areas – mostly in Auckland (approximately 66%) (Statistics New Zealand, 2014).

There are intra-Pacific diversities – within these nations, there are varying levels of acculturation into the dominant Western culture (particularly for children and young people). It is therefore important to acknowledge there is no generic "Pacific community", but rather Pacific people who align themselves variously depending on social and cultural circumstances. Overall however, there are underlying shared pan-Pacific socio-cultural universalities that allow a discussion of cultural competency and workforce development for Pacific populations in New Zealand.

Pasifika Health Profile

Pacific people have some of the worst health and social indicators in New Zealand and there is considerable unmet health needs in these communities (Tukuitonga, 2013). Pacific people have lower life expectancy and higher rates of mortality and hospitalizations for conditions that could have been avoided given timely access to effective healthcare (Ministry of Health, 2012). The leading contributors of poor health amongst Pacific peoples in New Zealand are cardiovascular disease, diabetes, injuries, respiratory diseases, cancers, and infectious diseases. Cardiovascular disease and diabetes are the major cause of amenable mortality for Pacific adults under the age of 75 years (Wright & Hornblow, 2008). Pacific children (age 0-14) have high rates of hospitalization for acute and chronic respiratory and infectious diseases and are 1.5 times more likely to be hospitalized due to asthma than children in the total population. The hospitalization rate for lower respiratory infection for Pacific children is twice the rate for children in the total population. Rates of meningococcal disease and rheumatic fever are also significantly higher. For Pacific young people (15-24 years), mental illness, alcohol abuse, and suicide are emerging concerns.

Poor health outcomes and ethnic disparities reflect the socioeconomic conditions under which Pacific people live and work. For Pacific people, poverty is a major contributor to poor health. The social determinants that impact on health status for Pacific families are low educational achievement and health literacy; high unemployment rates; crowded, cold and damp houses; and inequities in access to and quality of health care provided (Tukuitonga, 2013).

As a response to the unmet health needs of Pacific people, in recent times there has been investment in the development of "by Pacific for Pacific" health providers in New Zealand. There are examples showing that Pacific health providers have been successful in improving Pacific peoples' access to primary health care by delivering health services that are culturally responsive to Pacific families and communities (Tukuitonga & Finau, 1997). The challenge for Pacific providers is addressing issues effectively for Pacific young people. There is also an increasing number of young Pacific people identifying with more than one ethnicity, which bring client-centered and youth-centered approaches to service delivery to the fore. Pacific people access non-Pacific services the most, hence the challenge for non-Pacific health services is to be more responsive to the needs of Pacific peoples' in terms of providing culturally competent approaches to services delivery.

Pasifika Mental Health and Addiction Profile

New Zealand's national mental health survey – *Te Rau Hinengaro* (Oakley-Browne, Wells & Scott, 2006), identified that Pacific people have higher 12 month prevalence rates of mental disorder (25.0%) compared with the general New Zealand population (20.7%). Of the 25%, New Zealand-born (and younger) people were more than twice as likely to have had mental health issues than those who migrated to New Zealand after the age of 18 years. The most commonly reported lifetime disorders were anxiety (16.2%), mood (8.6%), and substance use disorders (5.3%). These findings were also reflected in *Te Rau Hinengaro*, where Pacific adults had the highest rates of anxiety or depressive disorder (12.9%) compared with Māori (10.8%), Asian (7.7%), and European/Other (6.1%) ethnic groups (Mental Health Commission, 2012). Perhaps most concerning was that Pacific people reported suicide attempts three times higher than the rate in the general population. The New Zealand born Pacific people had higher rates of suicide planning and attempts than their older Pacific migrants.

Pacific people feature disproportionately in addiction issues. Pacific have higher rates of substance use (5.3% for Pacific compared to 3.5% for the total population), also gambling-related harm. Data from the 2006/07 *New Zealand Health Survey* show that Pacific adults are approximately four times more likely to be problem gamblers compared to the total population (Ministry of Health, 2008).

Addiction related behavior appears to have reduced for young Pacific people over time. The *Youth 2012 Survey* is New Zealand's only nationally representative dataset for our Pacific youth population. Results indicate that most Pacific secondary students do not use alcohol or other drugs on a regular basis, and there have been significant drops in cigarette, alcohol, and marijuana use (Clark et al., 2013). Weekly cigarette use in 2012 has dropped to less than one-third since 2001, from 21.7%, to 6.8%. Weekly alcohol use similarly dropped nearly one-third from 14.3% in 2001 to 5.9% in 2012, and is below the 2012 New Zealand European rate of 9.5%. Binge drinking refers to five or more alcoholic drinks in one session (within 4 hours). For Pacific youth this has nearly halved, from 33.5% in 2001 to 18.4% in 2012, also below the 2012 New Zealand European rate of 24.9%. Marijuana use has dropped to one-third of 2001 rates, 8.8% to 2.8% in 2012 (Clark et al., 2013).

Suicide remains a significant concern and continues to be the leading cause of death among Pasifika young people aged 15-24 years. Pacific students have been more likely to have attempted suicide than

New Zealand European students in three national surveys (2000, 2007, and 2012) of high school students (Adolescent Health Research Group, in press). In the 2012 survey, Pasifika high school students were approximately three times more likely to attempt suicide at 8.6% compared to New Zealand European at 2.7% (Adolescent Health Research Group, in press).

THE CHALLENGE

The challenge is to address high rates of mental illness, substance abuse, and suicidal behavior, particularly for Pacific youth. This is exacerbated by contrasting cultural worldviews, low rates of access with high and complex needs, and a workforce that appears ill-equipped to deal with the situation.

Contrasting Cultural Worldviews

Cultural views, language, and history significantly influence the way in which Pacific peoples perceive, access, and use health services in New Zealand.

In order to understand the beliefs, ideas, and values that influence and inform the behavior and mental well-being, we need to understand the Pacific indigenous knowledge system these derive from. Traditionally Pacific cultures are inherently collective and relational with a holistic perspective of well-being where cognitive, emotional, spiritual, physical, environmental, and relational dimensions of the self are required to be in harmony for holistic well-being. The conceptualization of balanced relationships underpins many models of Pasifika well-being (Kingi-'Ulu'ave, Faleafa, Brown, & Daniela-Wong, in press).

Vā is a concept shared among many Pacific cultures which refers to a "space that relates" between people. *Teu le vā* is often translated as "making beautiful the vā": balance, symmetry, beauty, which are values strongly linked to well-being (Mila-Schaaf & Hudson, 2009). In terms of mental well-being, the idea that breeching *tapu* relationships may be a causal factor in sickness is common throughout the Pacific. The breaching of the *tapu* results in an unbalanced relationship which adds stress and may result in a person becoming unwell physically, spiritually, or mentally (Tamasese, Peteru, Waldegrave, & Bush, 2005). The cause of mental illness in a Pacific context may be also viewed as spiritual, such as a punishment from God, or inherited, such as a curse due to a family wrong. The treatment for this may thus be sought from spiritual healers of traditional methods of healing. The presence of "mental illness" may be shaming for Pacific families due to the spiritual or inherited explanations. It is important to acknowledge traditional Pacific beliefs and to be cognizant of the stigma surrounding mental illness, particularly among the older Pacific population (Kingi, Faleafa, & Brown, 2007).

Several Pacific approaches, models, and metaphoric frameworks have been developed that capture this holistic view of health and well-being. These frameworks include (but are not limited to): *Kakala* model (Thaman, 2004); *Tivaevae* model (Maua-Hodges, 2000), *Talanoa* framework (Vaioleti, 2006); *Fonua* model (Tu'itahi, 2007), and the *Popao* model (Tafa & Fotu, 2009). The *Nga Vaka o Kāiga Tapu: A Pacific Conceptual Framework to Address Family Violence in New Zealand* (Ministry of Social Development, 2012) includes seven ethnic specific conceptual frameworks and describes key cultural concepts and principles that promote family well-being, and the impact of violence on families.

Specific to mental health, Agnew et al. (2004) has identified six core values that are common to Pasifika groups and underpin relationships in a Pasifika context. The core values include *tapu* (sacred bonds), *alofa* (love and compassion), *fa'aaloalo* (respect and deference), *fa'amaualalo* (humility), *tautua* (reciprocal service), and *aiga* (family) (Agnew et al., 2004). The family is a key component of Pacific cultures and plays an important role in Pacific people's lives. The support of one's family and community are perhaps the areas most critical for an individual's recovery (Malo, 2000).

The first metaphoric framework specific to Pacific mental health and well-being that has been embraced by the Pacific mental health and addiction sector in New Zealand is the *Fonofale* model (Pulotu-Endemann, 1995). A Samoan *fale* or house is used as a metaphor, with the family as its foundation and the roof representing the cultural values and beliefs that shelter the family. The floor represents the genealogy that ties the family together. It also binds them to the land, the sea, the Gods of the Pacific, as well as to other cultures. The four *pou* or posts that hold up the roof connect culture and family. They are continuous and interactive with each other. They represent 1) spiritual well-being, 2) physical well-being, 3) the health of the mind, and 4) other elements that can affect health including gender, sexuality, age, and economic status.

The Fonofale approach is consistent with the recovery approach, which is supported by the Mental Health Commission (Malo, 2000). It embodies the cultural beliefs and value systems of Pacific people. It also provides important insights into how Pacific people view mental health. These perceptions influence their decision making and behavior surrounding the use of mental health services.

The mental health system in New Zealand for the most part, is informed by a paradigm dominated by secular, scientific, and empirical understandings of human behavior. Even the bio-psycho-social approach by mental health clinicians fails to take into account spirituality and cosmological beliefs connected to ancestry and *tapu* as "evidenced based", validated factors that require addressing for Pacific mental well-being (Mila-Schaaf & Hudson, 2009). This contrast in belief systems is likely to contribute to Pacific people's discomfort with using psychiatric services, and has been reported as a contributing factor to many being committed to psychiatric hospitals as involuntary consumers (Bathgate & Pulotu-Endemann, 1997).

Indigenous Māori challenges to the dominant medical paradigm in mental health came to the fore in the late 1980s with the *whakaruruhau* (cultural safety) movement amongst nurses, led by the late Dr Irihapeti Ramsden. The movement gave critical analyses to the impact of power structures, monoculturalism, the hegemony of *pakeha* worldview, the Treaty of Waitangi, poor health status, and racism for Māori. This was fueled by international black, feminist, and gay movements at the time. The *whakaruruhau* movement gave voice to issues for Pacific people too.

Over a decade later, with disparities worsening for Pacific populations, the New Zealand government began to invest in reducing inequalities for Pacific people with mental illness – recognizing the incongruent knowledge systems with an inequitable history of dominance and conflict, as well as the socio-cultural role in recovery and well-being for Pacific people.

Addressing the mental health and addiction needs of Pacific people requires acknowledgement that "one size does not fit all", and a commitment to flexibility and diversity. The balance between central control and diversity in service delivery is an ongoing challenge in the New Zealand health system (Wright & Hornblow, 2008).

Low Access, High Needs for Pacific

The Pacific population has a high prevalence of mental illness and substance abuse in New Zealand, yet are significantly less likely to access and utilize mental health services (25%) compared to the total New

Zealand population (58%) (Oakley-Browne, Wells, & Scott, 2006). Barriers to the utilization of health care for Pacific people have been well documented and include a lack of awareness of or discomfort with primary care services; cost, transport, language and communication difficulties; cultural norms, stigma and health beliefs; and a preference for traditional medicines and healers (Southwick, Kenealy, & Ryan, 2012).

When Pacific people do access mental health and addiction services, it is often at the severe end of the continuum, and in crisis. High rates of schizophrenia, paranoia and acute psychotic disorders among Pacific peoples are of particular concern. They account for two-thirds (66%) of Pacific inpatient episodes compared to 39% of New Zealand European episodes, and less than half (48%) of the overall population (Mila-Schaaf & Hudson, 2009; Pulotu-Endemann, Annandale, & Instone, 2004).

Furthermore, Pacific peoples' utilization of forensic psychiatric services is described by the Ministry of Health as "significantly elevated" (164%) compared to the general population. The Ministry of Health have identified that Pacific peoples are more likely to use acute inpatient units (198 versus 170, per 100,000) and stay longer compared to the total New Zealand population (Pulotu-Endemann et al., 2004).

At the severe end of the continuum, Pacific peoples have the highest average cost of adult inpatient and community episodes. The average (cost) weighting for Pacific peoples is 25% above the national average for inpatient episodes and 44% above the national average for community episodes (Pulotu-Endemann et al., 2004).

Inadequately Equipped Workforce

A key enabler for reducing health inequities around the world is developing the underrepresented ethnic minority health workforce. In New Zealand a culturally responsive workforce is also a key enabler to increasing access rates and better health outcomes across the board for Pasifika people and their families (Ministry of Health, 2014). A culturally responsive workforce means ensuring Pacific people are represented effectively in the workforce to reflect the population it serves, as well as upskilling in specialist skills to meet the needs of Pacific populations.

Pacific workers represent 5.0% (321 people) of the total adult mental health and addiction estimated workforce of 9,509 (Te Pou o te Whakaaro Nui, 2015).

Whilst there is no precise data available on the profile of the unregulated workforce, anecdotal evidence suggests that the majority of the Pacific health workforce consists of *unregulated* or *community* health workers. Research indicates that the ethnic minority community workforce makes a significant contribution to improving health outcomes for ethnic minorities. The benefits have included increased behavior change, improved health outcomes, and cost effectiveness. Pacific unregulated health workers who are culturally competent (either through their cultural heritage and/or training and support) are a substantial resource and a pool of talent that represent one of the most significant opportunities for enhancing the capacity and capability of the public health workforce. Key issues that the unregulated workforce face include a lack of appropriate supervision, education and training, formal processes, exploitation and misuse, and the effect all of these have on quality of care (Ministry of Health & Le Va, 2012).

The *Pacific Health Service Workforce Forecast* examined the composition and skills needed for the Pacific health workforce by 2020 identifying that:

The rapidly rising demand for services combined with constraints on funding and the availability of professional skills has led to the need for innovative thinking about how high quality health services can be delivered for Pacific communities… this will require a culturally competent workforce that understands how health services and health systems need to respond to the needs of culturally and socio-economically diverse populations is required to be developed. A key feature of a culturally competent workforce will be people of Pacific ethnicity – the Pacific health workforce. (Pacific Perspectives, 2013, p. 23)

The forecast noted that the most significant change facing the New Zealand market over the next 25 years is that many more workers will retire than will be recruited. Moreover, current projections suggest that Pacific people will make up a greater proportion of the workforce, and there will be increasing mobility of professionals in the global labor market. At present, of the 165,615 people working in healthcare in New Zealand, it is estimated that 2,090 (or 2.3%) are Pacific people in regulated positions (77.8% nurses, 8.6% doctors, and 13.5% other) (Ministry of Health & Le Va, 2012). To increase the number of Pacific health workers to ratios (per 1,000 people) that are consistent with the general population would require an additional 1,064 Pacific doctors, 3,657 Pacific nurses, and 1,412 other health professionals by 2020.

OUR RESPONSE TO THE CHALLENGE: LE VA

To improve mental health and addiction outcomes for Pacific people, and lift the performance of services to all in general, the New Zealand government recognizes the development of a workforce that can effectively engage with Pacific communities is required. Following a large feasibility study in 2005 (Te Pou o te Whakaaro Nui, 2007), the Ministry of Health produced robust evidence and a business case to invest targeted funding in Pacific-led mental health and addiction workforce development for Pacific people. This also included clinical and cultural competencies of the workforce that involved wide consultation with the Pacific mental health and addiction workforce and endorsement by Pacific mental health leadership. Growing the Pacific workforce, and enhancing the responsiveness and cultural competency of services in general, can also contribute to more timely access for Pacific people and communities. This scale of change takes time, and the investment was considered a long term strategy for meaningful and effective change that is measureable.

Le Va was the catalyst established in 2008 to bring about that change. Le Va is a national NGO charged with leading mental health and addiction workforce development in New Zealand, seeking to address disparities in outcomes for Pacific populations. The World Health Organisation's (WHO) approach to workforce development aims to have "the right number of people, with the right skills, in the right place, at the right time, with the right attitude, doing the right work, at the right cost, with the right work output" (World Health Organization, 2010, p. 1). Le Va aims to achieve this for Pacific communities by increasing the capacity and capability of the Pacific workforce, ensuring they are fit for purpose, and contribute to enhancing the cultural competency of the "mainstream" workforce as a whole.

Enhancing Cultural Responsiveness of the Workforce

Internationally, the field of cultural competence has emerged as part of a strategy to reduce disparities in access to, and quality of, health care. Clear links have been made between cultural competency programmes and reducing ethnic disparities. Promoting cultural competence among health care workers has been shown to help address barriers such as little or no access to quality health care, mistrust of the medical community, and/or cultural stereotyping of consumers. A plethora of international literature evidences cultural competency processes and the positive impact that clinical, organizational, and systemic cultural competence can have on outcomes for ethnic minorities (Betancourt, Green & Carrillo, 2002; Faleafa, Lua, & Tiatia, 2012).

There are significant legislative levers in New Zealand that enforce the need for a culturally competent health workforce. The *Health Practitioner Competency and Assurance Act 2004* requires that professional registration bodies set standards of cultural competency for professionals to adhere to. New Zealand's *Code of Health and Disability Services Consumers' Rights* also sets requirements related to cultural competence, such as taking into account a consumer's cultural needs, values and beliefs; that a consumer should be free from racial discrimination; and that information should be given in a form, language, and manner in which consumers can understand. *National Mental Health Sector Standards* require that services deliver culturally safe services for Pacific people and provide for the use of culturally acceptable treatment options – including cultural assessment, therapies, and audit. In mainstream services, there is now a growing acceptance of the importance of providing clinical services which meet defined standards of cultural safety and competence (Wright & Hornblow, 2008).

Generally, cultural competency in healthcare is recognized as a developmental process. It is an ongoing journey of discovery, acquiring awareness, knowledge, and the application of skills, rather than a time-limited process where competence is achieved on completion. Pacific cultural competence may be defined as the ability to understand and appropriately apply cultural values and practices that underpin Pacific peoples' worldviews and perspectives on health (Tiatia, 2008).

Betancourt and colleagues differentiate between individual and wider cultural competency - clinical cultural competence is referred to as training and upskilling in the knowledge, skills, and attitudes required to work cross culturally. Organizational cultural competence is focused more on systemic issues, such as ethnic minority leadership and career advancement programmes, or structural enablers, such as ensuring ethnicity data is being recorded and collected accurately (particularly for quality improvement and to monitor ethnic disparities), and culturally and linguistically appropriate health education material (Betancourt, Green, Carrillo & Ananeh-Firempong, 2003).

Le Va leads New Zealand's national *Engaging Pasifika* cultural competency training programme which helps ensure participants learn the foundational attitudes, knowledge, and skills for effectively engaging with Pasifika people and their families (Faleafa, Lua, & Tiatia, 2012). The government-funded, and sector-mandated national programme centres on the *va*, prioritizing the importance of relationships for Pasifika people (particularly at the first point of contact), as well as three essential themes critical for successful engagement with Pasifika families. Firstly, the *family* as a theme, is focussed on social structures, relationships, roles, and obligations. Secondly *language*, emphasizes effective communication, including non-verbal language and cultural nuance. Lastly *tapu* as a theme is primarily focused on understanding the Pasifika person as a relational being. This holistic and values-based approach to relationships with family, community, and environment has been evidenced in many approaches to working with Pacific people in care industries.

The *Engaging Pasifika* cultural competency training programme was developed over a 10 year period. This was an important part of its acceptability and uptake within New Zealand mental health and addiction services. Its essence is based on the Pacific clinical and cultural framework called *Seitapu* (Le Va, 2009), developed by Pacific mental health and addiction leaders, and endorsed by the Pacific mental health and addictions sector, as well as the government of the day.

Over 3,500 health workers voluntarily completed the *Engaging Pasifika* programme between 2010 and 2015. Based on international evidence, and local best practice, it is supported by Professor Betancourt from Harvard University, and acknowledged by the New Zealand Health and Disability Commission. Utilizing a blended learning approach, the programme consists of e-learning modules, face-to-face workshops, and post-training support via an online forum for continued support. Pre- and post-training evaluation results show that participants' awareness, understanding, knowledge, and confidence in engaging effectively with Pacific clients all increase significantly as a result of the programme. In addition, 95% of participants report that the overall programme is excellent. Results indicate the programme is highly effective. Two key success factors are 1) the practical and interactive action learning sets (online and face-to-face), and 2) a facilitation team with cultural, clinical, community, organizational, systems, and consumer expertise and experience.

Resources and tools to support the *Engaging Pasifika* programme have been developed due to demand from the workforce. For example, participants have access to ethnic-specific e-learning modules should they wish to know more about a specific ethnicity. *Talking Therapies for Pasifika Peoples* (Te Pou o te Whakaaro Nui, 2010) was developed to complement therapeutic approaches to mental health and addiction treatment by raising awareness of the importance of pre-engagement and engagement processes that will enhance therapeutic rapport and understanding in Pacific therapeutic conversations. The authors liken this process to metaphorically rolling out a mat – *fofola e fala* – which allows for a safe space for the therapeutic relationship. Factsheets in Pacific languages developed based on a health literacy approach are useful resources to support workers to better engage with Pacific people, and enable Pacific people to gain an equitable understanding of the issues.

To complement the *Engaging Pasifika* programme, Le Va developed organizational cultural competency guidelines (Le Va, 2014), whereby whole organizations and systems aim to increase access and provide the best care and support possible for Pacific families. The level of organizational cultural competence can be described as the degree of compatibility and adaptability between the characteristics of the Pasifika populations served, and the way Le Va's policies, structures, and processes work together to facilitate (or impede) access to and use of support services for Pacific communities (Harper et al., 2006). A culturally competent organization ensures commitment to culturally inclusive systems and services with Pacific cultural competency reflected in their philosophy, governance, vision, purpose, policy, structures, procedures, and practices.

The nine guidelines are depicted in Figure 1. The guidelines are inter-related and organized into three themes that are underpinned by four guiding principles. Together they form a cohesive cycle for improving organizational service delivery.

Growing the Size and Skills of the Pacific Workforce

Skilled Pacific workers bring connections with Pacific communities, personal understanding of Pacific issues, and Pacific cultural and language skills into the workplace (Ministry of Health & Le Va, 2012). A robust Pacific health workforce can positively influence Pacific equity in health outcomes by integrating cultural practices, concepts, and diverse worldviews into high-quality, evidence informed health services (Ministry of Health & Le Va, 2012). Le Va designed the *Futures that Work* programme to ensure the fit-for-purpose development of this robust Pacific mental health and addiction workforce. *Futures that Work* is targeted for Pacific people working in mental health and addiction services or

Figure 1. Nine organizational guidelines for Pasifika cultural competency

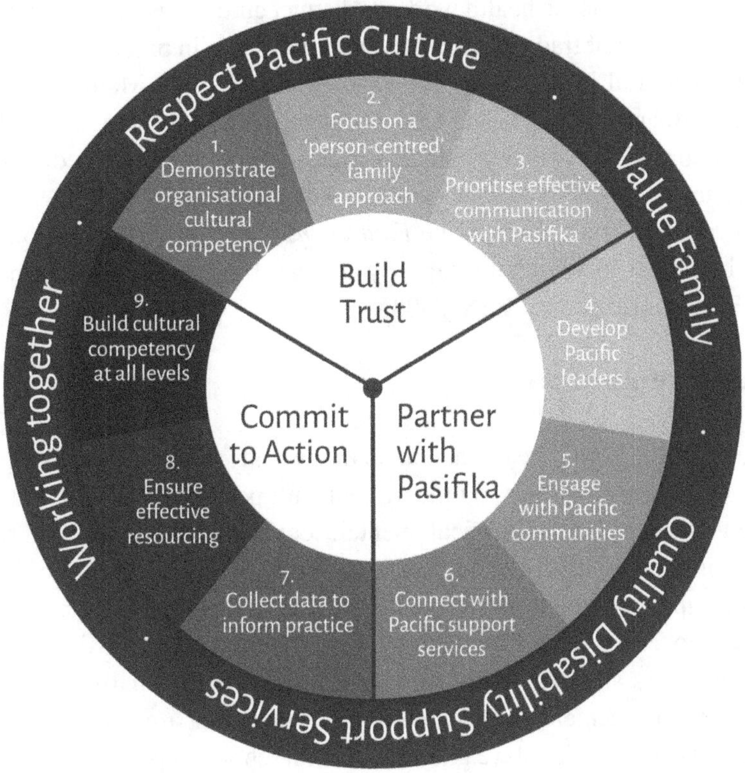

enrolled in relevant tertiary education courses. It is a three phased programme designed to upskill the Pacific workforce as outlined below.

1. **Get Your Fees Paid:** Provision of financial scholarships for targeted courses that align with consumer needs.
2. **Get Your Study Sorted:** Facilitation of a support programme to ensure completion of the qualification on time, involving: pastoral care, cultural support, education support, spiritual and peer support.
3. **Get Your Dream Job:** Career planning and connection with potential employers.

A review of the effectiveness of the programme showed that scholarships contributed to the successful completion of qualifications but success could not be solely attributed to financial support. The pastoral care, mentoring, coaching, and cultural support have also been key to the successful outcomes of the *Futures that Work* programme to date.

Taking a traditional workforce pipeline stance, once Pacific people are in the workforce, career advancement into leadership positions is crucial to influencing change in disparities for Pacific people. Growing Pacific leadership into influential positions in the workforce has potential to support retention rates, ensure appropriate models of service delivery, and enhance access rates for Pacific people.

Le Va developed the *Le Tautua* emerging leaders programme, which aims to equip participants with knowledge, skills, practical resources, and tools to become more effective Pacific leaders and managers in mental health and addiction services. This unique programme is currently the only one of its kind in New Zealand, addressing the Pacific health worker's distinct cultural leadership perspectives. The focus is on contemporary execution of traditional values and knowledge in practice – in clinical, cultural, and community contexts. Cultural leadership is provided by the Pasifika Matua Council of the northern region District Health Boards (DHBs). The Council members are all recognized chiefs (*Matua*) from each of the Pacific nations. The council provides spiritual and cultural knowledge, wisdom, protection, safety, and guidance for all of Le Va's projects, the organization and its staff.

By supporting over 350 people through the *Futures that Work* programme, combined with over 80 *Le Tautua* alumni, Le Va has increased the capacity and capability of the Pacific mental health and addiction workforce in a significant way since 2008.

Synergy Through Integration

Whilst Le Va has a focus on mental health and addiction workforce development, its purpose is to support Pasifika families and communities to unleash their full potential. Le Va takes a holistic approach to well-being, taking into account the physical, mental, social, environmental, and spiritual dimensions of a person, family, or community. This is reflected in Le Va's diverse portfolio across mental health, addiction, disability support, suicide prevention, violence prevention, public health, general health, sport, churches, local government, and education. Working nationally across sectors horizontally, and with a range of stakeholders vertically (from supporting grass roots initiatives to advising government policy), enables Le Va to implement multi-modal interventions that are conducive to synergistic gains. The interventions may be for individuals (e.g., mental health scholarships), families (e.g., suicide prevention training), organizations (e.g., organizational cultural competency guidelines), communities (e.g., disability awareness in churches), or wider society (e.g., Pasifika suicide prevention media guidelines). This ecological approach also supports Le Va's holistic and social determinants approach to reducing inequalities in outcomes for Pasifika.

Collaboration and co-design is key. Working with others to achieve a common purpose is beneficial not only for efficiencies regarding resources, but also to share complementary skills and knowledge, ensure cross sector coordination, promote seamless service delivery, gain wider reach, learn from cross-pollination, and measure collective impact.

CONCLUSION

With a vibrant history of residing in New Zealand for over 150 years, 300,000 Pasifika people now contribute to its international identity and economy in a significant way.

Le Va is addressing the challenges of over-representation of Pasifika people in negative social indicators associated with mental illness and addictions by increasing the capacity and capability of the Pacific workforce, ensuring they are fit for purpose, and also contributing to enhancing the cultural competency of the "mainstream" workforce as a whole. Le Va provides carefully developed, evidence-based and co-designed resources, tools, information, knowledge, and support services. These are all designed to contribute to the best outcomes possible for our Pacific families and communities to ensure they have every opportunity to unleash their potential and flourish well into the future.

Care is often expressed as alofa (love),
and is connected to another nuanced word: tausi - being a custodian and steward.
The Samoan word for nurse is tausi ma'i or tausi soifua.... tausi can be found in such concepts as
tausi aiga - custodian of aiga,
tausi nuu - custodian of village,
tausi faatoaga -custodian of agriculture,
tausi eleele - custodian of land,
tausi mavaega - custodian of inheritance,
tausi soifua - custodian of life and well-being.
Afioga Sister Vitolia Mo'a (2015)

REFERENCES

Adolescent Health Research Group. (in press). *Youth '12 the health and wellbeing of secondary students in New Zealand: Results for Pacific young people*. Author.

Agnew, F., Pulotu-Endemann, F. K., Robinson, G., Suaalii-Sauni, T., Warren, H., Wheeler, A., ... Schmidt-Sopoaga, H. (2004). Pacific models of mental health service delivery in New Zealand. Auckland, New Zealand: Health Research Council.

Bathgate, M., & Pulotu-Endemann, F. K. (1997). Pacific People in New Zealand. In P. M. Ellis & S. C. D. Collings (Eds.), *Mental health from a public health perspective*. Wellington, New Zealand: Ministry of Health.

Betancourt, J., Green, A., Carrillo, J. E., & Ananeh-Firempong, O. II. (2003). Defining cultural competence: A practical framework for addressing racial/ethnic disparities in health and health care. *Public Health Reports, 118*(4), 293–302. doi:10.1016/S0033-3549(04)50253-4 PMID:12815076

Betancourt, J. R., Green, A., & Carrillo, J. E. (2002). *Cultural competence in health care: Emerging frameworks and practical approaches*. The Commonwealth Fund.

Clark, T. C., Fleming, T., Bullen, P., Denny, S., Crengle, S., Dyson, B., ...Utter, J. (2013). Youth'12 overview: The health and wellbeing of New Zealand secondary school students in 2012. Auckland, New Zealand: The University of Auckland.

Durie, M. (1998). *Whaiora: Māori health development*. New Zealand: Oxford University Press.

Faleafa, M., Lua, M., & Tiatia, J. (2012). *Engaging Pasifika training programme: Engaging positively at the critical first point of contact. Unpublished document*. Auckland, New Zealand: Le Va.

Harper, M., Hernandez, M., Nesman, T., Mowery, D., Worthington, J., & Isaacs, M. (2006). *Organizational cultural competence: A review of assessment protocols*. Tampa, FL: University of South Florida.

Kingi, D. A., Faleafa, M., & Brown, T. (2007). A Pasifika perspective of psychology in Aotearoa. In I. M. Evans, J. J. Rucklidge, & M. O'Driscoll (Eds.), *Professional Practice of Psychology in Aotearoa New Zealand*. Wellington, New Zealand: New Zealand Psychological Society.

Kingi-'Ulu'ave, D., Faleafa, M., Brown, T., & Daniela-Wong, D. (in press). Connecting Culture and Care: Clinical Practice for Pasifika People. In I. M. Evans, J. J. Rucklidge, & M. O'Driscoll (Eds.), Professional Practice of Psychology in Aotearoa New Zealand. Academic Press.

Le Va. (2009). *Real skills plus seitapu: Working with Pacific peoples*. Auckland, New Zealand: Le Va.

Le Va. (2014). *Organisational guidelines for disability support services: Working with Pasifika people with disabilities and their families*. Auckland, New Zealand: Le Va.

Malo, V. (2000). *Pacific People in New Zealand talk about their experiences with mental illness*. Wellington, New Zealand: Mental Health Commission.

Maua-Hodges, T. (2000). *Ako pai ki aitutaki: Transporting or weaving cultures: Research report of field experiences to the Cook Islands*. Wellington, New Zealand: Wellington College of Education.

Mental Health Commission. (2012). *National indicators: Measuring mental health and addiction in New Zealand*. Wellington, New Zealand: Mental Health Commission.

Mila-Schaaf, K., & Hudson, M. (2009). *Negotiating space for indigenous theorising in mental health and addiction*. Auckland, New Zealand: Te Pou o te Whakaaro Nui.

Ministry of Health. (2008). *A portrait of health: Key results of the 2006/07 New Zealand health survey*. Wellington, New Zealand: Ministry of Health.

Ministry of Health. (2012). *Tupu ola moui Pacific health chart book*. Wellington, New Zealand: Ministry of Health.

Ministry of Health. (2014). *'Ala mo'ui: Pathways to Pacific health and wellbeing 2014-2018*. Wellington, New Zealand: Ministry of Health.

Ministry of Health & Le Va. (2012). *Taeao o tautai: Pacific public health workforce development implementation plan*. Wellington, New Zealand: Ministry of Health.

Ministry of Justice & Ministry of Pacific Island Affairs. (2000). *Pacific Peoples Constitution Report*. Wellington, New Zealand: Ministry of Justice and Ministry of Pacific Island Affairs.

Ministry of Social Development. (2012). *Nga vaka o kāiga tapu - The Pacific conceptual framework*. Wellington, New Zealand: Ministry of Social Development.

Mo'a, V. (2015, November). *Culture as foundation for care with particular reference to the multicultural context of life and health care for Pacific people in New Zealand.* Aniva Pacific workforce fono. Wellington, New Zealand.

Oakley-Browne, M. A., Wells, J. E., & Scott, K. M. (2006). *Te Rau Hinengaro: The New Zealand Mental Health Survey*. Wellington, New Zealand: Ministry of Health.

Pacific Perspectives. (2013). *Pacific health workforce service forecast: Report to Health Workforce New Zealand and the Ministry of Health*. Wellington, New Zealand: Pacific Perspectives.

Pulotu-Endemann, F. K., Annandale, M., & Instone, A. (2004). *A Pacific perspective on the NZ mental health classification and outcomes study (CAOS)*. Wellington, New Zealand: Mental Health Commission.

Pulotu-Endemann, K. (1995). *The fonofale Pacific model.* Retrieved from http://www.hauora.co.nz/resources/Fonofalemodelexplanation.pdf

Southwick, M., Kenealy, T., & Ryan, D. (2012). *Primary care for Pacific people: A Pacific and health systems approach.* Wellington, New Zealand: Pacific Perspectives.

Statistics New Zealand. (2014). *2013 quick stats about culture and identity: Pacific peoples ethnic group.* Auckland, New Zealand: Statistics New Zealand.

Tafa, T., & Fotu, M. (2009). *The Popao model: Folau ki he mo'ui lelei - Journey to wellness, a Pacific recovery and strength concept in mental health.* Auckland, New Zealand: The Popao Group.

Tamasese, K., Peteru, C., Waldegrave, C., & Bush, A. (2005). Ole taeao afua, the new morning: A qualitative investigation into Samoan perspectives of mental health and culturally appropriate services. *The Australian and New Zealand Journal of Psychiatry, 39*(4), 300–309. doi:10.1080/j.1440-1614.2005.01572.x PMID:15777368

Tamasese, T. A. T. (2002). *More on meaning, nuance and metaphor: Keynote speech. Pacific fono, Moving ahead together. Pataka Museum.* Porirua, Wellington: New Zealand: Capital Coast District Health Board.

Te Pou o te Whakaaro Nui. (2007). *Feasibility study into the establishment of a Pacific mental health workforce development organisation.* Auckland, New Zealand: Te Pou o te Whakaaro Nui.

Te Pou o te Whakaaro Nui. (2010). *Talking therapies for Pasifika peoples: Best and promising practice guide for mental health and addiction services.* Auckland, New Zealand: Te Pou o te Whakaaro Nui.

Te Pou o te Whakaaro Nui. (2015). *Overview of the adult mental health and addiction workforce: 2014 survey of vote health funded services.* Auckland, New Zealand: Te Pou o te Whakaaro Nui.

Thaman, H. (2004). Le'o e peau: Towards cultural and cognitive democracy in development in Pacific Islands communities. In *Changing islands – changing worlds:Proceedings from islands of the World VIII international conference* (pp. 36-47). Kinmen Island (Quemoy), Taiwan: Academic Press.

Tiatia, J. (2008). *Pacific Cultural Competencies: A literature review.* Wellington, New Zealand: Ministry of Health.

Tu'itahi, S. (2007). *Fonua: A model for Pacific health promotion.* Retrieved from http:// www.hauora.co.nz/resources/FonuaaPasifikmodel.pdf

Tukuitonga, C. (2013). Pacific people in New Zealand. In I. St George (Ed.), *Cole's medical practice in New Zealand* (12th ed.; pp. 66–73). Wellington, New Zealand: Medical Council of New Zealand.

Tukuitonga, C., & Finau, S. (1997). The health of Pacific peoples in New Zealand up to the early 1990s. *Pacific Health Dialog, 4*(2), 59–67.

Vaioleti, T. M. (2006). Talanoa research methodology: A developing position on Pacific research. *Waikato Journal of Education, 12*, 21–34.

World Health Organization. (2010). *Workload indicators of staffing need: User's manual.* Geneva, Switzerland: WHO Press.

Wright, S., & Hornblow, A. (2008). Emerging needs, evolving services: The health of Pacific peoples in New Zealand. *Kotuitui*, *3*(1), 21–33. doi:10.1080/1177083X.2008.9522430

KEY TERMS AND DEFINITIONS

Pacific People: There are 300,000 (7.4%) Pacific people residing in New Zealand according to the *2013 Census of Population and Dwellings* (Statistics New Zealand, 2014). This consists of Samoan as the largest ethnic group (48.7%), followed by Cook Islands (20.6%), Tongan (20.4%), Niuean (8.1%), Fijian (4.9%), Tokelauan (2.4%), and Tuvaluan (1.2%). These nations have their own specific languages, beliefs, customs, values, traditions, and lifestyles.

Tapu: Refers to sacred or forbidden in 38 Oceanic languages.

Tautua: "Service" in the Samoan language in reference to the Samoan proverb "*O le ala i le pule o le tautua*", "*the pathway to leadership is through service*".

Vā: A concept shared among many Pacific cultures which refers sacred relationships.

Section 3

Specific Workforce Development Applications

Chapter 9
Undergraduate Nursing Curriculum Content Focuses on Emerging Issues that Influence Health

Helen Mary Bingham
Western Institute of Technology, New Zealand

ABSTRACT

Undergraduate education content could hold the key to nursing workforce development. A professional's attitudes and beliefs are developed during these years, along with the ability to use knowledge and skills to promote mental health and well-being, and work with people experiencing mental health and addiction issues. Historically undergraduate education has targeted the support of illness as opposed to developing and supporting health and well-being. In the past decade research shows there is a close relationship between mental illness and addiction with physical health and early brain development. This chapter explores how the Modern Apprenticeship nursing curriculum prepares undergraduate nurses to critically think about a person or family's health at every encounter using a biopsychosocial framework by understanding that all of health is connected and the development of the brain in the early years is key to health and well-being.

INTRODUCTION

Workforce development to meet the needs of people experiencing mental illness or addiction issues has become critical as current structures and resources are unable to keep pace with society's mental illness needs. Adding to this idea is that future need is expected to increase (World Health Organization [WHO], 2001). This suggests the current approach to workforce development requires change in some way. WHO (2014) is of the opinion that health care systems have not been able to respond adequately to the need for treatment of mental illness and addiction issues, with 76%-85% of those who live in low to middle income countries receiving no treatment for their mental illness or addiction issues. In high income countries,

DOI: 10.4018/978-1-5225-1874-7.ch009

35%-50% do not receive adequate treatment. WHO (2014) note that mental illness and addiction issues are on the increase and impact not only on mental and physical health, but also have major implications for society. Research in the last decade shows a connection between brain development and the effect of stress on mental and physical health and illness. This implies that with increased mental illness and addictions issues there will be an associated increase in physical health issues across the life course.

This chapter explores workforce development strategies that aim to build skills within a nursing workforce to support preventative approaches to mental illness and addiction disorders. This would be achieved by concentrating on developing a workforce with knowledge and skills to work with people to make life choices that enhance well-being. Nursing education is often focused on an illness model. The supporting research shows brain development in infants is critical to both mental and physical health across the life span (Shonkoff & Phillips, 2000).

When Western Institute of Technology Taranaki, New Zealand was developing a nursing curriculum, the way mental health knowledge and skills were to be taught to undergraduate nurses was considered. There appeared to be a need to move from the traditional illness focus and provide undergraduates with the knowledge and skills to make a difference in the mental health and well-being of people that nurses would encounter in clinical environments. The ideas in this chapter are based on an undergraduate nursing curriculum but could also apply to other undergraduate training programs.

BACKGROUND

The nursing workforce for mental health and addictions has developed as a specialist area from an historical focus on treating illness. Undergraduate nursing education generally has mental illness and addiction knowledge and skills separated as a specialist topic. This separation supports not only a silo approach to learning but the silo use of knowledge and skills in clinical areas. In particular, neuroscience research has prompted a worldview change, with mental health increasingly being viewed from a well-being as well as an illness paradigm. This research indicates the importance of brain development as it "fits" in the development of resilience for optimum mental health and well-being.

Mental health nurses, who are part of a specialized workforce, appear to hold various views about the concepts of mental health and mental illness. This variation has led to a lack of consensus about the knowledge and skills required by nurses in undergraduate nursing curriculums (Patterson, Curtis & Reed, 2008). The result has been differences in skill level among nurses upon graduation depending on the undergraduate programmes that they have completed. Much of the literature sourced appears to be concerned with the role of nurses in treating people diagnosed with a major mental illness, as opposed to supporting mental health as a state of well-being. Nurses comprise a large proportion of multidisciplinary teams within the mental health and addictions workforce. The roles that nurses take, often allow them to spend more time with people with experience of mental illness and addiction than other health professionals (Barker, 2009). Therefore, nurses need to be prepared by their education to enter into a workplace and operate effectively in an increasingly complex, interdisciplinary health care environment, but also be able to use mental health knowledge and skill in any clinical area (Clinton & Hazelton, 2000).

Nurses play a critical role in the provision of timely, effective, and appropriate mental health and addiction promotion and care (WHO, 2007). Countries need to develop health care systems to support this. WHO (2014) argue the key to mental illness and addiction care is to provide nursing and social services that are capable of providing treatment. The nursing workforce can contribute to making this difference. In New Zealand, health policy also promotes an increased investment in whānau ora (family heath) within current budgetary restraints (Ministry of Health, 2011).

These ideas demonstrate there is a greater need for a strong mental health component within undergraduate nursing curricula (Moxham, McCann, Usher, Farrell, & Crookes, 2011). A nurse needs to be able to assess and provide timely interventions that may include health promotion and education, as well as care to those who are considered to have an illness. Using an interpersonal process nurses should be able to provide input into both mental and physical health or illness across the age span in a cultural context (New Zealand College of Mental Health Nurses, 2012). Nurses need to be able to nurse the ill if needed but more importantly promote the well-being of people to prevent the experience of mental health and addiction issues (McMurray & Clendon, 2011).

While Patterson et al. (2008) have argued there appears to be no consensus as to the knowledge and skills required by nurses, there are competency frameworks for professionals employed in mental health and addictions that could be adapted to guide mental health and addiction skills and content in undergraduate nursing curricula. These include *Let's Get Real* (Ministry of Health, 2008) and *Te Whare o Tiki – Co-existing Problems Knowledge and Skills Framework* (Matua Raki, & Te Pou, 2013). Consideration needs to be given also to *Real Skills Plus CAMHS* (The Werry Centre, 2008) as part of an undergraduate nursing curriculum. This is because programmes aimed at the prevention of mental illness and addiction issues need to focus on maximizing the brain architecture of infants and children, as is discussed later in the chapter.

If nurses use the medical model as an approach which focuses on symptom reduction and rapid stabilization, basing the interventions on the illness state of the person, workforce development will continue with an illness focus. The well-being model looks more towards developing the person's strengths, is centered on health, and empowers the person to manage life stressors. To achieve this undergraduate nursing education needs to be changed. There needs to be a focus on a biopsychosocial model of health, with an understanding of the interconnection between health, the life cycle, and the environment. The interaction between environment and age is essential to understand from a health development perspective as will be discussed further, along with brain development (Collins, Insel, Chockalingam, Daar, & Maddox, 2013).

Following an investigation of health care training providers, Avery and colleagues (2003) claimed there was a need to include new knowledge about the effect of stress on disease and an understanding of stress reduction skills within nursing curriculum. The base of this idea is that stress has been shown to have a relationship with such a wide range of disease states, including mental illness, addiction, and physical health or wellness states. They concluded that curriculum developers need to educate from a biopsychosocial model of health.

Undergraduate nurse training needs to produce graduates that are prepared to practice in all areas of nursing, including mental health (Cleary & Carlo, 2006). Roberts (2013) reports that due to the prevalence of mental health issues in all clinical areas nurses in all clinical encounters need to be to be able to respond appropriately. However, nurses often lack the knowledge and skills needed to provide holistic care, despite being in a unique position to detect mental health issues in all clinical practice areas (Roberts, 2013). Mental health and addiction issues are recognized as a global problem and nurses, because of the role they play in health, need to have the knowledge and skills to provide appropriate care for people in a range of clinical situations (Moxham et al., 2011).

NURSES AND MENTAL HEALTH KNOWLEDGE AND SKILLS

If workforce development is to meet the needs of society the *Blueprint II: Improving Mental Health and Well-being for all New Zealanders* (Mental Health Commission, 2012) indicates there needs to be an understanding of the role mental health and well-being has in achieving a productive society. The aspects supporting health and well-being which need to be part of nursing curriculum include the knowledge of stress, brain development, and how this fits with the encounters a nurse has with families and infants. It appears that what is included in undergraduate nursing curriculums is left to each individual education provider with no direction about content. The supporting knowledge that should be incorporated into an undergraduate nursing curriculum therefore includes:

- Understanding prenatal and infant brain development
- The connection between stress, health, well-being, and illness
- The development of resilience
- The role of the family
- The nursing role in health prevention and promotion.

Healthy Brain Development

While genetics provides instructions for an individual's brain development, the development of the brain is reliant on the environment for instructions (National Scientific Council on the Developing Child, 2010). This finding has caused a shift in the nature verses nurture debate, with the understanding that nurture has more of an impact on nature than thought in the past; in other words, genes are inherited but the expression of these is influenced by environment (Wilson, 2014). Nurses need to understand this as they are often in an infant's environment thus able to identify issues within the environment that may have a future impact. Nurses need to notice if the environment provides experiences that are going to enhance brain development. Nurses need to be able to connect knowledge to their assessment and use this to provide nursing responses that are supported by underpinning knowledge.

Brain and Stress

If nurses have knowledge of the complex relationship between the various parts of the brain, nervous system, and endocrine system that form the critical components of the body's stress response they will be able to use this in encounters with people when in professional practice. How a person reacts to stress as an adult is set during infancy. This is because when an infant experiences stress the responses of others influence the reaction of the brain and neuronal development (National Scientific Council on the Developing Child, 2004).

The flight and fight response which is designed to keep us safe by releasing the stress hormones, norepinephrine and cortisol, results in an increase in heart rate and blood pressure (Southwick & Charny, 2012). While some cortisol is essential to well-being, the balance is easily tipped (Arden, 2010). Negative emotional states tend to trigger the sympathetic nervous system which produces cortisol; while positive emotional states trigger the parasympathetic nervous system to neutralize the cortisol effect (Southwick & Charny, 2012).

The excessive and long term presence of cortisol can be corrosive to the brain and body with adverse effects on both mental and physical health (Arden, 2010). Cortisol when produced in excess can disrupt brain development along with the development of other organs increasing the risk of stress-related diseases like heart disease, diabetes, substance abuse, and depression (National Scientific Council on the Developing Child, 2008/2012). Toxic stress not only can disrupt the development of stress regulation but interferes with learning, memory, and social behavior (National Scientific Council on the Developing Child, 2010). Toxic stress is the prolonged unrelieved activation of the stress system in the body. This is largely the result of not having a protective adult to provide for the infant's needs (National Scientific Council on the Developing Child, 2008/2012). This increased activation of the stress response heightens vulnerability over a lifetime to behavior and physiological problems (National Scientific Council on the Developing Child, 2007).

Early childhood adversities increase the risk of not only mental illness and addiction issues but physical health issues as well. Early childhood adversities can have an enduring effect on the developing brain which in turn impacts on health across the life span. Stress in the developing brain can lead to the persistent activation of the biological stress system. When there is no buffering system that comes from supporting relationships, the levels of the stress hormones remain high and can damage the architecture of the brain (National Scientific Council on the Developing Child, 2008/2012).

Neuroplasticity

Knowledge of how the brain is wired during critical time periods is important. But there is also a need to understand that the brain has the ability to adapt and change according to the environment. With this knowledge nurses can support people to make changes in thinking and behavior at any stage of life (Wilson, 2014). There are crucial periods for some aspects of brain development and once passed, supporting healthier brain development is more difficult to achieve (Vimpani, 2001). This indicates that it is best to wire the brain in a healthy way during optimum time periods in life, which is during the first 1,000 days of life from conception (Southwick & Charney, 2012). Critical to the time frames of brain architecture is the dyad relationship between the infant and the adult that is the main caregiver.

The Dyad

The wiring of the brain with a secure attachment is predictive of a person feeling secure throughout life, thus allowing the development of meaningful relationships with high self-esteem, resilience, optimism, and being equipped to be intellectually curious (Arden, 2010). A dyad relationship is one between an infant and an adult who is attuned to the infant providing a safe, secure environment where the stressors of being an infant are buffered. This is usually the mother but could be any adult who spends the largest amount of time with the infant. This positive dyad relationship experience influences the development of the social brain with empathy development being the base of communication skills. These will have an impact on relationship building throughout life.

Those who build positive relationships will have a sense of well-being, and well developed mirror neurons which allow a person to be empathetic and compassionate which is essential for relationships that support well-being (Arden, 2010). The mirror neuron system develops as the infant is imitated by its caring adults helping connect actions to emotional states. The mirror neuronal system is directly connected to the emotional processing center of the brain, the limbic system. This forms the base for the development of empathy (Wilson, 2014).

With this knowledge as part of a nursing curriculum, nurses can use this understanding in encounters with families. It is essential these messages are passed on to those who are providing environments for infants. Allowing the infants to achieve brain development that leads to the development of resilience. This should include families or those who care for infants like child care providers.

Infants who are exposed to an environment that is consistent, predictable, and nurturing will develop the neurobiological capabilities that will increase their chances for well-being and resilience (Perry & Hambrick, 2008). Infants whose brains develop in a nurturing environment with adults who are attuned to their needs are more likely to develop attitudes that have a set point that allow for the management of stress. Research has largely focused on the attachment arising from the dyad relationship and suggests when there are issues with this relationship the risk of significant long term consequences is higher (Ministry of Health, 2011). If nurses learn about this within an undergraduate curriculum they will be able to support this concept by inter-sectorial co-ordination; not only across health but also education, justice, and social services to support families to grow resilient children (Ministry of Health, 2015).

Those who experience toxic stress are more likely to have lifelong effects including diabetes, hypertension, stroke, obesity, heart disease, and cancer. Adverse experiences in childhood increase the likelihood of physical and mental health problems in later life (National Scientific Council on the Developing Child, 2008/2012). WHO (2001) supports the connection between mental and physical health, and report the concept of mental health needs to be considered more broadly than the medical model to support prevention and recovery. Consideration of the social components of well-being should also be considered.

The neuroscience research supports the idea of human brain development in the first three years of life as being essential for sound mental health, which in turn supports all other aspects of human development and health. This gives clues to where the greatest impact on well-being and thus the prevention of illness can be achieved (Arden, 2010). Environmental and social exposures influence the risk of mental and physical illness across the life course (Collins et al., 2013).

Research from the National Scientific Council on the Developing Child (2008/2012) advocates that workforce development initiatives should consider how important the first 1,000 days are for health across the life span. The Brain Wave Trust in New Zealand suggests the dyad relationship is essential. The process of the baby's attachment to one key adult is now supported by research as the most important aspect in brain development in infancy (Brain Wave Trust Aotearoa, 2015). Support from that one adult develops a partnership for the infant to feel safe, loved, and adored, setting the scene for a successful and happy life (Wallis, 2015). O'Sullivan (2015) suggests that family is a key place to start. Schools are a meeting point for all families given all children attend. Schools could therefore provide the venue. To capture the needs of families and support them, nurses could take a more active part in schools by providing not only support for physical health but mental health and well-being for the whole family. To be successful this approach would need to be supported by more than the health care sector, and include the education and justice sectors as well. There would be a need to focus on what opportunities could be provided by whom to support people, families, and communities to be resilient and able to cope with adversity (Mental Health Commission, 2012). A nurse with a sound understanding of the knowledge that underpins the issues discussed above could make a difference and take a lead role.

Family as a Key

There is an increasing need for the nursing workforce to take on roles that understand the part family plays in mental health and well-being. A skilled nursing workforce working with families may support an understanding of how to minimize the effect of risk and maximize the effect of the protective factors in early childhood. The importance of multi-skilled professionals, who can assess and treat possible mental illness and addiction issues whilst understanding the importance of the relationship between the mother and infant in the context of family is essential (Ministry of Health, 2011).

Parenting is increasingly recognized as a key issue with the dyad relationship central to healthy development. There are aspects of an infants and child's environment which can expose them to risks that have a life course effect on all aspects of health and well-being. While it is unlikely that one risk factor will lead to a negative outcome there is a complex interaction between considered risk and protective factors and the timing of these exposures can predict outcomes on adult health (Vimpani, 2001).

Social policy drives initiatives and funding for health related projects. Those leading the development of social policy need to understand the importance of the dyad relationship during this critical period of brain development. Scandinavian countries for example have lower rates of absolute child poverty. These countries support parental leave and have provisions for high quality child care based on the underpinning knowledge of brain development. Despite a high rate of single parent families which could be considered a risk (Vimpani, 2001). An undergraduate nursing curriculum that recognizes the importance of this knowledge will produce graduates able to use this information in clinical encounters with families. This would not only help build resilient individuals but also prosperous and thriving communities (National Scientific Council on the Developing Child, 2010).

Happiness and positive emotions provide the key to physical and psychological health; achieving this is complex as it includes understanding the relationship between emotions, cognition, and behavior (Carruthers & Hood, 2004.) It appears cognition and literacy skills are focused on and tested by those involved in child care and education. But to develop infants and children whose brains are able to maximize emotional and social development there needs to be a shift in focus. Policymakers need to use this knowledge to underpin recommendations related to the development of educational programs. The key to resilience and well-being is emotional and social development (National Scientific Council on the Developing Child, 2004).

Workforce development strategies for nurses need to include knowledge and skills which allow nurses to support the early years of a child's life within a family. A meta-analysis of a range of preventive programs conducted by Durlak and Wells (1997) came to an interesting conclusion that the transition to first time motherhood is the best time to target interventions. This achieves the best outcomes for increasing resilience and decreasing risk factors for the first and subsequent children. During this interaction the behavior and skills which contribute to well-being could be shared with the family. For example, along with advice and behavior changes such as exercise and nutrition, information on how to develop bonding and positive supportive relationships can be shared (Brain Wave Trust Aotearoa, 2015).

The concept of providing a good start is supported by the Mental Health Commission (2012) who identified increasing the capability of families and communities to support positive infant and child development as a priority. The Ministry of Health (2015) recognizes that child health, development, and well-being sets the scene for an adult's health. Risks for heart disease, diabetes, and some mental health issues arise in childhood. There is also an understanding that broader effects on society are influenced by childhood development, health, and well-being.

Prevention and Promotion

To achieve improved long-term outcomes for society's mental health more resources need to concentrate on prevention and the promotion of well-being. Health promotion is concerned with enabling people and societies to increase control over and improve their health. These may be individual choices but are aimed at society in general (WHO, 2001). Preventative behaviors are those taken to prevent illness and maintain a wellness state (Pender, Murdaugh & Parson, 2006). A preventative behavior for example includes educating females attempting to conceive a baby not to use substances, such as nicotine and alcohol, by educating on the effect for baby's brain development. Health promotion is aimed at engaging individuals to behave in a way that increases well-being. This requires the engagement of people to promote change and growth (Pender et al., 2006).

However, the evidence for the success of health promotion strategies used to influence the population's mental health is difficult to assess as many programs have not been evaluated (Chesterson, 2009). Health promotion in the form of health education in the written form as pamphlets and posters are prolific in all health centers. There is some evidence that these documents are often of low or moderate quality and have a minimal effect on health behavior change. To be effective these materials need to be written in simple conversational language. They should be factual, include risk issues, and provide alternative behaviors (Crawford-Williams, Fielder, Mikocka-Walus, Esterman, & Steen-Greavs, 2015).

Mental health promotion needs to be aimed at a number of levels: individuals, families, organizations, communities, and society in general (WHO, 2001). Health skills need to be included in undergraduate nursing curriculum. There is a difference between health education and health promotion. Health education activities aim to give information but a partnership between nurse and patient is necessary for health promotion (Laverack, 2005). The skill of health promotion skills allows the nurse to empower people to improve their own health. By engaging people to gain increasing control over their own individual well-being. This would help raise the health status of communities (Ewles & Simnehi, 2004). Mental health promotion is described by Chesterson (2009) as measures used to strengthen the mental health and well-being of all people in society. There is an acknowledgement that this is not just the business of mental health professionals but needs to be addressed collectively by all professionals. However, nurses have frequent contact with families that provide opportunities to have health promotion conversations with people and as such can use opportunistic moments to make a difference (Pender et al., 2006).

Nurses are a group of professionals that often have opportunities to use health education to engage and motivate individuals to change and achieve better health outcomes. This skill involves more than giving education. Undergraduate nursing curriculums need to educate nurses to have the knowledge and skills required to assess if information was understood. They also need to be able to assess if the time is right for change. Knowledge and skills in using brief interventions and what supports are needed to sustain change are also essential (Matua Raki, 2012). To make the most of all opportunities to promote health in all encounters with people (Clinton & Hazelton, 2000), nurses need to be able to engage in a relationship that allows for health education to take place (Matua Raki, 2012). The professional skills and knowledge which allow this to happen are based in motivational interviewing and the understanding of the wheel of change (Matua Raki, & Te Pou, 2013).

As an example, the Cardiff Model of prevention of violence caused by alcohol could be used. All agencies in the community communicate with each other registering any people at risk. When the person is in an emergency department the nurses are trained to provide brief interventions and advice while other nursing care is completed. The aim is to motivate people to reduce their alcohol consumption.

Where this model has been used and researched it has been found to be effective in reducing violence in communities (Young, 2011). The concept of this model could be transferred to infant brain development with all professionals coming into contact with an infant and family offering a brief intervention and advice. Those that are at risk could be identified with all health, social, and justice agencies collaborating to put in place resources to manage the infant's risk to allow brain development that result in well-being as an adult.

In summary, undergraduate nursing education needs to include knowledge that optimizes the nurse's understanding of infant brain development; the connection between stress, health, well-being and illness; the development of resilience; the role of the family; and health prevention and promotion.

SOLUTIONS AND RECOMMENDATIONS

Undergraduate Nursing Curriculum: The Modern Apprenticeship

The Western Institute of Technology Taranaki, New Zealand is the base for a nursing school that has addressed workforce development by providing undergraduate nurses with an education to meet the changing needs of health care systems (Thorne, 2006). An undergraduate nursing curriculum has been developed which is based on the philosophies of a modern apprenticeship. This contemporary model combines the best of the old apprenticeship model with modern educational pedagogies. The Modern Apprenticeship is based on the work of Benner, Leonard, and Day (2010) and positions clinical practice as central to undergraduate nursing education (Tanner, 2008). The overall aim of the apprenticeship is to produce work-ready nurses who are lifelong learners (Western Institute of Technology Taranaki, 2012). The framework of learning consists of three apprenticeships that are served concurrently to support graduate nurses to act like, think like, and be a nurse (Tanner, 2008).

The three apprenticeships are taught simultaneously over the three years.

1. The apprenticeship of cognition and knowledge which is drawn from a range of sciences and used as part of learning to think like a nurse.
2. The apprenticeship of the technical nursing skills which are learnt throughout the three years, in simulation and clinical practice. Communication and the development of therapeutic relationships are key.
3. The apprenticeship of ethical and professional practice which is developed through clinical practice.

There is much discussion worldwide about the importance given to mental illness and addiction within nursing curricula with no consensus on the content of the knowledge and skills to be incorporated (Happell, 2010). The Modern Apprenticeship has an integrated approach to the curriculum design, which incorporates not only traditional views of mental illness, but also focuses on mental health and well-being (Western Institute of Technology Taranaki, 2012). The mental health, illness, and addictions knowledge and skills presented as learning opportunities have been designed and embedded into the curriculum to promote a biopsychosocial approach to mental health, illness, and addiction nursing. Undergraduates are encouraged to apply the knowledge and skills they learn at every encounter with others, not just in the traditional mental health and addiction nursing roles. This supports the Mental Health Commission's (2012) ideas that there needs to be a greater role for primary care in promoting early interventions.

The undergraduate curriculum at Western Institute of Technology Taranaki was designed so the knowledge and skills connected to mental health, illness, and addiction meet the following four aims for graduate nurses.

1. That graduates have the knowledge and skills to enter a specialist mental health and addiction clinical setting if they choose to (Clinton & Hazelton, 2000)
2. That graduates are able to provide complete mental health, illness, and addiction care in any other clinical setting in all encounters with people (Clinton & Hazelton, 2000).
3. That graduates consider the knowledge and skills of mental health, illness, and addiction in all encounters with people in their professional settings.
4. That graduates take every opportunity to promote well-being.

These aims are met by educational interventions aimed at maximizing the integrated learning for undergraduate nurses from the mental health, illness, and addiction field along with physical health.

The Modern Apprenticeship philosophies have clinical practice central to learning (Tanner, 2008). While traditional learning focuses on illness in mental health and addiction clinical settings, undergraduates are encouraged to apply the knowledge in all clinical settings. From a mental health, illness, and addiction specialty clinical perspective, year one undergraduate nurses experience clinical practice in an acute mental health unit. Using this time applying the weekly learning-focus and other mental health and addictions related learning to clinical experiences. In year two, all undergraduate nurses experience a mental health placement in secondary services; this could be in an inpatient or community setting. Year three is focused on placement choice, and is population and community based with some undergraduate nurses attending a community mental health placement, all experiencing an aged care residential placement, and another community health based placement with opportunities to promote health and well-being. During all clinical placements and in all settings, undergraduate nurses are encouraged to view all encounters with people from a biopsychosocial worldview, thus taking all opportunities to promote health and well-being.

An educational intervention was designed in year one to challenge assumptions and beliefs that support stigmatizing beliefs and discriminating behaviors. As undergraduate nurses can have stigmatizing beliefs towards people with experience of mental health issues as the general population does. This can result in undergraduate nurses experiencing anxiety during the first days of clinical practice. This anxiety impacts on the student nurse's ability to learn, as they do not feel safe or secure (Emrich, Thompson, & Moore, 2003).

Year one clinical practice is supported by specialist mental health nurses who are also lecturers. The lecturer uses encounters with people experiencing mental health and addiction issues to challenge and change these stigmatizing beliefs. By connecting underpinning knowledge to help the undergraduate nurse understand the person's experience. This experience results in undergraduate nurses feeling less anxious about clinical experience in the mental health setting, as anxiety driven by stigma and discrimination (Emerich et al., 2003) is challenged in year one. In order to transfer knowledge to practice and develop nursing skills, the benefit of experience cannot be over-emphasized (Tratnack, O'Neill, & Graham, 2011).

There is a risk that contact by nurses with people who have experienced mental illness or addiction issues early in undergraduate education can reinforce stigmatizing beliefs (Corrigan, 2002; Stuhlmiller, 2005). This risk is identified and understood by the accompanying lecturers who use a coaching approach to help undergraduate nurses make sense of the clinical experience and reframe their beliefs and assumptions in a recovery framework.

Another educational intervention used in the Modern Apprenticeship is having groups of people who are experiencing recovery and their family members spend time in the year two class room. This allows undergraduate nurses to understand the role of the nurse from the perspective of a person receiving care. This educational intervention is provided in a partnership with Supporting Families, a non-government organization (NGO). Supporting Families invite and prepare people with lived experience of mental illness or addiction and their family members to attend the learning sessions. This learning is not scripted and based on face-to-face interaction using small groups. Feedback indicates this educational intervention is positive for both the undergraduate nurses and those who have lived experience. The main point of difference is learning through the small group interaction and personal connection made by all participants.

The Modern Apprenticeship considers that all encounters with people no matter the clinical area should include the use of mental health knowledge and skills to promote well-being, support resilience, or assess and support illness (Western Institute of Technology Taranaki, 2012). For example, an undergraduate nurse providing a pre-employment check in a general practice notes an abnormally high blood pressure for a young male who appears otherwise healthy. Using communication skills, they discover his wife has left him, he has lost his job, has nowhere to live, and limited access to his children. Without this information medication may have been commenced as opposed to support to problem solve to reduce stress.

The three apprenticeships are structured so that each paper deepens the connection of knowledge to nursing practice and the ability to act like, think like, and be a nurse (Benner et al., 2010). Each year is structured to achieve these connections but framed from a different educational pedagogy that fits with the level of undergraduate nurse learning. The knowledge of brain development, well-being, self-care and resilience, along with mental health and addiction knowledge is threaded throughout the papers with well-being and therapeutic communication being a focus in year one; illness, recovery, and motivational interviewing a focus in year two; and development of the brain and brief intervention skills in year three. During all three years there is a focus on well-being based on learning about personal stress management and how to develop resilience.

Year one, learning is organized in concepts. Conceptual learning prepares nursing graduates who are skilled at conceptual thinking and learning which is necessary in health to be able to think critically to respond to the changing health care environment (Giddens & Brady, 2007). The following is an example of the learning connections that were applied by a year one undergraduate nurse in clinical practice who made the connection of the physiological affect that stress has on vital signs. An adolescent male experiencing a serious leg injury from rugby who was in hospital for the first time and was supported by the undergraduate nurse who sat and talked him through the process he was going to experience until he felt less anxious.

A visual aid displaying the concept learning as used in year one which are connected to the philosophies of the Modern Apprenticeship pedagogies and patient-centered care is illustrated in Figure 1. This framework is integrated across the three years of the nursing degree as a tool to demonstrate the scaffolding approach to developing critical thinking as a nurse. This aligns with a culturally responsive biopsychosocial model of person-centered care.

Year one, knowledge includes learning to reflect on self and how personal culture affects nursing interactions, with many challenging their own personal values and beliefs to fit with being a nurse. Communication and relationship building knowledge and skills are concentrated on in year one with this learning practiced in clinical practice each week. Much of the learning centers on well-being but there

Figure 1. Concept learning framework connecting the philosophies of the Modern Apprenticeship pedagogies and patient-centered care

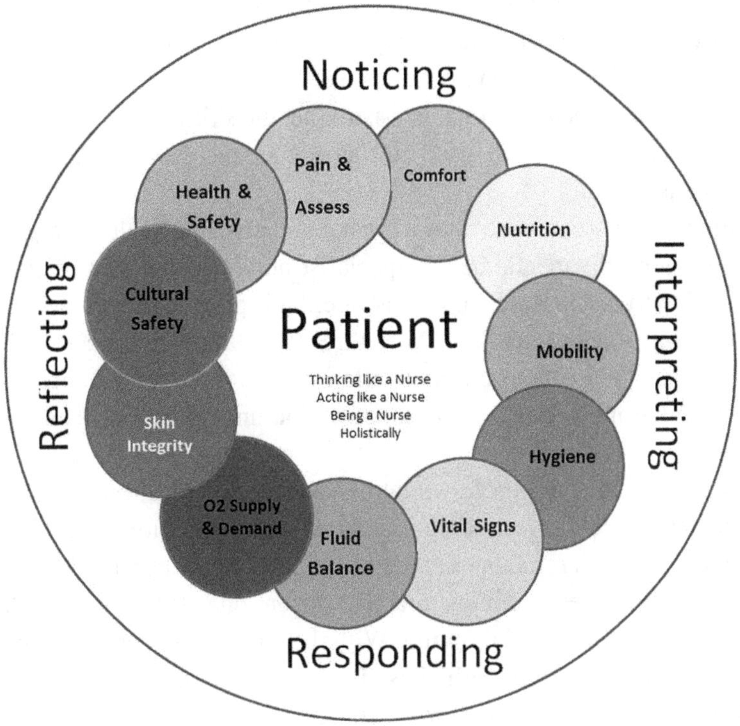

is also a focus on building undergraduate nurse's attitudes to people with experience of mental illness and addiction in a positive way. One week of year one has mental health as the concept; this learning is a mixture of wellness and illness perspectives which includes a stigma and discrimination workshop led by people with a lived experience.

Year two is case-based learning with six cases forming the base of the undergraduates' learning. Each issue is explored during the two weeks of class time, including face-to-face learning in an interactive learning based classroom, online, and simulation. Nurses in year two also learn about specific mental illness and addiction issues, as well as the use of pharmacological interventions. Case-based learning encourages the blending of all nursing knowledge and skills in all clinical areas. The year two cases included are outlined below.

1. Depression and diabetes.
2. Delirium, psychosis, and chronic obstructive pulmonary disease.
3. Addiction, alcohol, and cannabis use and trauma.
4. Bipolar and heart disease.
5. Suicide and trauma.

Year three learning objectives include preparing undergraduate nurses to be opportunistic in all clinical encounters to use their knowledge and skills to promote health and well-being. Learning includes cognitive behavioral therapy skills and how to use brief interventions to promote change to achieve optimum health, building on the knowledge and skill of year two. The talking therapy learnt in year two is motivational interviewing connected to the wheel of change and how this connects to health promotion.

The apprenticeship of nursing skills begins in the simulation laboratory. In all three years, simulation forms the base for facilitation of learning, with consolidation in clinical practice. In year one, each concept is connected to physical and mental health or illness. Nursing communication is practiced in simulation in preparation for clinical practice. For example, the skill of vital signs is connected to understanding how anxiety can affect the results, and how a brief anxiety lowering intervention like breathing can change the vital signs.

Year two simulation for each case study has a mental and physical health component. This continues the integrated approach with the mental health specialist nurses leading simulation skill sessions. For example, the conversation to assess a person who is suicidal is practiced with the lecturer acting the part of the person experiencing suicidal thinking. Year three simulation continues with the lecturer acting to allow the undergraduates to practice communication with those experiencing deregulated emotional states. Many of the simulation experiences are taped so the undergraduates can reflect on their use of knowledge and skills.

The apprenticeship of ethical and professional behavior is learnt throughout the three years. With the mental health specialist lecturers providing role modeling along with the nurses the undergraduates meet in clinical practice. The undergraduates experience the lecturers communicating with people experiencing acute mental health issues in clinical practice in year one. Tutorials provide the opportunity to discuss professional practice and ethical thinking. With the educational interventions aimed at challenging undergraduate nurses to develop strengths-based recovery attitudes towards people with experience of mental health issues and understanding how to enhance resilience to maintain well-being both on a personal and professional level.

While the mental health, illness, and addiction aims of the Modern Apprenticeship from a mental health and addictions workforce perspective have not been formally evaluated, anecdotal evidence collected through undergraduate nursing stories and assignment work show these aims are being met with the integrated approach.

CONCLUSION

Those interested in workforce development are becoming more aware that societal mental health conditions are complex. There is a relationship between the biological, cultural, and psychological dimensions of each individual and their social group that is becoming increasingly important in understanding health. Socioeconomic factors increase the likelihood of mental illness and addiction (Kahn, Wise, Kennedy, Kawachi, 2000; Oanh, Castro-Schilo, & Aguilar-Gaxiola, 2014). Taking these dimensions into account involves viewing health from a biopsychosocial perspective. This allows for the person, their biological makeup, cultural background, and experience of health, disease, or well-being to be the focus of health interventions (Fave, 2010).

With budget constraints on the delivery of health care, workforce development needs to be developed to promote mental health and well-being. Prevention is essential to change the growing demand for input from mental and addiction professionals. There is a need for the workforce to understand and target both states of mental health and mental illness.

In conclusion, the author asks the reader to consider two issues.

1. The knowledge and skills needed by the workforce to support the development of society's members who are resilient and able to cope with life stressors, and more importantly support each other to do so.
2. The timing of the use of resources. A young child's emotional well-being is dependent on the mental health of their caregivers and the wider environment they all live within (National Scientific Council on the Developing Child, 2008/2012). The first 1,000 days of a child's development is essential to adult well-being.

In the words of Frederick Douglass, an African American anti-slavery campaigner:

It is easier to build strong children than it is to repair broken men.

REFERENCES

Arden, J. (2010). Rewire your brain. Wiley. Hoboken, NJ.

Avery, H., Matheny, K., Robbins, A., & Jacobson, T. (2003). Health care providers' training, perceptions and practices regarding stress and health outcomes. *Journal of the National Medication Association, 95*(9), 833–838. PMID:14527051

Barker, P. (2009). *Psychiatric and mental health nursing: The craft of caring* (2nd ed.). London, UK: Hodder, Arnold.

Benner, P., Leonard, V., & Day, L. (2010). *Educating nurses: A call for radical transformation*. San Francisco, CA: Jossey-Bass.

Brain Wave Trust Aotearoa. (2015). Retrieved from www.brainwave.org.nz

Carruthers, C., & Hood, C. (2004). The power for the positive: Leisure and well-being. *Therapeutic Recreation Journal, 38*(2), 225–245.

Chesterson, J. (2009). Mental health promotion and prevention. In P. Barker (Ed.), *Psychiatric and mental health nursing: The craft of caring* (2nd ed.; pp. 571–586). London, UK: Arnold.

Child Health. (2015). Retrieved from www.health.govt.nz

Cleary, M., & Carlo, J. (2006). Improving student learning in the mental health settings: The view of clinical stakeholders. *Nurse Education in Practice, 6*(3), 141–148. doi:10.1016/j.nepr.2005.11.003 PMID:19040869

Clinton, M., & Hazelton, M. (2000). Scoping mental health nursing education. *The Australian and New Zealand Journal of Mental Health Nursing, 9*(1), 2–10. doi:10.1046/j.1440-0979.2000.00155.x PMID:11271010

Collins, P., Insel, T., Chockalingam, A., Daar, A., & Maddox, Y. (2013). Grand challenges in global mental health: Integration in research, policy and practice. *PLoS Medicine, 10*(4), e1001434. doi:10.1371/journal.pmed.1001434 PMID:23637578

Corrigan, P.W. (2002). Testing social cognitive models of mental illness stigma: The Prairie state stigma studies. *Psychiatric Rehabilitation Models, 6*(2), 232-254. doi:org/10.1080/109734302084084434

Crawford-Williams, F., Fielder, A., Mikocka-Walus, A., & Esterman, A. (2015). A critical review of public health interventions aimed at reducing alcohol consumption and/or increasing knowledge among pregnant women. *Drug and Alcohol Review, 34*(2), 154–161. doi:10.1111/dar.12152 PMID:24840708

Durlak, J. & Wells, A. (1997). Primary prevention mental health programs for children and adolescents: A meta-analytical review. *American Journal of Community Psychology, 25*(2), 115-152. doi:org/10.1023/a:1024654026640

Emrich, K., Thompson, T., & Moore, G. (2003). Positive attitude: An essential element for effective care of people with mental illnesses. *Journal of Psychosocial Nursing and Mental Health Services, 41*(5), 18–25. PMID:12743963

Ewles, L., & Simnett, I. (2004). *Promoting health: A practical guide.* London, UK: Baillere Tindal.

Fave, A. (2010). Development through disability. In G. Burns (Ed.), Happiness, healing and enhancement (pp. 88–123). Wiley. Hoboken, NJ

Giddens, J., & Brady, D. (2007). Rescuing nursing education form content saturation: The case for a concept based curriculum. *The Journal of Nursing Education, 46*(2), 65–68. PMID:17315564

Happell, B. (2010). Moving in circles: A brief history of reports and inquiries relation to mental health content in undergraduate nursing curricula. *Nurse Education Today, 30*, 643-648. doi.1016/jnedt.2009.12.108

Kahn, R., Wise, P., Kennedy, B., & Kawachi, I. (2000). State income inequality, household income and maternal mental and physical health: Cross sectional national survey. *British Medical Journal, 321*, 1311-1315. doi:org/10.1136/bjsm.34.1.73

Laverack, G. (2005). *Health promotion practice: Power and empowerment.* London, UK: Sage.

Matua Raki. (2012). *Brief intervention guide. Addressing risk and harm related to alcohol, tobacco, and other drugs and gambling*. Wellington, New Zealand: Matua Raki.

Matua Raki & Te Pou. (2013). *Te whare o tiki – Coexisting problems knowledge and skills framework.* Wellington, New Zealand: Matua Raki and Te Pou.

McMurray, A., & Clendon, J. (2011). *Community health and wellness: Primary health care in practice* (4th ed.). Sydney, Australia: Mosby Elsevier.

Mental Health Commission. (2012). *Blueprint II Improving mental health and wellbeing for all New Zealanders.* Wellington, New Zealand: Mental Health Commission.

Ministry of Health. (2008). *Let's get real: Real skills for people working in mental health and addiction.* Wellington, New Zealand: Ministry of Health.

Ministry of Health. (2011). *Healthy beginnings: Developing perinatal and infant mental health services in New Zealand.* Wellington: Ministry of Health.

Ministry of Health. (2015). *Supporting parents healthy children, supporting parents with mental illness and addiction and their children, A guideline for mental health and addiction services*. Wellington, New Zealand: Ministry of Health.

Moxham, L., McCann, T., Usher, K., Farrell, G., & Crooks, P. (2011). Mental health nursing in pre-registration nursing curricula. A national report. *International Journal of Mental Health Nursing, 20*(4), 232-236. doi:10.111. /j1447-0349-0349.2010. 00735.x

National Scientific Council on the Developing Child. (2004). *Children's emotional development is built in to the architecture of their brains: Working paper No 9*. Retrieved from http://www.developingchild.net

National Scientific Council on the Developing Child. (2007). *A science-based framework for early childhood policy: Using evidence to improve outcomes in learning, behavior, and health for vulnerable children*. Retrieved from http://www.developingchild.harvard.edu

National Scientific Council on the Developing Child. (2008/2012). *Establishing a level foundation for life: Mental health begins in early childhood: Working paper No 6* (Updated ed.). Retrieved from http://www.developingchild.harvard.edu

National Scientific Council on the Developing Child. (2010). *Persistent fear and anxiety can affect young children's learning and development. Working paper No 9*. Retrieved from http://www.develpingchild.net

New Zealand College of Mental Health Nurses. (2012). Standards of practice for mental health nursing in Aotearoa New Zealand (Standards No. 3rd ed.). Wellington, New Zealand: Te Maramatanga New Zealand College of Mental Health Nurses.

O'Sullivan, L. (2015). *The good doctor: Breaking the rules, making a difference*. Auckland, New Zealand: Penguin.

Oanh, L., Castro-Schilo, L., & Aguilar-Gaxiloa, S. (2014). Determinants of mental health and self-rated health: A model of socioeconomic status neighborhood safety and physical activity. *Research and Practice, 44*(9), 1734–1740. doi:10.2105/AJPH.2014.302003 PMID:25033151

Patterson, C., Curtis, J., & & Reid, A. (2008). Skills, knowledge, and attitudes expected of a newly graduated mental health nurse in an inpatient setting. *International Journal of Mental Health Nursing, 17*, 410-418. doi:101111/j.1447-0349,29-008. 00572.x

Pender, N., Murdaugh, C., & Parsons, M. (2006). *Health promotion in nursing practice*. Prentice Hall.

Perry, B., & Hambrick, E. (2008). The neurosequential model of therapeutics. *Reclaiming Children & Youth, 17*(3), 38-43. Retrieved from http://www.reclaiming.com

Roberts, D. (2013). *Psychosocial nursing care: A guide to nursing the whole person*. Berkshire, UK: Open Press.

Shonkoff, J., & Phillips, D. (Eds.). (2000). *From Neurons to neighborhood: The science of early childhood development*. Washington, DC: National Academy Press.

Southwick, S. M., & Charney, D. S. (2012). The science of resilience: Implications for the prevention and treatment of depression. *Science, 338*(6103), 79–82. doi:10.1126/science.1222942 PMID:23042887

Spence, D., Garrick, H., & McKay, M. (2012). Re building the foundations major renovations to the mental health component of an undergraduate nursing curriculum. *Journal of Mental Health Nursing*, 409-18. doi.111/j.1447-0349.201100806

Stuhlmiller, C. (2005). Rethinking mental health nursing education in Australia: A case for direct entry. *International Journal of Mental Health Learning*, *14*(3), 156–160. doi:10.1111/j.1440-0979.2005.00374.x PMID:16181151

Tanner, C. (2008). Thinking like a nurse: Research based model of clinical judgement in nursing. *The Journal of Nursing Education*, *45*(6), 204–2011. PMID:16780008

The Werry Centre. (2008). *Real skills plus: A competency framework for the infant, child and youth mental health and alcohol and other drug workforce*. Auckland, New Zealand: Werry Centre.

Thorne, S. (2006). Nursing education: Key issues for the 21st century. *Nurse Education Today*, *26*(8), 614–621. doi:10.1016/j.nedt.2006.07.010 PMID:17028072

Tratnack, S., ONeill, C., & Graham, P. (2011). Immersion experience in undergraduate psychiatric mental health nursing. *The Journal of Nursing Education*, *50*(9), 532–535. doi:10.3928/01484834-20110531-02 PMID:21627052

Vimpani, G. (2001). Health inequalities the seeds are sown in childhood, what about the remedies? In J. Dixon & B. Douglas (Eds.), *The social origins of health and well-being* (pp. 3–24). Melbourne, Australia: Cambridge University Press.

Wallis, N. (2015). Born to connect: How love grows babies' brains. *Porse Growing Little Minds at Home*. Retrieved from www.porse.co.nz

Western Institute of Technology Taranaki. (2012). *Program document for Bachelor of nursing*. New Plymouth, New Zealand: Western Institute of Technology.

Wilson, R. (2014). *Neuroscience for councilors*. London: Jessica Kingsley Publishers.

World Health Organization. (2001). *The world health report mental health: New understanding, new hope*. Geneva, Switzerland: WHO.

World Health Organization. (2007). *Atlas nurses in mental health*. Geneva, Switzerland: WHO.

World Health Organization. (2014). *Mental disorders fact sheet N396*. Geneva, Switzerland: WHO.

Young, H. (2011). *The Cardiff Model, Effective NHS contributes to violence prevention*. Retrieved from www.alchollearningcentre.org.uk

KEY TERMS AND DEFINITIONS

Addiction: Includes a wide range of behaviors but the connecting point is that the dopamine pathways involved in addiction are sculptured during childhood development.

Biopsychosocial: This implies that health and well-being are influenced by the complex relationship between biological factors especially a person's stress responses and the environment including cultural beliefs and the person's worldview. All aspects of the person's life, past and present, are influenced by subjective feelings influenced by emotional states.

Dyad: The person who spends the most time with a baby, providing a safe secure environment where because the adult is attuned to the baby all the babies' needs are met in a way that allows the baby to be as stress free as possible. Eye contact, touch, voice, rocking all provide that baby with an attachment that will form the basis of relationship building and optimal brain development to carry across the life span. This relationship is essential in the first 18 months.

Health: Often measured by mortality and life expectancy and the absence of illness. Increasingly well-being is being considered part of health and needs to be present to be healthy.

Illness: Related to symptomology and the effects these have on a person's well-being; this can be a chronic or an acute state. Illness is generally measured by signs and symptoms with diagnosis being applied accordingly by professionals.

Mental Health: More than the absence of illness, health includes being able to maximize potentials of life, having the resilience and relationships to cope with stressors or life crisis. The foundations are laid down during the first 1,000 days.

Mental Illness: The labels attached to symptomology that affects a person's ability to maintain mental health.

Modern Apprenticeship Nursing Curriculum: A nursing education that is based on clinical practice as in a traditional apprenticeship. Learning is organized and stepped in a way to transfer knowledge to practice in a timely way. The educational pedagogies that support the curriculum are based on an active learning environment where nursing learning is based on noticing, interpreting, responding, and reflecting like a nurse.

Stress: The physiological response to the environment and is controlled by the brain. Stress has implications for addiction, mental and physical health.

Resilience: Defined as the ability of a person to cope with adversity. Ten factors have a role in resilience, these include: a realistic optimistic attitude, facing fears, moral compass, religion and spirituality, social support, resilient role models, physical fitness, brain fitness, cognitive and emotional flexibility, and meaning and purpose in life. Stress experience and management along with genetics play a central role in the development of resilience. Those that are resilient, take personal reasonability to a life of purpose and growth.

Toxic Stress: Physiological responses to stress are needed to develop and keep safe, and if these are moderate or short lived in response to uncomfortable experiences they are part of healthy brain development. However, if the body's stress management system is not deactivated by a supporting environment the neurochemicals produced have a detrimental effect on the developing brain. This may affect the person across the life span from mental and physical health and addiction perspective in a negative way.

Well-Being: Based on an individual's values and beliefs and what makes them feel happy. There is a complex interplay between, genetics, environment, culture, personal circumstances, life events, culture, personality style, goals, and resilience. Those that report high life satisfaction or well-being are optimistic with positive social networks and relationships.

Chapter 10
Mental Health Support Workers: An Evolving Workforce

Julia L. Hennessy
Wellington Institute of Technology, New Zealand

Max Abbott
Auckland University of Technology, New Zealand

Liz Smythe
Auckland University of Technology, New Zealand

Frances A. Hughes
International Council of Nurses, Switzerland

ABSTRACT

This chapter provides the background for policy setting, educational preparation, and emergence of mental health support workers (MHSWs) in New Zealand and examines the work they do in mental health services. New Zealand formally introduced the MHSW role in the early 1990's to provide non-clinical services for mental health consumers or clients through either hospital or community-based services. The work MHSWs undertake and their relationship with other health professionals is discussed. Also discussed, is the relationship that MHSWs have with mental health consumers/clients and the attributes that the MHSW brings to the relationship. Consideration is given to the debate as to whether the role of the MHSW should be regulated, what it means to be considered a health professional, and the possibilities of expanding the scope of practice for MHSWs.

INTRODUCTION

In New Zealand the overall rates of psychiatric hospitalisation started to decline from the mid-1940s. However it was not until the late 1970s that the deinstitutionalization of large hospitals gathered momentum and total patient numbers fell appreciably (M. Abbott & Kemp, 1993; Haines & Abbott, 1985). Within the policy framework for the transition from hospital to community-based services limited attention was paid to the type of workforce needed to provide the new service design. The Central Regional Health Authority[1] produced a service implementation document *A Better Life* (Central Regional Health Authority, 1994), this set out the process for deinstitutionalization for the central region. While this document articulated a forward thinking approach it failed to identify the need to have an appropriate workforce to implement the policy shift. Services were moved from an institutional setting into the community with much of the support services required to be delivered by mental health support workers (MHSWs).

DOI: 10.4018/978-1-5225-1874-7.ch010

DeSouza (1997, p. 3) suggests that the role of the MHSW had evolved "in recognition of the gaps in community care provision", yet the nature of the work they do within the New Zealand health sector is largely unknown. New Zealand's health system is predominately funded through taxes, with 20 District Health Boards (DHBs) funding and delivering a range of primary, secondary, and tertiary health services, with policy direction for the funding being set by the Ministry of Health. MHSWs are primarily employed by non-government organizations (NGOs), however they are also employed within clinical acute or rehabilitation settings within DHB clinical services.

The Mental Health Foundation (n.d) described MHSWs as:

...non-clinicians who work with people with mental illness. The mental health support workforce is mainly employed in the non-government community support services sector. They provide support and practical assistance and deliver rehabilitation services or programmes that facilitate the recovery process for people experiencing serious mental illness or emotional distress.

This chapter will explore the manner in which the role of MHSW emerged and then go on to describe how the role is portrayed. Insights are drawn from Hennessy's (2015a) doctoral study, and other related literature.

A doctoral study by Hennessy, supervised by the co-authors, provides the foundation for this chapter. The study used an Appreciative Inquiry approach to reveal the work undertaken by MHSWs; and how this work contributed to mental health services and the well-being of mental health consumers.

BACKGROUND

The decade of the 1990s saw major policy changes which impacted on mental health services in New Zealand. *Looking Forward: Strategic Directions for the Mental Health Services* (Ministry of Health, 1994), was one of a number of plans by the Ministry of Health. This was followed by the *National Mental Health Plan, Moving Forward: The National Mental Health Plan for More and Better Services* (Ministry of Health, 1997). The first of these, *Looking Forward* (1994) saw the beginning of an approach that set benchmarks and targets for mental health service delivery to the population:

In New Zealand, benchmarks of 3 per cent have been established for the general adult population (and their families) and for youth (and their families). Benchmarks have yet to be set for other groups within the general population – the most important of which are children (and their families) older people, and those who require alcohol and drug treatment. (Ministry of Health, 1994, p. 7)

The policy changes and the move to community-based care required the closure of large psychiatric hospitals placing mental health consumers or service users[2] in either supported accommodation or in their own home with home-based support provided. This policy direction was generally accepted by most within the mental health sector including mental health consumers. What was absent from the planning was a requirement for training and education of a workforce required to deliver the services. Although Knapp et al. (1990) suggested that closure or downsizing of psychiatric hospitals provided a means to generate large savings in health care, Armitage (1994) provided a cautionary perspective by suggesting that moving psychiatric patients into the community was not a cheap alternative to inpatient care.

In the policy document *Looking Forward* (Ministry of Health, 1994), it was acknowledged that the process of community care had been relatively unplanned and that "mental health institutions were not well funded in the first place. As well, not enough funds were redirected to community services to deal with the increasing numbers of patients who were being transferred to community care" (Ministry of Health, 1994, p. 1). *Looking Forward* (Ministry of Health, 1994) also identified a number of requirements to ensure the success of community care; although it did suggest that specialist mental health services for people in the community, in their homes or in hospital, ought to be increased, it did not identify the need to develop another, more specialized, type of care provider (Ministry of Health, 1994). Studies by Abbott (1989ab) examined the results of a national survey of community mental health services. This study identified the perceived gaps and needs from different stakeholder perspectives.

In the early 1990s the MHSW emerged to meet service needs in a haphazard fashion. Contributing to this random approach was a lack of consistency in determining the educational preparation and service expectations resulting in differing models of mental health support work. At this time the majority of MHSWs did not have qualifications nor was there an agreed understanding of their roles and functions. Many educational providers worked with their local mental health services to develop local qualifications to fill the newly created gap in non-registered mental health service provision.

The Health Workforce Advisory Committee (2002a) undertook a stocktake of issues facing the health workforce, including its capacity to manage the strategic shift from institutional care to community-based mental health services. Data used by the committee saw MHSWs placed in the unregistered health workforce category and described as the part of the "workforce which provides support with everyday things" (Health Workforce Advisory Committee, 2002a, p. 88). The stocktake identified that the MHSW provided "support and delivers rehabilitation services or programmes that facilitate the recovery process for people experiencing serious mental or emotional distress" (Health Workforce Advisory Committee, 2002a, p. 124). Twelve percent of MHSWs in the report identified as Māori and 3.2% as Pasifika. This meant this particular workforce had the second highest proportion of Māori staff, surpassed only by alcohol and drug workers at 23% (Health Workforce Advisory Committee, 2002a). The need to train an ethnically appropriate workforce was recognised by the policy makers as "there are few Māori mental health workers. Training programmes are needed in all areas of mental health – in particular, to increase the number of Māori who can provide community mental health services" (Ministry of Health, 1994, p. 9).

Moving ahead nearly a decade, the unregistered mental health workforce had gained significant traction and visibility. By 2012 the importance of the MHSWs was realized when *Rising to the Challenge: The Mental Health and Addiction Service Development Plan* (Ministry of Health, 2012, p. 61), stated there is a need for the "strengthening use of the non-regulated workforce".

Mental Health Workforce Development

Looking Forward (Ministry of Health, 1994) identified a number of requirements to ensure the success of community services. This document however failed to identify the need to develop another type of service provider, although it did suggest that specialist mental health services for people in the community, in their homes, or in hospital ought to be increased (Ministry of Health, 1994); a significant omission when viewed retrospectively. Nonetheless, the NGO sector and with it MHSWs grew as qualifications were developed and positions made available.

In 2001, the then Minister of Health, the Right Honourable Annette King, addressed a MHSWs forum held at Hutt Valley District Health Board (HVDHB). She stated that "the National Certificate in Mental

Health Support Work was one of the most significant achievements in the last few years" (King, 2001). She went on to suggest that the national certificate was a vehicle through which the Māori workforce was being up-skilled and further, that government commitment to the ongoing development of the qualification was evident by the continued funding of the standards setting body and the goals set out in *Tauawhitia te Wero – Meeting the Challenges: National Mental Health and Addiction Workforce Development Plan 2000-2005* (Ministry of Health, 2005). By 2002 the *Mental Health (Alcohol and Other Drugs) Workforce Development Framework* (Ministry of Health, 2002) recognized the need to ensure access for MHSWs to the National Certificate in Mental Health (Mental Health Support Work) (Level 4), and to expand the range of training for support workers. The Health Workforce Advisory Committee (2002b, p. 125) recognized MHSWs as a separate occupational group and indicated that "there is a need for an increase of over 600 support workers to meet the increased service needs outlined in the Blueprint".

National Qualification for Mental Health Support Workers

The Ministry of Health (1997) identified in its policy document *Moving Forward* the need to have a workforce that was educated in a nationally consistent way with transferrable qualifications. By 1998, the National Certificate in Community Support Work (Mental Health) (Level 4) had been developed by a standards setting body accountable to the New Zealand Qualifications Authority (NZQA), with funding for the development coming from the four Regional Health Authorities. For the first time in the history of mental health services in New Zealand, a national qualification was available to support the education of the unregistered mental health workforce.

Platform (2007), an umbrella service supporting mental health NGOs in New Zealand, described the National Certificate in Mental Health (Mental Health Support Work) (Level 4) as an entry-level qualification for staff working in the newly developing NGO sector. With approximately one-third of mental health expenditure going into this sector, it was becoming one of the largest NGO mental health sectors in the developed world (Ministry of Health, 2004). Platform (2008, p. 2) also stated that "creating a new support work occupational grouping has been a great workforce achievement and has been specific to New Zealand innovation". Once the qualification was developed it was placed on the New Zealand Qualifications Framework (NZQF) for educators to deliver. When first developed the purpose of the national qualification was to educationally prepare MHSWs for employment in community mental health services, that is residential or home-based services. However there emerged a trend of employing MHSWs into other areas such as acute and rehabilitation services, a trend which has continued.

Both the Mental Health Commission (1998) and the Health Funding Authority (2000) prioritized the need for education and training of the mental health workforce, which now included MHSWs. The introduction of the MHSW role offered the opportunity to provide a different model of service delivery, one that freed other health professionals to take on additional, more complex roles within the service continuum. This would enable those health professionals prepared at degree level to divest themselves of tasks that were more in keeping with the educational preparation of the support worker and thus provide health care that was commensurate with their higher level of educational preparation. The Mental Health Commission (1998) recognized the need to invest in training for MHSWs as they saw many organizations resorting to employing untrained staff to deliver the increased volume of services being funded. The Mental Health Commission (1988) also identified that there were insufficient qualified support workers to deliver the expanded services.

The Mental Health Commission funded the report *Labour Market Constraints Affecting the Mental Health Sector* (Mental Health Commission, 2004). Although this report focused mainly on the clinical workforce it did acknowledge that "there is a dearth of data about the non-professional workers in the mental health workforce" (Mental Health Commission, 2004, p. 43).

Mental Health Support Worker

Studies undertaken in New Zealand with a focus specifically on MHSWs remain limited. The Mental Health Support Work Advisory Group commissioned three evaluative pieces of research: *Evaluation of the National Certificate in Mental Health* (Case Consulting, 2003), *Sei Tapu - O le Ala o le Ola An Evaluation of the National Certificate in Mental Health* (Annadale & Instone, 2004), and *Te Puawaitanga O Te Oranga Hinengaro* (Rangiaho, 2003). The focus of each piece of research was to evaluate the effectiveness of the National Certificate in Mental Health (Mental Health Support Work) (Level 4) from a different perspective, rather than evaluating the nature of the support work provided by MHSWs. The findings from the first report *Evaluation of the National Certificate in Mental Health* by Case Consulting (2003), were generally positive about mental health support work. However, the report identified that even though MHSWs were working towards a national qualification, there were significant regional variations in what was being taught. This report found the diversity of the work and the breadth of the roles meant the qualification was designed in such a way that the learning outcomes and graduate profile was narrower than the service reality. Māori were reported as noting that the qualification was so broad that its applicability to kaupapa Māori services[3] was restrictive. It is of note that Māori-specific services were not part of the service configuration when the national certificate was first developed in 1998. Furthermore, other health professionals interacting with MHSWs did not understand the support worker role. Concerns were raised by some respondents in regards to *qualification creep*, whereas others saw the need for a diploma level qualification. MHSWs were positive about an *earn and learn* structure so they could maintain their income. However, some respondents did not see the need for a qualification and felt that MHSWs only needed life skills and experience.

In the second evaluation report examining Pasifika MHSWs undertaken by Annadale and Instone (2004, p. 1), the key findings were that education provided a positive pathway for Pasifika mental health workers and went so far as to suggest "the health sector looks to mental health as a leader in workforce development". The report proposed the view that language competency is as valuable as other required competencies when working with Pasifika people and also identified other attributes such as: passion for the work, caring about people, listening, and involving the family in the person's recovery as critical. Another important finding was that while "there has been limited study done on the impact that community support workers have had on the mental health sector" (Annadale & Instone, 2004, p. 5), it was clear that "anecdotal evidence suggests that their contribution has been significant" (p. 5). Additionally the report recommended that there needed to be a qualification at levels higher than the current level 4 certificate.

Finally, *Te Puawaitanga o Te Oranga Hinengaro* (Rangiaho, 2003) found that Māori were generally positive about the national certificate as a qualification, but saw areas for improvement and suggested this could happen at the time the qualification was reviewed. One important point identified was the preference for the streaming of the qualification into separate Māori standards. The report also suggested that additional qualifications be developed to meet the needs of Māori progressing from a diploma to a degree. A number of recommendations were made in regard to what needed to change within the national certificate when it next underwent a review.

"New Zealand has one of the largest mental health and addiction NGO sectors in the world, delivering a wide range of community-based support services that account for one-third of the total national mental health expenditure" (Platform, n.d., p. 2). Rapp and Chamberlain (1985) believed the lack of community-based services and appropriately trained personnel had provided significant obstacles in the delivery of these types of services. Coop (2006) described mental health services as an area of health that was poorly understood by the public at large, including the role of MHSWs.

The Situation in 2014

A mental health and addictions stocktake of adult mental health services was undertaken by Te Pou (2015). This study found that MHSWs made up nearly one-third (31%), of the total adult mental health and addiction workforce, ahead of nurses (28%), the next largest group. These two groups "together comprise more than half the adult mental health and addictions workforce" (Te Pou, 2015, p. 45).

Models of Support Work

As mental health services have evolved, new categories of MHSWs have emerged. These include:

- Support worker roles for older persons with mental health issues
- Peer support workers (PSWs)
- Support time and recovery (STR) workers
- Primary mental health workers (PMHSWs).

Support Work for Older Person's Services

A study undertaken by McCrae, Banerjee, Murray, Prior, and Silverman (2008) examined the area of older person mental health services and its relationship with support workers. This study found the lack of role clarity caused confusion with other members of the health team with support workers reporting "their input was heavily influenced by professional practitioners' understanding of the role" (McCrae et al., 2008, p. 738). This lack of understanding then influenced the responsibilities they were given. The support workers reported they were "confident that they were making a valuable contribution to the services" (McCrae et al., 2008, p. 739); however, there was a mixed view of this from other members of the professional team. The other findings were that the ambiguity of the role had led to confusion with other health professionals and "new roles cannot be presumed to mean the same thing to all staff" (McCrae et al., 2008, p. 741). These findings are consistent with those of other writers when examining the role of support workers and the interface with other health professionals.

Peer Support Workers (PSWs)

The PSWs role is based on the premise that mental health and addiction problems "must be understood through the perspectives of those directly affected by them" (Tse, See, Wong, Kan, & Kwok, 2014, p. 211). The formal recognition of people with lived experience of mental health and addiction problems and recovery who are employed into the role of PSW is a recent development in mental health services in New Zealand. The study by Tse et al. (2014) explored aspects of this emerging workforce. Tse et al. (2014, p. 217) found there needed to be a relationship between "service providers and policy planners" and in order for PSWs to be successful in their role they required training that was "*learn as you practice* versus a set curriculum". The U.S. has recognized certified PSWs through a training programme that has resulted in this group of health workers being able to seek reimbursement through Medicaid and has allowed certified PSWs to work as "professional peer support workers" (Tse et al., 2014, p. 216). This suggests the need for training. An Australian study by Nestor and Galletly (2008) described a PSW as someone who brings "their experiential knowledge and understanding of mental illness". The findings from their study were that "[PSWs] can work in successful partnerships with other health professionals" (Nestor & Galletly, 2008, p. 347); however, the study identified that "ongoing support and supervision for PSW is essential and training programmes are needed for those people who are interested in qualifying as PSWs" (Nestor & Galletly, 2008, p. 347), again identifying the important contributors to professionalize.

A New Zealand study of PSW practice was undertaken by Scott, Doughty, and Kahi (2011) with the main key findings noting that while PSW is of a variable quality, so too was the available training. The study did not support a compulsory national qualification for PSW, instead arguing that adequate funding must be made available for supervision and training of PSWs. The study also recommended that "specific training in peer support needs to be offered to clinicians" (Scott et al., 2011, p. 127). Competencies for PSWs and a formal qualification in peer support have since been developed (Te Pou, 2014).

PSW in the Area of Addictions

People with experience of addiction problems have been supporting others for nearly 80 years in New Zealand (Alcoholics Anonymous, n.d.). A study by Norman et al. (2008) examining the PSW role in treatment for people who use injectable drugs was undertaken in Australia and identified the attributes that consumers found most helpful. These included: the ability of the PSW to empathise; being non-judgemental; able to listen; and to provide good advice. The concerns raised by the consumers in respect to PSW were issues over trustworthiness and "professional ramifications" for unprofessional behaviour (Norman et al., 2008, p. 5). This is an area that requires further consideration.

Support, Time, and Recovery (STR) workers

The introduction of the STR worker for mental health services in Britain in the late 1990s was one of the "more radical ideas to ensure that the workforce can be secured and sustained to deliver a mental health service fit for the 21st century" (Allock & Hollingsworth, 2009, p. 12). The introduction of STR resulted from the U.K.'s National Service Framework, which sought to introduce a new type of worker into mental health services (Allock & Hollingsworth, 2009). Allock and Hollingsworth (2009, p. 14) suggest the introduction of the STR worker has been "hugely rewarding… [and] the difference it has made is significant". The evaluation of this new workforce identified a number of themes these were: remuneration disparity of STR workers both within teams and across different services; the need for future career options; for a supportive infrastructure; education and training; and greater understanding of job titles and role clarity. This study also identified the importance of other staff within mental health services understanding these new and emerging roles. This would help to ensure existing staff did not have concerns of "their own roles being eroded"(Allock & Hollingsworth, 2009, p. 16).

Huxley, Evan, Beresford, Davidson, and King (2009) undertook a study that evaluated the relationship between STR workers in mental health services in England and people who accessed those services. The role was defined as, spending negotiated time with people, providing appropriate support, so aiding their recovery; having a specified education and training pathway (in practice this has taken a variety of forms); work in a variety of statutory or non-statutory service settings and across traditional service boundaries; supervised as part of a team; focused on practical help, promoting independence and integration into the community (Huxley et al., 2009, p. 100). The study's finding showed there were inconsistencies in the introduction of this new workforce, which was mainly composed of middle-aged people and included some people who had lived experience of mental health problems. The study found the service people received from the STR workers was of a superior quality (Huxley et al., 2009) compared to the service they had previously received from other health professionals. Other health professionals interviewed expressed concern about STR workers "breaching the boundaries between professional help and personal friendship" (Huxley et al., 2009, p. 113). The STR worker or the people accessing services did not support this concern, rather they reported an awareness of the boundaries and made "conscious efforts to avoid them" (Huxley et al., 2009, p. 113). Further questions raised in the study were around whether the attributes identified as positive by people accessing services can be taught or whether they are innate in workers who are drawn to this type of employment. This study and similar studies have shown that people place a high value on "the nature and quality of the relationship with the worker in social care practice and the importance of positive human qualities in workers" (Huxley et al., 2009, p. 114).

An earlier study by James, Chadwick, and Rushforth (2006) provided the rationale for the development of a new category of worker in mental health as being not only to look at new models of delivery but also noting that "frontline professionally qualified staff were burdened by increasing workloads" (James et al., 2006, p. 31). The introduction of the STR worker would "promote recovery and social inclusion/community engagement as being implicit in the role of the STR worker" (James et al., 2006, p. 31). The initial concerns associated with this new health worker related to terms and conditions within the employment contract, ensuring service users were involved in the planning and delivery of services, as well as target driven managers, and the need for education and training (James et al., 2006).

Primary Mental Health Work Role

A study by Hickey, Kramer, and Garralda (2010) investigated the role of primary MHSWs (PMHSWs) and found that, despite the expansion of this workforce, very little research had been undertaken to determine its effectiveness. This study specifically focused on MHSWs employed in child and adolescent mental health services. One of the key aims for the introduction of this role was to "broaden the range of children and adolescents accessing mental health services" (Hickey et al., 2010, p. 26). The study reported that the numbers of PMHSW had rapidly expanded with the most likely referrers being general practitioners (Hickey et al., 2010). The study also found that key to the role was flexibility and where the support worker was employed by a clinical service, those relationships were strong within those services; this is similar to the findings for those employed, in a primary health service. Positive job satisfaction was linked to good working relationships. In addition, the study found that no matter where the support worker was employed, there was a need for interagency understanding and this would benefit from training (Hickey et al., 2010). This need for continued training not only for the MHSWs but also for other health professionals to understand the role was considered essential for the role.

WORKING EFFECTIVELY: POSITIVE CHARACTERISTICS OF MENTAL HEALTH SUPPORT WORKERS

Unregistered roles within mental health services have continued to evolve. The emergence of differing roles has been described in the previous section. This section examines what it is that MHSWs bring to the relationship.

Hennessy, Abbott and Hughes, authors of this chapter, were all involved in the development of New Zealand's mental health services. Hennessy in particular has a deep interest in how the role of the MHSW was being enacted. Using an Appreciative Inquiry approach, and supervised by her co-authors, she undertook a doctoral study exploring the nature of the work of MHSWs throughout New Zealand. This involved interviewing 18 MHSWs and 16 stakeholders (including PSWs). The study identified a number of characteristics displayed by MHSWs that were valued by people with lived experience of mental health problems. These characteristics include the nature of the relationship, positive support, care, hope, trust, faith, happiness, and intrinsic fulfilment.

Appreciative Inquiry's roots can be found in post-modernist European philosophy. The foundation on which Appreciative Inquiry is built is the crafting of an environment so that the opportunity for individual stories to be told enables "a unique climate for collective dreaming where the forces of ridicule and repression are momentarily suspended" (Bushe, 1998, p. 2).

What do Mental Health Support Workers do?

Hennessy's (2015) research uses the term *life ballast* as a way to describe the stability and ordinariness that MHSWs bring into the relationships with people they work with. This creates evenness within the lives of people with lived experience of mental health problems (Hennessy, 2015). This study (Hennessy, 2015a) found that MHSWs:

- **Use Self:** The importance of using one's self in order to build and maintain relationships and rapport with people; with this relationship built on reciprocated and mutual respect.
- **Create Choice**: Able to work with people in order to provide the space to enable them to make choices; this frequently requires the MHSW to advocate on behalf of people.
- **Keep People Connected**: Have a role of keeping people connected as appropriate with their families, community, friends, and significant others.
- **Know the Consumer:** Build rapport with people in order to gain trust and that by acquiring trust the relationship continues to develop.
- **Create Ordinariness:** Bring an ordinariness to the relationship, those everyday conversations that take place in every walk of life enables people to be connected to part of an ordinary world.

The Relationship

Hennessy's research (2015a) revealed that people who experience mental health problems have a number of services provided for them by an assortment of health professionals within a variety of settings. A feature of the MHSW's relationship with people with lived experience that is not shared by others in the mental health sector is the closeness of the relationship. This closeness is a result of the time that the MHSW spends with the person and takes place in a number of settings including the person's home.

This makes the identification of desirable characteristics important when employing MHSWs. These are positive characteristics that educators and trainers need to build on in order to get the best out of MHSWs. This will ensure that even better services are provided to people. MHSWs bring to the relationship the characteristics associated with hope, trust, faith, happiness, and fulfilment; they are able to create space for mental health consumers.

Spending Time, Creating Space

A key finding in Hennessy's (2015a) study related to the time and space that is created by the MHSW for the benefit of people with mental health problems. MHSWs have the time to spend with the person; the interactions that occur during that time are important as they bring another dimension to the total health care and support being provided. This aspect of their role enables MHSWs to be the eyes and ears for the clinical team. In order for mental health services to maximise these benefits, MHSWs need to be seen as integral to the services provided to people, not separate and ignored.

MHSWs create space through the use of time. They bring support mechanisms to the relationship with people with mental health problems, which enable them to manage the provision of care. This type of relationship is one of closeness. It places a high emotional demand on the worker, particularly as it frequently operates in the person's environment. That closeness is a relationship favoured by people with mental health problems. It is not only founded on the traits that people value but also relates to the longevity of the relationship, which can remain over years rather than months. They spoke about the opportunities they create for people so the person's hopes for the future can be realized.

Positive Support

The importance of relationship for people with mental health problems is evident in other research findings. Evans and Moltzen's (2000) study identified six characteristics for effective support for people in the community. These are acceptance, positive atmosphere, expectation of change, incidental learning, responsiveness, normalization, and educative functions. These findings were based on empirical evidence provided within a broad range of literature. The researchers found there was "a paucity of information on the support staff behaviors most habilitative for patients with PSMI (persistent and serious mental illness)" (Evans & Moltzen, 2000, p. 637). While this study posed the question "what would an ideal therapeutic environment look like?" (p. 642) and sought to be future focused, the language used in this study (for example, "patient") is very traditional and has the unintended consequence of disempowering the therapeutic relationship.

Aubry, Flynn, Gerber, and Dostaler (2005) undertook a study to identify the competencies that people considered were required by MHSWs. The study recruited 34 people with mental health problems and 34 MHSWs. It sought to differentiate the competencies required "prior to assuming the position versus those that could be learned on the job" (p. 352). Aubry et al. (2005) identified that the competencies required of a support worker before starting the job "involved mostly personal attributes and that these reflected individual qualities that are consonant with a respectful, optimistic, accepting and sincere approach". They observed the main requirement for MHSWs, once in employment, was the need to develop more skills, although they noted this requirement was not limited to any one discipline and support work generally drew its skills from a range of other disciplines (Aubry et al., 2005).

Care in the Relationship

Finfgeld-Connett (2007) explored the concept of caring in comparison with social support. While they primarily took a nursing focus, they found caring and social support are intrinsically linked concepts. They also suggested the precursor to caring is *professional maturity*, which is defined as a protective mechanism that provides the nurse with the ability to "cope with the routine stresses of clinical practice" (p. 60). However Finfgeld-Connett (2007) suggests that there is no evidence supporting the notion that social support requires professional maturity. It is for this reason that Finfgeld-Connett (2007, p. 60) defines social support as being provided by lay people and may include family members and suggests that social support is provided by "healthcare professionals only when lay providers are unable". Finfgeld-Connett's (2007) study suggests that social support falls into two categories, "emotional and instrumental" (p. 59) and that the situational context of the relationship is more important than professional expertise. The other characteristics identified were that "unconditional positive regard is highly valued along with reliable availability, mutuality and reciprocity" (p. 62). Finfgeld-Connett (2007, p. 65) also puts forward the view that "psychic growth is associated with caring, whereas a feeling of normalcy and decreased isolation are more common to social support" and that nurses are "urged to remember that they are not the preferred providers of social support" (Finfgeld-Connett, 2007, p. 65).

Millet (2011) extends the concept of care that occurs within professional relationships and suggests that "a living thing ought to be looked after or cared for simply because it exists as a living thing". The relationship MHSWs have with mental health consumers transcends beyond that of a professional relationship in the purist sense of the word; that is not to say their relationship is not professional but rather their relationship and the nature of that relationship is one of professional care.

Give Hope

In an early exploration, Deegan (1988, p. 11) argued the concept of recovery is synonymous with the "concept of hope". More recently, Deegan's research was considered by Adeponle, Whitley, and Kirmayer (2012). Their interpretation of the work suggests recovery is both individual and community focused with an aspiration for a fullness of life (Adeponle et al., 2012). This adds the dimension of hope when considering the concept of recovery.

Building Trust Relationships

While numerous studies have been undertaken regarding the relationship between other health professionals and "patients"[4], the literature regarding the relationship between MHSWs and mental health consumers is scarce.

A study undertaken by Verhaeghe and Bracke (2011), found people with mental health problems have a distrust of mental health professionals that is "due to stigma expectations and self-stigma despite an absence of any concrete negative reaction from other people". The study went on to suggest this sense of distrust by people of health professionals is one of the identified factors that "impedes the positive relationship between stigma expectations and satisfaction" (Verhaeghe & Bracke, 2011, p. 300). Thus indicating the stigma related to having a mental illness is a barrier for mental health professionals (including MHSWs) even before they engage with people.

A study of relationships by Gilburt, Rose, and Slade (2008), within an acute mental health inpatient unit, identified one of the main themes in attending to positive relationships was the concept of trust. Mental health consumers' "attribution of *trust* or *mistrust* was described only in relation to other staff" (p. 6). The attributes that people described in this study and used for those staff they saw as trustworthy were "described as being professional, able to manage situations in which the safety of patients was at risk, flexible, non-coercive, committed, and caring about patients" (p. 6). This study also identified a connection between trust and professionalism and those staff who fell short of the people's expectation of professionalism were deemed to be untrustworthy (Gilburt et al., 2008).

McDonald, Cox, Paterson, and Lafrenière (2008) investigated the trust within the relationships of health workers. The study found there was a strong, positive correlation between high levels of trust and the status of the health worker. However, the participants conveyed that although they did have a high level of trust associated with certain health workers this was not "blind trust" (McDonald et al., 2008, p. 39); the "creation of trust is a reciprocal process" (p. 40).

Faith

Illingworth (2008) identified that *trust* and *hope* have been extensively researched as key factors in developing a therapeutic relationship. However this study focused on the concept of *faith* in the therapeutic relationship. Illingworth (2008, p. 10) suggests:

Faith is not knowledge or a weak belief, but a conviction about that not yet proven. Faith is rational when based upon knowledge and comprehension of past experience. Faith, it could be suggested, is paradoxical as it is not certainty in the sense of unquestionable predictability, but is the certainty of the unknown.

When studying faith, Illingworth (2008, p. 11) suggests it "is not bound by time and space and does not need to be based on past experiences". Further examination of the concept of faith reveals proximity to recovery; aspirational and future-focused aspects of faith can enable this concept to be embedded into aspirational futures that can be created through Appreciative Inquiry. Illingworth (2008) described faith as something that sustains one's conviction that what humans are doing is worth doing; faith that our actual existence has meaning; and faith that our concern for others reflects the concerns of others. Faith allows people to transport the future into the present.

Within the context of mental health, the concept of faith should not be confused with religious beliefs related to faith. However, if faith is applied in the broadest sense it provides a nexus between faith as a religious belief and faith as a concept interconnected with hope and trust. Illingworth's (2008) study focused on mental health consumers having faith in others and only in part touched on faith within the context of religious beliefs.

Intrinsic Fulfilment

Recovery and strength-based approaches can be found in the work of Aristotle. Bostock's (2000) interpretation of Aristotle's work uses the word *eudaimonia* to suggest that this has a similar connotation to the concept that has been referred to as intrinsic fulfilment. Eudaimonia has been referred to as greater than an immediate state of happiness and "requires more than mere contentment and satisfaction" (Bostock, 2000, p. 7). Haybron (2008, p. 22) suggested that certain goals are explicit and the "eudaimonistic theories share a teleological structure, grounding well-being in ideals of nature-fulfilment: we flourish by fulfilling our natures". Haybron (2008) then suggested there is a meaningful level of convergence between self-fulfilment and happiness and this is a reflection of an individual's temperament. The concept of existential fulfilment is described by Tomic and Tomic (2011, p. 469) as "a way of life that is full of meaning and purpose". Diener and Lucas (2000) suggested there is an implied need to test whether *needs* have a high correlation to resources and therefore the greater the resource the more likely the level of fulfilment. However, they did not define what those resources were.

Happiness

A study by Haybron (2008) examined the concept of happiness from the point of how happiness matters. Haybron examined the eudaimonistic theories, interpreting them to mean that "we flourish by fulfilling our natures" (Haybron, 2008, p. 22). The approach taken by Haybron was to examine some of the earlier concepts related to happiness such as well-being, welfare, flourishing, and eudaimonia. Haybron (2008) suggested that living in conflict with who we are and what we want to be places people in this conflicted position and that these values are misplaced (Haybron, 2008).

The term *mood propensity* was introduced by Haybron (2008, p. 30) who defined this as "when one is happy, bad moods can still occur in response to negative events, but they are less likely and will tend to yield quickly to positive ones. This sort of emotional resilience is one of the great benefits of being happy". Here Haybron introduces the concept of resilience from an emotional perspective. Haybron then linked the concepts of happiness to that of self-fulfilment so that "happiness has intrinsic prudential value as an aspect of self-fulfilment" (Haybron, 2008, p. 47). The concept of self-fulfilment has a strong link to recovery and how recovery has an individual meaning for people with mental health problems.

Endorsing the Work

Hennessy (2015a) suggests the relationship between MHSW and people with mental health problems is key; when this relationship works, support work works. Borg and Kristiansen (2004) suggested a measure for defining the quality of the relationship is through the interactions between consumers and MHSWs. The right environment is created when services are less illness-focused, more person-centered and strength-based, which is achieved by "developing the roles and competencies of helpers and services in general, towards a more open perspective of what actually helps (and also what hinders) recovery" (Borg & Kristiansen, 2004, p. 501). MHSWs in Hennessy's (2015a) study spoke of the importance of having support from their managers and other service providers, and of the need for their employers to provide them with relevant training and supervision. This support enables the work of MHSWs to be validated and endorsed.

Working Alongside Colleagues

Another significant issue identified by Hennessy (2015a) was the area of inter and intra professionalization.

The manner in which MHSW work is focused is that of building a human to human relationship with clients. Hennessy's (2015a) participants spoke of the positive impact of their work with people. However, how they worked with other colleagues varied with the MHSWs often feeling their contribution was not valued by the wider team. Duckett (2005) argues the need for teamwork across disciplines in order to meet the demands of the health sector.

Other literature discusses inter-professional collaborative practice within the health and social service sector described by Nancarrow and Borthwick (2005) as both *interdisciplinary* and *intra-disciplinary*. Thus suggesting the need for expansion of the role of the discipline being examined but also expanding the roles of other disciplines. This requires an environment where inter-professional practice or "working alongside colleagues" is a natural evolution of the role of the MHSW. A study by Kinnair, Anderson, and Thorpe (2012) demonstrated the value of introducing inter-professional education into the curriculum for mental health nursing students as the ultimate aim is how this improves outcomes for people.

MHSWs have suggested they have variable relationships with clinical teams. They suggested this variability was due primarily to the other health professionals not understanding their role (Hennessy, 2015; McCrae et al., 2008). If not addressed, this lack of understanding will continue to create unnecessary barriers in an area of health that is under serviced and under resourced.

MHSWs believe their knowledge gained through being with people in settings other than clinical settings help to inform the wider clinical team. Inclusion of the MHSW in the multi-disciplinary team ensures a more holistic view and informed decisions can be made (Hennessy, 2015a).

ISSUES

In considering MHSWs and the staff who undertake these roles, consideration needs to be given to the shadow of neoliberalism which exists when examining mental health services. The tension plays out in the fundamental questioning of the rights and responsibilities of the state for people with mental health problems versus the rights and responsibilities of the individual to provide for their own health and social service care. These tensions become magnified in the mental health sector due to the "clash of ideologies" (Carney, 2008, p. 105) between medicalization and therapeutic interventions. A humanistic public and socially good approach is in tension with the neoliberalism philosophy.

The 1990s was the period of New Zealand's health reforms that witnessed the growth of NGOs in providing mental health services, but also saw a move away from state control of services to private service providers. Esposito and Perez (2014) support the view that neo-liberalism reaches far beyond policies and regulations, it is a "vision of the world in which all aspects of social, cultural, and economic life are shaped". Resulting from such views is the assumption that there are inefficiencies in the state system that are not found in the private system and that "free functioning of the market forces leads to a better utilization and allocation of resources" (McGregor, 2001, p. 83). This approach suggests "social equity, participative democracy, sustainability and economic growth" (McGregor, 2001, p. 83) are not interconnected but economic growth should be the overarching driver for policies. The conflict that then exists between the ideology of mental health services and MHSWs if taken from a neoliberalism view is the challenge in placing an economic and monetary value on MHSWs.

It could be viewed that if it were not for the low wages they receive, MHSWs would become an unaffordable commodity due to the amount of time they spend with clients. Furthermore, there is the issue of what they do with people with mental health problems. From a neoliberalism approach individuals are responsible for finding "their own solutions to their lack of health care" (McGregor, 2001, p. 84). From such a perspective it could be argued that clients need to find their own support people from within their own family and social circles. Ramon (2008, p. 121) suggests the neoliberalism movement takes away the collective responsibility towards the individual and has contributed "to the continuation of perceiving mental health service users as social and personal failures in the twenty-first century".

Generally governments in first world countries continue to maintain control of individuals through legislation while rationing resources, thereby creating unachievable barriers for "clinicians, consumers and carer interests to win the sufficient share of resources needed to realize the promise of dignified community based care of the mentally ill" (Carney, 2008, p. 111). This goes back to the heart of people having the rights of citizenship. While research findings tend to address questions of role and function, it is important to remember that mental health support work is enabled or constrained by political ideology.

CONSIDERATIONS

Being Professional

When the role of support worker was established many MHSWs viewed themselves as *professional*. However, Chambers (2006) suggests this was not a universally held view and that MHSWs were more likely to have a similar status to health care assistants, another unregistered health worker, by virtue that their educational preparation was not at degree level. This finding, which relates status and professionalism only with degree-prepared health workers, is supported by Sutcliffe (2006) and the Health Workforce Advisory Committee (2002a). Their findings identified MHSWs as feeling disempowered as the people they provide support too and are viewed by other health professionals as having a low status. This finding was supported in Hennessy's (2015a) study.

Being Regulated

The Health Practitioners Competence Assurance (HPCA) Act (2003), provides a framework for regulation of some health professionals in New Zealand, where it is considered there may be public safety issues. By the time the Act was passed, there were 15 groups of health professionals operating under it. One of the overarching principles of the legislation is the protection of the public receiving health care from health professionals; MHSWs are not a designated group under the Act. This does raise some important questions as to how the public is protected when care is delivered by an unregulated health care worker. Holloway, Baker, and Lumby (2009) reported there is an expectation by people that care providers are knowledgeable in assisting with their health care needs. While it is accepted that this principle was being applied to the profession of nursing, this could also be an expectation of MHSWs. The Health and Disability Commissioner Act (1994) provides some protection for those health practitioners who are not regulated under the HPCA Act (2003). Gilmore (2005) argues that workers who provide aspects of what is seen as nursing care and who work closely with nurses should be regulated and suggests competency standards are required to ensure practice boundaries are identified. While the National Certificate in Mental Health (Mental Health Support Work) (Level 4) is a competency-based programme, the mechanism in place to ensure ongoing competencies is generally through the contractual process of employment agreements. MHSWs provide support to some of the most vulnerable sections of our community, yet they are not regulated – this raises the question of whether they should be.

In a study of the healthcare support workforce, Griffiths and Robinson (2010) postulate the establishment of a professional body for otherwise unregulated healthcare workers facilitates guidance and support as well as contributing to the area of workforce planning. The MHSWs in Hennessy's (2015a) study were anxious to establish some form of professional identity and protection, a similar issue raised by unregulated workers in the aged care sector.

Expanded Boundaries

Abbott (1998), MacDonald (1995), and Burrage and Torstendahl (1990) identified that occupational conflict could occur in the workplace as a result of emerging health professionals, particularly for aspirational health professionals who were seeking to legitimize their roles. Nancarrow and Borthwick (2005) suggest "disciplinary boundaries have come under pressure as a result of staffing shortages". The area of boundary stretch could also be considered a result of economic expediency, as it is usually cheaper to employ a health worker with no or minimal educational preparation than to employ a degree-prepared or registered health professional. Duckett (2005) suggests there needs to be significant changes in the health workforce and this needs to be done by way of substitution of roles suggesting that a small shift "would yield a substantial increase in the supply services".

CONCLUSION

MHSWs, in terms of their numbers and the work they do, are a significant and integral part of the mental health workforce. The movement away from institutional-based services into services provided in the community has created a mechanism which allows services to be progressive and client-facing. Legislation, inter-professional suspicion, lack of education and risk aversion has, however, meant that the full extent of this workforce's positive potentials has not yet been realized.

As well the issue of the professionalization of this workforce continues to be in question and heavily debated, as assurances are sought that the public is protected through the care provided by MHSWs.

Hennessy's (2015b, p. 17) study of MHSWs found:

the relationship with consumers is time-intensive, and provides care and support. It affords a non-judgmental and non-clinical way of working. Because the [MHSW] is free from formal assessment and treatment responsibilities, they are able to engage at a level that engenders trust and openness with consumers.

The MHSW therefore offers a unique and valuable contribution towards recovery and people with mental health problems have clearly and consistently voiced the difference MHSWs have made to their lives.

The contribution of MHSW to people's well-being still needs to be better understood and recognized by other professionals in the health sector. Through the MHSW's lens, a different perspective about the person's world is uncovered which therefore can inform the practice of other professionals and creates a more realistic and holistic view of the person. There is indeed significant potential for the future of mental health services through recognition of the work that MHSWs do with people and their family and whānau and the contribution they make to mental health services in New Zealand.

REFERENCES

Abbott, A. (1988). *The system of professions - A study of the divisions of expert labour*. London, UK: University of Chicago Press.

Abbott, M. (1989a). Community treatment and support of the mentally disabled in New Zealand. In *Cure and care for the mentally disabled in the community* (pp. 39–55). Tokyo: Japanese Association for Mental Health.

Abbott, M. (1989b). Current issues in mental health and developmental disabilities: Challenges for health professionals. *Mental Health in Australia*, *20*, 19–32.

Abbott, M., & Kemp, D. R. (1993). New Zealand. In D. R. Kemp (Ed.), *International handbook on mental health policy* (pp. 217–252). Westport, CT: Greenwood Press.

Adeponle, A., Whitley, R., & Kirmayer, L. (2012). Cultural contexts and construction of recovery. In A. Rudnick (Ed.), *Recovery of people with mental iIllness* (pp. 109–132). London, UK: Oxford Press. doi:10.1093/med/9780199691319.003.0008

Alcoholics Anonymous. (n.d.). *A brief history of AA in New Zealand.* Retrieved from http://www.aa.org.nz/about/history

Allock, J., & Hollingsworth, N. (2009). The non-professionally qualified workforce: A focus on the new roles of the support, time and recovery worker and the community development worker. *Journal of Mental Health Training. Education and Practice*, *4*(4), 12–17.

Annadale, M., & Instone, A. (2004). *Sei Tapu: Evaluation of the National Certificate in Mental Health Support Work.* Wellington, New Zealand: Platform.

Armitage, P. (1994). Long term mental health care in three European cities. *The Australian and New Zealand Journal of Mental Health Nursing*, *3*(2), 42–58.

Aubry, T. D., Flynn, R. J., Gerber, G., & Dostaler, T. (2005). Identifying the core competencies of community support providers working with people with psychiatric disabilites. *Psychiatric Rehabilitation Journal*, *28*(4), 346–353. doi:10.2975/28.2005.346.353 PMID:15895918

Borg, M., & Kristiansen, K. (2004). Recovery-orientated professionals: Helping relationships in mental health services. *Journal of Mental Health (Abingdon, England)*, *13*(5), 493–505. doi:10.1080/09638230400006809

Bostock, D. (2000). *Aristotle's ethics.* New York: Oxford University Press.

Burrage, M., & Torstendahl, R. (1990). *The formation of professions: Knowledge, state strategy*. London, UK: Sage.

Bushe, G. R. (1998). *Five theories of change embedded in appreciative inquiry*. Paper presented at the 18th Annual World Congress of Organization Development, Dublin, Ireland. Retrieved from www.gervasebushe.ca

Carney, T. (2008). The mental health service crisis of neoliberalism - An antipodean perspective. *International Journal of Law and Psychiatry, 31*(2), 173–175. doi:10.1016/j.ijlp.2008.02.001 PMID:18314192

Case Consulting. (2003). *Evaluation of the national certificate in mental heath support work.* Wellington, New Zealand: Platform Mental Health Support Worker Advisory Group.

Central Regional Health Authority. (1994). *A better life: Report of the greater Wellington mental health services review.* Wellington, New Zealand: Author.

Chambers, R. (2006). How healthcare assistants fit into a practice. *GP*, 52.

Coop, C. F. (2006). Balancing the balanced scorecard for a New Zealand mental health service. *Australian Health Review, 30*(2), 174–180. doi:10.1071/AH060174 PMID:16646766

Deegan, P. (1988). Recovery: The lived experience of rehabilitation. *Psychosocial Rehabilitation Journal, 11*(4), 11–19. doi:10.1037/h0099565

DeSouza, R. (1997). Improving collaboration between nursing professionals and support workers in the New Zealand mental health system. *Professional Leader, 4*(2), 16–17.

Diener, E., & Lucas, R. E. (2000). Explaining differences in societel levels of happiness: Relative standards, need fulfillment, culture, and evaluation theory. *Journal of Happiness Studies, 1*(1), 41–78. doi:10.1023/A:1010076127199

Duckett, S. J. (2005). Health workforce design for the 21st century. *Australian Health Review, 29*(2), 201–210. doi:10.1071/AH050201 PMID:15865571

Esposito, L., & Perez, M. (2014). Neoliberalism and the commodification of mental health. *Humanity & Society, 38*(4), 414–442. doi:10.1177/0160597614544958

Evans, I. M., & Moltzen, N. L. (2000). Defining effective community support for long-term psychiatric patients according to behavioural principles. *The Australian and New Zealand Journal of Psychiatry, 34*(4), 637–644. doi:10.1080/j.1440-1614.2000.00745.x PMID:10954395

Finfgeld-Connett, D. (2007). Concept comparison of caring and social support. *International Journal of Nursing Terminologies and Classifications, 18*(2), 58–68. doi:10.1111/j.1744-618X.2007.00051.x PMID:17542862

Gilburt, H., Rose, D., & Slade, M. (2008). The importance of relationships in mental health care: A qualitative study of service users' experiences of psychiatric hospital admissions in the U.K. *BMC Health Services Research, 8*(92), 1–12. PMID:18173837

Gilmore, V. (2005). Licensing of unregulated assistants urgent. *Australian Nursing Journal, 13*(1), 11. PMID:16502940

Griffiths, R., & Robinson, S. (2010). *Moving forward with healthcare support workforce.* London, UK: National Nursing Research Unit.

Haines, H., & Abbott, A. (1985). Deinstitutionalisation and social policy in New Zealand: Historical trends. *Community Mental Health in New Zealand,* (1), 44-56.

Haybron, D. M. (2008). Happiness, the self and human flourishing. *Utilitas, 20*(1), 21–49. doi:10.1017/S0953820807002889

Health and Disability Commissioner Act. New Zealand Statute (1994).

Health Funding Authority. (2000). *Tuutahitia te wero-meeting the challenges: Mental health workforce development plan 2000–2005*. Wellington, New Zealand: Author.

Health Practitioners Competence Assurance Act. New Zealand Statute (2003).

Health Workforce Advisory Committee. (2002a). *Framing future directions*. Wellington, New Zealand: Ministry of Health. Retrieved from http://www.hwac.govt.nz

Health Workforce Advisory Committee. (2002b). *The New Zealand health workforce: A stocktake of issues and capacity 2001*. Wellington, New Zealand: Ministry of Health.

Hennessy, J. (2015). The contribution of the mental health support worker to the mental health services in New Zealand: An Appreciative Inquiry approach (Doctoral thesis). Auckland, New Zealand: Auckland University of Technology. Retrieved from http://aut.researchgateway.ac.nz/handle/10292/9192

Hickey, N., Kramer, T., & Garralda, E. (2010). Developing the primary mental health worker role in England. *Child and Adolescent Mental Health, 15*(1), 23–29. doi:10.1111/j.1475-3588.2008.00524.x

Holloway, K., Baker, J., & Lumby, J. (2009). Specialist nursing framework for New Zealand: A missing link in workforce planning. *Policy, Politics & Nursing Practice, 10*(4), 269–275. doi:10.1177/1527154409357628 PMID:20042419

Huxley, P., Evan, S., Beresford, P., Davidson, B., & King, S. (2009). The principles and provisions of relationships findings from an evaluation of support, time and recovery workers in mental health services in England. *Journal of Social Work, 9*(1), 99–117. doi:10.1177/1468017308098434

Illingworth, P. (2008). Faith: An untapped mental health nursing resource. *Mental Health Nursing, 28*(4), 9–11.

James, A., Chadwick, S., & Rushforth, D. (2006). Implementing a new national role in mental health: The support, time and recovery worker. *Journal of Mental Health Workforce Development, 1*(1), 30–36.

Kinnair, D., Anderson, S., & Thorpe, L. (2012). Development of interprofessional education in mental health practice: Adapting the Leicester model. *Journal of Interprofessional Care, 26*(3), 189–197. doi:10.3109/13561820.2011.647994 PMID:22250705

Knapp, M. B., Dayson, D., Leff, J., Margolius, O., O'Driscoll, C., & Wills, W. (1990). The TAPs project 3: Predicting the community costs of closing psychiatric hospitals. *British Medical Journal, 157*, 661–670. PMID:2126218

MacDonald, K. M. (1995). *The sociology of the profession*. London, UK: Sage.

McCrae, N., Banerjee, S., Murray, J., Prior, S., & Silverman, A. M. (2008). An extra pair of hands? A case study of the introduction of support workers in community mental health teams for older adults. *Journal of Nursing Management, 16*(6), 734–743. doi:10.1111/j.1365-2834.2008.00929.x PMID:18808468

McDonald, M., Cox, S. M., Paterson, N. D., & Lafrenière, D. (2008). Trust in health relationships: Accounts of human subjects. *Journal of Empirical Research on Human Research Ethics; JERHRE, 3*(4), 35–47. doi:10.1525/jer.2008.3.4.35 PMID:19385755

McGregor, S. (2001). Neoliberalism and health care. *International Journal of Consumer Studies, 25*(2), 82–89. doi:10.1111/j.1470-6431.2001.00183.x

Mental Health Commission. (1998). *Blueprint for mental health services in New Zealand: How things need to be*. Wellington, New Zealand: Author.

Mental Health Commission. (2004). *Labour market constraints affecting the mental health sector*. Auckland, New Zealand: Auckland University.

Mental Health Foundation. (n.d.). *Glossary: Mental health support worker.* Retrieved from https://www.mentalhealth.org.nz/home/glossary/

Millet, S. (2011). *Aristotle's power and responsibilities for nature*. Pieterlen, Switzerland: Peter Lang.

Ministry of Health. (1994). *Looking forward*. Wellington, New Zealand: Author.

Ministry of Health. (1997). *Moving forward: The national mental health plan*. Wellington, New Zealand: Author.

Ministry of Health. (2002). *Mental health (alcohol and other drugs) workforce development framework*. Wellington, New Zealand: Author.

Ministry of Health. (2004). *Te Tahuhu - improving mental halth: The second national mental health and addiction plan 2005-2015*. Wellington, New Zealand: Author.

Ministry of Health. (2005). *Tauawhitia te Wero: Embracing the challenge: National mental health and addiction workforce development plan 2006-2009*. Wellington, New Zealand: Author.

Ministry of Health. (2012). *Rising to the challenge -The mental health and addiction service development plan*. Wellington, New Zealand: Author.

Nancarrow, S. A., & Borthwick, A. M. (2005). Dynamic professional boundaries in the healthcare workforce. *Sociology of Health and Illness, 27*(7), 897-919. doi: 10:.1111/j.1467-9566.2005.00463.x

Nestor, P., & Galletly, C. (2008). The employment of consumers in mental health services: Politically correct tokenism or genuinely useful? *Royal Australian and New Zealand College of Psychiatrists, 16*(5), 344–347. doi:10.1080/10398560802196016 PMID:18615343

Norman, J., Walsh, N., Mugavin, J., Stoove, M., Kelsall, J., Austin, K., & Lintzeris, N. (2008). The acceptability and feasibility of peer worker support role in community based HCV treatment for injecting drug users. *Harm Reduction Journal, 5*(8), 1–9. doi:10.1186/1477-7517-5-8 PMID:18298862

Platform. (2007). *NgOIT: Workforce survey*. Retrieved from: http://www.platform.org.nz

Platform. (2008). *Performance story report 2007*. Wellington, New Zealand: Author.

Platform. (n.d.). *Fair funding fact sheet*. Retrieved from www.platform.org.nz

Ramon, S. (2008). Neoliberalism and its implications for mental health in the UK. *International Journal of Law and Psychiatry*, *31*(2), 116–125. doi:10.1016/j.ijlp.2008.02.006 PMID:18342370

Rangiaho, A. (2003). *Te Puawaitanga o Te Oranga Hinengaro - An evaluation of the National Certificate in Mental Health Support Work from a Maori perspective*. Wellington, New Zealand: Mental Health Support Work Advisory Group.

Rapp, C., & Chamberlain, R. (1985). Case management services for the chronically mentally ill. *Social Work*, *30*(5), 417–422. PMID:10273981

Scott, A., Doughty, C., & Kahi, H. (2011). *Peer support practice in Aotearoa New Zealand*. Christchurch, New Zealand: University of Canterbury.

Sutcliffe, R. (2006). What is the meaning of supervison for mental health support workers? A critical hermeneutic inquiry (Master Thesis). Auckland, New Zealand: Auckland University of Technology. Retrieved from http://aut.researchgateway.ac.nz/handle/10292/88

Te Pou. (2014). *Competencies for the mental health and addiction service user, consumer and peer workforce*. Auckland, New Zealand: Author.

Te Pou. (2015). *Adult mental health and addiction workforce - 2014 survey of Vote Health funded services*. Auckland, New Zealand: Author.

Tomic, M., & Tomic, E. (2011). Existential fulfilment, work and workload engagement in nurses. *Journal of Research in Nursing*, *16*(4), 468–479. doi:10.1177/1744987110383353

Tse, S., See, E. W., Wong, S., Kan, A., & Kwok, C. (2014). Training of mental health peer support workers in a non-western high-income city: Preliminary evaluation and experience. *The International Journal of Social Psychiatry*, *60*(3), 211–218. doi:10.1177/0020764013481427 PMID:23539546

Verhaeghe, M., & Bracke, P. (2011). Stigma and trust among mental health service users. *Archives of Psychiatric Nursing*, *25*(4), 294–304. doi:10.1016/j.apnu.2011.02.001 PMID:21784287

KEY TERMS AND DEFINITIONS

Habilitative: Acquire, keep or improve skills of daily living.
Neo-Liberalism: Ideas associated with privatization.
Non-Judgmental: Not judging a person one one's own beliefs.
Peer: Someone from your own level.
Professional: Engaging in an occupation that requires training, skills or regulation.
Recovery: Having a meaningful life despite having a serious mental illness.
Strength-Based: A positive way of viewing ones workd through resilience and self-determination.

ENDNOTES

1 The 1990s saw health planning and funding divided into four regional health authorities.

2 *Consumer* and *service users* are interchangeable terms and refer to a person accessing mental health services.

3 Kaupapa Māori services refer to the delivery of services based on philosophies of the indigenous people of New Zealand.

4 Patients is a term still used in much of the literature when referring to service users/health consumers outside of mental health services.

Chapter 11
The Emerging Field of Peer Support within Mental Health Services

Lisa Carol St George
Recovery Innovations and Recovery Opportunity Center, USA

Mary O'Hagan
PeerZone, New Zealand

Simon Bradstreet
University of Glasgow, UK

Michael Burge
Mental Health Advocate, Australia

ABSTRACT

The Centre for Medicaid Services has identified that "peer support services are an evidence-based mental health model of care" (2007, August 15, p. 1). Although an evidence-based practice, peer support remains an emerging discipline in mental health. Peer supporters help individuals seeking mental wellness by inspiring hope, using their recovery story, and by developing mutual relationships. Peer supporters believe in each individual's ability to recover. They know recovery is possible, because they have experienced it themselves. Understanding what peer support is, and how peer supporters work within their unique discipline is important to those wishing to include peer supporters in their service systems. Peer support is more than simply sharing stories; systems guided by licensing requirements and quality management teams require effective, well-trained individuals, with lived experience to work within peer support. With effective training, and a strong footing in their own recovery, peer supporters can be exceptional contributors within behavioral health systems of care.

INTRODUCTION

The inclusion of peer support workers in behavioral health systems of care has created a profound change in the way mental health and addictions are understood. When peer support providers join service system teams, they help those teams to truly understand that recovery happens. Peer supporters demonstrate the reality of recovery and the people they serve quietly understand, "If she/he can do it, so can I" (St. George, Rider, Zeeb, Smithers, & Long, 2015).

DOI: 10.4018/978-1-5225-1874-7.ch011

Understanding the nature of peer support work and how a strong peer workforce can be developed is imperative if organizations are to move forward and include peers in their teams. Sometimes, what holds organizations and systems back are concerns for individual well-being and beliefs about recovery.

Positive outcomes are beginning to emerge from peer support work. Understanding the value of, and how to prepare teams and services to employ peers, is imperative for the development of strong and sustainable teams.

While many peer support workers volunteer or work within strictly peer run services, this chapter will focus on paid peer support within integrated teams, and on the development of a strong peer support workforce.

The objectives of this chapter are to provide an overview of:

- The emergence of peer support within multidisciplinary teams.
- Training available to prepare peer supporters to work in behavioral health.
- Key aspects of recovery oriented systems and services.
- Key components required to build a strong and sustainable peer workforce.
- Peer support experiences in the U.S., New Zealand, Scotland, and Australia.

BACKGROUND

Peer support and recovery has had strong supporters such as Sally Zinman, Judy Chamberlin, Shery Mead, Larry Fricks, Mary O'Hagan, Harvey Rosenthal, Patricia Deegan, Lisa St. George, Sue Bergeson, and many others. Each one has contributed to the belief that recovery is possible for people with diagnoses of serious mental illnesses and those with co-occurring substance use and mental health challenges. There has also been a view that recovery from substance use is possible since the emergence of Alcoholics Anonymous in 1935.

During the 1970s, consumer/survivors of mental health treatment boldly reclaimed their "madness" and their lives during the period of "deinstitutionalization" in the U.S. (Shapiro, 2010). Early leaders like Sally Zinman (Zinman, 2013), Judy Chamberlain (National Empowerment Centre, 2010), and Howie the Harp (Van Gelder, 1995) set the stage for the new discipline of peer support within mental health services to emerge.

Some mental health professionals had difficulty believing that recovery from serious mental health or co-occurring challenges was possible. Dr William Anthony has championed recovery and the belief that recovery is possible and that this is possible among many more people than previously thought (Anthony, 1993). Since the increased visibility and hiring of peer supporters within multidisciplinary teams in the mid-2000s, behavioral health providers and team members can see firsthand that recovery is possible everyday through the peers that work alongside them.

Today, more funders are requiring the use of peer support within service programs (Swarbrick, Brice, Jenkins-Tucker, & Miccio, 2011). There are not enough mental health professionals, such as psychiatrists, social workers, and advance practice nurses, to meet current and future demand and many positions remain unfilled. While peer supporters cannot replace licensed professionals, they can improve the engagement with people being served by systems of care (OptumHealth, 2016).

The idea of mutual help and support is not new in healthcare fields. In the U.S., Alcoholics Anonymous has used mutual (peer) support to help people for more than 80 years. Sponsors act in the role of a peer supporter (sponsor) as someone who has walked a similar path, and understands the struggle of recovery from addictions. Support groups exist for individuals with cancer, diabetes, survivors of rape, veterans and many others who come together using shared experiences to develop trust, relationship, and hope.

THE EMERGING FIELD OF PEER SUPPORT WITHIN MENTAL HEALTH

Peer Support Definitions

It is important to understand what is meant by the words "peer support". While there are many different definitions and ideas about peer support, below are three definitions. The International Association of Peer Supporters (2016) defines peer support providers as follows:

Peer support providers are people with a personal experience of recovery from mental health, substance use, or trauma conditions who receive specialized training and supervision to guide and support others who are experiencing similar mental health, substance use or trauma issues toward increased wellness.

Shery Mead (2003, p. 1) defined peer support as:

...a system of giving and receiving help founded on key principles of respect, shared responsibility, and mutual agreement of what is helpful. Peer support is not based on psychiatric models and diagnostic criteria. It is about understanding another's situation empathically through the shared experience of emotional and psychological pain.

In New Zealand, Scott and colleagues (2011, p. 18) have defined peer support as being:

...person-centered and underpinned by recovery and strength-based philosophies. The life experience of the worker creates common ground from which the trust relationship with the person is formed. Empowerment, empathy, hope, and choice along with mutuality are the main drivers in purposeful peer support work.

Three Core Principles and Values of Peer Support

The above definitions of peer support include some core principles. The first core principle is mutuality and shared experiences of peer supporters. The person being served and the peer supporter are both experts in the relationship. Their lives have taken a similar path, which creates an almost instant connectedness and trust.

The second core principle refers to the shared responsibility with the individual seeking wellness. Working within peer support values, both the peer supporter and the individual seeking wellness share responsibility for the outcomes of the work they do together. If an individual seeking wellness identifies specific hopes, dreams, or goals, these determine the process and the timeframe they require or need to reach these. In this working relationship, peer supporters do not tell the individual what to do. The individual receiving peer support identifies what they want to accomplish and what success looks like.

The next core value is of experiences being self-defined. Each person has the right to decide what their experience means to them. It is not about a diagnosis, it is about self-acceptance and self-definition. Everyone's life is a journey and they have the right to decide what is important.

There is an additional core principle that does not appear in the above definitions. It is the principle of measured sharing. This value means that peer supporters share their stories of challenges and recovery in measured doses. They share their own story when the individual seeking wellness might be helped by it, and the context of the discussion lends itself to a brief story connection. The peer supporter can use small portions of their journey when needed to demonstrate they understand the individual's experience at a personal level. The peer supporter's story must never usurp the discussion so the focus changes to the peer supporter from the person being served.

Trained peer support providers are a new discipline in behavioral health care. Their work within behavioral health systems, using their lived experience of mental distress, trauma, and addiction challenges, as well as recovery inspires hope. It is peer supporters who are the focus of this chapter.

History

In 2000, an organization founded in 1990 in Phoenix, Arizona - META Services (now RI International), moved in the direction of combining peer support work with traditional mental health care services (St. George, 2003a).

Until then, most peer support work with people seeking wellness from mental health or addiction challenges had been provided through non-traditional consumer directed services (CDS). The gentle atmosphere and comforting surroundings found in non-traditional peer run services have been valued by individuals seeking wellness, comfort, and belonging. In 2014, Shery Mead (p. 14) wrote about peer run respites and CDS, and how they engage in the process of "sharing stories, strategies, and ways of making meaning" of each person's experiences, especially while people are in crisis. Peer run services typically do not operate within the medical model of behavioral health services.

Other people with lived experience have acted in the roles of advocates. They have brought a consumer perspective to systems through program development, large-scale system changes, and informed decision-making when projects affect the experiences of people receiving treatment. With increased understanding that service improvement is necessary, the voices of people with lived experience have become important. These people have been able to help leaders understand perspectives they might not otherwise fully grasp.

META Services was originally a traditional mental health provider. The organization provided services in two urgent crisis centers and multiple outpatient service programs. They engaged in traditional treatment behaviors present in many psychiatric inpatient provider services at that time. They used seclusion and restraint regularly to manage patients. However, they also provided unique in-home and community crisis services, which were staffed by clinicians, doctors, and nurses.

During a discussion with Marianne Long (personal communication, June 14, 2016) who was one of the first peer leaders hired at META services, she recalled a trip to Vermont to learn about WRAP. After leaders visited Mary Ellen Copeland and become WRAP Facilitators and then Facilitator Trainers she said "things began to change at META". The visits to Mary Ellen Copeland inspired a profound transformation in how services were provided to the individuals served by META Services. The organization decided it would add people with mental health challenges (peer support specialists) to their service teams, as providers. As the number of peer support specialists grew, and their inclusion in teams strengthened, it helped provide the foundation for widespread use of peer support providers in Maricopa County, Arizona.

META decided to identify team members with lived experience using the job title "peer support specialist". Job titles have diversified as the profession has grown and career ladders have emerged. Some of the job titles for peer providers now include, but are not limited to: peer, peer supporter, peer recovery coach, recovery coach, crisis recovery coach, recovery services administrator, recovery educator, recovery facilitator, peer mentor, peer counselor, peer respite supporter, and team leader. Depending on the settings and services provided, there are likely to be more additional titles.

In addition to embarking on a journey towards zero restraint, another important part of the work carried out in META, was the hiring of a large number of peer supporters. As a result, the service system began to experience peer support and its effectiveness to a much larger degree than before. By 2002, META had trained 146 peer supporters, most of which were employed by the organization. The presence of these trained peer support providers in clinics across the county facilitating WRAP classes, and providing in-home and community services, helped community-based organizations and clinics begin to embrace the work of peer supporters. Recovery, wellness, and peer support began to be included in Requests for Proposals (RFPs) as core service components within Arizona.

Recovery Pathways

In 2003, RI International started describing the principles being used to guide the organization's transformation toward recovery based services as "recovery pathways". The pathways listed below reflect aspects of the system or organization which can create safety and an atmosphere that effectively supports recovery when implemented.

- **Hope:** An energy and a belief that things can change, get better, and create great results.
- **Choice:** The option of choice as a required component of recovery environments, identifies the right of people using services to identify which options work for them (choices should be credible and not just an invitation to choose for instance medications or jail).
- **Empowerment:** This creates an understanding that each individual served has a right to self-determination over their circumstances, and must hold a powerful and respected position within their treatment team.
- **Recovery Culture/Environment:** This concept identifies that individuals who receive services must be able to walk into beautiful and respectful surroundings for their care, and that individuals who work within the service system or organization treat them with kindness, respect, and caring, which prevents the infantilization of the individuals served.
- **Spirituality/Meaning and Purpose:** The inclusion of spirituality and/or meaning and purpose within the recovery pathways is not just about religion, it is about being invested in something more that ourselves, and service systems must increase awareness of this vital piece of a recovery oriented system of care and support it as part of an individual's recovery.

The inclusion of peer support in traditional settings began to spread throughout the U.S., Canada, New Zealand, and the rest of the world, in the mid-2000s. Attached in the appendices are overviews of peer support in New Zealand, Scotland and Australia by Mary O'Hagan, Simon Bradstreet, and Michael

Burge. While the idea of peer support did not emerge from the META Maricopa Model (St. George, 2003a), the high number of paid positions held by peer supporters at META Services created the most solidly built example of a large team of peer support workers in the world for more than a decade. With 650 or more employees working in peer support and leadership positions throughout the organization, the use of peer support became integral to service provision at META (St. George & Smithers, 2016). Due to the large and continuous amount of peer work provided in multiple services by the organization, leaders from the U.K., Scotland, Ireland, Australia, Italy, Canada, Singapore, New Zealand, and across the U.S. have visited the organization to learn about establishing strong teams of peer supporters.

Dr Sue Hallwright, the director of funding and planning at Counties Manukau District Health Board (DHB) during the mid-2000's, described the experience of Counties Manukau's visit in 2003.

A bunch of people from our DHB went off to see the services in Phoenix, Arizona, which were then called META Services, now Recovery Innovations. The team came back saying "We are going to do this inside our own services". (Hallwright & McPherson, 2010)

Peer Support Training

The use of specific training to develop the particular skills needed to engage in mutually respectful, person driven, and hopeful services is an important part of the development of any peer support workforce. There are now a number of peer support trainings available internationally.

One well-known, respected, and comprehensive training is RI International's Peer Employment Training: A Peer/Recovery Support Specialist Certified Training (PET). This tool was written and developed in 2000 when META Services embarked on its transformation to a recovery focused mental health service infused with peer support (St. George, 2003a). The PET is a comprehensive 76-hour training over 10 days. PET views peer support as integral to systems and services providing behavioral health care. The training prepares individuals to be part of systems and services, and to keep their focus on mutuality and person directed services. It also encourages teamwork and provides ethical practice guidelines. PET is used as a certifying training in 18 U.S. states and to train peer specialists in most states.

PET training is used by England's Cambridgeshire-Peterborough NHS Foundation Trust (2016). The Trust has used PET from RI International since 2010 as their core training for peer supporters. Since 2005, PET has also been used in New Zealand. Additionally, training has been provided in Ireland, Scotland, Greece, and Italy (St. George, 2015). PET is also the preferred peer training used by the Veteran's Administration (VA) in the U.S. since 2013. Overall, PET has prepared over 8,000 people with lived experience to work as peer supporters. Many companion trainings have also been developed to provide peer support workers with continuing education specific to their unique roles (see https://riinternational.com/consulting/training).

Intentional Peer Support (IPS) is another well-known and respected training used in the U.S. and internationally. It has been used in China, Japan, Australia, and New Zealand. IPS focuses on training individuals in the narrative and development of alternative ways of exploring people's experiences. IPS has a three-step approach to implementing skills into peer support services. The steps consist of a 5-day Core Training, Practice of Co-Reflection, and Advanced Training for IPS Providers (see http://www.intentionalpeersupport.org/trainings/).

The Georgia Model is another important peer training developed in the state of Georgia and used in various states. The Georgia Model began as a 3-day training program in 2001 and was integral to the

Georgia Certified Peer Specialist Project (Georgia CPS Project, 2016). Today, the Georgia Certified Peer Specialist training is approximately eight days long.

Depression Bi-Polar Support Alliance (DBSA, 2016) also provides a peer specialist core training. This well-known 40-hour training was developed in affiliation with the Georgia Certified Peer Specialist Project and has been used in various states across the U.S.

Other in-house peer trainings have been developed by agencies to educate peer support specialists. Having various training options available is vital to the recovery pathway of choice. However, in the U.S. the four above mentioned peer trainings are some of the most widely used.

Increasing Opportunities for Peer Support Providers

Prior to the use of peer support within integrated teams, most of the services provided by peer supporters occurred in non-traditional settings, like peer run respites. These are places of recovery for people seeking wellness following an intense and distressful experience (psychiatric crisis). These services are however underfunded. A U.S. survey shows over one-third of the 38 peer-run respite services receive less than $500,000 in funding each year (Ostrow & Croft, 2016). In addition, there a low number of CDS and peer run respite services, and these are often inaccessible for people who do not live in the area where they are located. In 2013, there were only 13 peer run crisis alternative services across the U.S. (Ostrow, 2013). Moreover, if peer run services were the only location in which peer support was delivered then people who are unaware of, or not in need of, alternative crisis or respite services might never have the opportunity to experience the hope that comes from the peer support relationship (National Action Alliance for Suicide Prevention: Crisis Services Task Force, 2016).

Despite the enormous value of peer respite programs and CDS, the expansion of peer support into traditional service provider systems has allowed many more people to experience the mutuality, relationship, and caring of peer support providers. With the addition of peer support workers in traditional clinics, emergency psychiatric facilities, and crisis centers, the relationship building skills of peer support workers have inevitably gained increased visibility.

According to SAMHSA (2009, p. 8), "mental health crisis services should afford opportunities for contact with others whose personal experiences with mental illness and past mental health crises allow them to convey a sense of hopefulness first-hand". This hopefulness develops, in part, by meeting an individual who has recovered and is now working and providing peer support.

The inclusion of peer support in traditional services creates increased opportunities for people to work as peer support providers. Additionally, peer supporters are now able to provide Medicaid funded services in some U.S. systems. In fact, the CMS (2007, August 15, p. 1) states that it is committed to "State flexibility, increased innovation, consumer choice, self-direction, recovery, and consumer protection of these services". CMS offers the option of peer support as part of a comprehensive mental health and substance use service delivery system. Each state has the responsibility of deciding whether or not to include peer support. While all "peer support providers must complete training and certification … the training required is also decided by each State" (CMS, 2007, August 15, p. 3).

Differing Schools of Thought

While most leaders in the peer movement agree the work of peer supporters is needed and is effective, there are various schools of thought among leaders and groups. Both perspectives have value and inspire meaningful discussion about what mutuality in peer support is, and how, where, and when services should occur.

The first school of thought to emerge was that of peer support being separate and apart from the treatment system. This philosophy emerged from the consumer survivor movement in the 1970s. This group asserts that individuals can make their own meaning of their experiences rather than looking at these experiences as an illness or diagnosable condition using the Diagnostic and Statistical Manual (DSM) IV (or any previous DSM). In addition, peer-run self-help services, and CDS "do not adopt a treatment orientation, do not generate and keep individual treatment plans and records, and do not formally monitor side effects, progress, and problems" (Salzer, 2002, p.7). They work from a narrative perspective. This group is often opposed to the classification and labelling of the unique experiences that human beings may encounter, which in a medical model is referred to as illness.

Some believe that "the success of the CDS is furthered by non-consumer professional collaboration and support that appreciates the unique contributions" (Salzer, 2002, p.6). However, caution is needed so that these unique services do not rely too strongly on these professional collaborations. If there is too much dependence, there is a risk that peer employees will step back from taking the lead in directing services and will acquiesce to the professional organization (Salzer, 2002). In order for services to remain independent the leadership and 51% of the board in peer run respites and CDS must have lived experience.

Studies have demonstrated that individuals served by self-help groups and peer-run respite services, experience better outcomes than they would from traditional services alone. These outcomes include reduced substance use and mental distress, and increased coping skills and life satisfaction (Salzer, 2002). As alternatives to hospitals, they also offer significant cost savings (Swarbrick, et al., 2011).

The first school of thought would assert that peer support providers who are paid for their services may disrupt the integrity of the mutual relationship that is fundamental to the role of peer supporters (Walsh, Crozier, Roennfeldt, & Wheeler, 2015; Mead & MacNeil, 2006). This group believes the power imbalances that come with paid work must be taken into account (Walsh et al., 2015). Shery Mead (Mead & MacNeil, 2006, p. 36) states, "one can't both work for the medical system and refute its very foundation" as she describes the need to change the diagnostic language to one focused on "meaning" that the person might find in the experience that is unrelated to illness, or medicalization.

The second school of thought believes there is a need to increase access to peer supporters by creating specific roles within traditional behavioral health provider systems and non-government organizations (NGOs). These peer supporters must receive training to help them work in effective and ethical ways with the people they serve. Training is imperative for these peer providers as they work within licensed services, which are typically made up of multidisciplinary teams. In contrast to CDS, the peer supporters working within NGO's, community-based organizations, licensed facilities, or funding entities, create documentation and participate in the development of recovery or treatment plans with the individuals they serve. They also work alongside others who provide services, and are part of the treatment team.

The latter school of thought believes peer support work deserves employment and wages. These peer supporters understand the work of multidisciplinary teams made up of doctors, nurses, clinicians, behavioral health technicians, and peer supporters. These teams bring the strengths of each team member, including peer supporters, in service to the individual. However, peer supporters maintain their mutuality, use of story, and the development of an honest, trusting relationship. Peers often act as a connector back to the service team, helping the individuals they work with gain an increased understanding of how to get the most out of available services and work with their teams in meaningful ways. Outcomes for these integrated services are discussed later.

Peer Support and the Fact of Recovery

Recovery happens it happens to everyone in one way or another. Even though Dr Courtney Harding and others (1987) have challenged old ideas about the chronic nature of severe mental illness, the belief that recovery *does not* happen perpetuates. However, Dr William Anthony has made two assertions about recovery. The first, recovery from mental illness is not the same as cure. This means regaining control over one's life, if not one's illness (Anthony, 1993). It means "living a satisfying, hopeful, and contributing life even with limitations caused by the illness" (Anthony, 1993, p. 7).

The second guiding idea put forward by Anthony (1993, p. 16) was the notion that "recovery from severe mental illness is possible for many more people than was previously believed". Having a vision like this creates hope. If peer supporters, family, and friends believe in an individual's ability to recover, it is highly likely they will. Recovery is not about never experiencing a symptom again, it is about experiencing symptoms and learning to manage them, working with them, and still living life fully.

There is still a long way to go until the use of peer support is seen in every NGO, system, and hospital around the world. Creating recovery-focused systems that are welcoming is important when bringing peer supporters into any integrated team. One of the first steps in the process involves developing a plan. Dr Anthony and others have created a plan that provides a roadmap for engaging all team members in the process of change (Anthony, 2000). The authors identify the characteristics that are important to a recovery-focused system, including an environment in which all service providers work from a mission driven perspective of recovery that includes input from the people served (Anthony, 2000). The presence of a strong mission and set of values will engage the team in the process of transformation.

Another aspect of the recovery change process is a focus on outcomes. The measurement of outcomes is not based upon the number of people served or followed up with appointments. While those measures are important, recovery based services track the number of people who have reached the goals they have set for themselves, and those actively engaged in their treatment planning process. Additionally, outcomes measurement might look at support systems and the inclusion of family members (by blood or choice) that people want as part of their care team (Anthony, 2000).

From the top down, organizations need to realize and value the idea of recovery. Leadership must set the tone and guide the organization's recovery practice. Leaders need to inspire employees to connect to hope for what is possible, the mission and values, and people served (Anthony, 2000).

Training is vital to help teams understand the work of peer supporters and the philosophy of recovery. Helping team members understand what peer supporters do, how to work together, and use everyone's strengths to create the best outcomes for the individual being served is invaluable (St. George & Smithers, 2016).

An organization strongly engaged in the use of recovery-focused practice ensures its policies and procedures support the people receiving services to achieve the best possible results. Organizations must have a medical record that tracks the service provision for timeliness, but is also refined enough to identify the attainment of individual goals. Each of these plans should be developed with the person using a collaborative process. Their preferences, hopes, and dreams should be recorded and become the focus of the clinical plan (Anthony, 2000).

No matter how small a goal, an individual's goal should receive support. The treatment plan becomes a living document and every time a goal or dream is reached, there is a celebration. Words, high fives, or a certificate of progress acknowledges each achievement. Then, the process begins again. In this way, the treatment plan becomes a joyful document that is full of examples of success. It no longer remains a management tool for compliance to a regime established by the team, consisting only of goals like medication adherence, time management, and clinic visits.

The individual in charge of planning goals is the person receiving services. The teams, including the peer supporter, help with implementation by way of ensuring services are available (Anthony, 2000). The value of this reciprocal planning process is not intended to create hardship or control team members (St. George & Smithers, 2016), rather, it is meant to include everyone in the team as responsible parties.

The individual may have goals and perhaps requirements they need meet. A person may want to take a walk to a local café where people play board games three times a week to increase their social connectedness. A team may be responsible for helping to arrange transportation to all clinic visits because the bus is overwhelming for the person. This reciprocal planning process of all parties involves working together on the development of goals, requirements, and timeframes and making treatment planning a "we" rather than "you" process.

As organizations begin to work with people and build these plans, a shift must necessarily take place. That shift involves the inclusion of specific goals that are not part of mental health systems of care. The plan may include identified goals to find a faith community. It may identify a need to build friendships and support systems outside the clinic. A plan may state a need to engage in meaningful work or a dance class. Any goal is documented and tracked, except those that involve illegal behavior or self-harm. The expectation that people receiving services will identify goals with no merit may happen. However, most individuals want to be part of the planning process and take it seriously. For example, an individual who wants money to buy a car identifies a goal of selling marijuana out of his garage. Rather than assuming they are rejecting the process or disrespecting it, take a moment to ask some questions. It could be that there is confusion about the legalization of marijuana dispensaries. It is important to provide information, listen, and work with the individual to find other ways of achieving their goals.

It may take time for many individuals to understand they are a valuable contributor to their own planning. They may be slow to take the lead. Many individuals are not used to being included in treatment planning, so don't give up. Once people realize their thoughts and goals are important, they will begin to engage in the process. The recognition of goals that fall outside those typically expected within a strictly medical model will lead to the development of a person who is part of something much larger, and provide a holistic view of their life.

Easy In and Easy Out

Peer support can help recovery-focused ideals come into a team's practice in an expedited manner. Their shared recovery stories will help teams try new things. Peer supporters often have stories of things that helped them recover. Some stories talk about services that helped, but they may also include healing activities that had nothing to do with traditional medical services. As teams begin to try new ways of working with people, the processes and procedures begin to shift. It will be necessary to change the way teams engage with people in mental health systems of care. These changes may include more intense yet gentle care for people in short-term crisis response centers, rather than long stays in hospitals. They might include helping people to exit systems of care and engage with their primary care physician for medication management.

However, there must be ease of access to a mental health clinical team if well-being declines. It may be that benefits (including Social Security and Medicare) grow more responsive and expeditious. Integrated teams and health homes can help people to receive full and complete care with easy access to both physical and behavioral health care as needed. When an individual has recovered from a mental health crisis they can exit the system without fear of not receiving services in the future.

A shift towards a belief in recovery and that people with even the most significant clinical diagnosis can recover and reclaim their lives, requires a more flexible and responsive system of care. These individuals can have long periods of wellness, or a lifetime, and systems of care must be able to meet this new paradigm. Implementing an easy in-easy out system, or a "rolling system" (St. George, 2016), will help people seeking wellness from being afraid of working, and going off social security and other benefits when they are recovering. Peer supporters will play an important role in this change process.

Outcomes of Peer Support

Evidence of the effectiveness of peer support services is beginning to emerge. One study out of Washington State looked at the results of bringing peer supporters into teams. They found reductions of 32% in hospitalizations over five years and in 30-day admissions (Optum, 2016). Average inpatient days were also 23% below the state average (Optum, 2016). Transitioning services, in which peer supporters help people exit the hospital, have been found to improve engagement and activation of service recipients. Significant decreases in the use of inpatient services have also been associated with these services.

Figure 1 and Figure 2 show the results of a transition programme using peer support in Washington State. Within the initial cohort of 125 people there were 202 hospitalizations in the year before the programme. In the year following implementation there were 42 hospitalizations for 35 people. Similarly, the use of inpatient services in New York was found to reduce by about half from 93% to 48% (Optum, 2016). In line with this, inpatient hospital service use in Wisconsin reduced from 72% to 44% (Optum, 2016). Both New York and Wisconsin also saw significant decreases in the number of inpatient days (Optum, 2016).

Figure 1. Hospitalizations before and after hospital transition services
Source: OptumHealth, 2016. Used with permission.

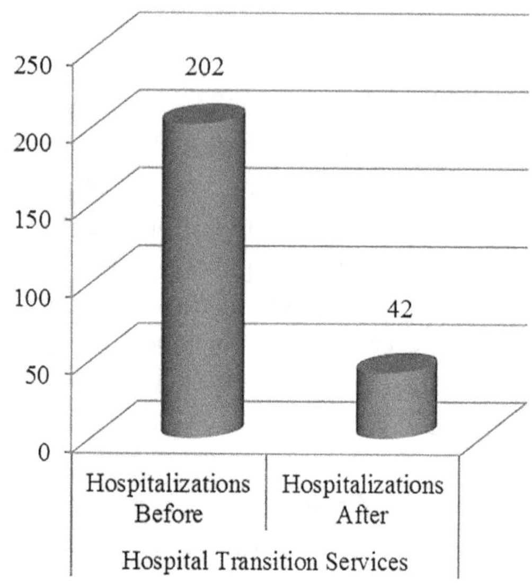

Figure 2. Number of individuals hospitalized before and after hospital transition services
Source: OptumHealth, 2016. Used with permission.

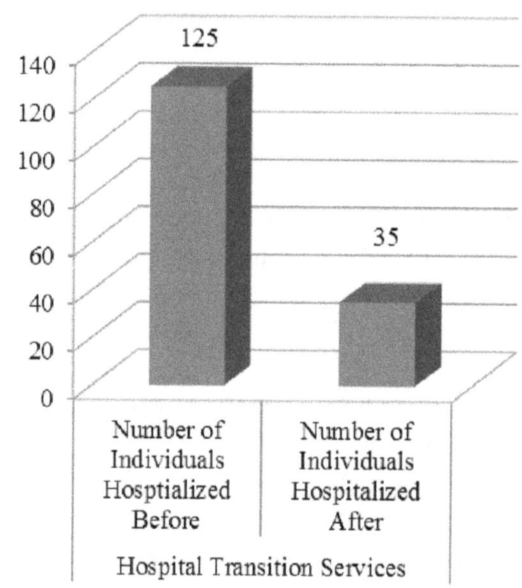

These reductions are consistent with the outcomes found in Phoenix by RI International. In 2003, peer supporters from RI International were brought into two large hospitals. They served everyday on each of the nine units for three hours and worked with people who were hospitalized against their will (committed). After the first year of their placement with two peer supporters on each of the nine units, the hospital's clinical director identified reductions of 36% in seclusion events, 48% in restraint events, and 56% in hospital readmission rates (Stevens & St. George, 2004).

Another study by Repper and Carter (2011) found some great outcomes associated with peer support work. People served by peer supporters started to have a greater understanding of their challenges, increased their sense of self value and personal acceptance, and experienced less social stigma. The experience of hope created energy to focus on their recovery. Furthermore, they felt higher levels of empowerment and took steps in their recovery, improved their problem-solving skills, and found solutions in the community.

Inclusion

In order to improve systems of care and achieve better outcomes for people with experiences of mental health challenges, the inclusion of peer supporters as providers must expand. Peer supporters, family members, and individuals who are receiving services must be included in every system of care planning meeting so they can provide input into changes being considered. Information from these key informants will offer guidance about new services from the perspective of someone who has used them. These individuals must not be invited as token consumers, family members, or peer supporters. Rather, their input must be viewed as essential and coming from subject matter experts. Participants, families, and peer supporters provide unique insights and information to leaders, policy makers, and system planners.

Systems of care have been using advocates for many years, but these advocates must be at all tables of discussion (Anthony, 2000). It is important that their input is shared at even the highest level of meetings. As systems become more aware of the vital need for transparency, advocates can support the development of programs that truly demonstrate an understanding that recovery is real.

Further strides will be made as inclusion and cultural humility (cultural competency) continue to play a vital part in service delivery (Anthony, 2000). Team members are expected to provide culturally sensitive programs and services to individuals from a wide range of cultures and differing abilities. Organizations led by funder expectations will participate in workshops and trainings that encourage increased cultural knowledge. Team members are encouraged to ask questions about what people need in the way of culturally appropriate services so they learn how to help each individual in ways that work for them (St. George et. al, 2015).

Another benefit that peer supporters bring to systems of care or CDS, is that they come from the community being served. As they begin to go through training, gain specific peer support skills, and join teams, the system will see that they mirror the diversity within the community (Hallwright & McPherson, 2010).

Team members need to be open and humble as they engage in continuous learning about the specific cultural needs of each person they serve. They need to ask questions, listen, and be open to the wonderful differences between people. Cultural trainings can include different perspectives from many individuals, various cultures, belief systems, genders and gender identities, as well as sexual preferences. Understanding individuals with invisible disabilities and from differently abled cultures will become part of the expected cultural groups that providers must understand. "People want to be viewed as unique treasures each possessing qualities and culture that comes from their ancestors" (St. George, 2003, p. 23).

Wherever possible, individuals should be brought in to participate in trainings and share expertise about their culture. This collaboration will ensure that assumptions and actions within a group will not be misinterpreted as team members look at differences through their own cultural lens. The lived experiences of all people can enrich the cultural wisdom of team members from both a heart and an intellectual level.

Developing a Recovery Culture within Services

Training about the recovery process should be available to all providers within mental health systems. As everyone begins to work with individuals in a manner that demonstrates their belief in them, and that recovery is possible for each individual served, a change in the culture of systems will occur. Systems will move towards a recovery culture (St. George, 2009). A recovery culture means the environment is welcoming, that staff work with individuals in ways that demonstrate respect, kindness, and a belief in recovery (St. George, 2009), within surroundings which also convey these ideals (Anthony, 2000). There are many ways to create a strong recovery environment and a culture of recovery (St. George, 2009). Some examples of recovery environments compared to non-recovery environments are included in Table 1.

Table 1. Non-recovery vs. recovery environments

Non-Recovery Environments	Recovery Environments
Stability/maintenance is the goal	Living a full life even though symptoms may still exist periodically is the goal
Compliance is valued	Self-determination, critical thinking as the individuals increase their independence are respected and valued
One size fits all	Each person's plan is self-directed and the entire support team encourages the individual to take charge
People are protected from trial and error learning	People have the right to make decisions, to succeed and to fail, they have the right to learn about life
Medication is the primary tool for symptom management	Medication is one of many tools used for symptom management
Emphasis is on treatment	Emphasis is on working with the person
Clinical knowledge is valued	Peer support and self-help are also valued
Individuals are signed in	Individuals are welcomed in
Individuals are patients, clients, consumers	Individuals are people, guests, citizens, people seeking wellness, but most of all they are Bob, Susan, Clara, Shahrukh, Tien, Mikala, in other words, people with names
Individual's gifts and strengths go unrecognized and do not guide their treatment planning	Individual's gifts and strengths are brought into every person-directed treatment planning meeting
Spaces are without decorations, painted in dull colors in an effort to reduce stimulation	Spaces are full of sunshine, art is on the walls, colors on the wall are cheerful and warm, plants and current magazines are present
There are staff restrooms, which the individuals being served cannot use	Restrooms are available to all and there is understanding that separate restrooms are a form of discrimination
Patient areas have hard washable plastic furniture	The furniture is sturdy, even washable, but still comfortable and soft

Source: St. George, Rider, & Long, 2003, p. 32

Training might be needed to provide guidance to organizations about hiring peer support team members. Specific training from knowledgeable organizations that have experience working with peer supporters will support quicker development of strong teams. Ongoing training and supervision about recovery, peer support, and collaboration can help maintain effective teamwork and support strong collegiality.

Understanding the Unique Role of Peer Support Workers

The contribution of every team member is important. When peer supporters work in blended teams, it is important to understand their unique role. Peer support workers follow similar ethics as other clinical team members. However, there are some aspects to their work that must be understood and valued.

Peer support workers engage in mutual relationships with the people they serve. Both individuals have important information to share. Both individuals are the experts about their own life and experiences. The peer supporter and the individual seeking wellness can share beneficial and helpful information. However, neither the peer supporter, nor the individual being served directs or leads the other (St. George et al., 2003; St. George et al., 2015; Mead & MacNeil, 2006).

The relationship is mutually beneficial in terms of both individuals seeking wellness and increasing their confidence. Both individuals gain expertise as strong self-advocates within the peer support relationship where all ideas are valued. Both individuals share next steps toward life goals, and see themselves as independent individuals with increased self-efficacy (St. George et al., 2015). Peer support workers share their lived experience of recovery as a tool for hope. One of the most important aspects of peer support is the sharing of stories. The peer support worker and the person seeking wellness use storytelling to communicate their understanding of their life experiences (Mead, 2003).

Unlike clinical team members who share little, if anything, about their personal life, peer supporters discuss aspects of their lives as a key component of their work, including hardships they have overcome, as well as their hopes and dreams (St. George, Rider, & Long, 2000). However, the peer supporter's personal story input is minimal, using only enough to show understanding and shared experience (St. George et al., 2000). Sharing personal stories is not helpful when told in a competitive fashion. A peer supporter's story should always be secondary and never center-stage.

Peer supporters are not therapists. Even if they might have been a therapist in the past, when they are working in the role of peer support, they do not use a clinical perspective. Additionally, peer supporters are not counselors, they are not guiding people unless all other options are exhausted or their opinion in a given situation is necessary. They "are the expert on not being the expert" (St. George et al., 2003, p. 28).

If a peer supporter worked as an MD, social worker, counselor, or therapist in the past, their role as a peer supporter does not encompass any suggestions on medication, therapies, or treatment. Offering these kinds of assistance would be unethical and is outside the scope of work for a peer support worker (St. George, 2003). Peer supporters use recovery language (common human language) that supports everyone's understanding of what is happening (St. George et al., 2015). Peer support is not about diagnosing, classifying, or describing situations in clinical terms. It is about hope and possibility being discussed on a mutual level.

A peer supporter's documentation of meetings with the people they serve contains necessary information to meet requirements, but it is written using recovery language and describes, rather than diagnoses, an individual's experience. They quote the person they are working with, and they create the note with the person whenever possible.

Peer support notes use the person's name rather than the distance creating "clt" for client, or "pt." for patient. During the beginning of META's journey, trainings helped clinical team members to embrace new peer support team members. Especially vexing to team members was the idea that they too could say "I" rather than "this writer" in their documentation. Additionally, they were worried about using the person's name in the body of the note (St. George, 2009). When one of those team members attended training six months later, she stated:

I was not happy about the last training when you told us to use the name of the consumer on our documentation rather than patient or "pt." I left vowing never to change my way of documentation. However, I decided to try one thing you had taught us in an effort to prove you wrong. I decided to use the individual's name in each note. I wrote things like, "Susan slept through the night." rather than "Pt. slept through the night."

Then, she said:

I would not have believed it, but every time I wrote a person's name, I saw their face, their face, not letters and it made all the difference. I felt more connected to the person, I could not just block myself off from the fact that I was working with a person, an individual who needed kindness and caring.

Peer supporters work with an individual with the intention they will not need them once their work together is complete. Peer supporters encourage the individual to take the lead in everything they do together. They affirm the individual's wisdom and capabilities. They cheer the individual on as they try new things, and push through feelings and thinking that has held them back. With utmost respect and kindness, peer supporters encourage those they serve as they seek to try new things, find new connections in their community, or strengthen family ties that may have been broken. These are fundamental aspects of peer support work. Some of these aspects have merged into traditional services, but others remain in the realm of peer support service provision.

Peer Support and Self-Care[1]

Peer support workers must be able to stay well on the job, just like everyone else. One of the best tools for increasing a person's wellness, and building a sturdy foundation for recovery is the WRAP (Wellness Recovery Action Plan). WRAP was developed by Mary Ellen Copeland. Mary Ellen conducted research and held a 3-day work group to find out "how people recover" (Copeland, 2015).

Mary Ellen developed a user friendly, easy to create, wellness plan that has changed the lives of hundreds of thousands of people around the world. The tool helps people identify how they are and what it feels like when they are well. It guides them to identify the things they do to stay in that well place and then helps them make plans for every area of symptom progression so they are able to pull themselves back into a better state of well-being (Copeland, 2015).

WRAP is provided in a group, which is called upon to be a safe place to share and be open through the development and use of a "trust agreement." In the class, participants learn about each part of the WRAP, and work together sharing knowledge and reading the materials to develop a complete plan to support their wellness. In Counties Manukau, New Zealand, the system, and the people seeking wellness within the system of care speak the language of WRAP. The DHB has supported widespread use of WRAP and because of this, many individuals have had the opportunity to build a WRAP.

WRAP is a prerequisite for people interested in undergoing training as peer supporters in Counties Manukau. WRAP helps people develop tools to stay well, and manage challenges (symptoms) that might arise while working. WRAP helps people gain knowledge about the signs their challenges are increasing (symptom progression) and can even alert them when a crisis is coming. One individual in New Zealand stated: "What used to be a point just before crisis, has become an early warning sign now". Any individual, who has developed a WRAP plan for themselves, speaks the language of WRAP. Discussions of toolboxes, triggers, and early warning signs are shared between individuals and no explanation is needed.

Other tools for maintaining wellness might include yoga, tai chi, walking, talking with friends and much more. However, no tools for wellness will work unless the peer supporter uses them. They must be aware of their stress levels, just as the rest of the team must. They must actively engage in developing strategies for managing stress, getting enough rest, and eating healthy food. Peer supporters are no different to other team members.

In the workplace, it is not the responsibility of team members to provide counseling and support to the peer worker. In the workplace, most colleagues support each other in small ways. They may help a colleague who is a friend through a difficult time in life, but should they choose not to, it would be fine. Some organizations have concerns about hiring peer support workers; they worry the person may continuously seek support for their mental health challenges. This is not helpful to other team members and is certainly not helpful to the peer provider. It places them in a vulnerable position with other team members because they take on the role of a person being served, rather than a colleague. If the peer is seeking too much support, it is important to talk with them and establish guidelines. Be forthright, kind, and clear.

A working relationship that includes counseling to the peer may cause them to connect back to being a patient needing help, rather than a person who works as an equal member of the team. In essence, they become a patient who happens to have a job, rather than an employee who has some challenges, just like everyone else. The role shift from being a patient to being a colleague is imperative.

Peer supporter's accommodations should include time off for counseling or visits to their clinical services within reason. However, whenever possible these appointments should occur outside scheduled work hours. Peer supporters are strong and resilient individuals who have travelled through many difficulties in their lives. Their strength, determination, and hard work will make their services invaluable to a team.

CONCLUSION

Peer supporters help systems save money through reduced service use. They help individuals by supporting them to grab hold of their recovery. They inspire the people they serve to gain confidence and build solution-seeking skills, engage with them in reciprocal planning, and support them to take the lead. Peer providers help teams and organizations recover by simply being there and reminding team members that recovery happens. As these teams begin to change long held beliefs about the chronic nature of behavioral health challenges, they emerge from roles that have put the responsibility for another's life and well-being solely on their shoulders. As they release that sole responsibility, they can enter into a partnership with the people they serve, and the peer supporters. This collaboration creates a strong working relationship where shared decision-making occurs and the individual being served drives goal identification.

The peer supporters themselves grow in confidence by understanding and embracing the knowledge that they have strengths and gifts to contribute to the world. The peer worker gains connectedness through the belonging that comes from being part of a team. Their healthcare may improve due to increased income and their ability to access insurance or pay for needed medical, dental, and vision care. Their connectedness to the world increases as they expand their circle of friends and acquaintances. It is time for behavioral health systems of care to step forward, to lead the way in the development of new ways of working with people who are challenged with mental health and addiction concerns. It is time to help our systems recover. A major stepping-stone on the pathway of recovery is the inclusion of peer support specialists.

An overview of the journeys in three countries in which peer support is gaining recognition is included in the appendices. Mary O'Hagan, Simon Bradstreet, and Michael Burge provide valuable perspectives on peer support in New Zealand, Scotland, and Australia.

REFERENCES

Alcoholics Anonymous. (n.d.). *A brief history of AA in New Zealand*. Retrieved from http://www.aa.org.nz/about/history

Anthony, W. A. (1993). Recovery from mental illness: The guiding vision of the mental health service system in the 1990s. *Psychosocial Rehabilitation Journal*, *16*(4), 11–23. doi:10.1037/h0095655

Anthony, W. A. (2000). Recovery-oriented service system: Setting some system level standards. Boston, MA: Centre for Psychiatric Rehabilitation. Retrieved from http://www.michigan.gov/documents/anthony2000_1_83536_7.pdf

Bradstreet, S. (2006). Harnessing the lived experience: Formalising peer support approaches to promote recovery. *The Mental Health Review*, *11*(2), 33–37. doi:10.1108/13619322200600019

Cambridgeshire and Peterborough NHS Foundation Trust. (2016). Retrieved from http://www.cpft.nhs.uk/patients/peer-support.htm

Centre for Medicaid Services. (2007, August 15). *Letter to State Medicaid Director*. Retrieved from https://downloads.cms.gov/cmsgov/archiveddownloads/SMDL/downloads/SMD081507A.pdf

Copeland, M. E. (2015). *Wellness recovery action plan. What is WRAP? Mental health recovery*. Retrieved from http://mentalhealthrecovery.com/

DBS Alliance. (2016). Core peer specialist training.(2016). Retrieved from http://www.dbsalliance.org/site/PageServer?pagename=education_training_peer_specialist_core

Georgia C. P. S. Project. (2016). Retrieved from http://www.gacps.org/

Gordon, J., & Bradstreet, S. (2015). So if we like the idea of peer workers, why aren't we seeing more? *World Journal of Psychiatry*, *5*(2), 160–166. PMID:26110117

Hallwright, S., & McPherson, I. (2010). *Interview*. Retrieved from (https://vimeo.com/10673116)

Harding, C. M., Brooks, G. W., Asolaga, T. S. J. S., & Breier, A. (1987). The Vermont longitudinal study of persons with severe mental illness. *The American Journal of Psychiatry*, *144*(6), 718–726. doi:10.1176/ajp.144.6.718 PMID:3591991

International Association of Peer Supporters. (2016). *Definition-Peer supporter.* Retrieved from www.inaops.org

McLean, J., Biggs, H., Whitehead, I., Pratt, R., & Maxwell, M. (2009). *Evaluation of the delivering for mental health peer support worker pilot scheme*. Edinburgh, UK: Scottish Government.

Mead, S. (2003). *Defining peer support.* Retrieved from http://www.intentionalpeersupport.org/wp-content/uploads/2014/02/Defining-Peer-Support.pdf

Mead, S. (2014). *Crisis as an opportunity for growth and change*. Retrieved from http://www.intentionalpeersupport.org/wp-content/uploads/2014/04/Crisis-as-an-Opportunity-for-Growth-and-Change.pdf

Mead, S. (2016). *Defining peer support*. Retrieved from http://www.intentionalpeersupport.org/trainings/

Mead, S., & MacNeil, C. (2006). Peer support: What makes it unique? *International Journal of Psychosocial Rehabilitation.*, *10*(2), 29–37.

Mental Health Commission. (1998). *The blueprint for mental health services in New Zealand.* Wellington, New Zealand: Mental Health Commission.

Ministry of Health. (2012). *Rising to the challenge: The mental health and addiction service development plan 2012-2017.* Wellington, New Zealand: Ministry of Health.

National Action Alliance for Suicide Prevention Crisis Services Task Force. (2016). Crisis now: Transforming services is within our reach. Washington, DC: Education Development Centre.

National Empowerment Center. (2010). Retrieved from http://www.power2u.org/judi-chamberlin.html

Optum. (2016). *Peer support services improve clinical outcomes by fostering recovery and promoting empowerment.* Retrieved from https://www.optum.com

OptumHealth. (2016). *Peer bridger programs.* Retrieved from https://www.leaders4health.org/images/uploads/files/OptumHealth_Peer_Bridgers.pdf

Ostrow, L. (2013). *Peer respite programs for mental health crisis: Research and practice initiatives in the United States*. Baltimore, MD: Lived Experience Research Network, Johns Hopkins.

Ostrow, L., & Croft, B. (2016). *Results from the 2016 peer respite essential features survey.* Retrieved from http://www.power2u.org/downloads/PREF-Report-05.05.16.pdf

Peer2peer. (2016). *Peer2peer vocational training course.* Retrieved from http://p2p.intras.es/index.php/trainingmaterials

Repper, J., & Carter, T. (2011). A review of the literature on peer support in mental health services. *Journal of Mental Health (Abingdon, England)*, *20*(4), 392–411. doi:10.3109/09638237.2011.583947 PMID:21770786

Salzer, M. (2002). Consumer-delivered services as a best practice in mental health care and delivery and the development of practice guidelines. University of Pennsylvania. Retrieved from http://www.cdsdirectory.org/SalzeretalBPPS2002.pdf

SAMHSA. (2009). *What is a peer support worker?* Retrieved from http://www.samhsa.gov/brss-tacs/core-competencies-peer-workers

SAMHSA. (n.d.). *Practice guidelines: Core elements of responding to mental health crises*. Rockville, MD. *SAMHSA*.

Scott, A., Doughty, C., & Kahi, H. (2011). *Peer support practice in Aotearoa, New Zealand*. Christchurch, New Zealand: University of Canterbury.

Scottish Executive. (2006). *Delivering for mental health*. Edinburgh, UK: Scottish Executive.

Scottish Qualifications Authority. (2010). *Arrangements for mental health peer support at SCQF level 7*. Glasgow, UK: Scottish Qualifications Authority.

Scottish Recovery Network. (2011). *Experts by experience implementation guidelines*. Glasgow, UK: Scottish Recovery Network.

Scottish Recovery Network. (2012). *Experts by experience: Values framework for peer working*. Glasgow, UK: Scottish Recovery Network.

Scottish Recovery Network. (2013). *Reviewing peer working: A new way of working in mental health*. Glasgow, UK: Scottish Recovery Network.

Shapiro, J. (2010). *Advocate for people with mental illnesses dies*. Retrieved from http://www.narpa.org/chamberlin.htm

Smith-Merry, J., Freeman, R., & Sturdy, S. (2011). Implementing recovery: An analysis of the key technologies in Scotland. *International Journal of Mental Health Systems*, *5*(11). PMID:21569633

St. George, L. (2003). *History and outcomes of the peer support project in Maricopa County, Arizona*. Arizona, AZ: Arizona State University.

St. George, L. (2009). *Culture of recovery training*. Phoenix, AZ: RI International.

St. George, L. (2015). *History and results of peer employment training*. Phoenix, AZ: RI International.

St. George, L., Rider, A., & Long, M. (2000). *Peer support training* (1st ed.). Phoenix, AZ: META Services.

St. George, L., Rider, A., & Long, M. (2003). *Peer support training* (2nd ed.). Phoenix, AZ: META Services.

St. George, L., Rider, A., Zeeb, M., Smithers, T., & Long, M. (2015). *Peer employment training: A peer/recovery support specialist certification course* (5th ed.). Phoenix, AZ: RI International.

St. George, L., & Smithers, T. (2007). *Advanced peer practices*. Phoenix, AZ: RI International.

St. George, L., & Smithers, T. (2016). *Peer/recovery support specialist supervisor training: Developing and sustaining a peer workforce* (2nd ed.). Phoenix, AZ: RI International.

Stevens, T., & St. George, L. (2004). *Changing a culture: Moving from custodial care to recovery focused treatment.* San Diego, CA: International Association of Psychosocial Rehabilitation, META Services.

Swarbrick, P., Brice, G. H., Tucker, S. J., & Miccio, S. (2011). *Peer support wellness respite centres.* Retrieved from https://cms.centerforintegratedhealthsolutions.org/images/res/PDF,%20PSWRC.pdf

Te Pou o te Whakaaro Nui & Matua Raki. (2015). *More than numbers workforce stocktake.* Auckland, New Zealand: Te Pou.

Te Pou o te Whakaaro Nui. (2014). *Competencies for the mental health and addiction service user, consumer and peer workforce.* Auckland: Te Pou, Auckland Regional Alliance and Midland Mental Health and Addiction Regional Network.

The Alcoholism Guide. (n.d.). *History of Alcoholics Anonymous.* Retrieved from http://www.the-alcoholism-guide.org/history-of-alcoholics-anonymous.html

Van Gelder, L. (1995). *Howard Geld, 42, Advocate for mentally ill, dies.* Retrieved from http://www.nytimes.com/1995/02/14/obituaries/howard-geld-42-advocate-for-mentally-ill-dies.html

Walsh, P., Stewart, V., Crozier, M., Roennfeldt, H., & Wheeler, A. J. (2015). *Paid peer support in mental health.* Brisbane, Australia: Griffith University.

Zinman, S. (2013). *Interview.* Retrieved from http://www.peersnet.org/videos/2014/may/sally-zinman

KEY WORDS AND DEFINITIONS

Easy In: This concept identifies a system in which it is easy to obtain help, including social services (housing, food stamps), when they are needed, thereby reducing the number of people who wait until they become a danger to themselves or others, succumb to suicide, or become destitute.

Easy Out: Easy out means that a person can exit when they are doing well, and that if they take that path, they know that they can return again for services because of the nature of "Easy In."

Hope: Hope is the energy that comes from a belief things can change for the better and that one has options available that can support them to create the life of their choosing.

Lived Experience: The idea of lived experience began to gain popularity in the mid-2000s when it occurred to those who were driving peer support forward that people's lived experience (of mental illness, recovery, substance use, jail, prison, homelessness, poverty etc.) gave them specific skill sets that contributed to the mutuality of peer support relationships and gave them hands-on knowledge and wisdom that is of great importance to the people served and the systems of care themselves.

Mental Health Challenges: This refers to the experience of emotional or mental unwellness, trauma experiences, and co-occurring challenges, as well as voice hearing, alternate realities, and seeing things that others do not see or hear. In diagnostic language, these are the diseases identified in the DSM, for use in categorizing different mental illnesses.

Mutuality: The idea of mutuality is the core of peer support, and means both people have expertise, they share, and learn from each other.

Peer Recovery Coaching: Peer recovery coaching is a tool developed by META Services (RI International) that is a foundation for a recovery-focused conversation, and is helpful to peer supporters as they support an individual they are serving to begin to identify solutions and engage in planning (St. George. & Smithers, 2007).

Peer Supporters: Peer supporters are people who have engaged in their own recovery process and with effective training, have learned to work with individuals in a compassionate and supportive manner. Peers do not take the lead in service provision by telling people what they should do to recover, rather, they relate to people in ways that support them to try new things, reclaim their strengths, and develop skills that can help them maintain their wellness. In this chapter, all references to peers can include family members.

Reciprocal Planning: Reciprocal planning is a process whereby each member of the team including the person receiving services contributes to the treatment planning process and everyone walks away with specific tasks to support the identified goals. Reciprocal planning creates a "we" process rather than a "you" process.

Recovery: Recovery refers to the process and experience of gaining new well-being and regaining or maintaining connections to and participation in important life activities even with the challenges that arise from a serious mental health challenge.

Recovery Culture: A recovery culture means that surroundings in which people are cared for are bright, hopeful, welcoming, well decorated, and respectful. In addition, the individuals providing support or care within these locations are joyful, positive, and have a high belief of recovery for each individual. They see each individual served as deserving of respect and kindness.

Recovery Language: Recovery language is common human language that creates clarity and understanding for all individuals on the team as well as the person served. It is also language that intentionally veers away from pathologizing illness-focused language, towards language that creates a space for the normalization of emotions, experiences, and the idea of recovery.

Recovery Pathways: This refers to five aspects of support from providers that will enhance the opportunity for individuals to recover. Developed by META Services (RI International) in 2003 (St. George et al., 2003), these pathways of hope, choice, empowerment, recovery culture, and spirituality/meaning and purpose can create a foundation for the work of recovery with each individual.

Rolling Systems: A system in which people have access to needed services without barriers due to income, insurance, lack of insurance, or ability to pay making the services easy to access. Within the rolling system, one would be able to exit to a lower level of services or return to work, because they would understand that the services are there if needed and are accessible.

Systems of Care: Systems of care are the organizations, funding entities, services and people that provide behavioral health care to individuals with serious mental health challenges.

ENDNOTE

1 Written by Lisa St. George with permission from Mary Ellen Copeland.

APPENDIX 1

Peer Support in New Zealand

Mary O'Hagan, writer, speaker, and consultant from New Zealand provides an overview of peer support in New Zealand.

History

New Zealand has 4.5 million inhabitants and was first settled by the Polynesian Māori just 1,000 years ago. European settlers, mainly from mainland Britain and Ireland, colonized New Zealand from the mid-19th century on. The first New Zealand lunatic asylum was opened in 1862. Since then New Zealand has developed a typical western mental health system based around hospitals, controlled by medical professionals and funded by taxpayers. New Zealand is one of the only Western countries that closed all its large psychiatric hospitals in the 1980s and 1990s. One-third of mental health funding now goes into community based support services. New Zealand has 20 District Health Boards (DHBs), which fund and provide virtually all mental health clinical services. The DHBs also fund community support services provided by non-government organizations (NGOs).

Peer support in mental health has its roots in the informal sharing and support among inmates as they struggled with their internal experiences, with psychiatric coercion, and social exclusion in the dormitories and day rooms of psychiatric hospitals and clinics. The first formalized peer support began in addiction with the development of Alcoholics Anonymous in the 1930s. Alcoholics Anonymous (n.d.) was introduced to New Zealand in 1947 after a psychiatric hospital inmate read about it in the *Readers Digest* and "identified with the article in a way that he had never identified with anyone before". In 1957, an Australian priest with lived experience of mental distress developed GROW, a peer support 12 step program inspired by AA, which has been in New Zealand since the 1960s. The 12 step programs were deliberately apolitical; they located the source of people's distress and addiction in the "wrongs" or "maladjustment" of the individual and sought recovery through peer support, belief in a higher power, and entering a process of personal reform.

In the 1970s, the international mental health consumer/survivor movement emerged on the same historical wave as other movements of that era, such as feminism, civil rights, indigenous movements, and gay rights. These movements were inherently political; they all located the source of their constituents' marginalization in society and advocated for equality and self-determination. The early consumer/survivor movement protested against psychiatric coercion and social exclusion and established peer-run alternatives to mainstream mental health services. In New Zealand, several local, independent peer-run alternatives were established by the late 1980s, including Psychiatric Survivors in Auckland and Madness Anonymous in Wellington. They provided peer support, peer advocacy, and input into local service development. They brought a new voice to the table – one that argued from a platform of human rights and equality rather than paternalism and social exclusion. This voice was fully recognized in 1998, on paper at least, when an official government document heralded the adoption of recovery as the guiding principle for mental health services in New Zealand (Mental Health Commission, 1998).

Between the 1990s and 2000s, many of New Zealand's peer led alternatives closed down due to a tighter contracting environment in health, management or governance failures, and as new work opportunities for people with lived experience in mainstream services emerged. These new opportunities began with the introduction of consumer advisors in mental health services in the 1990s and continued with the employment of peer support workers, mainly in the new community support services, from the 2000s on. It is difficult to estimate the number of peer support workers in New Zealand today due to lack of definitional consensus and inconsistent reporting systems. However, a recent survey indicates that there are more than 300 peer support workers working in adult mental health and addiction services in New Zealand (Te Pou o te Whakaaro Nui & Matua Raki, 2015).

National Developments

In recent years, the emergence of the peer support workforce has been recognized in national initiatives and policy.

Rising to the Challenge: The Mental Health and Addiction Service Development Plan 2012-2017 (Ministry of Health, 2012), the government's current mental health and addiction action plan, highlights the need for expanded peer support training and the development of peer support and self-management services for people of all ages with "high and low prevalence" conditions.

In 2014, *Competencies for the Mental Health and Addiction Service User, Consumer and Peer Workforce* (Te Pou o te Whakaaro Nui, 2014) was published to inform training curricula, job descriptions, performance management systems, self-assessment processes, service specifications, and auditing. It consists of seven core competencies across all lived experience roles and three peer support competencies.

In 2008, the New Zealand Qualifications Authority (NZQA) approved the first formal New Zealand-specific tertiary level peer support (mental health) qualification, as developed by Mind and Body. From that early start, a national NZQA qualification was later approved in 2015. Careerforce, an Industry Training Organisation, is currently developing a broader national certificate course to replace the 2008 version. The replacement qualification will cover peer support work in various health and social service contexts.

Local Developments

Health System-Funded Peer Support Positions

In 2006, Counties Manukau DHB, the South and East Auckland service funder and clinical service provider, embarked on a major project to establish over 20 peer support full time equivalent positions in local clinical services and 40 in community support services. This initiative was driven by the leadership within Counties Manukau with expert input from the Arizona based mental health provider META Services (now RI International). Counties Manukau has one of the largest health system-funded peer support initiatives outside of North America. The peer support workers are employed in clinical teams, a peer-led residential alternative to hospital, Māori and Pacific services, alcohol and drug services, and mobile support services. Prospective peer support workers receive peer employment training, (through RI International and Connect Supporting Recovery) as a pre-requisite to gaining employment. The Counties Manukau funded peer support work has been a success. Evaluations have shown that service users experience high satisfaction and good outcomes from peer support and the presence of peer support workers in professional teams has brought about some recovery-based culture change. Unfortunately,

Counties Manukau is an outlier in New Zealand and other health service funders have not funded many peer support positions.

Mainstream Community Support Services

Various mainstream community support services throughout New Zealand employ peer support workers. Sometimes the peer support positions are specified in their contracts with the funders, or the provider decides to replace other positions with peer support workers. These peer support workers often work one-to-one with people in a mobile community support service, but some work in residential crisis services, housing, and employment services.

Independent Peer Support Agencies and Initiatives

Some of the most successful and enduring peer led alternatives in New Zealand include Mind and Body, Balance Whanganui, the Mental Health Advocacy and Peer Support Trust in Christchurch, and the Otago Mental Health Trust. These initiatives are largely funded through health services and provide support, advocacy, training, evaluation, and other services.

Three peer support programs from the U.S. have been used in New Zealand: WRAP developed by Mary-Ellen Copeland, Intentional Peer Support (IPS) developed by Shery Mead, and Peer Employment Training (PET) developed by Recovery Innovations. New Zealand has also developed some of its own peer support programs including training offered by Mind and Body and PeerZone developed by Mary O'Hagan. PeerZone has certified 160 facilitators in New Zealand, Australia, and Canada since 2013, and is going into the U.S. in 2016.

Some Issues

Peer support is the fastest growing mental health and addiction workforce in New Zealand. However, its development has coincided with a fairly static national mental health budget since a change of government and the global financial crisis in 2008. Despite its prominence in national policy, growth in the number of peer support workers appears to be slow. There is little national infrastructure to support development, such as a peer support worker association, training standards, or career pathways. Funder accountability measures and processes are not always tailored to peer support work. A tiny percentage of people who use mental health services in New Zealand have access to peer support workers.

There is still no universal understanding of what peer support is, and is not. Some providers believe it is sufficient to place someone with lived experience in any support role to call them a peer support worker without specific training and supervision. Peer support is yet to be seen by all as a unique specialty with its own values, training needs, and practices. There is still a lack of explicit peer support models that clarify its unique features and differentiate it from other occupations. Non-peer colleagues in mainstream services who do not understand peer support may regard peer support workers as low-status helpers. On the other hand, they may view peer support workers more as service users than as colleagues. This blurs boundaries and creates an unsafe and discriminatory environment for affected peer support workers.

New Zealand has come a long way in recent decades but there is still much work to do in developing a peer support infrastructure, securing peer support as a valued part of the mental health and addiction system, growing the peer support workforce, and making it accessible to more people. There is also a danger that the essence and values of peer support will be lost as it becomes more professionalized and more absorbed into the medicalized, paternalistic, risk-averse cultures of mainstream mental health and addiction services.

Many people have contributed to the development of peer support in New Zealand. Some of the lived experience leaders include Mary O'Hagan who initiated the New Zealand survivor movement in the late 1980s and recently developed PeerZone; Jim Burdett who set up Mind and Body in the 1990s and developed a peer support qualification; Frank Bristol who has been a major force in Balance; Cassandra Laskey the professional lead at the Counties Manukau peer support service; Magdel Hammond who managed the largest peer support team in an NGO; and Carolyn Swanson the service user lead in New Zealand's adult mental health workforce development center – Te Pou o te Whakaaro Nui. Some professionals have also been actively involved in the development of peer support, including Sue Hallwright and Jo Chiplin who established the Counties Manukau peer support service; Lorna Murray, an NGO leader who developed a large peer support team; and Marge Jackson of Kites Trust who led the development of a peer support evaluation tool.

APPENDIX 2

Peer Support Working in Scotland

Simon Bradstreet, Empower Research Manager, former Network Director of Scottish Recovery Network, provides and overview of peer support in Scotland.

Scotland has been identified as a country in which significant progress has been made in the re-orientation of services towards a recovery approach and peer support working has been described as one of the "recovery technologies" that have supported the change process (Smith-Merry, Freeman & Sturdy, 2011). The Scottish Recovery Network (SRN) has led efforts to encourage the development of peer worker roles in Scotland, arguing strongly that their availability is an essential part of the drive to develop recovery-oriented systems (Bradstreet, 2006). Despite significant development of infrastructure, the pace of peer role development has been disappointing (Gordon & Bradstreet, 2015).

Developing the Infrastructure for a New Professional Role

The role was formally introduced in Scotland at a 2005 event, which featured speakers from established U.S. peer providing services. This ultimately led to a policy commitment to pilot the development of peer worker roles in five Scottish Health Boards (Scottish Executive, 2006; McLean, Biggs, Whitehead, Pratt & Maxwell, 2009). Further support for role creation at a national level has included the development of an accredited training award (Scottish Qualifications Authority, 2010) and its adaptation for use across Europe (Peer2peer, 2016). Guidelines have also been created to support the development of peer worker roles (SRN, 2011), as well as a framework of values and behaviors developed with those currently involved in peer working to increase understanding of the role and maintain its distinctiveness (SRN, 2012). SRN also host a vibrant network of people involved in the delivery or development of peer services, which meets regularly offering mutual support and shared learning opportunities.

Current Peer Worker Provision

A 2013 review paper, developed as part of a commitment in the Scottish Government's mental health strategy, detailed progress in role development reporting a slow but steady growth in the number of peer workers since the initial pilot projects (SRN, 2013). At that time it was estimated that the number of paid peer workers was somewhere in the region of 50 and it is estimated that in the intervening period this has risen to around 80. At the time of the review, 75% of peer workers were employed in third sector organizations (NGOs), with the majority of peer workers working between 20-30 hours per week. Peer worker roles and responsibilities in Scotland vary and are dependent upon their working environment, ranging from the delivery of specific interventions and supports (including wellness planning), to group work, information provision, and general support work. While efforts have been made to articulate the distinctiveness and unique contribution of peer roles, there is anecdotal evidence to suggest that a lack of role clarification has slowed role development and more work is recommended in this area.

Evidence of Blocks and Facilitators

Despite being a small country, the rate of role development is disappointing particularly in the light of long-term policy commitment and the supports available for role development. A small study to examine the views of decision makers with regards to role development identified a variety of relevant factors (Gordon & Bradstreet, 2015). Participants reported that role development within current systems and frameworks was complex and potentially daunting for planners and policy makers already under pressure because of economic restraints to maintain existing services let alone develop new models of provision. Where roles were developed, an impetus was found to be that the development of paid peer roles was seen as part of a natural progression, which fitted with an existing values base, and direction of travel, and the importance of local champions were highlighted. Findings also suggested that new evidence on effective implementation and cost effectiveness should be prioritized to support potentially complex role development in times of reduced resources. However, if that evidence was available it was argued that a number of other factors would likely still hinder role development. These included a sense that developing peer roles was not seen as a national policy priority. Where peer roles had not been developed there was a sense that it was seen as being hard to prioritize and as a complex and risky process of role development.

Moving Forward

Clearly, the question of "why bother" has to be emphatically answered to ensure that peer workers are routinely employed and available across Scotland. Evidence and experience suggests that for many people making decisions about the development of mental health services, peer worker roles are seen to fall into the "nice but not essential" category. SRN will continue to champion peer support in all its forms including peer support working but are limited in their influence. For peer working to develop fully in Scotland, it will require a stronger push from national and local policy makers backed by new evidence on successful role development.

Further Information

Further information on peer working in Scotland see www.scottishrecovery.net

APPENDIX 3

Australian Peer Worker Overview

Michael Burge, a mental health advocate from Australia, provides an Australian peer worker overview.

Peer work is a relatively new approach to service delivery in many organizations in Australia. It is not possible to say with any precision how many peer workers are currently employed in Australian mental health services. However, there is evidence that the workforce is growing and services in the public, private, and NGO sectors appear keen to employ peer workers. It should be noted that the first recruitment of people with personal lived experience in mental health support roles (that specified lived experience as a criterion of appointment) was in 1993.

Challenges

Some of the challenges faced since the introduction of peer workers into the Australia peer workforce are outlined below.

- No consistent industrial or employment agreements, nor requirements for peer work to be professionally paid work.
- No nationally recognized Australian Standards of peer practice.
- No national framework for peer workers.
- No nationally recognized peer worker values and ethics.
- Unclear roles and responsibilities of peer workers.
- No one nationally accepted definition of a peer worker.
- No agreed entry level to employment in mental health services for peer workers.
- Inconsistent clarity and understanding of peer worker roles within organizations.
- Lack of organizational readiness and awareness of how peer workers can add value to service delivery.
- The concerns some people have about the capacity of peer workers to contribute to service delivery, which results in the role being under-utilized and under-appreciated.
- Uncertainty regarding the boundaries of peer workers.
- Lack of appropriate leadership, supervision, and career pathways.
- Isolation and the lack of networking opportunities with other peer workers for support in rural and remote areas.

Training and Education

In 2012, development of a nationally accredited qualification, Certificate IV in Mental Health Peer Work, was completed. During 2013-2015, the Mental Health Peer Work Qualification Development Project was funded by the National Mental Health Commission (NMHC) and coordinated by the Mental Health Coordinating Council on behalf of Community Mental Health Australia. A national network of peer work expertise shaped this project.

The development of the qualification involved a rigorous process with input from technical and advisory groups including peer workers and people with lived experience. The Certificate IV offers an opportunity to move towards nationally consistent training for peer workers. The six core units cover:

- Applying peer work practices in the mental health sector.
- Contributing to continuous improvement of mental health services.
- Applying lived experience in mental health peer work.
- Working effectively in trauma informed care.
- Promoting and facilitating self-advocacy.
- Contributing to work health and safety processes.

In addition to the six units above, a further nine elective units must be completed. To complement peer workforce development directions, two nationally recognized skill sets have been developed for peer leadership and peer management. The peer leadership skill set provides an early career pathway for peer workers who have completed the Certificate IV. The peer management skill set is intended for line managers of peer workers (both peer and non-peer).

Some Australian organizations have developed their own training, or utilized peer worker/peer support training from overseas. Much of the training for peer workers occurs in-house or is outsourced to Registered Training Organizations (RTOs) or other providers.

Peer Worker Roles

Peer workers are providing support for people who may be experiencing mental health crises, and are walking alongside people who do not wish to, or are unable to, engage with mental health services upon discharge from emergency departments or hospital. Whilst not completely peer run, a number of organizations offer services that are staffed by a significant number of peer workers, and provide step up- step down services and other alternatives to hospitalization. They also provide peer support during hospitalization and upon discharge and transition into community living.

Many other duties performed by peer workers include, but are not limited to: providing individual support; delivering education programs; home visits; assisting people with wellness plans; assisting with monitoring progress and managing well-being; training and education; role modelling; face-to-face assessments; respite support; telephone warm lines; peer facilitated groups; referral to other services; providing support for housing and employment; advocating for systemic improvements; support in acute settings and emergency departments.

Peer Work Value Recognized

Service managers have indicated that peer workers are a highly valued asset, and some services are seeking to expand the number of peer workers employed. An increasing number of managers are experiencing positive outcomes for people using services; carers and families; services and systems; other workers; and peer workers themselves. However, it should be noted that the uptake of peer workers is still slow in many areas.

Future

Facilitating and supporting new ways of working, including greater use of peer workers, is an important task for mental health leaders. Associated with this is the need to provide others with the knowledge and skills necessary for change; to provide an environment where change happens; and to acknowledge and address the risks of change.

Leadership is needed to overcome barriers to the peer workforce and support organizational change. We need to continue to develop leadership capacity at all levels to support and lead the mental health peer workforce innovation and reform. Recognition of, and support for, peer leaders promotes people-centered services and system improvements in mental health. Their advice and expertise can contribute to better policies, services, and programs with a greater recovery orientation.

Chapter 12
Supporting People Who Experience Co-Existing Mental Health and Addiction Problems:
A National Approach to Improving Responsiveness in Aotearoa New Zealand

Ashley Koning
Matua Raki, New Zealand

Suzette Janet Poole
Te Pou o te Whakaaro Nui, New Zealand

ABSTRACT

Meeting the needs of people with co-existing mental health and addiction problems is a challenge faced by many mental health and addiction services and providers. A compounding factor has been the separation of mental health and addiction services which has meant that many people with co-existing mental health and addiction problems have fallen through the cracks between services or had issues not recognized or responded to, leading to poor health outcomes. This chapter describes the approach taken by New Zealand's workforce development centers to support services to improve responsiveness and workforce capability to work with people with co-existing mental health and addiction problems. International research on implementation is briefly summarized before discussion about the impact of the national approach and the barriers to implementation that have emerged. Recommendations for next steps conclude this chapter.

INTRODUCTION

Aotearoa New Zealand has recognized for the past two to three decades that people with co-existing mental health and addiction problems are likely to have the poor outcomes in terms of well-being, engagement with treatment, physical health, employment and housing (Minister of Health, 2006; The Mental Health Commission, 2007). Integrated care has been recognized as the best practice approach to meet the needs of people with co-existing mental health and addiction problems (Chow, Wieman,

DOI: 10.4018/978-1-5225-1874-7.ch012

Cichocki, Qvicklund, & Hiersteiner, 2013; Priester, Browne, Iachini, Clone, DeHart, & Seay, 2015). Integrated care is the provision of care for both mental health and addiction problems at the same time by individuals who have the knowledge and skills to work with mental health and addiction problems and/or teams working collaboratively to provide holistic care based on a single plan. Providing integrated care requires a workforce that has both mental health and addiction knowledge and skills, or the ability to work collaboratively, in systems that support and encourage person-centered care (Addiction and Mental Health Collaborative Project Steering Committee, 2014).

The separation of mental health services and addiction services and the development of specialist workforces with specific knowledge, skills and treatment approaches in each area has meant that many people with co-existing mental health and addiction problems have fallen through the cracks or have not had issues recognized or responded to when they have tried to access assistance. For example, people might go to a mental health service for assistance with depression to be told that they needed to deal with their drinking problem before they would get help for depression. On the other hand, they might receive treatment for their depression without ever being asked about substance use or gambling. People might also go to an addiction service for help about their cannabis use and their problems with anxiety might never be recognized or it may be considered likely that they will resolve on abstinence.

In New Zealand prior to 2010 the general approach to developing a workforce capable of addressing both mental health and addiction problems was to provide local and regional training and clinical practice guidelines. This approach came from a supposition that it was lack of knowledge and skills about addiction in the mental health workforce, and mental health in the addiction workforce, that reduced responsiveness. This approach had little apparent impact as it was piecemeal, uncoordinated, voluntary, and did not fully take into account systemic barriers to workers being able to practice in a way that integrates mental health and addiction knowledge and skills (Ministry of Health, 2010).

In 2010, a nationwide approach was taken to address systemic issues alongside workforce development needs. As part of this process the term *co-existing problems*, often abbreviated to CEP, has been coined in New Zealand to encompass the issues that in the past have been described as co-occurring disorders, co-morbidity, and dual diagnosis. The broadening of the definition to include *problems* rather than disorders, morbidities, or diagnoses, was in recognition of the need to take a more holistic view of well-being. This definition encompasses the social determinants of health and also takes into account the impact of sub-clinical mental health and addiction problems which have a negative impact on a person's well-being when they occur simultaneously.

This chapter will explore the approach taken to improve the responsiveness of mental health and addiction services and enhance the capability of the mental health and addiction workforce to support people with co-existing mental health and addiction problems in New Zealand. It will examine how this is related to international implementation research and the impact of the approach taken. Support provided by the mental health and addiction workforce development centers, barriers to implementation, and suggestions for steps to continue the momentum for change will also be discussed.

BACKGROUND

The separation of mental health and addiction treatment delivery appears to be a function of philosophical, funding and systemic differences and professional silos (Todd, 2010). Mental health and addiction problems, however, clearly share common aetiological pathways (Eaton, Rodriguez-Seijas, Carragher,

& Krueger, 2015; World Health Organization [WHO] & Calouste Gulbenkian Foundation, 2014). The development of substance use and/or gambling problems has been seen as a self-initiated process with treatment mainly limited to psycho-social interventions. Mental health problems on the other hand are seen as having a biological basis and thus more deserving of help and potentially responsive to pharmacological treatment. While it is now recognized that addiction also has a biological basis, the moral judgement and stigma has persisted. The divergent development and funding of services and treatment for mental health and addiction problems has reflected this and it is only more recently that the overlap and commonality between the disorders has come to be recognized.

The artificial separation of problems has also been reflected in training and education for the mental health and addiction workforces, with quite different models of care evolving over time. Much of the addiction model of care initially came from people with lived experience of addiction, while the mental health model of care developed out of the medical model. While the models of care have been converging, workers in services have become increasingly more specialized in order to be able to work with either mental health or addiction problems. However, as a consequence they are less able to work across both areas. While most practitioners in both fields are aware they are often working with people who have co-existing mental health and addiction problems, the perceived division of responsibility can be seen starkly in the following comments taken from an unpublished report (MacEwan, 2007) that was commissioned by Matua Raki to better understand the perspectives in each workforce.

Eighty percent of my patients have alcohol and drug problems and no, we don't address these problems. (Clinical director, mental health DHB service)

Mental health nurses are so medication focused. There is a hell of a lot more about people than giving them a pill. (Alcohol and other drug [AOD] practitioner, NGO service)

I am here to treat her depression. If she is using cannabis what am I supposed to do? Depression is my business. (Nurse, mental health, talking about a service user)

Theories about how best to provide care for people with co-existing mental health and addiction problems include sequential, parallel, and integrated care as described below.

- Sequential care is prioritizing one issue and treating that before initiating treatment for the other (this is not much different from the current model of care provided by many New Zealand services).
- Parallel care is separate services providing treatment according to their own models of care with or without a shared plan.
- Integrated care is when a treatment or intervention plan is developed in consultation with the person to address both issues in one service, or two or more services providing treatment, on the basis of that plan, collaborating to provide a seamless episode of care.

While the evidence for the effectiveness of any of these approaches is limited, integrated care has been accepted as being best practice and has been promoted internationally (Priester et al., 2015; Todd, 2010). However, as mentioned above, the separation of services and/or models of care has hindered the adoption of integrated care as a standard practice in mental health and addiction services.

Studies of the implementation of integrated care in services for people with co-existing mental health and addiction problems have tended to focus on organizational-level factors that support change in service delivery (Sylvain & Lamothe, 2013). Reviews point out that despite growing awareness of the importance of integrated care for people with mental health and addiction problems, the availability of services that provide integrated care remains limited and/or in localized pockets due to difficulties associated with implementation (Drake & Bond, 2010; McGovern, Lambert-Harris, Gotham, Claus, & Xie, 2014; Sylvain & Lamothe, 2013; Torrey, Tepper, & Greenwold, 2011).

In a review of implementation strategies used to support the use of evidence-based practice for people with CEP in the U.S., Drake and Bond (2010) observed that high quality health care requires the following three core elements.

- Taking account of the preferences of people who use services.
- The use of research evidence.
- Excellent clinical skills.

Based on evidence from implementation studies in other areas of healthcare, Drake and Bond (2010) suggested the use of information technology is likely to help the implementation of integrated care for people with CEP. This could include the use of distance learning and electronic decision support systems as promising service and workforce development strategies.

Factors for Successful Implementation

The literature about CEP capability implementation is scant. However, reviews by Torrey et al. (2011) and Sylvain and Lamothe (2013) provide some direction on success factors.

Torrey et al. (2011) reviewed published studies on organizational factors that supported the implementation of integrated care/treatment for people with CEP as part of the National Implementing Evidence-Based Practice Project in the U.S. This project utilized an implementation model that was developed for integrated dual disorders treatment (IDDT). The model for IDDT included a multidisciplinary team approach to assessments and treatment for people with substance use and mental health problems. It also includes a toolkit with educational resources, training for clinicians, and expert implementation consultation for one year. Torrey et al. (2011) also examined the implementation of less intensive and comprehensive programmes. The programmes either used standardized indexes to measure the capability of services to respond to people with mental health and addiction problems (for example, the Dual Diagnosis Capable Addiction Treatment and the Dual Diagnosis Capable Mental Health Treatment indices [Substance Abuse and Mental Health Services Administration, 2011]), or a case study design to explore the factors that supported the implementation of integrated care delivery.

Torrey et al. (2011) observed that it is possible to implement integrated care in services for people with CEP but success may take years. This may be due to the complex nature of developing services that are capable of providing integrated care as this requires changes in the culture, the workforce, clinical processes, skills development, and outcomes monitoring. Torrey et al. (2011) identified three common factors that support successful implementation.

- Effective leadership: Leaders who understand, are committed to, and actively promote integrated care make the most progress with implementation.

- Effective management of staff turnover: A focus on staff recruitment, training, and supervision supports implementation due to the long time frame.
- Organizational support for service providers: For example, requiring results from leaders, providing incentives for quality, targeted funding streams, and "technical support" including training, supervision, fidelity measurement, and feedback.

Torrey et al. (2011) also identified that implementation in the IDDT programmes was helped by the following factors.

- State support, including funding and technical support.
- Committed service leadership, for example providing space, training, financial support, and a mandate for the project.
- Use of the consultant, for example for strategy planning, to address implementation barriers, train staff, and reinforce key principles.
- Practice proficiency that is supported by training and supervision.
- Practice evaluation, including regular measurement of fidelity, outcomes and practice penetration (reach).

The IDDT programmes that did not sustain implementation cited a lack of funding and staff turnover as barriers.

Sylvain and Lamothes' (2013) review observed that, while almost all of the high quality implementation studies used fidelity scales to measure implementation, the scales used were designed for specific service contexts. This meant that the fidelity scales were not necessarily applicable and easily transferable across services and jurisdictions.

The Canadian Centre for Substance Abuse (CCSA) recently published a guidance document to support effective service level collaboration by mental health, addiction, and other service providers to provide integrated care (Addiction and Mental Health Collaborative Project Steering Committee, 2014). Six key actions to support collaboration between service providers were identified.

- Supporting change, that is using formal change management models and strategies informed by implementation science, and approaching collaboration as an organizational change initiative.
- Engagement and relationship building by developing collaborative relationships that include people who use services, both horizontally and vertically within and across organizations.
- Screening and assessment by increasing the use of screening and assessment (and brief interventions) outside of specialist services supported by clear response and referral pathways.
- Treatment and recovery that reinforces person-centered and person-directed care as the goal of service delivery.
- Building capacity for collaboration, which requires both workforce development and technology.
    - Focusing on collaboration in professional curricula, linked to core competencies for CEP capability and responsiveness.
    - Expectation for collaboration needs to be part of job descriptions and programme deliverables.
    - Service leaders should support cross-discipline education and skills training, job shadowing and mentoring.
    - Service providers need time and space, and dedicated clinical supervision, to work through the challenges associated with change.

- Technology to support effective collaboration by increasing access to services through web-based applications, using algorithms to enhance collaboration, shared data collection, analysis and information about people using services.

The CCSA commented that it is important to appropriately evaluate collaboration initiatives so that knowledge about what does, and what does not work, can inform future efforts.

In addition, research generally has found that treatment providers do not implement new therapies and strategies simply because they are provided evidence that treatments improve outcomes for the people who use services. Below are two key factors that support implementation.

- The observation by workers implementing new treatments that outcomes are improving for the people who use their service.
- Monitoring how new treatments are being implemented to ensure that fidelity to the original model is maintained (Substance Abuse and Mental Health Services Administration, 2011).

In summary, there is evidence the following factors support the development of CEP responsiveness and capability in mental health and addiction services.

- Committed, results-focused, on-site leadership.
- Strategies to manage the impact of staff turnover (including recruitment, training and supervision).
- Organizational support.
- A supportive funding environment.

The following factors have also been identified as likely to support the development of CEP responsiveness and capability.

- Comprehensive electronic decision support systems.
- Distance (or online) learning.
- Collaboration and shared models of integrated care.

INTEGRATED SOLUTIONS: THE NEW ZEALAND EXPERIENCE

In 2010, the Director of Mental Health outlined the New Zealand Ministry of Health's expectation that mental health and addiction services would become *CEP capable* (Ministry of Health, 2010). While the Ministry of Health and other agencies had previously commented on the need to address co-existing mental health and addiction problems (Minister of Health, 2006; The Mental Health Commission, 2007), this was the first national directive which clearly stated that services were expected to change how they responded to people with CEP and suggested strategies to achieve this. Using the tagline "any door is the right door", the intent was that people seeking help would be welcomed and assisted to connect with services that could help them, regardless of whether their first contact was with a mental health or addiction service. Each of the 20 New Zealand District Health Boards (DHBs), which are funded on a regional population basis by the Ministry of Health, were encouraged to decide how to do this within their region. There was an expectation to work collaboratively with local non-governmental organisation (NGO), primary, and secondary service providers. This work was seen as part of a significant culture shift towards the development and provision of integrated systems of care which ensure that people are cared for seamlessly within mental health and addiction services regardless of their diagnoses.

Figure 1. Factors supporting development of co-existing problems responsiveness and capability in mental health and addiction services

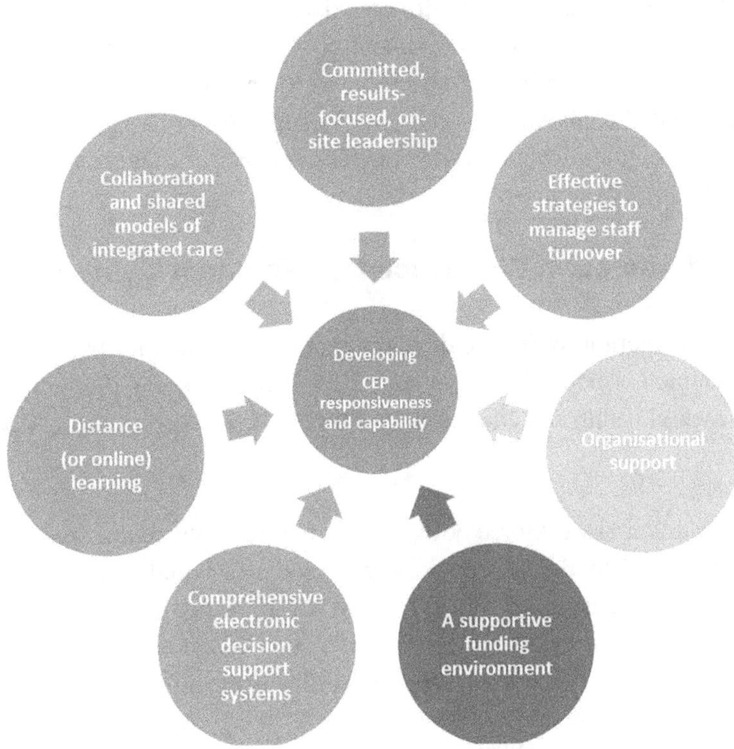

Service Delivery for People with Co-existing Mental Health and Addiction Problems: Integrated Solutions (Ministry of Health, 2010) was published as a guidance document for funders, service managers, and leaders. This guide outlined the Ministry of Health's expectations that all mental health and addiction services would become CEP capable. The guide provided tips, tools and links to other resources with the aim of increasing the responsiveness and capability of mental health and addiction services to people with co-existing mental health and addiction problems.

Integrated Solutions (Ministry of Health, 2010) recommended that mental health and addiction services become more CEP capable by focussing on the following.

- Being client-centered: Services and practitioners need to focus on the needs of the people who use mental health and addiction services.
- Service development: CEP responsiveness needs to be included as part of systems and processes.
- Developing integrated systems of care: Addiction (substance use and gambling) and mental health services and practitioners need to collaborate to provide integrated care.
- Workforce development: Services need to enhance CEP knowledge, skills, attitudes and capability across the respective workforces.

In addition, the Director of Mental Health formally advised all DHB mental health and addiction services, and funders to develop organizational and/or regional plans to improve CEP responsiveness within both specialist DHB and NGO providers in their region.

In the same year, *Te Ariari o te Oranga: the Assessment and Management of People with Co-existing Mental Health and Substance Use Problems* (Todd, 2010) was also published. This outlined a clinical framework for health professionals working with co-existing substance use and mental health problems and was an update to a previous guidance document published in 1999 (Todd, Sellman & Robertson, 1999). The primary focus of *Te Ariari o te Oranga* was to encourage the workforce to take a person-centered, well-being oriented stance when working with people. It emphasized the importance of drawing on evidence-based and or culturally appropriate practices to enhance engagement and provide integrated care for mental health and addiction problems.

Mental Health and Addiction Workforce Development Centers

The mental health and addiction workforce development centers are a fairly recent innovation in New Zealand, having come into existence during the mid-2000s, in response to the need identified for a well-trained and capable mental health and addiction workforce (Minister of Health, 2006). The five centers are listed below.

- Matua Raki, the addiction workforce development centre; www.matuaraki.org.nz.
- Te Pou o te Whakaaro Nui, the national center of evidence-based workforce development for the mental health, addiction, and disability sectors; www.tepou.co.nz.
- Te Rau Matatini, the Māori health workforce development center; www.matatini.co.nz.
- Werry Centre, the child and adolescent mental health and alcohol and other drug workforce development center; www.werrycentre.org.nz.
- ABACUS, a private training establishment funded to provide problem gambling workforce development; www.acts.co.nz.

The workforce centers provide training, scholarship support for under-graduate and post-graduate education, practice resources, and clinical guideline development. In addition, they promote leadership and systemic changes to support best practice in terms of having a workforce that has the right skills, with the right attitude, in the right place, at the right time (Te Pou o te Whakaaro Nui, 2014).

While no additional funding was made available to services to initiate and maintain systemic and/or workforce development to meet the goals of *Integrated Solutions,* a national mental health and addiction workforce development programme was initiated by the Ministry of Health. This national workforce development programme, led by Matua Raki, drew together expertise from the existing mental health and addiction workforce development centers.

Below are the aims for the CEP joint workforce development programme.

- Support mental health and addiction funders, service managers, and clinical leaders to focus on systems-level changes required to support CEP responsiveness, the provision of integrated care, and the ongoing development of workforce capability.
- Facilitate professional development within the mental health and addiction workforce to ensure people with CEP receive person and whānau-centred care that is responsive and capable.

At the start of the CEP programme, Matua Raki developed a CEP training framework for the mental health and addiction workforce (Matua Raki, 2009). The CEP training framework described the initial implementation strategy for the project and expected outcomes. Morris, Wooding, and Grant (2011) estimated that sustainable culture change and knowledge transfer into practice takes approximately 17 years to be fully implemented as "business as usual" within health services. Therefore, the programme of activities to support the development of CEP responsive and capable services has been seen as a long term investment and commitment.

The CEP programme of work has evolved over time and new initiatives have been included in response to knowledge exchange theory and sector requests. To support the evolution of the programme, a logic model describing the overall outcomes for the CEP programme was developed in 2013. The model identifies the progressive steps needed in terms of service provision, workforce development, and integrated systems of care to achieve the ultimate goal of people using mental health and addiction services having an improved quality of life.

It is important to acknowledge that a workforce development programme cannot be solely responsible for the achievement of these outcomes as there are multiple factors that influence whether or not services can develop CEP responsiveness and capability. These factors include committed leadership, funding, having CEP champions, and a stable skilled workforce.

Service Provision

The first joint workforce development center activity occurred in 2010 when representatives of the Ministry of Health, Matua Ra<u>k</u>i, Te Pou o te Whakaaro Nui, and Dr Fraser Todd (author of *Te Ariari o te Oranga*), toured the country promoting the goals of *Integrated Solutions* to managers, leaders, and funders of services. As part of these workshops, managers and clinical leaders were asked to nominate CEP champions to support both systemic and local workforce development. At that time, *enhanced* practitioners who were able to work at advanced levels of clinical practice with people who have co-

Figure 2. CEP programme logic model

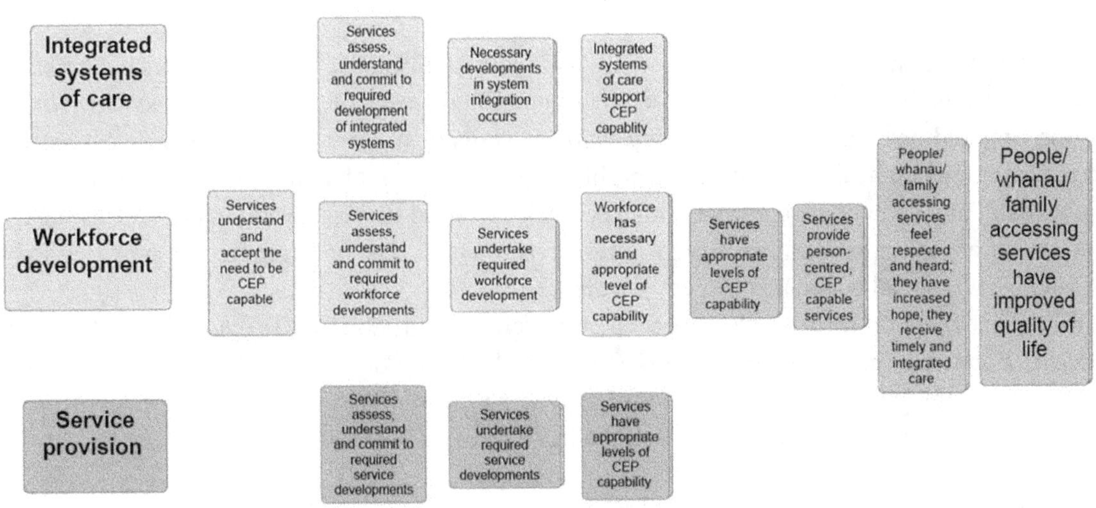

existing mental health and addiction problems, were considered to be suitable champions. Following these workshops, the regions were asked to provide plans for developing local CEP responsiveness and capability as described in *Integrated Solutions*, with the expectation that progress on the plans would be reviewed regularly by the Ministry of Health. To date, progress on the submitted plans have yet to be reviewed. As a consequence, each area was left to decide for themselves the importance of completing the actions described in the plans with no accountability for failing to do so or acknowledgement of significant progress.

Integrated Systems of Care

In 2012, the CEP Service Checklist (see Appendix 1) was developed by Matua Raki, Te Pou o te Whakaaro Nui, and the Werry Centre to assist service managers and clinical leaders to map out the steps needed to become CEP capable as described in *Integrated Solutions*. The CEP Service Checklist was based on a similar checklist developed in Australia (Croton, 2009). Managers and clinical leaders were able to self-rate their services' CEP capability and rapidly identify areas where service development and/or workforce development was needed to meet the goals of *Integrated Solutions*. Matua Raki and Te Pou o te Whakaaro Nui were also available to jointly facilitate workshops for organizations that requested support to carry out a self-assessment using the service checklist. From the outset it was considered important to model collaboration between mental health and addiction providers, demonstrating the principles of CEP responsiveness through joint facilitation.

To develop integrated systems of care, collaborative relationships between mental health and addiction services are necessary. For this reason regions have been encouraged and supported to use the service checklist as a larger group with managers and leaders from a range of DHB specialist and NGO primary and secondary mental health and addiction providers. These have been facilitated by Matua Raki and Te Pou o te Whakaaro Nui on request and have served to quickly identify strengths and gaps in local CEP capability and integrated systems of care, and to support the development of a local district or regional action plan.

Workforce Development

In 2011, following the initial promotion of CEP nationally to planners, funders, leaders and managers, a day-long training programme was provided by Matua Raki in each of the 20 DHB districts. This programme centered on developing *problem formulation* skills to support the comprehensive assessment of co-existing mental health and addiction problems and treatment planning for integrated care by the mental health and addiction workforce. This approach was used to raise awareness of CEP and engage the minds of as large a proportion of the workforce as possible. The programme was provided to both DHB and NGO mental health and addiction workers.

In 2013, the five workforce development centers developed and published *Te Whare o Tiki: Co-existing Problems Knowledge and Skills Framework* (Matua Raki & Te Pou o te Whakaaro Nui, 2013) which describes the knowledge and skills needed by a worker to be able to respond appropriately to people with CEP. Three tiers of capability are described in *Te Whare o Tiki* as listed below.

- *Foundation* knowledge and skills for the entire workforce, including primary care and support workers.

- *Capable* knowledge and skills expected from anyone who works routinely with people who have mental health and or addiction problems.
- *Enhanced* knowledge and skills for the secondary and specialist workforce.

Following publication of *Te Whare o Tiki*, an electronic version was developed to help self-assessment and to aggregate service and organizational results. This was to help with whole of service workforce development priority setting. This has since been incorporated into an online knowledge and skills tool that includes a range of other knowledge and skills frameworks for the mental health, addiction, and disability sectors. The online tool supports the generation of aggregated regional and national reports on workforce capability (http://realskills.tepou.co.nz).

The CEP champions/enhanced practitioner group, which had its beginnings at the *Integrated Solutions* workshops, has continued to recruit members from across the country and from various disciplines and workplaces. Initial efforts to establish an online *community of practice* were not successful and the group has evolved into a forum for knowledge exchange with regular mail-outs of current opinions, research and resources about the aetiology, impact and treatment of CEP. Some regions of New Zealand have established groups of champions who continue to support systemic and workforce responsiveness to CEP. The workforce development centers actively support these groups on request. More recently, the Werry Centre has supported a group of champions who work with young people and adolescents to develop a community of practice using video-conferencing to share their work and resources.

Train-the-trainer workshops for enhanced practitioners and CEP champions have been a feature of the workforce development centers approach to ensuring access to suitable training options for a wide cross-section of the mental health and addiction workforce. The train-the-trainer model has been used to maximize the impact of specialist training in a person-centered, well-being oriented model of care. The content of these workshops has been adapted to the needs of participants who were given the resources to provide the training to colleagues.

More recently, e-learning modules have been developed to introduce the rationale and philosophy of working in a CEP responsive manner, and to provide practical knowledge for working with young people. Advanced CEP skills based e-learning modules are in development. These modules complement the work of champions who provide face-to-face training rather than aiming to replace it. Face-to-face training has been identified as necessary to concretise any e-learning approach in New Zealand (www.werrycentre.org.nz; www.matuaraki.org.nz).

Scholarships to complete post-graduate health science qualifications are also available to support the development of a specialized, CEP enhanced workforce. These qualifications have been specifically developed to provide and enhance the knowledge and skills of health providers to work with people who have CEP. There are two post-graduate programmes that are funded to support 20 places each year (www.tepou.co.nz). These programmes aim to support an integrated approach to working with co-existing mental health and addiction problems.

Impact

In 2014, the joint workforce development group carried out an evaluation of the impact of the work carried out by the centers, champions, and others over the previous five years. The evaluation consisted of two parts. The first part was carried out in partnership with the Ministry of Health and consisted of a survey of managers of service providers in DHB and NGO settings, and a survey of planners and funders.

In the absence of reviews of the regional plans for development of CEP responsiveness and capability, the content of the surveys was based on the goals of *Integrated Solutions*. The managers' survey, which asked respondents to self-evaluate their current organizational capability from low to high against a range of criteria that were developed to reflect the spectrum of current capability, is shown in Appendix 2. The second part of the evaluation consisted of an analysis of records of discussions with champions attending workshops, and a survey of champions asking what worked, what did not, and what helped or hindered them in their roles as champions.

Service managers on average rated their organizations as generally providing CEP responsive and capable services, but not at an enhanced level as described in the questionnaire (see Appendix 2). Planners and funders were also asked about progress on their regional plans. The majority reported their region had an active plan. Many also stated their plan was progressing on schedule. The responses to both questionnaires indicated that organizational development of CEP capability was thought to be progressing well in some organizations, with pockets of excellent clinical practice. However, this was not yet "business as usual" across all services within an organization. In other cases, the implementation of CEP action plans had stalled or was progressing more slowly, in part due to competing demands on organizations.

While examples of excellent and good practice existed, integrated care for people with CEP was not being consistently provided within mental health and addiction services across the country. A small number of organizations reported that collaborative agreements were in place to provide integrated care across services and this was reflected in treatment plans.

From the survey of CEP champions it was apparent that many had been very active in their services and organizations providing in-service training, mentoring, and supervision. Some champions also reported that the services and practitioners they worked with were becoming more CEP responsive and capable.

When asked about the contribution of the workforce development centers to the development of CEP responsive and capable services and workforces, many survey respondents were positive about the effectiveness of raising the mental health and addiction sector's awareness and understanding of CEP. In a substantial proportion of New Zealand services this had translated to, and/or supported progress on the goals of *Integrated Solutions*. The strategies the workforce development centers adopted, as described above, to achieve this had by and large been effective where organizations and services had utilized them.

Barriers

From the responses to the questionnaires, surveys, and workshop discussions, some of the most common barriers to the development of CEP responsive and capable services and workforce are outlined below.

- The historical separation of mental health and addiction services.
- Limited leadership support at a regional level.
- Inadequate resourcing and support for workforce development.
- The need for workforce development and training across the broader workforce, including training for the non-clinical and NGO workforces.
- Lack of time available due to:
    - Multiple service development priorities and demands on services
    - The difficulty for people to commit time to specific project work.

- Organizational attitudes including:
    - A lack of buy-in from middle management
    - A lack of monitoring and follow through despite support from senior leaders
    - Expectations in some areas that addiction services will be the primary services to see people with CEP
    - Problems with services working collaboratively to develop person-centered integrated treatment plans.
- Resistance to change on the part of some clinicians who do not want to invest time in retraining.
- Limited engagement of clinically qualified people.
- Professional boundaries and specific roles.

Many of these barriers remain the same as those identified in earlier research in New Zealand (Todd, 2010) and have been observed in other countries (Padwa, Guerrero, Braslow, & Fenwick, 2015).

SOLUTIONS AND RECOMMENDATIONS

The New Zealand approach to developing the capability of mental health and addiction services and the workforce to respond effectively to co-existing mental health and addiction problems appears unique from a review of the literature. While it is apparent from the evaluation undertaken that there has not been a nationally consistent culture change, there are indications that, at the least, awareness has increased and CEP is still a priority area for workforce development. This was highlighted in a national survey of health-funded services in which over three-quarters of managers of DHB and NGO mental health and addiction services indicated there was a need for an increase in the capability and skills of the workforce to work with CEP (Te Pou o te Whakaaro Nui, 2015).

Based on survey feedback and a review of the literature, recommendations for future development of CEP responsive and capable organizations and workforce in New Zealand have been developed. The recommendations included below are likely to be relevant to mental health and addiction workforce development outside of New Zealand and recommendations specific to the New Zealand context have been omitted. The recommendations are grouped under the four focus areas of *Integrated Solutions.*

Client (Person)-Centred

- Strategies to enhance the ability of services and practitioners to work collaboratively in order to provide integrated care are developed and promoted.
- The use of feedback from people using services to reinforce and support buy-in for adoption of CEP responsive and capable practices is explored.
- Aggregated feedback is used at regular intervals to evaluate the overall effectiveness of the CEP programme in terms of making a difference for people with CEP, asking questions such as:
    - "Were you asked about other possible issues including substance use, gambling and mental health problems?"
    - "Were you offered support to access services to help with other problems?"
    - "Did the service supporting you know what other services were doing for you?".

- Services and the workforce are encouraged and supported to record mental health and addiction diagnoses and use this information to inform workforce planning and service development.
- Mental health and addiction services are supported to adopt a standardised and consistent approach to screening and comprehensive assessment.

Service Development

- Commissioning frameworks:
  - Take into account the need for standardised and consistent screening and assessment practices across services
  - Consider the resource implications of a significant culture change for some organisations
  - Establish clear guidelines to advise those in commissioning roles.
- Workforce development centres:
  - Encourage and support the development of CEP responsive services and a CEP capable workforce with a focus on enhancing the capability of those in leadership roles
  - Support CEP enhanced practitioners and champions with a focus on the evidence around implementation and change management
  - Explore options and develop strategies to influence clinical leaders and other service managers and leaders
  - Support a small number of organisations intensively
  - Develop and promote CEP responsive service exemplars.

Integrated Systems of Care

- Paradigms, or exemplars, of what a CEP responsive and capable service and workforce looks like are developed and promoted.
- A benchmark for effective CEP service delivery is developed.
- Quality assurance and audit processes are developed and used to support the development of nationally consistent CEP responsive services.
- Regional CEP enhanced practitioner and champion groups are supported to meet and develop local networks.

Workforce Development

- CEP training packages are:
  - Sustainably available nationally
  - Supported by a range of readily available CEP eLearning courses
  - Regularly reviewed and further developed to ensure their currency and efficacy.
- Workforce planning includes awareness of systemic and organizational culture changes that may be needed to ensure readiness for training so that new knowledge and skills can be integrated into practice.
- The needs of the Māori and Pasifika workforce in terms of developing CEP responsive and capable services and workforce are identified.

CONCLUSION

As in many other jurisdictions, New Zealand has struggled over the past two decades to fully embed a sustainable culture change to ensure mental health and addiction services and the workforce respond appropriately to co-existing mental health and addiction problems. It has been observed that training in isolation is unlikely to lead to sustained practice changes, and the adoption of evidence-based practice can take up to 17 years (Morris et al., 2012). Workforce development is about more than training and skills acquisition and, in the case of developing responsiveness to CEP, includes advocacy and recognition of the need for systemic and culture changes to support a workforce able to provide integrated care for mental health and addiction problems. While it may be considered that New Zealand has potential advantages in terms of achieving change at a national level due to having a smaller workforce than many other countries, this is offset by a wide geographical spread with a corresponding diversity in terms of size and funding of organizations and services providing mental health and addiction care. The impact of the diversity of providers on their ability to easily work together and collaborate was initially underestimated and a significant learning for the workforce development centers has been that there is a need to pay more attention to the skills and attitudes that are needed for effective collaboration that supports integrated care. What appears to have had a significant impact in New Zealand is the national focus, ongoing support from the Ministry of Health, and the joint workforce development centers approach to workforce development. The consistent commitment to change over several years has kept the need for service and practice change alive in the face of competing priorities. Evaluation of the impact of the mental health and addiction workforce development centers approach to developing CEP responsiveness and capacity has supported the approach taken to date and helped to identify areas for further development and enhancement.

REFERENCES

Addiction and Mental Health Collaborative Project Steering Committee. (2014). *Collaboration for addiction and mental health care: Best advice.* Ottawa, Canada: Canadian Centre on Substance Abuse.

Chow, C. M., Wieman, D., Cichocki, B., Qvicklund, H., & Hiersteiner, D. (2013). Mission impossible: treating serious mental illness and substance use co-occurring disorder with integrated treatment: a meta-analysis. *Mental Health and Substance Use, 6*(2), 150–168. doi:10.1080/17523281.2012.693130

Croton, G. (2009). *Checklist- Agency dual diagnosis capability.* Retrieved from http://www.dualdiagnosis.org.au

Drake, R. E., & Bond, G. R. (2010). Implementing integrated mental health and substance abuse services. *Journal of Dual Diagnosis, 6*(3-4), 251–262. doi:10.1080/15504263.2010.540772

Eaton, N. R., Rodriguez-Seijas, C., Carragher, N., & Krueger, R. F. (2015). Transdiagnostic factors of psychopathology and substance use disorders: A review. *Social Psychiatry and Psychiatric Epidemiology, 50*(2), 171–182. doi:10.1007/s00127-014-1001-2 PMID:25563838

MacEwan, I. (2007). *Mental health and alcohol and drug co-existing disorders: An integrated experience for whai ora?* Christchurch, New Zealand: Matua Raki.

McGovern, M. P., Lambert-Harris, C., Gotham, H. J., Claus, R. E., & Xie, H. (2014). Dual diagnosis capability in mental health and addiction treatment services: An assessment of programs across multiple state systems. *Administration and Policy in Mental Health and Mental Health Services Research*, *41*(2), 205–214. doi:10.1007/s10488-012-0449-1 PMID:23183873

Minister of Health. (2006). *Te kōkiri: The mental health and addiction action plan 2006–2015*. Wellington, New Zealand: Ministry of Health.

Ministry of Health. (2010). *Service delivery for people with co-existing mental health and addiction problems: Integrated solutions*. Wellington, New Zealand: Ministry of Health.

Morris, Z. M., Wooding, S., & Grant, J. (2011). The answer is 17 years, what is the question: Understanding time lags in translational research. *Journal of the Royal Society of Medicine*, *104*(12), 510–520. doi:10.1258/jrsm.2011.110180 PMID:22179294

Padwa, H., Guerrero, E. G., Braslow, J. T., & Fenwick, K. M. (2015). Barriers to serving clients with co-occurring disorders in a transformed mental health system. *Psychiatric Services (Washington, D.C.)*, *66*(5), 547–550. doi:10.1176/appi.ps.201400190 PMID:25686812

Priester, M. A., Browne, T., Iachini, A., Clone, S., DeHart, D., & Seay, K. D. (2016). Treatment access barriers and disparities among individuals with co-occurring mental health and substance use disorders: An integrative literature review. *Journal of Substance Abuse Treatment*, *61*, 47–59. doi:10.1016/j.jsat.2015.09.006 PMID:26531892

Matua Raki (2009). A co-existing problems training framework for the addiction and mental health workforce. Wellington, New Zealand: Matua Raki.

Matua Raki & Te Pou o te Whakaaro Nui. (2013). *Te whare o tiki: Co-existing problems knowledge and skills framework*. Auckland, New Zealand: Matua Raki and Te Pou o te Whakaaro Nui.

Substance Abuse and Mental Health Services Administration. (2011). *Dual diagnosis capability in mental health treatment toolkit version 4.0*. Rockville, MD: SAMHSA.

Sylvain, C., & Lamothe, L. (2013). Studying implementation of dual diagnosis services: *A review. Journal of Dual Diagnosis*, *9*(2), 195–207. doi:10.1080/15504263.2013.771809

Te Pou o te Whakaaro Nui. (2014). *Getting it right – workforce planning guide*. Auckland, New Zealand: Te Pou o te Whakaaro Nui.

Te Pou o te Whakaaro Nui. (2015). *Overview of the adult mental health and addiction workforce: 2014 survey of vote health funded services*. Auckland, New Zealand: Te Pou o te Whakaaro Nui.

The Mental Health Commission. (2007). *Te haererenga mo te whakaòranga 1996–2006: The journey of recovery for the New Zealand mental health sector*. Wellington, New Zealand: The Mental Health Commission.

Todd, F. C. (2010). *Te ariari o te oranga: The assessment and management of people with co-existing mental health and substance use problems*. Wellington, New Zealand: Ministry of Health.

Todd, F. C., Sellman, J. D., & Robertson, P. J. (1999). *The assessment and management of people with co-existing substance use and mental health disorders*. Wellington, New Zealand: Alcohol Advisory Council.

Todd, F. C., Sellman, J. D., & Robertson, P. J. (2002). Barriers to optimal care for patients with coexisting substance use and mental health disorders. *The Australian and New Zealand Journal of Psychiatry*, *36*(6), 792–799. doi:10.1046/j.1440-1614.2002.01049.x PMID:12406122

Torrey, W. C., Tepper, M., & Greenwold, J. (2011). Implementing integrated services for adults with co-occurring substance use disorders and psychiatric illnesses: A research review. *Journal of Dual Diagnosis*, *7*(3), 150–161. doi:10.1080/15504263.2011.592769

World Health Organization & Calouste Gulbenkian Foundation. (2014). *Social determinants of mental health*. Geneva, Switzerland: World Health Organization.

KEY TERMS AND DEFINITIONS

Aotearoa New Zealand: Acknowledges the Māori people who are the tāngata whenua or indigenous people.

Co-Existing Problems: Co-occurring, complex mental health, gambling and substance use disorders, often also referred to as dual diagnosis, co-existing disorders, or comorbidity.

District Health Board (DHB): Responsible for providing or funding, via planners and funders, the provision of health services in their district/region. Funding for DHBs comes from the government via the national Ministry of Health and is based on population demographics.

Pasifika: Describes people, and their descendants, from the Pacific Islands.

Planners and Funders: Located within DHBs and responsible for the allocation of funding, based on government and Ministry of Health priorities, for both mental health and addiction services based in the DHB and local NGOs. This role is similar to that usually described as a commissioner in other countries.

Tāngata Whai Ora: A Māori term used to refer to people who access mental health and addiction services, including children, youth and adult service users, clients, and consumers.

Whānau: A Māori term used to refer to the wider network and hierarchy of relationships that support a person and can include immediate and extended family and important relationships outside of direct familial links.

APPENDIX 1

Co-Existing Problem (CEP) Service Checklist

Table 1 is a simplified version for use in workshops. The complete version is available online at http://www.matuaraki.org.nz

Table 1. Co-existing problem (CEP) service checklist

Service Objectives	Consistently happening	Not routinely happening	Not happening at all
CEP responsiveness is identified as core business Service plans, service descriptions and mission statements reflect a CEP focus and responsiveness that reflects that any door is the right door for tāngata whai ora and family and whānau seeking help.			
Effective partnerships and agreed mechanisms to ensure 'any door is the right door' to support and treatment Formal agreements are in place between and with local DHB, NGO and PHO addiction/AOD, gambling and mental health services defining pathways of care and primary responsibility for support and treatment for tāngata whai ora, family and whānau.			
Screening All people seeking assistance from services are screened for mental health, substance use and gambling, using standardised and validated screening tools where appropriate			
Assessment Mental health services carry out a thorough alcohol and other drug and gambling assessment, including where necessary information from family, whānau and other relevant agencies, when screening indicates the presence of co-existing problems. Addiction/AOD and gambling services carry out a thorough Mental State Examination when screening indicates the presence of co-existing problems.			
Use of outcomes information Outcomes information is used by individual staff and teams to inform support and treatment.			
Integrated Treatment Either one case manager or team provide/co-ordinate treatment and support for people presenting with co-existing problems **or** staff of separate services work together to formulate, implement and monitor a single documented plan in consultation and in partnership with tangata whai ora, their family and whānau.			
Follow-up Tāngata whai ora with identified co-existing problems are prioritised for proactive follow-up following self or planned discharge and community agencies are actively engaged to provide ongoing support.			
Co-existing problem champion The service has at least one practitioner with appropriate experience, training and seniority who is the identified CEP champion.			
Workforce co-existing problem capability The service routinely carries out internal audits or inventories of the team's and individual staff member's CEP knowledge and skills in order to inform workforce development needed to meet service objectives.			
Outcomes and service responsiveness for tāngata whai ora with co-existing problems are recorded, monitored, and regularly reviewed Outcomes information about problematic substance use and gambling among tāngata whai ora who use mental health services and mental health problems among tāngata whai ora who use addiction/AOD and gambling services is routinely collected and systematically analysed to inform team and service development.			

APPENDIX 2

National Co-Existing Problems (CEP) Questionnaire

The following questionnaire/self-rating tool in Table 2 was developed based on the goals of *Integrated Solutions* (Ministry of Health, 2010) and formed the basis of an evaluation of current mental health and addiction service responsiveness to people with co-existing mental health and addiction problems. The questionnaire was disseminated to all 20 DHB services and 38 of the largest NGO providers in New Zealand.

Table 2. National co-existing problems (CEP) questionnaire

Client (Person and Whānau) Centred Care Please indicate how you believe your organisation is meeting each goal using the criteria provided				
1. All people seeking assistance from mental health and addiction services are screened for mental health, substance use and gambling				
There is no evidence of routine screening for addiction problems in mental health services or mental health problems in addiction services	Standardised screening tools are available but are only used depending on the judgement of the worker	Standardised screening tools are used with most people presenting and results recorded in clinical files	Standardised screening tools are used with all people presenting and results recorded in clinical files	Advanced screening tools are used when indicated
2. Treatment pathways are clearly documented and utilised in response to the results of screening				
Screening tools are used to determine access to services	Screening tool results are entered into clinical files but no evidence of follow-up on the results of screening	Screening tool results are used to make referrals to other services	The results of screening are documented and form the basis of brief interventions, treatment planning and or referral for all tāngata whai ora	The results of screening are documented and form the basis of collaborative integrated care plans
3. Tāngata whai ora have documented comprehensive assessments				
Mental health or addiction assessments are carried out	Mental health or addiction assessments are carried out along with screening for co-existing mental health or addiction problems	Both mental health and addiction problems are assessed and documented	Assessments include documented information about mental health, addiction and other CEP	Assessments include holistic information about CEP, strengths and well-being goals which are used to develop treatment plans
4. Family and whānau are involved in assessment and treatment planning with documented permission from tangata whai ora				
Family and whānau are not involved	Family and whānau are only involved in discharge planning	Family and whānau are only involved in initial assessment	Family and whānau are involved in treatment planning on their own request	Family and whānau are invited to attend all appropriate stages of the treatment process
Service Development Please indicate how you believe your organisation is meeting each goal using the criteria provided				
5. CEP responsiveness and appropriate workforce capability is identified in service plans, policies and procedures, service descriptions, mission statements and position descriptions				
CEP is not recognised in any service documentation	CEP is recognised in service plans	CEP is recognised in service plans and mission statements	Specific roles have CEP knowledge, skills and capability included in position descriptions	All position descriptions include reference to CEP knowledge, skills and capability
6. Service leaders promote and support organisational and culture change to embed sustainable CEP responsiveness and capability across mental health and addiction services				
Organisational and culture change is not being considered or prioritised	Organisational and culture change is being discussed	Organisational and culture change is happening at a clinical team level	Organisations respond collaboratively and effectively to the needs of tāngata whai ora with CEP	Organisational and culture change is translating into effective local policies and MDT practices

<table>
<tr><td colspan="5">7. Primary, secondary and provisional diagnoses are recorded in file notes and entered into PRIMHD for all tāngata whai ora</td></tr>
<tr><td>Only a primary diagnosis recorded in clinical files, if at all</td><td>Primary and secondary diagnoses recorded on 50% of clinical files</td><td>Primary, secondary and provisional diagnoses recorded in the majority of clinical files</td><td>Primary diagnoses entered on all clinical files and also recorded in PRIMHD</td><td>Primary, secondary and provisional diagnoses recorded in all clinical files and PRIMHD</td></tr>
<tr><td colspan="5">8. MultiDisciplinary Team (MDT) case review documents assessment and treatment of coexisting problems in clinical files</td></tr>
<tr><td>There is no evidence of MDT consultation</td><td>MDT case reviews referred to but CEP specific outcomes not documented in file notes</td><td>Service specific MDT case reviews have CEP assessments documented in clinical file</td><td>Organisation specific MDT case reviews have treatment plans for CEP documented in clinical file</td><td>Cross service, agency and organisation MDT case reviews have CEP assessments and treatment plans documented in clinical files</td></tr>
<tr><td colspan="5">9. Risk assessment includes recognition of the impact of substance use and gambling on mental health symptoms and vice versa</td></tr>
<tr><td>Each service has a service specific risk assessment format</td><td>Risk assessments includes recognition of substance use, gambling or mental health problems as possible risk factors</td><td>Risk assessments includes recognition of substance use, gambling or mental health problems as possible risk factors</td><td>Risk assessments document known risks for the individual with co-occurring substance use, gambling and mental health symptoms</td><td>Risk assessments include documented reference to known and potential risky interactions between mental health symptoms, substance use and gambling</td></tr>
<tr><td colspan="5">Integrated Systems of Care
Please indicate how you believe your organisation is meeting each goal using the criteria provided</td></tr>
<tr><td colspan="5">10. Tāngata whai ora models of care are underpinned by agreements that support collaborative and integrated care that extends across services and sectors</td></tr>
<tr><td>No service agreements between services and sectors for people who need more than one service</td><td>Referrals are made if people need more than one service but this means another assessment for the person</td><td>A process to identify and develop agreements with services/sectors for people who need more than one service is under development</td><td>Collaborative agreements to provide integrated care are currently being trialled</td><td>Collaborative agreements are in place to provide integrated care across services and are reflected in treatment plan</td></tr>
<tr><td colspan="5">11. The model of care for tāngata whai ora with CEP includes interagency communication and collaboration to provide integrated care</td></tr>
<tr><td>No interagency communication</td><td>Prior conversation with case-manager and other agency mentioned in MDT and or discharge meetings</td><td>Tangata whai ora is asked to inform other agency service providers about what role they will play in the treatment plan. This is added to plan by case manager</td><td>Other agency attends home or outpatient service with tangata whai ora and case manager as part of the assessment and treatment plan but does not attend MDT</td><td>Other agency attends home or outpatient service with tangata whai ora and case manager and the MDT as part of the assessment and treatment plan</td></tr>
<tr><td colspan="5">12. Discharge summaries for key stakeholders include details of coexisting problems and specific treatment plans</td></tr>
<tr><td>Only primary diagnosis documented</td><td>Primary and secondary diagnoses documented</td><td>Screening tool results reflected in the summary and note made when brief intervention delivered or referral made to other services and agencies</td><td>CEP diagnoses and treatment plan noted in the summary</td><td>Full formulation and treatment plan reflected in discharge summary with CEP specific recovery plan attached</td></tr>
<tr><td colspan="5">Workforce Development
Please indicate how you believe your organisation is meeting each goal using the criteria provided</td></tr>
<tr><td colspan="5">13. The training and development needs for the mental health and addiction workforce to develop appropriate CEP capability have been identified</td></tr>
<tr><td>There has been no review of the existing CEP knowledge and skills of the workforce</td><td>Specialist clinicians have carried out self-assessments of their CEP knowledge and skills</td><td>Training and development needs are identified for specialist clinicians</td><td>Service wide CEP knowledge and skills self-assessments have been carried out</td><td>Training and development needs are identified for all staff members</td></tr>
<tr><td colspan="5">14. The mental health and addiction workforce has the knowledge and skills to respond to people with mental health and addiction problems and their families and whānau</td></tr>
<tr><td>There is no workforce plan to develop knowledge or skills</td><td>A workforce plan has entered discussion stage</td><td>The workforce plan has been developed</td><td>The workforce plan to develop CEP capable and enhanced clinicians is in action</td><td>A plan is in place to sustain and maintain a CEP capable and enhanced workforce</td></tr>
</table>

Chapter 13
Workforce Development in the Child and Adolescent Mental Health Sector:
The Challenge of Rolling out a Specialist Eating Disorders Treatment in New Zealand

Rachel Lawson
South Island Eating Disorders Service, CDHB, New Zealand

Bronwyn Dunnachie
The Werry Centre for Child and Adolescent Mental Health Workforce Development, New Zealand

ABSTRACT

Eating disorders are serious illnesses with both physical and psychological symptoms. In the case of anorexia nervosa, the evidence suggests the earlier one identifies and treats the illness, the greater the chance of full recovery. In 2010 the New Zealand Ministry of Health provided funding to roll out the evidence based, Family Based Therapy (also known as Maudsley Family Based Therapy [MFBT]), treatment for anorexia nervosa, to specialist eating disorders services and clinicians in child and family services. The main focus of this chapter is the planning behind the implementation and sustainability processes, the evaluation, and the initial outcomes of the implementation of MFBT. Finally, lessons learned and recommendations from the implementation process will be outlined.

INTRODUCTION

Implementation science is a relatively new discipline which seeks to understand the factors that influence the uptake of specific evidence based interventions in natural settings (Bernfeld, Farrington & Leschied, 2001; Durlak & DuPre, 2008). This developing body of knowledge has informed how specific interventions can be implemented to achieve the best well-being outcomes for consumers engaged with health services. In New Zealand, The Werry Centre is funded to provide workforce development sup-

DOI: 10.4018/978-1-5225-1874-7.ch013

port by offering technical assistance to the infant, child and adolescent mental health (ICAMH) sector. This activity focuses on activities such as training, research, assistance with recruitment and retention, service and infrastructure development. The Werry Centre utilizes implementation science to support the implementation of specific interventions within ICAMH services in New Zealand.

Health services in New Zealand are, for the most part, publically funded, and administered locally by 20 District Health Boards (DHBs). The New Zealand specialist ICAMH services sit within the DHB structure and are delivered by multidisciplinary teams of health professionals. They are considered secondary level services and sit between primary health services, for example those delivered by general practitioners, and tertiary level services such as in-patient services. In 2014, there were 1086 full time equivalent positions employed within ICAMH services across a range of disciplines (The Werry Centre, 2015).

In 2010, the Werry Centre led the implementation of Maudsley Family Based Therapy (MFBT) to support the treatment of young people who had been clinically diagnosed with anorexia nervosa based on the *Diagnostic and Statistical Manual of Mental Disorders IV* (American Psychiatric Association, 2000). This chapter provides a brief description of the principles used for the roll out of the Real Skills Plus CAMHS competency framework in ICAMH services, coupled with implementation science to inform the implementation of the MFBT within New Zealand Aotearoa. The implementation process of the MFBT is discussed in detail, alongside some of the successes and lessons learned thus far.

Objectives:

- To explain the concept of implementation science translated into a framework for implementation of a specific programme (Durlak & DuPre, 2008).
- To describe evidence-based interventions for young people in New Zealand Aotearoa experiencing anorexia nervosa with a specific focus on MFBT.
- To describe the implementation process of the MFBT in ICAMH services in New Zealand Aotearoa.
- To provide recommendations for the future implementation of evidence-based therapies in ICAMH services in New Zealand Aotearoa.

BACKGROUND

The literature on implementation science consistently identifies a range of factors which contribute to implementation outcomes (Durlak & DuPre, 2008; Dymnicki, Wandersman, Osher, Grigorescu & Huang, 2014; Fixsen, Naoom, Blasé, Friedman, & Wallace, 2005). Fixsen et al. (2005, p.vi) describe specific components as including:

- The selection of specific practitioners who are supported with training, coaching and assessment.
- The provision of skilful supervision and coaching, and regular process and outcome evaluations.
- Communities and consumers are fully involved in the selection and evaluation of programs and practices.
- State and federal funding avenues, policies, and regulations create a hospitable environment for implementation and program operations.

Durlak and DuPre's (2008) review of the implementation of promotion and prevention programmes identified 23 contextual factors influencing implementation. These included:

- Provider characteristics
- The perceived need for and benefit of the innovation
- Organizational capacity
- Leadership
- Specific staffing considerations
- Issues of training and technical assistance.

The Werry Centre have used these implementation science components to support the implementation of specific programmes within ICAMH services in New Zealand. One example of this is the development of a knowledge and skills framework called Real Skills Plus CAMHS (The Werry Centre, 2009). This competency framework can be used to identify the skill and knowledge levels of practitioners and teams within ICAMH services. An implementation package was informed by the likely successful components of programme implementation (Durlak & DuPre, 2008). This included extensive promotion of the framework and engagement with service executive groups inclusive of consumers. Once this high-level engagement was secured, this buy-in was used to progressively engage with clinical teams. The clinical managers of these teams then identified skilled clinicians to *drive* the implementation of the skills and knowledge framework and assessment process. The Werry Centre provided ongoing support of the implementation process by resourcing the service-based *drivers* to coordinate implementation activity within their local services. In addition, the Werry Centre facilitated ongoing communication at all levels over a one-year period of implementation. This implementation process was then used to support successful uptake of programmes or interventions of other Werry Centre projects such as the implementation of MFBT in 2010.

The treatment of eating disorders in New Zealand is provided within a *hub and spoke* model as illustrated in Figure 1 (McKinley et al., 2002). The *hubs* are three specialist regional eating disorders services based in major centers that are contracted to provide training, supervision and inpatient beds to other services within their regions or *spokes*.

With this support, these other services are in a position to provide treatment for people experiencing eating disorders, and their families. For example, the South Island Eating Disorders Service caters for approximately one million people. They provide training, supervision and consultation by monthly telemedicine using a national health video-conferencing service, along with twice yearly site visits, and telephone consultations as required to the range of services within the five DHBs in the South Island (the Southern Region). They also provide inpatient specialist care for those unable to make treatment gains as an outpatient for any person within the Southern Region.

There is evidence that suggests for people with anorexia nervosa, the earlier the intervention the greater the chance of recovery (Treasure & Russell, 2011). The underpinnings of MFBT sit within the structural and strategic models of family therapy, with an added focus of the role of the parent taking a key role in focusing on the return to normal body weight of their child (Loeb & Le Grange, 2009). Research supports MFBT as the treatment of choice for those 18 years and under with a duration of illness of less than three years. Recovery was shown to be maintained at 12 months and at five year follow up (Loeb & Le Grange, 2009). In the absence of interventions that have shown such positive outcomes,

Figure 1. The hub and spoke model

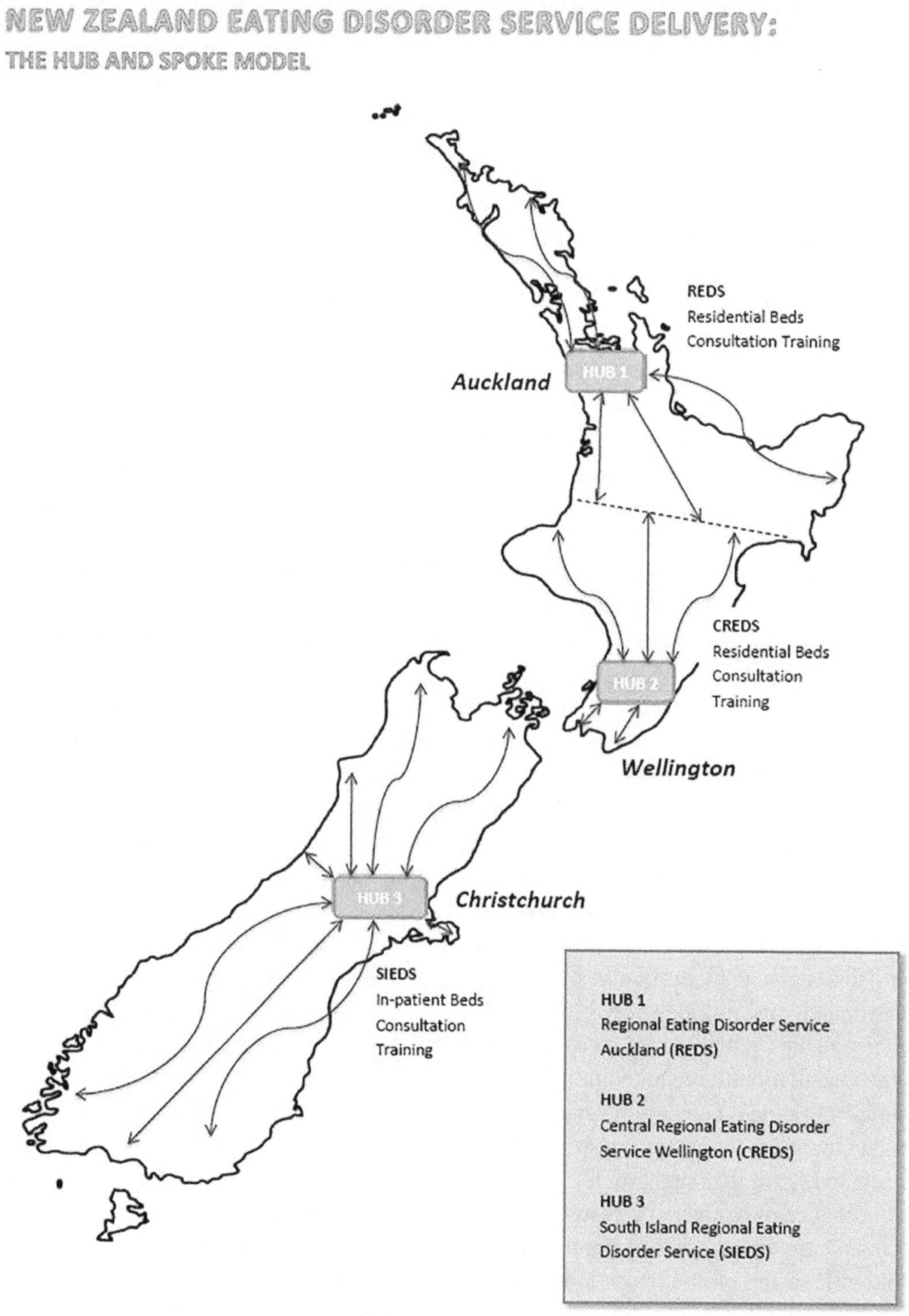

MFBT was chosen by the Ministry of Health, as an intervention to be implemented throughout New Zealand, as part of a broader workforce development initiative. The workforce goal was to strengthen the capacity and capability of service-providers working with people who experience eating disorders, with an emphasis on those working with young people and their family and whānau.

THE MFBT IMPLEMENTATION PROCESS

Fixsen et al. (2005, p. 2) stated that "implementation is a decidedly complex endeavor… every aspect of implementation is fraught with difficulty, from system transformation to changing service provider behavior and restructuring organization contexts". Therefore, these factors indicate the implementation process is often complex and multi-layered. This section looks at the stages of implementation, alongside the factors affecting its success.

Pre-Implementation

Step One: Know Your Community

For the successful implementation of a programme, Fixsen et al. (2005) highlighted the importance of knowing your community and in particular its current strengths and needs. In the New Zealand example, the community sits within 20 separate DHBs. Given the number of local governing authorities and associated complexities, the Ministry of Health contracted The Werry Centre to lead the implementation of the MFBT. The Werry Centre has well established relationships with the relevant community, that is the broader ICAMH sector which includes funders and planners, service managers, clinicians, Māori advisors, and consumer and family/whānau representatives. The Real Skills Plus CAMHS (The Werry Centre, 2009) model describes both *essential skills* (core skills) and *specialist skills* that are needed by a competent workforce to provide mental health services to infants, children, young people and their families. The specialist skills level is where clinicians are able to provide specific evidenced-based treatments. Therefore, this established competency framework provided the platform for CAMHS clinical and service leaders to be open to supporting team members to develop further *specialist skills* such as MFBT.

Step Two: Appoint a Project Leader with Credibility

To further broaden the knowledge of the community, the Werry Centre employed a project leader who was well embedded in the eating disorders sector and recognized for her highly advanced knowledge and skills in the area of eating disorders, and leadership qualities. The project leader held a leadership role in one of the specialist services and thus had an established understanding of the sector or community. For example, New Zealand has a "do it yourself" culture and in this context when MFBT training was unavailable some clinicians had sought their own training overseas and/or purchased and followed the manual. This meant MFBT did exist in New Zealand with some expertise. However, this was established in a fragmented capacity across the country, and with some concerns about fidelity to the key components of the model. In addition, people with eating disorders present with both psychiatric and physical symptoms. This necessitates an understanding of the broad systems across the health and education sector where these disorders may be encountered, plus a capacity to engage the wide ranging workforces including general practitioners, paediatricians, general medicine staff, school counselors, and teachers. Finally, the choice of this specialist practitioner as project leader was important to get buy-in from the clinical community who would recognise their expertise in the sector and who would "speak their language".

Step Three: Understand your External Implementation Levers

As an external implementation lever, the Ministry of Health required all DHBs to document the presence of an eating disorder programme/intervention in their Annual District Plans. This implementation process was further strengthened when the treatment of eating disorders became a key performance indicator for each service. Failure to meet this key performance indicator may incur financial penalty.

Step Four: Consider the Needs of Cultural Groups

A further requirement for service delivery is the responsibility services must take to ensure specific cultural groups, in particular Māori, are offered accessible and appropriate services. The Werry Centre therefore has a responsibility of ensuring that the implementation of programmes/interventions fits within this cultural context. For the implementation of the MFBT model, the Werry Centre's kaumatua (Māori elder) and Māori advisor ensured that the intervention/model met the principles of whānau ora (family/whānau focused health and well-being). Consultation on the cultural fit of this model was then extended to other Māori groups within each region. Extensive consultation with relevant DHB funders and planners and project leader service leaders was also conducted.

Step Five: Involve Clinicians and Managers

Clinicians and managers were consulted via an eating disorder conference facilitated by the project leader. The MFBT implementation project was also presented at the Werry Centre sector days. The Werry Centre sector days provide an opportunity for the Ministry of Health and DHB managers and clinical leaders of ICAMH services to share information on key priorities, training, and education. It also provides an opportunity for relationship building across services throughout New Zealand. This forum provided a key opportunity for the Ministry of Health to outline the expectations of the sector including reporting, and for the project leader to describe the intervention, the implementation plan, and resources which would be available to the sector.

Implementation

The MFBT training roll-out was based on a *train the trainer* model. This model is defined as the provision of training by someone possessing specialist skills and knowledge in a specific subject area to people with lesser skills and knowledge, to enable them to share the knowledge and skills to a broader audience (Orfaly, Frances, Campbell, Whittemore, Joly, & Koh, 2005). The implementation of the MFBT training in New Zealand followed this method. In 2010, 50 clinicians attended a national training in Auckland, New Zealand.

The training was extended to two distinct groups of clinicians. The first group consisted of clinicians from the specialty eating disorders services (the hubs for their region): the South Island Eating Disorders Service, the Central Regional Eating Disorders Service, and the Regional Eating Disorders Services. They were to become trainers and supervisors for the services within their region (the spokes) within the hub and spoke model.

The second group consisted of ICAMH service clinicians who were identified by their DHBs as having some experience in the MFBT model. This would allow for a strengthening of the *hub and spoke* model by having additional clinicians with specialist skills in the delivery of MFBT located within ICAMH services across the region. For those in this group with no experience in eating disorders, a 20 hour online training course was provided prior to the MBFT training.

The MBFT training was conducted over two days with an additional day dedicated for participants to consider and discuss how service development for the treatment of eating disorders could best occur in their regions. This day also provided an opportunity for the participants to network with their regional and national colleagues. Time was set aside for each region to discuss service development as a group and to develop clinical-supervision processes that would best fit with the existing mechanisms in the hub services. For example, clinicians from the Central Region Eating Disorders Service, in consultation with their *spoke* colleagues, developed slightly different supervision strategies to the South Island Eating Disorders Service.

Once these clinicians were trained, they were offered the opportunity to participate in a closed online forum via the Werry Centre web-site (www.werrycentre.org.nz). This forum was used for case discussion, technical questions, emotional support, and service development issues. The online national forum had 54 participants. It was driven by four specialist service eating disorders clinicians who posted questions and also answered queries. As the implementation process continued, two of the three regions were strongly established in MFBT, and as the need for close contact with the initial clinicians trained in MFBT was less, the forum ended. Finally, participants were provided with two follow up supervision days in March 2011 and November 2011.

To enhance the understanding of MFBT across the country, the trainers provided two *Introduction to MFBT* sessions consisting of an hour lecture in the evenings, with a further 30 minutes for questions. To make the sessions more accessible they were *broadcast* live across the internet and held in the evenings. The rationale behind these sessions was to explain the model to the broader community. Anyone could attend and thus self-select as the *broader community* however these sessions were also targeted at certain groups who would be supporting the model. These groups included, other members of the CAMHS teams, paediatric teams, those in primary health care, and the education sector. For those in primary care and the education sector the need was for them to understand the importance of early detection and referral, and their part in the model. For example, general practitioners who may be involved in medically monitoring their patient whilst in treatment, and school counselors who may be supporting the young person whilst they are in treatment.

Additionally, findings from a review of two areas in New Zealand identified that due to workforce attrition (that is parental leave and clinician movement), more clinicians needed to be trained to make this intervention sustainable. Therefore, extra training was provided. In one example, a collaborative approach was used to fund and provide this extra training. The region that hosted the training (Nelson/Marlborough DHB) worked with The Werry Centre project leader to extend the training to other areas of New Zealand, filling the available remaining places.

Post Implementation

Each component of the training implementation roll-out was evaluated to establish its effectiveness.

The evaluation of the intensive training session indicated a good coverage of the DHBs and professions had been attained. Participants reported:

- Enthusiastic praise for the trainers.
- Valuing the opportunity to think about service development, and network with their colleagues.
- That their understanding of the MFBT and confidence in using the intervention had increased as a result of the training.

In addition, the majority of participants (87%) reported an increase in their practical skills, and the majority of those (78%) who were trained in the initial group reported an increase in their level of confidence in supervising others.

The evaluation of the follow-up supervision days indicated that 60% of participants had an opportunity to work with young clients presenting with anorexia nervosa and their caregivers. All respondents indicated that they had a better understanding of how MFBT translated into clinical decision making for anorexia nervosa as a result of the training. Respondents reported that the most useful parts of the supervision days were the discussion of *real cases*, case complexities, consolidation of their skills, networking and strengthening links with other clinicians (particularly those who worked in rural areas), and the opportunity to have an ongoing discussion about service provision.

The effectiveness of the MFBT was also evaluated in a national audit, with data collected from 18 DHBs. This audit consisted of a review of all cases where MFBT had been the treatment of choice seen over a one year period. From the 18 DHBs, 107 people were identified and data was collected on 88 of them (82%). Results indicated a statistically significant increase in clients' weight and percentage of ideal body weight from baseline to follow up, or the client becoming weight restored from the MFBT treatment. Results from one specialist hub also showed that only a small number of people were receiving MFBT, although there were pockets of their spokes that were providing effective MFBT.

In summary, the audit provided preliminary evidence that this training model had been effectively disseminated, although the implementation was not fully established across the entire country. This outcome is in line with Durlak and Dupre's (2008) notable finding where they state that expecting perfect or near perfect implementation is unrealistic.

Factors Affecting Implementation

Durlak and Dupre (2008) outline at least 23 contextual factors that influence implementation, although they acknowledge there may be some overlap between these factors. The factors are grouped into five categories including variables related to communities, providers, innovations, organizational functioning, and the prevention support system (that is training and technical assistance). In the areas where the roll out of MFBT was successful, it appears there were a number of these factors which positively influenced this. In the areas where the implementation roll-out was ineffective, it was considered that there were a multitude of factors impacting negatively on each other, therefore compromising the success of the implementation. Factors related to the successful implementation of MFBT are discussed further below.

Engaging the Community

A key factor identified was the engagement of community or people across the country contributing to the delivery of eating disorder services. As discussed previously, positive engagement with people at all levels of service delivery is required for successful implementation of a programme/intervention. In this example, most, but not all, of the service leaders and clinicians across the country had buy-in as highlighted by the audit. Factors contributing to the buy-in likely included the previously established relationships with The Werry Centre and the service leaders, and the relationship skills of the project leader.

Funding

The provision of MFBT training in New Zealand was funded by the Ministry of Health. This meant clinicians only had to be released from their roles within their workplaces to attend training as all attendance costs were covered. Therefore, this provision of funding was an important enabler for the MBFT implementation. Additionally, those DHBs who perceived positive long term benefits from the MFBT training contributed extra funding to ensure its success. The Ministry of Health also provided extra funding to the region where MFBT had not been successfully implemented. This regional service made significant team changes to progress the implementation of MFBT. They brought in another trainer who tightly supervised their work with the clinicians who could see the benefits of implementing MFBT, and the funded access to training within their service. This led to the successful operation of the model in the hub.

The Absence or Presence of Innovative Service Delivery

While the implementation of MBFT was mandated as a priority by the Ministry of Health, Durlak and Dupre (2008) highlighted that an organization's positive perception of innovation within their mission, priorities and values, affected implementation. Therefore, successful implementation of MBFT was seen in those services where evidence-based and effective practice was an important part of their mission and values.

In discussion with the single *hub* that was unable to implement the MFBT, one of the factors that led to the failure of implementation was a resistance to give up the old model of practice. This component of the implementation process was identified as the lack of *readiness* of the service to implement MFBT. Prior to the training, this service had not identified MFBT as a treatment of choice, compared to the other two *hub* services. For this service, other contributing factors included a lack of perceived need and potential benefits of the innovation, and a lack of self-efficacy and skill proficiency when compared with other service areas. Contrary to this service's lack of *readiness*, the roll-out to those areas where a systemic intervention with some of the core elements of MFBT was in place, were excited about the prospect of refining their work to improve their client outcomes, fidelity of the model, and skill base. Therefore, clinicians in these areas were willing to use all aspects of the training which included supporting each other on the national discussion forum. These clinicians also had a strong existing skill base. The majority of these clinicians (69%) reported having specialist family therapy skills and therefore were able to integrate the MFBT training into their existing strengths. This also explained the existence of pockets of excellence in MFBT delivery in some of the regions of the *hub* where all of the resources offered in the implementation of MFBT had not been accessed. In two such areas, clinicians who were experienced in family therapy were confident to implement the treatment with limited support from the *hub*.

Positive Leadership

In the areas of New Zealand where examples of positive leadership at multiple levels of the system (including funders and planners, service and clinical management) were identified, there was a direct correlation with successful implementation of the MFBT intervention. The success of the implementation was also attributed to having strong clinical leadership where specialist clinicians with leadership qualities were identified and supported to be service *champions*. These clinicians within services found innovative ways to achieve the implementation of MFBT.

Organizational Functioning

Other factors that Dupre and Durlak (2008) described as having an impact on the implementation process included organizational capacity and more specifically, general organizational factors such as a positive work climate, an openness to change, capacity to integrate new programmes, and a shared vision. For example, the successful implementation of MFBT in the South Island of New Zealand was a result of a shared vision for a regional eating disorders service from all of the DHBs involved. The *hub* that was unable to implement MFBT reported experiencing a significant amount of other systems-level-change. Therefore, too much change at once was unmanageable and impeded implementation of the MFBT intervention.

Sustainability

Sustainability is a key factor in maintaining a skilled workforce, and an indicator of positive functioning of the organization. A programme/intervention is considered effective if there are contingences for sustainability in place. A degree of attrition within the trained workforce is an accepted part of a functioning system of service delivery and must be considered as part of workforce development planning. For instance, of the 50 clinicians who were trained in MFBT, 17 went on parental leave within four years of the initial training. This highlighted the need for succession planning and the provision of ongoing training for new recruits. In this example, two trainers were selected by the South Island Eating Disorders Service hub to provide skilled training for their region. To ensure the sustainability of the MFBT, they provide an annual two day training in their region. They also extend this training to the Central Region when spaces are available. Their task is to respond flexibly to the needs of their region. As an example, in 2015, an extra training was provided for the Southern part of the South Island due to high workforce attrition in this area. This training is set within the context of a well-established supervision structure both within local teams and by telemedicine from the hub.

The Central Region has continued to maintain and develop a MFBT supervision structure. In a follow-up interview in 2013, they stated that "the focus for MFBT is strong in the region and clinicians have a real passion and commitment to work with families in this way". They continue to work collaboratively with the Southern Region to train further clinicians.

Training and Technical Assistance

Finally Dupre and Durlak (2008) highlighted that successful implementation of a programme/intervention also requires adequate support from particular training and technical assistance in combination with other factors as above. The provision of technical support as part of the implementation process has been described elsewhere and in essence includes the resourcing provided to services by the Werry Centre and the project leader. Furthermore, the audit results showed the provision of this technical support was deemed to be viewed positively. There is however a suggestion that longer term sustainability of the national delivery of MFBT would be enhanced with ongoing technical support offered through a funded coordinating role positioned externally to services delivering the intervention. This would ensure ongoing training needs and mechanisms for knowledge transfer are identified and supported.

SOLUTIONS AND RECOMMENDATIONS

Durlak and Dupre (2008 , p. 327) state that "transferring effective programs into real world settings and maintaining them there is a complicated, long term process that requires dealing effectively with the successive complex phases of programme diffusion". Whilst considering the process of the implementation of MFBT across regions in New Zealand services, and reviewing this in the context of the factors outlined by Durlak and Dupre (2008), there are several recommendations that can be offered to others undertaking similar initiatives. These are presented below.

Pre-Implementation

The effects of external levers such as governing and funding body's reporting requirements on specific service provision influence successful implementation.

External motivators such as the need to report to the governing funding body (Ministry of Health) on the establishment of a treatment programme for eating disorders as part of an annual planning process potentially influencing ongoing funding was an important lever in this implementation process, and therefore needs to be considered when implementation processes are being scoped.

Buy-in and engagement in the implementation process will be influenced by the appointment of a project leader who has specialist clinical and leadership skills and can establish credibility across the regions.

Success in the pre-implementation phase is likely to have been influenced by the appointment of a funded national project team and a project leader chosen for their specialist knowledge and skills in the area of eating disorders. In addition to strong leadership qualities and sound project management skills, their knowledge of the sector and established relationships enabled the identification of services and mechanisms of approach to service-leads to gain buy-in. This contributed to strategic relationship development and engagement with service leaders. The project leader was also able to establish credibility within services by having thoroughly scoped the project which included a literature review of the evidence and examples of successful implementation from the international literature. This was also necessary to secure the confidence of services identified for the implementation process. Meeting with service leaders and promoting the evidence-based treatment, implementation plan, resources and supports available were also important elements of this phase.

Services being able to access funding for an implementation process will contribute to the success of a process.

The ability of services to access funding for their specialist clinicians to attend training and access ongoing support such as supervision and discussion forums also enhanced buy-in.

Implementation

Services open to innovative practice supported by positive organizational functioning will influence successful implementation.

Specific organizational features contributed to successful implementation. These included a strong leadership and existing support for innovative practices with a strong evidence-base. The identification of *champions* within services supported the embedding and successful implementation of the use of MFBT. The champions require dedicated time and support to attend training, and to share their expertise. Funded opportunities for champions to *meet* with their peers is also important for successful implementation. Evaluation is an important factor of successful implementation processes.

Formative evaluation throughout the implementation process contributes to an understanding of the efficacy of the implementation and provides opportunities to review and refine the implementation process. This contributes to the sustainability of the provision of the programme.

Post Implementation

Mechanisms of evaluation are key to enabling review and re-direction of the implementation plan if required.

Opportunities to review and evaluate the implementation process both during and at the end of the implementation process using data from contact with the managers and clinicians involved in the delivery of MFBT, and the audit, contributed to the project's success. The review opportunities were taken by the project leader to fine-tune implementation where this was required.

Dedicated and on-going funding for a coordinating role, external to current services will enhance the opportunity for ongoing sustainability of the implementation of MFBT.

Whilst not specifically explored during the immediate evaluation of this implementation process, an additional recommendation focuses on longer term sustainability. In maintaining programme fidelity and sustaining effective delivery of MFBT, the provision of enduring support for a coordinating role, and a mechanism for this (for example, a Service Level Agreement) to be firmly in place before the end of a project is recommended.

REFERENCES

American Psychiatric Association. (2000). *Diagnostic and statistical manual of mental disorders* (4th ed.). Washington, DC: Author.

Bernfeld, G. A., Farrington, D. P., & Leschied, A. W. (2001). *Offender rehabilitation in practice: Implementing and evaluating effective programs*. New York, NY: John Wiley & Sons.

Durlak, J. A., & DuPre, E. (2008). Implementation matters: A review of research on the influence of implementation on program outcomes and the factors affecting implementation. *American Journal of Community Psychology*, *41*(3-4), 327–350. doi:10.1007/s10464-008-9165-0 PMID:18322790

Dymnicki, A., Wandersman, A., Osher, D., Grigorescu, V., & Huang, L. (2014). *Willing, able ready: Basics and policy implications of readiness as a key component for implementation of evidence-based practices*. Washington, DC: Office of Human Services Policy, US Department of Health and Human Services.

Fixsen, D. L., Naoom, S. F., Blase, K. A., Friedman, R. M., & Wallace, F. (2005). *Implementation research: A synthesis of the literature*. Tampa, FL: University of South Florida, Louis de la Parte Florida Mental Health Institute, The National Implementation Research Network.

Loeb, K., & Le Grange, D. (2009). Family-based treatment for adolescent eating disorders: Current status, new applications and future directions. *International Journal of Child and Adolescent Health*, *2*(2), 243–254. PMID:20191109

McKinley, K. E., Bryan-Smith, L., Dosch, T. L., Hamory, B. H., & Fillipo, B. H. (2002). A hub-and-spoke model of care: Providing specialty care in patients' own communities. *The Joint Commission Journal on Quality Improvement*, *28*(10), 574–575. PMID:12369160

Ministry of Health. (2008). *Future directions for eating disorders*. Wellington, New Zealand: Author.

Orfaly, R. A., Frances, J. C., Campbell, P., Whittemore, B., Joly, B., & Koh, H. (2005). Train-the-trainer as an educational model in public health preparedness. *Journal of Public Health Management and Practice*, *11*(6Supplement), 123–127. doi:10.1097/00124784-200511001-00021 PMID:16205531

The Werry Centre. (2009). *Real skills plus CAMHS*. Auckland, New Zealand: Author.

The Werry Centre. (2015). *2014 stocktake of infant, child and adolescent mental health and alcohol and other drug services in New Zealand*. Auckland, New Zealand: The Werry Centre, University of Auckland.

Treasure, J., & Russell, G. (2011). The case for early intervention in anorexia nervosa: Theoretical explanations of maintaining factors. *The British Journal of Psychiatry*, *199*(1), 5–7. doi:10.1192/bjp.bp.110.087585 PMID:21719874

KEY TERMS AND DEFINITIONS

Eating Disorders: A group of mental health disorders characterized by severe disturbance in eating behaviours.

Maudsley Family Based Therapy: A specific treatment for people experiencing the eating disorder anorexia nervosa.

Implementation: The process of embedding an evidence-based intervention into practice.

Infant Child and Adolescent Mental Health: An area of mental health service delivery which focuses on the age spectrum of infancy to late adolescence.

Real Skills Plus CAMHS Competency Framework: A competency framework designed to support health professionals working in infant, child and adolescent mental health services to estimate their knowledge and skills levels at two levels.

Chapter 14
Workforce Development and E-Competency in Mental Health Services

Simone N. Rodda
Auckland University of Technology, New Zealand

Nicki A. Dowling
Deakin University, Australia

Max W. Abbott
Auckland University of Technology, New Zealand

Dan I. Lubman
Turning Point and Monash University, Australia

ABSTRACT

Online chat and email are two of the most popular ways of providing e-mental health. Online chat is synchronous communication in a virtual chat room where client and counselor meet at the same time. In contrast, email is referred to as asynchronous because it can be accessed without the synchronous presence of client and counselor. There has been a rapid increase in the demand for chat and email over recent years and much of the demand has been met by services that have traditionally provided helplines or crisis support. This chapter provides an overview of the key issues associated with the delivery of e-mental health services and workforce development. This includes an examination of the range of options for providing e-mental health and key issues to consider when working online. The chapter concludes with a brief exploration of issues associated with client suitability for e-mental health via chat and email.

INTRODUCTION

E-mental health (or e-therapy) involves the provision of mental health services via computer mediated communication. E-mental health via chat and email provides many benefits to clients, as well as to the mental health worker. For the client, they provide easy access to expertise without the need to travel or attend appointments. There are no technical barriers in that no special software is required to send or receive messages. These options are increasingly popular with clients because of the increased flexibility they provide. Services around the world are reporting increased numbers of clients accessing help by chat or email. Although online counseling has been available for more than 10 years for a range of mental

DOI: 10.4018/978-1-5225-1874-7.ch014

health conditions, including depression, anxiety, and addictive behaviors, there is limited information to guide mental health services in the development and delivery of chat and email.

The aim of this chapter is to provide an overview of the key issues associated with the delivery of e-mental health services and workforce development. This includes an examination of the range of options for providing e-mental health from single session work through to follow-up and after care, as well as identification of the potential pathways into online services. The chapter then describes key issues to consider when working online, including a discussion on how to develop good working relationships in the absence of verbal and non-verbal cues. The chapter concludes with a brief exploration of issues associated with client suitability for e-mental health via chat and email.

Background

E-mental health can be accessed anonymously to ask about a mental health concern that a person might find embarrassing. It appears especially attractive where there are barriers to help-seeking due to associated stigma. It can be an effective treatment approach in its own right or can be used to build confidence in help-seeking and counseling or therapy. Indeed, e-mental health can provide a means for the client to become familiar with the service or service system, and can provide an easy place to start before moving to telephone or face-to-face options if needed or wanted (Car & Sheikh, 2004). For the novice or new help-seeker, e-mental health is less confronting than face-to-face or phone counseling, in that it allows the person to control how quickly they engage with the content (i.e., how quickly they write) and how much information is made known to the clinician (i.e., the client can delete content that they have written prior to sending the text information) (King et al., 2006). Moreover, there is a great deal of research indicating that writing has a therapeutic effect (Pennebaker, 1997). E-mental health allows clients to re-read their sessions as well as reflect on responses by the clinician. Having access to a hard copy transcript of the session may also prevent memory bias or forgetting (Gilat & Shahar, 2007).

Email, which is the most common of all online activities generally, is an integral part of our daily lives. Email is asynchronous in that it can be used to communicate with individuals or groups regardless of where they are located, or the time of day. Email has been a part of our lives for the last 15 to 20 years since internet service providers first began allocating email addresses as a component of service connection. Every day, billions of emails are sent and received around the world. Most of us send and receive emails for professional and personal reasons.

In addition to professional and personal communication, email is used for consulting and counseling and to provide support to clients of mental health services. As the most frequently used electronic modality in mental health (Chester & Glass, 2006), it can be used to provide administrative information, such as appointment reminders, as well as initial screening or assessment, information on services, and referral through to low-intensity interventions. Compared with other regularly used technologies, such as text messaging for appointment reminders, email is used to provide a broader range of interventions. A systematic review of 24 studies involving email communications in primary healthcare settings found that medical and medication information was the most common topic discussed, followed by updates on medical conditions to patients (Ye, Rust, Fry-Johnson, & Strothers, 2010).

In the mental health field, chat and email have been used to provide low-intensity interventions including counseling, information and support, as well as a whole host of other novel programs. In addition to delivery of treatment, chat and email can be provided as an adjunct to telephone or face-to-face treatment. Chat and email can also be an easy way to provide post-care follow-up. Research into this area has to date focused on the following.

- Personalised feedback on self-assessments (Te Poel, Bolman, Reubsaet, & de Vries, 2009).
- Single session question and answers (Nieuwboer, Fukkink, & Hermanns, 2014).
- Prompt to access resources as part of a prevention program (Cremers et al., 2014).
- Delivery of psycho-education and self-help messages (Morgan, Jorm, & Mackinnon, 2012).
- Tailored one-way information (Abroms, Gill, Windsor, & Simons-Morton, 2009).
- Unstructured support or advice (Finn & Barak, 2010).
- Single session consultations (Nieuwboer et al., 2014).
- Guidance for self-directed programs (Cuijpers, Donker, van Straten, Li, & Andersson, 2010).
- Relapse prevention, such as providing support at critical times (e.g., quit date) (Lenert, Muñoz, Perez, & Bansod, 2004).

Synchronous chat (also called text chat, instant messaging or IM) is available through multiple platforms such as Facebook and Skype. Chat more closely replicates the traditional face-to-face environment than email, as it involves a back and forward conversation between at least two people at the same time and in the same virtual space. Chat based counseling has been offered since the 1990s, and is often delivered as a stand-alone intervention similar to helpline interventions (Urbis, Keys, & Young, 2003). Similar to helpline interventions, chat can be provided anonymously and as a single-session intervention or multiple sessions by appointment. A recent systematic review of chat based interventions found that chat was effective in reducing client-reported distress and perceived burden, as well as improving well-being and global functioning for a range of issues, including depression, work place issues, and anxiety (Dowling & Rickwood, 2013).

How Online Services Are Provided

There are two ways generally in which clients access an email or chat program. These are through the "contact us" tab or via a specific entry point for email or chat, such as a "sign up here" or "send an email here" tab. The "contact us" tab usually requires the provision of an email address, name, and issue or concern that may or may not be selected from a drop down list. This method of access is delivered to administrative or reception personnel and the email is then forwarded to a clinician. In contrast, when signing up for email or chat via an organized program, clients are usually presented with a series of terms and conditions which must be agreed to before accessing counseling or support (Urbis et al., 2003).

Terms and conditions specific to electronic communication may include client use of email, such as not forwarding communication to another party or using materials derived from the session in a way that was not intended. The benefit of this approach is that screening and/or assessment can be built into the registration, and the registration details can be presented at the start of the session to the mental health worker. In addition, terms and conditions can guide client expectations in regards to the duration of the program, frequency of the exchange, and responsiveness of the clinician (i.e., when a response can be expected) (Roy & Gillett, 2008). Clients should be advised whether they will be allocated a clinician (which is common with email exchange) or whether they can access any available clinician. Where the client is allocated a clinician, contingency planning should be in place when the clinician is on leave or out of the office (Cartwright, Gibbon, McDermott, & Bor, 2005).

An issue to be considered in service provision is speed of clinician response. Services that are synchronous may be offered with or without an appointment but this can mean wait times of up to an hour. It also means that people can get help when they really need it (i.e., in the evening when they are thinking about the problem). In contrast, email can be responded to at any time of the day or night, and response times are usually within 24 hours (Urbis et al., 2003). These response times depend on the organizational capacity to respond, which is dependent on the amount of funding (and staff) available. Given the nature of working with people with mental health conditions, there is a risk that emails may contain indicators or harm to self or others. This means the content of emails should be monitored, even if they are not responded to until a later time or date.

Help-seeking email content received through administrative pathways is not unusual. Receiving a clinical contact via administration, however, means that the client has not undertaken screening or agreed to the organization's terms and conditions of service use. Even when clients have disclosed important information, it is a good idea to gently help them complete the registration pathway.

E-COMPETENCY

Developing competency in an online environment requires the same communication skills as face-to-face or telephone counseling, but there are at least five differences that need to be considered. These include:

1. Developing therapeutic alliance in an online space.
2. The use of language, abbreviations, and emoticons.
3. Client and clinician multi-tasking.
4. The use of email templates, especially for the first response.
5. Integrating screening and self-help into chat and email.

Practice Element 1: Developing a Therapeutic Relationship Online

Empathy, warmth trust, liking, and congruence play a pivotal role in the development of a therapeutic relationship (Lambert & Barley, 2001). In online environments, being warm and empathic are arguably more challenging because counselors and clients cannot see each other smile, hear emotion in each other's voices or send or receive positive non-verbal cues. Perhaps surprisingly, recent research suggests that not only can the helping relationship be developed when interacting online, but that it can be developed in such a way that it is rated similarly to face-to-face settings (Sucala et al., 2012). This is important because the therapeutic relationship has been shown to predict client outcomes (Lambert & Barley, 2001), and feelings of warmth and liking towards a clinician are reasons that people recommend online services to others (Rodda, Lubman, Dowling, Bough, & Jackson, 2013).

There are both disadvantages and advantages of online environments in the development of a therapeutic relationship. Clients (and clinicians) can forget to attend a session because they physically do not have to go to an office. The absence of travel can make e-mental health accessible to people who are in rural or remote areas, are time poor, do not wish to travel, or lack requisite transport to access services. While travel becomes less of an issue, some clients may find that the need to type to express and convey emotions can be difficult especially in times of distress. However, the lack of physical presence can mean greater spontaneity and less self-censorship (King et al., 2006). This is different to other settings, in that the client can delete or add to their disclosure before pressing "send" and more easily control exactly what is disclosed. Clients can also read and review their sessions and consider the interaction and advice provided within online sessions at a later date.

For the clinician, the characteristics of the online environment can make the development of a positive helping relationship challenging. Online sessions start with fewer pleasantries and clients tend to develop a sense of trust and rapport earlier on in the session (i.e., right from the start) (Urbis et al., 2003). This process, which is the opposite to the normal order of counseling, is possibly due to the client being in a familiar environment (e.g., their home), or at a time that they are ready to talk (e.g., emails can be written at any time of the day or night). Furthermore, clients engage and disclose serious issues more quickly online.

This disinhibition effect, which is characterised by reduced self-censorship, likely occurs because of the lack of physical presence between client and counselor, and the feeling of being anonymous (Suler, 2004). This effect places clients in a position of greater power in that they have more control over the message and flow of information (Bambling, King, Reid, & Wegner, 2008). They also have more control over the time spent in the session and the amount of reflection in which they engage. In email or chat based counseling, clients can discontinue by clicking on the close screen button, which makes terminating a session much easier than physically walking out of a face-to-face counseling session. Sometimes sessions end prematurely because it has proceeded slower or faster than the client is comfortable. This situation can mean clinicians feel frustrated, guilty, disappointed or annoyed. The content of sessions should be reviewed in supervision and include review of the events leading up to the end of the session.

When working with chat, clinicians are likely to be speaking to a younger cohort, and people who might not otherwise engage in a clinical intervention. This can be challenging, especially when the client types quickly. Line by line communication is the way people, particularly young people, deliver their thoughts in this environment. This provides an opportunity for the clinician to allow the client to take control and contribute the greatest amount of content and gives the clinician space to think about their responses. Clients writing one line at a time may appear that they are pausing for a response, but it can be difficult for the clinician to identify when the client has stopped talking. The clinician really needs to listen to identify the best time to contribute (e.g., when there is a natural pause). Being able to scroll back and review the interaction is also a good tool for the clinician as this can provide useful content for reflecting back to the client.

In the online environment, the challenge for the clinician is to provide a sense of social presence (or telepresence). Social presence is the moment-by moment awareness of the other person (Tu & McIsaac, 2002). In face-to-face or video settings, the sense of social presence is strongest because the person is physically present. In telephone or online communication, however, the social presence is more difficult to establish. Being engaged and present to the other person requires a different set of skills than face-to-face settings. One of the most common criticisms of clinicians working online is the sense that they emulate a computer, by using drop-down pre-prepared responses, speaking to multiple clients at once, or generally not paying attention (Bambling et al., 2008).

Social presence can be enhanced by adapting writing style, punctuation, emotional expression, tempo, and flow. Practical options for creating social presence suggested for counselors during online communication are outlined below.

- Use simple language, and avoid misunderstandings by explaining things simply.
- Stay engaged in the session. This means avoiding long periods of silence. If reflecting or considering your response, use trailer dots to indicate pause or thinking, or say that you are thinking and need a moment. Long periods of silence are often viewed by clients as disengagement and may lead to them ending the session abruptly.
- Write frequently and often to indicate encouragement and engagement.
- Move at the same pace as the client and avoid rushing forward to give advice or provide solutions to problems that have not been fully articulated.
- Overtly express emotions. This can be through the use of capitals (I feel HAPPY for you), punctuation (you showed such strength!!!!) or emoticons (☺).
- Swearing is generally not permitted according to the terms and conditions of most services and should be avoided.
- Be ready to jump into the session and be where the client is from the start. Research suggests online clients are ready to take action but need help in developing their skills and confidence (Rodda, Lubman, Iyer, Gao, & Dowling, 2015).
- Describe your own thoughts, emotions, or physicality [big smile on my face]. Alternatively, use emotional bracketing, which involves placing feelings in square brackets to convey concern or warmth [feeling happy for you] (Murphy & Mitchell, 1998).
- Ask directly about distress or other emotions the client might be experiencing. Readiness rulers can aid this process. For example, "On a scale of 1 to 10, 1 being not distressed at all and 10 being very distressed, where would you be right now?"
- Ask questions that move the client forward and are relevant to their current readiness. For example, asking about the past when the client has asked for help developing strategies for change may not be helpful.
- Change pace to make a point through the use of shorter sentences or reflections. Avoid getting into a question and answer session.

To manage space, it can be tempting to ask multiple questions at once. While this information gathering technique is perhaps efficient, it interrupts the flow of the conversation and means that the clinician then has to provide reflections or feedback to multiple responses received concurrently. Clients respond best to one question at a time (Bambling et al., 2008). Indeed, one study found that young people found it frustrating when the session became out of sync due to the clinician asking a follow-up question before waiting for a response to the first question (Haberstroh, Duffey, Evans, Gee, & Trepal, 2007). This imposes another challenge in terms of giving the client the space to reflect while also retaining social presence.

Client non-responsiveness can occur during a chat session and may be a consequence of technology problems, interruptions, or client distress. It is helpful to have a policy on how long to wait for the client and also appropriate wording to let them know that you are still there. Non-responsiveness can also occur in email communication. This could be due to a whole range of issues related to client attrition that are relevant to any kind of intervention, such as sufficient treatment having been received, the client being focused on other priorities, or the treatment moving too fast. It might be, however, that the email has been delivered to a spam mailbox or has been missed. In any case, contacting the client to offer support and providing details of how to re-engage when they are ready or willing to continue is recommended.

Practice Element 2: Language, Abbreviation and Emoticons

Working in an online environment requires the clinician to be aware of language rules specific to text-based interactions. Online communication is guided by an explicit list of rules (sometimes referred to as net etiquette). These rules are related to language characterised by abbreviations, phonetic spelling, and low use of rules related to grammar. Mobile phone text messaging and social media sites such as Twitter that impose character limits (<120 characters) mean abbreviations and acronyms have developed for common phrases (e.g., HTH means hope this or that helps). These have been applied for faster communication in terms of typing speed, while also using as few words as possible to communicate the message.

Text speak can be a challenge for the clinician in terms of the language of their response. Client sentences may be brief and may not follow traditional conversation rules. For example, traditional conversations involve turn taking, where one person says something and the other responds. This goes back and forward until the theme is extinguished and another is started. In e-mental health, clients will often type a statement and present it to the clinician in the chat window (usually by pushing the enter key). This statement will be quickly followed by another statement without waiting for a response from the clinician. This can be challenging for the clinician to know when to respond, and it can be difficult to get into the flow of the conversation. An option is to allow the client to take the lead by letting them use the space therapeutically by writing out their concerns. The role of the clinician in this situation is to ask very good questions that help clients solve their own problems. This is congruent with counseling approaches such as Egan's Skilled Helper Model (Egan, 2009), which place clients as the experts on their own problems.

In face-to-face settings, non-verbal posturing, such as facial expressions and body movements, are associated with rapport (Trout & Rosenfeld, 1980). In online settings, spelling and abbreviations are part of the non-verbal vernacular. Facial expressions can be expressed as emoticons (e.g., faces created from colons and parentheses ☺). The text-based facial expressions are as important when communicating online to reflect, mirror, and convey emotion (Derks, Bos, & Von Grumbkow, 2007). Neuroscience research has found that the brain responds in the same way as seeing an actual face when we look at emoticons (Churches, Nicholls, Thiessen, Kohler, & Keage, 2014).

Multiple qualitative studies have reported the use of formal language and even the clinician's speed of typing can impact on feelings or warmth and connection between the client and clinician (Gibson & Cartwright, 2014; King et al., 2006). A study of text messages sent and received from the New Zealand agency Youthline reported young people preferred texting over talking because it was more private ("Cn I jus txt cos I don wanna b heard"), and because it was an easier way to communicate when distressed ("I cnt talk wen I cry") (Haxell, 2015). How the clinician responds is influenced by their service provider's clinical guidelines and their own personal style and preferences. For example, a typical Youthline response was "Hi there, sounds like things r bit rough 4 u right now. Since there r thngs ur wanting 2 get clearer about, u culd call us free @0800Youthline NZ to tlk" (Haxell, 2015). This response mirrors the client's language in terms of abbreviation, spelling, and punctuation.

Practice Element 3: Client and Clinician Multi-Tasking

Chat based environments are susceptible to multi-tasking. This is because chat based sessions do not generally occur in the clinician's office, but can occur in any place where there is internet access (e.g., on a bus, at work or in private spaces such as at home or in bed). Research suggests young people are heavy multi-taskers in the same medium (swapping between windows and programs), as well as switching between media (like watching television while using a computer or mobile device) (Prensky, 2001). This means that during an e-mental health session, the client might be watching television, browsing other websites, going to the toilet or getting a drink, on the phone, texting, or consuming alcohol, drugs, or engaged in gambling activity.

There are two ways clinicians can determine if the client is multi-tasking. The first is to ask directly (e.g., "Is there something else happening for you at the moment?"). This, however, could negatively impact on the client's sense of comfort as they always engage in multiple activities when they are online. The second is to notice change in session speed or tempo. Multi-tasking becomes apparent in the session when the pace or speed of the client's responses change (Bambling et al., 2008). There might be long gaps or a period of inactivity that is punctuated by multiple responses or questions directed back to the clinician as a means of filling the space. Clinicians may not notice the change in tempo (or their own change in tempo) when they multi-task. Some online services, especially those offering services provided by volunteers, require clinicians to respond to multiple clients at the same time. Clinicians also consult with colleagues, surf the net, or multi-task themselves while in an online session. In addition, the move towards open plan environments means clinicians are often not in a closed room but in a similar shared space as the client.

Research suggests that when attention is split between multiple activities, the cognitive load increases. Multi-tasking while using a computer can therefore be related to reduced efficiency and increased distractedness (Ophir, Nass, & Wagner, 2009). This means that when counseling in this environment, it may be helpful to reaffirm conversations by providing attachments or handouts following the session, or encouraging clients to print or save their transcripts. Another option is to set up expectations prior to the session by providing videos or information on how to get the most out of an online session. This should include being physically located in a safe quiet space.

Practice Element 4: Email Template for the First Response

Email provides mental health workers with multiple benefits in terms of session preparation and responsiveness. Clinicians can also benefit by having additional time to construct responses and consult with peers or supervisors. In addition, there is time to locate other resources and information before responding. However, some clinicians are wary of having a written record of their therapeutic exchange. This is because each email correspondence is a permanent record of the conversation that could be examined outside of the context in which the conversation occurred (e.g., subpoenaed by a court or examined by a third party).

Email provides the option to increase or decrease client contact as required. The client can access more care when needed (e.g., when at risk for relapse), and easily step down from more intensive treatment (e.g., face-to-face therapy). In general, email counseling is shorter-term than face-to-face counseling, with around five sessions provided per client (Chester & Glass, 2006). There is very limited research in this area, but some studies suggest that around 20% of sessions are provided as a single email (session), and around 20% as more than 10 emails (Finn & Barak, 2010).

The asynchronous nature of email means that materials can be prepared prior to the session. A way to do this is through the use of structured templates. Templates can be developed and then tailored for the individual (Abroms et al., 2009), and other resources can be appended to the communication (e.g., referral or homework sheets). Templates are more efficient than starting a response with a blank page every time a new client presents. They can be prepared in advance and this can mean a faster response time. Templates can also be developed in response to common presenting issues (e.g., crisis response, counseling, or information).

Structured emails developed from a template require around 15 minutes for the clinician to prepare, but can range up to 60 minutes depending on the amount of personalization (Abroms et al., 2009). This is a significant time saving for the clinician. A review of services using unstructured emails suggests the average email takes around 20 minutes to compose, with around 10% of emails taking more than 30 minutes to write. A risk of structured emails is that they may appear less personal. This can be overcome through tailoring which means adapting content to reflect individual needs and their use of language (e.g., formal or informal).

Structured emails are especially helpful for the first client response. There are a number of important components of the initial email including what, how often, how long, and what no response means. An ideal way to structure emails is with a beginning, middle, and end.

Beginning of the email.

- The beginning of the email should identify yourself by name, your organization, and your role. It should then explicitly congratulate and reinforce help seeking and normalize the approach indicating that reaching out can be both challenging but exciting.
- To reduce the chance of misunderstanding, it is helpful to restate the client's words from their initial email. In the absence of minimal encouragers (e.g., nodding and utterances that encourage continued disclosure), this can also indicate that you are listening and have heard what has been said.

Middle of the email.

- The middle part of the email should integrate the results of any screening into the response. This could be feedback on the level of severity of the problem, readiness to change, or treatment goals. This really depends on the types of screening tools offered during the registration process.
- At this time, it is tempting to ask a lot of questions. Usually the first email from the client will be brief and this leaves the clinician with many more questions than there are answers. It is helpful to focus on the data that is available (i.e., screening) and the content of the client's email.
- A strengths based approach can be used in terms of highlighting the client's identified strengths rather than weaknesses. For example, responding to the first email with a request for information on how the problem developed may move the client backwards rather than forwards.
- A benefit of templates is that key questions which are important can be decided both at an agency and individual level in advance. Given that there is so little room for questions, it is important to only ask those that you think are important to respond to and move your client forward.

End of the email.

- At the end of the email, it is helpful to offer hope and reflect that the majority of people do improve after they access your service. It is helpful to revisit the terms and conditions and check on suitability and treatment preferences. For example, clinicians can say "there are many ways to get help and I am wondering if email is your preferred option?".

- It is then helpful to provide an overview of the service and set up expectations. This might include the length of the program (often six weeks), how many emails might be exchanged each week (perhaps 1-2), and how often the client might send emails to the clinician (usually this is as often as required, but they would only be responded to once or twice a week).
- There are a whole range of other online resources, tools, and materials that can support email counseling. It is helpful to point the client in the direction of relevant resources that might include self-help materials or peer support groups. The agency might also have additional reading or resources that can also be appended to the email. When appending to the email, the clinician should introduce the resource in the email and explain why it is relevant.
- Lastly, invite further contact and provide a warm sign off. Remember that using this modality means the client cannot see the clinician smiling or gesturing warmth, so it is important to convey this both in the email and at the email conclusion.

A challenge when communicating via email as a clinician is word length. Years ago, when we received an email it was often composed like a letter and this was appreciated as we did not receive emails very frequently. Today, emails are shorter and people are sensitive to their length. This is mostly due to the number of emails people receive a day which is estimated to be upwards of 120 or more (Jenkin, 2014). Generally, the absolute maximum words per email should be around 250, which is about a page of text. A good rule of thumb is that an email should be not more than 2-3 times the length of the client's initial email. This process of mirroring can help to avoid placing the client in a position where they feel overwhelmed and less powerful in the therapeutic exchange.

Practice Element 5: Integrating Screening and Self-Help

A chat counseling session is often around an hour in duration, but the amount of content that is shared is much less than in phone or face-to-face settings. Only around half the total words expressed verbally are shared in an online session, because typing is slower than talking and significantly reduces the amount of content that can be covered. Research indicates clients spend a great deal of time telling their story, and given the constraints of the medium, this seems to be at the expense of a range of other online options that could be incorporated into the session (Rodda et al., 2015). Options that are known to improve outcomes such as online screening (or self-assessment) and self-directed options such as self-help could be offered before, during, or after an episode of care (Rodda, Lubman, Cheetham, Dowling, & Jackson, 2015).

Most services conduct screening or assessment as part of intake into their service. Screening provides a consistent method of collecting information about how much the identified behavior is a problem. In comparison, assessment defines the nature of the problem, determines a diagnosis, and develops specific treatment recommendations. In online work, screening and assessment may be used for:

1. Administrative purposes.
2. Background information to inform the session.
3. Assessment of problem and areas to work on.
4. Assessment with tailored feedback that is integrated into the session.

In practice, the different ways screening and assessment are incorporated into online sessions can mean that the client:

- Is asked the same questions that they have previously answered in a screening tool
- Is invited to tell their story without reference to screening information
- Information is reflected, but in such a way as to check whether the information is correct
- Responds to here and now information in the screening tool (such as levels of distress), but this is not responded to even when the client says that they are upset
- Asks what their score means but the clinician is unable to readily interpret the responses
- Information is reflected and integrated into the session (such as linked to goal setting or session planning).

How clinicians respond to screening sets the tone for the session. Firstly, it is important to let the screening tool do the work of gathering information and use the information to provide feedback. Self-assessment has also been shown to elicit change and tailored personal feedback can increase the impact of assessments (Morrison, Moss-Morris, Michie, & Yardley, 2014). To do this, clinicians need to know the purpose of screening, be aware of the cut-off scores for interpretation, and be able to provide feedback on where the person is compared to others of a similar demographic. This information should be pre-prepared and ready for the session. There is no need to check the correctness of client responses as the relative anonymity can actually elicit more honest answers than may be reported in other settings.

The clinician should then work with the information that has been provided. It is helpful to recognize that the client has started the intervention before you meet in the virtual chat room. They have already thought about the responses to the assessment items and this may have increased their awareness of their situation. It is therefore important to integrate this information into the session. The example below demonstrates how screening can be reflected and used to reaffirm readiness and importance to change. This example demonstrates how to identify past strengths and capabilities and then sought to provide focus for the session.

You say it's a high priority to change & very important to you, and you are moderately confident that you can deal with it. Since you've done so well in the past staying off it for years you clearly have the strength & capacity to do it again. I'm wondering what prompted this last relapse...

The above example also used abbreviations and punctuation to render the response briefer, avoided questions, demonstrated positive regard, and shared an internal process. In addition to screening at the start of the session, clinicians might also consider checking in at the end of the session. The example below demonstrates how this can be integrated into the initial response.

I can hear that you are feeling pretty stressed about it all and have read that you are not feeling confident about addressing it, perhaps we can talk some more tonight about what has been happening and see how you feel at the end of our chat - how does that sound?

Online screening need not only include formal or forced choice questionnaires and screening instruments. Given that writing can be therapeutic and clients want to tell their story, an option may be to assist clients to tell their story more efficiently. For example, templates could be developed that prompt a history taking narrative. This could be offered to the client while waiting for the session to commence. The clinician could then provide feedback and guidance on the text. This approach would significantly reduce the amount of time spent on history taking in the session. This is important because wait times, data gathering, and reduced session content are the main sources of client dissatisfaction with this modality (King et al., 2006).

In addition to screening, self-directed options can be integrated into chat and email. Self-directed options include online tools and resources that the client can undertake before, during, or after the session. Self-directed programs (also called internet therapy) are available for almost every mental health condition. These programs offer self-paced access to motivational or cognitive-behavioral treatment over around six sessions. Other options include smart phone applications (that can support self-monitoring or goal setting) and community forums (that can offer peer-to-peer support). A list of suitable options can be appended to emails or chat sessions for clients to follow-up. However, client outcomes might be improved if the clinician works to integrate these options into the session.

Integrating self-directed options into the email or chat session requires some planning. First, as a source of information, the clinician should be familiar with self-directed options. They should know the range of options available, how they work (in terms of content and technology), and whether there is research indicating they are effective (Baguley et al., 2010). It is helpful to know whether there are any costs associated with access and the amount of disclosure required of the client (some programs may require disclosure of personal details such as name or address). Associated with this is the likelihood of shame or embarrassment (i.e., community forums involve other people and this could be challenging for new clients). Indeed, comfort in contributing in an online forum may be improved if moderated well and this can provide an important source of support and understanding. The clinician should also provide guidance and instruction in the use of self-directed materials. Guidelines for the use of self-directed materials suggest strategies such as planning and allocating a time each day for the activity can improve outcomes (Williams, 2006). Throughout the use of self-directed options, it is helpful to support and encourage change through regular review of the client's progress. Review may include supporting the client's self-efficacy and motivation to continue as well as re-administration of assessment tools to monitor progress.

ISSUES, CONTROVERSIES, PROBLEMS

Client Suitability

There has been a great deal of discussion and debate over the years on client suitability for seeking help online. The debate has been influenced by guidelines written for the International Society for Mental Health Online (Suler, 2001). This paper identified three key issues related to suitability - technical expertise, treatment preferences, and text-based skills. Technical expertise refers to whether the client has access to the internet in a private or convenient setting. It also refers to the client's experience of talking online, especially in the selected modality (i.e., "have they tried chat previously if wanting to use chat?").

A frequent concern when working online is the interplay between client anonymity and client safety. E-mental health is attractive to at least some clients because they can access it without disclosing any personal information. A dilemma faced here is when working with clients evidencing risk of harm to self or others is whether to request contact details other than an email address (Pollock, 2006). Some advocate contact details such as phone number, address, or next of kin contact details. Alternatively, the initial assessment could be conducted by telephone. These are methods to increase physicality with the client, but this approach arguably detracts from some of the known benefits of this modality. Some clients will not want to provide contact details and being asked to do so could be unwelcome. The limits of anonymity can be outlined in the terms and conditions of service use and links provided to online services that can provide greater anonymity.

All types of treatment can now be delivered online via video conferencing, chat, email, or self-directed modules. It is helpful to determine whether the client prefers in the moment communication (such as chat), or to reflect and edit or think before they speak (such as email). For some people, there could be benefits of using online options even when they are not the preferred modality (such as relapse prevention), and this should also be considered when determining suitability.

Suler (2004) suggests clients may not be suitable for online work if differences in language or culture impede the flow of communication. In New Zealand, chat and email could be viewed as an appealing option for Māori and Pasifika especially given the perceived stigma, shame, and confidentiality issues associated with accessing mental health services. Care should be taken however in ensuring screening tools and other written communication is culturally appropriate and that misunderstandings in wording are minimized. Given the importance of non-verbal communication and visual diagrams to enhance learning, chat and email may need to be delivered with greater flexibility and creativity. For example, clients and counselors could upload videos, photos of drawings, or other images as part of the therapeutic exchange.

Workforce Issues

Almost all of the competencies required for telephone and face-to-face counseling apply online. However, online communication has special challenges in terms of how emotions and thoughts are conveyed and the use of relevant and accessible language becomes even more important in the text-based environment. There is an urgent need to develop and make widely accessible workforce development initiatives and resources for this modality. Translation of practice from a face-to-face environment to online delivery is complex and requires supervision that is informed by the best available evidence. Postgraduate counseling programs need to include e-mental health in curriculums to ensure graduates have the requisite counseling competencies to work in this new environment.

Clinicians should also be informed by guidelines developed by their professional associations. There are multiple guidelines that can guide clinicians in providing ethical e-mental health. E-mental health guidelines are available for members of the American Psychological Association, the American Counselling Association, The Australian Psychological Society, and the British Association of Counselling and Psychotherapy (usually available in the members only area of each site). The main areas covered in these guidelines are related to confidentiality (e.g., sharing of information for supervision or professional purposes), disclosure of personal information (e.g., how far does anonymity extend), as well as client use of emails and the security of correspondence (e.g., providing information to clients on how to safeguard and save their correspondence). It is also recommended that information on the limits of e-therapy is provided at the outset and this is discussed as the treatment proceeds.

FUTURE RESEARCH DIRECTIONS

E-mental health has been offered to people for a range of mental health conditions for more than 10 years in New Zealand and around the world. To date however, there has been limited longer-term evaluation and much of the evidence is based on descriptive studies, case studies, or clinical observations. The exponential growth of e-mental health has meant that few services have been evaluated. This is due to the speed of growth in a relatively short time period. This is challenging for treatment providers as well as the mental health field more broadly, as practice is moving faster than the evidence base can be established. Ideally all new e-mental health services are established with funding for longer-term evaluation and this evaluation is embedded in everyday service delivery.

Longer-term evaluation is also required so that evidence-informed workforce development programs and clinical governance frameworks are relevant to online settings. This chapter presents evidence that skills obtained in face-to-face training and delivered in face-to-face settings may not always be sufficient when working online. There is a great need to identify specific online skills and to test whether clinical observations described in the literature are correct. For example, there is currently no longer-term evaluation demonstrating that the development of therapeutic rapport is required when working online. To inform training programs, information is also required on whether processes such as developing social presence, using pre-prepared email templates, and the use of text speak impact on client outcomes. Clinicians also need to feel confident in recommending e-mental health to clients. Knowing what works and for who is a key priority so that clinicians are better informed on client suitability.

CONCLUSION

Chat and email provide unprecedented opportunities for mental health workers to expand their client base and reach people who otherwise would not access help. The aim of this chapter was to provide an overview of the key issues associated with the delivery of e-mental health services and workforce development. Formal and informal pathways into chat and email have been described along with an outline of several considerations for service planners and developers.

For clinicians, e-mental health may pose new challenges in terms of developing therapeutic rapport, and warm and trusting helping relationships. The use of writing style, punctuation, emotional expression, tempo and flow can be adapted to the online environment to overcome the absence of both non-verbal and verbal cues. The physical environment for text-based counseling is completely different to face-to-face, in that the client is usually in their own home or other familiar space. While this can support more open and honest dialogue, there is a risk of multi-tasking and becoming distracted or otherwise occupied during online sessions.

Clinicians can integrate pre-prepared materials to overcome time constraints. By far, the biggest disadvantage for clients is the slowness of the typing medium, but this can be overcome through clever integration and the use of evidence-based tools. This includes screening and assessment tools adapted for online environments and self-directed materials. Services can also develop templates for email contact that can be tailored to the client's specific situation. This may be especially helpful for the first contact.

E-mental health is providing services in a way that many people now want and expect, when help is required. Not all people, however, will be suitable for e-mental health. It is therefore important to provide clients with information on a range of treatment options, so they can choose the option that is most suited to their needs.

REFERENCES

Abroms, L. C., Gill, J., Windsor, R., & Simons-Morton, B. (2009). A process evaluation of e-mail counselling for smoking cessation in college students: Feasibility, acceptability and cost. *Journal of Smoking Cessation*, *4*(1), 26–33. doi:10.1375/jsc.4.1.26

Baguley, C., Farrand, P., Hope, R., Leibowitz, J., Lovell, K., Lucock, M., . . . Richards, D. (2010). *Good practice guidance on the use of self-help materials within IAPT services.* Technical Report. Improving Access to Psychological Therapies (IAPT). Retrieved January 13, 2016, http://www.iapt.nhs.uk

Bambling, M., King, R., Reid, W., & Wegner, K. (2008). Online counselling: The experience of counsellors providing synchronous single-session counselling to young people. *Counselling & Psychotherapy Research*, *8*(2), 110–116. doi:10.1080/14733140802055011

Car, J., & Sheikh, A. (2004). Email consultations in health care: 1—scope and effectiveness. *British Medical Journal*, *329*(7463), 435–438. doi:10.1136/bmj.329.7463.435 PMID:15321902

Cartwright, M., Gibbon, P., McDermott, B. M., & Bor, W. (2005). The use of email in a child and adolescent mental health service: Are staff ready? *Journal of Telemedicine and Telecare*, *11*(4), 199–204. doi:10.1258/1357633054068865 PMID:15969796

Chester, A., & Glass, C. (2006). Online counselling: A descriptive analysis of therapy services on the Internet. *British Journal of Guidance & Counselling*, *34*(2), 145–160. doi:10.1080/03069880600583170

Churches, O., Nicholls, M., Thiessen, M., Kohler, M., & Keage, H. (2014). Emoticons in mind: An event-related potential study. *Social Neuroscience*, *9*(2), 196–202. doi:10.1080/17470919.2013.873737 PMID:24387045

Cremers, H.-P., Mercken, L., Crutzen, R., Willems, P., de Vries, H., & Oenema, A. (2014). Do email and mobile phone prompts stimulate primary school children to reuse an internet-delivered smoking prevention intervention? *Journal of Medical Internet Research*, *16*(3), 96–106. doi:10.2196/jmir.3069 PMID:24642082

Cuijpers, P., Donker, T., van Straten, A., Li, J., & Andersson, G. (2010). Is guided self-help as effective as face-to-face psychotherapy for depression and anxiety disorders? A systematic review and meta-analysis of comparative outcome studies. *Psychological Medicine*, *40*(12), 1943–1957. doi:10.1017/S0033291710000772 PMID:20406528

Derks, D., Bos, A. E., & Von Grumbkow, J. (2007). Emoticons and online message interpretation. *Social Science Computer Review*, *26*(3), 379–388. doi:10.1177/0894439307311611

Dowling, M., & Rickwood, D. (2013). Online Counseling and Therapy for Mental Health Problems: A Systematic Review of Individual Synchronous Interventions Using Chat. *Journal of Technology in Human Services*, *31*(1), 1–21. doi:10.1080/15228835.2012.728508

Egan, G. (2009). The skilled helper: A problem-management and opportunity-development approach to helping.Belmont, CA: Brooks/Cole.

Finn, J., & Barak, A. (2010). A descriptive study of e-counsellor attitudes, ethics, and practice. *Counselling & Psychotherapy Research*, (1): 1–10.

Gibson, K., & Cartwright, C. (2014). Young peoples experiences of mobile phone text counselling: Balancing connection and control. *Children and Youth Services Review*, *43*, 96–104. doi:10.1016/j.childyouth.2014.05.010

Gilat, I., & Shahar, G. (2007). Emotional first aid for a suicide crisis: Comparison between telephonic hotline and internet. *Psychiatric*, *70*(1), 12–18. doi:10.1521/psyc.2007.70.1.12 PMID:17492908

Haberstroh, S., Duffey, T., Evans, M., Gee, R., & Trepal, H. (2007). The experience of online counseling. *Journal of Mental Health Counseling*, *29*(3), 269–282. doi:10.17744/mehc.29.3.j344651261w357v2

Haxell, A. J. (2015). On becoming textually active at Youthline, New Zealand. *British Journal of Guidance & Counselling*, *43*(1), 144–155. doi:10.1080/03069885.2014.922163

Jenkin, C. (2014). *Emails expected to rise to 140 a day in 2018*. Retrieved from news.com.au

King, R., Bambling, M., Lloyd, C., Gomurra, R., Smith, S., Reid, W., & Wegner, K. (2006). Online counselling: The motives and experiences of young people who choose the Internet instead of face to face or telephone counselling. *Counselling & Psychotherapy Research*, *6*(3), 169–174. doi:10.1080/14733140600848179

Lambert, M. J., & Barley, D. E. (2001). Research summary on the therapeutic relationship and psychotherapy outcome. *Psychotherapy (Chicago, Ill.)*, *38*(4), 357–361. doi:10.1037/0033-3204.38.4.357

Lenert, L., Muñoz, R. F., Perez, J. E., & Bansod, A. (2004). Automated e-mail messaging as a tool for improving quit rates in an internet smoking cessation intervention. *Journal of the American Medical Informatics Association*, *11*(4), 235–240. doi:10.1197/jamia.M1464 PMID:15064291

Manhal-Baugus, M. (2001). E-therapy: Practical, ethical, and legal issues. *Cyberpsychology & Behavior*, *4*(5), 551–563. doi:10.1089/109493101753235142 PMID:11725648

Morgan, A. J., Jorm, A. F., & Mackinnon, A. J. (2012). Email-based promotion of self-help for subthreshold depression: Mood memos randomised controlled trial. *The British Journal of Psychiatry*, *200*(5), 412–418. doi:10.1192/bjp.bp.111.101394 PMID:22442102

Morrison, L., Moss-Morris, R., Michie, S., & Yardley, L. (2014). Optimizing engagement with Internet-based health behaviour change interventions: Comparison of self-assessment with and without tailored feedback using a mixed methods approach. *British Journal of Health Psychology*, *19*(4), 839–855. doi:10.1111/bjhp.12083 PMID:24308806

Murphy, L., & Mitchell, D. (1998). When writing helps to heal: E-mail as therapy. *British Journal of Guidance & Counselling*, *26*(1), 21–32. doi:10.1080/03069889808253835

Nieuwboer, C. C., Fukkink, R. G., & Hermanns, J. M. (2014). Single session email consultation for parents: an evaluation of its effect on empowerment. *British Journal of Guidance & Counselling*, 1-13.

Ophir, E., Nass, C., & Wagner, A. D. (2009). Cognitive control in media multitaskers. *Proceedings of the National Academy of Sciences of the United States of America*, *106*(37), 15583–15587. doi:10.1073/pnas.0903620106 PMID:19706386

Pennebaker, J. W. (1997). Writing about emotional experiences as a therapeutic process. *Psychological Science*, *8*(3), 162–166. doi:10.1111/j.1467-9280.1997.tb00403.x

Pollock, S. L. (2006). Internet counseling and its feasibility for marriage and family counseling. *The Family Journal (Alexandria, Va.)*, *14*(1), 65–70. doi:10.1177/1066480705282057

Prensky, M. (2001). Digital natives, digital immigrants part 1. *On the Horizon*, *9*(5), 1–6. doi:10.1108/10748120110424816

Rodda, S. N., Lubman, D. I., Cheetham, A., Dowling, N. A., & Jackson, A. C. (2015). Single session web-based counselling: A thematic analysis of content from the perspective of the client. *British Journal of Guidance & Counselling*, *43*(1), 117–130. doi:10.1080/03069885.2014.938609

Rodda, S. N., Lubman, D. I., Dowling, N. A., Bough, A., & Jackson, A. C. (2013). Web-Based Counseling for Problem Gambling: Exploring Motivations and Recommendations. *Journal of Medical Internet Research*, *15*(5), e99. doi:10.2196/jmir.2474 PMID:23709155

Rodda, S. N., Lubman, D. I., Iyer, R., Gao, C., & Dowling, N. (2015). Subtyping based on readiness and confidence: The identification of help-seeking profiles for gamblers accessing web-based counselling. *Addiction (Abingdon, England)*, *110*(3), 494–501. doi:10.1111/add.12796 PMID:25393315

Roy, H., & Gillett, T. (2008). E-mail: A new technique for forming a therapeutic alliance with high-risk young people failing to engage with mental health services? A case study. *Clinical Child Psychology and Psychiatry*, *13*(1), 95–103. doi:10.1177/1359104507086344 PMID:18411868

Sucala, M., Schnur, J. B., Constantino, M. J., Miller, S. J., Brackman, E. H., & Montgomery, G. H. (2012). The Therapeutic Relationship in E-Therapy for Mental Health: A Systematic Review. *Journal of Medical Internet Research*, *14*(4), e110. doi:10.2196/jmir.2084 PMID:22858538

Suler, J. (2001). Assessing a persons suitability for online therapy: The ISMHO clinical case study group. *Cyberpsychology & Behavior*, *4*(6), 675–679. doi:10.1089/109493101753376614 PMID:11800174

Suler, J. (2004). The online disinhibition effect. *Cyberpsychology & Behavior*, *7*(3), 321–326. doi:10.1089/1094931041291295 PMID:15257832

Te Poel, F., Bolman, C., Reubsaet, A., & de Vries, H. (2009). Efficacy of a single computer-tailored e-mail for smoking cessation: Results after 6 months. *Health Education Research*, *24*(6), 930–940. doi:10.1093/her/cyp036 PMID:19574405

Trout, D. L., & Rosenfeld, H. M. (1980). The effect of postural lean and body congruence on the judgment of psychotherapeutic rapport. *Journal of Nonverbal Behavior*, *4*(3), 176–190. doi:10.1007/BF00986818

Tu, C.-H., & McIsaac, M. (2002). The relationship of social presence and interaction in online classes. *American Journal of Distance Education*, *16*(3), 131–150. doi:10.1207/S15389286AJDE1603_2

Urbis, Keys, & Young. (2003). *National review of tele counselling and web counselling services: Final report.* Canberra, Australia: Australian Government Department of Health and Ageing.

Williams, C. (2006). *Overcoming depression and low mood.* London, UK: Hodder Arnold.

Ye, J., Rust, G., Fry-Johnson, Y., & Strothers, H. (2010). E-mail in patient–provider communication: A systematic review. *Patient Education and Counseling*, *80*(2), 266–273. doi:10.1016/j.pec.2009.09.038 PMID:19914022

KEY TERMS AND DEFINITIONS

Chat Counseling: A text based therapeutic exchange between a clinician and individual or groups that is synchronous. Interactions require the clinician and client to be present in the same virtual room at the same time.

Email Counseling: A text based therapeutic exchange between a clinician and individual or groups that is asynchronous. Interactions do not require clinician and client to be present in the session at the same time.

Email Templates: Structured emails that have been prepared prior to the session that can be tailored for the client.

e-Mental Health: Any therapeutic exchange that occurs via technology including chat, email, video conferencing or text messaging.

Social Presence: The feeling of being in the presence of another person. In text based settings, social presence can be enhanced by adapting writing style, punctuation, emotional expression, tempo and flow.

Text Speak: Social conventions for online communication related to the use of language including sentence length, abbreviations, phonetic spelling and low use of rules related to grammar.

Therapeutic Alliance Online: The development of a positive helping relationship in the absence non-verbal cues.

Chapter 15
Routine Outcome Measurement and the Development of the Australian Mental Health Workforce:
The First 25 Years of Implementation Are the Hardest

Tim Coombs
Australian Mental Health Outcomes and Classification Network, Australia

Rosemary Dickson
Australian Mental Health Outcomes and Classification Network, Australia

Philip Burgess
School of Public Health Faculty of Medicine and Biomedical Sciences, University of Queensland, Australia

Roderick McKay
New South Wales Institute of Psychiatry, Australia

ABSTRACT

This chapter provides an overview of the implementation of routine outcome measurement in mental health services in Australia. It describes the preparation necessary to enable the collection of these measures, including policy development. It then identifies the training, benchmarking, communication, and other workforce development activities necessary to initiate and sustain the collection. The chapter concludes by outlining the future development of the collection and the implication for continued workforce development.

DOI: 10.4018/978-1-5225-1874-7.ch015

INTRODUCTION

The policy and workforce development activities necessary to support the introduction of routine outcome measurement to public mental health services in Australia are examined in this chapter. The chapter provides an overview of:

- Specific workforce development challenges associated with the introduction of a suite of standard measures
- The way in which Australia has sought to overcome these challenges.

BACKGROUND

National Mental Health Strategy

In April 1992, all Australian Health Ministers endorsed the *National Mental Health Strategy* (Australian Health Ministers, 1992) as the framework to guide mental health reform. This was initially for the period between 1993 and 1998.

Australian states and territories agreed to undertake reform activity within their respective jurisdictions. To also collaborate on policy and service development issues requiring a national focus. This was the first attempt at national coordination of public mental health services, whilst recognizing the complementary but different roles of the Australian state and territory governments.

Broadly, the *National Mental Health Strategy* (Australian Health Ministers, 1992) aimed to:

- Promote the mental health of the Australian community, and prevent the development of mental health disorders where possible.
- Reduce the impact of mental disorders on individuals, families, and the community.
- Assure the rights of people with mental illness.

The *National Mental Health Strategy* has been articulated through national mental health plans. These set out the strategic directions and priorities for national mental health reform. The strategy gave priority to improving the quality and availability of mental health data to inform the reform, resourcing, planning, and management of quality mental health services.

An evaluation of the first plan (Mental Health Branch Commonwealth Department of Health and Family Services [CDHFS), 1997) found information use in mental health was grossly under developed. There was also a need to build an information infrastructure at a clinical services level. This infrastructure needed to contribute to:

- Individual consumer care
- Assessment, care planning, and transfer of care activities
- Service quality improvement activities.

This clinical service level activity would contribute to the collection and reporting of material and support higher level planning and policy review (CDHFS, 1997).

Priority Areas for Mental Health Information Development

Ten priority areas for mental health information development in Australian mental health services have been identified as outlined below (Department of Health and Aged Care, 2005).

1. Using outcome measurement to improve mental health care.
2. Further development of mental health casemix classification.
3. Using information to improve safety in mental health care.
4. Establishing performance indicators and benchmarking in mental health services.
5. Strengthening workforce uptake and capacity to use information.
6. Improving the minimum data sets for mental health care.
7. Information to support mental health care provided external to the specialist sector.
8. Monitoring population mental health and well-being.
9. Information to support mental health prevention and promotion.
10. Monitoring and reporting progress under the *National Mental Health Strategy*.

The *Australian National Standards for Safety and Quality in Health Care* (Australian Commission on Safety and Quality in Health Care, 2011) also requires the effective use of data and information to monitor and report on organizational performance. This aims to support good clinical and corporate governance within mental health services.

Infrastructure and Workforce Development

Information Systems

All members of the workforce should be able to access information that identifies areas for improvement, which is reliable, useful, timely and not a burden to collect (Australian Commission on Safety and Quality in Health Care, September, 2011). To enable this to occur, information systems need to be developed and staff require training in their use. Information systems are not static. They undergo modifications and correction. This can have a significant impact on both the user's experience, and the quality of the data being collected. Staff retraining is therefore also an issue.

Information systems can be used for a variety of purposes, including the creation of electronic medical records. This enables both the documentation of clinical practice and access to consumer records including: past history, pathology results, and resources to support consumer assessment. Information systems can also be used for incident monitoring and management (Travaglia, Westbrook, & Braithwaite, 2009), as well as administrative reporting and staff management (Hegney et al., 2006). Additionally, systems can be used to access information on policy, evidence-based practice guidelines, and support professional development.

In Australia, information systems have been developed to support these activities, either in stand-alone or combined systems. For example, an electronic medical record that allows the documentation of clinical practice, collection of administrative data, and access to information to support clinical decision making at the point of care. These information systems have posed a challenge to an increasingly aged workforce. Some members have limited experience or a desire to engage with electronic systems. Ensuring workforce competence with clinical information systems has been further complicated by the introduction of either a fully electronic system, or a hybrid approach (combing both electronic and paper based systems). Variations exist across states and territories in their development and adoption of electronic systems.[1] Both approaches require a workforce with the knowledge, skills, and attitudes necessary to embrace the use of clinical information systems.

In Australian mental health services these information systems have been developed to enable the implementation, collection, and use of routine outcome measurement as part of clinical practice and service development. Work has been undertaken in this area for a number of years within private psychiatric hospitals in Australia. Also more recently in the community managed or non-government sector. However, this chapter will focus on the infrastructure and associated workforce development activities that have occurred to support routine outcome measurement in specialist public sector mental health services managed by states and territories. Focusing on this aspect of information system development will provide an exemplar of the workforce development initiatives necessary to support the sustainable implementation of information systems and their use.

Workforce Development

Work has been undertaken over the last 20 years in Australia under a series of four national mental health plans. A 5th plan is in development and due for release in 2016. Initially, much effort was directed towards introducing clinicians to new information collections, such as a national minimum data set or a set of routine outcome measures introduced under the Mental Health National Outcomes and Casemix Collection (MH-NOCC). Within three years, nearly 10,000 clinical staff had participated in MH-NOCC training events.

There was a need to develop a workforce who engaged with the information being collected. It was imperative the workforce saw the collection as more than simply an administrative activity and as an essential part of practice. The need to develop the capacity of the workforce to access, interpret, and apply the information being collected to support quality improvement and good governance also became clear. This required the development of training resources that extended the basic skills necessary to collect accurate information. Resources to also use the information to support the development of care plans, monitor consumer progress, or inform risk management.

Beyond the individual clinician, it has been necessary to equip team leaders and service managers with skills to use information to better understand their service performance. To also understand how the information can be used to support quality improvement projects.

The focus in Australia has been on the development of a more "information literate" workforce. However, this is only possible if information collected is reported in a way that is meaningful and useful to stakeholders.

ROUTINE OUTCOME MEASUREMENT IN MENTAL HEALTH SERVICES

The Mental Health National Outcomes and Casemix Collection (MH-NOCC)

A protocol to guide the collection of the MH-NOCC was released in 2002 (Department of Health and Ageing, 2002b). This was most recently updated in 2016 (Department of Health, 2016). The MH-NOCC protocol requires clinician-rated and consumer-rated measures to be completed by clinicians or offered to consumers at particular "collection occasions" (admission, review, and discharge) during each episode of care. Each episode of care is a more or less continuous period of contact between a consumer and a mental health service organization that occurs within the one inpatient or community mental health service setting. The MH-NOCC measures summarized in Table 1 vary according to the age group targeted by the particular service setting. Since 2002, states and territories have begun work to implement the MH-NOCC collection.

The Australian Mental Health Outcomes and Classification Network

In late 2003, the Australian Government's Department of Health and Ageing began the process of creating the Australian Mental Health Outcomes and Classification Network (AMHOCN). This is a consortium of organizations which aims to support:

- Implementation of the MH-NOCC collection through national data management.
- Training and service development in relation to the measures within the collection.
- Analysis and reporting of the collection.

The initial AMHOCN program of work was shaped by a key question posed by Leginski and U.S. colleagues in 1989: "Who receives what services from whom, at what cost, and with what effect?"

Development of Training Materials

Mental Health National Outcomes and Casemix Collection (MH-NOCC)

Training materials were developed to equip the workforce to collect measures within the MH-NOCC. The materials were adapted from a number of pre-existing documents including technical reports (Department of Health and Ageing, 2002ab), glossaries (Wing, Curtis, & Beevor, 1999), and training manuals (Eagar et al., 2000).

Initially, AMHOCN aimed to produce one set of nationally consistent training materials. However, there was no agreement nationally between states and territories about which consumer rated measure should be used. Some states and territories modified their collection protocol to meet their own information development needs. So, for example, while the consumer rated measure the Kessler-10 (Kessler et al., 2002) was excluded from the national protocol, New South Wales required it to be offered in inpatient units.

The solution to differences in the collection of measures was to create a core group of training materials which could be modified to meet local needs. Following the initial training, however, stakeholders consistently called for training materials that could demonstrate the utility of the measures in clinical practice. Consumers indicated that rather than just offering the measures and collecting the information, they wanted the measures to be used in care planning and to support consumer-carer-clinician dialogue (Black et al., 2009). As a result, AMHOCN collaborated with Barwon Mental Health Services in Victoria and developed a set of training materials focused on use of the consumer rated measure.

An evaluation of these training materials found they contributed to altering clinicians' attitudes towards the measures, particularly in relation to their clinical potential (Willis, Deane, & Coombs, 2009). Training materials were also developed that explored use of the measures as part of team review

Table 1. Data to be reported at each "collection occasion" within each "episode service setting", for consumers in each "age group"[1]

Episode Service Setting *Collection Occasion*	**Inpatient A R D**	**Community Residential A R D**	**Ambulatory A R D(2,3)**
Children and Adolescents			
HoNOSCA [4]	● ● ●	● ● ●	● ● ●
CGAS	● ● ✗	● ● ✗	● ● ✗
FIHS	✗ ● ●	✗ ● ●	✗ ● ●
Parent/consumer self-report (SDQ)[5, 6]	● ● ●	● ● ●	● ● ●
Principal and additional diagnoses	✗ ● ●	✗ ● ●	✗ ● ●
Mental health legal status	✗ ● ●	✗ ● ●	✗ ● ●
Adults			
HoNOS [4]	● ● ●	● ● ●	● ● ●
LSP-16 [7]	✗ ✗ ✗	● ● ●	✗ ● ●
Consumer self-report (MH38I, BASIS32, K10[6])	● ● ●	● ● ●	● ● ●
Principal and additional diagnoses	✗ ● ●	✗ ● ●	✗ ● ●
Focus of care [8]	✗ ✗ ✗	✗ ✗ ✗	✗ ● ●
Mental health legal status	✗ ● ●	✗ ● ●	✗ ● ●
Older persons			
HoNOS 65+ [4]	● ● ●	● ● ●	● ● ●
LSP-16 [7]	✗ ✗ ✗	● ● ●	✗ ● ●
RUG-ADL	● ● ✗	● ● ✗	✗ ✗ ✗
Consumer self-report (MHI38, BASIS32, K10) [6]	● ● ●	● ● ●	● ● ●
Principal and additional diagnoses	✗ ● ●	✗ ● ●	✗ ● ●
Focus of care [8]	✗ ✗ ✗	✗ ✗ ✗	✗ ● ●
Mental health legal status	✗ ● ●	✗ ● ●	✗ ● ●

Notes.

A = Admission to Mental Health Care, **R** = Review of Mental Health Care, **D** = Discharge from Mental Health Care.

● = Reporting of data on this occasion is mandatory, ✗ = No reporting requirements apply.

(1) This table identifies the national reporting requirements and is not intended to restrict a state or territory from the collection of additional data at specific collection occasions.

(2) Discharge ratings for the clinician and consumer-rated measures (i.e., the HoNOS/CA/65+, LSP-16, FIHS, CGAS, Focus of Care, the SDQ, BASIS-32/K10/MHI-38) are *not completed* by the ambulatory service or the consumer respectively, when the reason for the closure of the ambulatory episode is transfer to a bed-based treatment service setting of that organisation (i.e., psychiatric inpatient or community residential service). Where possible, the clinician and consumer measure ratings for the admission NOCC in the inpatient unit or the community residential care setting are reported as the consumer's discharge ratings from the ambulatory episode. Details are required, however, regarding Principal and Additional Diagnoses and Mental Health Legal Status relevant to the ambulatory episode of care.

(3) Discharge ratings for the clinician and consumer-rated measures (i.e., the HoNOS/CA/65+, LSP-16, FIHS, CGAS, Focus of Care, the SDQ, BASIS-32/K10/MHI-38) are not required for brief ambulatory episodes. Brief ambulatory episodes are those where the number of days between admission to and discharge from the episode of care is 14 days or less duration. Details are required, however, regarding Principal and Additional Diagnoses and Mental Health Legal Status relevant to the ambulatory episode of care.

(4) Discharge ratings for the HoNOS, HoNOS65+ and HoNOSCA are not required for inpatient episodes of 3 days or less duration.

(5) Discharge ratings for the SDQ are not required for any episode of less than 21 days duration because the rating period used at discharge (previous month) would overlap significantly with the period rated at admission.

(6) The classification of consumer self-report measures as mandatory is intended only to indicate the expectation that consumers will be invited to complete self-report measures at the specified *Collection Occasions*, not that such measures will always be appropriate. Special considerations applying to the collection of self-report measures are described in section 7.4.

(7) The LSP-16 is not included as a measure for use in inpatient settings as, in its current form, it requires ratings to be based on the consumer's functioning over the previous three months. This is difficult for the majority of inpatient episodes which are relatively brief.

(8) Restriction of the Focus of Care only to ambulatory care episodes for adults and older persons is based on experience in the MH-CASC study which found it to be of limited value in inpatient and community residential settings and with child/adolescent consumers.

processes. These materials were used during numerous face-to-face training sessions to support their further development and were modified for delivery via an online format.

Reporting

AMHOCN has worked to maximize the utility of collected information by developing ways of reporting information that is readily accessible to clinicians, consumers, and carers. To that end, AMHOCN developed a website which makes resources, training materials, and MH-NOCC based reports publically available (see http://www.amhocn.org).

Decision Support Tool

In 2007, AMHOCN developed a web Decision Support Tool (wDST) which enables clinicians to compare consumers with others from around Australia. In 2012, this reporting was enhanced so users could view state and territory reference material. AMHOCN also explored ways of aligning the wDST functions with clinical prompts or a library of information, and its incorporation within local information systems to add value to the information collected and reported. This was seen as particularly useful junior clinicians' work (McKay et al., 2008).

Online Training for Registrars

AMHOCN worked with the Royal Australian and New Zealand College of Psychiatrists (RANZCP) to develop an online training resource for registrars. The online training exposes registrars to the clinical and service development utility of routine outcome measurement. These materials are an elective unit and contribute to registrars' educational preparation necessary for college fellowship. The training materials focused on:

- Improving knowledge of the collection.
- The development of skills in the completion of the measures.
- Promoting positive attitudes towards the collection and use of clinical and administrative information.

Using Measures in Clinical Practice

A great deal of work has been undertaken to identify the usefulness of the routinely collected measures in clinical practice. While the way in which this information is shared across the mental health sector is outlined below (see Sector Communication), some examples from practice have proven particularly useful.

In Noarlunga, South Australia, the Health of the Nation Outcome Scales (HoNOS) (Wing et al., 1998) has been used to support decision-making in the Mobile Assertive Care (MAC) team that provides an intensive case management service. Also within the Shared Care Team which provides a low intensity clinical service to people who are relatively stable but who require long-term support. The HoNOS acts as a summary of the clinician's assessment and, as such, is used as a tool to aid clinical decision-making. High scores on individual HoNOS items are used to focus attention on particular problems or areas that may require clinical intervention. Total scores on the HoNOS are used as flags to prompt decisions regarding discharge from or transfer between teams. For example, for the MAC team, a HoNOS total score of eight or lower would prompt consideration of discharge from the team, while a score of 12 or lower would prompt consideration of a transfer to the Shared Care Team. The flag does not compel practice but simply raises the issue for consideration. There are legitimate reasons for some consumers to remain in care, regardless of HoNOS scores. However, the flags have proven a valuable way of using routinely collected information to influence the process of service delivery (Prowse & Coombs, 2009).

In the Adult Community Mental Health Team Bundaberg in Queensland (Coombs, Stapley, & Pirkis, 2011), the MH-NOCC measures are routinely used as a standard component of multi-disciplinary case reviews. Case review procedures have been modified, with the support of the consultant psychiatrist, to provide daily review meetings, also ensuring reviews are presented to the consumer's treating psychiatrist. A laptop computer and data projector enable team members to access the mental health information application live and to view the previous and current outcome measure collections for consumers during the reviews. Discussion is focused on all clinically significant HoNOS ratings, which then become a target of treatment planning. An important inclusion in the review is consideration of the adult consumer self-rated measure which must be offered to the consumer prior to the review process. These changes to the team review process have ensured that the focus of the review is on sharing and reflecting upon both clinician and consumer-rated information. As a consequence, reviews are both more productive and more rigorous, allowing approximately 10 minutes review time per consumer.

The case studies described above show that outcome measurement has clinical utility at a local level and is being used to:

- Guide clinical decision-making.
- Engage consumers in treatment.
- Foster a collaborative approach to care planning and goal setting.
- Review consumers' progress with treatment.
- Inform questions about consumers' eligibility for given programs.
- Assist with discharge planning.
- Improve the evidence base on which services are founded.
- Evaluate particular models of service delivery.

However, clinicians' views about outcome measurement are quite mixed and there are indications that clinical utility may tip the balance for many of them. When outcome measurement is seen as an aid to their clinical practice, clinicians are positive; when outcome measurement is seen as a time consuming process of collecting data that goes into a "black hole", clinicians are negative. Consumers also hold a range of views about outcome measurement and tend to be more sanguine when they see outcome measurement encouraging dialogue between themselves and clinicians, and leading to improved care (Guthrie, McIntosh, Callaly, Trauer, & Coombs, 2008). The development of these training materials has been an iterative process and takes time as the workforce matures and moves from simply collecting information to using that information for various purposes.

Benchmarking Mental Health Services

Australia has a set of nationally agreed indicators that can be used to monitor a variety of aspects of organizational performance and can be aggregated to report nationally (Australian Health Ministers

Advisory Council's Mental Health Drug and Alcohol Principal Committee [MHDAPC] by the National Mental Health Performance Subcommittee [NMHPSC], 2013). These indicators include the proportion of completed outcome measures and the outcomes of care as indicated by HoNOS change scores.

Benchmarking was a process originally designed to improve the efficiency of a business through the introduction of best practice with a desire to standardize care, reduce costs, and improve the outcome of care (Joint Commission on Accreditation of Healthcare Organizations, 2000). In 2005, states and territories, supported by AMHOCN, collaborated on a National Mental Health Benchmarking Project (NMHBP) (Coombs, Walter, & Brann, 2011). The project explored the value of the benchmarking process within the four main program areas of public sector mental health organizations (general adult, child and adolescent, older persons, and forensic). The objective was to run a series of forums at which organizations could benchmark themselves against each other, with a view to understanding variability in performance against the National Mental Health Performance Framework's (NMHPF) key performance indicators (KPIs). Participants took part in up to eight face-to-face meetings, and made use of online forums that were developed to facilitate discussion outside of these meetings.

To ensure active participation in these benchmarking forums, mental health organizations had to build a culture where the benchmarking process was established as the norm and data was routinely made available to contribute to improved clinical practice and better service management. For benchmarking to become routine, it is necessary to invest resources in developing organizational infrastructure and capacity, and in fostering the skills of individuals to collate, analyze, and interpret local data.

The information needs to be relevant to service providers. They need to see the value in using KPI data to understand inter-organizational variability and how this data can assist in identifying areas for improvement in local practices. The NMHBP has shown that benchmarking is possible, and that mental health organizations can do this in a collaborative fashion, rather than a competitive one. Managers and clinical leaders need to champion benchmarking and highlight its utility in relation to quality improvement and service development if the accountability goals of national reform initiatives are to be realized.

One of the lessons learned from benchmarking has been the amount of time necessary to maximize participation. The development of technical specifications and the collecting, reporting, and sharing of information takes time, before a benchmarking forum can even take place. It takes even more time to make substantial changes to organizational performance and have these reflected in the information collected. Benchmarking provides tremendous opportunities for quality improvement and service development. It is important to note that these opportunities are not realized overnight.

Sector Communication

One of the first activities undertaken by AMHOCN was a multi-way communication about outcome measurement that involved a series of consultation sessions with stakeholders from all states and territories (Pirkis et al., 2005). In total, 123 individuals attended consultation sessions (policymakers, personnel from central mental health units, mainstream health information sections, service managers, clinicians, individuals responsible for reporting routine outcome measurement at a site level, consumers and carers, and members of nationally convened expert groups). These consultations indicated that there was considerable variability across states and territories in their progress and approach to the implementation of routine outcome measurement in mental health. AMHOCN quickly realized it needed to adopt a tailored approach to support the endeavors of individual jurisdictions.

Communicating with the sector has been supported by the creation of "expert panels". Originally known as Outcome Expert Groups, they have developed into Mental Health Information Development Expert Advisory Panels because of an acknowledgement that routine outcome measurement is not independent of the mental health information development agenda. Routine outcome measurement is essential to understanding the relationship between the routine activity of services and the outcomes of care those services provide. These expert panels are made up of clinicians, managers, academics, consumers, and carers and provide advice on information development within the mental health sector. Importantly, they also provide a mechanism for broader consultation with the sector and a way of disseminating information, including developments around routine outcome measurement.

AMHOCN has held forums and workshops in all states and territories every year since its inception. While these workshops have focused on training and the development of training materials, the forums have been opportunities for service providers, consumers, and carers to share experiences in the use of routine outcome measurement. During forums, consumers share their views on completing a consumer self-assessment measure, highlighting how it can be an opportunity for personal reflection and to motivate change. Clinicians describe how they have used the clinician rated measures to inform care planning or monitoring change over time. Service managers share how they have used the measures for business case development or understanding the workload within teams. These forums provide an opportunity for the mutual sharing of knowledge of the opportunities that the use of routine outcome measurement can bring to the mental health field.

Since its inception, AMHOCN has given presentations on the MH-NOCC to over 10,000 people (clinicians, consumers, and carers) and over 4,000 people have registered for online training. AMHOCN estimates that it has probably had contact with at least 20% of the mental health clinical workforce in Australia (Burgess, Coombs, Clarke, Dickson, & Pirkis, 2012). It is important to note that states and territories have also undertaken their own communication and training activities, so the number of service providers who are not aware of the collection of outcome measures is expected to be very limited.

Awareness of the MH-NOCC has been promoted by AMHOCN through a biannual Outcomes and Information Conference. This event has been a collaborative initiative with colleagues from Te Pou (New Zealand's National Centre of Mental Health Research, Information and Workforce Development). The conference has run for over 10 years and brings together national and international speakers sharing their experience and expertise on the use of routine outcome measurement in mental health services. After 10 years of sharing information in this way, the conversations taking place during the conference have gradually changed from "this is what we should do", to "this is what we have done", to "this is what we want to do". The implementation of routine outcome measurement is sustained by the ongoing development of the collection and its use. At the start of the journey in Australia, we thought we knew what the answer was going to be, what we learned was to ask better questions.

FUTURE DIRECTIONS

A strategic review of the MH-NOCC has been undertaken and a series of recommendations have been produced aimed at improving the efficiency and effectiveness of the collection along with maximizing its clinical and service management utility. The review process began in 2011 with the Mental Health Information Strategy Standing Committee (MHISSC) tasking the National Mental Health Information Development Expert Advisory Panel (NMHIDEAP) and AMHOCN with a stocktake of the progress to date on the implementation of the MH-NOCC. This work also encompassed the identification of strategies to promote routine outcome measurement and the use of the data in public mental health services. The review focused on the measures that make up the MH-NOCC, the protocols for the collection of measures, along with the identification of implementation and capacity issues that impact upon the introduction and ongoing collection of the measures.

The MH-NOCC review, known as *NOCC Strategic Directions 2014 – 2024* (National Mental Health Information Development Expert Advisory Panel, 2013), involved an extensive consultation with over 1500 individual participants. These consultations included forums and face-to-face consultations with consumers, carers, health service clinicians and managers, and services managed by non-government organizations (NGOs). From May to September 2012, 866 participants attended consultations, including 47 forums, 22 consultation meetings, 25 site visits, and 5 videoconference consultations. In addition, consultations were held with national peak bodies such as the Australian National Mental Health Commission (NMHC), the Australian College of Mental Health Nurses, and the RANZCP. Presentations and consultations were also undertaken at The Mental Health Services Conference, held annually in Australia, and other forums as became available. Finally, two online surveys were conducted with responses received from 511 clinicians, and 134 consumers and carers.

Overall, the consultations indicated a need for continued investment in a routine outcome measure collection. Feedback indicated this was important because the collection enabled services to understand, improve, and be accountable for the effectiveness of their care. The extensive consultation resulted in some 25 recommendations. Specifically, work should be undertaken to develop guidelines to support the use, analysis, and reporting of outcome measures that would support good practice by jurisdictions, services, consumers, carers, and clinicians. These guidelines should include the use of outcome measures with culturally and linguistically diverse (CALD) consumers and consumers who identify as Aboriginal or Torres Strait Islander people. The practical use of the guidelines would be reinforced through workshops, forums, educational activities, and other events undertaken in partnership with consumers, carers, clinicians, and service managers.

Recommendations from *NOCC Strategic Directions 2014 – 2024* also highlight that work should be undertaken to develop decision support tools that build upon the clinical prompts project, mentioned previously, along with the exploration of technology to enable the use of these prompts within local information systems. The consultation process, undertaken as part of the review, highlighted the difficulties that clinical staff and service managers have in translating the information collected to their clinical practice. The consultations identified the need for more work to be undertaken in this area, harnessing the decision support opportunities provided by routine outcome measures. The consultations also highlighted the need for more work to be undertaken to ensure that the usefulness of the measures is shared more broadly across the sector.

CONCLUSION

In conclusion, the process of implementing and supporting routine outcome measurement in the Australian mental health workforce has been a long term and complex activity. It started with strong ongoing policy development and support. It continued with the provision of clear guidance, in particular a nationally consistent collection protocol. There has been significant investment, both nationally and at a state and territory level, in the implementation of routine outcome measurement through the development of training resources, and their dissemination, both face-to-face and online. There has been investment in communication with the sector, via workshops, forums and conferences, which enable the sharing of information on the implementation and use of measures to improve the outcomes of care. There has been a necessary, significant investment in workforce development over a number of years to provide the foundation upon which the benefits of routine outcome measurement can be realized. A vision for the development of the collection of outcome measures into the future has also been articulated. This includes ensuring services improve the outcomes that matter to consumers and their families, and increasing the focus on how best to use the measures in practice.

Workforce development within the mental health sector should be seen through the lens of significant, overarching reform initiatives – ones that focus on quality improvement, transparency and accountability, and most importantly, the active engagement of consumers and carers in service delivery and service development. Improving service delivery to the people served is always the aim. These long term efforts involve changing the culture of mental health services, including the practices, values, and skills of staff. Routine outcome measurement therefore provides an example of the need to undertake significant investment over the long term to ensure meaningful development of the mental health workforce. Routine outcome measurement continues in Australian public mental health services because stakeholders indicate that the first 25 years of implementation have been worthwhile, supporting the focus of service delivery on consumers and carers. It is the next 25 that pose the real challenge.

REFERENCES

Australian Commission on Safety and Quality in Health Care. (2011). *National Safety and Quality Health Service Standards*. Retrieved from http://www.safetyandquality.gov.au/

Australian Health Ministers. (1992). *National mental health policy*. Retrieved from http://www.health.gov.au/internet/main/publishing.nsf/Content/mental-pubs-n-pol08

Australian Health Ministers Advisory Council's Mental Health Drug and Alcohol Principal Committee (MHDAPC) by the National Mental Health Performance Subcommittee (NMHPSC). (2013). *Key performance indicators for Australian public mental health services* (3rd ed.). Retrieved from https://mhsa.aihw.gov.au/indicators/nkpi/

Black, J., Lewis, T., McIntosh, P., Callaly, T., Coombs, T., Hunter, A., & Moore, L. (2009). Its not that bad: The views of consumers and carers about routine outcome measurement in mental health. *Australian Health Review*, *33*(1), 93–99. doi:10.1071/AH090093 PMID:19203338

Burgess, P., Coombs, T., Clarke, A., Dickson, R., & Pirkis, J. (2012). Achievements in mental health outcome measurement in Australia: Reflections on progress made by the Australian Mental Health Outcomes and Classification Network (AMHOCN). *International Journal of Mental Health Systems*, *6*(1), 4. doi:10.1186/1752-4458-6-4 PMID:22640939

Coombs, T., Stapley, K., & Pirkis, J. (2011). The multiple uses of routine mental health outcome measures in Australia and New Zealand: Experiences from the field. *Australasian Psychiatry*, *19*(3), 247–253. doi:10.3109/10398562.2011.562507 PMID:21682624

Coombs, T., Walter, G., & Brann, P. (2011). Overview of the National Mental Health Benchmarking Project. *Australasian Psychiatry*, *19*(1), 37–44. doi:10.3109/10398562.2010.539221 PMID:21303275

Department of Health. (2016). *Mental health national outcomes and casemix collection: Technical specification of state and territory reporting requirements* (version 1.9). Retrieved from http://www.amhocn.org/publications/mh-nocc-technical-specifications-ver-19-consolidated-document

Department of Health and Aged Care. (2005). *Mental health information development: National information priorities* (2nd ed.). Retrieved from https://www.health.gov.au/internet/main/publishing.nsf/Content/AA5F407938FC9D2FCA257BF000209AA9/$File/infopri2.pdf

Department of Health and Ageing. (2002a). *National outcomes and casemix collection: Overview of clinical measures and data items* (version 1.02). Retrieved from http://www.amhocn.org/publications/mental-health-national-outcomes-and-casemix-collection-overview-clinician-rated-and

Department of Health and Ageing. (2002b). *National outcomes and casemix collection: Technical specification of state and territory reporting requirements for the outcomes and casemix components of 'agreed data' under national mental health information development funding Agreement* (version 1.0). Retrieved from http://www.amhocn.org/what-collected/nocc-technical-specifications

Eagar, K., Buckingham, W., Coombs, T., Trauer, T., Graham, C., Eagar, L., & Callaly, T. (2000). *Outcome measurement in adult area mental health services: Implementation resource manual*. Victoria, Australia: Department of Human Services.

Guthrie, D., McIntosh, M., Callaly, T., Trauer, T., & Coombs, T. (2008). Consumer attitudes towards the use of routine outcome measures in a public mental health service: A consumer-driven study. *International Journal of Mental Health Nursing*, *17*(2), 92–97. doi:10.1111/j.1447-0349.2008.00516.x PMID:18307597

Hegney, D., Eley, R., Buikstra, E., Fallon, T., Soar, J., & Gilmore, V. (2006). Australian nurses access and attitudes to information technology- A national survey. *Studies in Health Technology and Informatics*, *122*, 688–692. PMID:17102351

Joint Commission on Accreditation of Healthcare Organizations. (2000). *Benchmarking in health care: Finding and implementing the best practices*. Oakbrook Terrace, IL: Joint Commission on Accreditation of Healthcare Organizations.

Kessler, R. C., Andrews, G., Colpe, L. J., Hiripi, E., Mroczek, D. K., Normand, S. L. T., & Zaslavsky, A. M. et al. (2002). Short screening scales to monitor population prevalences and trends in non-specific psychological distress. *Psychological Medicine*, *32*(6), 959–976. doi:10.1017/S0033291702006074 PMID:12214795

Leginski, W., Croze, C., Driggers, J., Dumpman, S., Geertsen, D., Kamis-Gould, E., & Wurster, C. et al. (1989). *Data standards for mental health decision support systems: A report of the task force to revise the data content and system guidelines of the mental health statistics improvement program*. Washington, DC: US Department of Health and Human Services.

McKay, R., Coombs, T., Burgess, P., Pirkis, J., Christo, J., & Delle-Vergini, A. (2008). *Development of clinical prompts to enhance decision support tools related to the national outcomes and casemix collection* (version 1.0). Retrieved from http://www.amhocn.org/publications/development-clinical-prompts-enhance-decision-support-tools-related-national-outcomes

Mental Health Branch Commonwealth Department of Health and Family Services. (1997). *National Mental Health Strategy Evaluation Steering Committee, for the Australian Health Ministers Advisory Council, Evaluation of the National Mental Health Strategy: Final report*. Retrieved from https://www.health.gov.au

National Mental Health Information Development Expert Advisory Panel. (2013). *NOCC strategic directions 2014-2024*. Canberra, Australia: Commonweath of Australia. Retrieved from http://www.amhocn.org/special-projects/nocc-strategic-directions-2014-2024

Pirkis, J., Burgess, P., Coombs, T., Clarke, A., Jones-Ellis, D., & Dickson, R. (2005). Routine measurement of outcomes in Australian public sector mental health services. *Australia and New Zealand Health Policy*, *2*(1), 8. doi:10.1186/1743-8462-2-8 PMID:15840170

Prowse, L., & Coombs, T. (2009). The use of the Health of the Nation Outcome Scales(HoNOS) to inform discharge and transfer decisions in community mental health services. *Australian Health Review*, *33*(1), 13–18. doi:10.1071/AH090013 PMID:19203329

Travaglia, J. F., Westbrook, M. T., & Braithwaite, J. (2009). Implementation of a patient safety incident management system as viewed by doctors, nurses and allied health professionals. *Health*, *13*(3), 277–296. doi:10.1177/1363459308101804 PMID:19366837

Willis, A., Deane, F., & Coombs, T. (2009). Improving clinicians attitudes toward providing feedback on routine outcome assessments. *International Journal of Mental Health Nursing*, *18*(3), 211–215. doi:10.1111/j.1447-0349.2009.00596.x PMID:19490232

Wing, J., Curtis, R., & Beevor, A. (1999). Health of the Nation Outcome Scales (HoNOS). Glossary for HoNOS score sheet. *The British Journal of Psychiatry*, *174*(5), 432–434. doi:10.1192/bjp.174.5.432 PMID:10616611

Wing, J. K., Beevor, A. S., Curtis, R. H., Park, S. B., Hadden, S., & Burns, A. (1998). Health of the Nation Outcome Scales (HoNOS). Research and development. *The British Journal of Psychiatry*, *172*(1), 11–18. doi:10.1192/bjp.172.1.11 PMID:9534825

KEY TERMS AND DEFINITIONS

Benchmarking: Using key indicators to compare organizational performance and improve the quality of care.

Carer: A family member, partner or friend of a person with a lived experience of mental illness.

Casemix: Literally means the "mix of cases" that a health service treat.

Change Management: The use of tools, techniques and process to manage people to achieve a desired outcome.

Consumer: A person with the lived experience of mental illness who receives mental health services.

Key Performance Indicator: The means by which an objective can be judged to have or have not been achieved.

Outcome: A change in health status attributable to an intervention.

Web Decision Support Tool: A web based portal providing access to, and manipulation of, national aggregate statistics to inform clinical and service development decision making.

ENDNOTE

1 The introduction of fully electronic systems on occasion has resulted in frustration within the workforce as these complex systems are introduced and refined. These refinements often require changes in business rules, workflow, or documentation and can significantly impact upon the engagement of the workforce in the use of the information system. There have been similar experiences with the introduction of hybrid (electronic and paper based) systems. In this case, the workforce had been exposed to the ease of access to information but frustrated by the lack of a complete record.

Compilation of References

Abbott, A. (1988). *The system of professions - A study of the divisions of expert labour.* London, UK: University of Chicago Press.

Abbott, M. (1989a). Community treatment and support of the mentally disabled in New Zealand. In *Cure and care for the mentally disabled in the community* (pp. 39–55). Tokyo: Japanese Association for Mental Health.

Abbott, M. (1989b). Current issues in mental health and developmental disabilities: Challenges for health professionals. *Mental Health in Australia, 20,* 19–32.

Abbott, M., & Kemp, D. R. (1993). New Zealand. In D. R. Kemp (Ed.), *International handbook on mental health policy* (pp. 217–252). Westport, CT: Greenwood Press.

Abroms, L. C., Gill, J., Windsor, R., & Simons-Morton, B. (2009). A process evaluation of e-mail counselling for smoking cessation in college students: Feasibility, acceptability and cost. *Journal of Smoking Cessation, 4*(1), 26–33. doi:10.1375/jsc.4.1.26

Adams, A. M., Ahmed, T., El Arifeen, S., Evans, T. G., Huda, T., & Reichenbach, L. (2014). Innovation for universal health coverage in Bangladesh: A call to action. *Lancet, 382*(9910), 2104–2111. doi:10.1016/S0140-6736(13)62150-9 PMID:24268605

Addiction and Mental Health Collaborative Project Steering Committee. (2014). *Collaboration for addiction and mental health care: Best advice.* Ottawa, Canada: Canadian Centre on Substance Abuse.

Adeponle, A., Whitley, R., & Kirmayer, L. (2012). Cultural contexts and construction of recovery. In A. Rudnick (Ed.), *Recovery ofpeople with mental iIllness* (pp. 109–132). London, UK: Oxford Press. doi:10.1093/med/9780199691319.003.0008

Adolescent Health Research Group. (in press). *Youth '12 the health and wellbeing of secondary students in New Zealand: Results for Pacific young people.* Author.

Agnew, F., Pulotu-Endemann, F. K., Robinson, G., Suaalii-Sauni, T., Warren, H., Wheeler, A., … Schmidt-Sopoaga, H. (2004). Pacific models of mental health service delivery in New Zealand. Auckland, New Zealand: Health Research Council.

Ahmed, S. M., Hossain, M. A., Chowdhury, A. M. R., & Bhuiya, A. U. (2011). The health workforce crisis in Bangladesh: Shortage, inappropriate skill-mix and inequitable distribution. *Human Resources for Health, 9*(1), 3. doi:10.1186/1478-4491-9-3 PMID:21255446

Ajzen, I. (1991). The theory of planned behavior. *Organizational Behavior and Human Decision Processes, 50*(2), 179–211. doi:10.1016/0749-5978(91)90020-T

Alcohol and Drug Treatment Workforce Development Advisory Group. (2001). Practitioner competencies for alcohol and drug workers in Aotearoa-New Zealand. Wellington, New Zealand: Alcohol Advisory Council of New Zealand (ALAC).

Alcoholics Anonymous. (n.d.). *A brief history of AA in New Zealand.* Retrieved from http://www.aa.org.nz/about/history

Alem, A., Pain, C., Araya, M., & Hodges, B. D. (2010). Co-creating a psychiatric resident program with Ethiopians, for Ethiopians, in Ethiopia: The Toronto Addis Ababa Psychiatry Project (TAAPP). *Academic Psychiatry, 34*(6), 424–432. doi:10.1176/appi.ap.34.6.424 PMID:21041465

Allock, J., & Hollingsworth, N. (2009). The non-professionally qualified workforce: A focus on the new roles of the support, time and recovery worker and the community development worker. *Journal of Mental Health Training. Education and Practice, 4*(4), 12–17.

American Academy of Nursing. (2012). Essential psychiatric, mental health and substance use competencies for the registered nurse. *Archives of Psychiatric Nursing, 26*(2), 80–110. doi:10.1016/j.apnu.2011.12.010 PMID:22550669

American Hospital Association. (2005). Aligning hospital and physician interests: Broadening the concept of gain sharing to allow care improvement incentives. Chicago, IL: Author.

American Psychiatric Association. (2000). *Diagnostic and statistical manual of mental disorders* (4th ed.). Washington, DC: Author.

American Psychiatric Association. (2013). *Diagnostic and statistical manual of mental disorders: DSM-5.* Washington, DC: American Psychiatric Association.

American Psychological Association. (2015). *Demographics of the U.S. psychology workforce: Findings from the American community survey.* Washington, DC: Author.

Anderson, P., Kaner, E., Wutzke, S., Funk, M., Heather, N., Wensing, M., & Pas, L. et al. (2004). Attitudes and managing alcohol problems in general practice: An interaction analysis based on findings from a WHO collaborative study. *Alcohol and Alcoholism, 39*(4), 351–356. doi:10.1093/alcalc/agh072 PMID:15208170

Andolsek, K., Padmore, J., Hauer, K. E., & Holmboe, E. (2015). *Clinical competency committees: A guidebook for programs.* Retrieved from https://www.acgme.org/acgmeweb/Portals/0/ACGMEClinicalCompetencyCommitteeGuidebook.pdf

Annadale, M., & Instone, A. (2004). *Sei Tapu: Evaluation of the National Certificate in Mental Health Support Work.* Wellington, New Zealand: Platform.

Anthony, W. A. (2000). Recovery-oriented service system: Setting some system level standards. Boston, MA: Centre for Psychiatric Rehabilitation. Retrieved from http://www.michigan.gov/documents/anthony2000_1_83536_7.pdf

Anthony, W. A. (1993). Recovery from mental illness: The guiding vision of the mental health service system in the 1990s. *Psychosocial Rehabilitation Journal, 16*(4), 11–23. doi:10.1037/h0095655

Araya, R., Rojas, G., Fritsch, R., Gaete, J., Rojas, M., Simon, G., & Peters, T. J. (2003). Treating depression in primary care in low-income women in Santiago, Chile: A randomised controlled trial. *Lancet, 361*(9362), 995–1000. doi:10.1016/S0140-6736(03)12825-5 PMID:12660056

Archer, R. P., Nunn, S., & Regan de Bere, S. (2015). *The evidence and options for medical revalidation in the Australian context.* Retrieved from http://www.medicalboard.gov.au/Registration/Revalidation.aspx

Arden, J. (2010). Rewire your brain. Wiley. Hoboken, NJ.

Armitage, P. (1994). Long term mental health care in three European cities. *The Australian and New Zealand Journal of Mental Health Nursing, 3*(2), 42–58.

Aron, L., Honberg, R., Duckworth, K., Kimball, A., Edgar, E., Carolla, B., & Fitzpatrick, M. (2009). *Grading the States 2009: A report on America's health care system for adults with serious mental illness*. Retrieved from https://www.nami.org/getattachment/About-NAMI/Publications/Reports/NAMI_GTS2009_FullReport.pdf

Aronson, D. (1996). *Overview of systems thinking*. Retrieved from http://resources21.org/cl/files/project264_5674/OverviewSTarticle.pdf

Asante, A., & Hall, J. J. (2011). *A review of health leadership and management capacity in Papua New Guinea*. Sydney, Australia: Human Resources for Health Knowledge Hub, University of NSW.

Ashton, T., King, D., & McRae, S. (2004). *Labour market constraints affecting the mental health sector: Report to the Mental Health Commission*. Auckland, New Zealand: Centre for Health Services Research and Policy, University of Auckland.

Astho. (n.d.). *Workforce development plan toolkit: Guidance and resources to assist state and territorial health agencies to create a workforce training and development plan*. Arlington, VA: Astho. Retrieved from http://www.astho.org/Accreditation-and-Performance/Workforce-Development-Plan-Toolkit/Home/

Aubry, T. D., Flynn, R. J., Gerber, G., & Dostaler, T. (2005). Identifying the core competencies of community support providers working with people with psychiatric disabilites. *Psychiatric Rehabilitation Journal*, *28*(4), 346–353. doi:10.2975/28.2005.346.353 PMID:15895918

Australian College of Mental Health Nurses. (2016a). *National framework for mental health nursing course accreditation*. Retrieved from http://www.acmhn.org/about-us/course-accreditation

Australian College of Mental Health Nurses. (2016b). *National framework for postgraduate mental health nursing education*. Retrieved from http://www.acmhn.org/acmhn-national-framework

Australian Commission for Safety and Quality in Healthcare. (2015). *Australian atlas of healthcare variation*. Sydney, Australia: ACSQHC. Retrieved from http://www.safetyandquality.gov.au/atlas

Australian Commission on Safety and Quality in Health Care. (2011). *National Safety and Quality Health Service Standards*. Retrieved from http://www.safetyandquality.gov.au/

Australian Commission on Safety and Quality in Health Care. (2015). Australian atlas of healthcare variation. Sydney, Australia: Australian Commission on Safety and Quality in Health Care Australian Government.

Australian Government Department of Health. (2016a). *Health Workforce Australia transition to the Department of Health*. Retrieved from http://www.health.gov.au/internet/main/publishing.nsf/Content/hwa-archived-publications

Australian Government Department of Health. (2016b). *Health workforce programs*. Retrieved from http://www.health.gov.au/internet/main/publishing.nsf/Content/work-prog

Australian Health Ministers Advisory Council's Mental Health Drug and Alcohol Principal Committee (MHDAPC) by the National Mental Health Performance Subcommittee (NMHPSC). (2013). *Key performance indicators for Australian public mental health services* (3rd ed.). Retrieved from https://mhsa.aihw.gov.au/indicators/nkpi/

Australian Health Ministers. (1992). *National mental health policy*. Retrieved from http://www.health.gov.au/internet/main/publishing.nsf/Content/mental-pubs-n-pol08

Australian Health Ministers. (1992). *National mental health strategy*. Canberra, Australia: Mental Health Branch, Commonwealth Department of Health and Family Services.

Australian Health Ministers' Advisory Council. (2013) *A national framework for recovery-oriented mental health services: Guide for practitioners and providers*. Retrieved from http://www.health.gov.au/internet/main/publishing.nsf/Content/mental-pubs-n-recovfra

Australian Institute of Health and Welfare. (2016). *Mental health services in Australia*. Retrieved from https://mhsa.aihw.gov.au

Australia, O. T. (1999). *Australian competency standards for occupational therapists in mental health*. Melbourne, Australia: Occupational Therapy Australia.

Avery, H., Matheny, K., Robbins, A., & Jacobson, T. (2003). Health care providers' training, perceptions and practices regarding stress and health outcomes. *Journal of the National Medication Association*, *95*(9), 833–838. PMID:14527051

Baguley, C., Farrand, P., Hope, R., Leibowitz, J., Lovell, K., Lucock, M., . . . Richards, D. (2010). *Good practice guidance on the use of self-help materials within IAPT services*. Technical Report. Improving Access to Psychological Therapies (IAPT). Retrieved January 13, 2016, http://www.iapt.nhs.uk

Baker, A., & Roche, A. (2002). Editorial: From training to work-force development: A large and important conceptual leap. *Drug and Alcohol Review*, *21*(3), 205–207. doi:10.1080/0959523021000002642 PMID:12270069

Ballew, P., Castro, S., Claus, J., Kittur, N., Brennan, L., & Brownson, R. C. (2013). Developing web-based training for public health practitioners: What can we learn from a review of five disciplines? *Health Education Research*, *28*(2), 276–287. doi:10.1093/her/cys098 PMID:22987862

Bambling, M., King, R., Reid, W., & Wegner, K. (2008). Online counselling: The experience of counsellors providing synchronous single-session counselling to young people. *Counselling & Psychotherapy Research*, *8*(2), 110–116. doi:10.1080/14733140802055011

Barkat, A., & Maksud, A. (2003). Private sector health services in Bangladesh: An exploratory study. Dhaka, Bangladesh: Human Development Research Centre (HDRC), EngenderHealth.

Barker, P. (2009). *Psychiatric and mental health nursing: The craft of caring* (2nd ed.). London, UK: Hodder, Arnold.

Barker, P. J., & Buchanan-Barker, P. (2011). Mental health nursing and the politics of recovery: A global reflection. *Archives of Psychiatric Nursing*, *25*(5), 350–358. doi:10.1016/j.apnu.2011.03.009 PMID:21978803

Barrett, T., Boeck, R., Fusco, C., Ghebrehiwet, T., Yan, J., & Saxena, S. (2009). Nurses are the key to improving mental health services in low-and middle-income countries. *International Nursing Review*, *56*(1), 138–141. doi:10.1111/j.1466-7657.2008.00687.x PMID:19239528

Bathgate, M., & Pulotu-Endemann, F. K. (1997). Pacific People in New Zealand. In P. M. Ellis & S. C. D. Collings (Eds.), *Mental health from a public health perspective*. Wellington, New Zealand: Ministry of Health.

Becker, A. E., & Kleinman, A. (2013). Mental health and the global agenda. *The New England Journal of Medicine*, *369*(1), 66–73. doi:10.1056/NEJMra1110827 PMID:23822778

Beinecke, R., Minas, H., Goldsack, S., & Peters, J. (2010). Global mental health leadership training programmes. *International Journal of Leadership in Public Services*, *6*(0suppl), 63–72. doi:10.5042/ijlps.2010.0575

Bell, M., & MacDougall, K. (2013). Adapting online learning for Canada's Northern public health workforce. *International Journal of Circumpolar Health*, 72. PMID:23971012

Benner, P., Leonard, V., & Day, L. (2010). *Educating nurses: A call for radical transformation*. San Francisco, CA: Jossey-Bass.

Bennett, J., Lehman, W., & Forst, J. (1999). Change, transfer climate, and customer orientation: A contextual model and analysis of change driven training. *Group & Organization Management*, *24*(2), 188–216. doi:10.1177/1059601199242004

Ben-Zeev, D., Schueller, S., Begale, M., Duffecy, J., Kane, J., & Mohr, D. (2014). Strategies for mHealth research: Lessons from 3 mobile intervention studies. *Administration and Policy in Mental Health and Mental Health Services Research*, *42*(2), 157–167. doi:10.1007/s10488-014-0556-2 PMID:24824311

Bergeson, S. (2015). *Patient issues that get in the way of treatment adherence: Surprising survey findings.* Retrieved from http://slideplayer.com/slide/3885538/

Bernfeld, G. A., Farrington, D. P., & Leschied, A. W. (2001). *Offender rehabilitation in practice: Implementing and evaluating effective programs*. New York, NY: John Wiley & Sons.

Betancourt, J. R., Green, A., & Carrillo, J. E. (2002). *Cultural competence in health care: Emerging frameworks and practical approaches*. The Commonwealth Fund.

Betancourt, J., Green, A., Carrillo, J. E., & Ananeh-Firempong, O. II. (2003). Defining cultural competence: A practical framework for addressing racial/ethnic disparities in health and health care. *Public Health Reports*, *118*(4), 293–302. doi:10.1016/S0033-3549(04)50253-4 PMID:12815076

Biswas, T., Islam, A., Rawal, L., & Islam, S. (2016). Increasing prevalence of diabetes in Bangladesh: A scoping review. *Public Health*, *138*, 4–11. doi:10.1016/j.puhe.2016.03.025 PMID:27169347

Black, J., Lewis, T., McIntosh, P., Callaly, T., Coombs, T., Hunter, A., & Moore, L. (2009). Its not that bad: The views of consumers and carers about routine outcome measurement in mental health. *Australian Health Review*, *33*(1), 93–99. doi:10.1071/AH090093 PMID:19203338

Bluestone, J., Johnson, P., Fullerton, J., Carr, C., & Alderman, J., & BonTempo, J. (2013). Effective in-service training design and delivery: Evidence from an integrative literature review. *Human Resources for Health*, *11*(51), 1–26. PMID:24083659

Blume, B., Ford, J., Baldwin, T., & Huang, J. (2010). Transfer of training: A meta analytic review. *Journal of Management*, *36*(4), 1065–1105. doi:10.1177/0149206309352880

Bobrow, K., Farmer, A. J., Springer, D., Shanyinde, M., Yu, L.-M., Brennan, T., & Tarassenko, L. et al. (2016). Mobile phone text messages to support treatment adherence in adults with high blood pressure (SMS-text adherence support [StAR]): A single-blind, randomized trial. *Circulation*, *133*(6), 592–600. PMID:26769742

Borg, M., & Kristiansen, K. (2004). Recovery-orientated professionals: Helping relationships in mental health services. *Journal of Mental Health (Abingdon, England)*, *13*(5), 493–505. doi:10.1080/09638230400006809

Bostock, D. (2000). *Aristotle's ethics*. New York: Oxford University Press.

Bradstreet, S. (2006). Harnessing the lived experience: Formalising peer support approaches to promote recovery. *The Mental Health Review*, *11*(2), 33–37. doi:10.1108/13619322200600019

Brain Wave Trust Aotearoa. (2015). Retrieved from www.brainwave.org.nz

Bramwell, A. (2011). *Training policy for the 21st Century. In Decentralization and workforce development programs for unemployed working-age adults in Canada*. Toronto, Canada: Mowat Centre for Policy Innovation.

Briggs, L. (2012). *Tackling wicked problems: A public policy perspective*. Retrieved from http://www.apsc.gov.au/publications-and-media/archive/publications-archive/tackling-wicked-problems

Broyles, L., Binswanger, I., Jenkins, J., Finnell, D., Faseru, B., Cavaiola, A., & Gordon, A. et al. (2014). Confronting inadvertent stigma and pejorative language in addiction scholarship: A recognition and response. *Substance Abuse*, *35*(3), 217–221. doi:10.1080/08897077.2014.930372 PMID:24911031

BRSS TACS. (2015, November). *Core competencies for peer workers in behavioral health services.* Rockville, MD: Substance Abuse and Mental Health Services Administration.

Bruckner, T., Scheffler, R., Shen, G., Yoon, J., Chisholm, D., Morris, J., & Saxena, S. et al. (2011). The mental health workforce gap in low-and middle-income countries: A needs-based approach. *Bulletin of the World Health Organization*, *89*(3), 184–194. doi:10.2471/BLT.10.082784 PMID:21379414

Buchan, H., Sewell, J., & Sweet, M. (2004). Translating evidence into practice. *The Medical Journal of Australia*, *180*(6Suppl), S43. PMID:15012577

Bunch, K. (2007). Training failure as a consequence of organizational culture. *Human Resource Development Review*, *6*(2), 142–163. doi:10.1177/1534484307299273

Burgess, P., Coombs, T., Clarke, A., Dickson, R., & Pirkis, J. (2012). Achievements in mental health outcome measurement in Australia: Reflections on progress made by the Australian Mental Health Outcomes and Classification Network (AMHOCN). *International Journal of Mental Health Systems*, *6*(1), 4. doi:10.1186/1752-4458-6-4 PMID:22640939

Burke, L. A., & Hutchins, H. M. (2007). Training transfer: An integrative literature review. *Human Resource Development Review*, *6*(3), 263–296. doi:10.1177/1534484307303035

Burrage, M., & Torstendahl, R. (1990). *The formation of professions: Knowledge, state strategy.* London, UK: Sage.

Bushe, G. R. (1998). *Five theories of change embedded in appreciative inquiry.* Paper presented at the 18th Annual World Congress of Organization Development, Dublin, Ireland. Retrieved from www.gervasebushe.ca

Bywood, P., Lunnay, B., & Roche, A. (2008a). *Effective dissemination: A systematic review of implementation strategies for the AOD field.* Adelaide, Australia: National Centre for Education and Training on Addiction, Flinders University.

Bywood, P., Lunnay, B., & Roche, A. (2008b). *Effective dissemination. An examination of the costs of implementation strategies for the AOD field.* Adelaide, Australia: National Centre for Education and Training on Addiction, Flinders University.

Callister, P., Badkar, J., & Didham, R. (2011). Globalisation, localisation and implications of a transforming nursing workforce in New Zealand: Opportunities and challenges. *Nursing Inquiry*, *18*(3), 205–215. doi:10.1111/j.1440-1800.2011.00528.x PMID:21790871

Cambridgeshire and Peterborough NHS Foundation Trust. (2016). Retrieved from http://www.cpft.nhs.uk/patients/peer-support.htm

Campbell, J., Dussault, G., Buchan, J., Pozo-Martin, F., Guerra Arias, M., Leone, C., & Cometto, G. (2013). *A universal truth: No health without a workforce.* Geneva, Switzerland: World Health Organization.

Campion, M. A., Fink, A. A., Ruggeberg, B. J., Carr, L., Phillips, G. M., & Odman, R. B. (2011). Doing competencies well: Best practices in competency modelling. *Personnel Psychology*, *64*(1), 225–262. doi:10.1111/j.1744-6570.2010.01207.x

Car, J., & Sheikh, A. (2004). Email consultations in health care: 1—scope and effectiveness. *British Medical Journal*, *329*(7463), 435–438. doi:10.1136/bmj.329.7463.435 PMID:15321902

Carney, T. (2008). The mental health service crisis of neoliberalism - An antipodean perspective. *International Journal of Law and Psychiatry*, *31*(2), 173–175. doi:10.1016/j.ijlp.2008.02.001 PMID:18314192

Carruthers, C., & Hood, C. (2004). The power for the positive: Leisure and well-being. *Therapeutic Recreation Journal, 38*(2), 225–245.

Cartwright, M., Gibbon, P., McDermott, B. M., & Bor, W. (2005). The use of email in a child and adolescent mental health service: Are staff ready? *Journal of Telemedicine and Telecare, 11*(4), 199–204. doi:10.1258/1357633054068865 PMID:15969796

Case Consulting. (2003). *Evaluation of the national certificate in mental heath support work.* Wellington, New Zealand: Platform Mental Health Support Worker Advisory Group.

Cassels, S. (2006). Overweight in the Pacific: Links between foreign dependence, global food trade, and obesity in the Federated States of Micronesia. *Globalization and Health, 2*(1), 1–8. doi:10.1186/1744-8603-2-10 PMID:16834782

Cassie, F. (2015). NETP: A decade of growth. *Nursing Review, 15*(4). Retrieved from http://www.nursingreview.co.nz/issue/august-2015/netp-a-decade-of-growth/#.V-TxoE0cT84

Center for Health Care Strategies. (2013). *Family and youth peer support literature review.* Retrieved from http://www.chcs.org/media/FYPS_Literature_Review_FINAL.pdf

Center for Substance Abuse Treatment. (2006). *Addiction counseling competencies: The knowledge, skills, and attitudes of professional practice (Technical Assistance Publication Series 21, HHS Publication No. 08-4171).* Rockville, MD: Substance Abuse and Mental Health Services Administration.

Center for Substance Abuse Treatment. (2007). *Competencies for substance abuse treatment clinical supervisors (Technical Assistance Publication Series 21-A, HHS Publication No. 12-4243).* Rockville, MD: Substance Abuse and Mental Health Services Administration.

Centers for Disease Control and Prevention, National Center for Health Statistics System, Mortality File. (2015). *Number and age-adjusted rates of drug-poisoning deaths involving opioid analgesics and heroin: United States, 2000-2014.* Atlanta, GA: Center for Disease Control and Prevention. Retrieved from https://www.cdc.gov/nchs/data/health_policy/AADR_drug_poisoning_involving_OA_Heroin_US_2000-2014.pdf

Central Intelligence Agency. (2013). *The world factbook 2013-14.* Washington, DC: Central Intelligence Agency.

Central Regional Health Authority. (1994). *A better life: Report of the greater Wellington mental health services review.* Wellington, New Zealand: Author.

Centre for Medicaid Services. (2007, August 15). *Letter to State Medicaid Director.* Retrieved from https://downloads.cms.gov/cmsgov/archiveddownloads/SMDL/downloads/SMD081507A.pdf

Chambers, R. (2006). How healthcare assistants fit into a practice. *GP*, 52.

Chan, W., Lam, L., & Chen, E. (2015). Hong Kong: Recent development of mental health services. *Advances in Psychiatric Treatment, 21*(1), 71–72. doi:10.1192/apt.bp.113.012278

Chester, A., & Glass, C. (2006). Online counselling: A descriptive analysis of therapy services on the Internet. *British Journal of Guidance & Counselling, 34*(2), 145–160. doi:10.1080/03069880600583170

Chesterson, J. (2009). Mental health promotion and prevention. In P. Barker (Ed.), *Psychiatric and mental health nursing: The craft of caring* (2nd ed.; pp. 571–586). London, UK: Arnold.

Cheverton, J., & Janamian, T. (2016). The Partners in Recovery program: Mental health commissioning using value co-creation. *The Medical Journal of Australia, 204*(7), S38. doi:10.5694/mja16.00124 PMID:27078791

Child Health. (2015). Retrieved from www.health.govt.nz

Chisholm, D. (2007). Mental health system financing in developing countries: Policy questions and research responses. *Epidemiology and Psychiatric Sciences*, *16*(04), 282–288. PMID:18333422

Chisholm, D., Lund, C., & Saxena, S. (2007). Cost of scaling up mental healthcare in low-and middle-income countries. *The British Journal of Psychiatry*, *191*(6), 528–535. doi:10.1192/bjp.bp.107.038463 PMID:18055957

Chow, C. K., Redfern, J., Hillis, G. S., Thakkar, J., Santo, K., Hackett, M. L., & Barry, T. et al. (2015). Effect of lifestyle-focused text messaging on risk factor modification in patients with coronary heart disease: A randomized clinical trial. *Journal of the American Medical Association*, *314*(12), 1255–1263. doi:10.1001/jama.2015.10945 PMID:26393848

Chow, C. M., Wieman, D., Cichocki, B., Qvicklund, H., & Hiersteiner, D. (2013). Mission impossible: treating serious mental illness and substance use co-occurring disorder with integrated treatment: a meta-analysis. *Mental Health and Substance Use*, *6*(2), 150–168. doi:10.1080/17523281.2012.693130

Churches, O., Nicholls, M., Thiessen, M., Kohler, M., & Keage, H. (2014). Emoticons in mind: An event-related potential study. *Social Neuroscience*, *9*(2), 196–202. doi:10.1080/17470919.2013.873737 PMID:24387045

Clark, T. C., Fleming, T., Bullen, P., Denny, S., Crengle, S., Dyson, B., … Utter, J. (2013). Youth'12 overview: The health and wellbeing of New Zealand secondary school students in 2012. Auckland, New Zealand: The University of Auckland.

Cleary, M., & Carlo, J. (2006). Improving student learning in the mental health settings: The view of clinical stakeholders. *Nurse Education in Practice*, *6*(3), 141–148. doi:10.1016/j.nepr.2005.11.003 PMID:19040869

Clemens, S., & Ritter, A. (2008). Estimating the prevalence of individuals likely to use publicly funded alcohol treatment services: An indirect estimation technique. *Drug and Alcohol Review*, *27*(5), 504–508. doi:10.1080/09595230802093752 PMID:18696297

Clinton, M., & Hazelton, M. (2000). Scoping mental health nursing education. *The Australian and New Zealand Journal of Mental Health Nursing*, *9*(1), 2–10. doi:10.1046/j.1440-0979.2000.00155.x PMID:11271010

Colby, S. L., & Ortman, J. M. (2014). *Projections of the size and composition of the U.S. population: 2014 to 2060, current population reports*. Washington, DC: U.S. Census Bureau.

Collins, P., Insel, T., Chockalingam, A., Daar, A., & Maddox, Y. (2013). Grand challenges in global mental health: Integration in research, policy and practice. *PLoS Medicine*, *10*(4), e1001434. doi:10.1371/journal.pmed.1001434 PMID:23637578

Commonwealth of Australia. (2009). *Fourth national mental health plan*. Retrieved from https://www.health.gov.au/internet/main/publishing.nsf/

Commonwealth of Australia. (2015). *Australian government response to Contributing Lives, Thriving Communities – Review of mental health programmes and services*. Retrieved from http://www.health.gov.au/internet/main/publishing.nsf/Content/mental-review-response

Connell, J. (2010). *Migration of health workers in the Asia Pacific region*. Sydney, Australia: Human Resources for Health Knowledge Hub, University of New South Wales.

Conway, J., McMillan, M., & Becker, J. (2006). Implementing workforce development in health care: A conceptual framework to guide and evaluate health service reform. *Human Resource Development International*, *9*(1), 129–139. doi:10.1080/13678860500522975

Coombs, T., Stapley, K., & Pirkis, J. (2011). The multiple uses of routine mental health outcome measures in Australia and New Zealand: Experiences from the field. *Australasian Psychiatry*, *19*(3), 247–253. doi:10.3109/10398562.2011.562507 PMID:21682624

Coombs, T., Walter, G., & Brann, P. (2011). Overview of the National Mental Health Benchmarking Project. *Australasian Psychiatry*, *19*(1), 37–44. doi:10.3109/10398562.2010.539221 PMID:21303275

Coop, C. F. (2006). Balancing the balanced scorecard for a New Zealand mental health service. *Australian Health Review*, *30*(2), 174–180. doi:10.1071/AH060174 PMID:16646766

Copeland, M. E. (2015). *Wellness recovery action plan. What is WRAP? Mental health recovery*. Retrieved from http://mentalhealthrecovery.com/

Corrigan, P.W. (2002). Testing social cognitive models of mental illness stigma: The Prairie state stigma studies. *Psychiatric Rehabilitation Models, 6*(2), 232-254. doi:org/10.1080/109734302084084434

Cotten, A. (2007). *Seven steps of effective workforce planning*. Washington, DC: IBM Center for the Business of Government.

Crawford-Williams, F., Fielder, A., Mikocka-Walus, A., & Esterman, A. (2015). A critical review of public health interventions aimed at reducing alcohol consumption and/or increasing knowledge among pregnant women. *Drug and Alcohol Review*, *34*(2), 154–161. doi:10.1111/dar.12152 PMID:24840708

Cremers, H.-P., Mercken, L., Crutzen, R., Willems, P., de Vries, H., & Oenema, A. (2014). Do email and mobile phone prompts stimulate primary school children to reuse an internet-delivered smoking prevention intervention? *Journal of Medical Internet Research*, *16*(3), 96–106. doi:10.2196/jmir.3069 PMID:24642082

Croft, B., & Parish, S. L. (2013). Care integration in the Patient Protection and Affordable Care Act: Implications for behavioral health. *Administration and Policy in Mental Health and Mental Health Services Research*, *40*(4), 258–263. doi:10.1007/s10488-012-0405-0 PMID:22371190

Croton, G. (2009). *Checklist- Agency dual diagnosis capability*. Retrieved from http://www.dualdiagnosis.org.au

Cuijpers, P., Donker, T., van Straten, A., Li, J., & Andersson, G. (2010). Is guided self-help as effective as face-to-face psychotherapy for depression and anxiety disorders? A systematic review and meta-analysis of comparative outcome studies. *Psychological Medicine*, *40*(12), 1943–1957. doi:10.1017/S0033291710000772 PMID:20406528

Dailey, W. F., Morris, J. A., & Hoge, M. A. (2015). Workforce development innovations with direct care workers: Better jobs, better services, better business. *Community Mental Health Journal*, *51*(6), 647–653. doi:10.1007/s10597-014-9798-4 PMID:25535046

Dal Poz, M. R., Quain, E. E., ONeil, M., McCaffery, J., Elzinga, G., & Martineau, T. (2006). Addressing the health workforce crisis: Towards a common approach. *Human Resources for Health*, *4*(1), 1–4. doi:10.1186/1478-4491-4-21 PMID:16887029

Damschroder, L. J., Aron, D. C., Keith, R. E., Kirsh, S. R., Alexander, J. A., & Lowery, J. C. (2009). Fostering implementation of health services research findings into practice: A consolidated framework for advancing implementation science. *Implementation Science; IS*, *4*(1), 50. doi:10.1186/1748-5908-4-50 PMID:19664226

Davis, D., Davis, M., Jadad, A., Perrier, L., Rath, D., Ryan, D., & Wowk, M. et al. (2003). The case for knowledge translation: Shortening the journey from evidence to effect. *British Medical Journal*, *327*(7405), 33–35. doi:10.1136/bmj.327.7405.33 PMID:12842955

DBS Alliance. (2016). Core peer specialist training.(2016). Retrieved from http://www.dbsalliance.org/site/PageServer?pagename=education_training_peer_specialist_core

De Crespigny, C., Grønkjær, M., Liu, D., Moss, J., Cairney, I., Procter, N., & Banders, A. (2015). Service provider barriers to treatment and care for people with mental health and alcohol and other drug comorbidity in a metropolitan region of South Australia. *Advances in Dual Diagnosis*, *8*(3), 120–128. doi:10.1108/ADD-05-2015-0007

Deegan, P. (1988). Recovery: The lived experience of rehabilitation. *Psychosocial Rehabilitation Journal*, *11*(4), 11–19. doi:10.1037/h0099565

Deering, D., Robinson, G., Wheeler, A., Pulford, J., Frampton, C., Dunbar, L., & Black, S. (2009). *Preliminary work towards validating a draft outcome measure for use in the alcohol and drug sector.* Auckland, New Zealand: Te Pou o te Whakaaro Nui.

Demyttenaere, K., Bruffaerts, R., Posada-Villa, J., Gasquet, I., Kovess, V., Lepine, J., & Morosini, P. et al. (2004). Prevalence, severity, and unmet need for treatment of mental disorders in the World Health Organization World Mental Health Surveys. *Journal of the American Medical Association*, *291*(21), 2581–2590. doi:10.1001/jama.291.21.2581 PMID:15173149

Department of Developmental Disability Neuropsychiatry, University of NSW. (2016). *The intellectual disability mental health core competency framework: A manual for mental health professionals.* NSW, Australia: Ministry of Health. Retrieved from https://3dn.unsw.edu.au/content/intellectual-disability-mental-health-core-competency-framework-%E2%80%93-download-page

Department of Health and Aged Care. (2005). *Mental health information development: National information priorities* (2nd ed.). Retrieved from https://www.health.gov.au/internet/main/publishing.nsf/Content/AA5F407938FC9D2FCA257BF000209AA9/$File/infopri2.pdf

Department of Health and Ageing. (2002a). *National outcomes and casemix collection: Overview of clinical measures and data items* (version 1.02). Retrieved from http://www.amhocn.org/publications/mental-health-national-outcomes-and-casemix-collection-overview-clinician-rated-and

Department of Health and Ageing. (2002b). *National outcomes and casemix collection: Technical specification of state and territory reporting requirements for the outcomes and casemix components of 'agreed data' under national mental health information development funding Agreement* (version 1.0). Retrieved from http://www.amhocn.org/what-collected/nocc-technical-specifications

Department of Health and Human Services. (2015). *Health Resource Service Administration, Find shortage areas: HPSA by state and county.* Retrieved from www.hpsafind.hrsa.gov

Department of Health. (2008). *Kimberley mental health and drug service.* Retrieved from http://www.health.wa.gov.au/services/detail.cfm?Unit_ID=267

Department of Health. (2016). *Australia's future health workforce – Psychiatry.* Retrieved from http://www.health.gov.au/

Department of Health. (2016). *Mental health national outcomes and casemix collection: Technical specification of state and territory reporting requirements* (version 1.9). Retrieved from http://www.amhocn.org/publications/mh-nocc-technical-specifications-ver-19-consolidated-document

Derks, D., Bos, A. E., & Von Grumbkow, J. (2007). Emoticons and online message interpretation. *Social Science Computer Review*, *26*(3), 379–388. doi:10.1177/0894439307311611

DeSouza, R. (1997). Improving collaboration between nursing professionals and support workers in the New Zealand mental health system. *Professional Leader*, *4*(2), 16–17.

Devane, M., & Leahy-Warren, P. (2015). Mental health nurses on prescribing in Ireland: Although in its infancy in Ireland, nurse prescribing has helped patients. Here, Michelle Devane and Patricia Leahy-Warren discuss conflicting views and practical concerns. *Mental Health Practice*, *19*(3), 14–22. doi:10.7748/mhp.19.3.14.s16

Dewit, D., & Rush, B. (1996). Assessing the need for substance abuse services: A critical review of needs assessment models. *Evaluation and Program Planning*, *19*(1), 41–64. doi:10.1016/0149-7189(95)00039-9

Dey, S., Standing, C., & Islam, S. (2009). A framework for offering professional certifications worldwide. *INTED2009 Proceedings*, 1227-1235.

Diener, E., & Lucas, R. E. (2000). Explaining differences in societel levels of happiness: Relative standards, need fulfillment, culture, and evaluation theory. *Journal of Happiness Studies*, *1*(1), 41–78. doi:10.1023/A:1010076127199

Dowling, M., & Rickwood, D. (2013). Online Counseling and Therapy for Mental Health Problems: A Systematic Review of Individual Synchronous Interventions Using Chat. *Journal of Technology in Human Services*, *31*(1), 1–21. doi:10.1080/15228835.2012.728508

Drake, R. E., & Bond, G. R. (2010). Implementing integrated mental health and substance abuse services. *Journal of Dual Diagnosis*, *6*(3-4), 251–262. doi:10.1080/15504263.2010.540772

Drake, R. E., Goldman, H. H., Leff, H. S., Lehman, A. F., Dixon, L., Mueser, K. T., & Torrey, W. C. (2001). Implementing evidence-based practices in routine mental health service settings. *Psychiatric Services (Washington, D.C.)*, *52*(2), 179–182. doi:10.1176/appi.ps.52.2.179 PMID:11157115

Duckett, S. J. (2005). Health workforce design for the 21st century. *Australian Health Review*, *29*(2), 201–210. doi:10.1071/AH050201 PMID:15865571

Duffy, M. R., Chen, T.-H., Hancock, W. T., Powers, A. M., Kool, J. L., Lanciotti, R. S., & Hayes, E. B. et al. (2009). Zika virus outbreak on Yap Island, Federated States of Micronesia. *The New England Journal of Medicine*, *360*(24), 2536–2543. doi:10.1056/NEJMoa0805715 PMID:19516034

Duraisingam, V. (2005a). Recruitment and Selection. In N. Skinner, A.M. Roche, J. O'Connor, Y. Pollard, & C. Todd (Eds.), Workforce development TIPS (theory into practice strategies): A resource kit for the alcohol and other drugs field. Adelaide, Australia: National Centre for Education and Training on Addiction (NCETA), Flinders University.

Duraisingam, V. (2005b). Retention. In N. Skinner, A.M. Roche, J. O'Connor, Y. Pollard, & C. Todd (Eds.), Workforce development TIPS (theory into practice strategies): A resource kit for the alcohol and other drugs field. Adelaide, Australia: National Centre for Education and Training on Addiction (NCETA), Flinders University.

Durie, M. (1994). *Whaiora: Māori health development*. Auckland, New Zealand: Oxford University Press.

Durlak, J. & Wells, A. (1997). Primary prevention mental health programs for children and adolescents: A meta-analytical review. *American Journal of Community Psychology, 25*(2), 115-152. doi:org/10.1023/a:1024654026640

Durlak, J. A., & DuPre, E. P. (2008). Implementation matters: A review of research on the influence of implementation on program outcomes and the factors affecting implementation. *American Journal of Community Psychology*, *41*(3-4), 327–350. doi:10.1007/s10464-008-9165-0 PMID:18322790

Dymnicki, A., Wandersman, A., Osher, D., Grigorescu, V., & Huang, L. (2014). *Willing, able ready: Basics and policy implications of readiness as a key component for implementation of evidence-based practices*. Washington, DC: Office of Human Services Policy, US Department of Health and Human Services.

Eagar, K., Buckingham, W., Coombs, T., Trauer, T., Graham, C., Eagar, L., & Callaly, T. (2000). *Outcome measurement in adult area mental health services: Implementation resource manual*. Victoria, Australia: Department of Human Services.

Eaton, N. R., Rodriguez-Seijas, C., Carragher, N., & Krueger, R. F. (2015). Transdiagnostic factors of psychopathology and substance use disorders: A review. *Social Psychiatry and Psychiatric Epidemiology*, *50*(2), 171–182. doi:10.1007/s00127-014-1001-2 PMID:25563838

Eby, L., Burk, H., & Maher, C. (2010). How serious of a problem is staff turnover in substance abuse treatment? A longitudinal study of actual turnover. *Journal of Substance Abuse Treatment*, *39*(3), 264–271. doi:10.1016/j.jsat.2010.06.009 PMID:20675097

Egan, G. (2009). The skilled helper: A problem-management and opportunity-development approach to helping.Belmont, CA: Brooks/Cole.

Elwyn, G., Taubert, M., & Kowalczuk, J. (2007). Sticky knowledge: A possible model for investigating implementation in healthcare contexts. *Implementation Science; 2*(1), 44. doi:10.1186/1748-5908-2-44 PMID:18096040

Emrich, K., Thompson, T., & Moore, G. (2003). Positive attitude: An essential element for effective care of people with mental illnesses. *Journal of Psychosocial Nursing and Mental Health Services*, *41*(5), 18–25. PMID:12743963

Ergo, A., Eichler, R., Koblinsky, M., & Shah, N. (2011). *Strengthening health systems to improve maternal neonatal and child health outcomes: A framework*. Washington, DC: Maternal and Child Health Integrated Progam.

Esposito, L., & Perez, M. (2014). Neoliberalism and the commodification of mental health. *Humanity & Society*, *38*(4), 414–442. doi:10.1177/0160597614544958

Evans, I. M., & Moltzen, N. L. (2000). Defining effective community support for long-term psychiatric patients according to behavioural principles. *The Australian and New Zealand Journal of Psychiatry*, *34*(4), 637–644. doi:10.1080/j.1440-1614.2000.00745.x PMID:10954395

Evans, S., Huxley, P., Gately, C., Webber, M., Mears, A., Pajak, S., & Katona, C. et al. (2006). Mental health, burnout and job satisfaction among mental health social workers in England and Wales. *The British Journal of Psychiatry*, *188*(1), 75–80. doi:10.1192/bjp.188.1.75 PMID:16388074

Ewer, P., Teesson, M., Sannibale, C., Roche, A. M., & Mills, K. (2015). The prevalence and correlates of secondary traumatic stress among alcohol and other drug workers in Australia. *Drug and Alcohol Review*, *34*(3), 252–258. doi:10.1111/dar.12204 PMID:25355060

Ewles, L., & Simnett, I. (2004). *Promoting health: A practical guide*. London, UK: Baillere Tindal.

Faleafa, M., Lua, M., & Tiatia, J. (2012). *Engaging Pasifika training programme: Engaging positively at the critical first point of contact. Unpublished document*. Auckland, New Zealand: Le Va.

Fave, A. (2010). Development through disability. In G. Burns (Ed.), Happiness, healing and enhancement (pp. 88–123). Wiley. Hoboken, NJ

Field, A. (2015). *New entry to specialist practice: Mental health and addiction nursing*. Retrieved from http://www.tepou.co.nz/resources/an-analysis-of-the-skills-matter-new-entry-to-specialist-practice-programme/640

Finfgeld-Connett, D. (2007). Concept comparison of caring and social support. *International Journal of Nursing Terminologies and Classifications*, *18*(2), 58–68. doi:10.1111/j.1744-618X.2007.00051.x PMID:17542862

Finn, J., & Barak, A. (2010). A descriptive study of e-counsellor attitudes, ethics, and practice. *Counselling & Psychotherapy Research*, (1): 1–10.

Fisher, E. S., & McClellan, M. B. (2009). *Report to the Congress: Improving incentives in the Medicare program - Accountable care organizations*. Washington, DC: Medicare Payment Advisory Commission.

Fixsen, D. L., Naoom, S. F., Blase, K. A., Friedman, R. M., & Wallace, F. (2005). *Implementation research: A synthesis of the literature*. Tampa, FL: University of South Florida, Louis de la Parte Florida Mental Health Institute, The National Implementation Research Network.

Forrester, J. (1987). Lessons from system dynamics modeling. *System Dynamics Review*, *3*(2), 136–149. doi:10.1002/sdr.4260030205

Francis, K. (2012). Health and health practice in rural Australia: Where are we, where to from here? *Online Journal of Rural Nursing and Health Care*, *5*(1), 28–36.

Freeman, E., McGuire, C. A., Thomas, J. W., & Thayer, D. A. (2014). Factors affecting costs in Medicaid populations with behavioral health disorders. *Medical Care*, *52*(3Suppl 2), S60–S66. doi:10.1097/MLR.0000000000000075 PMID:24561760

Ftanou, M., Machlin, A., Nicholas, A., King, K., Fletcher, J., Harvey, C., & Pirkis, J. (2014). Mental health professional online development (MHPOD): A web-based training tool for the non-government community mental health workforce. *The Journal of Mental Health Training Education and Practice*, *9*(3), 177–189.

Fulton, B. D., Scheffler, R. M., Sparkes, S. P., Auh, E. Y., Vujicic, M., & Soucat, A. (2011). Health workforce skill mix and task shifting in low income countries: A review of recent evidence. *Human Resources for Health*, *9*(1), 1–11. doi:10.1186/1478-4491-9-1 PMID:21223546

Gaines, P., Bower, A., Buckingham, W., Eager, K., Burgess, P., & Green, J. (2003). *New Zealand mental health classification and outcome study: Final report*. Auckland, New Zealand: Health Research Council of New Zealand.

Gausia, K., Fisher, C., Ali, M., & Oosthuizen, J. (2009). Antenatal depression and suicidal ideation among rural Bangladeshi women: A community-based study. *Archives of Womens Mental Health*, *12*(5), 351–358. doi:10.1007/s00737-009-0080-7 PMID:19468825

Gawande, A. (2009, January 26). Getting there from here: How should Obama reform healthcare. *Annals of Public Policy/The New Yorker*. Retrieved from http://www.newyorker.com/magazine/2009/01/26/getting-there-from-here

Georgia C. P. S. Project. (2016). Retrieved from http://www.gacps.org/

Gibson, K., & Cartwright, C. (2014). Young peoples experiences of mobile phone text counselling: Balancing connection and control. *Children and Youth Services Review*, *43*, 96–104. doi:10.1016/j.childyouth.2014.05.010

Gibson, N. (2015). Mental health: Mental health act 2014: Doc, are you ready? *Medicus*, *55*(9), 7–9.

Giddens, J., & Brady, D. (2007). Rescuing nursing education form content saturation: The case for a concept based curriculum. *The Journal of Nursing Education*, *46*(2), 65–68. PMID:17315564

Gilat, I., & Shahar, G. (2007). Emotional first aid for a suicide crisis: Comparison between telephonic hotline and internet. *Psychiatric*, *70*(1), 12–18. doi:10.1521/psyc.2007.70.1.12 PMID:17492908

Gilburt, H., Rose, D., & Slade, M. (2008). The importance of relationships in mental health care: A qualitative study of service users' experiences of psychiatric hospital admissions in the U.K. *BMC Health Services Research*, *8*(92), 1–12. PMID:18173837

Gilmore, V. (2005). Licensing of unregulated assistants urgent. *Australian Nursing Journal*, *13*(1), 11. PMID:16502940

Glasgow, R., Lichtenstein, E., & Marcus, A. (2003). Why dont we see more translation of health promotion research to practice? Rethinking the efficacy-to-effectiveness transition. *American Journal of Public Health*, *93*(8), 1261–1267. doi:10.2105/AJPH.93.8.1261 PMID:12893608

Global Health Workforce Alliance. (2011). *Outcome statement of the second global forum on human resources for health*. Geneva, Switzerland: WHO.

Glover, L. (2016). The Australian health care system, 2015. *2015 International Profiles of Health Care Systems*, 11.

Goldberg, S. B., Rousmaniere, T., Miller, S. D., Whipple, J., Nielsen, S. L., Hoyt, W. T., & Wampold, B. E. (2016). Do psychotherapists improve with time and experience? A longitudinal analysis of outcomes in a clinical setting. *Journal of Counseling Psychology*, *63*(1), 1–11. doi:10.1037/cou0000131 PMID:26751152

Gordon, S., Ellis, P., Haggerty, C., O'Connor, S., Pere, L., Foster, C., & Walkey, F. (2009). *Taku reo taku mauri ora: My voice, my life*. Auckland, New Zealand: Te Pou o te Whakaaro Nui.

Gordon, J., & Bradstreet, S. (2015). So if we like the idea of peer workers, why aren't we seeing more? *World Journal of Psychiatry*, *5*(2), 160–166. PMID:26110117

Gordon, S., Ellis, P., Haggerty, C., Pere, L., Platz, G., & McLaren, K. (2004). *Preliminary work towards the development of a self-assessed measure of consumer outcomes*. Auckland, New Zealand: Health Research Council of New Zealand.

Gotham, H. (2006). Advancing the implementation of evidence-based practices into clinical practice: How do we get there from here? *Professional Psychology, Research and Practice*, *37*(6), 606–613. doi:10.1037/0735-7028.37.6.606

Government of Western Australia Mental Health Commission. (2015). *The Western Australian mental health, alcohol and other drug services plan 2015-2025*. Retrieved from http://www.mentalhealth.wa.gov.au/ThePlan.aspx

Greenhalgh, T., Robert, G., Macfarlane, F., Bate, P., & Kyriakidou, O. (2004). Diffusion of innovations in service organizations: Systematic review and recommendations. *The Milbank Quarterly*, *82*(4), 581–629. doi:10.1111/j.0887-378X.2004.00325.x PMID:15595944

Green, J., & Mears, J. (2014). The implementation of the NDIS: Who wins, who loses? *Cosmopolitan Civil Societies: An Interdisciplinary Journal*, *6*(2), 25–39.

Green, L., & Kreuter, M. (1999). *The precede–proceed model. Health promotion planning: An educational approach* (4th ed.). New York: McGraw-Hill.

Griffiths, R., & Robinson, S. (2010). *Moving forward with healthcare support workforce*. London, UK: National Nursing Research Unit.

Grimshaw, J., & Eccles, M. (2004). Is evidence-based implementation of evidence-based care possible? *The Medical Journal of Australia*, *180*(6), S50. PMID:15012580

Grimshaw, J., Eccles, M., Lavis, J., Hill, S., & Squires, J. (2012). Knowledge translation of research findings. *Implementation Science; 7*(50). PMID:22651257

Grimshaw, J., Eccles, M., Walker, A., & Thomas, R. (2002). Changing physicians behavior: What works and thoughts on getting more things to work. *The Journal of Continuing Education in the Health Professions*, *22*(4), 237–243. doi:10.1002/chp.1340220408 PMID:12613059

Grimshaw, J., Shirran, L., Thomas, R., Mowatt, G., Fraser, C., Bero, L., & O'Brien, M. et al. (2001). Changing provider behavior: An overview of systematic reviews of interventions. *Medical Care*, II2–II45. PMID:11583120

Grol, R., & Wensing, M. (2004). What drives change? Barriers to and incentives for achieving evidence-based practice. *The Medical Journal of Australia*, *180*(6Suppl), S57. PMID:15012583

Gureje, O., & Alem, A. (2000). Mental health policy development in Asia. *Bulletin of the World Health Organization*, *78*(4), 475–482. PMID:10885166

Gureje, O., Hollins, S., Botbol, M., Javed, A., Jorge, M., Okech, V., & Jenkins, R. et al. (2009). Report of the WPA task force on brain drain. *World Psychiatry; Official Journal of the World Psychiatric Association (WPA)*, *8*(2), 115–118. doi:10.1002/j.2051-5545.2009.tb00225.x PMID:19516936

Gurvis, J. P., & Grey, M. T. (1995). The anatomy of a competency. *Journal of Nursing Staff Development*, *11*(5), 247–252. PMID:7562071

Guthrie, D., McIntosh, M., Callaly, T., Trauer, T., & Coombs, T. (2008). Consumer attitudes towards the use of routine outcome measures in a public mental health service: A consumer-driven study. *International Journal of Mental Health Nursing*, *17*(2), 92–97. doi:10.1111/j.1447-0349.2008.00516.x PMID:18307597

Gutiérrez-Maldonado, J., & Caqueo-Urízar, A. (2007). Effectiveness of a psycho-educational intervention for reducing burden in Latin American families of patients with schizophrenia. *Quality of Life Research: An International Journal of Quality of Life Aspects of Treatment, Care and Rehabilitation*, *16*(5), 739–747. doi:10.1007/s11136-007-9173-9 PMID:17286192

Gutiérrez-Maldonado, J., Caqueo-Urízar, A., & Ferrer-García, M. (2009). Effects of a psychoeducational intervention program on the attitudes and health perceptions of relatives of patients with schizophrenia. *Social Psychiatry and Psychiatric Epidemiology*, *44*(5), 343–348. doi:10.1007/s00127-008-0451-9 PMID:18982233

Haberstroh, S., Duffey, T., Evans, M., Gee, R., & Trepal, H. (2007). The experience of online counseling. *Journal of Mental Health Counseling*, *29*(3), 269–282. doi:10.17744/mehc.29.3.j344651261w357v2

Hacker, K., & Walker, D. K. (2013). Achieving population health in accountable care organizations. *American Journal of Public Health*, *103*(7), 1163–1167. doi:10.2105/AJPH.2013.301254 PMID:23678910

Haggerty, C., McEldowney, R., Wilson, D., & Holloway, K. (2009). *Growing our own: An evaluation of nurse entry to practice programmes in New Zealand 2006-2009*. Wellington, New Zealand: Clinical Training Agency, Ministry of Health.

Haines, H., & Abbott, A. (1985). Deinstitutionalisation and social policy in New Zealand: Historical trends. *Community Mental Health in New Zealand*, (1), 44-56.

Hallwright, S., & McPherson, I. (2010). *Interview*. Retrieved from (https://vimeo.com/10673116)

Happell, B. (2010). Moving in circles: A brief history of reports and inquiries relation to mental health content in undergraduate nursing curricula. *Nurse Education Today*, *30*, 643-648. doi.1016/jnedt.2009.12.108

Harding, C. M., Brooks, G. W., Asolaga, T. S. J. S., & Breier, A. (1987). The Vermont longitudinal study of persons with severe mental illness. *The American Journal of Psychiatry*, *144*(6), 718–726. doi:10.1176/ajp.144.6.718 PMID:3591991

Harper, M., Hernandez, M., Nesman, T., Mowery, D., Worthington, J., & Isaacs, M. (2006). *Organizational cultural competence: A review of assessment protocols*. Tampa, FL: University of South Florida.

Harris, M., Diminic, S., Burgess, P., Carstensen, G., Stewart, G., Pirkis, J., & Whiteford, H. (2014). Understanding service demand for mental health among Australians aged 16 to 64 years according to their possible need for treatment. *The Australian and New Zealand Journal of Psychiatry*, 1–14. PMID:24810872

Hauff, E. (1996). The Cambodian mental health training programme. *Australasian Psychiatry*, *4*(4), 187–188. doi:10.3109/10398569609080486

Hawai`i State Epidemiological Outcomes Workgroup. (2014a). *State epidemiological profile: Selected youth and adult drug indicators*. Retrieved from http://health.hawaii.gov/substance-abuse/survey/hiepi-profile2014/

Hawai`i State Epidemiological Outcomes Workgroup. (2014b). *State epidemiological profile: Selected youth and adult alcohol indicators*. Retrieved from http://health.hawaii.gov/substance-abuse/survey/hiepi-profile2014/

Hawaii Workforce Infonet. (2015a). *State of Hawaii: Employment projections for industries & occupations 2012-2022*. Retrieved from https://www.hiwi.org/gsipub/index.asp?docid=423

Hawaii Workforce Infonet. (2015b). *Hawaii County: Employment projections for industries & occupations 2012-2022*. Retrieved from https://www.hiwi.org/gsipub/index.asp?docid=423

Hawaii Workforce Infonet. (2015c). *Honolulu County: Employment projections for industries & occupations 2012-2022*. Retrieved from https://www.hiwi.org/gsipub/index.asp?docid=423

Hawaii Workforce Infonet. (2015d). *Kauai County: Employment projections for industries & occupations 2012-2022*. Retrieved from https://www.hiwi.org/gsipub/index.asp?docid=423

Hawaii Workforce Infonet. (2015e). *Maui County: Employment projections for industries & occupations 2012-2022*. Retrieved from https://www.hiwi.org/gsipub/index.asp?docid=423

Hawaii/Pacific Basin AHEC. (2014). Report of findings from the Hawaii Physician Workforce Assessment project. Honolulu, HI: University of Hawaii, John A. Burns School of Medicine (JABSOM).

Haxell, A. J. (2015). On becoming textually active at Youthline, New Zealand. *British Journal of Guidance & Counselling*, *43*(1), 144–155. doi:10.1080/03069885.2014.922163

Haybron, D. M. (2008). Happiness, the self and human flourishing. *Utilitas*, *20*(1), 21–49. doi:10.1017/S0953820807002889

Health and Disability Commissioner Act. New Zealand Statute (1994).

Health Funding Authority. (2000). *Tuutahitia te wero-meeting the challenges: Mental health workforce development plan 2000–2005*. Wellington, New Zealand: Author.

Health Practitioners Competence Assurance Act. New Zealand Statute (2003).

Health Practitioners Competency Assurance Act, 48 (2003).

Health Resources and Services Administration, National Center for Health Workforce Analysis. (2013, November). *The U.S. health workforce chartbook Part IV: Behavioral and allied health*. Rockville, MD: U.S. Department of Health and Human Services.

Health Resources and Services Administration. (2010). *The registered nurse population: Findings from the 2008 national sample survey of registered nurses*. Retrieved from http://bhpr.hrsa.gov/healthworkforce/rnsurveys/rnsurveyfinal.pdf

Health Resources and Services Administration. (2015). *Mental health HPSA designation criteria*. Retrieved from http://bhpr.hrsa.gov/shortage/hpsas/designationcriteria/mentalhealthhpsacriteria.html

Health Resources and Services Administration. (2016a). *Health professional shortage areas (HPSA) and medically underserved areas/populations (MUA/P)*. Retrieved from http://datawarehouse.hrsa.gov/topics/shortageareas.aspx#chart

Health Resources and Services Administration. (2016b). *Area health education centers*. Retrieved from http://bhpr.hrsa.gov/grants/areahealtheducationcenters/

Health Resources and Services Administration. (2016c). *Health workforce, area health education centers (AHEC) program directory*. Retrieved from http://datawarehouse.hrsa.gov/topics/healthprofessions.aspx

Health Workforce Advisory Committee. (2002a). *Framing future directions*. Wellington, New Zealand: Ministry of Health. Retrieved from http://www.hwac.govt.nz

Health Workforce Advisory Committee. (2002b). *The New Zealand health workforce: A stocktake of issues and capacity 2001*. Wellington, New Zealand: Ministry of Health.

Health Workforce Australia. (2012). *Leadership for the sustainability of the health system*. Adelaide: Health Workforce Australia.

Health Workforce Australia. (2013). *Mental health workforce planning data inventory*. Retrieved from http://pandora.nla.gov.au/pan/133228/20150419-0017/www.hwa.gov.au/our-work/mental-health-workforce-reform/mental-health-workforce-study.html

Health Workforce Australia. (2014a). *Mental health peer workforce study*. Retrieved from http://pandora.nla.gov.au/pan/133228/20150419-0017/www.hwa.gov.au/our-work/mental-health-workforce-reform/mental-health-peer-workforce.html

Health Workforce Australia. (2014b). *National mental health core capabilities*. Retrieved from http://pandora.nla.gov.au/pan/133228/20150419-0017/www.hwa.gov.au/our-work/mental-health-workforce-reform/mental-health-capabilities.html

Heath, B., Wise Romero, P., & Reynolds, K. (2013, March). *A review and proposed standard framework for levels of integrated healthcare*. Washington, DC: SAMHSA-HRSA Center for Integrated Health Solutions. Retrieved from http://www.integration.samhsa.gov/integrated-care-models/CIHS_Framework_Final_charts.pdf

Hedegaard, H., Chen, L., & Warner, M. (2015, March). *Drug-poisoning deaths involving heroin: United States, 2000-2013* (NCHS Data brief, Number 190). Hyattsville, MD: National Center for Health Statistics.

Hegney, D., Eley, R., Buikstra, E., Fallon, T., Soar, J., & Gilmore, V. (2006). Australian nurses access and attitudes to information technology- A national survey. *Studies in Health Technology and Informatics*, *122*, 688–692. PMID:17102351

Heisler, E. J., & Bagalman, E. (2015, April). *The mental health workforce: A primer*. Washington, DC: Congressional Research Service.

Heisler, E., & Bagalman, E. (2015). *The mental health workforce: A primer*. Washington, DC: Congressional Research Service.

Held, R. F., DePue, J., Rosen, R., Bereolos, N., Nuusolia, O., Tuitele, J., & McGarvey, S. (2010). Patient and health care provider views of depressive symptoms and diabetes in American Samoa. *Cultural Diversity & Ethnic Minority Psychology*, *16*(4), 461–467. doi:10.1037/a0020089 PMID:21058808

Helzer, J., Bucholz, K., & Gossop, M. (2007). Dimensional option for the diagnosis of substance dependence in DSM-V. *International Journal of Methods in Psychiatric Research*, *16*(S1), S24–S33. doi:10.1002/mpr.210 PMID:17623392

Hemingway, S., Clifton, A., & Edward, K.-L. (2016). The future of mental health nursing education in the United Kingdom: Reflections on the Australian and New Zealand experience. *Journal of Psychiatric and Mental Health Nursing*, *23*(5), 331–337. doi:10.1111/jpm.12312 PMID:27307264

Hendry, P., Hill, T., & Rosenthal, H. (2014). *Peer services toolkit: A guide to advancing and implementing peer-run behavioral health services*. Retrieved from https://acmha.org/images/uploads/files/Peer_Services_Toolkit.pdf

Hennessy, J. (2015). The contribution of the mental health support worker to the mental health services in New Zealand: An Appreciative Inquiry approach (Doctoral thesis). Auckland, New Zealand: Auckland University of Technology. Retrieved from http://aut.researchgateway.ac.nz/handle/10292/9192

Hickey, N., Kramer, T., & Garralda, E. (2010). Developing the primary mental health worker role in England. *Child and Adolescent Mental Health*, *15*(1), 23–29. doi:10.1111/j.1475-3588.2008.00524.x

Hickton, D. J., & Leary, M. L. (2015, December). *National heroin task force final report and recommendations.* Washington, DC: U.S. Department of Justice, White House Office of National Drug Control Policy.

Hoge, M. A., Morris, J. A., Laraia, M., Pomerantz, A., & Farley, T. (2014). Core competencies for integrated behavioral health and primary care. Washington, DC: SAMHSA-HRSA Center for Integrated Health Solutions. Retrieved from http://www.integration.samhsa.gov/workforce

Hoge, M. A., McFaul, M., Cauble, L. L., Craft, K. L., Paris, M., & Calcote, R. M. (2016). Building the skills of direct care workers: The Alaskan core competencies initiative. *Journal of Rural Mental Health, 40*(1), 31–39. doi:10.1037/rmh0000045

Hoge, M. A., Migdole, S., Cannata, E., & Powell, D. J. (2014). Strengthening supervision in systems of care: Exemplary practices in empirically supported treatments. *Clinical Social Work Journal, 42*(2), 171–181. doi:10.1007/s10615-013-0466-x

Hoge, M. A., Morris, J. A., Daniels, A. S., Stuart, G. W., Huey, L. Y., & Adams, N. (2007). *An action plan for behavioral health workforce development: A framework for discussion.* Rockville, MD: Substance Abuse and Mental Health Services Administration.

Hoge, M. A., Morris, J. A., & Paris, M. (Eds.). (2005). Workforce competencies in behavioral health. *Administration and Policy in Mental Health, 32*(5/6), 481–671.

Hoge, M. A., Morris, J. A., Stuart, G. W., Huey, L. Y., Bergeson, S., Flaherty, M., & Madenwald, K. (2009). A national action plan on workforce development in behavioral health. *Psychiatric Services (Washington, D.C.), 60*(7), 883–887. doi:10.1176/ps.2009.60.7.883 PMID:19564217

Hoge, M. A., & Paris, M. (2006). *Recruitment and retention in behavioral health: Background research for the national action plan on behavioral health workforce development.* Cincinnati, OH: The Annapolis Coalition on the Behavioral Health Workforce.

Hoge, M. A., Wolf, J., Migdole, S., Cannata, E., & Gregory, F. (2016). Workforce development and mental health transformation: A state perspective. *Community Mental Health Journal, 52*(3), 323–331. doi:10.1007/s10597-015-9953-6 PMID:26410216

Hoge, M., Stuart, G., Morris, J., Flaherty, M., Paris, M., & Goplerud, E. (2013). Mental health and addiction workforce development: Federal leadership is needed to address the growing crisis. *Health Affairs, 32*(11), 2005–2012. doi:10.1377/hlthaff.2013.0541 PMID:24191093

Holland, B. (2015). A workforce development systems model for unemployed job seekers. *Journal of Adult and Continuing Education, 21*(2), 55–76.

Holloway, K., Baker, J., & Lumby, J. (2009). Specialist nursing framework for New Zealand: A missing link in workforce planning. *Policy, Politics & Nursing Practice, 10*(4), 269–275. doi:10.1177/1527154409357628 PMID:20042419

Hope, R. (2004). *The ten essential shared capabilities. A framework for the whole of the mental health workforce.* London, U.K.: Sainsbury Centre for Mental Health. doi:10.1037/e543012011-001

Hosman, C., Jané-Llopis, E., & Saxena, S. (2004). *Prevention of mental disorders: Effective interventions and policy options: Summary report.* Geneva, Switzerland: WHO.

Huey, L., Alford, D., Flaherty, M., & Socklingham, S. (2016, March). *Addressing America's opioid overdose crisis through education: Breaking the cycle through workforce development at CME, GME, and UME levels.* Poster presentation at the World Congress on Continuing Professional Development, San Diego, CA.

Huntington, A., Bidewell, J., Gilmour, J., Chang, E., Daly, J., Wilson, H., & Lambert, C. et al. (2008). The relationship between workplace stress, coping strategies and health status in New Zealand nurses. *Journal of Occupational Health and Safety*, *24*, 131–141.

Hurley, J., Cashin, A., Mills, J., Hutchinson, M., & Graham, I. (2016). A critical discussion of Peer Workers: Implications for the mental health nursing workforce. *Journal of Psychiatric and Mental Health Nursing*, *23*(2), 129–135. doi:10.1111/jpm.12286 PMID:26914867

Hu, W., McColl, G., Thistlethwaite, J., Schuwirth, L., & Wilkinson, T. (2013). Where is the next generation of medical educators. *The Medical Journal of Australia*, *188*(1), 8–9. doi:10.5694/mja12.11654 PMID:23330743

Huxley, P., Evan, S., Beresford, P., Davidson, B., & King, S. (2009). The principles and provisions of relationships findings from an evaluation of support, time and recovery workers in mental health services in England. *Journal of Social Work*, *9*(1), 99–117. doi:10.1177/1468017308098434

Hyde, J. (2014). Lessons from Australia in the public funding of mental health services. *Canadian Psychology*, *55*(2), 139–143. doi:10.1037/a0036237

Illingworth, P. (2008). Faith: An untapped mental health nursing resource. *Mental Health Nursing*, *28*(4), 9–11.

Institute of Medicine. (2000). *To err is human: Building a safer health system*. Washington, DC: National Academy Press.

Institute of Medicine. (2001). *Crossing the quality chasm: A new health system for the 21st century*. Washington, DC: National Academy Press.

Institute of Medicine. (2006). *Improving the quality of health care for mental and substance-use conditions*. Washington, DC: The National Academies Press.

Institute of Medicine. (2012). *The mental health and substance abuse workforce for older adults: In whose hands?* Washington, DC: The National Academies Press.

Intergovernmental Committee on Drugs. (2014). *National alcohol and other drug workforce development strategy 2015–2018*. Canberra, Australia: Intergovernmental Committee on Drugs.

Intergovernmental Committee on Drugs. (2015). *National alcohol and other drugs workforce development strategy 2015-2020*. Retrieved from http://www.nationaldrugstrategy.gov.au/internet/drugstrategy/publishing.nsf/Content/home

International Association of Peer Supporters. (2016). *Definition-Peer supporter.* Retrieved from www.inaops.org

Islam, S. (2010). *Demographic situation of population ageing in Bangladesh.* Paper presented at the Asian Population Association. Geneva: World Health Organization.

Islam, S. M. S., Mainuddin, A., Islam, M. S., Karim, M. A., Mou, S. Z., Arefin, S., & Chowdhury, K. N. (2015). Prevalence of risk factors for hypertension: A cross-sectional study in an urban area of Bangladesh. *Global Cardiology Science & Practice, 2015*(4), 43. doi: 10.5339/gcsp.2015.43

Islam, S., & Moreau, A. (2009). Traditional healers in preventing HIV/AIDS: Roles and scopes. UNDP program on HIV/AIDS prevention in Bangladesh. *Bulletin of Medicus Mundi Switzerland, 2009*(113), 39-43.

Islam, A., & Biswas, T. (2014). Health system in Bangladesh: Challenges and opportunities. *American Journal of Health Research*, *2*(6), 366–374. doi:10.11648/j.ajhr.20140206.18

Islam, A., & Biswas, T. (2015). Mental health and the health system in Bangladesh: Situation analysis of a neglected domain. *Journal of Psychiatry & Neuroscience*, *3*(4), 57–62. doi:10.11648/j.ajpn.20150304.11

Islam, M. A., Rahman, A., Aleem, M. A., & Islam, S. M. S. (2016). Prevalence and associated factors of depression among posts-stroke patients in Bangladesh. *International Journal of Mental Health and Addiction, 14*(2), 154–166. doi:10.1007/s11469-015-9582-x

Islam, S. M. S., Ferrari, U., Seissler, J., Niessen, L., & Lechner, A. (2015). Association between depression and diabetes amongst adults in Bangladesh: A hospital based case–control study. *Journal of Global Health, 5*(2), 020406. doi:10.7189/jogh.05.020406 PMID:26649173

Islam, S. M. S., & Niessen, L. W. (2014). Population based cancer registry in the developing countries: A first step towards cancer control programs and research. *Journal of Cancer Therapeutics and Research, 11*(4), 1044. doi:10.4103/0973-1482.140989 PMID:26881677

Islam, S. M. S., Niessen, L. W., Ferrari, U., Ali, L., Seissler, J., & Lechner, A. (2015). Effects of mobile phone SMS to improve glycemic control among patients with type 2 diabetes in Bangladesh: A Prospective, Parallel-Group,Randomized Controlled Trial. *Diabetes Care, 38*(8), 112–113. doi:10.2337/dc15-0505

Islam, S. M. S., Purnat, T. D., Phuong, N. T. A., Mwingira, U., Schacht, K., & Fröschl, G. (2014). Non-communicable diseases (NCDs) in developing countries: A symposium report. *Globalization and Health, 10*(1), 1–8. doi:10.1186/s12992-014-0081-9 PMID:25498459

Islam, S. M. S., Rawal, L. B., & Niessen, L. W. (2015). Prevalence of depression and its associated factors in patients with type 2 diabetes: A cross-sectional study in Dhaka, Bangladesh. *Asian Journal of Psychiatry, 17*, 36–41. doi:10.1016/j.ajp.2015.07.008 PMID:26259893

Islam, S. M. S., & Tabassum, R. (2015). Implementation of information and communication technologies for health in Bangladesh. *Bulletin of the World Health Organization, 93*(11), 806–809. https://dx.doi.org/10.2471/BLT.15.153684 doi:10.2471/BLT.15.153684 PMID:26549909

Jacob, K., Sharan, P., Mirza, I., Garrido-Cumbrera, M., Seedat, S., Mari, J. J., & Saxena, S. et al. (2007). Mental health systems in countries: Where are we now? *Lancet, 370*(9592), 1061–1077. doi:10.1016/S0140-6736(07)61241-0 PMID:17804052

Jacobs, R., & Hawley, J. (2009). The emergence of 'workforce development': Definition, conceptual boundaries and implications. In R. MacLean & D. Wilson (Eds.), *International handbook of education for the changing world of work* (pp. 2537–2552). New York: Springer. doi:10.1007/978-1-4020-5281-1_167

JAMA Network Journals. ScienceDaily. (2015, November). *Prevalence of lifetime drug use disorders nearly 10 percent in US.* Retrieved from http://www.sciencedaily.com/releases/2015/11/151118125314.htm

James, A., Chadwick, S., & Rushforth, D. (2006). Implementing a new national role in mental health: The support, time and recovery worker. *Journal of Mental Health Workforce Development, 1*(1), 30–36.

Jansen, P. (2009). Non-financial barriers to primary health care services for Maori. *Journal of Primary Health Care, 1*(3), 240. PMID:20690390

Jansen, P., Bacal, K., & Crengle, S. (2008). *He ritenga whakaaro: Maori experiences of health services*. Auckland, New Zealand: Mauri Ora Associates.

Jenkin, C. (2014). *Emails expected to rise to 140 a day in 2018.* Retrieved from news.com.au

Jenkins, R., Kydd, R., Mullen, P., Thomson, K., Sculley, J., Kuper, S., & Brownie, S. et al. (2010). International migration of doctors, and its impact on availability of psychiatrists in low and middle income countries. *PLoS ONE, 5*(2), e9049. doi:10.1371/journal.pone.0009049 PMID:20140216

Joint Commission on Accreditation of Health Care Organizations. (1999). *Comprehensive accreditation manual for hospitals: The official handbook*. Oak Park, IL: Author.

Joint Commission on Accreditation of Healthcare Organizations. (2000). *Benchmarking in health care: Finding and implementing the best practices*. Oakbrook Terrace, IL: Joint Commission on Accreditation of Healthcare Organizations.

Joint Learning Initiative. (2004). *Human resources for health: Overcoming the crisis*. Retrieved from http://www.who.int/hrh/documents/JLi_hrh_report.pdf

Jones, D. R., Macias, C., Barreira, P. J., Fisher, W. H., Hargreaves, W. A., & Harding, C. M. (2004). Prevalence, severity, and co-occurrence of chronic physical health problems of persons with serious mental illness. *Psychiatric Services (Washington, D.C.)*, *55*(11), 1250–1257. doi:10.1176/appi.ps.55.11.1250 PMID:15534013

Jorm, A. F. (2012). Mental health literacy: Empowering the community to take action for better mental health. *The American Psychologist*, *67*(3), 231–243. doi:10.1037/a0025957 PMID:22040221

Jorm, A. F. (2014). Why hasnt the mental health of Australians improved? The need for a national prevention strategy. *The Australian and New Zealand Journal of Psychiatry*, *48*(9), 795–801. doi:10.1177/0004867414546387 PMID:25147289

Kahn, R., Wise, P., Kennedy, B., & Kawachi, I. (2000). State income inequality, household income and maternal mental and physical health: Cross sectional national survey. *British Medical Journal, 321*, 1311-1315. doi:org/10.1136/bjsm.34.1.73

Kahn, J., Yang, J., & Kahn, J. (2010). Mobilehealth needs and opportunities in developing countries. *Health Affairs*, *29*(2), 252–258. doi:10.1377/hlthaff.2009.0965 PMID:20348069

Kakuma, R., Minas, H., van Ginneken, N., Dal Poz, M. R., Desiraju, K., Morris, J. E., & Scheffler, R. W. et al. (2011). Human resources for mental health care: Current situation and strategies for action. *Lancet*, *378*(9803), 1654–1663. doi:10.1016/S0140-6736(11)61093-3 PMID:22008420

Karim, M. A., Majumder, A. A. S., Islam, K. Q., Alam, M. B., Paul, M. L., Islam, M. S., & Islam, S. M. S. et al. (2015). Risk factors and in-hospital outcome of acute ST segment elevation myocardial infarction in young Bangladeshi adults. *BMC Cardiovascular Disorders*, *15*(73). PMID:26197888

Kathol, R. G., Butler, M., McAlpine, D. D., & Kane, R. L. (2010). Barriers to physical and mental condition integrated service delivery. *Psychosomatic Medicine*, *72*(6), 511–518. doi:10.1097/PSY.0b013e3181e2c4a0 PMID:20498293

Kaufman, L., Brooks, W., Bellinger, J., Steinley-Bumgarner, M., & Stevens-Manser, S. (2014). *Peer specialist training and certification programs: A national overview*. Austin, TX: Texas Institute for Excellence in Mental Health, School of Social Work, University of Texas at Austin.

Kessler, R. C., Aguilar-Gaxiola, S., Alonso, J., Chatterji, S., Lee, S., Ormel, J., & Wang, P. S. et al. (2009). The global burden of mental disorders: An update from the WHO World Mental Health (WMH) Surveys. *Epidemiology and Psychiatric Sciences*, *18*(1), 23–33. doi:10.1017/S1121189X00001421 PMID:19378696

Kessler, R. C., Andrews, G., Colpe, L. J., Hiripi, E., Mroczek, D. K., Normand, S. L. T., & Zaslavsky, A. M. et al. (2002). Short screening scales to monitor population prevalences and trends in non-specific psychological distress. *Psychological Medicine*, *32*(6), 959–976. doi:10.1017/S0033291702006074 PMID:12214795

Kessler, R. C., Matthias, A., Anthony, J. C., De Graaf, R., Demyttenaere, K., Gasquet, I., & Haro, J. (2007). *Lifetime prevalence and age-of-onset distributions of mental disorders in the World Health Organization's World Mental Health Survey Initiative*. Geneva, Switzerland: World Health Organization.

Kingi-'Ulu'ave, D., Faleafa, M., Brown, T., & Daniela-Wong, D. (in press). Connecting Culture and Care: Clinical Practice for Pasifika People. In I. M. Evans, J. J. Rucklidge, & M. O'Driscoll (Eds.), Professional Practice of Psychology in Aotearoa New Zealand. Academic Press.

Kingi, D. A., Faleafa, M., & Brown, T. (2007). A Pasifika perspective of psychology in Aotearoa. In I. M. Evans, J. J. Rucklidge, & M. O'Driscoll (Eds.), *Professional Practice of Psychology in Aotearoa New Zealand*. Wellington, New Zealand: New Zealand Psychological Society.

Kingi, T. K., & Durie, M. (2000). *Hua oranga: A Maori measure of mental health outcomes*. Palmerston North, New Zealand: Te Pumanawa Hauora School of Māori Studies, Massey University.

King, R., Bambling, M., Lloyd, C., Gomurra, R., Smith, S., Reid, W., & Wegner, K. (2006). Online counselling: The motives and experiences of young people who choose the Internet instead of face to face or telephone counselling. *Counselling & Psychotherapy Research*, *6*(3), 169–174. doi:10.1080/14733140600848179

Kinnair, D., Anderson, S., & Thorpe, L. (2012). Development of interprofessional education in mental health practice: Adapting the Leicester model. *Journal of Interprofessional Care*, *26*(3), 189–197. doi:10.3109/13561820.2011.647994 PMID:22250705

Knapp, M. B., Dayson, D., Leff, J., Margolius, O., O'Driscoll, C., & Wills, W. (1990). The TAPs project 3: Predicting the community costs of closing psychiatric hospitals. *British Medical Journal*, *157*, 661–670. PMID:2126218

Knowles, M. (1984). *Andragogy in action: Applying modern principles of adult learning*. San Francisco: Jossey-Bass.

Kohn, R., Saxena, S., Levav, I., & Saraceno, B. (2004). The treatment gap in mental health care. *Bulletin of the World Health Organization*, *82*(11), 858–866. PMID:15640922

Koivu, B., Drummond, A., Battersby, M., & Cromarty, P. (2016). Large reductions in depression and anxiety via low-intensity cognitive behavioural therapy delivered by novice coach. *The Australian and New Zealand Journal of Psychiatry*, *50*(6), 202. doi:10.1177/0004867415624971 PMID:26764369

KPMG. (2012). *Value walks: Successful habits for improving workforce motivation and productivity*. Zurich: KPMG.

Kulhara, P., Chakrabarti, S., Avasthi, A., Sharma, A., & Sharma, S. (2009). Psychoeducational intervention for caregivers of Indian patients with schizophrenia: A randomised-controlled trial. *Acta Psychiatrica Scandinavica*, *119*(6), 472–483. doi:10.1111/j.1600-0447.2008.01304.x PMID:19032700

Lambert, M. J., & Barley, D. E. (2001). Research summary on the therapeutic relationship and psychotherapy outcome. *Psychotherapy (Chicago, Ill.)*, *38*(4), 357–361. doi:10.1037/0033-3204.38.4.357

Laverack, G. (2005). *Health promotion practice: Power and empowerment*. London, UK: Sage.

Le Va. (2009). *Real skills plus seitapu: Working with Pacific peoples*. Auckland, New Zealand: Le Va.

Le Va. (2014). *Organisational guidelines for disability support services: Working with Pasifika people with disabilities and their families*. Auckland, New Zealand: Le Va.

Leginski, W., Croze, C., Driggers, J., Dumpman, S., Geertsen, D., Kamis-Gould, E., & Wurster, C. et al. (1989). *Data standards for mental health decision support systems: A report of the task force to revise the data content and system guidelines of the mental health statistics improvement program*. Washington, DC: US Department of Health and Human Services.

Lenert, L., Muñoz, R. F., Perez, J. E., & Bansod, A. (2004). Automated e-mail messaging as a tool for improving quit rates in an internet smoking cessation intervention. *Journal of the American Medical Informatics Association, 11*(4), 235–240. doi:10.1197/jamia.M1464 PMID:15064291

Liu, J., Ma, H., He, Y., Xie, B., Xu, Y., Tang, H., & Zhang, M. et al. (2011). Mental health system in China: History, recent service reform and future challenges. *World Psychiatry; Official Journal of the World Psychiatric Association (WPA), 10*(3), 210–216. doi:10.1002/j.2051-5545.2011.tb00059.x PMID:21991281

Livermore, P., & Renu, A. (2011). *SMHSOP core competencies for beginning community clinicians – A clinician resource booklet to aid implementation.* Retrieved from https://www.google.com.hk/url?sa=t&rct=j&q=&esrc=s&source=web&cd=2&cad=rja&uact=8&ved=0ahUKEwiizMvEtMfMAhUGHKYKHX8HB1QQFgghMAE&url=http%3A%2F%2Fwww.health.nsw.gov.au%2Fmhdao%2Fprograms%2Fmh%2FDocuments%2Fcore-comp-measurecrit-comclinbklet.pdf&usg=AFQjCNHeEAPq4J6n5zR5F5LNETJOdzcLaw

Loeb, K., & Le Grange, D. (2009). Family-based treatment for adolescent eating disorders: Current status, new applications and future directions. *International Journal of Child and Adolescent Health, 2*(2), 243–254. PMID:20191109

Lyon, A., Stirman, S. W., Kerns, S., & Bruns, E. (2011). Developing the mental health workforce: Review and application of training approaches from multiple disciplines. *Administration and Policy in Mental Health and Mental Health Services Research, 38*(4), 238–253. doi:10.1007/s10488-010-0331-y PMID:21190075

MacDonald, K. M. (1995). *The sociology of the profession.* London, UK: Sage.

Macduff, C., Gass, J., Laing, A., Williams, H., Coull, M., Addo, M., & Mackay, R. (2010). *An evaluation of the impact of the dissemination of educational resources to support values-based and recovery-focused mental health practice.* Aberdeen, Scotland: NHS Education for Scotland.

MacEwan, I. (2007). *Mental health and alcohol and drug co-existing disorders: An integrated experience for whai ora?* Christchurch, New Zealand: Matua Raki.

Malo, V. (2000). *Pacific People in New Zealand talk about their experiences with mental illness.* Wellington, New Zealand: Mental Health Commission.

Manderscheid, R., & Kathol, R. (2014). Fostering sustainable, integrated medical and behavioral health services in medical settings. *Annals of Internal Medicine, 160*(1), 61–65. doi:10.7326/M13-1693 PMID:24573665

Manhal-Baugus, M. (2001). E-therapy: Practical, ethical, and legal issues. *Cyberpsychology & Behavior, 4*(5), 551–563. doi:10.1089/109493101753235142 PMID:11725648

Mason, J. (2013). *Review of Australian government health workforce programs.* Canberra, Australia: Department of Health and Ageing.

Matua Raki & Te Pou o te Whakaaro Nui. (2013). *Te whare o tiki: Co-existing problems knowledge and skills framework.* Auckland, New Zealand: Matua Raki and Te Pou o te Whakaaro Nui.

Matua Raki & Te Pou. (2013). *Te whare o tiki – Coexisting problems knowledge and skills framework.* Wellington, New Zealand: Matua Raki and Te Pou.

Matua Raki (2009). A co-existing problems training framework for the addiction and mental health workforce. Wellington, New Zealand: Matua Raki.

Matua Raki. (2012). *Brief intervention guide. Addressing risk and harm related to alcohol, tobacco, and other drugs and gambling.* Wellington, New Zealand: Matua Raki.

Maua-Hodges, T. (2000). *Ako pai ki aitutaki: Transporting or weaving cultures: Research report of field experiences to the Cook Islands*. Wellington, New Zealand: Wellington College of Education.

Mazmanian, P., Johnson, R., Zhang, A., Boothby, J., & Yeatts, E. (2001). Effects of a signature on rates of change: A randomized controlled trial involving continuing education and the commitment-to-change model. *Academic Medicine*, *76*(6), 642–646. doi:10.1097/00001888-200106000-00018 PMID:11401812

McClintock, K., Sokratov, A., Mellsop, G., & Kingi, T. K. (2013). Hua oranga: Service utility pilot of a mental health outcome measurement for an indigenous population. *International Indigenous Policy Journal*, *4*(3), 1–14. doi:10.18584/iipj.2013.4.3.7

McCrae, N., Banerjee, S., Murray, J., Prior, S., & Silverman, A. M. (2008). An extra pair of hands? A case study of the introduction of support workers in community mental health teams for older adults. *Journal of Nursing Management*, *16*(6), 734–743. doi:10.1111/j.1365-2834.2008.00929.x PMID:18808468

McDonald, M., Cox, S. M., Paterson, N. D., & Lafrenière, D. (2008). Trust in health relationships: Accounts of human subjects. *Journal of Empirical Research on Human Research Ethics; JERHRE*, *3*(4), 35–47. doi:10.1525/jer.2008.3.4.35 PMID:19385755

McGovern, M. P., Lambert-Harris, C., Gotham, H. J., Claus, R. E., & Xie, H. (2014). Dual diagnosis capability in mental health and addiction treatment services: An assessment of programs across multiple state systems. *Administration and Policy in Mental Health and Mental Health Services Research*, *41*(2), 205–214. doi:10.1007/s10488-012-0449-1 PMID:23183873

McGregor, S. (2001). Neoliberalism and health care. *International Journal of Consumer Studies*, *25*(2), 82–89. doi:10.1111/j.1470-6431.2001.00183.x

McKay, R., Coombs, T., Burgess, P., Pirkis, J., Christo, J., & Delle-Vergini, A. (2008). *Development of clinical prompts to enhance decision support tools related to the national outcomes and casemix collection* (version 1.0). Retrieved from http://www.amhocn.org/publications/development-clinical-prompts-enhance-decision-support-tools-related-national-outcomes

McKinley, K. E., Bryan-Smith, L., Dosch, T. L., Hamory, B. H., & Fillipo, B. H. (2002). A hub-and-spoke model of care: Providing specialty care in patients' own communities. *The Joint Commission Journal on Quality Improvement*, *28*(10), 574–575. PMID:12369160

McKinnon, B., & Cross, W. (2008). Occupational violence and assault in mental health nursing: A scoping project for a Victorian Mental Health Service. *International Journal of Mental Health Nursing*, *17*(1), 9–17. doi:10.1111/j.1447-0349.2007.00499.x PMID:18211399

McLean, J., Biggs, H., Whitehead, I., Pratt, R., & Maxwell, M. (2009). *Evaluation of the delivering for mental health peer support worker pilot scheme*. Edinburgh, UK: Scottish Government.

McMurray, A., & Clendon, J. (2011). *Community health and wellness: Primary health care in practice* (4th ed.). Sydney, Australia: Mosby Elsevier.

Mead, S. (2003). *Defining peer support*. Retrieved from http://www.intentionalpeersupport.org/wp-content/uploads/2014/02/Defining-Peer-Support.pdf

Mead, S. (2014). *Crisis as an opportunity for growth and change*. Retrieved from http://www.intentionalpeersupport.org/wp-content/uploads/2014/04/Crisis-as-an-Opportunity-for-Growth-and-Change.pdf

Mead, S. (2016). *Defining peer support*. Retrieved from http://www.intentionalpeersupport.org/trainings/

Meadows, D., & Wright, D. (2008). *Thinking in systems: A primer*. White River Junction, VT: Chelsea Green Publishing.

Meadows, G., Enticott, J., Inder, B., Russell, G., & Gurr, R. (2015). Better access to mental health care and the failure of the Medicare principle of universality. *The Medical Journal of Australia*, *202*(4), 190–194. doi:10.5694/mja14.00330 PMID:25716601

Mead, S., & MacNeil, C. (2006). Peer support: What makes it unique? *International Journal of Psychosocial Rehabilitation.*, *10*(2), 29–37.

Medicare Payment Advisory Commission. (2008, June). *Report to the Congress: Reforming the delivery system - A path to bundled payment around a hospitalization*. Washington, DC: Author.

Mellsop, G., & Smith, M. (2010). Outcome measures in New Zealand. In T. Trauer (Ed.), *Outcome measurement in mental health: Theory and practice* (pp. 26–31). New York, NY: Cambridge University Press. doi:10.1017/CBO9780511760686.004

Mental Health Branch Commonwealth Department of Health and Family Services. (1997). *National Mental Health Strategy Evaluation Steering Committee, for the Australian Health Ministers Advisory Council, Evaluation of the National Mental Health Strategy: Final report*. Retrieved from https://www.health.gov.au

Mental Health Commission. (1998). *Blueprint for mental health services in New Zealand: How things need to be*. Wellington, New Zealand: Author.

Mental Health Commission. (1998). *The blueprint for mental health services in New Zealand*. Wellington, New Zealand: Mental Health Commission.

Mental Health Commission. (2001). *Recovery competencies for the mental health workforce*. Wellington, New Zealand: Mental Health Commission.

Mental Health Commission. (2004). *Labour market constraints affecting the mental health sector*. Auckland, New Zealand: Auckland University.

Mental Health Commission. (2011). *National indicators 2011: Measuring mental health and addiction*. Wellington, New Zealand: Mental Health Commission.

Mental Health Commission. (2012). *Blueprint II Improving mental health and wellbeing for all New Zealanders*. Wellington, New Zealand: Mental Health Commission.

Mental Health Commission. (2012). *National indicators: Measuring mental health and addiction in New Zealand*. Wellington, New Zealand: Mental Health Commission.

Mental Health Coordinating Council. (2016). *Sector development*. Retrieved from http://www.mhcc.org.au/sector-development.aspx

Mental Health Foundation. (n.d.). *Glossary: Mental health support worker*. Retrieved from https://www.mentalhealth.org.nz/home/glossary/

Mental Health Workforce Advisory Committee. (2011). *National mental health workforce strategy*. Melbourne, Australia: Mental Health Workforce Advisory Committee.

Mental Health Workforce Advisory Committee. (2011a). *National mental health workforce plan*. Melbourne, Australia: Victorian Government Department of Health. Retrieved from http://webarchive.nla.gov.au/gov/20141216070238/http://www.health.gov.au/internet/mhsc/publishing.nsf/Content/pub-mhwac-plan

Mental Health Workforce Advisory Committee. (2011b). *National mental health workforce strategy*. Melbourne, Australa: Victorian Government Department of Health Retrieved from http://webarchive.nla.gov.au/gov/20141216070240/http://www.health.gov.au/internet/mhsc/publishing.nsf/Content/pub-mhwac-strat

Metz, A., Blase, K., & Bowie, L. (2007). *Implementing evidence-based practices: Six "drivers" of success. Child Trends: Research-to-Results Brief.* Washington, DC: The Atlantic Philanthropies.

Meurk, C., Leung, J., Hall, W., Head, B., & Whiteford, H. (2016). Establishing and governing e-mental health care in Australia: A systematic review of challenges and a call for policy-focussed research. *Journal of Medical Internet Research, 18*(1), e10. doi:10.2196/jmir.4827 PMID:26764181

Michie, S., Johnston, M., Abraham, C., Lawton, R., Parker, D., & Walker, A. (2005). Making psychological theory useful for implementing evidence based practice: A consensus approach. *Quality & Safety in Health Care, 14*(1), 26–33. doi:10.1136/qshc.2004.011155 PMID:15692000

Migration Policy Institute. (2011). *2008 American Community Survey and census data on the foreign born by State.* Retrieved from http://migrationinformation.org/dataHub/acscensus.cfm#

Mila-Schaaf, K., & Hudson, M. (2009). *Negotiating space for indigenous theorising in mental health and addiction.* Auckland, New Zealand: Te Pou o te Whakaaro Nui.

Millet, S. (2011). *Aristotle's power and responsibilities for nature.* Pieterlen, Switzerland: Peter Lang.

Minas, H. (2012). The Centre for International Mental Health approach to mental health system development. *Harvard Review of Psychiatry, 20*(1), 37–46. doi:10.3109/10673229.2012.649090 PMID:22335181

Minister of Health. (2006). *Te kōkiri: The mental health and addiction action plan 2006–2015.* Wellington, New Zealand: Ministry of Health.

Ministerial Council on Drug Strategy. (1998). *The national drug strategic framework. 1998-99 to 2002-02: Building partnerships. A strategy to reduce harm caused by drugs in our community.* Canberra, Australia: AusInfo.

Ministry for Culture and Heritage. (2015). *Read the Treaty.* Retrieved from http://www.nzhistory.net.nz/politics/treaty/read-the-treaty/english-text

Ministry of Health & Le Va. (2012). *Taeao o tautai: Pacific public health workforce development implementation plan.* Wellington, New Zealand: Ministry of Health.

Ministry of Health. (1994). *Looking forward.* Wellington, New Zealand: Author.

Ministry of Health. (1997). *Moving forward: The national mental health plan.* Wellington, New Zealand: Author.

Ministry of Health. (1998). *Report of the Ministerial Taskforce on nursing: Releasing the potential of nursing.* Wellington, New Zealand: Ministry of Health.

Ministry of Health. (2002). *Mental health (alcohol and other drugs) workforce development framework.* Wellington, New Zealand: Ministry of Health.

Ministry of Health. (2004). *Te Tahuhu - improving mental halth: The second national mental health and addiction plan 2005-2015.* Wellington, New Zealand: Author.

Ministry of Health. (2005). *Tauawhitia te Wero: Embracing the challenge: National mental health and addiction workforce development plan 2006-2009.* Wellington, New Zealand: Author.

Ministry of Health. (2005). *Tauawhitia te wero: Embracing the challenge: National mental health and addiction workforce development plan 2006-2009.* Wellington, New Zealand: Ministry of Health.

Ministry of Health. (2008). *A portrait of health: Key results of the 2006/07 New Zealand health survey.* Wellington, New Zealand: Ministry of Health.

Ministry of Health. (2008). *Future directions for eating disorders*. Wellington, New Zealand: Author.

Ministry of Health. (2008). *Let's get real: Real skills for people working in mental health and addiction*. Wellington, New Zealand: Ministry of Health.

Ministry of Health. (2010). *Service delivery for people with co-existing mental health and addiction problems: Integrated solutions*. Wellington, New Zealand: Ministry of Health.

Ministry of Health. (2011). *Healthy beginnings: Developing perinatal and infant mental health services in New Zealand*. Wellington: Ministry of Health.

Ministry of Health. (2012). *Rising to the challenge -The mental health and addiction service development plan*. Wellington, New Zealand: Author.

Ministry of Health. (2012). *Rising to the challenge: The mental health and addiction service development plan 2012-2017*. Wellington, New Zealand: Ministry of Health.

Ministry of Health. (2012). *Tupu ola moui Pacific health chart book*. Wellington, New Zealand: Ministry of Health.

Ministry of Health. (2014). *'Ala mo'ui: Pathways to Pacific health and wellbeing 2014-2018*. Wellington, New Zealand: Ministry of Health.

Ministry of Health. (2015). *Supporting parents healthy children, supporting parents with mental illness and addiction and their children, A guideline for mental health and addiction services*. Wellington, New Zealand: Ministry of Health.

Ministry of Health. (2016a). *New Zealand health strategy: Future direction*. Wellington, New Zealand: Ministry of Health.

Ministry of Health. (2016b). *Commissioning framework for mental health and addictions: A New Zealand guide*. Wellington, New Zealand: Ministry of Health.

Ministry of Justice & Ministry of Pacific Island Affairs. (2000). *Pacific Peoples Constitution Report*. Wellington, New Zealand: Ministry of Justice and Ministry of Pacific Island Affairs.

Ministry of Social Development. (2012). *Nga vaka o kāiga tapu - The Pacific conceptual framework*. Wellington, New Zealand: Ministry of Social Development.

Mo'a, V. (2015, November). *Culture as foundation for care with particular reference to the multicultural context of life and health care for Pacific people in New Zealand*. Aniva Pacific workforce fono. Wellington, New Zealand.

Mojtabai, R., & Crum, R. (2013). Perceived unmet need for alcohol and drug use treatments and future use of services: Results from a longitudinal study. *Drug and Alcohol Dependence*, *127*(1), 59–64. doi:10.1016/j.drugalcdep.2012.06.012 PMID:22770461

Morgan, A. J., Jorm, A. F., & Mackinnon, A. J. (2012). Email-based promotion of self-help for subthreshold depression: Mood memos randomised controlled trial. *The British Journal of Psychiatry*, *200*(5), 412–418. doi:10.1192/bjp.bp.111.101394 PMID:22442102

Morris, J., McFaul, M., Madenwald, K., & Hoge, M. A. (2008). *Iowa mental health and disability services workforce review*. Cincinnati, OH: The Annapolis Coalition on the Behavioral Health Workforce.

Morrison, L., Moss-Morris, R., Michie, S., & Yardley, L. (2014). Optimizing engagement with Internet-based health behaviour change interventions: Comparison of self-assessment with and without tailored feedback using a mixed methods approach. *British Journal of Health Psychology*, *19*(4), 839–855. doi:10.1111/bjhp.12083 PMID:24308806

Morris, Z. M., Wooding, S., & Grant, J. (2011). The answer is 17 years, what is the question: Understanding time lags in translational research. *Journal of the Royal Society of Medicine*, *104*(12), 510–520. doi:10.1258/jrsm.2011.110180 PMID:22179294

Moxham, L., McCann, T., Usher, K., Farrell, G., & Crooks, P. (2011). Mental health nursing in pre-registration nursing curricula. A national report. *International Journal of Mental Health Nursing, 20*(4), 232-236. doi:10.111. /j1447-0349-0349.2010. 00735.x

Murphy, D. M., & Hubbard, R. L. (2009). *Understanding America's substance use disorders treatment workforce*. Kansas City, MO: ATTC Network Coordinating Office.

Murphy, L., & Mitchell, D. (1998). When writing helps to heal: E-mail as therapy. *British Journal of Guidance & Counselling*, *26*(1), 21–32. doi:10.1080/03069889808253835

Murthy, R. S., Kumar, K. K., Chisholm, D., Thomas, T., Sekar, K., & Chandrashekar, C. (2005). Community outreach for untreated schizophrenia in rural India: A follow-up study of symptoms, disability, family burden and costs. *Psychological Medicine*, *35*(03), 341–351. doi:10.1017/S0033291704003551 PMID:15841870

Nancarrow, S. A., & Borthwick, A. M. (2005). Dynamic professional boundaries in the healthcare workforce. *Sociology of Health and Illness, 27*(7), 897-919. doi: 10:.1111/j.1467-9566.2005.00463.x

National Action Alliance for Suicide Prevention Crisis Services Task Force. (2016). Crisis now: Transforming services is within our reach. Washington, DC: Education Development Centre.

National AHEC Organization. (2016). *AHEC mission*. Retrieved from http://www.nationalahec.org/About/AHECMission.html

National Empowerment Center. (2010). Retrieved from http://www.power2u.org/judi-chamberlin.html

National Health Workforce Planning & Research Collaboration. (2011). *Mental health non-government organisation workforce project final report.* Retrieved from http://pandora.nla.gov.au/pan/133228/20150419-0017/www.hwa.gov.au/sites/uploads/Mental Health NGO Workforce Project Final Report.pdf

National Institute on Drug Abuse. (1999, October 25). *Magnitude.* Retrieved from http://archives.drugabuse.gov/about/welcome/aboutdrugabuse/magnitude/

National Institute on Drug Abuse. (2004, February). *Beyond the brain: The medical consequences of abuse and addiction* (NIDA Notes 18, No. 6). Retrieved from http://archives.drugabuse.gov/NIDA_Notes/NNVol18N6/DirRepVol18N6.html

National Mental Health Commission. (2014). *The national review of mental health programmes and services*. Sydney, Australia: National Mental Health Commission.

National Mental Health Information Development Expert Advisory Panel. (2013). *NOCC strategic directions 2014-2024.* Canberra, Australia: Commonweath of Australia. Retrieved from http://www.amhocn.org/special-projects/nocc-strategic-directions-2014-2024

National Panel for Psychiatric Mental Health NP Competencies. (2003). *Psychiatric-mental health nurse practitioner competencies*. Washington, DC: National Organization of Nurse Practitioner Faculties.

National Scientific Council on the Developing Child. (2004). *Children's emotional development is built in to the architecture of their brains: Working paper No 9.* Retrieved from http://www.developingchild.net

National Scientific Council on the Developing Child. (2007). *A science-based framework for early childhood policy: Using evidence to improve outcomes in learning, behavior, and health for vulnerable children.* Retrieved from http://www.developingchild.harvard.edu

National Scientific Council on the Developing Child. (2008/2012). *Establishing a level foundation for life: Mental health begins in early childhood: Working paper No 6* (Updated ed.). Retrieved from http://www.developingchild.harvard.edu

National Scientific Council on the Developing Child. (2010). *Persistent fear and anxiety can affect young children's learning and development. Working paper No 9.* Retrieved from http://www.develpingchild.net

National Service Framework Library. (2015). *Mental health ring fence trends 2015/16.* Retrieved from http://nsfl.health.govt.nz/dhb-planning-package/201516-planning-package/supplementary-information-201516-planning-guidelines--3

Nestor, P., & Galletly, C. (2008). The employment of consumers in mental health services: Politically correct tokenism or genuinely useful? *Royal Australian and New Zealand College of Psychiatrists, 16*(5), 344–347. doi:10.1080/10398560802196016 PMID:18615343

New Zealand College of Mental Health Nurses. (2012). Standards of practice for mental health nursing in Aotearoa New Zealand (Standards No. 3rd ed.). Wellington, New Zealand: Te Maramatanga New Zealand College of Mental Health Nurses.

Ng, C., Herrman, H., Chiu, E., & Singh, B. (2009). Community mental health care in the Asia-Pacific region: Using current best-practice models to inform future policy. *World Psychiatry; Official Journal of the World Psychiatric Association (WPA), 8*(1), 49–55. doi:10.1002/j.2051-5545.2009.tb00211.x PMID:19293961

Nicholas, R., Adams, V., Roche, A., White, M., & Battams, S. (2013). *The development of Australia's alcohol and other drug workforce development strategy: A discussion paper.* Adelaide, Australia: National Centre for Education and Training on Addiction, Flinders University.

Nieuwboer, C. C., Fukkink, R. G., & Hermanns, J. M. (2014). Single session email consultation for parents: an evaluation of its effect on empowerment. *British Journal of Guidance & Counselling,* 1-13.

Norman, J., Walsh, N., Mugavin, J., Stoove, M., Kelsall, J., Austin, K., & Lintzeris, N. (2008). The acceptability and feasibility of peer worker support role in community based HCV treatment for injecting drug users. *Harm Reduction Journal, 5*(8), 1–9. doi:10.1186/1477-7517-5-8 PMID:18298862

NSW Department of Health. (2009). *Clinical guidelines for the care of persons with comorbid mental illness and substance use disorders in acute care settings.* NSW, Australia: Better Health Centre. Retrieved from http://www.health.nsw.gov.au/mhdao/programs/mh/Publications/comorbidity-report.pdf

NSW Ministry of Health. (2011). *NSW child and adolscent mental health services (CAMHS) competency framework.* NSW, Australia: Better Health Centre.

O*Net Online. (2015a). *Summary report for: 21-1023.00 mental health and substance abuse social workers.* Retrieved from http://www.onetonline.org/link/summary/21-1023.00

O*Net Online. (2015b). *Summary report for: 19-3031.02 clinical psychologists.* Retrieved from http://www.onetonline.org/link/summary/19-3031.02

O*Net Online. (2015c). *Summary report for: 21-1013.00 marriage and family therapists.* Retrieved from http://www.onetonline.org/link/summary/21-1013.00

O*Net Online. (2015d). *Summary report for: 29-1066.00 psychiatrists.* Retrieved from http://www.onetonline.org/link/summary/29-1066.00

O*Net Online. (2015e). *Summary report for: 29-1141.02 advanced practice psychiatric nurses*. Retrieved from http://www.onetonline.org/link/summary/29-1141.02

O'Sullivan, L. (2015). *The good doctor: Breaking the rules, making a difference*. Auckland, New Zealand: Penguin.

Oakley Browne, M. A., Wells, J. E., & Scott, K. M. (Eds.). (2006). *Te Rau Hinengaro: The New Zealand mental health survey*. Wellington, New Zealand: Ministry of Health.

Oakley-Browne, M. A., Wells, J. E., & Scott, K. M. (2006). *Te Rau Hinengaro: The New Zealand Mental Health Survey*. Wellington, New Zealand: Ministry of Health.

Oanh, L., Castro-Schilo, L., & Aguilar-Gaxiloa, S. (2014). Determinants of mental health and self-rated health: A model of socioeconomic status neighborhood safety and physical activity. *Research and Practice*, *44*(9), 1734–1740. doi:10.2105/AJPH.2014.302003 PMID:25033151

OConnell, M. J., Morris, J. A., & Hoge, M. A. (2004). Innovations in behavioral health workforce education. *Administration and Policy in Mental Health*, *32*(2), 131–165. doi:10.1023/B:APIH.0000042744.48923.8c PMID:15586848

OECD. (2015). *Health at a glance 2015: OECD indicators*. Retrieved from http://www.who.int/hrh/news/2015/oecd_analysis/en/

Office of National Drug Control Policy. (2013). *National drug control strategy*. Retrieved from https://www.whitehouse.gov//sites/default/files/ondcp/policy-and-research/ndcs_2013.pdf

Okpaku, S. O. (2014). *Essentials of global mental health*. Cambridge: University Press. doi:10.1017/CBO9781139136341

Olfson, M. (2016). Building the mental health workforce capacity needed to treat adults with serious mental illnesses. *Health Affairs*, *35*(6), 983–990. doi:10.1377/hlthaff.2015.1619 PMID:27269013

Ono, T., Lafortune, G., & Schoenstein, M. (2013). *Health workforce planning in OECD countries. A Review of 26 Projection Models from 18 Countries, OECD Health Working Papers*, No. 62, OECD Publishing. Retrieved from http://www.oecd-ilibrary.org/docserver/download/5k44t787zcwb.pdf?expires=1472475496&id=id&accname=guest&checksum=83A91B5474CF0B62984A4A8B8F5A2E2E

Ophir, E., Nass, C., & Wagner, A. D. (2009). Cognitive control in media multitaskers. *Proceedings of the National Academy of Sciences of the United States of America*, *106*(37), 15583–15587. doi:10.1073/pnas.0903620106 PMID:19706386

Optum. (2016). *Peer support services improve clinical outcomes by fostering recovery and promoting empowerment*. Retrieved from https://www.optum.com

OptumHealth. (2016). *Peer bridger programs*. Retrieved from https://www.leaders4health.org/images/uploads/files/OptumHealth_Peer_Bridgers.pdf

Orfaly, R. A., Frances, J. C., Campbell, P., Whittemore, B., Joly, B., & Koh, H. (2005). Train-the-trainer as an educational model in public health preparedness. *Journal of Public Health Management and Practice*, *11*(6Supplement), 123–127. doi:10.1097/00124784-200511001-00021 PMID:16205531

Ostrow, L., & Croft, B. (2016). *Results from the 2016 peer respite essential features survey*. Retrieved from http://www.power2u.org/downloads/PREF-Report-05.05.16.pdf

Ostrow, L. (2013). *Peer respite programs for mental health crisis: Research and practice initiatives in the United States*. Baltimore, MD: Lived Experience Research Network, Johns Hopkins.

Owen, J., Wampold, B. E., Kopta, M., Rousmaniere, T., & Miller, S. D. (2016). As good as it gets? Therapy outcomes of trainees over time. *Journal of Counseling Psychology*, *63*(1), 12–19. doi:10.1037/cou0000112 PMID:26751153

Owens, P., Myers, M., Elixhauser, A., & Brach, C. (2007). *Care of adults with mental health and substance abuse disorders in U.S. community hospitals, 2004.* Retrieved from Agency for Healthcare Research and Quality website: http://archive.ahrq.gov/data/hcup/factbk10/factbk10.pdf

Pacific Perspectives. (2013). *Pacific health workforce service forecast: Report to Health Workforce New Zealand and the Ministry of Health.* Wellington, New Zealand: Pacific Perspectives.

Padwa, H., Guerrero, E. G., Braslow, J. T., & Fenwick, K. M. (2015). Barriers to serving clients with co-occurring disorders in a transformed mental health system. *Psychiatric Services (Washington, D.C.)*, *66*(5), 547–550. doi:10.1176/appi.ps.201400190 PMID:25686812

Papa Ola Lokahi. (2015a). *Hawaiian health master plan, 2013.* Retrieved from http://www.papaolalokahi.org/wp-content/uploads/2015/01/NH-Health-Overview-FINAL-Master-Planning.pdf

Papa Ola Lokahi. (2015b). *Nā leo I mauli ola – Native Hawaiian health discussion webinars.* Retrieved from http://www.papaolalokahi.org/na-leo-i-mauli-ola-native-hawaiian-health-discussion-webinars/

Paris, M., & Hoge, M. (2012). *Improving workforce diversity & cultural and linguistic competency: Implications for integrated healthcare.* Unpublished report prepared for SAMHSA-HRSA Center for Integrated Health Solutions.

Paris, M., & Hoge, M. (2010). Burnout in the mental health workforce: A review. *The Journal of Behavioral Health Services & Research*, *37*(4), 519–528. doi:10.1007/s11414-009-9202-2 PMID:20013066

Paris, M., Silva, M. A., Diaz, E., Bedregal, L. E., Cole, R. A., & Añez-Nava, L. (2016). The Connecticut Latino behavioral health system: A culturally informed community-academic collaboration. *Psychological Services*, *13*(2), 140–147. doi:10.1037/ser0000065

Parks, J., Svendsen, D., Singer, P., & Foti, M. E. (2006). Morbidity and mortality in people with serious mental illness. Alexandria, VA: National Association of State Mental Health Program Directors (NASMHPD) Medical Directors Council.

Patel, V., & Saxena, S. (2014). Transforming lives, enhancing communities — Innovations in global mental health. *The New England Journal of Medicine*, *370*(6), 498–501. doi:10.1056/NEJMp1315214 PMID:24428425

Pathman, D., Konrad, T., Freed, G., Freeman, V., & Koch, G. (1996). The awareness-to-adherence model of the steps to clinical guideline compliance: The case of pediatric vaccine recommendations. *Medical Care*, *34*(9), 873–889. doi:10.1097/00005650-199609000-00002 PMID:8792778

Patterson, C., Curtis, J., & & Reid, A. (2008). Skills, knowledge, and attitudes expected of a newly graduated mental health nurse in an inpatient setting. *International Journal of Mental Health Nursing, 17*, 410-418. doi:101111/j.1447-0349,29-008.00572.x

Peer2peer. (2016). *Peer2peer vocational training course.* Retrieved from http://p2p.intras.es/index.php/trainingmaterials

Pender, N., Murdaugh, C., & Parsons, M. (2006). *Health promotion in nursing practice.* Prentice Hall.

Pennebaker, J. W. (1997). Writing about emotional experiences as a therapeutic process. *Psychological Science*, *8*(3), 162–166. doi:10.1111/j.1467-9280.1997.tb00403.x

Perry, B., & Hambrick, E. (2008). The neurosequential model of therapeutics. *Reclaiming Children & Youth, 17*(3), 38-43. Retrieved from http://www.reclaiming.com

Peters, D. (2014). The application of systems thinking in health: Why use systems thinking? *Health Research Policy and Systems*, *12*(1), 51. doi:10.1186/1478-4505-12-51 PMID:25160707

Petty, R., & Cacioppo, J. (1986). *The elaboration likelihood model of persuasion.* New York: Springer.

Phalen, J., & Paradis, R. (2015, January 16). How community health workers can reinvent health care delivery in the US. *Health Affairs Blog*. Retrieved from http://healthaffairs.org/blog/2015/01/16/how-community-health-workers-can-reinvent-health-care-delivery-in-the-us/

Pillay, I., Best, D., & Lubman, D. I. (2014). Exploring clinician attitudes to addiction recovery in Victoria, Australia. *Alcoholism Treatment Quarterly*, *32*(4), 375–392. doi:10.1080/07347324.2014.949126

Pirkis, J., Burgess, P., Coombs, T., Clarke, A., Jones-Ellis, D., & Dickson, R. (2005). Routine measurement of outcomes in Australias public sector mental health services. *Australia and New Zealand Health Policy*, *2*(1), 8. doi:10.1186/1743-8462-2-8 PMID:15840170

Pirkis, J., Harris, M., Hall, W., & Ftanou, M. (2011). *Evaluation of the better access to psychiatrists, psychologists and general practitioners through the medicare benefits schedule initiative: Summative evaluation*. Melbourne, Australia: Centre for Health Policy, Programs and Economics, University of Melbourne.

Platform. (2007). *NgOIT: Workforce survey*. Retrieved from: http://www.platform.org.nz

Platform. (2008). *Performance story report 2007*. Wellington, New Zealand: Author.

Platform. (n.d.). *Fair funding fact sheet*. Retrieved from www.platform.org.nz

Pollock, S. L. (2006). Internet counseling and its feasibility for marriage and family counseling. *The Family Journal (Alexandria, Va.)*, *14*(1), 65–70. doi:10.1177/1066480705282057

Prensky, M. (2001). Digital natives, digital immigrants part 1. *On the Horizon*, *9*(5), 1–6. doi:10.1108/10748120110424816

Priester, M. A., Browne, T., Iachini, A., Clone, S., DeHart, D., & Seay, K. D. (2016). Treatment access barriers and disparities among individuals with co-occurring mental health and substance use disorders: An integrative literature review. *Journal of Substance Abuse Treatment*, *61*, 47–59. doi:10.1016/j.jsat.2015.09.006 PMID:26531892

Prince, M., Patel, V., Saxena, S., Maj, M., Maselko, J., Phillips, M. R., & Rahman, A. (2007). No health without mental health. *Lancet*, *370*(9590), 859–877. doi:10.1016/S0140-6736(07)61238-0 PMID:17804063

Prochaska, J., & DiClemente, C. (1986). *Toward a comprehensive model of change*. New York: Springer. doi:10.1007/978-1-4613-2191-0_1

Prowse, L., & Coombs, T. (2009). The use of the Health of the Nation Outcome Scales(HoNOS) to inform discharge and transfer decisions in community mental health services. *Australian Health Review*, *33*(1), 13–18. doi:10.1071/AH090013 PMID:19203329

Public Service Commission. (2013). *Workforce planning explained*. Retrieved from http://www.apsc.gov.au/publications-and-media/current-publications/workforce-planning-guide/workforce-planning-explained

Pulotu-Endemann, K. (1995). *The fonofale Pacific model*. Retrieved from http://www.hauora.co.nz/resources/Fonofale-modelexplanation.pdf

Pulotu-Endemann, F. K., Annandale, M., & Instone, A. (2004). *A Pacific perspective on the NZ mental health classification and outcomes study (CAOS)*. Wellington, New Zealand: Mental Health Commission.

Rahman, M. M., Rahaman, M. M., Hamadani, J. D., Mustafa, K., & Islam, S. M. S. (2016). Psycho-social factors associated with relapse to drug addiction in Bangladesh. *Journal of Substance Use*, *21*(6), 1–4. doi:10.3109/14659891.2015.1122099

Ramon, S. (2008). Neoliberalism and its implications for mental health in the UK. *International Journal of Law and Psychiatry*, *31*(2), 116–125. doi:10.1016/j.ijlp.2008.02.006 PMID:18342370

Rangiaho, A. (2003). *Te Puawaitanga o Te Oranga Hinengaro - An evaluation of the National Certificate in Mental Health Support Work from a Maori perspective*. Wellington, New Zealand: Mental Health Support Work Advisory Group.

Rapp, C. A., & Goscha, R. J. (2011). *The strengths model: A recovery-oriented approach to mental health service* (3rd ed.). Oxford University Press.

Rapp, C., & Chamberlain, R. (1985). Case management services for the chronically mentally ill. *Social Work, 30*(5), 417–422. PMID:10273981

Rawal, L. B., Joarder, T., Islam, S. M. S., Uddin, A., & Ahmed, S. M. (2015). Developing effective policy strategies to retain health workers in rural Bangladesh: A policy analysis. *Human Resources for Health, 13*(1), 1–10. doi:10.1186/s12960-015-0030-6 PMID:25990240

Rawal, L., Mahmud, K., Islam, S., Mahumud, R., Nuruzaman, M., & Ahmed, S. (2016). Training mid-level health cadres to improve health service delivery in rural Bangladesh. *Primary Health Care Research and Development, 17*(5), 503–513. doi:10.1017/S1463423616000104 PMID:27029790

Repper, J., & Carter, T. (2011). A review of the literature on peer support in mental health services. *Journal of Mental Health (Abingdon, England), 20*(4), 392–411. doi:10.3109/09638237.2011.583947 PMID:21770786

Reynolds, G. (1975). *A primer of operant conditioning*. Oxford, UK: Scott Foresman & Co.

Reynolds, J., Griffiths, K. M., Cunningham, J. A., Bennett, K., & Bennett, A. (2015). Clinical practice models for the use of e-mental health resources in primary health care by health professionals and peer workers: A conceptual framework. *JMIR Mental Health, 2*(1), e6. doi:10.2196/mental.4200 PMID:26543912

Rhydderch, M., Elwyn, G., Marshall, M., & Grol, R. (2004). Organizational change theory and the use of indicators in general practice. *Quality & Safety in Health Care, 13*(3), 213–217. doi:10.1136/qshc.2003.006536 PMID:15175493

Riemsma, R., Pattenden, J., Bridle, C., Sowden, A., Mather, L., Watt, I., & Walker, A. (2002). A systematic review of the effectiveness of interventions based on a stages-of-change approach to promote individual behaviour change in health care settings. *Health Technology Assessment, 6*(24), 1–242. doi:10.3310/hta6240 PMID:12433313

Rimer, B., & Glanz, K. (2005). *Theory at a glance: A guide for health promotion practice*. Bethesda, MD: National Institutes of Health.

Ritter, A., Berends, L., Chalmers, J., Hull, P., Lancaster, K., & Gomez, M. (2014). *New Horizons: The review of alcohol and other drug treatment services in Australia*. Sydney, Australia: Drug Policy Modelling Program, National Drug and Alcohol Research Centre, University of NSW.

Roberts, D. (2013). *Psychosocial nursing care: A guide to nursing the whole person*. Berkshire, UK: Open Press.

Roberts, L., Smith, J., McFaul, M., Paris, M., Speer, N., Boeckmann, M., & Hoge, M. A. (2011). Behavioral health workforce development in rural and frontier Alaska. *Journal of Rural Mental Health, 35*(1), 10–16. doi:10.1037/h0094780

Roche, A. M. (2001). *What is this thing called workforce development?* Retrieved from nceta.flinders.edu.au/files/7712/5548/1891/EN91.pdf

Roche, A. M. (2002). Workforce development: Our national dilemma. In *Catching clouds: Exploring diversity in workforce development in the alcohol and other drugs field* (pp. 7-16). Adelaide, Australia: Academic Press.

Roche, A. M., & Skinner, N. (2005). An introduction to workforce development. In N. Skinner, A.M. Roche, J. O'Connor, Y. Pollard, & C. Todd (Eds.), Workforce development TIPS (theory into practice strategies): A resource kit for the alcohol and other drugs field. Adelaide, Australia: National Centre for Education and Training on Addiction (NCETA), Flinders University.

Roche, A. M. (2002). *Workforce development: Our national dilemma. In Catching clouds: Exploring diversity in workforce development in the alcohol and other drugs field.* Adelaide, Australia: National Centre for Education and Training on Addiction, Flinders University.

Roche, A. M. (2013). Looking to the future: The challenges ahead. *Substance, 11*(1), 17.

Roche, A. M., Adams, V., & White, M. (2014). Up in smoke: Cannabis content in alcohol and other drug qualifications. *Drugs Education Prevention & Policy, 21*(2), 140–146. doi:10.3109/09687637.2013.819567

Roche, A. M., Duraisingam, V., Trifonoff, A., Battams, S., Freeman, T., Tovell, A., & Bates, N. et al. (2013). Sharing stories: Indigenous alcohol and other drug workers' well-being, stress and burnout. *Drug and Alcohol Review, 32*(5), 527–535. PMID:23675893

Roche, A. M., & Pidd, K. (2010). *Alcohol and other drugs workforce development issues and imperatives: Setting the scene.* Adelaide, Australia: National Centre for Education and Training on Addiction, Flinders University.

Roche, A. M., Pidd, K., & Freeman, T. (2009). Achieving professional practice change: From training to workforce development. *Drug and Alcohol Review, 28*(5), 550–557. doi:10.1111/j.1465-3362.2009.00111.x PMID:19737213

Roche, A., Todd, C., & OConnor, J. (2007). Clinical supervision in the alcohol and other drugs field: An imperative or an option? *Drug and Alcohol Review, 26*(3), 241–249. doi:10.1080/09595230701247780 PMID:17454013

Rodda, S. N., Lubman, D. I., Cheetham, A., Dowling, N. A., & Jackson, A. C. (2015). Single session web-based counselling: A thematic analysis of content from the perspective of the client. *British Journal of Guidance & Counselling, 43*(1), 117–130. doi:10.1080/03069885.2014.938609

Rodda, S. N., Lubman, D. I., Dowling, N. A., Bough, A., & Jackson, A. C. (2013). Web-Based Counseling for Problem Gambling: Exploring Motivations and Recommendations. *Journal of Medical Internet Research, 15*(5), e99. doi:10.2196/jmir.2474 PMID:23709155

Rodda, S. N., Lubman, D. I., Iyer, R., Gao, C., & Dowling, N. (2015). Subtyping based on readiness and confidence: The identification of help-seeking profiles for gamblers accessing web-based counselling. *Addiction (Abingdon, England), 110*(3), 494–501. doi:10.1111/add.12796 PMID:25393315

Rogers, E. (1995). Diffusion of innovations: Modifications of a model for telecommunications. *Die Diffusion von Innovationen in der Telekommunikation, 17*, 25–38. doi:10.1007/978-3-642-79868-9_2

Rogers, E. M. (1995). *Diffusion of innovations* (4th ed.). New York, NY: The Free Press.

Rossi, A., Cetrano, G., Pertile, R., Rabbi, L., Donisi, V., Grigoletti, L., & Amaddeo, F. et al. (2012). Burnout, compassion fatigue, and compassion satisfaction among staff in community-based mental health services. *Psychiatry Research, 200*(2), 933–938. doi:10.1016/j.psychres.2012.07.029 PMID:22951335

Ross, J. D., Clarke, A., & Kettles, A. (2014). Mental health nurse prescribing: Using a constructivist approach to investigate the nurse–patient relationship. *Journal of Psychiatric and Mental Health Nursing, 21*(1), 1–10. doi:10.1111/jpm.12039 PMID:23413877

Rössler, W. (2012). Stress, burnout, and job dissatisfaction in mental health workers. *European Archives of Psychiatry and Clinical Neuroscience, 262*(2), 65–69. doi:10.1007/s00406-012-0353-4 PMID:22926058

Royal Australian and New Zealand College of Psychiatrists. (2016a). *RANZCP 2012 (competency-based) fellowship program.* Retrieved from https://www.ranzcp.org/Pre-Fellowship/2012-Fellowship-Program.aspx

Royal Australian and New Zealand College of Psychiatrists. (2016b). *Faculty of Addiction Psychiatry.* Retrieved from https://www.ranzcp.org/Membership/Faculties-sections/Addiction-Psychiatry.aspx

Roy, H., & Gillett, T. (2008). E-mail: A new technique for forming a therapeutic alliance with high-risk young people failing to engage with mental health services? A case study. *Clinical Child Psychology and Psychiatry, 13*(1), 95–103. doi:10.1177/1359104507086344 PMID:18411868

Ruggeri, K., Farrington, C., & Brayne, C. (2013). A global model for effective use and evaluation of e-learning in health. *Telemedicine Journal and e-Health, 19*(4), 312–321. doi:10.1089/tmj.2012.0175 PMID:23472702

Rush, K. L., Adamack, M., Gordon, J., Lilly, M., & Janke, R. (2013). Best practices of formal new graduate nurse transition programs: An integrative review. *International Journal of Nursing Studies, 50*(3), 345–356. doi:10.1016/j.ijnurstu.2012.06.009 PMID:22795800

Ryan, O., Murphy, D., & Krom, L. (2012). Vital signs: Taking the pulse of the addiction treatment workforce, a national report (version 1). Kansas City, MO: Addiction Technology Transfer Center National Office in residence at the University of Missouri-Kansas City.

Ryan, R., & Deci, E. (2000). Self-determination theory and the facilitation of intrinsic motivation, social development, and well-being. *The American Psychologist, 55*(1), 68–78. doi:10.1037/0003-066X.55.1.68 PMID:11392867

Ryder, D., & Ryder, D. (2008). Political and legal institutions and their influence on drug policy: An Australian perspective. *Drug and Alcohol Review, 27*(4), 374–379. doi:10.1080/09595230802090774 PMID:18584386

Rydon, S. E., Rolleston, A., & Mackie, J. (2008). Graduates and initial employment. *Nurse Education Today, 28*(5), 610–619. doi:10.1016/j.nedt.2007.10.002 PMID:18226841

Safety and Quality Partnerships Committee. (2013). *National practice standards for the mental health workforce 2013.* Melbourne, Australia: Victorian Government Department of Health.

Salas, E., Tannenbaum, S. I., Kraiger, K., & Smith-Jentsch, K. A. (2012). The science of training and development in organizations: What matters in practice. *Psychological Science in the Public Interest, 13*(2), 74–101. doi:10.1177/1529100612436661 PMID:26173283

Saldivia, S., Vicente, B., Kohn, R., Rioseco, P., & Torres, S. (2004). Use of mental health services in Chile. *Psychiatric Services (Washington, D.C.), 55*(1), 71–76. doi:10.1176/appi.ps.55.1.71 PMID:14699204

Sal-sabil, T., Islam, A., & Islam, S. M. S. (2016). Risk factors for type 2 diabetes in Bangladesh: A systematic review. *Journal of Diabetology, 2*(4), 1–12.

Salzer, M. (2002). Consumer-delivered services as a best practice in mental health care and delivery and the development of practice guidelines. University of Pennsylvania. Retrieved from http://www.cdsdirectory.org/SalzeretalBPPS2002.pdf

SAMHSA. (2009). *What is a peer support worker?* Retrieved from http://www.samhsa.gov/brss-tacs/core-competencies-peer-workers

SAMHSA. (2013). *Behavioral health, United States, 2012. HHS Publication No. (SMA) 13-4797.* Rockville, MD: SAMHSA.

SAMHSA. (2015a). *Behavioral health barometer: Hawaii, 2014. HHS Publication No. SMA–15–4895HI.* Rockville, MD: SAMHSA.

SAMHSA. (2015b). *SAMHSA – Fiscal year 2015 discretionary funds: Hawaii*. Retrieved from http://www.samhsa.gov/grants-awards-by-state/details/Hawaii

SAMHSA. (n.d.). *Practice guidelines: Core elements of responding to mental health crises*. Rockville, MD. *SAMHSA*.

Savin, D. (2000). Developing psychiatric training and services in Cambodia. *Psychiatric Services (Washington, D.C.)*, *51*(7), 935–935. doi:10.1176/appi.ps.51.7.935 PMID:10875964

Saxena, S., Sharan, P., & Saraceno, B. (2003). Budget and financing of mental health services: Baseline information on 89 countries from WHO's Project Atlas. *The Journal of Mental Health Policy and Economics*, *6*(3), 135–143. PMID:14646006

Saxena, S., Thornicroft, G., Knapp, M., & Whiteford, H. (2007). Resources for mental health: Scarcity, inequity, and inefficiency. *Lancet*, *370*(9590), 878–889. doi:10.1016/S0140-6736(07)61239-2 PMID:17804062

Schiffbauer, J., OBrien, J. B., Timmons, B. K., & Kiarie, W. N. (2008). The role of leadership in HRH development in challenging public health settings. *Human Resources for Health*, *6*(1), 1–7. doi:10.1186/1478-4491-6-23 PMID:18983671

Scott, A., Doughty, C., & Kahi, H. (2011). *Peer support practice in Aotearoa New Zealand*. Christchurch, New Zealand: University of Canterbury.

Scott, A., Doughty, C., & Kahi, H. (2011). *Peer support practice in Aotearoa, New Zealand*. Christchurch, New Zealand: University of Canterbury.

Scottish Executive. (2006). *Delivering for mental health*. Edinburgh, UK: Scottish Executive.

Scottish Qualifications Authority. (2010). *Arrangements for mental health peer support at SCQF level 7*. Glasgow, UK: Scottish Qualifications Authority.

Scottish Recovery Network. (2011). *Experts by experience implementation guidelines*. Glasgow, UK: Scottish Recovery Network.

Scottish Recovery Network. (2012). *Experts by experience: Values framework for peer working*. Glasgow, UK: Scottish Recovery Network.

Scottish Recovery Network. (2013). *Reviewing peer working: A new way of working in mental health*. Glasgow, UK: Scottish Recovery Network.

Senge, P. (1990). *The fifth discipline: The art and practice of the learning organization*. NSW, Australia: Random House Australia Pty Ltd.

Shane Solomon & Associates. (1996). *MH-CASC study manual*. Victoria, Australia: Mental Health Research Institute.

Shapiro, J. (2010). *Advocate for people with mental illnesses dies*. Retrieved from http://www.narpa.org/chamberlin.htm

Shea, P., & Shern, D. (2011). *Primary prevention in behavioral health: Investing in our nation's future*. Alexandria, VA: National Association of State Mental Health Program Directors.

Sherk, K. E., Nauseda, F., Johnson, S., & Liston, D. (2009). An experience of virtual leadership development for human resource managers. *Human Resources for Health*, *7*(1), 1–3. doi:10.1186/1478-4491-7-1 PMID:19133140

Shmulewitz, D., Heath, S. C., Blundell, M. L., Han, Z., Sharma, R., Salit, J., … Friedman, J.M. (2006). Linkage analysis of quantitative traits for obesity, diabetes, hypertension, and dyslipidemia on the island of Kosrae, Federated States of Micronesia. *Proceedings of the National Academy of Sciences of the United States of America*, *103*(10), 3502-3509. doi:10.1073/pnas.0510156103

Shonkoff, J., & Phillips, D. (Eds.). (2000). *From Neurons to neighborhood: The science of early childhood development.* Washington, DC: National Academy Press.

Silins, E., Conigrave, K., Rakvin, C., Dobbins, T., & Curry, K. (2007). The influence of structured education and clinical experience on the attitudes of medical students towards substance misusers. *Drug and Alcohol Review*, *26*(2), 191–200. doi:10.1080/09595230601184661 PMID:17364855

Simpson, D., & Flynn, P. (2007). Moving innovations into treatment: A stage-based approach to program change. *Journal of Substance Abuse Treatment*, *33*(2), 111–120. doi:10.1016/j.jsat.2006.12.023 PMID:17434704

Singh, B., & Ng, C. H. (2008). Psychiatric education and training in Asia. *International Review of Psychiatry (Abingdon, England)*, *20*(5), 413–418. doi:10.1080/09540260802397362 PMID:19012125

Skeen, S., Kleintjes, S., Lund, C., Petersen, I., Bhana, A., & Flisher, A. J.The Mental Health and Poverty Research Programme Consortium. (2010). Mental health is everybodys business: Roles for an intersectoral approach in South Africa. *International Review of Psychiatry (Abingdon, England)*, *22*(6), 611–623. doi:10.3109/09540261.2010.535510 PMID:21226649

Skinner, N. (2005). Workplace support. In N. Skinner, A.M. Roche, J. O'Connor, Y. Pollard, & C. Todd (Eds.), Workforce development TIPS (theory into practice strategies): A resource kit for the alcohol and other drugs field. Adelaide, Australia: National Centre for Education and Training on Addiction (NCETA), Flinders University.

Skinner, N., & Roche, A. M. (2005). Stress and burnout: A prevention handbook for the alcohol and other drugs workforce. Adelaide, Australia: National Centre for Education and Training on Addiction (NCETA), Flinders University.

Skinner, N., Roche, A. M., O'Connor, J., Pollard, Y., & Todd, C. (2005). *Workforce development 'TIPS': Theory into practice strategies.* Retrieved from http://nceta.flinders.edu.au/index.php?cID=111

Skinner, N., Feather, N., Freeman, T., & Roche, A. M. (2007). Stigma and discrimination in health-care provision to drug users: The role of values, affect, and deservingness judgments. *Journal of Applied Social Psychology*, *37*(1), 163–186. doi:10.1111/j.0021-9029.2007.00154.x

Skinner, N., Roche, A., Freeman, T., & Addy, D. (2005). Responding to alcohol and other drug issues: The effect of role adequacy and role legitimacy on motivation and satisfaction. *Drugs Education Prevention & Policy*, *12*(6), 449–463. doi:10.1080/09687630500284281

Smith, M., & Baxendine, S. (2015). Outcome measurement in New Zealand. *International Review of Psychiatry (Abingdon, England)*, *27*(4), 276–285. doi:10.3109/09540261.2015.1023783 PMID:25832565

Smith-Merry, J., Freeman, R., & Sturdy, S. (2011). Implementing recovery: An analysis of the key technologies in Scotland. *International Journal of Mental Health Systems*, *5*(11). PMID:21569633

Social Work Registration Act, 17 (2003).

South Estern Sydney Local Health District. (2016). *South Eastern Sydney Recovery College.* Retrieved from http://www.seslhd.health.nsw.gov.au/Recovery_College/

Southwick, M., Kenealy, T., & Ryan, D. (2012). *Primary care for Pacific people: A Pacific and health systems approach.* Wellington, New Zealand: Pacific Perspectives.

Southwick, S. M., & Charney, D. S. (2012). The science of resilience: Implications for the prevention and treatment of depression. *Science*, *338*(6103), 79–82. doi:10.1126/science.1222942 PMID:23042887

Spence, D., Garrick, H., & McKay, M. (2012). Re building the foundations major renovations to the mental health component of an undergraduate nursing curriculum. *Journal of Mental Health Nursing*, 409-18. doi.111/j.1447-0349.201100806

St. George, L. (2003). *History and outcomes of the peer support project in Maricopa County, Arizona*. Arizona, AZ: Arizona State University.

St. George, L. (2009). *Culture of recovery training*. Phoenix, AZ: RI International.

St. George, L. (2015). *History and results of peer employment training*. Phoenix, AZ: RI International.

St. George, L., Rider, A., & Long, M. (2000). *Peer support training* (1st ed.). Phoenix, AZ: META Services.

St. George, L., Rider, A., Zeeb, M., Smithers, T., & Long, M. (2015). *Peer employment training: A peer/recovery support specialist certification course* (5th ed.). Phoenix, AZ: RI International.

St. George, L., & Smithers, T. (2007). *Advanced peer practices*. Phoenix, AZ: RI International.

St. George, L., & Smithers, T. (2016). *Peer/recovery support specialist supervisor training: Developing and sustaining a peer workforce* (2nd ed.). Phoenix, AZ: RI International.

Standards Australia. (2015). *Workforce planning AS 5620:2015*. NSW, Australia: Standards Australia.

State of Hawaii. (2012). *Primary care needs assessment databook 2012*. Retrieved from http://health.hawaii.gov/about/files/2013/06/pcna2012databook.pdf

State of Hawaii. (2015). *Department of Health, Tuberculosis control program, data and statistics, 2014*. Retrieved from http://health.hawaii.gov/tb/data-statistics/#CaseRate_HI

Statistics New Zealand. (2013). *2013 census*. Retrieved from http://stats.govt.nz/Census/2013-census.aspx

Statistics New Zealand. (2014). *2013 quick stats about culture and identity: Pacific peoples ethnic group*. Auckland, New Zealand: Statistics New Zealand.

Stevens, T., & St. George, L. (2004). *Changing a culture: Moving from custodial care to recovery focused treatment*. San Diego, CA: International Association of Psychosocial Rehabilitation, META Services.

Stokes, T., & Baer, D. (1977). An implicit technology of generalization. *Journal of Applied Behavior Analysis*, *10*(2), 349–367. doi:10.1901/jaba.1977.10-349 PMID:16795561

Stuart, G. W., Tondora, J., & Hoge, M. A. (2004). Evidence-based teaching practice: Implications for behavioral health. *Administration and Policy in Mental Health*, *32*(2), 107–130. doi:10.1023/B:APIH.0000042743.11286.bc PMID:15586847

Stuhlmiller, C. (2005). Rethinking mental health nursing education in Australia: A case for direct entry. *International Journal of Mental Health Learning*, *14*(3), 156–160. doi:10.1111/j.1440-0979.2005.00374.x PMID:16181151

Substance Abuse and Mental Health Services Administration. (2009). *Integrated treatment for co-occurring disorders: Training frontline staff (DHHS Pub. No. SMA-08-4366)*. Rockville, MD: Author.

Substance Abuse and Mental Health Services Administration. (2011). *A provider's guide: How to use core competencies in behavioral health*. Rockville, MD: SAMHSA.

Substance Abuse and Mental Health Services Administration. (2011). *Dual diagnosis capability in mental health treatment toolkit version 4.0*. Rockville, MD: SAMHSA.

Substance Abuse and Mental Health Services Administration. (2011). Results from the 2010 national survey on drug use and health: Summary of national findings (NSDUH Series H-41, HHS Publication No. (SMA) 11-4658). Rockville, MD: Author.

Substance Abuse and Mental Health Services Administration. (2013). *Report to Congress on the nation's substance abuse and mental health workforce issues*. Rockville, MD: SAMHSA.

Substance Abuse and Mental Health Services Administration. (2014a). Improving cultural competence (Treatment Improvement Protocol (TIP) Series No. 59, HHS Publication No. (SMA) 14-4849). Rockville, MD: Author.

Substance Abuse and Mental Health Services Administration. (2014b). Leading change 2.0: Advancing the behavioral health of the nation 2015-2018 (HHS Publication No. [PEP] 14-LEADCHANGE2). Rockville, MD: Author.

Sucala, M., Schnur, J. B., Constantino, M. J., Miller, S. J., Brackman, E. H., & Montgomery, G. H. (2012). The Therapeutic Relationship in E-Therapy for Mental Health: A Systematic Review. *Journal of Medical Internet Research*, *14*(4), e110. doi:10.2196/jmir.2084 PMID:22858538

Suler, J. (2001). Assessing a persons suitability for online therapy: The ISMHO clinical case study group. *Cyberpsychology & Behavior*, *4*(6), 675–679. doi:10.1089/109493101753376614 PMID:11800174

Suler, J. (2004). The online disinhibition effect. *Cyberpsychology & Behavior*, *7*(3), 321–326. doi:10.1089/1094931041291295 PMID:15257832

Sunderland, A., & Findlay, L. (2013). *Perceived need for mental health care in Canada: Results from the 2012 Canadian community health survey-Mental health*. Ottawa, Canada: Statistics Canada.

Sutcliffe, R. (2006). What is the meaning of supervison for mental health support workers? A critical hermeneutic inquiry (Master Thesis). Auckland, New Zealand: Auckland University of Technology. Retrieved from http://aut.researchgateway.ac.nz/handle/10292/88

Swarbrick, P., Brice, G. H., Tucker, S. J., & Miccio, S. (2011). *Peer support wellness respite centres*. Retrieved from https://cms.centerforintegratedhealthsolutions.org/images/res/PDF,%20PSWRC.pdf

Sylvain, C., & Lamothe, L. (2013). Studying implementation of dual diagnosis services: *A review. Journal of Dual Diagnosis*, *9*(2), 195–207. doi:10.1080/15504263.2013.771809

Tafa, T., & Fotu, M. (2009). *The Popao model: Folau ki he mo'ui lelei - Journey to wellness, a Pacific recovery and strength concept in mental health*. Auckland, New Zealand: The Popao Group.

Tamasese, K., Peteru, C., Waldegrave, C., & Bush, A. (2005). Ole taeao afua, the new morning: A qualitative investigation into Samoan perspectives of mental health and culturally appropriate services. *The Australian and New Zealand Journal of Psychiatry*, *39*(4), 300–309. doi:10.1080/j.1440-1614.2005.01572.x PMID:15777368

Tamasese, T. A. T. (2002). *More on meaning, nuance and metaphor: Keynote speech. Pacific fono, Moving ahead together. Pataka Museum*. Porirua, Wellington: New Zealand: Capital Coast District Health Board.

Tanner, C. (2008). Thinking like a nurse: Research based model of clinical judgement in nursing. *The Journal of Nursing Education*, *45*(6), 204–2011. PMID:16780008

Tansella, M., & Thornicroft, G. (2009). Implementation science: Understanding the translation of evidence into practice. *The British Journal of Psychiatry*, *195*(4), 283–285. doi:10.1192/bjp.bp.109.065565 PMID:19794192

Te Ao Maramatanga NZ College of Mental Health Nurses. (2004). Standards of practice for mental health nursing in New Zealand (2nd ed.). Auckland, New Zealand: Te Ao Maramatanga (NZCMHN).

Te Poel, F., Bolman, C., Reubsaet, A., & de Vries, H. (2009). Efficacy of a single computer-tailored e-mail for smoking cessation: Results after 6 months. *Health Education Research*, *24*(6), 930–940. doi:10.1093/her/cyp036 PMID:19574405

Te Pou o te Whaakaro Nui & Matua Raki. (2015). *More than numbers workforce stocktake.* Auckland, New Zealand: Te Pou.

Te Pou o te Whaakaro Nui. (2009b). *Data to information report.* Auckland, New Zealand: Te Pou.

Te Pou o te Whaakaro Nui. (2012). *Technical review of the psychometric properties of the HoNOS family of measures.* Auckland, New Zealand: Te Pou.

Te Pou o te Whaakaro Nui. (2012a). *Mental health outcomes information collection protocol.* Auckland, New Zealand: Te Pou.

Te Pou o te Whakaaro Nui & Matua Raki. (2015). *More than numbers workforce stocktake.* Auckland, New Zealand: Te Pou.

Te Pou o te Whakaaro Nui. (2007). *Feasibility study into the establishment of a Pacific mental health workforce development organisation.* Auckland, New Zealand: Te Pou o te Whakaaro Nui.

Te Pou o te Whakaaro Nui. (2009). *Let's get real overview.* Auckland, New Zealand: Te Pou.

Te Pou o te Whakaaro Nui. (2010). *Talking therapies for Pasifika peoples: Best and promising practice guide for mental health and addiction services.* Auckland, New Zealand: Te Pou o te Whakaaro Nui.

Te Pou o te Whakaaro Nui. (2012b). *Skills Matter 2012 student survey: Evaluation report.* Auckland, New Zealand: Te Pou.

Te Pou o te Whakaaro Nui. (2012c). *Briefing paper on management of post entry clinical training funding for the mental health and addiction workforce.* Auckland, New Zealand: Te Pou.

Te Pou o te Whakaaro Nui. (2014). *Competencies for the mental health and addiction service user, consumer and peer workforce.* Auckland: Te Pou, Auckland Regional Alliance and Midland Mental Health and Addiction Regional Network.

Te Pou o te Whakaaro Nui. (2014). *Getting it right – workforce planning guide.* Auckland, New Zealand: Te Pou o te Whakaaro Nui.

Te Pou o te Whakaaro Nui. (2015). *Adult mental health and addiction nursing roles: 2014 survey of vote health funded services.* Auckland, New Zealand: Te Pou.

Te Pou o te Whakaaro Nui. (2015). *Overview of the adult mental health and addiction workforce: 2014 survey of vote health funded services.* Auckland, New Zealand: Te Pou o te Whakaaro Nui.

Te Pou o te Whakaaro Nui. (2016a). *National PRIMHD outcomes report (September 2016).* Retrieved from www.tepou.co.nz

Te Pou o te Whakaaro Nui. (2016b). *Skills Matter provider feedback 2016.* Auckland, New Zealand: Te Pou.

Te Pou. (2014). *Competencies for the mental health and addiction service user, consumer and peer workforce.* Auckland, New Zealand: Author.

Te Pou. (2015). *Adult mental health and addiction workforce - 2014 survey of Vote Health funded services.* Auckland, New Zealand: Author.

Thaman, H. (2004). Le'o e peau: Towards cultural and cognitive democracy in development in Pacific Islands communities. In *Changing islands – changing worlds:Proceedings from islands of the World VIII international conference* (pp. 36-47). Kinmen Island (Quemoy), Taiwan: Academic Press.

The Alcoholism Guide. (n.d.). *History of Alcoholics Anonymous*. Retrieved from http://www.the-alcoholism-guide.org/history-of-alcoholics-anonymous.html

The Mental Health Commission. (2007). *Te haererenga mo te whakaòranga 1996–2006: The journey of recovery for the New Zealand mental health sector*. Wellington, New Zealand: The Mental Health Commission.

The Werry Centre. (2008). *Real skills plus: A competency framework for the infant, child and youth mental health and alcohol and other drug workforce*. Auckland, New Zealand: Werry Centre.

The Werry Centre. (2009). *Real skills plus CAMHS*. Auckland, New Zealand: Author.

The Werry Centre. (2015). *2014 stocktake of infant, child and adolescent mental health and alcohol and other drug services in New Zealand*. Auckland, New Zealand: The Werry Centre, University of Auckland.

The White House, Office of the Press Secretary. (2015, October). *Fact sheet: Obama administration announces public and private sector efforts to address prescription drug abuse and heroin use*. Retrieved from https://www.whitehouse.gov/the-press-office/2015/10/21/fact-sheet-obama-administration-announces-public-and-private-sector

Thomas, K. C., Ellis, A. R., Konrad, T. R., Holzer, C. E., & Morrissey, J. P. (2009). County-level estimates of mental health professional shortage in the United States. *Psychiatric Services (Washington, D.C.)*, *60*(10), 1323–1328. doi:10.1176/ps.2009.60.10.1323 PMID:19797371

Thorne, S. (2006). Nursing education: Key issues for the 21st century. *Nurse Education Today*, *26*(8), 614–621. doi:10.1016/j.nedt.2006.07.010 PMID:17028072

Tiatia, J. (2008). *Pacific Cultural Competencies: A literature review*. Wellington, New Zealand: Ministry of Health.

Todd, F. C. (2010). *Te ariari o te oranga: The assessment and management of people with co-existing mental health and substance use problems*. Wellington, New Zealand: Ministry of Health.

Todd, F. C., Sellman, J. D., & Robertson, P. J. (1999). *The assessment and management of people with co-existing substance use and mental health disorders*. Wellington, New Zealand: Alcohol Advisory Council.

Todd, F. C., Sellman, J. D., & Robertson, P. J. (2002). Barriers to optimal care for patients with coexisting substance use and mental health disorders. *The Australian and New Zealand Journal of Psychiatry*, *36*(6), 792–799. doi:10.1046/j.1440-1614.2002.01049.x PMID:12406122

Tomic, M., & Tomic, E. (2011). Existential fulfilment, work and workload engagement in nurses. *Journal of Research in Nursing*, *16*(4), 468–479. doi:10.1177/1744987110383353

Torrey, W. C., Tepper, M., & Greenwold, J. (2011). Implementing integrated services for adults with co-occurring substance use disorders and psychiatric illnesses: A research review. *Journal of Dual Diagnosis*, *7*(3), 150–161. doi:10.1080/15504263.2011.592769

Tratnack, S., ONeill, C., & Graham, P. (2011). Immersion experience in undergraduate psychiatric mental health nursing. *The Journal of Nursing Education*, *50*(9), 532–535. doi:10.3928/01484834-20110531-02 PMID:21627052

Travaglia, J. F., Westbrook, M. T., & Braithwaite, J. (2009). Implementation of a patient safety incident management system as viewed by doctors, nurses and allied health professionals. *Health*, *13*(3), 277–296. doi:10.1177/1363459308101804 PMID:19366837

Treasure, J., & Russell, G. (2011). The case for early intervention in anorexia nervosa: Theoretical explanations of maintaining factors. *The British Journal of Psychiatry*, *199*(1), 5–7. doi:10.1192/bjp.bp.110.087585 PMID:21719874

Treasury. (2016). *The budget economic and fiscal update 2016*. Wellington, New Zealand: Treasury. Retrieved from http://www.treasury.govt.nz/budget/forecasts/befu2016

Trout, D. L., & Rosenfeld, H. M. (1980). The effect of postural lean and body congruence on the judgment of psychotherapeutic rapport. *Journal of Nonverbal Behavior*, *4*(3), 176–190. doi:10.1007/BF00986818

Tse, S., See, E. W., Wong, S., Kan, A., & Kwok, C. (2014). Training of mental health peer support workers in a non-western high-income city: Preliminary evaluation and experience. *The International Journal of Social Psychiatry*, *60*(3), 211–218. doi:10.1177/0020764013481427 PMID:23539546

Tu'itahi, S. (2007). *Fonua: A model for Pacific health promotion*. Retrieved from http:// www.hauora.co.nz/resources/FonuaaPasifikmodel.pdf

Tu, C.-H., & McIsaac, M. (2002). The relationship of social presence and interaction in online classes. *American Journal of Distance Education*, *16*(3), 131–150. doi:10.1207/S15389286AJDE1603_2

Tukuitonga, C. (2013). Pacific people in New Zealand. In I. St George (Ed.), *Cole's medical practice in New Zealand* (12th ed.; pp. 66–73). Wellington, New Zealand: Medical Council of New Zealand.

Tukuitonga, C., & Finau, S. (1997). The health of Pacific peoples in New Zealand up to the early 1990s. *Pacific Health Dialog*, *4*(2), 59–67.

U.S. Department of Health and Human Services. (2013). *National standards for culturally and linguistically appropriate services in health and health care: A blueprint for advancing and sustaining CLAS policy and practice*. Rockville, MD: Office of Minority Health.

Uchtenhagen, A., Stamm, R., Huber, J., & Vuille, R. (2008). A review of systems for continued education and training in the substance abuse field. *Substance Abuse*, *29*(3), 95–102. doi:10.1080/08897070802219263 PMID:19042211

University of Hawaii at Manoa. (2016). *Lokahi program*. Retrieved from http://www.hawaii.edu/shs/health_promotion/lokahi_program.php

Unutzer, J., Schoenbaum, M., Druss, B. G., & Katon, W. J. (2006). Transforming mental health care at the interface with general medicine: Report for the Presidents commission. *Psychiatric Services (Washington, D.C.)*, *57*(1), 37–47. doi:10.1176/appi.ps.57.1.37 PMID:16399961

Urbanoski, K., Cairney, J., Bassani, D., & Rush, B. (2008). Perceived unmet need for mental health care for Canadians with co-occurring mental and substance use disorders. *Psychiatric Services (Washington, D.C.)*, *59*(3), 283–289. doi:10.1176/ps.2008.59.3.283 PMID:18308909

Urbis, Keys, & Young. (2003). *National review of tele counselling and web counselling services: Final report*. Canberra, Australia: Australian Government Department of Health and Ageing.

US Census Bureau. (2015a). *American factfinder, ACD demographic and housing estimates, 2013*. Retrieved from http://factfinder.census.gov/faces/tableservices/jsf/pages/productview.xhtml?src=CF

US Census Bureau. (2015b). *American factfinder, Annual population estimates, 2014*. Retrieved from http://factfinder.census.gov/faces/nav/jsf/pages/index.xhtml

Ustun, B. D., & Von Korff, M. (1995). Primary mental health service access and provision of care. In T. B. Ustun & N. Sartorius (Eds.), *Mental Illness in general health care: An international study*. Chichester, UK: John Wiley.

Vaioleti, T. M. (2006). Talanoa research methodology: A developing position on Pacific research. *Waikato Journal of Education*, *12*, 21–34.

Van Gelder, L. (1995). *Howard Geld, 42, Advocate for mentally ill, dies*. Retrieved from http://www.nytimes.com/1995/02/14/obituaries/howard-geld-42-advocate-for-mentally-ill-dies.html

Verhaeghe, M., & Bracke, P. (2011). Stigma and trust among mental health service users. *Archives of Psychiatric Nursing, 25*(4), 294–304. doi:10.1016/j.apnu.2011.02.001 PMID:21784287

Vimpani, G. (2001). Health inequalities the seeds are sown in childhood, what about the remedies? In J. Dixon & B. Douglas (Eds.), *The social origins of health and well-being* (pp. 3–24). Melbourne, Australia: Cambridge University Press.

Vincent, L. (2008). Differentiating competence, capability and capacity. *Innovating Perspectives, 16*(3).

Volker, R., Bernhard, B., Anna, K., Fabrizio, S., Robin, R., Jessica, P., & Franz, H. et al. (2010). Burnout, coping and job satisfaction in service staff treating opioid addicts—from Athens to Zurich. *Stress and Health, 26*(2), 149–159. doi:10.1002/smi.1276

Walker, L. E. A., Pann, J. M., Shapiro, D. L., & Van Hasselt, V. B. (2016). *Best practices for the mentally ill in the criminal justice system*. Springer International Publishing. doi:10.1007/978-3-319-21656-0

Wallis, N. (2015). Born to connect: How love grows babies' brains. *Porse Growing Little Minds at Home*. Retrieved from www.porse.co.nz

Walsh, P., Stewart, V., Crozier, M., Roennfeldt, H., & Wheeler, A. J. (2015). *Paid peer support in mental health*. Brisbane, Australia: Griffith University.

Wang, P. S., Angermeyer, M., Borges, G., Bruffaerts, R., Chiu, W. T., De Girolamo, G., & Huang, Y. (2007). *Delay and failure in treatment seeking after first onset of mental disorders in the World Health Organization's World Mental Health Survey Initiative*. Geneva, Switzerland: World Health Organization.

Wardhani, V., Utarini, A., van Dijk, J. P., Post, D., & Groothoof, J. W. (2009). Determinants of quality management systems implementation in hospitals. *Health Policy (Amsterdam), 89*(3), 239–251. doi:10.1016/j.healthpol.2008.06.008 PMID:18752866

Werner, J. M., & DeSimone, R. L. (2012). *Human resource development* (6th ed.). Mason, OH: Cengage Learning.

Western Institute of Technology Taranaki. (2012). *Program document for Bachelor of nursing*. New Plymouth, New Zealand: Western Institute of Technology.

Whiteford, H. A., & Buckingham, W. J. (2005). Ten years of mental health service reform in Australia: Are we getting it right? *The Medical Journal of Australia, 182*(8), 396–400. PMID:15850436

Whiteford, H. A., Degenhardt, L., Rehm, J., Baxter, A. J., Ferrari, A. J., Erskine, H. E., & Vos, T. et al. (2013). Global burden of disease attributable to mental and substance disorders: Findings from the Global Burden of Disease *Study 2010. Lancet, 382*(9904), 1575–1586. doi:10.1016/S0140-6736(13)61611-6 PMID:23993280

Whiteford, H. A., Ferrari, A. J., Degenhardt, L., Feigin, V., & Vos, T. (2015). The global burden of mental, neurological and substance use disorders: An analysis from the global burden of disease study 2010. *PLoS ONE, 10*(2), e0116820. doi:10.1371/journal.pone.0116820 PMID:25658103

Whittaker, L. (2013). *New Zealand nurse migration to the United States: What makes them go? What will bring them back?* (Master's thesis). Retrieved from http://mro.massey.ac.nz/handle/10179/5471#sthash.PmH7F03a.dpuf

WHO. (2010). Pacific islanders pay heavy price for abandoning traditional diet. *Bulletin of the World Health Organization, 88*(7), 481–560. Retrieved from http://www.who.int/bulletin/volumes/88/7/10-010710/en/ PMID:20616964

WHO. (2015). *Marshall Islands: WHO statistical profile (January 2015)*. Retrieved from http://www.who.int/gho/countries/mhl.pdf

Williams, C. (2006). *Overcoming depression and low mood*. London, UK: Hodder Arnold.

Williams, T. M., & Smith, G. P. (2014). Can the National Disability Insurance Scheme work for mental health? *The Australian and New Zealand Journal of Psychiatry*, *48*(5), 391–394. doi:10.1177/0004867414530007 PMID:24671233

Willis, A., Deane, F., & Coombs, T. (2009). Improving clinicians attitudes toward providing feedback on routine outcome assessments. *International Journal of Mental Health Nursing*, *18*(3), 211–215. doi:10.1111/j.1447-0349.2009.00596.x PMID:19490232

Wilson, R. (2014). *Neuroscience for councilors*. London: Jessica Kingsley Publishers.

Wing, J. K., Beevor, A. S., Curtis, R. H., Park, S. B. G., Hadden, S., & Burns, A. (1998). Health of the nation outcomes scales (HoNOS) research and development. *The British Journal of Psychiatry*, *172*(1), 11–18. doi:10.1192/bjp.172.1.11 PMID:9534825

Wing, J., Curtis, R., & Beevor, A. (1999). Health of the Nation Outcome Scales (HoNOS). Glossary for HoNOS score sheet. *The British Journal of Psychiatry*, *174*(5), 432–434. doi:10.1192/bjp.174.5.432 PMID:10616611

Withy, K. (2015). *Hawaii Physician Workforce Assessment, Act 18, SLH, 2009. University of Hawaii system report to the Hawaii State Legislature*. Retrieved from http://ahec.hawaii.edu/workforce/html

Wolanski, E., Richmond, R. H., & McCook, L. (2004). A model of the effects of land-based, human activities on the health of coral reefs in the Great Barrier Reef and in Fouha Bay, Guam, Micronesia. *Journal of Marine Systems*, *46*(1), 133–144. doi:10.1016/j.jmarsys.2003.11.018

Wolff, J., Maula, E., & Padron, J. (2015, October). *Education pays! 2.0: Peer career development strategies*. Presentation at the Alternatives Conference, Memphis, TN.

Woltmann, E., Whitley, R., McHugo, G., Brunette, M., Torrey, W., Coots, L., & Drake, R. et al. (2008). The role of staff turnover in the implementation of evidence-based practices in mental health care. *Psychiatric Services (Washington, D.C.)*, *59*(7), 732–737. doi:10.1176/ps.2008.59.7.732 PMID:18586989

Wood, D., & Klassen, T. (2009). Bilateral federalism and workforce development policy in Canada. *Canadian Public Administration*, *52*(2), 249–270. doi:10.1111/j.1754-7121.2009.00074.x

World Health Organization & Calouste Gulbenkian Foundation. (2014). *Social determinants of mental health*. Geneva, Switzerland: World Health Organization.

World Health Organization & International Council of Nurses. (2007). *Atlas: Nurses in mental health 2007*. Geneva, Switzerland: World Health Organization.

World Health Organization. (1948). *Constitution of the World Health Organization*. Retrieved from http://www.who.int/about/mission/en/

World Health Organization. (1978). Declaration of Alma-Ata. *International Conference on Primary Health Care*. Retrieved from http://www.who.int/publications/almaata_declaration_en.pdf

World Health Organization. (2001). *The world health report mental health: New understanding, new hope*. Geneva, Switzerland: WHO.

World Health Organization. (2004). *International statistical classification of diseases and related health problems* (Vol. 1). Geneva, Switzerland: World Health Organization.

World Health Organization. (2005). *Human resources and training for mental health: Mental Health Policy and Guidance Package*. Geneva, Switzerland: WHO.

World Health Organization. (2006). *Quality of care: A process for making strategic choices in health systems.* Geneva, Switzerland: WHO. Retrieved from http://apps.who.int/iris/handle/10665/43470

World Health Organization. (2006). *The world health report: 2006: Working together for health.* Geneva, Switzerland: WHO.

World Health Organization. (2006). *The world health report: Working together for health.* Geneva, Switzerland: WHO. Retrieved from http://www.who.int/whr/2006/whr06

World Health Organization. (2007). *Atlas nurses in mental health.* Geneva, Switzerland: WHO.

World Health Organization. (2007a). *Towards better leadership and management in health: report on an international consultation on strengthening leadership and management in low-income countries.* Accra, Ghana: Department for Health Policy, Development and Services Health Systems and Services WHO.

World Health Organization. (2007b). *Workers' health: global plan of action. Sixtieth world health assembly.* Geneva, Switzerland: World Health Organization.

World Health Organization. (2010). *Models and tools for health workforce planning and projections.* Geneva, Switzerland: World Health Organization.

World Health Organization. (2010). *Workload indicators of staffing need: User's manual.* Geneva, Switzerland: WHO Press.

World Health Organization. (2011). mental health atlas 2011. Geneva, Switzerland: WHO.

World Health Organization. (2011). *Transformative scale up of health professional education: An effort to increase the numbers of health professionals and to strengthen their impact on population health.* Geneva, Switzerland: World Health Organization.

World Health Organization. (2014). *Global status report on alcohol and health.* Geneva, Switzerland: World Health Organization.

World Health Organization. (2014). *Mental disorders fact sheet N396.* Geneva, Switzerland: WHO.

World Health Organization. (2015). *mental health atlas 2014.* Geneva, Switzerland: WHO.

World Health Organization. (2015). *Mental health atlas 2014.* Geneva, Switzerland: WHO.

World Health Organization. Western Pacific Region. (2012). Human resources for health: Action Framework for the Western Pacific Region (2011–2015). Geneva, Switzerland: World Health Organization.

World Psychiatric Association & World Health Organization. (2005). *Atlas: Psychiatric education and training across the world: 2005.* Geneva, Switzerland: World Health Organization.

Wright, S., & Hornblow, A. (2008). Emerging needs, evolving services: The health of Pacific peoples in New Zealand. *Kotuitui*, *3*(1), 21–33. doi:10.1080/1177083X.2008.9522430

Ye, J., Rust, G., Fry-Johnson, Y., & Strothers, H. (2010). E-mail in patient–provider communication: A systematic review. *Patient Education and Counseling*, *80*(2), 266–273. doi:10.1016/j.pec.2009.09.038 PMID:19914022

Yip, W., Hsiao, W., Chen, W., Hu, S., Ma, J., & Maynard, A. (2012). Early appraisal of Chinas huge and complex health-care reforms. *Lancet*, *379*(9818), 833–842. doi:10.1016/S0140-6736(11)61880-1 PMID:22386036

Young, H. (2011). *The Cardiff Model, Effective NHS contributes to violence prevention*. Retrieved from www.alchol-learningcentre.org.uk

Zinman, S. (2013). *Interview*. Retrieved from http://www.peersnet.org/videos/2014/may/sally-zinman

About the Contributors

Mark Smith, co-editor of this book with Angela Jury, is employed as a clinical lead with Te Pou o te Whakaaro Nui, New Zealand's national mental health, disability and addiction workforce center for adults. In this role he is responsible for the national implementation of outcome measures into New Zealand's mental health services. By background a registered psychiatric nurse he was registered as New Zealand's first mental health Nurse Practitioner in 2002 and has worked extensively in many clinical roles and services along with working as a Lecturer at the University of Auckland on their clinical Masters programme. He has a keen interest in academic philosophy in which he has a PhD.

Angela Jury, PhD is the co-editor of this book. She is a researcher at Te Pou o te Whakaaro Nui – New Zealand's adult mental health, addiction and disability workforce centre. As a researcher she has been involved in a range of workforce development initiatives including the review and synthesis of evidence to inform workforce development activities, workforce planning, national workforce stocktakes, psychometric evaluation of outcome measures, and evaluation of training and other workforce development initiatives. She has an interest in knowledge translation and the transfer of training into practice.

* * *

Max Abbott is Dean of AUT's Faculty of Health and Environmental Sciences, Pro Vice-chancellor (North Campus) and Professor of Psychology and Public Health. Max is also Co-director of the National Institute for Public Health and Mental Health Research and directs the Institute's Gambling and Addictions Research Centre and Centre for Migrant and Refugee Research. He was previously National Director of the Mental Health Foundation and President of the World Federation for Mental Health (WFMH). He remains the WFMH Senior Advisor. Max has been a board member of Waitemata District Health Board since 2001 and was Deputy Chair for nine years. He is a director on a variety of other boards including the AUT Millennium Trust and Brain Research New Zealand. He has advisory roles with Health Workforce New Zealand and Te Pou. In January 2016 Max was made Companion of the New Zealand Order of Merit (CNZM) for services to health, science and education.

Julie Anderson is a lived experience leader in Australia. Julie has completed the National Mental Health Commission's Future Leaders program. She provides advice to Federal and State governments from a lived experience perspective, currently on the National NDIS Mental Health Sector Reference Group, 5th National Mental Health Plan Writers Group, and the Digital Gateway co design group. Julie has published articles on recovery, presented at conferences on peer group programs, consumer participation and recovery. Julie is a Board Director for Forensicare, Victoria including the Clinical Governance and Research Sub Committees. Julie is a former President of the Board at Neami National.

Rex Billington, Ph.D., is a Professorial Fellow and Adjunct Professor of Psychology at Auckland University of Technology. To the year 2000 he served 10 years as a scientist in the World Health Organization's (WHO's) Eastern Mediterranean Region substantially involved in health personnel education, followed by 8 years in WHO headquarters in Geneva where he held senior posts in the Global Program on HIV/AIDs and in the Division of Mental Health and Substance Abuse. His present research interest is in health outcomes assessment, particularly in the mental health sector.

Helen Bingham is a New Zealand registered nurse with a masters in nursing who has practiced in mental health for the past four decades. When practicing as nurse educator in an acute mental health unit an interest was sparked in how undergraduate nurses react to and learn about mental health. At this time an observation was made that nurses in other clinical areas tended to not use mental health knowledge and skills but considered this the role of specialist mental health nurses. The opportunity to be part of designing a curriculum that would allow the integration of mental health into the whole of the curriculum saw a move from clinical practice to an academic role. The author is currently a lecturer and clinical practice tutor for the Western Institute of Technology's nursing school in New Zealand.

Simon Bradstreet is a Research Fellow at the University of Glasgow managing research on digital technology to support wellbeing. He has a strong personal and professional interest in peer support developed during his time as the Director of the Scottish Recovery Network where he played a lead role in the introduction of peer support workers to the professional workforce in Scotland. He has written extensively on peer support working and recovery and has a personal research interest in internalized stigma.

Michael Burge, OAM, has been advocating for Australian consumers and carers for approx 21 years. He has been a representative on numerous state, national and international committees and written articles for Mental Health Magazines. Michael is a member of the International Initiative for Mental Health Leadership (IIMHL) and has participated in exchanges to America, Canada, England, Ireland, Scotland, and New Zealand. Michael is former chair of National Mental Health Consumer/Carer Forum a combined national voice for mental health consumers/carers. In June 2014, Michael received an Order of Australia (OAM) for his dedication as a Mental Health Advocate in the community.

Philip Burgess has a background in clinical psychology. Previously, he has worked in a variety of roles including managing psychiatric information services and the Victorian Psychiatric Case Register, Head of the Policy & Analysis Group at the Mental Health Research Institute of Victoria, and the Principal Researcher for the Mental Health Classification and Service Costs (MH-CASC) project. Since 2003, he has led the Analysis and Reporting Component of the Australian Mental Health Outcomes and Classification Network (AMHOCN).

Paolo C. Colet received his BS and Master in Nursing from Union Christian College and his doctorate (educational management) at Saint Jude College, Philippines. Earlier to his career, he worked as a clinical nurse instructor in the Philippines, before he moved to Saudi Arabia as a lecturer in Shaqra University. While in Saudi, he further developed his research interest in human resources for health. He is a fellow of the International Society of Quality, a vice director of one of the scholar's programs of American Medical Students Association, and a member of Sigma Theta Tau International.

Tim Coombs has worked in health care for over 25 years, starting as a general nurse before moving into mental health services. As a Divisional Nurse Manager, Tim has been responsible for nursing clinical governance and professional standards. Tim has also been Director, Training and Service Development of, then consultant to, the Australian Mental Health Outcomes and Classification Network (AMHOCN). He has contributed to AMHOCN's leadership of sustainable implementation of routine outcome measurement to public mental health services and managed nationally significant special projects. Tim is a surveyor for the Australian Council of Health Care Standards.

Jonas Preposi Cruz is a registered nurse from the Philippines. He is currently working as a lecturer in the nursing department of the College of Applied Medical Sciences of Shaqra University in Saudi Arabia. He has been working as a nurse educator since 2008. He has a Ph.D. in Educational Management and a master's in nursing with specialization in Medical and Surgical nursing. He is a member of the Psi Beta Chapter of Sigma theta Tau International and an advanced member of the Philippine Nursing Research Society, Inc. At present, he is involved in various research studies on topics related to nursing education and practice.

Sukhen Dey serves as an Associate Professor of Computer Science at Bellarmine University, Louisville, KY. He served as an Associate Professor of Computer Science and Informatics at Indiana University, SE. He holds a doctorate degree in System Sciences, an Education Specialist degree in Higher Education and an MBA, all from the University of Louisville. He is an expert in systems analysis, database development, cyber security, analytics and health informatics. He has published and presented numerous articles in his areas of expertise. He serves in various editorial review boards. Dr. Dey is a Life Member of Cambridge Who's Who.

Rosemary Dickson has worked in health care for over 20 years, in roles such as managing mental health information lines, Deputy CEO of the NSW Mental Health Association and as the Network Coordinator for the Australian Mental Health Outcomes and Classification Network (AMHOCN). Rosemary has participated in work on several nationally significant special projects, including the development of the Living in the Community Questionnaire, the Mental Health Carer Experiences Survey, the review of the National Outcomes and Casemix Collection and the development of guidelines for the use of outcome measures in the mental health community managed organization sector.

Nicki Dowling is an Associate Professor of Psychology in the School of Psychology at Deakin University, with honorary positions at the University of Melbourne and the Australian National University. Her track record includes 125 publications and 140 conference presentations and professional development seminars, most of which have been in the field of gambling research. She has been a Chief Investigator on multiple grants and tenders in the field of gambling. She is a registered clinical psychologist and a member of the Australian Psychological Society (Clinical College). She has had significant experience in the treatment of problem gambling in her part-time employment as a problem gambling counselor over a 12 year period. Recently, Nicki established an online CBT program that has been integrated into everyday service delivery in Victoria, Australia.

Bronwyn Dunnachie is a Senior Advisor at The Werry Centre. Bronwyn is a part of the Senior Management Team, supporting the governance structure of the Centre and contributes to key strategic and operational decision making. Based in Christchurch, Bronwyn leads the Christchurch office team, and has oversight for the Werry Centre projects delivered to the Central and Southern regions. Bronwyn has a background in mental health nursing. She has also completed a Masters in Education, Counselling Certificate (dist), and a PhD which focused on depression during adolescence. Bronwyn has held senior nursing and management roles in child and adolescent mental health (CAMHS) services over a 25-year period.

Monique Faleafa has served Pacific communities in the not-for-profit sector, district health boards, academia and social services for over 17 years as a clinician, and as an advocate for improving health and social outcomes for Pacific communities. Of Samoan descent, Dr Faleafa is the founding Chief Executive of Le Va and a registered clinical psychologist. She also contributes to her communities at governance levels, currently serving on Crown Entity, the Health Promotion Agency, MBIE Science Challenge Board, the Westpac External Stakeholder panel, and has been the Deputy Chair of regulatory authority, the New Zealand Psychologists' Board since 2009. Internationally she serves on the Pacific Advisory Group and is a mental health advisor to Australia's National Rugby League, is an Alumni of the commonwealth Emerging Pacific Leaders Dialogue, and an Associate Member of Global Women.

Michael Flaherty, PhD, is a clinical psychologist with 35 years in policy, research and practice in mental health, substance use and recovery. He has led hospital and community health systems, a behavioral managed care organization, and works with local communities to build recovery oriented systems of care. In 1999 he founded the Institute for Research Education and Training in the Addictions (IRETA) to align science and practice to outcomes. He regularly consults with the U.S. Department of Justice and White House Office of National Drug Control Policy on America's substance use policies and its overdose prevention response.

Julia Hennessy, prior to becoming the Director Teaching and Learning, was Executive Dean at Wellington Institute of Technology. She currently represents the tertiary vocational education sector on the unregulated health workforce group. Previous experience includes General Manager, Mental Health and Addiction Service for Hutt Valley DHB and Senior Advisor (Nursing) with the Ministry of Health. She worked in the tertiary education sector before being appointed Contracts and Relationship Manager for the Central Regional Health Authority. She has taught on health related programmes in the tertiary sector and has worked in a range of clinical settings as a registered nurse. She has an interest in workforce development of mental health services. She is a Fellow of the College of Nurses Aotearoa (New Zealand), Member of the College of Mental Health Nurses and was a member of Nursing Council of New Zealand from 2008-2011. PhD (AUT), M.Ed (Victoria), M.Mgmt (Massey), P.G. Dip H.S.M (Massey), BA (Victoria), Dip N, RN.

Christopher Hill is a public health researcher and workforce development professional with the University of Hawaii John A. Burns School of Medicine, the University of Hawaii Office of Public Health Studies: Public Health Training Hui, and the Research Corporation of the University of Hawaii. He managed the development of a health career planning book for youth and recruits health care professions to work in under-served areas in Hawaii and the US-Affiliated Pacific Islands. He is also a Certified Health Education Specialist.

Michael A. Hoge, PhD, is a Professor and Director of Clinical Training in Psychology within the Department of Psychiatry at the Yale University School of Medicine. He is also the Director of Yale Behavioral Health and the Yale Program on Supervision. Dr. Hoge serves as the Senior Science and Policy Advisor for the Annapolis Coalition on the Behavioral Health Workforce and has lectured and published widely on mental health and substance use workforce development. He has consulted on behavioral health workforce issues to the President's New Freedom Commission on Mental Health, the Institute of Medicine, and to numerous states and organizations.

Leighton Y. Huey, MD, is the Associate Dean for Community & Continuing Medical Education and Birnbaum/Blum Professor of Psychiatry at the University of Connecticut School of Medicine. He has an interest in health care reform and innovation with a particular focus on integrated care and quality improvement of clinical systems and the workforce.

Frances Hughes was awarded the Harkness Fellowship in Health Care Policy from the Commonwealth Fund in New York and working with Dr Linda Aitken on research relating to nurse practitioners, costing nursing turnover and the effects of nursing on patient outcomes. The first professor of nursing at Auckland University, chair of mental health nursing, Frances established the Centre for Mental Health Policy, Research and Service Development. Visiting professorship at the University of Sydney. Facilitator for the Pacific Island Mental Health Network (PIMHNet) and worked for World Health Organization (WHO). Officer of the New Zealand Order of Merit (ONZM). Executive officer for a national disability group in New Zealand. Acting deputy director of mental health for New Zealand. A Fulbright New Zealand Senior Scholar spending five months based at Rutgers University College of Nursing in Piscataway, New Jersey, USA researching the preparation of health professionals for psychosocial response to natural disasters. Received a Distinguished Alumni Service Award from Massey University in New Zealand. Chief Nursing and Midwifery Officer for the Queensland Department of Health, Queensland Health, Australia. Frances is currently the CEO for the International Council of Nurses. RN, Dip. Nursing, BA, MA, Doctorate in Nursing, Fellow of Te Ao Māramatanga New Zealand College of Mental Health Nurses, Officer of the New Zealand Order of Merit.

Anwar Islam, with a PhD in Sociology from the University of Alberta (Edmonton, Alberta, Canada), has thirty years of professional experience as a specialist in health systems, international development, public health, public policy/planning and program monitoring and evaluation. He worked for the Ottawa-based International Development Research Centre (IDRC), the then Canadian International Development Agency (CIDA), the Aga Khan University (Karachi, Pakistan) and the James P Grant School of Public Health, BRAC University (Dhaka, Bangladesh). Currently, he is serving as an Adjunct Professor with the School of Health Policy and Management, York University in Toronto, Ontario, Canada.

Shariful Islam is a postdoctoral research fellow at The George Institute for Global Health in Australia. He serves as a faculty and principal investigator at the non-communicable diseases unit, International Center for Diarrhoeal Disease Research, Bangladesh. Shariful completed his PhD in International Health from Ludwig-Maximilians-Universität (LMU), Munich, Germany. Shariful has professional experience with UNDP, WHO, GiZ and Texas Tech University, Lubbock, USA. He has received several awards, including gold-medal for academic excellence, Fogarty Fellowship, Packard Award and DAAD Fellowship. His main areas of interests are using innovative technologies for health, specially diabetes and cardiovascular diseases.

Ashley Koning's primary focus as Project Lead with Matua Raki is supporting services and the wider mental health and addiction workforce to develop co-existing problems responsiveness and capability. Alongside that he also helps to develop resources and guidelines for the sector, including elearning, and facilitates workshops on request. He has worked with Matua Raki for the past six years drawing on his experience as an addiction practitioner and also his previous experience as a counsellor, social worker, psychologist, youth worker, child care worker and psychiatric assistant. He also has post graduate qualifications in psychology and social work.

Rachel Lawson is a Consultant Clinical Psychologist and Clinical Head of the South Island Eating Disorders Service, Christchurch, New Zealand. She has extensive experience in the treatment of eating disorders in both New Zealand and the United Kingdom. She has co-authored two books on the treatment of eating disorders and published research in this area. She speaks to local, national and international audiences about eating disorders and provides workshops. She is the New Zealand representative on the committee for the Australia and New Zealand Academy for Eating Disorder. She has an interest in workforce development and has worked as a project leader for the eating disorders for the Werry Centre for Child and Adolescent Mental Health.

Dan Lubman is a Psychiatrist and Addiction Medicine Specialist. He has worked across mental health and addiction treatment settings in both the UK and Australia. He is Director of Turning Point and Professor of Addiction Studies and Services at Monash University. Dr Lubman's research is wide-ranging and includes investigating the impact of alcohol and drug use on brain function, the relationship between substance use, gambling and mental disorder, as well as the development of targeted intervention programs within school, primary care, mental health and drug treatment settings.

Roderick McKay is a psychiatrist who has specialised in working with older people, postgraduate education of mental health professionals, and the use of information to improve mental health care. Rod is the Director of Psychiatry and Mental Health Programs at the New South Wales Institute of Psychiatry and conjoint senior lecturer at the University of New South Wales. He is a clinical advisor regarding policy development in older people's mental health, chair of the Australian National Mental Health Information Development Expert Advisory Group, and chair of the Royal Australian and New Zealand College of Psychiatrists Community Collaboration Committee.

John A. Morris, MSW, is Executive Director of the Annapolis Coalition on the Behavioral Health Workforce. He retired in 2007 from the University of South Carolina School of Medicine, where he served as Professor of Clinical Neuropsychiatry and Behavioral Sciences; he also served as the Director of Health Policy Studies in the Department of Psychiatry. Prior to his time at the University, he had an extensive career in public behavioral health, having served as Deputy State Director of Mental Health for nearly a decade, including a two-year interim appointment as State Director.

Roger Nicholas is the Senior Project Manager at the National Centre for Education and Training on Addiction at Flinders University where he is involved in a number of national alcohol and other drug-related projects. He has twenty-eight years' experience in working in the alcohol and other drugs field including 10 years with the Australasian Centre for Policing Research (Australian Federal Police) and 2 years with SA Police (National Drug Law Enforcement Research Fund). He has numerous publications in this area. Roger also holds a Master's Degree in Public Policy. His research and policy interests include: substance use problems among older people, regulatory and law enforcement responses to alcohol-related crime and disorder; and pharmaceutical drug misuse.

Mary O'Hagan was a key initiator of the psychiatric survivor movement in New Zealand in the late 1980s, and was the first chairperson of the World Network of Users and Survivors of Psychiatry between 1991 and 1995. She has been an advisor to the United Nations and the World Health Organization. Mary was a full-time Mental Health Commissioner in New Zealand between 2000 and 2007. Mary is now director of the international social enterprise PeerZone, which provides peer-led workshops, an online recovery toolkit, support to employers and consultancy. Mary has written an award-winning memoir called 'Madness Made Me'. She was made a Member of the New Zealand Order of Merit in 2015. All Mary's work has been driven by her quest for social justice for one of the most marginalized groups in our communities.

Manuel Paris, PsyD, is an Associate Professor of Psychiatry at the Yale University School of Medicine and Deputy Director of Hispanic Services for the Connecticut Mental Health Center (CMHC). He also serves as Director of Training for the Latino Track of the Yale Psychology Pre and Post-Doctoral Fellowship Program at the Hispanic Clinic/CMHC. His research and scholarly interests focus on the evaluation of cultural/linguistic adaptations of evidence based assessments and interventions, multisite training and fidelity monitoring, and workforce development.

Suzette Poole is a registered psychiatric nurse with over 30 years of nursing experience in roles such as: clinical nurse educator, clinical nurse director, nurse advisor-health (Nursing Council), practice board chair and Fellow of Te Ao Māramatanga, New Zealand College of Mental Health Nurses, honorary lecturer at the University of Auckland. Her current role is Clinical lead for Te Pou o te Whakaaro Nui-national center of evidence based workforce development for the mental health, addiction and disability sectors in New Zealand. Suzette leads the 'Co-existing problem project' stream of work alongside Ashley Koning from Matua Raki and three other workforce centers. Suzette is co-editor of 'Handover- a mental health and addiction nursing newsletter'. Suzettes' research includes her thesis on 'New Zealand Mental Health Nurses' Perceptions of Structural and Psychological Empowerment' and a study about violence towards nurses in their first year of practice. She contributed to the book 'Changing Times, Changing Places: From Tokanui Hospital to Mental Health Services in the Waikato, 1910-2012'.

Richie Poulton is Director of the Dunedin Multidisciplinary Health and Development Research Unit which conducts the Dunedin longitudinal study, one of the most detailed studies of human health and development ever undertaken. A multidisciplinary, longitudinal study of 1,037 babies born in Dunedin during 1972/73. In 2007, Professor Poulton established and became a Co-Director of the National Centre for Lifecourse Research, a research center based at the University of Otago in Dunedin, but with partners located at universities across New Zealand and internationally. He has published 200+ peer-reviewed scientific papers, with many appearing in leading international journals. His research interests include: mental health, nature-nurture interplay, and psychosocial determinants of chronic physical disease. In 2014, he was named as a Highly Cited Researcher by Thomson-Reuters (one of only four New Zealanders so designated) and was listed in *2015 World's Most Influential Scientific Minds,* Thomson-Reuters.

Fuimaono Karl Pulotu-Endemann is the first Pacific person to be registered as a Psychiatric nurse leading to comprehensive nurse registration in New Zealand. Fuimaono is a high chief/title from Samoa. A pioneer in Pacific mental health sector in New Zealand. He has represented Pacific people on various boards including Mental Health Commission of New Zealand, Alcohol Advisory Council of New Zealand, The Parole Board, The Psychologist Board, The Drug Foundation and is active in Pacific community development, for example establishment of the Pacific Trust Canterbury NGO and Pacific Island AIDS Trust. Fuimaono in partnership with Pava, a contract with the Ministry of Health, produced a number of outcomes that led to the establishment of Le Va, the Pacific mental health workforce organization.

Lal B. Rawal is a Public Health Professional having received PhD from Australia, MPH from Thailand and MEd (Health Ed.) from Nepal. Currently, Rawal works with icddr,b Bangladesh, as Senior Associate. He is also an Adjunct Faculty at JPG School of Public Health, BRAC University. He has over 15 years of experience working in the health sector and has led several health and related projects and consultancies and has published a number of papers in peer-reviewed inter (national) journals. His current projects focused on NCDs prevention and management; Universal health coverage; Human resources for health and Health policy and systems strengthening.

Ann Roche has over 30 years' experience in public health. She has worked as a policy analyst, researcher, and educator. For the past 15 years she has been the Director of the National Centre for Education and Training on Addiction (NCETA), Flinders University. Previously, she was Director of the Queensland Alcohol and Drug Research and Education Centre (QADREC). She has held academic posts at several universities, and has worked in clinical, public health and community settings. Ann's professional activities have primarily focused on alcohol and other drug issues, particularly policy development, best practice, workforce development, and research dissemination.

Simone Rodda has worked for more than a decade in the education and treatment of addictive behaviors. Dr Rodda is a Lecturer at AUT University in New Zealand (Psychology) and an Honorary Senior Research Fellow with Turning Point (Melbourne, Australia). She is currently involved in multiple investigations involving the use of e-therapy and brief interventions for problem gambling. Dr Rodda has provided many workforce development sessions and workshops across Australia and New Zealand in the use of e-therapy for addictive behaviors and established the first national online gambling help service in Australia in 2009.

Liz Smythe is an experienced hermeneutic researcher. Her doctoral thesis explored the meaning of being safe in childbirth, drawing on the philosophies of Heidegger and Gadamer. She has since done studies in the thinking of postgraduate education, leadership, the rise of postgraduate education, and professional supervision while also continuing her writing in midwifery. She has supervised over 25 masters theses/dissertations and 25 doctoral studies, most using hermeneutic methodology. To date, she has 70 peer review journal and book publications. PhD:(Massey University), Post-graduate Diploma in Social Science (1995), (Massey University) BA Social Science (Nursing), RN, RM.

Lisa St. George is the Director of Recovery Practices at RI International leading RI Consulting and RI's New Zealand services. Since 2000, Lisa has developed peer teams for more than 20 programs. Service programs developed by Ms. St. George are widely replicated. She is an expert in supporting system change towards recovery-focused services. Ms. St. George is leading a multi-county training project developing peer support workers throughout California. She has authored books, many tools, trainings, and articles. Lisa also co-authored RI's internationally recognized Peer Employment Training and a Peer Support Training for NASMHPD. Ms. St. George serves on the Board of Directors for iN-APS, NARPA, and the Arizona Peer and Family Career Academy. She works with the Cross Disability Crisis Intervention workgroup in Phoenix, and CHAMP NGO Leadership Group in Counties Manukau, New Zealand, and the Maricopa County Veteran's Administration Clay Hunt Collaboration Leadership Group. Lisa was the 2010 California Health Hero.

Gail W. Stuart, PhD, RN, FAAN, is Dean and a tenured Distinguished University Professor in the College of Nursing and a Professor in the College of Medicine in the Department of Psychiatry and Behavioral Sciences at the Medical University of South Carolina. Prior to her appointment as Dean, she was the Associate Director of the Center for Health Care Research at MUSC and the administrator and Chief Executive Officer of the Institute of Psychiatry at the Medical University where she was responsible for all clinical, fiscal, and human operations across the continuum of psychiatric care. Dr. Stuart is best known for her significant contributions to psychiatric mental health nursing. She is a prolific writer and has published numerous articles, chapters, textbooks, and media productions. Most notable among these is her textbook, Principles and Practice of Psychiatric Nursing, now in its 10th edition, which has been honored with four Book of the Year Awards from the American Journal of Nursing and has been translated into 5 languages. She has taught in undergraduate, graduate, and doctoral programs in nursing and serves on numerous academic, corporate and government boards. She has represented nursing on a variety of National Institute of Mental Health and National Institute of Nursing Research policy and research panels. She has received many awards, including the American Nurses Association Distinguished Contribution to Psychiatric Nursing Award, the Psychiatric Nurse of the Year Award from the American Psychiatric Nurses Association, and the Hildegard Peplau Award from the American Nurses Association. She was the co-chair of the AACN Joining Forces Tool Kit. She is a fellow in the American Academy of Nursing, a member of Sigma Theta Tau, a past president of the American College of Mental Health Administration, a past president of the American Psychiatric Nurses Association, and currently President of the Annapolis Coalition on the Behavioral Health Workforce. Dr. Stuart has been a van Ameringen fellow at the Beck Institute of Cognitive Therapy and Research and was a visiting professor at King's College, Institute of Psychiatry, at the Maudsley in London.

Reshman Tabassum served as 'Human Resources Generalist' and 'Research Associate' for Peoples Radio Ltd and North South University respectively. She graduated from Macquarie University, with a master's degree in human resources management in 2015. She is currently doing Master of Research in human resources management and health at Macquarie University. She also has affiliations with Australian Human Resources Institute (AHRI), and Macquarie Graduate School of Management (MGSM).

Kelley Withy is an experienced family medicine doctor and workforce researcher. She is the Director of the Hawaii/Pacific Basin AHEC, a member of the faculty at the University of Hawaii John A. Burns School of Medicine, and participates in health and medical workforce initiatives across the entire Pacific Region. Her expertise is internationally known for her work on physician workforce shortage research and her innovative workforce development methodologies.

Index

Y

www.ingramcontent.com/pod-product-compliance
Lightning Source LLC
LaVergne TN
LVHW060407300926
849162LV00006B/1364